S0-ADX-474

OCCUPATIONAL LITERATURE

OCCUPATIONAL LITERATURE
OCCUPATIONAL LITERATURE
OCCUPATIONAL LITERATURE
OCCUPATIONAL LITERATURE
OCCUPATIONAL LITERATURE

An Annotated Bibliography

OCCUPATIONAL LITERATURE
OCCUPATIONAL LITERATURE
OCCUPATIONAL LITERATURE
OCCUPATIONAL LITERATURE
OCCUPATIONAL LITERATURE
OCCUPATIONAL LITERATURE
OCCUPATIONAL LITERATURE
OCCUPATIONAL LITERATURE
OCCUPATIONAL LITERATURE
OCCUPATIONAL LITERATURE
OCCUPATIONAL LITERATURE
OCCUPATIONAL LITERATURE
OCCUPATIONAL LITERATURE
OCCUPATIONAL LITERATURE

OCCUPATIONAL LITERATURE
OCCUPATIONAL LITERATURE
OCCUPATIONAL LITERATURE
OCCUPATIONAL LITERATURE
OCCUPATIONAL LITERATURE
OCCUPATIONAL LITERATURE

OCCUPATIONAL LITERATURE
OCCUPATIONAL LITERATURE
OCCUPATIONAL LITERATURE
OCCUPATIONAL LITERATURE
OCCUPATIONAL LITERATURE
OCCUPATIONAL LITERATURE
OCCUPATIONAL LITERATURE
OCCUPATIONAL LITERATURE
OCCUPATIONAL LITERATURE
OCCUPATIONAL LITERATURE
OCCUPATIONAL LITERATURE
OCCUPATIONAL LITERATURE
OCCUPATIONAL LITERATURE
OCCUPATIONAL LITERATURE

1971 EDITION

OCCUPATIONAL LITERATURE

An Annotated Bibliography

GERTRUDE FORRESTER

FORMERLY HEAD COUNSELOR
WEST SIDE HIGH SCHOOL
Newark Public Schools, New Jersey

The H.W. Wilson Company New York 1971

Occupational Literature: An Annotated Bibliography
Copyright © 1946, 1948, 1954, 1958, 1964, 1971
By GERTRUDE FORRESTER

The 1946 and 1948 editions of this work were entitled, respectively,

Occupations: A Selected List of Pamphlets
and
Occupational Pamphlets: An Annotated Bibliography

PRINTED IN THE UNITED STATES OF AMERICA

Library of Congress Catalog Card No. 79-149382

International Standard Book Number 0-8242-0437-9

016.607
F771o
1971
cop 3

Contents

PART I. Introduction 7

PART II. Publications Issued in Series, Arranged According to Publisher of Series 13

PART III. Annotated Bibliography

A. Books and Pamphlets Listed Alphabetically by Occupation 45

B. Books and Pamphlets Describing More than One Occupation 503

C. Apprenticeship 512

D. Bibliographies and Indexes 513

E. Charts, Posters, and Display Materials 516

F. Foreign Study or Employment 520

G. Information about Colleges, Schools for Vocational Training, and Other Educational Institutions 532

H. Job Seeking 539

I. Legislation and Social Security 550

J. Occupations for the Handicapped 554

K. Package Purchases 558

L. Periodicals 560

M. Planning a Career 563

N. Preparing for Examinations 567

O. Professional Counseling Services 570

P. Scholarships 571

Q. Textbooks for Pupils 577

R. Use of Occupational Information and the Counselor's Professional Bookshelf 580

DIRECTORY OF PUBLISHERS AND DISTRIBUTORS 589

INDEX 617

Part I

Introduction

This bibliography has been prepared to assist in acquainting youth with sources of information about occupations—information that has become increasingly important in the complex world of career opportunities. In order that young people may make their career choices wisely, they must be aware of the changing trends in manpower demand. The increasing use of automation and the emergence of new jobs resulting from scientific developments point up the need for current occupational information.

Recent events have indicated that the United States has need of manpower in many occupations, particularly in those requiring exceptional talent and specialized training. To meet this situation in the years ahead, teachers and counselors must be alert to help every young person discover his talents and interests and to encourage him to develop his best capabilities. They must be able to show the student how to relate these capabilities to opportunities in our society and how to relate the occupational information realistically to his needs. It is hoped that this bibliography will provide access to some of the sources of occupational information necessary in this task.

In compiling this bibliography, several other purposes have been borne in mind. One is to assist teachers, counselors, and librarians in selecting materials for occupational collections. The second is to serve as a reader's guide to occupational literature, so that an inquirer may determine what to look for in the library or select materials he may wish to purchase. An individual may refer to the descriptions of available material on a specific topic and pursue his examination of the occupational literature with relatively little help. Another purpose is to list the best of the current material on the various subjects so that librarians and counselors may refer students to appropriate sources of information. An obvious aim is to point out the existence of available publications which may be used by research workers.

This bibliography brings together in a central index approximately six thousand selected references to available occupational literature. It includes more than books and pamphlets which simply describe occupations. Since the preparation for a career often involves the selection of a school for training, one section describes the school and college information. Other sections annotate charts, posters, and graphic aids; textbooks for courses in occupations; materials designed to assist youth to evolve a sound vocational plan; references on the techniques of job seeking and job advancement; and publications devoted to the counselors' use of occupational information. Additional sections describe the references to information about scholarships and the publications on studying and working abroad.

Selected titles have been cited in the occupations and fields of work on which useful and authentic material has been found. An attempt has been made to describe as completely as possible the available references which have value and which meet the objectives of vocational and educational guidance.

The fifty-five series published by thirty-two publishers are described in Part II. In the annotated bibliography, Part III, the publications are arranged alphabetically by subject. The data given for each book or pamphlet include the title, author if known, name of publisher, date of publication, number of pages, and price. A reference to a section of a book is indicated by the title of the chapter or section followed by the page reference and the name of the publication. The index then will refer the reader to the page of the full annotation.

Titles of Government publications are followed by the name of the bureau or department which prepared the material. However, if there is a charge for the publication and if the designation "Supt. of Documents" follows, the order should be sent to the Superintendent of Documents, Government Printing Office, Washington 25, D.C.

The references are briefly annotated to indicate the general content of the publication and the major topics included. Most of the publications are prepared for use of students in secondary school and early college years. Otherwise, the annotations point out the age level or special group to which the material is addressed. A limited number of books and pamphlets has been included for graduate students, adult workers, and elementary school pupils.

The prices given are those quoted at the time the publications were examined; because of increasing printing costs, they are subject to change without advance notice. The cost stated is for single copies only; frequently special prices are quoted for large orders. Also there is usually a charge for free publications when ordered in quantity.

Approximately 4,500 pamphlets have been included in this bibliography; there are about 1,500 references to books. The publications have been classified under about 500 occupational titles. For the most part, the headings are the base titles to which code numbers have been assigned in Volume I of the second edition of the *Dictionary of Occupational Titles* and the industry titles given in Volume II of the *Dictionary*. In some cases a general title has been used when it has been convenient to group under one label publications describing a range of occupations, several kinds of work, or related occupations.

For the convenience of users who may wish to arrange their occupational files according to the *Dictionary of Occupational Titles*, the *Dictionary* code numbers have been added to the titles in the annotated bibliography in Part III of this book. The title at the head of each group of entries is the title under which the occupation is defined in the *Dictionary*. Opposite the title, at the right-hand side of the same line, is the code number. This "base" title is the one by which the occupation is most commonly known, or the one which is considered most descriptive of the occupation. Other titles by which the occupation may be designated are given in their proper alphabetical order in the list with a "see" reference to the "basic" title.

Users who assemble the complete collection may find it advisable to classify further the titles with an unwieldy number of pamphlets. Titles with the largest number of references in this book are as follows:

Titles	Number of References	Titles	Number of References
Nurse (professional)	65	Police officer	31
Engineer	55	Home economist	30
Librarian	54	Photographer	30
Physician	49	Insurance industry worker	29
Teacher	49	Architect	29
Scientist	44	Forester	28
Salesman	40	Writer	28
Social worker	39	Accountant	27
Medical service worker	37	Journalist	27
Secretary	34	Hospital administrator	27
Lawyer	32	Hotel industry worker	27

A star marks the publications recommended for first purchase in small libraries; a double star indicates those most highly recommended.

The criteria given below were used in selecting the literature and in affixing the stars and double stars for special recommendation:

1. *Content*—The topics covered should include those recommended by the National Vocational Guidance Association in its reprints, *Standards for Use in Preparing and Evaluating Occupational Literature* and the 1964 revision, *Guidelines for Preparing and Evaluating Occupational Materials*, listed on page 583.
2. *Authenticity*—Authoritative sources; accurate information; thoroughness of data.
3. *Objectivity*—Unbiased, unprejudiced, and balanced presentation.
4. *Availability of publication.*
5. *Recency of publication*—Date of publication or revision given.
6. *Recency of research or printed sources used.*
7. *Suitability*—Appropriateness for the age, interests, and understanding of individuals who will use them.

8. *Inclusion of information not found elsewhere.*
9. *Style and readability*—Interesting, clear, and concise presentation.
10. *Format and physical features*—Typography and artistic appearance.
11. *Cost*—Effort made to include many free and inexpensive materials.
12. *Motivation for further reading and inquiry*—References for additional information.
13. *Helpfulness in meeting objectives*—Contents aid counselor in meeting goals set forth in many of the authoritative statements listed in the section on "Use of Occupational Information."

Beyond the criteria enumerated above, contents of educational guidance literature, especially, should provide encouragement and assistance to the student in establishing goals commensurate with his abilities, in planning an appropriate course of action to achieve these goals, and in formulating suitable career choices which will mean ultimate satisfaction, success, and increased contributions to society.

This bibliography may be supplemented by the current issues of the *Career Index* (Chronicle Guidance Publications), the *Career Guidance Index* (Careers), the *Counselor's Information Service* (B'nai B'rith Vocational Service, "Current Career Literature" in the *Vocational Guidance Quarterly*, and the *Guidance Exchange*. These are listed in the section on bibliographies and indexes.

The 6,000 references annotated and classified in this bibliography are issued by 670 publishers, professional organizations, and government agencies. These sources are listed in the Directory of Publishers and Distributors, at the end of the book. Approximately 1,000 publications are available free of charge.

Although an effort has been made to include the available materials of unusual merit, some helpful publications have doubtless been omitted. It is inevitable that between the time the manuscript is prepared and the purchase of the book by the user, some publications should go out of print or be repriced. The author and publisher invite users of the bibliography to assist in correcting any shortcomings. Suggestions for improvements in future editions will be appreciated.

OCCUPATIONAL LITERATURE

OCCUPATIONAL LITERATURE
OCCUPATIONAL LITERATURE
OCCUPATIONAL LITERATURE
OCCUPATIONAL LITERATURE
OCCUPATIONAL LITERATURE

An Annotated Bibliography

OCCUPATIONAL LITERATURE
OCCUPATIONAL LITERATURE
OCCUPATIONAL LITERATURE
OCCUPATIONAL LITERATURE
OCCUPATIONAL LITERATURE
OCCUPATIONAL LITERATURE
OCCUPATIONAL LITERATURE
OCCUPATIONAL LITERATURE
OCCUPATIONAL LITERATURE
OCCUPATIONAL LITERATURE
OCCUPATIONAL LITERATURE
OCCUPATIONAL LITERATURE
OCCUPATIONAL LITERATURE
OCCUPATIONAL LITERATURE

Part II

Publications Issued in Series Arranged According to Publisher of Series

ALUMNAE ADVISORY CENTER, INC., Box A.C., 541 Madison Avenue, New York, N.Y. 10022

Mademoiselle College and Career Reprints. 102 reprints. 35c each

This series consists of reprints of charts and articles which have appeared in *Mademoiselle,* prepared by the College and Careers Department of the magazine. They are available from the Alumnae Advisory Center, a nonprofit organization which publishes some vocational pamphlets and counsels women college graduates on jobs in New York City.

Written in lively style, these four- to ten-page articles are intended to arouse interest in the vocation. Vocational information is often presented through case histories of young women who have succeeded in their specialized fields of work. Because of the attractive illustrations, photographs, and brief biographical sketches of prominent women, these articles are decidedly stimulating in tone. Although the disadvantages of each career are discussed briefly in some of the articles, the approach is intended to create confidence and to encourage further investigation.

Timely information on requirements, opportunities, salaries, and the changing outlook in work for women are considered in many of the series, especially those based on interviews with several young women engaged in the work. However, these reprints are more useful in supplying introductory or supplementary information than in providing complete factual data. The job fields usually are those of interest to college women and high school girls who expect to attend college. Some specialized fields for women such as photo journalism, puppeteering, wire service reporting, lecture management, and fund raising are included in this series. Some articles contain discussions of job seeking, college information, working abroad, and creative jobs.

The reprints may be ordered either individually or through a subscription of $3 per year for the next ten articles as they are issued. Only prepaid orders accepted.

A list of the current reprints may be obtained from the Alumnae Advisory Center. About thirty-five titles are described in this bibliography. Typical examples are as follows:

Free-lance photography. 1968
Job hunters' bibliography. 1969
Jobs in ecology. 1970
Job hunting in New York. 1967
Jobs in zoos. 1967
Museum jobs. 1966
Reporting jobs. 1968
Running a business after marriage. 1963
Travel industry jobs. 1964
Your own business. 1966

B'NAI B'RITH VOCATIONAL SERVICE, 1640 Rhode Island Ave., N.W., Washington, D.C. 20036

B'nai B'rith Occupational Brief Series. 40 briefs. 35c each

The B'nai B'rith Vocational Service conducts occupational and educational research and engages in a broad publications program. It aims to provide up-to-date information for the regional offices conducted in many of the major population centers in cooperation with local Jewish Vocational Service agencies. The service has issued sixty-seven publications on occupations and broad fields of work, college information, job finding, and career planning, as well as charts, research studies, reading lists, and a quarterly bibliography, *Counselor's Information Service.*

The briefs average from four to eighteen pages in length. They are written to interest young people, and contain information on outlook, duties, preparation and entry, qualifications, earnings and advancement, and sources of further information. Where information is available, a section is added giving data of interest to Jewish youth. Ten briefs are devoted specifically to careers in Jewish communal service.

Most of the briefs are illustrated. They are frequently revised. They are comparatively inexpensive. A B'nai B'rith Guidance Kit is available for $40. This consists of the sixty-seven publications listed in the annual catalog which, if purchased separately, would cost $60.85. Typical titles are:

Occupational Brief Series

Biological sciences. 1970
City management. 1968
Corporate management. 1969
Medicine. 1970
Memorial counseling. 1968
Optometry. 1968
Pharmacy. 1970
Psychology. 1968

Careers in Jewish Communal Service

Careers in the cantorate. 1968
Careers in Jewish education. 1968
Careers in the rabbinate. 1969
Careers in synagogue and temple administration. 1968

Directories and Research
College guide for Jewish youth. 1968
Prep school guide for Jewish youth. 1966
"Starter file" of free occupational literature. 1970
Studying for success in high school and college. 1968

CAREERS, INC., Box 135, Largo, Florida 33540

Career Guidance Service. September through May. $35 per subscription

This publishing company distributes a monthly packet of material to subscribers from September through May. Under the editorship of Raymond M. Handville, the material is practical and up to date. All of the booklets and posters appearing in the service may be purchased individually or they may be obtained as they are published through an annual subscription. A junior high school service is available for $30. Counselors and librarians may send for a composite sample of the service, including one of each of the items listed below. Subscription to one year's service includes the following:

45 career briefs. Single copies 35c
80 career summaries or thumbnail sketches. Single copies 20c
45 reprints of selected career articles. Single copies 15c
9 career guidance indexes, listing references to free and inexpensive career materials. Yearly subscription $6
18 training guides, listing training opportunities for specific careers, $3 per set
18 posters, stimulating students to think about their future careers. $10 per set
9 timely professional reprints, reports from professional publications, $5.50 per set
9 college guides, listing entrance requirements, costs, etc. $3 per set

Career Briefs. 200 titles. Yearly subscription to 45 new and revised briefs per year, $10. 35c each

These briefs are published at the rate of forty-five per year and are revised every four years. They contain information on the history and development of the occupation, duties, working conditions, training requirements, training opportunities, personal qualifications, employment prospects, hours and earnings, advancement prospects, measuring one's interests and abilities, and a suggested high school program. Most of the briefs contain references to four or more suggested readings.

Eight pages in length, the briefs are 5½ by 8½ inches, and are designed to fit Careers' desk-top file. The titles and code numbers are placed on the top in the upper right-hand corner. The information is timely and well presented. Typical titles in this series are:

Aerospace engineer. 1970
Air traffic controller. 1970
Auto mechanic. 1967
Biochemist. 1970
Botanist. 1970
Carpenter. 1968
Dental hygienist. 1968
Draftsman. 1968
Earth scientist. 1970
Flight engineer. 1970
Geophysicist. 1970
Industrial designer. 1970
Peace Corps volunteer. 1970
Programmer. 1966
Tailor. 1970
Wildlife specialist. 1970

Career Summaries. Total of 345 titles. Yearly subscriptions to 80 new and revised titles, $10. Single copies 20c each

The summaries contain shorter and more concise information than the career briefs, and the filing plan suggested for them makes them convenient to use. They are printed on card stock, both sides, size 5½ by 8½ inches, the same size as the career briefs and career reprints, to fit into the desk-top metal file box. The titles and code numbers are placed on the top in the upper right hand corner. Because of the large number of titles, this series covers many occupations not found in book-length discussions.

An up-to-date list of current titles may be secured from the publisher. Typical titles are:

Cashier. 1970
Cattle farmer. 1970
Cement mason. 1970
Coal miner. 1970
Comparison shopper. 1970
Court reporter. 1970
Fingerprint classifier. 1968
Food scientist. 1970
Horticulturist. 1972
Mail carrier. 1970
Meter reader. 1966
Park naturalist. 1970
Poultry farmer. 1970
Roofer. 1970
Safety engineer. 1970
Securities salesman. 1967
Taxi driver. 1970
Traffic manager. 1969
Truck farmer. 1970
Urban planner. 1970

CHANGING TIMES, THE KIPLINGER MAGAZINE, 1729 H Street, N.W., Washington 6, D.C. 20006

Changing Times Reprints. 20 booklets. 15c to 75c each

Collections of related material on careers from *Changing Times* are reprinted in booklet form, size 8½ by 6 inches. Some research bulletins on college and employment information are larger, size 8½ by 11 inches. The style is clear, concise, direct, and convincing, obviously the work of trained writers. The career reprints are three or four pages in length. Examples of titles are:

Careers in planning. 1963. 15c
Colleges with room for students. Annually. 75c
Do you have what it takes to be a boss some day? 1966. 15c

Good jobs in the health field. 1966. 15c
Good jobs waiting for men who learn a trade. 1966. 15c
No, you don't have to go to college. 1966. 15c
Tomorrow's jobs—where the best will be. 1966. 15c

CHILDRENS PRESS, INC., and MELMONT PUBLISHERS, 1224 W. Van Buren Street, Chicago, Illinois 60607

"I Want To Be" Series. 42 books. $2.25 each

This series, designed to encourage independent reading on the beginner level, is prepared for readers with a reading level of upper first grade. Many of the books were written by Carla Greene and Eugene Baker, with the consultation of Dr. Paul Witty of the Psycho-Educational Clinic, Northwestern University. He states that all but about ten to twenty of the approximately two hundred words used in each book are from the first thousand words for children's reading. The books are thirty-two pages in length, size 8 by 9½ inches, and are illustrated in color.

These books are frequently used as social studies material to acquaint children in lower elementary grades with services provided in the community. Only a few titles in this series are included in the main bibliography of this book, as examples of available simple materials for young readers:

I want to be an architect. 1969
I want to be a beauty operator. 1969
I want to be a forester. 1969
I want to be a sales clerk. 1969
I want to be a secretary. 1969
I want to be a ship captain. 1962
I want to be a taxi driver. 1969
I want to be a zoo keeper. 1961

Primary Social Studies Enrichment Materials. 68 books. $2.25 each

This series is similar to the "I Want To Be" books described above, but is prepared to appeal to grades two through four. It is distributed by Melmont Publishers, subsidiary of Childrens Press. Examples of titles are:

About the driver of a bus
About the engineer of a train
About men at work
About policemen
At the bakery
At the bank
At the dairy
At the post office

"Come to Work With Us" Series. 12 books. $3.38 each

This series is announced as a career awareness series for grades kindergarten through three. Each occupation is illustrated through a full color photograph showing a young child at work in an adult job situation. On the page opposite the photograph is a four-line rhyme explaining the job. Each book is forty-eight pages in length and contains an introduction by Sam Levenson. The career information has been developed by Sextant Systems, Inc., and the series is distributed by Melmont Publishers and Childrens Press.

COME TO WORK WITH US IN A (OR AN)

Aerospace
Airport
Dairy
Department store
Bank
Hospital
Hotel
House construction
Newspaper
Telephone company
Toy factory
Television station

CHRONICLE GUIDANCE PUBLICATIONS, INC., Moravia, N.Y.

Chronicle 3-in-1 Service. Subscription, September through April. $46.50 per year for single subscription. Quantity prices on request. Price subject to change

This service offers a package of occupational, educational, and professional guidance material each month from September through April. The items may be ordered separately or obtained as they are published through an annual subscription. Several of the services are described in this book in the section on "Package Purchases." An annual subscription consists of the following materials:

90 job briefs. $20.25 per year. 35c for single copies
24 reprints. $6 per year. Set of 150 best for $25
48 pieces of professional information. $10 per year
Career index. Annual compilation of references with 4 supplements. $10
Posters suitable for bulletin board use. $12 per year
Educational books containing information about colleges, student aid, etc. $17.50

Chronicle Occupational Brief Service. 90 new briefs each year $20.25 Single copies 35c each. Full set of 395 titles, $67.50 unbound; $72.50 bound in 3 volumes with vinyl covers. Cash is required with orders totaling less than $5

These briefs are included in the Chronicle 3-in-1 Service, the Occupational Service, and the Pamphlet Service. They may be purchased separately or on an annual subscription basis. Most of them have been prepared or revised within the last four years; the publishers plan to issue ninety new titles each year and to revise about sixty. On request, the publishers will send a list of the 395 titles followed by the year of publication.

Each four-page brief, 8½ by 11 inches, contains information on the following topics: duties, working conditions, hours, earnings, personal qualifications, training requirements and opportunities, employment outlook, where employed, and references for further reading. All of the briefs acknowledge the assistance of three or more recognized authorities in the field, whose names are given, and who have approved the manuscript. Examples of titles in this series are:

Biologist. 1970
Claims adjuster. 1970
Correspondence clerk. 1970
Court clerk. 1970
Executive housekeeper. 1970
Historian. 1970
Hospital attendant. 1970
Hunting and fishing guide. 1969
Lawyer. 1970
Marine corps. 1970
Radiologic technician. 1970
Travel counselor. 1970
Truck driver. 1967
Usher. 1970

Several collections of occupational briefs, reprints, and posters are described in the section "Package Purchases." One is called *Chronicle Occupational Library;* another *Chronicle's Ready Reference to Occupations.*

COWARD, McCANN and GEOGHEGAN, INC., 200 Madison Ave., New York, N.Y. 10016

The Colby Books. 65 titles. $3.29 each

In this series, written by Carroll B. Colby, numerous photographs and brief text provide an introduction to a wide variety of subjects. Some of the books give a picture of the training, equipment, and nature of the work done in a number of fields. These books are of special interest to boys in grades three through seven and to older, reluctant readers. They average forty-eight pages in length. This series has proved very popular with elementary grades. Some of the titles are:

Air Force Academy
Annapolis
Special Armed Forces
Coast Guard Academy
Communications
Countdown: rockets and missiles
Fish and wildlife
Night people
Our space age Navy
Park ranger
Smoke eaters
Soil savers
Trucks on the highway
West Point today

Let's Go Community Books. 21 books. $2.43 each

This publisher also distributes a series of books designed to make more meaningful the learning experience of classroom trips for grades one through three. They are prepared for reading as preparation for a trip or as an added interest-building exercise after returning to the classroom. Many of these books describe various kinds of work. They are not included in the main bibliography of this book, but typical of the titles are the following:

Let's go to a court. 1961
Let's go to a hospital. 1968
Let's go to a post office. 1964
Let's go to build a highway. 1970
Let's go to stop air pollution. 1969
Let's go to stop water pollution. 1969

Community Helper Series. 18 books. $2.68 each

This is a recent series designed for first and second graders who are applying their reading skills to learning about and identifying with their immediate environment. The subject matter is confined to very simple introductions to essential community services. All books are illustrated with color drawings and include helpful picture glossaries:

I know an airline pilot. 1969
I know an animal doctor. 1970
I know a baker. 1969
I know a dairyman. 1970
I know a farmer. 1970
I know a fireman. 1967
I know a garageman. 1968
I know a grocer. 1970
I know a mayor. 1967
I know a nurse. 1968
I know a policeman. 1967
I know a postman. 1967
I know a telephone operator. 1970
I know a truck driver. 1970

DODD, MEAD AND COMPANY, 79 Madison Avenue, New York, N.Y. 10016

Dodd, Mead Career Books. 33 books. $3 to $3.75 each

The Dodd, Mead career books have numbered over eighty, but many of them are now out of print. Some of them are fiction. Whereas the authors of some of the other series are professional writers trained in journalism, the writers of these books are required by the publisher to "have lived the careers they write about and be able to discuss them enthusiastically and with understanding." In addition, the authors of this series must have the special ability to evaluate their personal experiences and to use these to the advantage of readers who want sound advice.

Consequently, many of these books appear to be semiautobiographical. Reading about interviews or discussions of advantages and disadvantages of various types of work, one has the impression that the author is expressing his personal opinions gained from his own experience. The authors are also expressing the opinions of other successful career people in their respective fields, based on actual case records which are woven into the story. The plots may not hold the suspense of the traditional novel, but these books offer considerable occupational information.

The editors of this series have also stipulated that the titles chosen must be careers which offer "plenty of opportunities." As a result, practical rather than glamorous occupations are included in the series. For example, the titles include librarianship, physical therapy, and public relations, in addition to nursing. The following are examples of these career fiction titles:

Angela in public relations. 1964
I, the airline pilot. 1966
I, the lawyer. 1966
Janet Moore, physical therapist. 1965
Midshipman plowright. 1969
Nat Love, Negro cowboy. 1969
Susan, hospital aide. 1964
Vicky Barnes, candy striper. 1966

Juvenile Titles. 16 titles. $3.50; Dodd durable binding $3.23 each

Dodd, Mead and Company also publishes a series of juvenile titles, suitable for grades three to seven. By means of photographs and simple text, each portrays the work done in a variety of fields in a number of situations. The books are approximately sixty-four pages each. The titles include:

What does a airline crew do? 1965
What does an astronaut do? 1961
What does a coast guardsman do? 1968
What does a congressman do? 1965
What does a cowboy do? 1963
What does a driver do? 1961
What does a forest ranger do? 1964
What does a librarian do? 1963
What does an oceanographer do? 1970
What does a parachutist do? 1960
What does a Peace Corpsman do? 1964
What does a photographer do? 1965
What does a secret service agent do? 1962
What does a senator do? 1967
What does an UN soldier do? 1964
What does a veterinarian do? 1964

E. P. DUTTON AND COMPANY, INC., 201 Park Avenue South, New York, N.Y. 10003

Dutton Books on Careers. 24 books. $3.50 to $4.95 each

These books contain narrative descriptions of various fields of work and the opportunities for work in them. Although some of the books include biographical sketches of well-known people who have attained prominence in their specialty, the authors do not attempt to dramatize a few incidents in the lives of the workers; rather they aim to present detailed information about the various kinds of work, the qualifications, the promotional steps, and the opportunities. The books are illustrated.

This series contains thorough and penetrating information, yet is written in simple nontechnical language. It is suitable for the senior high school and the college student. Many of these books are double starred in this bibliography because of the quality and quantity of occupational information presented. The titles in this series include:

CAREERS AND OPPORTUNITIES IN OR FOR:

Accounting. 1965
Astronautics. 1969
Chemistry. 1960
Commercial art. 1963
Computer science. 1967
Fashion. 1964
How to get into college. 1967
International service. 1965
Journalism. 1966
Music. 1964
Sports. 1964
Teaching. 1969
Theatre. 1969
Women in business. 1963

FINNEY COMPANY, 3350 Gorham Avenue, Minneapolis, Minnesota 55426

Occupational Guidance Series: Five units with eight volumes in each unit and twenty monographs in each volume. $39.50 per unit

About two thirds of these titles have been prepared for students terminating their education with high school graduation and the other one third for students going on for additional training. Each monograph is four pages in length, size 8½ by 11 inches. In fairly simple language, the following topics are discussed briefly in each: Description of Work; earnings; history of occupation; working conditions; hours of work; ability required; temperament required; education and training required; finances required before earning; Financial aids; attractive features; disadvantages; outlook for the future; licensing, unions, organizations; suggested courses in high school; suggested high school activities; methods to enter work; free information material; purchasable material; visual aids; and testing your interests.

Each unit contains 160 job descriptions; the total number of titles covered is 800 and includes a wide range of occupations. An alphabetical index is available indicating which unit and volume contains a specific title. A display rack with pockets to accommodate the units is distributed by the publisher to stimulate reading and minimize supervision of the materials. Among the 800 titles are some unusual ones not frequently found in series of career briefs. Examples are:

Baseball umpire
Bridal consultant
Circus clown
Golf professional
Hearing aid consultant
House mover
Information desk clerk
Jail matron
jockey
Music arranger
Music critic
Ship's purser
Store detective
trapper
Travel agent
Weaver (repairing)

The *Occupational Guidance Workbook* is designed for use with the *Occupational Guidance* series and is intended to help students reach personal career decisions. $1.50 per copy.

Finding Your Job Series: Six units with five volumes in each unit and twelve monographs in each volume. $22.50 per unit

This series has been developed in response to the needs of students in special education classes. The publisher states that the materials are prepared for young people ". . . with limited attention spans, limited comprehensions and limited vocabularies."

One unit consists of job descriptions bound in sets of twelve, with five such books representative of a complete unit. One unit consists of sixty job descriptions of unskilled or semiskilled occupations, arranged in five volumes. The total number of titles covered is 360 and includes a wide range of occupations. An alphabetical index is available, indicating which unit and volume contains a specific job title. A display rack with pockets to accommodate the units is distributed by the publisher to stimulate reading and minimize supervision of the materials.

Each job description is four pages in length, size 8½ by 11 inches. The following topics are discussed briefly in simple language: The kind of job this is; what this job pays; what to expect; working hours; what a worker must be able to do; what a worker must be like; schooling needed; money needed before starting work; good things about this job; bad things about this job; what's ahead; groups to join; helpful subjects in school; things to do at school; ways to get this job; free information; books to buy; movies about this job; and is this the job for you?

The materials are presented in a manner easy to understand for the purpose of helping potential dropouts, slow learners, retarded children and special education classes consider specific jobs within their capabilities. The descriptions represent occupations requiring limited amounts of training, for example:

Bakery stock man
Busboy
Cafeteria server
Candy packer
Carhop
Car washer
Dog groomer
Farmhand
Florist's helper
Hospital cleaning lady
Hotel maid
Laundry marker
Messenger (telegraph)
Night watchman
Nurses' aide
Powder room attendant
Service station attendant
Stock clerk's helper

GOLDEN PRESS, Division of Western Publishing Company, Inc., 850 Third Avenue, New York, N.Y. 10022

"Busy People" Books. Six tall books, 6¾ by 16¼ inches. 69 cents each

The six titles listed below are the first in a series of tall picture books, sixteen inches tall, prepared for nursery school and kindergarten children. They contain vivid color illustrations of the uniforms, equipment, and some work-a-day activities, explained in simple caption texts. Each book contains 24 pages and has glossy hard covers.

The aim is to describe, very basically, different occupations and the duties of each, indicating that these workers are busy and helpful people.

Andy Astronaut. Illustrated by Leonard Shortail. 1968
Captain Charlie. Illustrated by Bill Dugan. 1968
Danny Driver. Illustrated by J. P. Miller. 1968
Fred Fireman. Illustrated by Joe Kaufman. 1968
Peter Policeman. Illustrated by Craig Pineo. 1968
Zeke Zookeeper. Illustrated by Joe Kaufman. 1968

GUIDANCE CENTRE, The College of Education, University of Toronto, 1000 Yonge Street, Toronto 289, Ontario, Canada

Guidance Centre Occupational Information Monographs. 195 monographs. Speical quantity prices. Single copies are 25c plus 15% handling and delivery charges, postpaid

These monographs present information about workers in Canada. Each monograph is prepared by an authority actively associated with the occupation under consideration and checked by the centre's research staff before publication. Each booklet starts with a short definition of the occupational title and gives information under the following headings: history and importance; nature of the work; working conditions; qualifications necessary for entry and success; preparation needed; employment; advancement; outlook; remuneration; related occupations; advantages; disadvantages; how to get started toward the occupation; and sources of additional information.

Four pages in length, containing from 2,500 and 3,500 words, they are printed on heavy, coated stock. One picture is used in each monograph. The information on employment opportunities and wages is based on Canadian statistics; certain sections of many of the monographs apply equally to Canada and the United States.

The monographs are revised about every three years. A check list and order form is updated and republished bimonthly October to June. School guidance workers may obtain, without charge, copies of the check list in any desired quantity for distribution to students. All orders coming from outside of Canada must be accompanied by a complete remittance.

There are 195 titles included in the following pages. Typical examples are:

Accountant. 1968
Auctioneer. 1969
Auto mechanic. 1968
Baker. 1969
Beekeeper. 1966
Bricklayer. 1969
Court reporter. 1969
Electronic technician. 1969
Horticulturist. 1966
Medical laboratory technologist. 1969
Mushroom grower. 1968
Oil-burner serviceman. 1966
Truck farmer. 1969
Woodworker. 1969

J. B. LIPPINCOTT COMPANY, East Washington Square, Philadelphia, Pennsylvania 19105

Informal Vocational Studies by John J. Floherty. 15 books. $3.00 to $4.95 each

Most of these are dramatic stories about the work of men in adventurous and hazardous occupations. The excitement and heroism behind the scenes are described in the daring exploits of the secret service men, policemen, fire fighters, Coast Guardsmen and other sentries of the sea. Mr. Floherty is a good reporter and his accounts are full of human interest stories. For example, to gather the material for books about the Coast Guard, he visited many of the Coast Guard stations and accompanied the men on a number of their expeditions. All facts were taken from the official records of the United States Coast Guard.

These books describe many kinds of work and the daring, danger, and adventure implicit in them. They do not contain discussion of the employment outlook, supply and demand of workers, or training. They seem to be intended for the general reader more than the aspiring career inquirer. However, they are useful because they are well liked by high school boys, especially in grades 8 to 11. Also, they are supplemented by excellent action photographs taken by the authors.

Some of the recent books have been written by or with Mike McGrady. Examples of titles in this series are:

Aviation from the ground up. 1960
Behind the silver shield. 1957
Crime scientists. 1961
Man against earth. 1961
Skin-diving adventures. 1962
Rockets, missiles and space. 1962
Whirling wings. 1961
Youth and the F.B.I. 1960

MACMILLAN COMPANY, 866 Third Avenue, New York, N.Y. 10022

Macmillan Career Books. 10 titles. $3.50, $3.95 and $4.95 each

This series contains rather full information as the books average about two hundred pages in length. They have been prepared by authors who have been successful in their careers and who are enthusiastic about helping young people avoid mistakes in choosing a profession. The general editor of the series is Charles W. Cole, former president of Amherst College. Each book includes a description of the history and importance of the career, duties, an average working day, personal characteristics and abilities needed, education and necessary preparation, kinds of work possible, rewards, and possible future developments in the field. Many of the books point to the tremendously varied opportunities open to the person with the necessary training. They are intended for the mature high school student as well as the college student. Though older than many of the other series, these books are especially well written.

Architect. 1962
Career diplomat. 1964
Journalist. 1962
Lawyer. 1961
Minister. 1963
Nurse. 1962
Physician. 1961
Professor. 1961
Scientist. 1964
Social worker. 1964

JULIAN MESSNER, a division of Simon and Schuster, Inc., 1 West 39th St., New York, N.Y. 10018

Career Romances for Young Moderns. 23 books. $3.50 each

These books combine adventurous romance fiction with facts about careers. The information about the kinds of work, qualifications, advantages, disadvantages, promotional steps, and working conditions of a special career is interwoven into the conversations of the main characters. One gets a feeling of the way of life of people engaged in the kind of work described. These fictionalized tales, therefore, may stimulate the reader to search for additional information of a more factual type. The plot and love theme usually are sufficiently strong to lure teen-age readers into reading several of the books, with the result that they receive some information about several fields of work.

In this series, the occupational information is exceptionally accurate and authentic. Well over half of the titles have been published since 1965. A few typical titles are:

Beth Donnis: Speech therapist. 1968
County agent. 1968
Flair for fashion. 1967
Jet stewardess. 1962
Navy nurse. 1968
Stephanie Lane: Editorial secretary. 1967
The young medics. 1968

Messner Biographies. 250 books. $3.95 each; Messner certified edition $3.64 each

The Messner biographies number more than 250 books. Uniform in size, 5⅝ by 8½ inches, clothbound, 192 pages in length, they are attractively printed and written for junior and senior high school boys and girls. They introduce young people to the personalities and achievements of men and women in many fields of endeavor and serve as inspirational reading for teen-agers. Many of them illustrate the triumphs over handicaps and frustrations. Biographies and autobiographies of successful workers have long been recognized as being a rich and stimulating branch of literature for those seeking knowledge about an occupation. Career fiction and inspirational accounts have, as many teachers and counselors will testify, an exceedingly useful function in stimulating the imagination and enthusiasm of the individual who has not seriously considered certain occupations. Many times, the young workers-to-be will learn to approach work as a satisfying way of life and to take courage from the early struggles of people they admire. In the publisher's catalog, each title is followed by symbols indicating recommendations in sources as the *Booklist, Library Journal, Standard Catalog, Children's Catalog,* etc. Following are examples of these biographies:

Battlefield president: Dwight D. Eisenhower. 1967
Discoverer of X-ray: Wilhelm Conrad Rontgen. 1968
Fighting journalist: Horace Greeley. 1966
Genius with a scalpel: Harvey Cushing. 1971
Incredible man of science: Irving Langmuir. 1968
Labor's advocate: Eugene V. Debs. 1966
Pioneer in blood plasma: Dr. Charles Drew. 1968
Plant detective: David Douglas. 1966
Science explorer: Roy Chapman Andrews. Revised 1968
The Sherlock Holmes of medicine: Dr. Joseph Goldberger. 1969
Spokesman for the free world: Adlai E. Stevenson. 1967

Messner Career Books. 35 books. Cloth $4.50 each; Messner certified edition $4.29

This is another series of nonfiction career books that is comprehensive in scope and presents a well-rounded picture of the various careers. These books offer practical advice on specific occupations with guides to colleges and schools for special training, salary range, growth opportunities, personal qualifications, and future outlook. Each contains photographs, bibliographies, sources of additional information, and index. The titles include:

Beauty as a career. 1969
Careers in biological science. 1968
Careers in the legal profession. 1970
Careers in social service. 1969
Careers in horticultural sciences. 1969
Careers in hotel management. 1971
Exciting careers for home economists. 1967
On the job training and where to get it. 1967
Wall Street careers. 1968
Your career in the aerospace industry. 1966
Your career in computer programming. 1967
Your career in film making. 1969
Your career in interior design. 1969
Your career in oceanology. 1968
Your career in parks and recreation. 1970
Your career in the world of travel. 1971

Books for Personal Counseling. 7 books. Cloth $3.95 and $4.95 each; Messner certified edition $3.64 and $4.64 each

Drugs and you. 1971
Teen-age diet book. Revised 1969
What about teen-age marriage? 1961

You and today's troubled world: talks to urban youth. 1970
Your career—if you're not going to college. Revised 1971
Your college education—how to pay for it. 1968
Your handicap—don't let it handicap you. 1967
Your personality and you. 1965

MICHIGAN EMPLOYMENT SECURITY COMMISSION, 7310 Woodward Avenue, Detroit, Michigan 48202

Job Briefs. 107 briefs. Free

The objective of the series is the presentation of accurate and authentic job information for the vocational guidance of youth and the placement of workers on jobs better suited to their abilities. In its employment work, the Commission found that one of the greatest weaknesses in vocational guidance programs has been the lack of up-to-date and reliable information about jobs. Consequently, it is trying to supply that need by providing occupational information necessary for wiser occupational choices.

Most of the briefs include the nature of the work, location of jobs, employment outlook, working conditions, earnings, requirements for entry, and references for further reading.

The briefs are prepared mainly from occupational information collected in Michigan. However, materials and publications from other areas are used in their preparation. Most of the information in each guide is applicable to other areas, especially nature of the work, requirements for entry, training needed, advantages, and disadvantages. However, the reader should realize that salaries, number of workers, and employment outlook apply chiefly to Michigan.

These briefs are objective and contain factual information for the use of employment interviewers as well as counselors. They are the result of careful research. Personal opinion is kept to a minimum. There is a limitation on the number distributed in states other than Michigan, but the job briefs may be reproduced in full without prior permission. Examples of titles are:

Airplane mechanic. 1967
Automotive draftsmen. 1965
Barber. 1960
Carpenter. 1966
Dental hygienist. 1967
Millwright. 1967

PARK PUBLISHING HOUSE, 516 Viewridge Drive, Angwin, California 94508

Vocational Monographs. 18 booklets. $1 each

Written by a former vocational educator and counselor, the monographs in this series are revised about every two years. Averaging twenty to thirty pages in length, the uniform size is six by nine inches. The price is $1 each.

The uniform outline followed in most of the monographs covers definition of the career, history, importance, nature of work, training, entrance requirements, expenses, qualifications, licensure, conditions of work, advancement, income, advantages, disadvantages, opportunities, where employed, how to begin, employment outlook, associations, and suggestions for further reading. Where appropriate, the requirements for licensure are given in detail and lists of accredited schools are included.

About half of the titles are those of professional careers; the other half requiring less preparation. For example:

Barber. 1969
Chiropractic. 1969
Cook-chef. 1969
Dental assistant. 1969
Funeral services. 1968
Hotel-motel housekeeper. 1968
Medical assistant. 1969
Nurse aide. 1969
Podiatry. 1969
Practical nurse. 1969
Receptionist. 1969
Waiter-waitress. 1966

PRATT INSTITUTE, Communications Department, De Kalb Avenue and Hall Street, Brooklyn, N.Y. 11205

Career Briefs. Free

These four-page illustrated leaflets are published as an educational service by Pratt Institute. They are devoted to timely information about a particular area of work for which the Institute offers career preparation. Curriculums leading to the bachelor's degree are offered in architecture, art education, advertising design, food science and management, fashion design and merchandising, chemistry, computer science, mathematics, physics, building science and chemical, electrical, industrial, and mechanical engineering. Transfer students may earn bachelor's degrees in humanities or social science in Pratt's Senior College. Sixteen master's programs are offered in architecture and urban planning, art and design, library and information science and engineering and science.

The briefs, punched for a ring binder, contain information on personal qualifications, preparation, a typical day's work and opportunities. The issues go out of print shortly after they are published and the titles are not listed here. However, the career briefs will be sent upon publication to any counselor or librarian who requests that his name be added to the mailing list. Requests should be addressed to the Editor, Career Briefs, Communications Department, Pratt Institute, Brooklyn, N.Y. 11205.

RICHARDS ROSEN PRESS, 29 East 21st Street, New York, N.Y. 10010

"Careers in Depth" Series. 93 books. $4 each; granite library edition, $3.78

The "Careers in Depth" series consists of full-book information on each of ninety-three careers. To help the reader determine whether the career would be a realistic choice, the authors present information to encourage one to weigh his own capabilities and ambitions in light of the requirements, advantages, and drawbacks of such work. A self-evaluation test is part of each book with questions which will lead to an analysis of one's abilities and interests. Each book of 160 pages contains description of the various kinds of work and specializations, desirable personal qualities, training, preparation, earnings, opportunities, related careers, and suggested reading material.

One strong feature of this series is that the books have been written recently, since 1960; and twenty-five were prepared in 1968 or 1969. The books published prior to 1965 were revised in 1969. Each has been written by a prominent man or woman who has been successful in his field of endeavor. Each stresses what the work requires and what it offers and gives special attention to educational facilities for training and what to expect during the period of preparation. This series contains few photographs. The publisher's catalog indicates which of the trade or professional associations or library reviewing publications have recommended each of the ninety-three career books.

YOUR FUTURE IN (OR AS):

Beauty business. 1969
Drafting. 1967
Fashion design. 1966
International service. 1969
Jobs abroad. 1968
Merchant marine. 1968
Museums. 1967
NASA. 1969
Nursery industry. 1966
Shortland reporter. 1969

Aim High Vocational Guidance Series. 14 books, $4 each; library edition $3.78

A new series has been initiated to provide career information for students not pursuing their education beyond high school. Special consideration is given to the high school dropouts by using especially selected vocabularies. The jobs available at the beginning level are described, followed by information concerning the increasingly better jobs with additional training and incentives. Announced are the following:

Air conditioning and refrigeration. 1968
Appliance service. 1969
Automotive service. 1968
Building trades. 1969
Graphic design art. 1968
Hospital jobs. 1968
Iron and steel industry. 1967
Pipe trades. 1969
Restaurants and food service. 1969
Textile industry. 1969

Arco-Rosen Career Guidance Series. 40 titles. $1.95 each

In cooperation with the Arco Publishing Company, forty of the "Careers in Depth" series are available in a special paperback edition at $1.95 each; complete set of forty titles $59.95. Examples are:

Air conditioning
Automotive service
Bakery industry
Beauty culture
Forestry
Medical technology
Oceanography
Restaurants and food service

ROCHESTER INSTITUTE OF TECHNOLOGY, Department of Public Relations, 65 Plymouth Avenue South, Rochester, N.Y. 14608

The Vocational Guidance Series. 10 titles. Free

These career bulletins are written to give information to prospective students about some of the fields of work for which the institute offers technological education. Authors of the pamphlets are members of the institute faculty.

There is a minimum amount of recruiting material. Information is given about the various branches of the vocation, the duties performed by persons employed, requirements for employment, wages, promotions, advantages, and disadvantages of employment in that field. An illuminating feature of certain pamphlets is a job chart prepared to aid students in visualizing the kinds of beginning jobs in those fields, as well as the kinds of jobs to which successful persons may be promoted. The chart also lists the training or beginning jobs, the intermediate jobs, and related and supplementary jobs to which persons with demonstrated ability, maturity, and experience may be promoted. The terminal jobs are those for which the curriculum does not specifically train but which may be attained by demonstrating special aptitudes and by profiting by experience and self-training.

The pamphlets are attractively bound in heavy paper covers, size 5½ by 7½ inches. They average about twenty-four pages. Considerable pertinent information is clearly presented. The titles include:

Careers in biology. 1966
Careers in business. 1963
Careers in chemistry. 1965
Careers in engineering. 1966
Careers in food services administration. 1966
Careers in photography. 1965
Careers in printing. 1965
Careers in retailing. 1963

SCIENCE RESEARCH ASSOCIATES, INC., 259 East Erie Street, Chicago, Illinois 60611

SRA Guidance Service Subscription Plan. Quarterly mailings $43.50 per year

Several kits and sets of materials are described in the appropriate sections of this book and in the section on "Package Purchases." The

SRA Guidance Service is a comprehensive subscription plan aimed to keep the counselor informed of the latest developments in academic, vocational, and personal guidance. The materials are mailed quarterly during the school year in September, November, January, and March. The components for a school year are 114 assorted guidance materials, 80 occupational briefs, 16 research reports, 8 guidance posters, 4 newsletters, 6 texts and booklets for pupil and professional use, and special prepublication bonus materials.

SRA Occupational Briefs. 400 titles. Complete set $83.50. Single copies 45c each. For 50 or more, 37c each

These illustrated briefs, four pages in length, contain information on 400 major occupations, which the publishers state represent the jobs held by 95 per cent of today's work force. For the most part, the titles are the base titles to which code numbers have been assigned in the *Dictionary of Occupational Titles.* Each brief includes a description of a specific kind of work, qualifications, training required, earnings, working conditions, and future employment outlook. Usually two authorities in trade associations or professional societies are named who have checked the information for accuracy.

The briefs each contain two illustrations. The occupational title and code number are placed on the side and upper right hand corner, for convenience in filing. They are of uniform size, 8½ by 11 inches. Titles are being revised constantly. Examples of titles are:

Airline dispatchers. 1969
Apartment house janitors. 1969
Bowling machine mechanics. 1969
Caterers. 1966
Composers. 1967
Correspondence clerks. 1969
Doormen. 1966
Economists. 1970
Foremen. 1967
Laborers. 1969
Mail carriers. 1969
Newsstand vendors. 1966
Pest control operators. 1965
Press photographers. 1969
Scene designers. 1967
Scriptwriters. 1967
Typists. 1970
Union business agents. 1967

SRA Junior Occupational Briefs. 400 titles. Complete set $89.50. Single copies 45c. For 50 or more, 37c each

These briefs for junior high school readers contain appealing stories about selected occupations. By encouraging young people to picture themselves in a variety of jobs, the aim is to broaden their occupational interests and orient their estimates of educational needs in terms of the career choices they must make at the appropriate time in later years. The first page of each brief contains a colored illustration. The two inside pages contain the narrative in which the worker throws some light on the kind of work he is doing, and its service to the community. The last page carries in capsule form some important facts about the job, in very simple language, under the headings: required education, high school courses, training, location of jobs, getting started, getting ahead, hours of work, earnings, number of workers, future labor requirements, and other ways of finding out about the job. There are usually only two or three sentences under each heading. They are suitable for grades 6 through 9 or for older reluctant readers.

This series is contained in the kit called the SRA Widening Occupational Roles Kit (WORK), which includes student workbooks, junior guidance booklets, and a teacher's handbook with detailed procedures for putting the program into operation. Total cost of kit is $141.75. The publisher will send a complete list of available titles to those requesting it. Typical titles are:

Bakers. 1967
Broadcast technicians. 1967
Building service workers. 1967
Chefs. 1967
Divers. 1967
Doormen. 1967
Draftsmen. 1967
Factory assemblers. 1967
Fishermen. 1967
Guards and watchmen. 1967
Hotel maids. 1967
Janitors. 1967
Lathers. 1967
Linemen. 1967
Mailing service workers. 1967
Parking attendants. 1967
Ship pilots. 1967
Shipping clerks. 1967
Sightseeing guides. 1967
Travel agents. 1967
Tree experts. 1967
Wildlife managers. 1967

SRA Guidance Series Booklets. 57 booklets. 75c each. Complete set $35

These booklets, prepared for young people by specialists in the various fields, aim to help them solve their problems in many areas—educational, social, personal, and vocational. Recommended especially for group work, they include such topics as adjusting to school, getting along with others, boy-girl relations, understanding and solving personal problems, learning how to study, how to take tests, and how to stay in college.

They are written in a simple style to appeal to teen-agers, are attractively bound in variously colored bright covers, and make considerable use of visual aids. There is a wide range of titles, including the following:

Facts about venereal disease. 1969
Finding part-time jobs. 1968
Getting along with others. 1969
How to live with parents. 1967
What tests can tell you about you. 1969
Understanding love. 1969
Understanding yourself. 1966
What good is high school? 1968

SEXTANT SYSTEMS, INC., 3048 North 34th Street, Milwaukee, Wisconsin 53210

Sextant Series for Exploring Your Future. 16 books. Complete set $159.50. Separate volumes $8.95. Wall charts $1.50 each. Library set of 16 volumes $110; 12 volumes $82.50

Each book in this series combines job descriptions with a method of "personal profiling" designed to give each student a more personal relationship with the jobs described. Each set contains one hundred personal profile forms for individual pupil use. Each book has 75 to 110 job descriptions and an organizational chart for the industry showing the students "where they can start and where they can go." Additional copies of the profile forms are available at $9.50 per hundred. Accompanying the set are a teacher's manual and instructions for use with opaque or transparency projectors.

One page is devoted to each of ninety-five jobs in each book, presenting the employment duties, requirements for entering, promotional outlook, and the pay and skill levels. Each book is approximately ninety-six pages long, size 8½ by 11 inches. Some users of this series report that they like it because of the profiling activity on the part of the student and others because of the simplicity of the career information. Description of other materials, used with this series in career planning, with price lists, will be sent upon request. Titles now available, with copyright dates, are:

EXPLORING YOUR FUTURE IN:

Air transportation. 1970
Agriculture. 1971
Banking. 1970
Construction. 1971
Graphic arts and publishing. 1971
Hospitals. 1971
Hotels and restaurants. 1971
Insurance. 1971
Manufacturing—salaried. 1968
Manufacturing—wage. 1970
Merchandising. 1970
Motor transporation. 1970
Professions. 1970
Protective agencies. 1970
Public utilities. 1971
Recreation, parks, and youth services. 1971

SMALL BUSINESS ADMINISTRATION, Office of Procurement and Management Assistance, Washington, D.C. Order from Supt. of Documents, Government Printing Office, Washington, D.C. 20402

Starting-and-Managing Series. 19 booklets. 25c to 60c each

This series consists of publications containing directions on how to establish various small businesses and service establishments in specific fields. The booklets cover opportunities, risks, problems involved, and suggestions to help the prospective owner-manager decide whether he can wisely enter the field. Practical standards are offered by which one can measure his personal qualifications and prospects of success, as well as gain an understanding of the operating problems involved. Considerable technical information is included, with suggestions concerning shop management, equipment, operating costs, captial outlay, location, legal requirements, and management practices whose application is necessary for the attainment of success.

Additional titles are announced for future publication at irregular intervals. Each will take the viewpoint of the prospective owner-manager and include suggestions for starting and managing a specific kind of small business. Some titles are:

STARTING AND MANAGING A SMALL:

Automatic vending business. 1967. 30c
Bookkeeping service. 1962. 30c
Carwash. 1967. 35c
Dry cleaning business. 1966. 35c
Duplicating and mailing service. 1963. 25c
Motel. 1963. 30c
Pet shop. 1970. 30c
Restaurant. 1964. 45c
Retail flower shop. 1970. 55c
Retail camera shop. 1969. 40c
Service station. 1961. 35c
Swap shop. 1968. 35c
Shoe service. 1968. 45c

STATE OF CALIFORNIA DEPARTMENT OF EMPLOYMENT, 800 Capitol Mall, Sacramento, California 95814

Occupational Guide Series. 413 guides. Single copies free

California occupational guides are designed primarily for vocational counseling in the department's local placement offices and in the state's secondary school system. Each guide is produced according to a prescribed pattern. Questionnaires are mailed to employers. The data secured are then summarized and added to other available information. Wage and other statistical data are the result of a broadly based sampling of employers' returns.

This series contains unusually clear descriptions of the nature of work and duties. Current information also is given on working conditions, employment outlook, wages, hours, promotional and training requirements, and how to find the job. Much of the information is applicable to many states. It clearly shows the result of an exceptionally broad research and statistical program.

Each guide consists of from two to eight printed 8½- by 11-inch sheets, stapled and punched for loose-leaf filing. The program is a continuing one. Each guide is revised periodically.

The department does not send multiple copies outside the state, but an interested enquirer may request a single copy of any one title.

Because the series now covers 413 titles, it includes material on many occupations found in few other publications, such as:

Employment counselor. 1967
Gunsmith. 1965
Job analyst. 1966
Outboard motor repairman. 1967
Plumber. 1965
Routeman. 1964
Sanitarian. 1968
Shipping clerk. 1968
Ski instructor. 1968
Swimming pool service technician. 1968
Telephone answering service operator. 1968
Sport fishing captain. 1968

UNITED STATES CIVIL SERVICE COMMISSION, Washington, D.C. 20415

The U.S. Civil Service Commission publishes several booklets describing the opportunities available in the Federal Government. For the most part, they contain information concerning the kinds of work, application procedures, requirements, advantages, and salary ranges. Single copies of publications for which no price is listed may be requested from the Commission; others are available at the prices listed from the Superintendent of Documents, Government Printing Office, Washington, D.C. 20402.

Some of the booklets described in the appropriate annotated sections of this book are as follows:

Federal careers for women. 1967. 10c
Federal career directory. 1968. $1.25
Federal jobs overseas. 1965. 10c
Federal office assistant examinations. 1964. 40c
Futures in the Federal Government. 1967. 20c
Go Government. 1968. Free
New directions: career opportunities for computer specialists in the Federal Government. 1969. Free
Occupations of Federal white-collar workers. 1968. $1.25
Opportunities for returning Peace Corps volunteers. 1969. 5c
Opportunities in trades and crafts with the Federal Government. 1964. Free
Science and engineering careers in Government. 1968. 35c
Summer jobs in Federal agencies. 1969. Free
Thinking about your first job? 1968. 10c

UNITED STATES DEPARTMENT OF LABOR, BUREAU OF LABOR STATISTICS

Occupational Outlook Handbook. 1970-71 Edition. Bulletin No. 1650. 859p. $6.25. Order from Supt. of Documents, U.S. Government Printing Office, Washington, D.C. 20402

The ninth revised edition of this Handbook is the most comprehensive source of occupational and industry career information available. Prepared every two years by the Bureau of Labor Statistics, it provides information on the nature of work, long-term employment outlook, and related topics for over seven hundred occupations and thirty major industries.

It is designed for use in counseling young people, veterans, and others in the choice of a career or course of training. The subtitle of the previous editions has been "Employment Information on Occupations for Use in Guidance." Based on information gathered from industry, labor organizations, trade organizations, trade associations, professional societies, Government agencies, and some educational institutions, it draws upon an extensive program of research in industrial and occupational trends in the United States. It discusses many future trends and conditions which are likely to affect employment outlook in the decade ahead. Based upon the extensive manpower research program of the Bureau of Labor Statistics, the long-range projections for each occupation include, for example, a discussion of employment growth and number of workers needed to take care of death, retirement, and transfers out of the occupation.

The occupations include the professions; skilled trades; clerical, sales, and service occupations; selected agricultural occupations; and occupations in government. Each report describes the nature of work, training and qualifications required, earnings, working conditions, and employment outlook. The first chapter, "Tomorrow's Jobs," provides a graphic overview of where people work today, what the manpower needs of tomorrow will be, and describes the supply of workers. An alphabetical index to occupations contains many cross-references. The book is illustrated with 310 photographs and 40 charts.

Congress in 1955 provided for a program of regular reappraisal of the employment outlook and for the maintenance of the *Occupational Outlook Handbook* and its related publications on an up-to-date basis. This action made possible the biennial revision of the handbook as well as the initiation of the periodical, the *Occupational Outlook Quarterly,* which is issued four times annually to provide a flow of current information between editions of the handbook.

Most of the reports and reprints are listed and annotated in this bibliography, because the information on employment trends and outlook contained therein is outstanding.

Reprints from the 1970-71 Occupational Outlook Handbook. 119 reprints. 5c to 20c each. $9.25 a set

One hundred and nineteen sections of the *Occupational Outlook Handbook,* separately bound, are available from the Superintendent of Documents. These reprints vary in length from two to twenty-four pages and range in price from 5c to 20c. A complete set of the 119 reprints may be obtained for $9.25.

The reprints of the various chapters are designed for use by the following:

Individuals interested in a particular field of work.
Industry, labor, or professional organizations desiring a supply of the chapters to inform the public about their fields.
Schools and other counseling organizations needing many copies of chapters on industries important in their communities.
Libraries desiring individual sections for their occupational vertical files.
Counselors who want extra copies of chapters to lend to persons interested in various fields.
Teachers who want publications on the career opportunities in fields related to their subjects.

Because of the importance of this series, all of the 119 reprints have been annotated in the appropriate sections of this book and most of them are double starred as being most highly recommended. A 25 per cent discount is given on orders of 100 or more copies of any single publication. A check or money order should be drawn payable to the Superintendent of Documents; no stamps are accepted.

Occupational Outlook Excerpts. 7 briefs. Free

Seven major occupational groups are described in excerpts from the 1970-71 edition of the *Occupational Outlook Handbook.* Contained in these reports in addition to occupational definitions, are national employment figures for the groups and for subdivisions of the groups. The necessary training requirements, chances for advancement, and employment outlook are reviewed. Some of the briefs include lists of further sources of information. While the supply lasts, the following excerpts are available from the regional offices of the Bureau of Labor Statistics:

Clerical and related occupations
Health service occupations
Managerial occupations
Professional and related occupations
Sales occupations
Service occupations
Skilled and other manual occupations

UNITED STATES DEPARTMENT OF LABOR, WAGE AND LABOR STANDARDS ADMINISTRATION, WOMEN'S BUREAU, Washington, D.C. 20210

Publications for which a price is indicated may be purchased from the Superintendent of Documents, U.S. Government Printing Office, Washington, D.C. 20402, at prices listed, with a discount of 25 per cent on orders of 100 copies or more of any single publication. Single copies of all Women's Bureau publications may be obtained from the Women's Bureau without charge.

The Women's Bureau has prepared a wide variety of pamphlets, bulletins, brochures, reports, leaflets, and fact sheets concerned with women's job opportunities. They also cover earnings, employment, legal status, labor laws, continuing education and training, counseling and guidance, discrimination in employment, standards for working conditions, day care for working mothers, and related subjects.

Some of these publications describe trends in occupations for which training at the college level prepares women. These reports are concerned primarily with changes and developments that affect the outlook for women's employment. A recent series of leaflets covers career opportunities often overlooked by women, such as mathematics, pharmacy, and optometry.

The publications provide information not only on the job outlook and opportunities for advancement, but also on training requirements, qualifications, job duties, conditions of employment, and earnings. They give minimum requirements to enter approved schools for training and for completion of approved courses, and note related professional associations.

Publications vary in size and many have appropriate illustrations. They provide up-to-date information based upon extensive research. They are recommended most highly. Some of the publications issued by the Women's Bureau are described on the following pages.

Why Not Be? Series. 10 leaflets. 5c and 10c each. Order from Supt. of Documents, Government Printing Office, Washington, D.C. 20402

In this series of ten leaflets, eight pages in length, illustrated, each contains brief sketches of the nature of work, duties, where employed, qualifications, earnings, and opportunities. They aim to encourage girls to consider indicated careers, at the same time pointing out the variety of exciting fields available. They suggest the qualifications needed and offer sources of further information.

WHY NOT BE (A OR AN):

Apprentice? Leaflet 52. 1970. In press
Conservation specialist? Leaflet 50. 1969. 10c
Engineer? Leaflet 41. 1967. 5c
Mathematician? Leaflet 45. 1968. 10c
Medical technologist? Leaflet 44. 1968. 10c
Optometrist? Leaflet 42. 1968. 10c
Pharmacist? Leaflet 43. 1968. 10c
Personnel specialist? Leaflet 48. 1968. 10c
Public relations worker? Leaflet 46. 1970. 10c
Technical writer? Leaflet 47. 1968. 5c

Career Opportunities for Women. Order from Supt. of Documents, Government Printing Office, Washington, D.C. 20402

Automation and women workers. 1970. In press
Continuing education programs and services for women. 1968. 40c

Expanding opportunities for girls. 1969. Free
Fact sheet on women in professional and technical positions. 1968. Free
Job horizons for college women. 1967. 35c
Job training suggestions for women and girls. 1968. 10c
Jobfinding techniques for mature women. 1970. 30c
Negro women in the population and in the labor force. 1967. 30c
1969 handbook on women workers. 1968. $1
Why women work? 1970. In press

VETERANS ADMINISTRATION, Forms and Publications Depot, Arlington, Virginia 22206

Career Pamphlets. 13 pamphlets. Free

The Veterans Administration has prepared a number of pamphlets giving information about the occupations in which they are recruiting workers. These pamphlets describe the opportunities for service, the nature of the work, educational and experience requirements, promotional possibilities, employment benefits, and procedure for making application.

With attractive colored covers, varying in size and in length from four to twenty-four pages, these pamphlets are generously illustrated. They are addressed primarily to the experienced professional workers and recent college graduates, although some are intended to provide health career information to high school and college students. The pamphlets listed below may be requested in small quantities from the address given above provided the number listed below is cited:

Audiologist and speech pathologist. Pamphlet No. 10-69
Dietitian. Pamphlet No. 10-55
Engineer and architect. Pamphlet 05-15
Librarian. Pamphlet No. 10-61
Manual arts therapist. Pamphlet 10-64
Nurse. Pamphlet No. 10-30
Occupational therapist. Pamphlet No. 10-58
Pharmacist. Pamphlet No. 10-62
Physical therapist. Pamphlet No. 10-59
Physician. Pamphlet No. 10-35
Practical nurse. Pamphlet No. 10-52
Psychologist. Pamphlet No. 10-57
Social Worker. Pamphlet No. 10-56

The series of publications listed below was prepared for use in the vocational rehabilitation, and also in education programs of the Veterans Administration. Number and title are needed when ordering from the Superintendent of Documents, U.S. Government Printing Office, Washington, D.C. 20402.

VA Pamphlet	Title	
7-10	Occupations of totally blinded veterans of WW II and Korea, 1956	25c
7-12	Occupations of paraplegic veterans of WW II and Korea, 1957	35c
22-6	Occupations of epileptic veterans of WW II and Korean Conflict, 1960	40c
22-9	They return to work—the job adjustment of psychiatrically disabled veterans of WW II and Korean Conflict. 1963	70c
21-64-1	Educational assistance for sons and daughters of disabled veterans	Free
21-65-1	To work again—to live again 1965	45c
20-67-1	Summary of benefits for veterans with service since January 31, 1955, and their dependents	Free

VOCATIONAL GUIDANCE MANUALS, a Division of Universal Publishing and Distributing Corporation, 235 East 45th Street, New York 17, N.Y. 10017

Vocational Guidance Manuals. 50 manuals. $1.95 each, less educational and library discounts. Clothbound library editions, $3.75 each

Averaging 120 pages in length, these manuals present a comprehensive picture of the vocations covered. About half of the space in each manual is devoted to technical information of interest to a beginner in the field, to methods of getting started, and to steps to advancement. In the remaining half, there are descriptions of the types of work, requirements, educational preparation, opportunities, and qualifications for success. In most of them there is a full discussion of the desirable and undesirable aspects and the future prospects. They are complete with glossaries, lists of approved schools, apprentice opportunities, high school and college requirements, names of trade and professional associations, publications, bibliographies, and indexes. For the most part, the bibliographies have been prepared for the reader in quest of technical information and do not include many references to the occupational literature.

In each volume a biographical note about the author establishes his intimate acquaintance with the occupation described. The publishers apparently seek authors who are experienced writers in the fields in which they also have held executive positions. For example, Shepard Henkin, author of the manual on public relations, is a former director of public relations for the Hotel New Yorker; Richard Pack (radio) has been director of publicity of WOR; Dick Moore (acting) is editor of *Equity Magazine;* and John Barry (newspaper careers) is the assistant editor of the *Guild Reporter.*

The variously colored bright covers, containing interesting designs symbolic of the specific careers, add to their attractiveness. Each title is available in both the regular paperbound edition and the clothbound library edition. Many of the earlier books have been revised. Among the fifty included in this bibliography are the following titles:

Architecture. 1966
Drafting. 1967
Food preparation and service. 1969
Graphic arts. 1968
Physical therapy. 1968
Speech pathology. 1968
Textile industry. 1966
Traffic engineering. 1966
Technical writing. 1964
Veterinary medicine. 1965

HENRY Z. WALCK, INC., 19 Union Square West, New York, N.Y. 10003

Careers for Tomorrow Series. 25 books. $4.50 each; institutional discounts to schools and libraries

This series of nonfiction books is about careers of interest to senior high school and college students. The books are written by authorities in their professions. The publisher's catalog lists the reviewing agencies which have recommended each of the twenty-five books. They contain good descriptions of work in the specializations within the broad categories, many case studies of people in the field, and detailed descriptions of a typical day's work. Personality and temperament factors, opportunities, and trends are also given special attention. The books average 108 pages in length and have a uniform grey-blue cover. Each book has an index and a recommended reading list.

This series contains a limited amount of factual career data such as supply and demand, salaries, outlook, and disadvantages, but stresses the environment within which the individual works. The descriptions of the major kinds of specializations and the various types of employment potentialities are forthrightly presented. There are about twenty half-page illustrations in each book. This is one of the more recent series, beginning in 1961.

Building trades. 1969
Biological sciences. 1963
Business management. 1964
College teaching. 1965
Computer programming. 1967
Foreign languages. 1963
Government. 1964
Hotels and restaurants. 1967
Music. 1968
Natural resource conservation. 1965
Public planning. 1967
Social work. 1965

FRANKLIN WATTS, INC., 845 Third Avenue, New York, N.Y. 10022

"The Professions and What They Do" Books. 15 books. $3.95 each; Watts guaranteed library bindings, $2.63 net

The purpose of this group of books, as announced by the publisher, is "to give information about the inner workings of a profession as well as the qualities, training, and experience to enter and succeed in that occupation." They are written with the grades 7 through 10 in mind. They average 196 pages. The words "and what they do" follow the name of the career and indicate the special feature of this series:

Archaeologists. 1960
Anthropologists. 1965
Clergy. 1961
Foresters. 1963
Forest fire fighters. 1962
Geographers. 1964
Lawyers. 1965
Nuclear submarine skippers. 1962
Nurses. 1968
Oilmen. 1965
Plant scientists. 1964.
Servicewomen. 1964

WORLD TRADE ACADEMY PRESS, INC., 50 East 42nd Street, New York, N.Y. 10017

Employment and Scholarship Handbooks and Directories. 23 books

The 1971 winter catalog lists twenty-three books, many of which are recent revisions, prepared by Juvenal L. Angel. Several of the handbooks and directories provide detailed information and suggestions on job hunting campaigns. Several of these include practical assistance to persons seeking employment in foreign countries. One offers suggestions to men and women over forty-five. Two of the directories are compilations of scholarship information. Examples are:

Employment opportunities for the handicapped. 1969. 411p. $12.50
Employment opportunities for men and women after 60. 1969. 282p. $10
Directory of professional and occupational licensing in the U.S. 1970. 530p. $25
Looking for employment in foreign countries. 1971. 425p. $17.50
Matching armed forces training to civilian jobs. 1971. 410p. $15
Matching college men to jobs. 1971. 265p. $12.50
Matching college women to jobs. 1970. 285p. $12.50
Matching technicians to jobs. 1971. 310p. $12.50
Modern vocational trends reference handbook. 7th edition. 1970. 815p. $17.50
National register of scholarships and fellowship. 5th edition. 1971. 700p. $25
Occupations for men and women after 45. 1964. 200p. $12.50
Students' guide to occupational earnings opportunities. 1967. 225p. $12.50
Why and how to prepare an effective résumé. 1965. 225p. $9
World directory of occupational, professional and labor organizations. 1971. 450p. $25

Part III

Annotated Bibliography

A. Books and Pamphlets Listed Alphabetically by Occupation

* Especially recommended
** Most highly recommended

ABLE SEAMAN 911.884

Able seaman. Careers. 1970. 2p. 20c

Career summary for desk-top file. This card, printed on both sides, describes duties, working conditions, personal qualifications, training required, salaries, recommended courses in high school, and employment outlook.

Able seaman. Chronicle Guidance Publications. 1969. 4p. 35c

Occupational brief summarizing kinds of work performed, working conditions, personal requirements, determination of aptitudes and interests, opportunities, where employed, unionization, training, methods of entry, and employment outlook.

Able seaman. Brief section in *Occupational Outlook Handbook*.†

Description of work of merchant seamen who constitute about one fifth of the unlicensed crew.

ACCOMPANIST. *See* Instrumental musician

ACCOUNTANT 160.188

Accountant. Chronicle Guidance Publications. 1969. 4p. 35c

Occupational brief containing definition, specialities, history, work performed, working conditions, personal qualifications, determination of aptitudes and interest, training requirements, opportunities, outlook, methods of entry, licensing, and suggested activities.

Accountant. Guidance Centre. 1968. 4p. 35c postpaid

Definition, history and importance, nature of work, qualifications, preparation, working conditions, employment, advancement, outlook, remuneration, and how to get started.

Accountants. Michigan Employment Security Commission. 1967. 2p. Single copy free

Job brief summarizing nature of work, location of jobs, working conditions, employment outlook, earnings, and requirements for entry.

† To locate the full entry for a title when only a section or chapter is given, consult the Index of this book.

ACCOUNTANT—*Continued*

Accountants. Science Research Associates. 1967. 4p. 45c

Occupational brief describing nature of work, training, qualifications, opportunities, advantages, disadvantages, and future outlook.

**Accountants. One section of *Occupational Outlook Handbook.*

Nature of work, where employed, training and other qualifications, employment outlook, earnings, and working conditions.

Accounting clerk. California State Department of Employment. 1966. 4p. Single copy free

Occupational guide describing work, requirements, training, and outlook.

Accounting clerk. Careers. 1967. 2p. 20c

Career summary for desk-top file. Description of duties, working conditions, personal qualifications, training required, salaries, related careers, recommended courses in high school, advantages, disadvantages, and employment outlook.

Accounting for your future. United Business Schools Association. 1962. 20p. Free

Description of various accounting services, personal qualifications, and opportunities.

A calculating miss. Cunningham, Virginia. Julian Messner. 1966. 192p. $3.50

Career fiction. Story of a young worker in an accounting department. Includes some basic information about office procedures and the duties of an assistant in accounting.

**Careers and opportunities in accounting. Cashin, James A. Dutton and Company. 1965. 224p. $4.95

Asserting that accounting is second only to engineering as America's largest profession for men, the author describes the nine basic branches of accounting. He advises on educational planning for various accounting careers and includes a chapter on opportunities for women. Gives list of collegiate schools of business offering programs in accounting. Illustrated.

* Careers in accounting. Ashworth, John. Henry Z. Walck, Inc. 1963. 109p. $4.50

Beginning with descriptions of the nature of work in business, public practice, government, and teaching, this book includes the personal and educational qualifications, employment outlook, rewards, and opportunities.

Careers in accounting. Changing Times. 1961. 3p. 15c

Discussion of preparation, future outlook, and earnings.

Careers in controllership. Aluminum Company of America. No date. 10p. Free

A recruiting brochure describing work and opportunities.

Cooperative work-study opportunities for accounting majors. Internal Revenue Service. 1968. 4p. Free

Describes the Internal Revenue Service's cooperative work-study program for accounting majors. Information given on opportunities throughout the United States in the field of Federal taxation.

Cost accountant. Careers. 1966. 2p. 20c

Career summary for desk-top file. Duties, qualifications, and outlook.

Employment opportunities for accountants. U.S. Securities and Exchange Commission. 1968. 2p. Free

Information about the location of positions, duties to be performed, salaries, career opportunities, fringe benefits, training, recruitment policy, and civil service examinations.

**Employment outlook for accountants. Bulletin No. 1650–2. Bureau of Labor Statistics, U.S. Department of Labor. Supt. of Documents. 1970. 8p. 10c

Reprint from the *Occupational Outlook Handbook.*

Finding out about accountants. Science Research Associates. 1967. 4p. 45c

Junior occupational brief containing concise facts about the job.

Industrial accountant. Guidance Centre. 1967. 4p. 35c postpaid

History and importance, nature of work, qualifications, working conditions, preparation, remuneration, outlook, related occupations, how to get started, and employment.

Junior accountant. California State Department of Employment. 1966. 3p. Single copy free

Occupational guide describing work, requirements, training, and outlook.

Management accounting opportunities unlimited. National Association of Accountants. 1968. 6p. Free

Describes work, training, advancement opportunities, and compensation.

No other career offers women more income and security than accounting. International Accountants Society. 1968. 8p. Free

Points out the growing opportunities in a number of accounting fields.

* Opportunities in an accounting career. Ankers, Raymond G. Vocational Guidance Manuals. 1967. 144p. $1.95 paper; $3.75 library edition

Work, qualifications, preparation, opportunities, and employment outlook.

What's it like to be an accountant. Accounting Careers Council. 1969. 24p. Single copy free

Educational preparation, work duties, earnings, and advancement are observed through interviews with six accountants working in major areas of accounting.

Your business success through accounting. International Accountants Society. 1968. 24p. Free

Description of opportunities and outlook in accounting and related fields.

ACCOUNTANT—*Continued*

**Your future in accounting. Locklear, Edmund, Jr. Richards Rosen Press. Revised 1969. 159p. $4; library edition $3.78

The importance of accounting in modern business is stressed, together with the educational preparation necessary for this career.

See also Auditor; Bookkeeper; Public accountant

ACROBAT-AERIALIST. *See* Circus performer

ACTOR AND ACTRESS 150.048

* Actor-actress. Careers. 1966. 8p. 35c

Career brief describing nature of work, working conditions, qualifications, training, earnings, and outlook.

Actor and actress. Chronicle Guidance Publications. 1968. 4p. 35c

Occupational brief summarizing work performed, working conditions, qualifications, training, earnings, methods of entry, and outlook.

Actor or actress. Guidance Centre. 1970. 4p. 35c postpaid

History and importance, nature of work, qualifications, working conditions, preparation, remuneration, related occupations, and how to get started.

Actors and actresses. Michigan Employment Security Commission. 1965. 2p. Single copy free

Job brief summarizing nature of work, location of jobs, working conditions, earnings, employment outlook, and requirements for entry.

Actors and actresses. Science Research Associates. 1969. 4p. 45c

Occupational brief describing nature of work, training, qualifications, opportunities, advantages, disadvantages, and future outlook.

**Actors and actresses. One section of *Occupational Outlook Handbook*.

Nature of work, where employed, training, other qualifications, employment outlook, earnings, and working conditions.

Actors on acting: the theories, techniques, and practices of the great actors of all times as told in their own words. Cole, Toby and Chinoy, Helen, eds. Crown Publishers. 1970. 715p. $8.95

The editors have assembled writings on the art of acting from the Greeks to the moderns. The editors preface each selection with further data. In some cases quotations from critics or authors supplement the actors' statements. This is a new revised edition with a good bibliography, arranged by country.

**Careers and opportunities in the theatre. Dalrymple, Jean. Dutton and Company. 1969. 256p. $5.95

Information for the theatrical aspirant from would-be actor to would-be producer. Includes training, kinds of work, lists of earnings, and case histories of some who have achieved. Illustrated. The appendix contains a list of school, producers, and Actor's Equity pay scales.

Curtain going up! The story of Katharine Cornell. Malvern, Gladys. Julian Messner. 1943. 244p. $3.95; library binding $3.64

Biography which includes information about acting and directing.

Finding out about actors and actresses. Science Research Associates. 1967. 4p. 45c

Junior occupational brief describing work and opportunities.

Finding out about theatrical directors. Science Research Associates. 1967. 4p. 45c

Junior occupational brief describing work and opportunities.

Jobs in children's entertainment. Van Gelder, Rosalind. Alumnae Advisory Center. 1968. 5p. 35c

Discussion of careers in entertaining children. Includes television stars and directors, toy designers, writers of children's books, and producers of children's theatre.

Madame Sarah. Skinner, Cornelia Otis. Houghton Mifflin Company. 1966. 256p. $6.95

Biography of Sarah Bernhardt, relating her many theatrical exploits. Of greatest appeal to girls.

**Opportunities in acting. Moore, Dick. Vocational Guidance Manuals 1963. 128p. $1.95 paper; library edition $3.75

Description of types of acting positions in the theatre, motion pictures, and television. Discussion of requirements, trends, training, related fields, advantages, and disadvantages.

**Stagestruck: your career in theatre. Hirschfeld, Burt. Julian Messner. 1963. 192p. $3.95; library binding $3.64

Presents the variety of theatrical jobs, as well as the arduous work and keen competition involved. Includes actor, business manager, choreographer, dancer, designer, playwright, producer, press agent, stagehand, and talent agent.

Theatre jobs(non-acting). Alumnae Advisory Center. 1967. 6p. 35c

Reprint from *Mademoiselle* describing several theatrical jobs such as producer, director, stage manager, casting director, property managers, and designers of art, costumes, and lighting.

ACTUARY 020.188

**The actuarial profession in the United States and Canada. Society of Actuaries. 1967. 16p. Single copy free to counselors

Booklet describing responsibilities, training, opportunities, and outlook.

Actuaries, Science Research Associates. 1969. 4p. 45c

Occupational brief describing nature of work, training, qualifications, opportunities, advantages, disadvantages, and future outlook.

**Actuaries. One section of *Occupational Outlook Handbook*.

Nature of work, training, other qualifications, employment outlook, earnings, and working conditions.

ACTUARY—*Continued*

Actuary. California State Department of Employment. 1965. 3p. Single copy free

Occupational guide describing work, requirements, training, and outlook.

Actuary. Careers. 1968. 2p. 20c

Career summary for desk-top file. Duties, qualifications, and outlook.

Actuary. Chronicle Guidance Publications. 1969. 4p. 35c

Occupational brief summarizing work performed, where employed, training requirements, opportunities, earnings, and outlook.

Actuary. Guidance Centre. 1967. 4p. 35c postpaid

Definition, qualifications, preparation, employment, advancement, earnings, how to get started, and working conditions.

Actuary. Michigan Employment Security Commission. 1962. 2p. Single copy free

Job brief summarizing occupational data for use in Michigan.

Finding out about actuaries. Science Research Associates. 1967. 4p. 45c

Junior occupational brief describing work and opportunities.

Preliminary actuarial examinations. Society of Actuaries. 1968. 49p. Free

Description of examinations, miscellaneous information for candidates, and sample examination questions. The appendix describes the character of actuarial work, qualifications, and opportunities.

Requirements for admission. Society of Actuaries. 1969. 27p. Free

General regulations, description of examinations, and a recommended course of reading.

See also Accountant; Insurance industry worker; Mathematician; Statistician

ADVERTISING AGENT 164.168

**Advertising: a career of action and variety for exceptional men and women. American Association of Advertising Agencies. 1969. 24p. 25c. Single copy free to counselors

A description of the career opportunities in advertising agencies, including examples of young people who have advanced rapidly to positions of responsibility in short periods of time. Also covered are suggested educational preparation and extra-curricular work for advertising careers. Illustrated.

Advertising account executives. Science Research Associates. 1966. 4p. 45c

Occupational brief describing work, training, qualifications, opportunities, and outlook.

Advertising assistant. Chronicle Guidance Publications. 1969. 4p. 35c

An occupational brief summarizing work performed, working conditions, personal qualifications, hours, earnings, training, where employed, opportunities, methods of entry, and outlook.

Advertising-space salesman. Careers. 1966. 2p. 20c

Career summary for desk-top file. Duties, qualifications, and outlook.

* Advertising workers. Science Research Associates. 1968. 4p. 45c

Occupational brief describing kinds of work, preparation, qualifications, opportunities, advantages, disadvantages, and future outlook.

** Advertising workers. One section of *Occupational Outlook Handbook.*

Nature of work, where employed, training, other qualifications, advancement, employment outlook, earnings, and working conditions.

** Careers and opportunities in advertising. Boland, Charles M. Dutton and Company. 1964. 224p. $4.50

Based on interviews with forty-nine top advertising executives. The author discusses the role of the advertising manager and account executive; the work of the copywriter, artist, production man; and opportunities in television, radio, marketing and research, sales promotion, and public relations.

* Careers in advertising. Ray, Royal H. Quill and Scroll Foundation. 1965. 12p. 35c

Discussion of the role of advertising, types of positions, opportunities, and outlook.

Careers in industrial advertising. Association of Industrial Advertisers. 1963. 22p. 10c. Single copy free

This booklet defines industrial advertising and gives information on salaries, major fields, qualifications, getting started, and applying for a job.

Confessions of an advertising man. Ogilvy, David. Atheneum Publishers. 1963. 172p. $5.95

Biography of a director of a New York advertising agency who gives a revealing picture of the work of members of a successful advertising staff.

** Employment outlook for advertising workers, marketing research workers, public relations workers. Bulletin No. 1650–3. Bureau of Labor Statistics, U.S. Department of Labor. Supt. of Documents. 1970. 12p. 15c

Reprint from the *Occupational Outlook Handbook.*

Finding out about advertising account executives. Science Research Associates. 1967. 4p. 45c

Junior occupational brief containing concise facts about the job.

Jobs in advertising. American Advertising Federation. 1962. 16p. $2.50 for 25. Single copy free

Description of work in twelve jobs, qualifications, and training.

Marketing as a career—a bibliography. American Marketing Association. 1964. 4p. Free

Sixteen references most of which pertain to careers in advertising.

** Opportunities in advertising careers. Clarke, George T. Vocational Guidance Manuals. 1968. 96p. $1.95 paper; $3.75 library edition

Types of positions in advertising agencies, with manufacturers, service organizations, institutions, magazines, newspapers, retail organizations, and in nonspecialist advertising positions. Educational pr paration and how to get

ADVERTISING AGENT—*Continued*

started. Describes the examination plan sponsored by the American Association of Advertising Agencies and the high school essay contest sponsored by the Advertising Federation of America.

Ten advertising jobs. Alumnae Advisory Center. 1962. 6p. 35c
Reprint from *Mademoiselle* describing ten typical jobs held by women.

**Your career in advertising. Johnson, George. Julian Messner. 1966. 160p. $3.95; library binding $3.64
Describing advertising as strenuous but exhilarating work, the owner of an advertising agency describes various kinds of job opportunities and offers suggestions for training and for getting a start. Good reading list.

**Your future in advertising. Singer, Jules B. Richards Rosen Press. Revised 1969. 160p. $4; library edition $3.78
Includes the importance of advertising, advantages, kinds of work, and opportunities in an advertising agency, department store, magazine, newspaper, radio-television network, and national advertising.

ADVERTISING-COPY WRITER. *See* Copy writer

AERONAUTICAL ENGINEER 002.081

Aeronautical engineer. Chronicle Guidance Publications. 1966. 4p. 35c
Occupational brief describing work performed, where employed, salary, personal qualifications, training, employment outlook, and related jobs.

Aeronautical engineering technician. Careers. 1970. 2p. 20c
Career summary for desk-top file. Duties, qualifications, and outlook.

Aeronautical engineers. One section of *Occupational Outlook Handbook*.
Nature of work, where employed, and employment outlook.

See also Aerospace industry worker; Air transportation industry worker; Aviator; Engineer

AEROSPACE ENGINEER 002.081

Aerospace engineer. Careers. 1970. 8p. 35c
Career brief describing duties, working conditions, qualifications, training, earnings, and outlook.

Aerospace engineer. Guidance Centre. 1967. 4p. 35c postpaid
History and importance, nature of the work, qualifications, preparation, advancement, outlook, remuneration, advantages, disadvantages, how to get started, and related occupations.

Aerospace engineers. Science Research Associates. 1969. 4p. 45c
Occupational brief describing nature of work, requirements, opportunities, earnings, and future prospects.

Aerospace technicians. Science Research Associates. 1966. 4p. 45c
Occupational brief describing work, training, qualifications, opportunities, and outlook.

Finding out about aerospace engineers. Science Research Associates, 1967. 4p. 45c

Junior occupational brief summarizing what the work requires and offers.

AEROSPACE INDUSTRY WORKER 621.281

Aerospace bibliography. Government Printing Office. Supt. of Documents. 1970. 102p. $1

Fifth edition, January, 1970.

Aerospace industries manufacturing workers. Science Research Associates. 1970. 4p. 45c

Occupational brief describing work, requirements, earnings, working conditions, and outlook.

**Employment outlook for aircraft, missile, and spacecraft manufacturing. Bulletin No. 1650–108. Bureau of Labor Statistics, U.S. Department of Labor. Supt. of Documents. 1970. 16p. 15c

Reprint from the *Occupational Outlook Handbook.*

Father of supersonic flight: Theodore von Karman. Halacy, D. S., Jr. Julian Messner. 1965. 192p. $3.25; library binding $3.19

Biography including accounts of many exploits and adventures on the challenging conquest of space.

From spinning wheel to space craft: the story of the industrial revolution. Neal, Harry Edward. Julian Messner. 1964. 192p. Library binding $3.64

Story of modern man's startling inventions and discoveries that have changed standards of living throughout the world. Includes accounts of many inventors who overcame handicaps to bring their discoveries into existence.

Men, rockets and space rats. Mallan, Lloyd. Simon and Schuster, Inc. 1961. 368p. $5.95

An account of the men and the research projects concerned with the conquest of outer space. Photographs.

**Occupations in aircraft, missile, and spacecraft manufacturing. One chapter of *Occupational Outlook Handbook.*

Nature and location of the industry, kinds of work, training, other qualifications, advancement, employment outlook, earnings, and working conditions.

Robert Goddard, space pioneer. Dewey, Anne Perkins. Little, Brown and Company. 1962. 154p. $4.25

Biography revealing the hard work and perseverance necessary in the work of the scientist who built and fired the first liquid-fuel rocket.

Rockets, missiles, and men in space. Ley, Willy. Viking Press. 1968. 640p. $8.95

This book traces the development of rocketry and its place in today's world, including the wonders and challenges of this growing field.

AEROSPACE INDUSTRY WORKER–*Continued*

Sky rangers; satellite tracking around the world. Engle, Eloise and Drummond, Kenneth H. John Day Company. 1965. 219p. $4.95

Describes the training of the satellite watchers and the building of a network of tracking stations all over the world. Includes the network that covered manned space flights.

United States aircraft, missiles, and spacecraft. National Aerospace Education Council. 1968. 224p. $3

Contains photographs and descriptions of current aircraft, missiles, and spacecraft produced in the United States. Ask for latest edition.

**Your career in the aerospace industry. Boyd, Waldo T. Julian Messner. 1966. 222p. Library binding $3.64

This is a guide scanning a wide variety of expanding career opportunities and the necessary preparation for industrial, government civil service, and military space activities. Also covers five secondary aerospace interests: ocean mining, commercial transportation, solar research, cryogenics, and electronics. Included is a list of aerospace positions and salaries for engineers, scientists, and skilled craftsmen.

**Your future in aerospace technology. Ely, Lawrence. Richards Rosen Press. Revised 1969. 153p. Library edition $3.78

A career study of the aerospace industry and its outlook.

**Your future in NASA. Levine, Sol. Richards Rosen Press. 1969. 190p. $4; library edition $3.78

Explanation of educational preparation, personal qualifications, and types of technical talent needed by the National Aeronautics and Space Administration. Explanation of the work done at the various centers.

See also Aeronautical engineer; Air transportation industry worker; Airplane pilot; Astronaut; Missileman

AGRICULTURAL AGENT (COUNTY). *See* Cooperative extension service worker

AGRICULTURAL ENGINEER 013.081

Agricultural engineer. California State Department of Employment. 1966. 6p. Single copy free

Occupational guide describing work, requirements, training, and outlook.

Agricultural engineer. Careers. 1969. 2p. 20c

Career summary for desk-top file. Duties, qualifications, and outlook.

Agricultural engineer. Chronicle Guidance Publications. 1969. 4p. 35c

Occupational brief summarizing work performed, working conditions, training, earnings, outlook, and opportunities.

Agricultural engineering and you. American Society of Agricultural Engineers. No date. 14p. 15c

Description of nature of work, kinds of employment available, preparation, and future outlook.

* Agricultural engineering serving the world's largest industry. American Society of Agricultural Engineers. No date. 6p. 25c

Illustrated in four colors, this brochure describes career opportunities, future outlook, and desirable qualifications.

Agricultural engineers. Science Research Associates. 1966. 4p. 45c

Occupational brief describing nature of work, requirements, methods of entering, earnings, advantages, disadvantages, and future outlook.

Agricultural engineers. One section of *Occupational Outlook Handbook.*

Nature of work, employment outlook, training and other qualifications.

** Agriculture engineering: the profession with a future. American Society of Agricultural Engineers. Revised 1968. 6p. $1 per 100. Single copy free

Description of five major areas of agricultural engineering: electric power and processing, farm structures and environment, power and machinery, soil and water conservation, and food engineering.

Finding out about agricultural engineers. Science Research Associates. 1967. 4p. 45c

Junior occupational brief containing concise facts about the job.

**Opportunities in agricultural engineering. Stone, Archie A. Vocational Guidance Manuals. 1963. 128p. $1.95 paper; library edition $3.75

Includes discussion of organizations and agencies that employ agricultural engineers, nature of work, employment outlook, training, and opportunities.

See also Engineer

AGRICULTURAL SPECIALIST 040.081 and 401.

**Agricultural, forestry, and oceanographic technicians: career opportunities for technicians and specialists. Sidney, Howard, ed. Ferguson Publishing Company. 1969. 344p. $8.95

The book is divided into sections on animal science, plant science, ornamental horticulture, forest and conservation, oceanography, and off-farm employment. Information is given about a variety of careers in each area concerning the type of work done, necessary personal qualities, educational requirements, entry-level jobs, advancement, working conditions, and benefits. Most careers are those for which two-year post high school educational programs exist.

Agricultural finance workers. One section of *Occupational Outlook Handbook.*

Nature of work, where employed, employment outlook, and sources of additional information.

**Agricultural occupations. One section of *Occupational Outlook Handbook.*

Employment opportunities on farms, significance of agriculture in the economy, farming opportunities, training available, description of the various types of farming, and a discussion of specialized agricultural occupations.

AGRICULTURAL SPECIALIST—*Continued*

* Agricultural research workers. Careers. 1969. 8p. 35c

Career brief describing specialized work in this field, working conditions, requirements, training, earnings, outlook, and places of employment. Additional readings.

Agricultural research workers. One section of *Occupational Outlook Handbook.*

Nature of work, where employed, employment outlook, and earnings.

Agriculture: earned degrees, by level, sex, and institution. One section of *Earned Degrees Conferred.*

Useful for judging the extent of a college's program in each of the following specialties: agronomy, animal husbandry, dairy husbandry, dairy technology, farm management, food technology, horticulture, poultry husbandry, soils, and general agriculture.

Agriculture U.S.A.; America's most basic industry. Lent, Henry B. Dutton and Company. 1968. 160p. $4.95; library edition $4.90

An overview of the modern American agriculture industry which covers farming methods, crop and livestock production, and food processing and marketing. The final chapter is on career opportunities. A list of state agriculture colleges is appended. Prepared for grades 5 to 9.

Careers in agribusiness and industry. Stone, Archie A. Interstate Printers and Publishers. 1965. 292p. $5.25

Stresses the need for business specialists and professional workers in agricultural business and industry. Gives the qualifications, training, and opportunities in selected industries.

Careers in agriculture. American Institute of Cooperation. 1964. 8p. Free

Brochure describes opportunities, job titles, and future outlook for agricultural specialists.

** Employment outlook for agriculture. Bulletin No. 1650–106. Bureau of Labor Statistics, U.S. Department of Labor. Supt. of Documents. 1970. 20p. 20c

Reprint from the *Occupational Outlook Handbook.* Includes cooperative extension service workers, soil scientists, soil conservationists, other professional workers, and farm service jobs.

Exploring agribusiness. Roy, Ewell Paul. Interstate Printers and Publishers. 1967. 295p. $6.95

Explains the need for trained persons to process and distribute agricultural products, to give special services to people who produce these products, and to do research that will make production and distribution more efficient.

Exploring your future in agriculture. Sextant Systems, Inc. 1971. 96p. $8.95

One page is devoted to each of ninety-five jobs, summarizing the duties, requirements for entering, promotional outlook, and pay and skill level.

**Guidance in agricultural education. Byram, Harold M. Interstate Printers and Publishers. 1966. 258p. $5.75

The purpose of this book is to provide help for the teacher of agriculture for carrying out the guidance activities he finds appropriate in his school. Includes information about occupations in agriculture.

**Handbook of agricultural occupations. Hoover, Norman K. Interstate Printers and Publishers. 1969. 400p. $5.95

Describes the opportunities which exist in the agricultural and agriculture-related fields of employment and gives specific information as to the education needed to get the jobs and the avenues for advancement. Occupational briefs are provided for fifty-five typical off-farm occupations in which farm backgrounds will be an asset. Includes a directory of colleges offering instruction in agriculture.

Jobs in agriculture. Science Research Associates. 1966. 32p. $1.15

Describes the variety of job prospects and opportunities within this field.

Opportunities on specific types of farms. One section of *Occupational Outlook Handbook,* 1961 edition.

Discussion of the outlook on dairy, poultry, livestock, corn and wheat, cotton, tobacco, peanut, and crop specialty farms.

Professional workers in state agricultural experiment stations and other cooperating state institutions. U.S. Department of Agriculture. Supt. of Documents. Revised 1970. 280p. $1.50

Information regarding the professional workers for the year 1969-70.

**Profiles: careers in the U.S. Department of Agriculture. Miscellaneous Publication 1071. Supt. of Documents. 1968. 190p. $3.25

Presenting a comprehensive view of the sixty-five types of careers, each profile gives the duties, qualifications, training, and employment specifications. One section describes the relation of college studies to the employment opportunities. Another section gives employment procedures, benefits, and salaries.

**Rewarding careers in a dynamic industry . . . agriculture. National Association of State Universities and Land-Grant Colleges. 1966. 24p. Free from land-grant colleges to students within the state.

Illustrated brochure describing fields of work, opportunities, and outlook.

A soil science career for you in Soil Conservation Service. U.S. Department of Agriculture. Miscellaneous Publication Number 716. Supt. of Documents. 1965. 8p. 5c

Illustrated folder describing nature of work in soil mapping, classification, correlation, laboratory research, soil investigation, and soil survey interpretation. Also contains employment facts such as work locations, advancement, and benefits.

Your opportunities in vocational agriculture. Phipps, Lloyd J. Interstate Printers and Publishers. 1962. 175p. $3.50

Describes opportunities in farming and nonfarm agricultural occupations for high school students.

See also Agricultural agent (county); Agronomist; Soil scientist

AGRONOMIST 040.081

Agronomist. California State Department of Employment. 1964. 5p. Single copy free

Description of work, training, promotion, working conditions, and employment outlook.

Agronomist. Careers. 1969. 2p. 20c

Career summary for desk-top file. Duties, qualifications, and outlook.

* Agronomist. Chronicle Guidance Publications. 1969. 4p. 35c

Occupational brief summarizing work performed, working conditions, qualifications, where employed, hours and wages, method of entry, related jobs, training, opportunities, and outlook.

**Careers in agronomy, crop science, and soil science. American Society of Agronomy. 1966. 22p. Single copy free

Illustrated brochure describing nature of work, opportunities, and training. Also contains list of 73 colleges and universities offering majors in agronomy.

Crop scientists. Science Research Associates. 1968. 4p. 45c

Occupational brief describing nature of work, requirements, training, getting started and advancing, earnings, and future outlook.

Finding out about crop and soil scientists. Science Research Associates. 1967. 4p. 45c

Junior occupational brief summarizing what the work requires and offers.

See also Agricultural specialist; Soil conservationist and scientist

AIR-CONDITIONING AND REFRIGERATION ENGINEER 007.081

**Aim for a job in air conditioning and refrigeration. Daly, Donald F. Richards Rosen Press. 1968. 140p. $4; library edition $3.78

The opportunities in home and industry for jobs in these fields. Stresses the value of technical education in enabling junior mechanics and technicians to keep pace with changes in industrial technology.

**Air-conditioning and refrigeration engineers. Science Research Associates. 1966. 4p. 45c

Occupational brief describing nature of work, training, qualifications, opportunities, advantages, disadvantages, and outlook.

Finding out about air-conditioning and refrigeration engineers. Science Research Associates. 1967. 4p. 45c

Junior occupational brief containing concise facts about the job.

Refrigerating engineer. Michigan Employment Security Commission. 1960. 2p. Single copy free

Job brief summarizing occupational data for use in Michigan.

You and your future in the air conditioning and refrigeration industry. Air Conditioning and Refrigeration Institute. 1968. 4p. Single copy free

Description of the industry, opportunities, and employment outlook.

* Your future in air-conditioning, heating, and refrigeration engineering. American Society of Heating, Refrigerating, and Air-Conditioning Engineers. 1968. 16p. Free

Emphasis on careers in air-conditioning, heating, refrigerating, and ventilating.

AIR-CONDITIONING, REFRIGERATION, AND HEATING MECHANIC 637.281 and 862.281

**Aim for a job in the pipe trades. Daly, Donald F. Richards Rosen Press. 1969. 158p. $4; library edition $3.78

Opportunities in the chief branches of the pipe trades which include automatic sprinkler, fire-control fitter, coppersmith, refrigeration and air-conditioning fitter, and steam fitter.

Air-conditioning and refrigeration mechanic. Chronicle Guidance Publications. 1968. 4p. 35c

Occupational brief summarizing work performed, working conditions, qualifications, hours, where employed, training, earnings, and outlook.

Air-conditioning, heating, and refrigeration technician. One section of *Occupational Outlook Handbook.*

Brief description of nature of work and employment outlook.

Air conditioning-heating technician. Careers. 1966. 2p. 20c

Career summary for desk-top file. Duties, qualifications, and outlook.

**Air-conditioning, refrigeration, and heating mechanics. One section of *Occupational Outlook Handbook.*

Nature of work, where employed, training, other qualifications, advancement, employment outlook, earnings, and working conditions.

* Air-conditioning technicians. Science Research Associates. 1967. 4p. 45c

Occupational brief describing nature of work, requirements, methods of getting started and advancing, earnings, advantages, disadvantages, and future outlook.

**Employment outlook for air-conditioning, refrigeration, and heating mechanics. Bulletin No. 1650–80. Bureau of Labor Statistics, U.S. Department of Labor. Supt. of Documents. 1970. 8p. 10c

Reprint from the *Occupational Outlook Handbook.*

Finding out about air-conditioning technicians. Science Research Associates. 1967. 4p. 45c

Junior occupational brief describing work and opportunities.

AIR-CONDITIONING, REFRIGERATION, AND HEATING MECHANIC—*Continued*

Finding out about refrigeration and air-conditioning mechanics. Science Research Associates. 1967. 4p. 45c

Junior occupational brief containing some concise facts about the job and listing ways of finding out about the nature of the work. Includes suggestions for reading and the titles of other occupational briefs on related topics.

Refrigeration and air-conditioning technician. Guidance Centre. 1966. 4p. 35c postpaid

Definition, history and importance, nature of work, preparation, qualifications, working conditions, employment, advancement, outlook, remuneration, and how to get started.

Refrigeration mechanic. California State Department of Employment. 1966. 3p. Single copy free

Duties, working conditions, finding the job, wages, hours, training, promotion, and employment prospects.

Refrigeration mechanic. Careers. 1970. 2p. 20c

Career summary for desk-top file. Duties, qualifications, and outlook.

AIR FORCE AIRMAN 378.

Air Force Academy: cadets, training and equipment. Colby, C. B. Coward-McCann, Inc. 1962. 48p. Library edition $2.97

Photographs and brief text show life while training. Written for grades 4 to 8.

Air Force careers. Careers. 1968. 8p. 35c

Career brief describing the aviation cadet program and the forty-two airmen career fields.

The Air Force: from civilian to airman. Landis, Lawrence C. Viking Press. 1962. 192p. $3

Explains the procedures for entrance, the life of the trainee at Lackland Air Force Base, the specialized training offered in the technical schools, and the opportunities for advancement.

Catalog of information. U.S. Air Force Academy. 1968-69. 208p. Free

Catalog describing training, eligibility requirements, entrance examinations, curriculum, and career information. Revised annually.

Counsel for prospective candidates. U.S. Air Force Academy. 1969. 8p. Free

Statistics of the entering class including comparative performance on college entrance examinations. Revised annually.

**Current career booklets. U.S. Air Force Recruiting Service. 1969. 10 booklets. Free

Frequently revised booklets are available from local recruiting offices or the above. Present titles include: *Look-ahead jobs on the aerospace team, Gateway to leadership,* and *Meet tomorrow's challenge.*

Gateway to leadership—the U.S. Air Force Officer Training School. U.S. Air Force Recruiting Service. 1967. 8p. Free

Illustrated brochure answering questions most frequently asked about the training.

Growth into leadership. U.S. Air Force Academy. 1969. 26p. Free

Pictorial brochure depicting many phases of the Academy curriculum and cadet life.

Meet tomorrow's challenge as a pilot or navigator. U.S. Air Force Recruiting Service. 1968. 19p. Free

A color brochure describing pilot and navigator training. Also shows the types of aircraft flown in the Air Force.

The new tigers. Mason, Herbert M. David McKay Company. 1967. 256p. $6.95

Portrayal of the life of the undergraduate pilot and trainee of the Tactical Air Command.

Officer training school pamphlet. U.S. Air Force Recruiting Service. 1968. 42p. Free

A reference publication describing utilization field in which the officer may serve and a section showing related academic subjects and degrees. Illustrated.

U.S. Air Force Academy. Engeman, Jack. Lothrop, Lee and Shepard Company. 1962. 128p. $4.95

Story showing the life of a cadet. Two hundred illustrations.

**United States airman occupational handbook. U.S. Air Force. 1968. 44p. Free to counselors.

A comprehensive manual for guidance counselors describing qualifications, training, and career fields for the Air Force. Also includes a school subject index to airman career fields and an index to related civilian occupations.

Women officers in the U.S. Air Force. U.S. Air Force Recruiting Service. 1968. 16p. Free

An illustrated brochure depicting opportunities for college women.

** Your future in the Air Force. MacCloskey, Monro. Richards Rosen Press. Revised 1969. 160p. $4; library edition $3.78

An experienced officer describes varied kinds of work, training, qualifications, and opportunities.

See also Armed Forces; Coast guardsman; Marine; Sailor; Soldier

AIR TRAFFIC CONTROLLER 193.168

Air traffic control specialist (controller). California State Department of Employment. 1968. 5p. Single copy free

Occupational guide describing work, requirements, training, and outlook.

* Air traffic controller. Chronicle Guidance Publications. 1967. 4p. 35c

Occupational brief summarizing definition, work performed, working conditions, qualifications, where employed, hours, and earnings.

AIR TRAFFIC CONTROLLER—*Continued*

Air traffic controllers. Careers. 1970. 8p. 35c

Career brief describing duties, working conditions, requirements, training, earnings, and outlook.

* Air traffic controllers. Science Research Associates. 1969. 4p. 45c

Occupational brief describing work, training, qualifications, opportunities, and outlook.

Air traffic controllers. One section of *Occupational Outlook Handbook.*

Outlook summary, duties, qualifications, and earnings.

Finding out about air traffic controllers. Science Research Associates. 1967. 4p. 45c

Junior occupational brief describing work and opportunities.

AIR TRANSPORTATION INDUSTRY WORKER 912.

Air transportation occupations. Chronicle Guidance Publications. 1966. 4p. 35c

Occupational brief summarizing work performed, employment conditions, educational requirements, methods of entry, and outlook.

Airline ticket agent (airline ticket reservation agent). California State Department of Employment. 1966. 5p. Single copy free

Occupational guide describing work, requirements, training, and outlook.

**Careers in airlines operations. Nathan, Raymond. Henry Z. Walck, Inc. 1964. 112p. $4.50

This is a survey of the air transportation industry describing the nature of work, preparation, qualifications, advancement possibilities, and rewards. Includes the pilots who man the controls, the flight attendants, the technicians in ground operations, the sales and service people, and other related personnel. Includes list of schools for training and addresses of domestic airlines. Reading list. Illustrated.

**Civil aviation occupations. One chapter of *Occupational Outlook Handbook.*

Nature of activities, kinds of work, employment outlook, earnings, and working conditions. Specific information is given concerning pilot, flight engineer, stewardess, aircraft mechanic, airline dispatcher, air traffic controller, ground radio operator, and traffic agent. Seven illustrations.

Exploring your future in air transportation. Sextant Systems, Inc. 1970. 96p. $8.95

One page is devoted to each of ninety-five jobs, summarizing duties, requirements for entering, promotional outlook, and pay and skill level. Accompanying the book is an organizational chart showing the beginning jobs and those to which one may be promoted.

Your career with the airlines. Air Transport Association of America. No date. 8p. Free

This brochure includes a listing, brief description, and salary range of twenty-eight airline jobs in flight operations, airline communications, airline maintenance, airline office and sales, and professional work. Included is a list of the member airlines.

See also Aerospace industry worker

AIRCRAFT MECHANIC 621.281

Aircraft and engine mechanic. Chronicle Guidance Publications. 1967. 4p. 35c

Occupational brief summarizing work performed, certification requirements, where employed, qualifications, training, earnings, opportunities, and outlook.

Aircraft maintenance engineer. Guidance Centre. 1969. 4p. 35c postpaid

Definition, qualifications, employment and advancement, earnings, advantages, disadvantages, and related occupations.

**Aircraft mechanics. One section of *Occupational Outlook Handbook.*

Nature of work, training, other qualifications, advancement, employment outlook, earnings, and working conditions.

Airplane mechanic. Careers. 1969. 8p. 25c

Career brief describing duties, working conditions, qualifications, training, earnings, places of employment, and outlook.

Airplane mechanic. Michigan Employment Security Commission. 1967. 2p. Single copy free

Job brief summarizing occupational data for use in Michigan.

**Airplane mechanics. Science Research Associates. 1968. 4p. 45c

Occupational brief describing nature of work, qualifications, training, getting started and advancing, earnings and hours, advantages, disadvantages, and future outlook.

**Aviation careers: jobs in the air and on the ground. Fenten, D. X. Lippincott Company. 1969. 224p. $4.98

Fully illustrated. Appendix has sample questions from different examinations.

**Career opportunities in aviation. National Aerospace Education Council. 1967. 24p. 50c

Detailed coverage of the aviation mechanic field, including related high school courses, how to get started, a list of certificated mechanic schools, and sample examination questions for the oral, practical, and written exams.

Certificated mechanic schools. Federal Aviation Administration. 1968. 8p. Free

Lists alphabetically within the regions of the Federal Aviation Administration the certificated aircraft mechanic schools with rating.

AIRCRAFT MECHANIC—*Continued*

Finding out about airplane ground servicemen. Science Research Associates. 1967. 4p. 45c

Junior occupational brief containing concise facts about the job.

Finding out about airplane mechanics. Science Research Associates, 1967. 4p. 45c

Junior occupational brief describing work and opportunities.

AIRCRAFT, MISSILE, AND SPACECRAFT MANUFACTURING INDUSTRY WORKER 807.

Aircraft assemblyman. Careers. 1966. 2p. 20c

Career summary for desk-top file. Duties, qualifications, and outlook.

Aircraft manufacturing industry. Chronicle Guidance Publications. 1967. 8p. 50c

Occupational brief summarizing nature of work, working conditions, where employed, outlook, hours and earnings, education, and training.

Aircraft plaster patternmaker. California State Department of Employment. 1964. 3p. Single copy free

Occupational guide summarizing duties, employment prospects, earnings, requirements for entry, and suggestions for locating a job.

**Occupations in aircraft, missile, and spacecraft manufacturing. One chapter of *Occupational Outlook Handbook*.

Nature and location of the industry, kinds of jobs, training, other qualifications, employment outlook, earnings, and working conditions.

AIRLINE DISPATCHER 912.168

**Airline dispatcher. Careers. 1970. 8p. 35c

Career brief describing duties, working conditions, training, qualifications, earnings, outlook, and where employed.

Airline dispatchers. Science Research Associates. 1969. 4p. 45c

Occupational brief describing work, training, qualifications, opportunities, and outlook.

**Airline dispatchers. One section of *Occupational Outlook Handbook*.

Nature of work, qualifications, training, advancement, employment outlook, earnings, and working conditions.

Airline traffic agents and clerks. Science Research Associates. 1965. 4p. 45c

Occupational brief describing nature of the work, requirements, getting started, earnings, working conditions, and future outlook. Selected references.

Dispatcher (air transportation). Chronicle Guidance Publications. 1968. 4p. 35c

Occupational brief describing work, qualifications, opportunities, and outlook.

Finding out about airline dispatchers. Science Research Associates. 1967. 4p. 45c

Junior occupational brief describing work and opportunities.

Finding out about airline reservationists. Science Research Associates. 1967. 4p. 45c

Junior occupational brief containing concise facts about the job.

AIRPLANE HOSTESS. *See* Airplane stewardess

AIRPLANE MECHANIC. *See* Aircraft mechanic

AIRPLANE PILOT 196.168 and 196.283

Aerospace pilot. Coombs, Charles Ira. William Morrow and Company. 1964. 224p. $4.50

Emphasizing the vigorous training required for a career as an aerospace pilot, this book describes the various phases of the preparation from entrance into officer training school to assignment as a test pilot. Illustrated. For grades 6 to 10.

Agricultural aircraft pilot. California State Department of Employment. 1964. 6p. Single copy free

Occupational guide describing work, requirements, training, and outlook.

Airline pilot. California State Department of Employment. 1964. 5p. Single copy free

Occupational guide describing work, requirements, training, and outlook.

Airline pilot. Guidance Centre. 1968. 4p. 35c postpaid

Definition, nature of work, qualifications, preparation, working conditions, earnings, advantages, disadvantages, and how to get started.

Airline pilots. Science Research Associates. 1968. 4p. 45c

Occupational brief describing work, training, opportunities, and outlook.

* Airplane pilot. Careers. 1968. 8p. 35c

Career brief describing duties, working conditions, qualifications, training, earnings, and outlook. Additional readings.

Arctic bush pilot. Helmericks, Bud. Little, Brown and Company. 1956. 180p. $3.75

Career fiction. Experiences in flying over frozen spaces and in rescuing and guiding hunters and fishermen in the Far North. Semiautobiographical story of the author and his experiences with the Arctic bush pilots.

Commercial airplane pilot. Chronicle Guidance Publications. 1966. 4p. 35c

Occupational brief describing duties, requirements, working hours, pay, training opportunities, and employment outlook.

AIRPLANE PILOT–*Continued*

Commercial pilot examination guide. Federal Aviation Agency. Supt. of Documents. 1966. 88p. 75c

Prepared to aid pilots in their preparation for the commercial pilot written examination. It explains the nature, scope, and content of the examination and recommends basic study materials. Also included is a sample examination.

Finding out about airline pilots. Science Research Associates. 1967. 4p. 45c

Junior occupational brief describing work and opportunities.

Girl pilot. Gay, Kathlyn. Julian Messner. 1966. 187p. $3.50

Career fiction. Experiences of a commercial pilot in a varied career of ferrying passengers and planes and performing aerial errands. Shows the problems and obstacles faced by a woman pilot.

I, the airline pilot. Lodeesen, Marius. Dodd, Mead and Company. 1966. 208p. $3.75

A master pilot with thirty years of experience sets down the needed qualifications, training, and opportunities. Illustrated.

Instrument pilot examination guide. Federal Aviation Agency. Supt. of Documents. 1966. 49p. 40c

The purpose of this booklet is to provide the applicant with a list of study materials, a study outline, and sample examination to prepare him to pass the pilot's examination.

Jet flier. Archibald, Joseph. David McKay Company. 1960. 182p. $4.25

Career fiction based on the forced wheels-up landing of a modern jet. Covers many aspects of aviation such as stunt flying, cargoes, the B-24's in World War II, and the big jets.

Jet pilot. Lent, Henry. Macmillan Company. 1958. 200p. $4.50

Career fiction. Story of a jet pilot from the time he joins the U.S. Air Force to the day he receives his overseas flight assignment. For ages 12 to 16.

Jet pilot overseas. Lent, Henry. Macmillan Company. 1959. 183p. $3

Career fiction. Story showing that an assignment to a combat-ready squadron and an overseas tour of duty means constant training. For ages 12 to 16.

The last of the bush pilots. Helmericks, Harmon. Alfred A. Knopf, Inc. 1969. 384p. $6.95

This is a narrative of aviation in Alaska's bush country.

Navigator-pilot, airplane. Careers. 1969. 2p. 20c

Career summary for desk-top file. Duties, qualifications, and outlook.

North Atlantic jet flight. Stevens, Leonard. Thomas Y. Crowell Company. 1968. 96p. $3.75

Written for ages ten to fourteen, this book explains the preflight preparations, the functions of the crew members, the navigational systems, and the steps of an instrument landing.

**Pilots and copilots. One section of *Occupational Outlook Handbook.*

Nature of work, where employed, qualifications, training, advancement, employment outlook, earnings, and working conditions.

Sabre pilot. Meader, Stephen W. Harcourt, Brace & World. 1956. 173p. $3.50

Story of the training and experiences of a jet fighter pilot in the Air Force.

What does an airline crew do? Ray, E. Roy. Dodd, Mead and Company. 1968. 64p. $3.25

Simple text accompanied by descriptive photographs describe the nature of work of members of the crew, the qualifications for the various positions, and preparation needed. For grades 4 to 7.

What does a jet pilot do? Wells, Robert and Lippman, Harvey. Dodd, Mead and Company. 1959. 58p. $2.99

Simple text and pictures portray various duties and explain how flying a jet differs from flying other planes. Written for grades 3 to 7.

Windmill pilot. Archibald, Joseph. David McKay Company. 1963. 256p. $3.95; library binding $3.59

Story of a young lieutenant who makes a career of helicopter piloting.

* Your future as a pilot. Scribner, Kimball. Richards Rosen Press. 1968. 154p. $4; library edition $3.78

Description of the many opportunities and how to qualify.

AIRPLANE STEWARDESS 352.878

The airline guide to stewardess careers. Morton, Alexander. Stewardess Careers. 1970. 120p. $3.50

An account of eligibility, pay scales, uniforms, training bases, and pass benefits of airlines employing stewardesses.

**Airline stewardess. Alumnae Advisory Center. 1967. 12p. 35c

Reprint from *Mademoiselle* describing typical work and qualifications. For fourteen airlines, a chart shows the specific specifications, training, base pay, and the base cities.

Airline stewardess. California State Department of Employment. 1965. 4p. Single copy free

Job duties, working conditions, entrance requirements, pay, hours, training, promotion, and employment outlook.

**Airline stewardess. Careers. 1968. 8p. 35c

Career brief describing history of the occupation, duties, working conditions, training requirements, training opportunities, personal qualifications, employment prospects, advantages, disadvantages, earnings, advancement prospects, where employed, related careers, suggested high school program, and unionization.

Airline stewardess. Guidance Centre. 1967. 4p. 35c postpaid

Definition, history and importance, nature of work, qualifications necessary for entry and success, opportunities for advancement, remuneration, advantages, disadvantages, how to get started, and related occupations.

AIRPLANE STEWARDESS—*Continued*

Airline stewardess. Michigan Employment Security Commission. 1967. 2p. Single copy free

Job brief summarizing occupational data for use in Michigan.

Airline stewardess: a picture story. Engeman, Jack. Lothrop, Lee and Shepard Company. 1960. 128p. $4.95

On-the-scene photographs, with informative text and captions, show the life of an airline stewardess from her training-school experiences to actual flights aboard modern planes. Many aspects of training are shown: how to apply, requirements for admission, special courses and studies, customs, and traditions.

**Airline stewardesses. Science Research Associates. 1968. 4p. 45c

Occupational brief describing nature of work, requirements, education, how to enter and advance, earnings and hours, advantages, disadvantages, and future outlook.

Airplane stewardess. Chronicle Guidance Publications. 1966. 4p. 35c

Occupational brief summarizing work performed, working conditions, personal requirements, training, earnings, opportunities, and outlook.

As a mainliner stewardess the future looks bright. United Air Lines. No date. 28p. Free

An attractively illustrated brochure describing qualifications, opportunities, and benefits.

Finding out about airline stewardesses. Science Research Associates 1967. 4p. 45c

Junior occupational brief summarizing what the work requires and offers

* Flying high; what it's like to be an airline stewardess. Rich, Elizabeth. Stein and Day Publishers. 1970. 189p. $5.95

Including many personal anecdotes, the author discusses both advantages and disadvantages of this work and gives details of qualifications, training, role in emergencies, and problems likely to be encountered by beginners. Specific information, including route maps, is given for twelve major air lines.

Jet stewardess. Gerard, Jane. Julian Messner. 1962. 192p. $3.50

Career fiction. The romance includes authentic information about work on international jet airlines.

So you want to be an airline stewardess. Saunders, Keith. Arco Publishing Company. 1967. 176p. $4.95

Includes the general qualifications, training, duties, and benefits of this work. Both advantages and disadvantages are discussed by the editor of *Air Travel* magazine.

Stewardesses (civil aviation). One section of *Occupational Outlook Handbook.*

Nature of work, places of employment, training, other qualifications, advancement, employment outlook, earnings, and working conditions.

**What you need to know for a career as an airline stewardess. Morton, Alexander C. Cowles Book Company. 1969. 281p. $4.95

A practical airline-by-airline guide to the merits and requirements of employment with the airlines in the United States, Canada, and the Caribbean. Each profile contains such information as eligibility requirements, training, pay scale, pass and travel benefits, union affiliation, and where and how to apply. Most include a photograph showing current uniforms. A useful aid to selecting an airline for a young woman interested in a career as a stewardess.

**Your future as an airline stewardess. Rudolph, Patricia. Richards Rosen Press. Revised 1969. 158p. $4; library edition $3.78

Contains description of the life of a stewardess, qualifications, opportunities, pluses and minuses, and how to apply for a stewardess job. Included is a self-evaluation test and a list of airlines with the locations of their stewardess bases and cities on their routes.

AIRPORT MANAGER 184.118

Airport manager. Careers. 1967. 2p. 20c

Career summary for desk-top file. Duties, qualifications, and outlook.

Airport managers. Science Research Associates. 1969. 4p. 45c

Occupational brief describing nature of work, training, qualifications, opportunities, advantages, disadvantages, and future outlook.

Finding out about airport managers. Science Research Associates. 1967. 4p. 45c

Junior occupational brief describing work and opportunities.

ALUMINUM INDUSTRY WORKER 630.884 and 559.885

Aluminum industry workers. Science Research Associates. 1969. 4p. 45c

Occupational brief describing nature of work, requirements, earnings, employment, opportunities, advantages, disadvantages, and future outlook.

A career for you with Alcoa. Aluminum Company of America. 1968. 30p. Free

An industrial brochure describing opportunities and personnel policies.

*Ceramics—today's technology, tomorrow's future. Aluminum Company of America. 1969. 22p. Single copy free

A picture of the promising opportunities in this field. Also lists sources of career information.

Employment outlook and occupations in the aluminum industry. One section of *Occupational Outlook Handbook.*

Occupations in the industry, training, qualifications, advancement, employment outlook, earnings, and working conditions.

Employment outlook for the aluminum industry. Bulletin No. 1650–109. Bureau of Labor Statistics, U.S. Department of Labor. Supt. of Documents. 1970. 12p. 15c

Reprint from the *Occupational Outlook Handbook.*

ANESTHETIST. *See* **Nurse anesthetist**

ANIMAL CARE WORKER 356.

**Animal care occupations. Chronicle Guidance Publications. 1968. 4p. 35c

Occupational brief summarizing nature of work, working conditions, earnings, opportunities, educational requirements, and opportunities.

Animal keeper. California State Department of Employment. 1968. 4p. Single copy free

Occupational guide describing work, requirements, training, and outlook.

Clyde Beatty: boy animal trainer. Wilkie, Katherine. Bobbs-Merrill Company. 1968. 200p. $2.50

This book describes how this animal trainer developed an interest in animals, how he started working in the circus, and how he advanced as an animal trainer. For grades 4 to 7.

Finding out about animal keepers. Science Research Associates. 1967. 4p. 45c

Junior occupational brief containing concise facts about the job.

Starting and managing a pet shop. Small Business Administration. 1970. 40p. 30c

An idea of the risks and responsibilities that go with owning and running a pet shop and the knowledge needed to make and keep it profitable.

ANIMAL HUSBANDMAN 040.081

Animal husbandman. Chronicle Guidance Publications. 1966. 4p. 35c

Occupational brief summarizing areas of work, where employed, training, working conditions, entry, and outlook.

Animal scientist. California State Department of Employment. 1964. 7p. Single copy free

Occupational guide describing work, requirements, training, and outlook.

Jobs for kids who love animals. Changing Times. 1966. 3p. 15c

Reprint giving information about the veterinarian, wildlife conservationist, zoo keeper, and operator of animal shelter.

Kennelmen. California State Department of Employment. 1965. 3p. Single copy free

Occupational guide describing work, requirements, training, and outlook.

Nobel prize winners in medicine and physiology, 1901-1965. Sourkes, T. L. Abelard-Schuman, Ltd. 1967. 464p. $8.50

Notable is how medical advance depends upon the laboratory and on animal experimentation.

Raymond L. Ditmars: his exciting career with reptiles, animals and insects. Wood, Laura N. Julian Messner. 1944. 256p. Library binding $3.64

Biography of a boy who turned a hobby into a profession and developed new insights into the habits of animals.

Saddles for breakfast. Randall, Janet. David McKay Company. 1961. 224p. $3.50

Career fiction. Robin's love of horses and willingness to work hard help bring the run-down stables back to their former popularity.

Your career in animal science. Virginia Polytechnic Institute. No date. 4p. Free

An example of a college recruiting brochure pointing out the varied opportunities in this field.

ANTHROPOLOGIST 055.088

Anthropologist. Careers. 1970. 2p. 20c

Career summary for desk-top file. Duties, qualifications, and outlook.

Anthropologist. Chronicle Guidance Publications. 1966. 4p. 35c

Occupational brief summarizing definition, nature of work, where employed, earnings, personal qualifications, training required, working conditions, and outlook.

**Anthropologists. Science Research Associates. 1969. 4p. 45c

Occupational brief describing nature of work, requirements, earnings, methods of getting started, advantages, disadvantages, and future outlook. Selected references.

Anthropologists. One section of *Occupational Outlook Handbook.*

Nature of work, where employed, training and other qualifications, and employment outlook.

Anthropologists and what they do. Mead, Margaret. Franklin Watts, Inc. 1965. 212p. $3.95

Discussion of the importance of anthropology and its relation to the present and future world. Suggests what students must do to prepare for work in this field. For grades 7 to 11.

Finding out about anthropologists. Science Research Associates. 1967. 4p. 45c

Junior occupational brief containing facts about the job.

Guide to graduate departments of anthropology. American Anthropological Association. 1968. 234p. $1.50

A listing of departments in United States, Canadian, and Mexican universities offering the Ph.D. in anthropology, as well as some of the departments conferring only the master's degree. Also included are staff specialities and departmental strengths.

APPAREL INDUSTRY WORKER 781.381

**Clothing manufacturing workers. Science Research Associates. 1966. 4p. 45c

Occupational brief describing some kinds of work, requirements, getting started and advancing, earnings and hours, advantages, disadvantages, and future outlook.

APPAREL INDUSTRY WORKER—*Continued*

**Employment outlook for the apparel industry. Bulletin No. 1650–110. Bureau of Labor Statistics, U. S. Department of Labor. Supt. of Documents. 1970. 12p. 15c

Reprint from the *Occupational Outlook Handbook.*

Finding out about garment cutters. Science Research Associates. 1967. 4p. 45c

Junior occupational brief describing work and opportunities.

Garment cutter. California State Department of Employment. 1966. 5p. Single copy free

Occupational guide describing work, requirements, training, and outlook.

Industry wage survey: women's and misses' dresses. Bureau of Labor Statistics. Supt. of Documents. 1966. 34p. 30c

Survey of wages and supplementary practices in eleven important areas of the women's and misses' dress manufacturing industry. Many tables. Includes cutter, inspector, presser, sewer, sewing machine operator, thread trimmer, and work distributor.

Knit goods industry. Chronicle Guidance Publications. 1967. 8p. 50c

Occupational brief summarizing nature of industry, work performed, training, working conditions, hours, earnings, and outlook.

**Occupations in the apparel industry. One chapter in *Occupational Outlook Handbook.*

Nature and location of the industry, kinds of jobs, training, other qualifications, advancement, employment outlook, earnings, and working conditions.

See also Clothes designer; Milliner

APPLIANCE REPAIRMAN. *See* Home appliance serviceman

ARCHAEOLOGIST 055.088

Archaeologist. Careers. 1968. 2p. 20c

Career summary for desk-top file. Duties, qualifications, and outlook.

**Archaeologist. Chronicle Guidance Publications. 1969. 4p. 35c

Occupational brief summarizing definition, work performed, personal and educational requirements, entry into field, and outlook.

Archaeologist. Guidance Centre. 1969. 4p. 35c postpaid

History and importance, nature of work, qualifications, preparation, employment outlook, remuneration, and how to get started.

**Archaeologists. Science Research Associates. 1967. 4p. 45c

Occupational brief describing nature of work, requirements, getting started, earnings, advantages, disadvantages, and future outlook.

Archaeologists and what they do. Braidwood, Robert. Franklin Watts, Inc. 1960. 180p. $3.95

Discussion of the varied kinds of work, specialized training, qualifications, and rewards. For grades 7 to 11.

Archaeology as a career. Archaeological Institute of America. 1968. 8p. 10c. Single copy free

Discussion of many opportunities in this field.

Finding out about archaeologists. Science Research Associates. 1967. 4p. 45c

Junior occupational brief summarizing what the work requires and offers.

4000 years under the sea: the story of marine archaeology. Diole, Philippe. Simon and Schuster, Inc. 1954. 237p. $4.50

An account of the discovery and exploration of sunken ships on the floor of the Mediterranean which bring to light new aspects of ancient cultural and economic history.

Underwater archaeology; treasures beneath the sea. Pinney, Roy. Hawthorn Books, Inc. 1970. 214p. $4.95

Following a brief outline of diving history, the author describes different techniques of underwater archaeological excavation and discusses future developments and career opportunities.

ARCHITECT 001.081

American architects directory. R. R. Bowker Company. 1962. 919p. $25

Appendix includes a list of schools of architecture, standards of professional practice, and state registration boards and officers.

**Architect. McLaughlin, Robert W. Macmillan Company. 1962. 201p. $4.95

The author discusses qualifications, registration and licensing, professional schools and apprenticeship, the contributions of renowned men in the field, and a typical week of a practicing architect.

Architect. California State Department of Employment. 1966. 7p. Single copy free

Occupational guide describing work, requirements, training, and outlook.

* Architect. Careers. 1967. 8p. 35c

Career brief describing history and importance of the work, duties, working conditions, training requirements, training opportunities, personal qualifications, employment prospects, advantages, disadvantages, earnings, advancement prospects, related careers, measuring one's interests and ability, suggested high school program, and license requirements.

Architect. Chronicle Guidance Publications. 1966. 4p. 35c

Occupational brief containing definitions, work performed, requirements, determination of aptitudes and interest, employment, opportunities, outlook, and suggested activities.

ARCHITECT—*Continued*

Architect. Guidance Centre. 1968. 4p. 35c postpaid
Definition, history and importance, nature of work, qualifications necessary for entry and success, preparation, earnings, advantages, disadvantages, and how to get started.

Architect. Michigan Employment Security Commission. 1959. 2p. Single copy free
Job brief summarizing occupational data for use in Michigan.

Architects. Science Research Associates. 1968. 4p. 45c
Occupational brief describing nature of work, training, qualifications, opportunities, advantages, disadvantages, and future outlook.

**Architects. One section of *Occupational Outlook Handbook.*
Nature of work, where employed, training and other qualifications, employment outlook, earnings, and working conditions.

Architectural draftsman. Chronicle Guidance Publications. 1967. 4p. 35c
Occupational brief summarizing nature of work, working conditions, personal qualifications, educational requirements, earnings, and outlook.

Architectural technician. Careers. 1966. 2p. 20c
Career summary for desk-top file. Duties, qualifications, and outlook.

Architectural technologist. Guidance Centre. 1966. 4p. 35c postpaid
History and importance, nature of work, qualifications, working conditions, preparation, remuneration, related occupations, and how to get started.

Architecture: earned degrees by level, sex, and institution. One section of *Earned Degrees Conferred.*
List of seventy-one schools and the number of bachelor's, master's, and doctor's degrees conferred by each.

A career as an architect. Changing Times. 1960. 3p. 15c
A reprint discussing the preparation and future outlook.

Careers for engineers and architects. New York State Department of Civil Service. 1968. 4p. Free
Illustrated leaflet describing opportunities and examination procedures.

**Designing a better tomorrow—a career in architecture. American Institute of Architects. No date. 20p. $5 per 100. Single copy free
Nature of work, training, specialization, and a list of member schools of the Association of Collegiate Schools of Architecture.

**Employment outlook for architects. Bulletin No. 1650–28. Bureau of Labor Statistics, U.S. Department of Labor. Supt. of Documents. 1970. 6p. 10c
Reprint from the *Occupational Outlook Handbook.*

Engineers and architects in the Veterans Administration. VA pamphlet 05-15. Veterans Administration Forms Depot. 1967. 24p. Free
Description of opportunities, training, qualifications, and benefits.

Finding out about architects. Science Research Associates. 1967. 4p. 45c
Junior occupational brief containing concise facts about the job.

List of accredited schools of architecture. National Architectural Accrediting Board. 1968. 4p. Free
List of sixty-three schools and the degrees conferred by each upon completion of their professional curricula in architecture. Revised annually.

The master builders. Blake, Peter. Knopf, Inc. 1961. 412p. $8
Biography of three architects who were pioneers in modern building design: France's Le Corbusier, Germany's Van der Rohe, and America's Frank Lloyd Wright.

Member and associate member schools. Association of Collegiate Schools of Architecture. 1970. 2p. Single copy free
List of schools offering training in architecture, frequently revised.

Men of modern architecture. Forsee, Aylesa. Macrae Smith Company. 1966. 224p. $4.75
Biographies of outstanding contemporary architects.

Naval architect. Careers. 1966. 2p. 20c
Career summary for desk-top file. Duties, qualifications, and outlook.

**Opportunities in an architecture career. Piper, Robert J. Vocational Guidance Manuals. 1966. 120p. $1.95 paper; library edition $3.75
Discussion of the nature of work, types of jobs available, educational preparation, qualifications, opportunities, rewards, and employment outlook.

**So you want to be an architect. Meinhardt, Carl and others. Harper and Row. 1969. 201p. $4.95; library edition $4.43
Stressing the complex training, the authors present the educational requirements from high school subjects through liberal arts college, architectural school, and advanced degrees. Specialized jobs, types of architectural firms, and the apprenticeship required for licensing also are described. Includes list of accredited schools of architecture.

Young women in architecture—a battleground of the spirit. Alumnae Advisory Center. 1966. 4p. 35c
Reprint from *Mademoiselle* describing the work and experiences of several young women who are progressing in this field.

**Your future in architecture. Roth, Richard. Richards Rosen Press. Revised 1969. 159p. $4; library edition $3.78
Nature of work, importance to society, qualifications, opportunities, places of employment, preparation, and how to get started. Includes list of schools and state architectural registration boards.

* Your future in naval architecture. Benford, Harry and Mathes, J. M. Richards Rosen Press. 1968. 160p. $4; library edition $3.78
A study of the training necessary, the specialties available in this field, and a list of schools where preparation is given. Marine engineering is also described.

See also Landscape architect; Scientist

ARCHIVIST 101.168

Archivist. Careers. 1967. 2p. 20c

Career summary for desk-top file. Duties, qualifications, and outlook.

Careers in archives. Society of American Archivists. 1966. 2p. Single copy free to counselors

Leaflet describing briefly the career possibilities in archives.

ARMED FORCES 378.

Armed forces. Science Research Associates. 1969. 4p. 45c

Occupational brief describing opportunities for training and education, advancement in the services, opportunities for women, earnings, and other benefits.

Armed Forces. One section of *Occupational Outlook Handbook.*

Brief discussion of the military service obligation. Included is a chart portraying the types of work performed by enlisted men in the Armed Forces in 1967.

Armed services occupations. Chronicle Guidance Publications. 1967. 4p. 35c

Occupational brief summarizing work performed, working conditions, basic training, methods of entry, hours and earnings, and outlook.

Background paper in National Service and young women. Women's Bureau, U.S. Department of Labor. 1967. 8p. Free

Discussion concerning the possible adoption of a program of national service and a possible draft status for women.

**Basic facts about military service. Volume 14, Number 1. U.S. Department of Defense, High School News Service. 1970. 64p. Free

This is a collection of articles on the opportunities and obligations of military service. Topics included are: explanations of the Selective Service system, enlistment programs, commissioning programs, women in the armed forces, basic facts of service life, advanced educational programs, and career fields. Published annually.

Draft act 1970. Scientific Manpower Commission. 1970. 15p. 50c

Questions about the new draft system are answered. Regulations governing selective service classifications, deferments, and appeals are explained. Lottery sequence numbers are included.

The draft and you. Rothberg, Leslie S. Doubleday and Company. 1968. 332p. Paper $1.45

Good explanation of young men's rights, obligations, and privileges. Includes history of the draft, possibilities of appeals, conscientious objection, deferments, and resistance.

The draft lottery and how it works. Summer issue of *Occupational Outlook Quarterly,* 1970. 4p. 45c

Explanation of the new selection system and the implications it has for young men planning their education and careers. Presents the 1970 draft lottery sequence numbers by month and day.

Greeting: you are hereby ordered for induction . . . the draft in America. Liston, Robert A. McGraw-Hill Book Company. 1970. 159p. $5.50; library edition $5.33

The author objectively explains the Selective Service System, traces the historical background of conscription, and describes the current operation of the draft.

Handbook for conscientious objectors. Central Committee for Conscientious Objectors. 1968. 110p. $1.00

Procedures under selective service law to obtain deferments (such as occupational) on assignment to noncombatan service or to civilian work. Information concerning criminal prosecution if one is not classified as an objector. Also includes a selected, annotated bibliography of conscientious objection to war.

How to fill in the form for conscientious objectors. 1969. 4p. 10c

Instructions for filling in the Selective Service form number 150.

Meet today's WAC officer. U.S. Army Recruiting Command. 1966. 40p. Free

Illustrated booklet for the college graduate describing life and opportunities in the Women's Army corps.

Military, naval, air science: earned degrees, by level, sex, and institution. One section of *Earned Degrees Conferred.*

List of sixteen institutions and the number of degrees conferred by each.

A new life, a new world of opportunities with today's Women's Army Corps. Army Opportunities, U.S. Army Recruiting Command. 1968. 28p. Free

Advantages and benefits. For high school graduates.

Pathways to military service for college men and women. U.S. Department of Defense, Manpower and Reserve Affairs. 1969. 64p. Free

In outlining the various military service alternatives, this handbook will assist the young person in selecting a program best adapted to his interests and needs.

Questions and answers on the classification and assignment of conscientious objectors. National Service Board for Religious Objectors. 1969. 40p. 35c

Procedures for obtaining proper classification and description of the civilian work program in lieu of induction into the armed services.

Selective service and you. Careers. 1966. 8p. 35c

Career brief describing the classification system, appeals, college deferment, other deferments, conscientious objection, and induction into the Armed Forces.

Servicewomen and what they do. Schuon, Karl and Lyons, Ronald. Franklin Watts, Inc. 1964. 288p. $3.95

Answers some questions for young women, eighteen of age or older, who are considering military duty in any of the four major services. For grades 7 to 11.

ARMED FORCES—*Continued*

Special forces trooper. Archibald, Joseph. David McKay Company. 1967. 192p. $3.95; library binding $3.67

Story of a private who undergoes special training for the Green Berets, sees combat in Vietnam, and learns the importance of teamwork.

**The student's guide to military service. Harwood, Michael. Meredith Press. 1968. 313p. $3.95 paper

Suggestions for choosing the method of deferred or present service from among the number of programs offered by the uniformed services. Contains information about obtaining specialized or professional education while fulfilling military obligations. The emphasis is on how to get as much value as possible out of one's tour of duty.

Who is a conscientious objector? National Service Board for Religious Objectors. No date. 8p. $3 per 100. Single copy free

One of several leaflets giving information on this subject.

The woman marine. U.S. Marine Corps. 1968. 20p. Free

Illustrated brochure describing specialist training and qualifications.

The woman officer. U.S. Marine Corps. 1968. 18p. Free

Illustrated brochure describing qualifications and opportunities for college graduates.

See also Air force airman; Coast guardsman; Marine; Military serviceman; Sailor; Soldier

ARMY OFFICER. ***See*** **Armed forces; Soldier**

ARTIST **970.381**

American art directory. Gilbert, Dorothy, ed. R. R. Bowker Company. 1967. 508p. $22.50

Complete information on education in the fine arts. Lists professional art schools and art departments of colleges and universities in the United States and Canada. Entries indexed by name and interest, such as architecture, archaeology, art, etc. Published triennially for the American Federation of Arts.

American artist art school directory. National Art Education Association. 1968. 16p. 25c

Names and locations of art schools.

**Art career guide. Holden, Donald. Watson-Guptill Publications. Revised 1967. 280p. $6.95

This book contains sections on planning one's education, choosing a career, finding a job, and schools for preparation. Includes discussions on planning a portfolio, conducting job interviews, and what to expect from school or college. Also, the major art fields are described.

**Art careers. Roth, Claire J. and Weiss, Adelle. Henry Z. Walck, Inc. 1963. 116p. $3.75

The authors describe many unique and satisfying careers in advertising, industrial design, interior design, museum work, scenic design, teaching, and illustrating. For each field there is given the nature of work, qualificatons, training, and outlook.

Artists, general. Careers. 1970. 8p. 35c

Career brief describing duties, working conditions, training, qualifications, salaries, outlook, and places of employment.

Careers in art. National Art Education Association. No date. 11p. 10c

This booklet describes some of the major art careers and what makes for success in them. Includes art education, advertising design, industrial design, graphic art and illustration, fashion design and illustration, and ceramic design.

College and university acceptance of high school art credits for admission. National Art Education Association. 1968. 16p. 40c

Statement concerning college entrance requirements.

Directory of member schools. National Association of Schools of Art. 1967. 6p. Single copy free

Information about professional study in art and design in member schools. Includes major programs and degrees or certificates offered.

**Employment outlook for commercial artists, industrial designers, interior designers and decorators. Bulletin No. 1650–30. Bureau of Labor Statistics, U.S. Department of Labor. Supt. of Documents. 1970. 12p. 15c

Reprint from the *Occupational Outlook Handbook.*

Exploring your future in graphic arts and publishing. Sextant Systems, Inc. 1963. 96p. $6.50

One page is devoted to each of ninety-five jobs, summarizing duties, requirements for entering, promotional outlook, and pay and skill level.

Famous American painters. McKinney, Roland J. Dodd, Mead and Company. 1955. 125p. $3.50

Biographies of thirteen American painters. List of art institutions at which the artist's works are located and a reproduction of a typical painting included for each artist.

Finding out about art teachers. Science Research Associates. 1967. 4p. 45c

Junior occupational brief describing work and opportunities.

Finding out about artists. Science Research Associates. 1967. 4p. 45c

Junior occupational brief summarizing what the work requires and offers.

Fine and applied arts: earned degrees, by level, sex, and institution. One section of *Earned Degrees Conferred.*

Useful for judging the extent of a college's program in general art, music, speech and dramatic arts, and fine and applied arts.

ARTIST—*Continued*

Fine arts. Science Research Associates. 1966. 4p. 45c

Description of work, requirements, training, opportunities, advancement, outlook, advantages, and working conditions.

A guide to art studies. National Association of Schools of Art. 1967. 3p. Single copy free

A statement concerning the objectives of professional education in art and design.

Teaching art as a career. National Art Education Association. No date. 4p. 15c

Challenges of teaching art, salaries and other benefits, and how to become an art teacher.

Young women artists. Alumnae Advisory Center. 1968. 8p. 35c

Reprint from *Mademoiselle*. Despite the warning that the young woman artist still struggles to survive, experiences are given of a dozen or more young artists who have successfully marketed their artistic talents.

**Your career in art. Philadelphia College of Art. 1969. 33p. Single copy free on receipt of self-addressed, stamped business-size envelope

Qualifications, duties, and working conditions are described for advertising; art teaching; fashion illustration; fine arts; illustration; and industrial, dimensional, interior, fabric, and fashion design. Also general opportunities and rewards for men and women are pointed out.

See also Cartoonist; Commercial artist; Industrial designer; Medical and scientific illustrator; Performing artist

ASBESTOS AND INSULATING WORKER 863.

Asbestos and insulating workers. Careers. 1967. 8p. 35c

Career brief describing duties, working conditions, training, places of employment, earnings, and outlook.

Asbestos and insulating workers. Science Research Associates. 1967. 4p. 45c

Occupational brief describing nature of work, training, earnings, things to consider, and future outlook.

Asbestos and insulating workers. One section of *Occupational Outlook Handbook*.

Nature of the work, where employed, training, other qualifications, advancement, employment outlook, earnings, and working conditions.

**Employment outlook of asbestos and insulating workers. Bulletin No. 1650–68. Bureau of Labor Statistics, U.S. Department of Labor. Supt. Documents. 1970. 12p. 15c

Reprint from the *Occupational Outlook Handbook*.

Finding out about asbestos and insulation workers. Science Research Associates. 1967. 4p. 45c

Junior occupational brief describing work and opportunities.

Insulation (and asbestos) workers. Chronicle Guidance Publications. 1968. 4p. 35c

Occupational brief summarizing definition, history, work performed, working conditions, training requirements, personal qualifications, method of entry, advancement, employment outlook, earnings, and hours.

ASTRONAUT 002.081

American astronauts and spacecraft. Knight, David C. Franklin Watts, Inc. 1970. 159p. $8.95

A pictorial history from Project Mercury through Apollo 13. Includes two hundred photographs and brief biographies of all of the U.S. astronauts.

America's space pilots. National Aerospace Education Council. 1963. 12p. 25c

Illustrated leaflet featuring the photographs and brief biographies of the nine astronaut candidates then in training. The booklet also describes the training of space pilots and discusses the prospects for women in the national space program.

Americans to the moon; the story of Project Apollo. Gurney, Miriam. Random House. 1970. 147p. $3.95

A brisk account of Project Apollo from its inception to the completion of the Apollo 12 mission. Includes the aims and achievements of the exploratory unmanned and manned missions and the moon-landing flight of Apollo 11. Copiously illustrated. For grades 5 to 9.

Andy astronaut. Davis, Daphne. Golden Press. 1968. 24p. 69c

A tall picture book, sixteen inches tall, prepared for nursery school and kindergarten children. Contains vivid color illustrations of typical activities, explained in simple caption texts. One of the series called "busy people" books.

**Careers and opportunities in astronautics. Zarem, Lewis. Dutton and Company. 1969. 290p. $6.95

An engrossing account of the work being done in the exploration of space by men and machines, the qualifications and educational background needed, salaries, and opportunities for advancement. Each of the nineteen specialized fields of astronautics is discussed, including astrodynamics, missiles and space vehicles, nuclear propulsion, propellants and combustion, space law and sociology, and structures and materials. Illustrated.

**Careers in astronautics and rocketry: training and opportunities in the space and missile fields. Adams, Carsbie, C. and Von Braun, Wernher. McGraw-Hill Book Company. 1962. 252p. $6.95

Written for persons interested in a career in astronautics, the book presents information on the evolution of astronautics and rocketry, astronautics and the natural sciences, astronautics and the engineering disciplines, training, and opportunities. Information is given concerning schools, universities, and technical institutes offering training in astronautics.

ASTRONAUT—*Continued*

Careers in space. Binder, Otto O. Walker and Company. 1963. 308p. $6.50

Stresses the need for trained scientists, engineers, and technicians and describes the types of positions open to men and women. Of special interest to college students is the listing of industrial firms engaged in astronautical research and construction, with descriptions of the opportunities they offer.

First on the moon: a voyage with Neil Armstrong, Michael Collins, and Edwin E. Aldrin, Jr. Armstrong, Neil and others. Little, Brown and Company. 1970. 434p. $7.95

This is a detailed story of Apollo 11, biographies of the astronauts and coworkers, and a short history of space flight.

NASA counsels the earthbound. Chronicle Guidance Publications. 1967. 7p. 50c

Reprinted article from *Occupational Outlook Quarterly* discusses some of the counseling and educational services offered by the Educational Programs Division of NASA.

The next decade in space; a report of the Space Science and Technology Panel of the President's Science Advisory Committee. Supt. of Documents. 1970. 63p. 65c

The recommendations of the panel for the seventies; the goals to be achieved, the technology to be developed, and the ways in which new scientific knowledge can add to the quality of life in the world.

What does an astronaut do? Wells, Robert. Dodd, Mead and Company. 1961. 64p. Library binding $2.99

Simple text and pictures portray varied activities, training, and equipment. Written for grades 3 to 7.

What the moon astronauts will do all day. Hill, Robert W. John Day Company. 1968. 64p. $3.86

In eighty-four photographs, with accompanying text, this book describes the plan of Project Apollo to put men on the moon. For grades 4 to 6.

See also Aerospace industry worker; Airplane pilot; Aviator; Missileman

ASTRONOMER **021.088**

America's first woman astronomer: Maria Mitchell. Baker, Rachel and Merlen, Joanna. Julian Messner. 1960. 192p. $3.50; library binding $3.34

Biography of the woman who discovered a comet in 1847 and was the first woman to be elected to the American Academy of Arts and Sciences.

Astronomer. California Department of Employment. 1964. 7p. Single copy free

Duties, working conditions, salaries, training, promotion, and employment outlook in California.

Astronomer. Careers. 1970. 2p. 20c

Career summary for desk-top file. Duties, qualifications, and outlook.

Astronomer. Chronicle Guidance Publications. 1969. 4p. 35c

Occupational brief summarizing work performed, working conditions, qualifications, training, earnings, and outlook.

Astronomer. Guidance Centre. 1969. 4p. 35c postpaid

History and importance, nature of work, qualifications, working conditions, preparation, remuneration, related occupations, and how to get started.

* Astronomers. Science Research Associates. 1967. 4p. 45c

Occupational brief describing nature of work, requirements, getting started, earnings, advantages, disadvantages, and future outlook.

**Astronomers. One section of *Occupational Outlook Handbook.*

Nature of work, where employed, training, other qualifications, employment outlook, earnings, and working conditions.

**A career in astronomy. American Astronomical Society. 1969. 17p. Single copy free

Discussion of broad general requirements, rewards, opportunities, and some recommendations. List of colleges that offer an undergraduate major in astronomy. Also included is a list of colleges that give the doctor's degree in astronomy, with their major fields of specializations.

Copernicus. Thomas, Henry. Julian Messner. 1960. 192p. $3.50; library binding $3.34

Biography of the sixteenth century astronomer who demonstrated that the sun, and not the earth, was the center of the solar system.

Finding out about astronomers. Science Research Associates. 1967. 4p. 45c

Junior occupational brief describing work and opportunities.

The men behind the man in the moon. Chronicle Guidance Publications. 1967. 4p. 35c

Reprinted article from *Occupational Outlook Quarterly* discusses the work force of the National Aeronautics and Space Administration.

The telescope makers; from Galileo to the space age. Land, Barbara. Crowell, Collier and Macmillan, Inc. 1969. 245p. $4.50

Profiles about the life and work of ten astronomers span the development of telescopes from the first primitive ones.

**Your future in astronomy. Bell, Raymond M. Richards Rosen Press. 1970. 160p. $4; library edition $3.78

Includes description of careers in the aircraft, spacecraft, missile, and rocket industries.

ATHLETE 153.348

Athletes. Chronicle Guidance Publications. 1967. 4p. 35c

Occupational brief summarizing work performed, personal qualifications, training, working conditions, earnings, opportunities for advancement, and outlook.

ATHLETE—*Continued*

Best sports stories; a panorama of the 1969 sports world, including the 1969 champions of all sports. Marsh, Irving T. and Enre, Edward, ed. Dutton and Company. 1970. 336p. $6.95

Baseball and football are the sports most heavily represented but others featured are basketball, golf, boxing, horse racing, track, tennis, hockey and automobile racing. Includes twenty-five of the year's notable sports photographs.

Broadway Joe and his super Jets. Fox, Larry. Coward-McCann, Inc. 1969. 255p. $5.95

Incorporating anecdotes and profiles of players and owners, a sportswriter covers Joe Namath's career and the history of the American Football League and the New York Jets. Includes analysis of important games and many records and statistics.

**Careers and opportunities in sports. Isaacs, Stan. Dutton and Company. 1964. 192p. $4.50

A guide to professional careers in the world of sports—as player, coach, official, "front office" executive, newspaper writer, or broadcaster. In individual chapters on the various sports, the author gives the qualifications and training needed and the best way of entering the field.

Famous American women athletes. Jacobs, Helen Hull. Dodd, Mead and Company. 1964. 160p. $3.50

The author analyzes what each woman contributed to her particular sport and the qualifications that made her a champion in swimming, skating, skiing, golf, bowling, or tennis.

Finding out about professional football players. Science Research Associates. 1967. 4p. 45c

Junior occupational brief summarizing what the work requires and offers.

Goal! My life on ice. Gilbert, Rod and others. Hawthorn Books, Inc. 1968. 181p. $4.95

Biography of a professional ice hockey player. Includes a lively analysis of ice hockey for the beginner.

Hockey player. Guidance Centre. 1968. 4p. 35c postpaid

Nature of work, qualifications, earnings, how to enter, advantages, disadvantages, and related occupations.

Hockey's greatest stars. Orr, Frank. Putnam's Sons. 1970. 192p. $3.64

Twenty-two biographical sketches covering the past four decades.

In the pocket: my life as a quarterback. Morall, Earl and Sullivan, George. Grosset and Dunlap. 1969. 210p. $5.95

Inspirational account of a player considered by many the most valuable quarterback of the year.

Professional athlete—golfer. California State Department of Employment. 1964. 6p. Single copy free

Occupational guide describing work, requirements, training, and outlook.

Professional athletes. Science Research Associates. 1967. 4p. 45c

Occupational brief describing nature of work, training, qualifications, opportunities, advantages, and future outlook.

The pros. Liston, Robert. Platt and Munk. 1968. 275p. $3.95

Thirteen professionals in the fields of baseball, football, basketball, hockey, and golf were interviewed. The author brings out why each man chose his career and how and why he did or did not succeed. The text is provocative and the individual personalities of the athletes well defined.

Rookie Goalie: Gerry Desjardins. Libby, Bill. Julian Messner. 1970. 192p. $3.95; library binding $3.64

The story of a major league hockey player as told through the trials and triumphs of his career.

Snow on Blueberry Mountain. Meader, S. T. Harcourt, Brace and World. 1961. 189p. $3.50

Career fiction. Story of a high school boy who dreams of turning a worthless strip of cutover mountainside into a commercial ski slope.

Sports. One chapter in Volume I of the *Encyclopedia of Careers and Vocational Guidance.*

Discussion of the work and opportunities of the sports performer, sportscaster, newspaper sportswriter, coach, talent scout, and sports columnist, statistician, announcer, official, and umpire.

Stan Mikita; the turbulent career of a hockey superstar. Fischler, Stan. Cowles Book Company. 1969. 213p. $3.95

Biography of the man who played center for ten seasons on the Chicago Black Hawks professional ice hockey team.

They play for money. Reprint from the *Occupational Outlook Quarterly,* December, 1967. Supt. of Documents. 1967. 3p. 45c

This reprint describes the nature of professional sports, qualifications, number and distribution of players, future prospects, advan es, and disadvantages of being a professional athlete.

See also Athletic coach; Baseball player; Physical education teacher

ATHLETIC COACH 099.228

Athletic coach (education). Chronicle Guidance Publications. 1968. 4p. 35c

Occupational brief summarizing work performed, working conditions, personal qualifications, training, earnings, disadvantages, and outlook.

**Athletic coaches. Science Research Associates. 1968. 4p. 45c

Occupational brief describing nature of work, training, qualifications, opportunities, advantages, disadvantages, and future outlook.

Coach. California State Department of Employment. 1966. 6p. Single copy free

Job duties, working conditions, pay, hours, entrance requirements, training, and employment outlook.

ATHLETIC COACH—*Continued*

Coach Tom Cahill, a man for the corps. White, Gordon and Hyman, Mervin. Macmillan Company. 1969. 181p. $5.95

A sports journalist and football editor portray the life and coaching career of the head football coach at West Point Military Academy. They show how his previous experience prepared him for his assignment.

Fighting coach. Archibald, Joseph. Macrae Smith Company. 1954. 192p. $3.75

Career fiction. A young coach refuses to compromise the ethics of amateur football for financial gains and public prestige.

Finding out about athletic coaches. Science Research Associates. 1967. 4p. 45c

Junior occupational brief summarizing what the work requires and offers.

See also Athlete; Physical education instructor

ATOMIC ENERGY INDUSTRY WORKER 982.

Atomic energy, careers in. Chronicle Guidance Publications. 1967. 4p. 35c

Occupational brief summarizing nature and geographic distribution, personal requirements, working conditions, specific occupations in the field, educational requirements, hours and earnings, and outlook.

Atomic Energy Commission special fellowships in nuclear science and engineering. Oak Ridge Associated Universities. 1968. 38p. Free

Description of the work, training, programs of study at the graduate level, and qualifications for fellowships.

Atomic Energy Commission special fellowships in radiation science and protection. Oak Ridge Associated Universities. 1969. 20p. Free

Qualifications for fellowships and description of training.

Atomic energy engineers and scientists. Careers. 1967. 8p. 35c

Career brief describing nature of work, training, working conditions, personal qualifications, places of employment, related careers, earnings, and outlook. Additional readings.

Atomic light: lasers—what they are and how they work. Sterling Publishing Company. 1967. 152p. $3.95

Clear explanation. No background is expected of readers. Illustrated.

**Careers in atomic energy—planning for scientific and technical professions. U.S. Atomic Energy Commission, Division of Technical Information. 1968. 27p. Free

Discussion of the work of the atomic scientists, college training, scholarships and other financial assistance, location of opportunities, and professional satisfactions. Good reading lists.

Educational programs and facilities in nuclear science and engineering. U.S. Atomic Energy Commission, Special Projects Office. 1968. 101p. Free to counselors

A summary of schools offering education in this field, including four-year colleges that offer at least one year of study in atomic and nuclear physics. The facilities and equipment tables list course offerings and equipment available for teaching and research in nuclear fields.

**Employment outlook for the atomic energy field. Bulletin No. 1650–111. Bureau of Labor Statistics, U. S. Department of Labor. Supt. of Documents. 1970. 15p. 15c

Reprint from the *Occupational Outlook Handbook.*

Guide to nuclear education activities. U.S. Atomic Energy Commission, Division of Nuclear Education and Training. 1966. 24p. Free

Includes grants, loans, research opportunities, fellowships, and other assistance to graduate students.

J. Robert Oppenheimer and the atomic story. Kugelmass, J. Alvin. Julian Messner. 1953. 192p. $3.50; library binding $3.34

Biography of a man who contributed to the development of atomic energy, containing many of the dramatic incidents at the Los Alamos Scientific Laboratory and the Institute for Advanced Study in Princeton, New Jersey.

**Occupations in the atomic energy field. One chapter in *Occupational Outlook Handbook.*

Applications and production of atomic energy, nature of the field, kinds of occupations, training, other qualifications, advancement, employment outlook, earnings, and working conditions.

**Your future in nuclear energy fields. Thompson, William E., Jr. Richards Rosen Press. Revised 1969. 160p. $4; library edition $3.78

Information and advice concerning the nature of work in government, industry, or teaching are followed by a discussion of training, opportunities, how to look for the first job, and employment information.

ATOMIC ENERGY TECHNICIAN 726.281

Atomic energy technicians. Science Research Associates. 1968. 4p. 45c

Occupational brief describing nature of work, requirements, methods of getting started, earnings, and future outlook.

Finding out about atomic energy technicians. Science Research Associates. 1967. 4p. 45c

Junior occupational brief containing concise facts about the job.

Nuclear technician. Chronicle Guidance Publications. 1970. 4p. 35c

Occupational brief summarizing nature of the work, requirements, training, opportunities, and employment outlook.

ATTORNEY. *See* Lawyer

AUCTIONEER 294.258

Auctioneer. Careers. 1969. 2p. 20c

Career summary for desk-top file. Duties, qualifications, and outlook.

Auctioneer. Chronicle Guidance Publications. 1969. 4p. 35c

Occupational brief summarizing work performed, working conditions, personal qualifications, training requirements, opportunities, and employment outlook.

Auctioneer. Guidance Centre. 1970. 4p. 35c postpaid

Nature of work, qualifications, preparation, working conditions, outlook, advantages, disadvantages, how to get started, and related occupations.

AUDITOR 160.188

Auditor. Careers. 1967. 2p. 20c

Career summary for desk-top file. Duties, qualifications, and outlook.

Internal auditor. Internal Revenue Service. 1969. 16p. Free

Information on professional accounting careers in management audit positions in the Internal Revenue Service. Describes qualifications requirements, promotion opportunities, job locations, training, and how to apply.

Your future in the field of internal auditing. Institute of Internal Auditors. 1968. 14p. 25c

Description of work, responsibilities, qualifications, and its place in the business world. Designed for use by college students and to assist audit managers to recruit graduates.

AUTHOR. *See* Writer

AUTOMOBILE-BODY REPAIRMAN 807.381

Automobile-body repairman. Careers. 1969. 2p. 20c

Career summary for desk-top file. Duties, qualifications, and outlook.

Automobile-body repairman. Michigan Employment Security Commission. 1962. 2p. Single copy free

Job brief summarizing occupational data for use in Michigan.

Automobile-body repairman. One section of *Occupational Outlook Handbook.*

Nature of work, places of employment, training, qualifications, employment outlook, earnings, and working conditions.

* Automobile body repairmen. Science Research Associates. 1966. 4p. 45c

Occupational brief describing work, training, working conditions, getting started, earnings and benefits, things to consider, and future outlook.

Automotive body repairman. Chronicle Guidance Publications. 1969. 4p. 35c

Occupational brief summarizing work performed, working conditions, personal qualifications, training requirements, opportunities, and employment outlook.

Finding out about automobile-body repairmen. Science Research Associates. 1967. 4p. 45c

Junior occupational brief describing work and opportunities.

AUTOMOBILE MANUFACTURING INDUSTRY WORKER. ***See*** **Motor vehicle and equipment manufacturing worker**

AUTOMOBILE MECHANIC **620.281**

**Aim for a job in automotive service. Taylor, Dawson and Bradley, James. Richards Rosen Press. 1968. 154p. $4; library edition $3.78; edition in large type $5.97

Many aspects of auto service are discussed with the training and skills needed for each.

Automobile and truck mechanics. Michigan Employment Security Commission. 1959. 2p. Single copy free

Job brief summarizing occupational data for use in Michigan.

Automobile brakeman. Careers. 1970. 2p. 20c

Career summary for desk-top file. Duties, qualifications, and outlook.

Automobile mechanic. California State Department of Employment. 1967. 3p. Single copy free

Duties, working conditions, wages, hours, preparation, promotion, and employment prospects.

* Automobile mechanic. Careers. 1967. 8p. 35c

Career brief describing duties, working conditions, training requirements, training opportunities, personal qualifications, employment prospects, earnings, advancement prospects, where employed, measuring one's interest and ability, suggested high school program, and unionization.

Automobile mechanic. Chronicle Guidance Publications. 1967. 4p. 35c

Occupational brief containing history, work performed, working conditions, personal requirements, training requirements, training opportunities, outlook, and where employed.

Automobile mechanic. Guidance Centre. 1968. 4p. 35c postpaid

Nature of work, history of the occupation, working conditions, qualifications, preparation, employment and advancement, earnings, how to get started, advantages, and disadvantages.

**Automobile mechanics. One section in *Occupational Outlook Handbook.*

Nature of work, where employed, training, other qualifications, advancement, employment outlook, earnings, and working conditions.

Automotive mechanic (automotive mechanic apprentice). California State Department of Employment. 1967. 5p. Single copy free

Occupational guide describing work, requirements, training, and outlook.

Automotive mechanics. Science Research Associates. 1967. 4p. 45c

Occupational brief describing nature of work, requirements, training, getting started and advancing, earnings, advantages, disadvantages, and future outlook.

AUTOMOBILE MECHANIC—*Continued*

Career opportunities in automotive service. Automobile Manufacturers Association. 1968. 8p. Free

Includes the wide range of opportunities in this industry and how to train for these jobs.

**Employment outlook for automobile service occupations. Bulletin No. 1650–79. Bureau of Labor Statistics, U.S. Department of Labor. Supt. of Documents. 1970. 20p. 20c

Reprint from the *Occupational Outlook Handbook*. Includes automobile body repairman, automobile mechanics, truck and bus mechanics, automobile painters, automobile trimmers and installation men, automobile parts countermen, automobile service advisors, and gasoline service station attendants.

Find a career in auto mechanics. Harrison, C. William. Putnam's Sons. 1964. 160p. $3.50

Emphasizing the broad range of skills needed, this book points out the vital role of the mechanic in safety and public relations. For grades 7 to 11.

Finding out about automotive mechanics. Science Research Associates. 1967. 4p. 45c

Junior occupational brief summarizing what the work requires and offers.

Job opportunities in automotive service. Chronicle Guidance Publications. 1967. 4p. 35c

Reprinted article from *Occupational Outlook Quarterly* discusses work performed by mechanics, body repairmen, painters, parts countermen, and service advisors.

New car get-ready man. California State Department of Employment. 1966. 3p. Single copy free

Occupational guide describing work, requirements, training, and outlook.

Tire builder (vulcanizer). Careers. 1967. 2p. 20c

Career summary for desk-top file. Duties, qualifications, and outlook.

Truck and bus mechanic. Careers. 1967. 2p. 20c

Career summary for desk-top file. Duties, qualifications, and outlook.

Truck and bus mechanics. Chronicle Guidance Publications. 1968. 4p. 35c

Occupational brief summarizing work performed, where employed, working conditions, hours and earnings, training requirements and opportunities, and outlook.

Truck mechanic and serviceman. California State Department of Employment. 1967. 3p. Single copy free

Occupational guide describing work, requirements, training, and outlook.

Truck mechanics and bus mechanics. One section of *Occupational Outlook Handbook*.

Nature of work, places of employment, qualifications, employment outlook, earnings, and working conditions.

AUTOMOBILE SALESMAN 280.358

Automobile dealer. California State Department of Employment. 1965. 3p. Single copy free

Occupational guide describing work, requirements, training, and outlook.

Automobile parts countermen. One section of *Occupational Outlook Handbook.*

Nature of work, places of employment, training, requirements, advancement, employment outlook, earnings, and working conditions.

Automobile salesman. Careers. 1969. 2p. 20c

Career summary for desk-top file. Duties, qualifications, and outlook.

Automobile salesman. Chronicle Guidance Publications. 1969. 4p. 35c

Occupational brief summarizing work performed, working conditions, earnings, personal qualifications, opportunities, methods of entry, and related jobs.

* Automobile salesmen. Science Research Associates. 1970. 4p. 45c

Occupational brief describing nature of work, qualifications, earnings, getting started and advancing, advantages, disadvantages, and future outlook.

Automobile salesmen. One section of *Occupational Outlook Handbook.*

Nature of work, places of employment, training, employment outlook, earnings, advancement, and working conditions.

Automobile service advisors. One section of *Occupational Outlook Handbook.*

Nature of work, where employed, employment outlook, and working conditions.

**Employment outlook for automobile salesmen. Bulletin No. 1650–56. Bureau of Labor Statistics, U.S. Department of Labor. Supt. of Documents. 1970. 8p. 10c

Reprint from the *Occupational Outlook Handbook.*

Finding out about automobile salesmen. Science Research Associates. 1967. 4p. 45c

Junior occupational brief summarizing what the work requires and offers.

Professional profile of an automobile salesman. General Motors Corporation. 1961. 31p. Free

Discussion of requirements, opportunities, and earnings. Indicates that a career in retail automobile selling can mean a good income and life-long security. Includes advice from a number of successful salesmen in this field.

Your career in the retail automobile industry. National Automobile Dealers Association. 1966. 25p. Free

Description of many career opportunities including service and sales occupations.

AUTOMOBILE SERVICE-STATION ATTENDANT 915.867

Automobile service-station attendant. Michigan Employment Security Commission. 1962. 2p. Single copy free

Job brief summarizing occupational data for use in Michigan.

AUTOMOBILE SERVICE STATION ATTENDANT—*Continued*

Automobile service station attendant (manager). Chronicle Guidance Publications. 1967. 4p. 35c

Occupational brief containing definition, work performed, working conditions, training opportunities, and private ownership.

* Automotive-service-station attendant. Careers. 1968. 8p. 35c

Career brief describing duties, working conditions, training, qualifications, earnings, and outlook.

Finding out about service station workers. Science Research Associates. 1967. 4p. 45c

Junior occupational brief containing concise facts about the job.

Garage service salesman. California State Department of Employment. 1964. 3p. Single copy free

Occupational guide describing work, requirements, training, and outlook.

** Gasoline service station attendants. One section of *Occupational Outlook Handbook.*

Nature of work, where employed, training, other qualifications, advancement, employment outlook, earnings, and working conditions.

The new look in service stations. Chronicle Guidance Publications. 1967. 4p. 35c

Reprinted article from the *The Distributor* discusses new products, services, and physical appearance of service stations.

* Opportunities in automotive service. Automobile Manufacturers Association. 1968. 8p. Free

This leaflet indicates the wide range of opportunities for young men in this field, the employment outlook, training, trainee-selection factors, and qualities needed for success.

Service station attendant. California State Department of Employment. 1968. 3p. Single copy free

Duties, working conditions, pay, training, promotion, and employment prospects.

Service station attendant. Guidance Centre. 1968. 4p. 35c postpaid

Nature of work, qualifications, working conditions, outlook, earnings, advantages, disadvantages, how to get started, and related occupations.

** Service station workers. Science Research Associates. 1969. 4p. 45c

Occupational brief describing nature of work, opportunities, advantages, disadvantages, and future outlook.

Starting and managing a service station. Small Business Administration. Supt. of Documents. 1961. 80p. 35c

This booklet describes the advantages and disadvantages of entering this particular business, the risks involved, the personal characteristics that will contribute to success, and some management practices.

AUTOMOTIVE ENGINEER. *See* Engineer

AVIATION MECHANIC. *See* Airplane mechanic

AVIATOR 196.168

Air drop: men, weapons and cargo by parachute. Colby, C. B. Coward-McCann, Inc. 1953. 48p. Library edition $2.97

Photographs and brief text reveal work and training. Written for grades 4 to 8.

**Aviation careers: jobs in the air and on the ground. Fenton, D. X. Lippincott Company. 1969. 208p. $4.95

This is a survey of job opportunities in three major areas of aviation—scheduled and supplemental airline service, general aviation activities, and the aerospace industry. Noting educational requirements and salary ranges, the author describes the work done by air and ground personnel, including flight engineers, dispatchers, mechanics and reservation agents. The appendix contains lists of institutions offering courses in aviation subjects and sample questions from aviation examinations. Illustrated.

Aviation—where career opportunities are bright. National Aerospace Education Council. 1968. 120p. $3

Current facts for many jobs in aviation including career pilots, aviation mechanics, airline jobs, and aviation careers in government.

**Civil aviation occupations. One section of *Occupational Outlook Handbook.*

Nature of work, training, qualifications, employment outlook, earnings, and working conditions.

**Employment outlook for civil aviation. Bulletin No. 1650–117. Bureau of Labor Statistics, U.S. Department of Labor. Supt. of Documents. 1970. 20p. 20c

Reprint from the *Occupational Outlook Handbook.* Includes pilots and co-pilots, flight engineers, stewardesses, aircraft mechanics, airline dispatchers, air traffic controllers, ground radio operators and teletypists, traffic agents and clerks.

Helicopters in action. Bergaust, Erik and Foss, William. Putnam's Sons. 1962. 96p. $3.29

An account of the development of this aircraft and information on helicopter flight schools in the United States and Canada. Written for ages 10 to 14.

SAC: men and machines of our Strategic Air Command. Colby, C. B. Coward-McCann, Inc. 1961. 48p. Library binding $2.97

Photographs and brief text reveal the work of maintaining a security vigil. Written for grades 4 to 8.

Skyblazers: your career in aviation. Neal, Harry Edward. Julian Messner. 1963. 192p. Library binding $3.64

Describes the many jobs involved in the aircraft industry, emphasizing the opportunities in military and naval aviation, commercial, and business flying. One chapter is devoted to aviation careers for women.

AVIATOR—*Continued*

Whirling wings. Floherty, John J. and McGrady, Mike. Lippincott Company. 1961. 160p. $3

Story of the helicopter and the men responsible for its invention and development. Illustrated.

See also Aerospace industry worker; Air force airman; Airplane pilot; Astronaut; Atomic energy industry worker

BABY-SITTER **307.878**

Baby-sitters' handbook. Flander, Judy. Science Research Associates. 1962. 48p. 75c

Written for teen-age sitters, the booklet includes qualifications for a sitter, the many problems concerning wages and employer-employee relations, duties of a sitter, the care of infants and older children. The book emphasizes that anyone can be a baby-sitter, but it is important to have the required skills and knowledge to be a good one.

A manual for baby sitters: Lowndes, Marion. Little, Brown and Company. 1961. 185p. $4.50

Description of the skills, desirable qualities needed, and obligations. Includes a list of twelve essentials for baby sitters. Also given are the responsibilities of those who hire sitters. Selected reading lists.

Au pair jobs abroad (mother's helper). Alumnae Advisory Center. 1969. 6p. 35c

Reprint from *Mademoiselle* recounting experiences of some young women who worked in a continental household in exchange for "bed, board, and pocket money." Information also is given concerning requirements and how to find this kind of a job.

When teenagers take care of children: a guide for baby sitters. Kraft, Ivor. Macrae Smith Company. 1965. 64p. $2.95

Discussion of duties, rights, and responsibilities.

When teenagers take care of children; a guide for baby sitters. Supt. of Documents. 1964. 60p. 25c

This guide provides information that will be helpful to young people in meeting their responsibilities in caring for children.

BACTERIOLOGIST. ***See*** **Microbiologist**

BAKER **526.781**

**Aim for a job in the bakery industry. O'Connell, Desmond. Richards Rosen Press. 1967. 146p. $4; library edition $3.78

Describes opportunities at various levels in the bakery industry.

Baker. Careers. 1969. 2p. 20c

Career summary for desk-top file. Duties, qualifications, and outlook.

Baker. Chronicle Guidance Publications. 1966. 4p. 35c
Occupational brief summarizing work performed, working conditions, training, opportunities, employment outlook, related jobs, and suggested activities.

Baker. Guidance Centre. 1969. 4p. 35c postpaid
History and importance of the work, qualifications, preparation, earnings, employment and advancement, how to get started, and related occupations.

Bakers. Michigan Employment Security Commission. 1963. 2p. Single copy free
Job brief summarizing occupational data for use in Michigan.

* Bakers. Science Research Associates. 1967. 4p. 45c
Occupational brief describing nature of work, preparation, qualifications, opportunities, advantages, disadvantages, and future outlook.

Bakery occupations. California State Department of Employment. 1968. 4p. Single copy free
Occupational guide describing work, requirements, training, and outlook.

The baking industry. One chapter in *Encyclopedia of Careers and Vocational Guidance.*
Growth of the industry, kinds of work, compensation, and opportunities in marketing and sales.

Finding out about bakers. Science Research Associates. 1967. 4p. 45c
Junior occupational brief describing work and opportunities.

Handbook on baking schools and scholarships. Allied Trades of the Baking Industry. 1962. 24p. Free
Stresses the need for more and better trained young bakers and provides information on training opportunities and scholarships.

**Occupations in the baking industry. One chapter of *Occupational Outlook Handbook,* 1966-67 edition.
Nature and location of the industry, kinds of jobs, training, other qualifications, advancement, employment outlook, earnings, and working conditions.

* There's a future for you in the baking industry. American Bakers Association. 1965. 22p. Free
Description of the baking industry, its composition, size, and importance in the economy. Shows the steps in production and marketing, the wide variety of jobs, and the skills required. Distributed through local wholesale bakers who are members of the American Bakers Association.

BALLET DANCER. *See* Dancer

BANK OFFICER 186.118

Bank manager. Guidance Centre. 1966. 4p. 35c postpaid
Definition, history and importance of work, qualifications, preparation, employment, outlook, earnings, and how to get started.

BANK OFFICER—*Continued*

Bank officers. Science Research Associates. 1970. 4p. 45c

Occupational brief containing description of work, qualifications, earnings, opportunities, things to consider, and outlook. Selected references.

**Bank officers. One section of *Occupational Outlook Handbook.*

Nature of work, training, other qualifications, advancement, and employment outlook.

**Banking—a career for today and tomorrow. American Bankers Association. 1967. 24p. Single copy free

Directed to the college student, this describes career opportunities in banking for the college graduate. Includes the importance of banks in today's world, wide range of jobs, typical bank positions, opportunities, and advantages.

College men in banking. American Bankers Association. 1967. 4p. Single copy free

Report of a survey concerning recruiting and promoting men graduating from colleges and universities.

Facts you should know about investment banking. Investment Bankers Association of America. 1967. 16p. Free

Explanation of the role of the investment banker in serving business, government, and the investor.

Finding out about bank officers. Science Research Associates. 1967. 4p. 45c

Junior occupational brief summarizing what the work requires and offers.

How to achieve success in investment banking. Davis, George W. Investment Bankers Association of America. 1968. 5p. Free

Advice given to graduates of a university course in this field.

To the young man who is interested in everything. Investment Bankers Association of America. 1965. 4p. Free

A description of opportunities in the investment business and the characteristics and requirements for persons seeking a career in this field.

Want to be a banker? Changing Times. 1959. 3p. 15c

A reprint describing the promising careers in banking.

BANK TELLER 212.368

* Bank teller. Careers. 1968. 8p. 35c

Career brief describing duties, working conditions, qualifications, training, earnings, and outlook.

Bank teller. Chronicle Guidance Publications. 1968. 4p. 35c

Occupational brief summarizing work performed, hours, earnings, personal requirements, training, methods of entry, promotion, and outlook.

Bank teller. Guidance Centre. 1969. 4p. 35c postpaid

Definition, nature of work, qualifications, preparation, how to get started, earnings, advantages, and disadvantages.

Bank teller. Michigan Employment Security Commission. 1962. 2p. Single copy free

Job brief summarizing occupational data for use in Michigan.

Finding out about bank tellers. Science Research Associates. 1967. 4p. 45c

Junior occupational brief containing concise facts about the job.

Teller (banking). California State Department of Employment. 1968. 4p. Single copy free

Occupational guide describing work, requirements, training, and outlook.

Tellers. One section of *Occupational Outlook Handbook.*

Nature of work, training, other qualifications, advancement, employment outlook, and earnings.

The work of the bank teller. Beaty, John Y. Bankers Publishing Company. 1952. 77p. $1

Intended as information for the beginning bank teller, the book includes descriptions of the various tasks and qualifications.

BANK WORKER 219.388

Bank accountant. Guidance Centre. 1966. 4p. 35c postpaid

History and importance, nature of work, qualifications, working conditions, preparation, remuneration, related occupations, and how to get started.

* Bank careers. Careers. 1968. 8p. 35c

Career brief describing the history and functions of banks, duties of typical bank workers, training, personal qualifications, earnings, advancement prospects, measuring one's interest and ability, and hours of work.

Bank clerks and related workers. One section of *Occupational Outlook Handbook.*

Nature of work, training, other qualifications, advancement, and employment outlook.

Bank workers. Science Research Associates. 1970. 4p. 45c

Occupational brief describing nature of work, training, qualifications, opportunities, advantages, disadvantages, and future outlook.

**Banking—an opportunity for you. American Bankers Association. 1966. 12p. Single copy free

Directed to high school students, this discusses the growth of banking, typical starting positions, qualifications, training, and desirable features.

A career for women in banking. National Association of Bank-Women, Inc. 1966. 12p. Single copy free

Information about the opportunities open to women in banking.

Careers in banking. Chronicle Guidance Publications. 1966. 4p. 35c

Occupational brief summarizing work performed, employment conditions, hours, earnings, personal requirements, educational requirements, where employed, and outlook.

BANK WORKER—*Continued*

**Employment outlook for banking. Bulletin No. 1650–124. Bureau of Labor Statistics, U.S. Department of Labor. Supt. of Documents. 1970. 12p. 15c

Reprint from the *Occupational Outlook Handbook*. Includes bank clerks, tellers, and bank officers.

Exploring your future in banking. Sextant Systems, Inc. 1970. 120p. $8.95

One page is devoted to each of ninety-five jobs, presenting the duties, requirements for entering, promotional outlook, and the pay and skill level.

Finding out about bank clerks. Science Research Associates. 1967. 4p. 45c

Junior occupational brief summarizing what the work requires and offers.

Free literature available to educators and vocational counselors. Bankers Association of America. 1969. 2p. Free

Description of available leaflets.

The new look in banking—careers for young women in banking and finance. David McKay Company. 1961. 210p. $3.50

Describes the increasing opportunities for women, nature of work, qualifications, and outlook.

Occupations in banking. One chapter in *Occupational Outlook Handbook*.

Nature of work, where employed, employment outlook, earnings, working conditions, and advancement. Specific information concerning bank clerk, teller, and bank officer.

Safe deposit work. Beaty, John Y. Bankers Publishing Company. 1952. 62p. $1

Includes an explanation of the duties and responsibilities involved in safe deposit work.

See also Securities salesman

BARBER **330.371**

Barber. California State Department of Employment. 1966. 5p. Single copy free

Duties, working conditions, wages, hours, promotion, training, and employment outlook.

Barber. Careers. 1968. 8p. 35c

Career brief describing duties, working conditions, training, personal qualifications, earnings, unionization, and outlook.

Barber. Chronicle Guidance Publications. 1969. 3p. 35c

Occupational brief describing work performed, working conditions, personal qualifications, training requirements, opportunities, outlook, methods of entry, and suggested activities.

Barber. Guidance Centre. 1969. 4p. 35c postpaid

Nature of work, qualifications necessary for entry and success, employment and advancement, earnings, advantages, disadvantages, and related occupations.

Barber. Michigan Employment Security Commission. 1960. 2p. Single copy free

Job brief summarizing occupational data for use in Michigan.

**Barbering as a career. Belleau, Wilfrid. Park Publishing House. 1969. 14p. $1

Importance and nature of work, qualifications, training, entrance requirements, expenses, apprenticeship, working conditions, advancement, income, employment outlook, and how to begin.

Barbers. Science Research Associates. 1966. 4p. 45c

Occupational brief describing duties, requirements, training, methods of getting started and advancing, earnings, advantages, disadvantages and future outlook.

**Barbers. One section of *Occupational Outlook Handbook.*

Nature of work, where employed, training, other qualifications, advancement, employment outlook, earnings, and working conditions.

**Employment outlook for barbers, cosmetologists. Bulletin No. 1650–61. Bureau of Labor Statistics, U.S. Department of Labor. Supt. of Documents. 1970. 8p. 10c

Reprint from the *Occupational Outlook Handbook.*

Finding out about barbers. Science Research Associates. 1967. 4p. 45c

Junior occupational brief describing work and opportunities.

* A profitable career in barbering awaits you! National Career Center. 1968. 8p. 10c

An illustrated brochure describing the nature of the work, trends, training, advantages, and income.

BASEBALL PLAYER (PROFESSIONAL) 153.348

Baseball player, professional. California State Department of Employment. 1963. 7p. Single copy free

Occupational guide describing work, requirements, training, and outlook.

Finding out about professional baseball players. Science Research Associates. 1967. 4p. 45c

Junior occupational brief describing work and opportunities.

Heroes behind the mask; America's greatest catchers. Shapiro, Milton J. Julian Messner. 1968. 191p. 3.95; library edition $3.64

Highlights from the careers of ten catchers.

Jackie Robinson the Brooklyn Dodgers. Shapiro, Milton J. Julian Messner. 1957. 192p. $3.50; library binding $3.34

Biography containing information about the struggles and triumphs of the first Negro baseball player in the major leagues.

BASEBALL PLAYER (PROFESSIONAL)—*Continued*

World series thrills. Bell, Joseph N. Julian Messner. 1962. 192p. $3.95; library binding $3.64

The author has selected ten of the top thrills in world series play from 1912 to 1960, each followed by a capsule biography of the player and his baseball record. Photographs.

See also Athlete

BEAUTY OPERATOR. *See* **Cosmetologist**

BEEKEEPER **419.181**

Beekeeper. Careers. 1966. 2p. 20c

Career summary for desk-top file. Duties, qualifications, and outlook.

Beekeeper. Guidance Centre. 1966. 4p. 35c postpaid

Definition, history and importance, nature of work, qualifications necessary for entry and success, preparation, employment and advancement, remuneration, advantages, disadvantages, how to get started, and related occupations.

BELLMAN AND BELL CAPTAIN **324.138**

Bellmen and bell captains. Chronicle Guidance Publications. 1967. 4p. 35c

Occupational brief summarizing nature of work, working conditions, earnings, hours, personal qualifications, where employed, education, training, and outlook.

Bellmen and bell captains. One section of *Occupational Outlook Handbook.*

Nature of work, training, other qualifications, advancement, and employment outlook.

BERRY FARMER. *See* **Fruit grower**

BIOCHEMIST **041.081**

** Biochemist. Careers. 1970. 8p. 35c

Career brief describing duties, working conditions, training, personal qualifications, places of employment, earnings, and outlook. Additional readings.

Biochemist. Chronicle Guidance Publications. 1969. 4p. 35c

Occupational brief summarizing work performed, working conditions, earnings, personal qualifications, ways of determining interest and ability, training, opportunities, methods of entry, and outlook.

Biochemists. Science Research Associates. 1968. 4p. 45c

Occupational brief describing work, training, opportunities, and outlook.

Biochemists. One section of *Occupational Outlook Handbook.*

Nature of work, places of employment, training and other qualifications, working conditions, and outlook.

* Careers in biochemistry. American Society of Biological Chemists. 1962. 24p. Single copy free

Discussion of the nature of work in chemistry of living things, opportunities, and training.

Finding out about biochemists. Science Research Associates. 1967. 4p. 45c

Junior occupational brief containing concise facts about the job.

BIOLOGIST 041.081

Biological sciences: earned degrees, by level, sex, and institution. One section of *Earned Degrees Conferred.*

Useful for judging the extent of a college's program in each of the following specialties: anatomy, bacteriology, biochemistry, biology, biophysics, botany, entomology, genetics, optometry, pathology, pharmacology, physiology, plant pathology, plant physiology, premedical sciences, and zoology.

Biological scientist. California State Department of Employment. 1964. 6p. Single copy free

Occupational guide describing work, requirements, training, and outlook.

* Biologist. Careers. 1968. 8p. 35c

Career brief describing duties, working conditions, training, personal qualifications, outlook, earnings, where employed and measuring one's interests and ability.

Biologist. Chronicle Guidance Publications. 1969. 4p. 35c

Occupational brief summarizing occupational specialties, outlook, salaries, working conditions, and training requirements.

Biologist. Guidance Centre. 1970. 4p. 35c postpaid

Definition, history and importance, nature of work, working conditions, qualifications necessary for entry and success, preparation, employment, advancement, outlook, remuneration, advantages, disadvantages, how to get started, and related occupations.

Biologist, assistant. Careers. 1968. 2p. 20c

Career summary for desk-top file. Duties, qualifications, and outlook.

Biologists. Michigan Employment Security Commission. 1959. 2p. Single copy free

Job brief summarizing occupational data for use in Michigan.

**Careers in biological science. Sarnoff, Paul. Julian Messner. 1968. 192p. $3.95; library binding $3.64

This book gives information about preparation, potential rewards, prospective employers, as well as the many opportunities in the inter-related fields that comprise biological science. Includes a list of biological societies and a list of recommended reading.

**Careers in biology. American Institute of Biological Sciences. 1967. 20p. 20c. Single copy free

A brochure for high school students presenting challenges and opportunities. Included is a list of sources of additional material in specific fields of the biosciences.

BIOLOGIST—*Continued*

* Careers in biology. Rochester Institute of Technology. 1966. 32p. Free

This illustrated bulletin gives information about various branches of the vocation, duties performed by persons employed, advantages, disadvantages, and requirements for initial employment and for promotions.

**Careers in the biological sciences. Fox, William W. Henry Z. Walck, Inc. 1963. 128p. $4.50

A survey which divides the subject into areas of related professions such as thoughtful sciences, science inside man, and wildlife biology, and then elaborates on one example of each as representative of the area. Discusses educational requirements, compensation, advancement, and outlook. Reading list. Illustrated.

Finding out about biological scientists. Science Research Associates. 1967. 4p. 45c

Junior occupational brief describing work and opportunities.

A guide to opportunities in cell biology. Satir, Birgit. American Society for Cell Biology. No date. 29p. 30c

Nature of the work, training, salaries, opportunities, and examples of job openings for cell biologists. Reading list.

**Opportunities in the biological sciences. Winter, Charles A. Vocational Guidance Manuals. 1969. 128p. $1.95 paper; library edition $3.75

Nature of work, types of jobs available, educational preparation, qualifications, opportunities, rewards, and employment outlook.

BIOPHYSICIST 041.081

Biophysicist. Careers. 1968. 2p. 20c

Career summary for desk-top file. Duties, qualifications, and outlook.

* Biophysics, an exciting new frontier science. Biophysical Society. 1963. 4p. Free

An explanation of biophysics, the need for specialists trained in this area, training, opportunities, and qualifications.

BLACKSMITH 356.381 and 610.381

Blacksmith. Careers. 1970. 2p. 20c

Career summary for desk-top file. Duties, qualifications, and outlook.

Blacksmith. Chronicle Guidance Publications. 1967. 4p. 35c

Occupational brief summarizing work performed, working conditions, personal requirements, where employed, hours, earnings, educational requirements, and outlook.

Blacksmith. Michigan Employment Security Commission. 1965. 2p. Single copy free

Job brief summarizing occupational data for use in Michigan.

Blacksmiths. Science Research Associates. 1969. 4p. 45c
Occupational brief describing the work of the modern blacksmith, working conditions, training, earnings, and outlook.

**Blacksmiths. One section of *Occupational Outlook Handbook.*
Nature of work, where employed, training, other qualifications, employment outlook, earnings, and working conditions.

**Employment outlook for blacksmiths. Bulletin No. 1650–91. Bureau of Labor Statistics, U.S. Department of Labor. Supt. of Documents. 1970. 8p. 10c
Reprint from the *Occupational Outlook Handbook.*

Finding out about blacksmiths. Science Research Associates. 1967. 4p. 45c
Junior occupational brief describing work and opportunities.

BOILERMAKER **805.281**

Boilermaker. Careers. 1969. 2p. 20c
Career summary for desk-top file. Duties, qualifications, and outlook.

Boilermaker. Chronicle Guidance Publications. 1966. 4p. 35c
Occupational brief summarizing nature of work, where employed, qualifications, training, earnings, related jobs, and employment outlook.

Boilermakers. Michigan Employment Security Commission. 1961. 2p. Single copy free
Job brief summarizing occupational data for use in Michigan.

Boilermakers. Science Research Associates. 1969. 4p. 45c
Occupational brief describing work, qualifications, training, opportunities, and outlook.

**Boilermaking occupations. One section of *Occupational Outlook Handbook.*
Nature of work, where employed, training, other qualifications, employment outlook, earnings, and working conditions.

**Employment outlook for boilermaking occupations. Bulletin No. 1650–92. Bureau of Labor Statistics, U.S. Department of Labor. Supt. of Documents. 1970. 8p. 10c
Reprint from the *Occupational Outlook Handbook.*

Finding out about boilermakers. Science Research Associates. 1967. 4p. 45c
Junior occupational brief summarizing what the work requires and offers.

BOOK ILLUSTRATOR. ***See*** **Artist; Commercial artist; Medical illustrator**

BOOKBINDER 977.884

Bindery worker. Chronicle Guidance Publications. 1967. 4p. 35c

Occupational brief summarizing work performed, where employed, working conditions, training required, earnings, personal qualifications, and outlook.

Bookbinder. Careers. 1969. 2p. 20c

Career summary for desk-top file. Duties, qualifications, and outlook.

Bookbinder and bindery woman. California State Department of Employment. 1966. 5p. Single copy free

Occupational guide describing work, requirements, training, and outlook.

Bookbinders. Science Research Associates. 1966. 4p. 45c

Occupational brief describing nature of work, training, qualifications, opportunities, advantages, disadvantages, and future outlook.

Bookbinders and related workers. One section of *Occupational Outlook Handbook.*

Nature of work, training and other qualifications, employment outlook, earnings, and working conditions.

Finding out about bookbinders. Science Research Associates. 1967. 4p. 45c

Junior occupational brief describing work and opportunities.

See also Printing industry worker

BOOKKEEPER 210.388

* Bookkeeper. Careers. 1968. 7p. 35c

Career brief describing duties, working conditions, training, requirements, qualifications, employment prospects, earnings, and related careers.

Bookkeeper. Chronicle Guidance Publications. 1967. 4p. 35c

Occupational brief containing history, work performed, working conditions, determination of aptitudes and interests, training requirements, training opportunities, outlook, methods of entry, advantages, and disadvantages.

Bookkeeper. Guidance Centre. 1968. 4p. 35c postpaid

Definition, qualifications necessary for entry and success, requirements, earnings, advantages, disadvantages, and related occupations.

Bookkeepers. Michigan Employment Security Commission. 1965. 2p. Single copy free

Job brief summarizing occupational data for use in Michigan.

**Bookkeeping workers. One section of *Occupational Outlook Handbook.*

Nature of work, where employed, training, other qualifications, advancement, earnings, and working conditions.

**Employment outlook for bookkeeping workers and office machine operators. Bulletin No. 1650–50. Bureau of Labor Statistics, U.S. Department of Labor. Supt. of Documents. 1970. 8p. 10c

Reprint from the *Occupational Outlook Handbook.*

Finding out about bookkeepers. Science Research Associates. 1967. 4p. 45c

Junior occupational brief summarizing what the work requires and offers.

Full charge bookkeeper. California State Department of Employment. 1968. 2p. Single copy free

Occupational guide describing work, requirements, training, and outlook.

Starting and managing a small bookkeeping service. Small Business Administration. Supt. of Documents. 1962. 64p. 30c

This booklet describes the advantages and disadvantages of this work, the risks involved, the personal characteristics that will contribute to success, and some management practices.

See also Accountant; Public accountant

BOOKKEEPING MACHINE OPERATOR 215.388

Bookkeeping machine operator. California State Department of Employment. 1966. 3p. Single copy free

Occupational guide describing work, requirements, training, and outlook.

Bookkeeping machine operator. Careers. 1970. 8p. 35c

Career brief describing duties, working conditions, training, earnings, related careers, and outlook.

* Bookkeeping machine operator. Chronicle Guidance Publications. 1969. 4p. 35c

Occupational brief summarizing definition, qualifications, preparation, earnings, working conditions, interest and ability tests, and outlook.

Bookkeeping machine operators. Science Research Associates. 1967. 4p. 45c

Occupational brief describing work, training, qualifications, opportunities, and outlook.

Calculating machine operator. Chronicle Guidance Publications. 1968. 4p. 35c

Occupational brief summarizing work performed, working conditions, where employed, earnings, qualifications, training, and outlook.

Finding out about bookkeeping machine operators. Science Research Associates. 1967. 4p. 45c

Junior occupational brief containing concise facts about the job.

See also Office-machine operator

BOTANIST 041.081

* Botanist. Careers. 1970. 8p. 35c

Career brief describing duties, working conditions, training, personal qualifications, places of employment, earnings, and outlook.

BOTANIST—*Continued*

Botanist. Guidance Centre. 1969. 4p. 35c postpaid

History and importance, nature of work, qualifications, working conditions, preparation, remuneration, outlook, related occupations, and how to get started.

Botanists. Science Research Associates. 1966. 4p. 45c

Occupational brief describing work in the special fields of botany, qualifications, places of employment, earnings, and outlook. Selected references.

**Botany as a profession. Botanical Society of America. 1967. 16p. 25c; single copy free

Illustrated booklet describing nature of work, sources of employment, requirements, salaries, and outlook.

Luther Burbank; plant magician. Beaty, John Y. Julian Messner. 1943. 251p. $3.95; library binding $3.64

Biography of the man whose amazing achievements in the development of plant varieties enriched the world.

* Plant detective: David Douglas. Young, Bob and Young, Jan. Julian Messner. 1966. 190p. $3.50; library binding $3.34

Biography which shows the relentless scientific detective work of a successful botanist.

Plant explorer: David Fairchild. Williams, Beryl and Epstein, Samuel. Julian Messner. 1961. 192p. $3.50; library binding $3.34

Biography of a botanist who brought many plant species into the United States and established the New Crops Research Branch of the U.S. Department of Agriculture.

The plant hunters. Tyler-Whittle, Michael Sidney. Chilton Book Company. 1970. 281p. $8.95

The subtitle describes this book: "Being an examination of collecting, with an account of the careers and the methods of a number of those who have searched the world for wild plants." Appended are essays on plant distribution, plant names, techniques of plant collecting, and a bibliography.

BOWLING-PIN-MACHINE MECHANIC 639.381

Bowling machine mechanics. Science Research Associates. 1969. 4p. 45c

Occupational brief describing work, training, opportunities, and outlook.

Bowling-pin-machine mechanics. One section of *Occupational Outlook Handbook.*

Nature of work, places of employment, outlook, earnings, and working conditions.

**Employment outlook for bowling-pin-machine mechanics. Bulletin No. 1650–82. Bureau of Labor Statistics, U.S. Department of Labor. Supt. of Documents. 1970. 8p. 10c

Reprint from the *Occupational Outlook Handbook.*

BOY SCOUTS PROFESSIONAL WORKER 159.228

Boy Scout district executive. Careers. 1963. 2p. 15c
Career summary for desk-top file. Duties, qualifications, and outlook.

On the job with a district Scout executive. Boy Scouts of America. 1968. 4p. Free
An illustrated reprint showing an executive at work.

**Your invitation to a career in the Boy Scouts of America. Boy Scouts of America. 1968. 6p. Free
Description of qualifications, opportunities, duties of a field scout executive, advancement, compensation, preparation, and how to place an application.

Your life job can be with the Boy Scouts of America. Boy Scouts of America. 1968. 6p. Free
Stresses the importance of a college education and activities in scouting as preparation.

BRICKLAYER 861.381

Bricklayer. Careers. 1968. 2p. 20c
Career summary for desk-top file. Duties, qualifications, and outlook.

Bricklayer. Chronicle Guidance Publications. 1965. 4p. 35c
Occupational brief summarizing work performed, employment conditions, qualifications, determination of aptitudes and interests, training requirements, opportunities, outlook, and related jobs.

Bricklayer. Guidance Centre. 1969. 4p. 35c postpaid
History and importance, nature of work, qualifications, preparation, advancement, outlook, remuneration, advantages, disadvantages, how to get started, and related occupations.

Bricklayer and bricklayer apprentice. California State Department of Employment. 1965. 5p. Single copy free
Occupational guide describing work, requirements, training, and outlook.

Bricklayer, apprentice. Careers. 1967. 2p. 20c
Career summary for desk-top file. Duties, qualifications, and outlook.

Bricklayers. Michigan Employment Security Commission. 1967. 2p. Single copy free
Job brief summarizing occupational data for use in Michigan.

* Bricklayers. Science Research Associates. 1968. 4p. 45c
Occupational brief describing work, qualifications, training, wages, opportunities, advantages, disadvantages, and outlook. Selected references.

**Bricklayers. One section of *Occupational Outlook Handbook.*
Nature of work, where employed, training, other qualifications, advancement, employment outlook, earnings, and working conditions.

* Bricklaying as a vocation. Structural Clay Products Institute. 1962. 4p. Free
Need for bricklayers, employment prospects, nature of work, working conditions, personal requirements, wage rates, and apprenticeship.

BRICKLAYER—*Continued*

**Employment outlook for bricklayers, stonemasons, marble setters, terrazo workers. Bulletin No. 1650–69. Bureau of Labor Statistics, U.S. Department of Labor. Supt. of Documents. 1970. 20p. 20c
Reprint from the *Occupational Outlook Handbook.*

Finding out about bricklayers. Science Research Associates. 1967. 4p. 45c
Junior occupational brief containing concise facts about the job.

BROADCAST TECHNICIAN **963.168**

Broadcast technician (television). California State Department of Employment. 1967. 6p. Single copy free
Occupational guide describing work, requirements, training, and outlook.

Broadcast technicians. Science Research Associates. 1966. 4p. 45c
Occupational brief describing nature of work, training, qualifications, getting started, earnings, advantages, disadvantages, and future outlook. Selected references.

**Broadcast technicians. One section of *Occupational Outlook Handbook.*
Nature of work, training, other qualifications, employment outlook, earnings, and working conditions.

Finding out about broadcast technicians. Science Research Associates. 1967. 4p. 45c
Junior occupational brief describing work and opportunities.

BROADCASTING ENGINEER. ***See*** **Radio and television engineer**

BUILDING CONSTRUCTION INDUSTRY WORKER. ***See*** **Construction industry Worker**

BUILDING CONTRACTOR **182.168**

Building contractors. Science Research Associates. 1967. 4p. 45c
Occupational brief describing nature of work, requirements, getting started and advancing, earnings, advantages, disadvantages, and future outlook.

Finding out about building contractors. Science Research Associates. 1967. 4p. 45c
Junior occupational brief summarizing what the work requires and offers.

House builder. Chronicle Guidance Publications. 1968. 4p. 35c
Occupational brief summarizing organization of the industry, work performed, education and training, personal characteristics, working conditions, and outlook.

BUILDING CUSTODIAN AND JANITOR 187.168 and 382.

Apartment house janitors. Science Research Associates. 1969. 4p. 45c
Occupational brief describing work, training, qualifications, opportunities, and outlook.

Apartment manager. California State Department of Employment. 1966. 3p. Single copy free
Occupational guide describing work, requirements, training, and outlook.

Building custodians. One section of *Occupational Outlook Handbook.*
Nature of work, places of employment, training, qualifications, earnings, and working conditions.

**Building service workers. Science Research Associates. 1970. 4p. 45c
Occupational brief describing duties, requirements, personal qualifications, earnings, advantages, disadvantages, and future outlook. Describes the work of maintenance workers, school custodians, elevator operators, and building superintendents.

Custodian (janitor). Chronicle Guidance Publications. 1966. 4p. 35c
Occupational brief summarizing work performed, where employed, qualifications, earnings, advantages, disadvantages, and methods of entering.

**Employment outlook for building custodians. Bulletin No. 1650–62. Bureau of Labor Statistics, U.S. Department of Labor. Supt. of Documents. 1970. 8p. 10c
Reprint from the *Occupational Outlook Handbook.*

Finding out about apartment building managers. Science Research Associates. 1967. 4p. 45c
Junior occupational brief containing facts about the job.

Finding out about building service workers. Science Research Associates. 1967. 4p. 45c
Junior occupational brief containing concise facts about the job.

Finding out about building superintendents. Science Research Associates. 1967. 4p. 45c
Junior occupational brief describing work and opportunities.

Finding out about janitors. Science Research Associates. 1967. 4p. 45c
Junior occupational brief containing concise facts about the job.

Janitor (porter). California State Department of Employment. 1966. 4p. Single copy free
Occupational guide summarizing duties, working conditions, employment prospects, earnings, training, requirements for entry, and suggestions for locating a job.

School custodian (janitor). Careers. 1969. 2p. 20c
Career summary for desk-top file. Duties, qualifications, and outlook.

BUS BOY 311.878

Bus boy and bus girl. Careers. 1966. 2p. 20c
Career summary for desk-top file. Duties, qualifications, and outlook.

BUS BOY—*Continued*

Finding out about bus boys. Science Research Associates. 1967. 4p. 45c
Junior occupational brief summarizing what the work requires and offers.

BUS DRIVER **913.463**

Bus driver. California State Department of Employment. 1968. 3p. Single copy free
Duties, working conditions, entrance requirements, and employment prospects.

Bus driver. Chronicle Guidance Publications. 1966. 4p. 35c
Occupational brief describing work performed, working conditions, requirements, opportunities, outlook, and methods of entry.

Bus driver. Michigan Employment Security Commission. 1962. 2p. Single copy free
Job brief summarizing occupational data for use in Michigan.

Bus facts. National Association of Motor Bus Owners. 1966. 48p. Free
A summary of facts and figures on the intercity-bus industry, including number of employees and wages.

Finding out about local bus drivers. Science Research Associates. 1967. 4p. 45c
Junior occupational brief describing work and opportunities.

Finding out about long-distance bus drivers. Science Research Associates. 1967. 4p. 45c
Junior occupational brief containing concise facts about the job.

**Intercity bus drivers. One section of *Occupational Outlook Handbook.*
Nature of work, where employed, qualifications, employment outlook, earnings, and working conditions.

**Local bus drivers. Science Research Associates. 1968. 4p. 45c
Occupational brief describing kinds of jobs, requirements, training, getting started, earnings, advantages, and future outlook.

**Local transit bus drivers. One section of *Occupational Outlook Handbook.*
Nature of work, where employed, qualifications, training, employment outlook, earnings, and working conditions.

Street car operator, bus and trolley coach operator, subway motorman, and guard. Guidance Centre. 1966. 4p. 35c postpaid
Duties, employment, earnings, working conditions, advantages, disadvantages, and related occupations.

See also Motor vehicle transportation worker; Truck driver

BUSINESS EXECUTIVE **050. and 165.**

Achieving executive success. Alpha Kappa Psi Fraternity. 1968. 18p. 10c
Opinions of successful business executives as expressed in panel discussions.

Big business leaders in America. Atheneum Publishers. 1963. 243p. $1.25

A discussion of the economic levels, educational backgrounds, geographic locations, marriage status, occupations of parents, and mobility of business leaders.

**Business administration and related professions. One section of *Occupation Outlook Handbook.*

Nature of work, training, advancement, employment outlook, and earnings for each of the following: accountant, advertising worker, marketing research worker, personnel worker, and public relations worker.

Business agent—labor union. California State Department of Employment. 1965. 8p. Single copy free

Occupational guide describing work, requirements, training, and outlook.

Business proprietor, retail. Chronicle Guidance Publications. 1966. 4p. 35c

Occupational brief summarizing work performed, personal qualifications, opportunities, and entry into business.

**Careers and opportunities in retailing. Wilinsky, Harriet. Dutton and Company. 1970. 251p. $5.95

The vice-president of a large specialty store offers an account of the advantages and enjoyment of careers in retailing. Included is a description of the training and preparation needed, the compensation, chances for advancement, and the variety of jobs in different kinds of retail stores. Practical advice is also given on owning a retail store.

* Careers in business. Rochester Institute of Technology. 1963. 28p. Free

This career bulletin gives information about the various branches of the vocation, duties performed by persons employed, advantages, disadvantages, and requirements for initial employment and for promotions.

**Careers in business management. Mann, Roland. Henry Z. Walck, Inc. 1963. 111p. $4.50

Presenting a picture of the industrial enterprise and modern business management as an expanding career field, this book describes the various management functions, requirements, basic skills needed, opportunities, and outlook.

Careers in corporate management. B'nai B'rith Vocational Service. 1969. 2p. 35c

Description of nature of work and fields of specialization, educational and personal requirements, opportunities for women and minority group youth, remuneration, employment outlook, and how to seek the job.

Club management: a path to a rewarding future. Club Managers Association of America. 1968. 14p. Single copy free

Illustrated booklet describing job requirements, training, and advancement opportunities. Also includes a list of colleges offering training programs in club management.

Do you have what it takes to be a boss some day? Changing Times. 1966. 6p. 15c

Discussion of qualities looked for by business executives.

BUSINESS EXECUTIVE—*Continued*

The executive breakthrough. Uris, Auren. Doubleday and Company. 1967. 421p. $5.95

Biographies of twenty-one men and women who have built their businesses by their own efforts. Each sketch contains a short analysis of the personal qualities contributing to the success.

Executive junior. Careers. 2p. 20c

Career summary for desk-top file. Duties, qualifications, and outlook.

The executives. Fullerton, Alexander. Putnam's Sons. 1970. 319p. $6.95

Career fiction. Story of the hero's meteoric rise from obscurity to corporate success. The account probes his personal and professional career from his earliest minor job after service to his place as chief executive.

Executives. Science Research Associates. 1968. 4p. 45c

Occupational brief describing the function of management, nature of work, requirements, training, getting started, earnings, advantages, disadvantages, and future outlook.

F. W. Woolworth: five and ten boy. Myers, Elisabeth P. Bobbs-Merrill Company. 1962. 200p. $2.25

Biography prepared for third to seventh grades, showing how the founder of the five and ten cent stores got started.

Industrial management technologist. Guidance Centre. 1966. 4p. 35c postpaid

Definition, history and importance, nature of work, outlook, qualifications, preparation, advancement, remuneration, and how to get started.

Junior executive. Chronicle Guidance Publications. 1969. 4p. 35c

Occupational brief summarizing work performed, working conditions, earnings, personal qualifications, training requirements, opportunities, and employment outlook.

Lessons of leadership. Doubleday and Company. 1968. 271p. $4.95

Twenty-one giants of the business world tell their own success stories in revealing interviews. Includes Conrad Hilton, Howard Johnson, Samuel Goldwyn, and David Sarnoff.

Manager or executive. Guidance Centre. 1966. 4p. 35c postpaid

Definition, history and importance, nature of work, qualifications, working conditions, preparation, remuneration, advancement, outlook, related occupations, and how to get started.

Managers, general. Careers. 1969. 8p. 35c

Career brief describing advertising, industrial relations, personnel, plant, production, public relations, purchasing, sales, and traffic manager.

My years with General Motors. Sloan, Alfred Pritchard. Doubleday and Company. 1964. 472p. $7.95

The history of a major American business firm by the man who was its chief executive for twenty-three years.

Practice program produces managers. Chronicle Guidance Publications. 1966. 4p. 35c

Reprinted article from *Petroleum Management* discusses an oil company's program for increasing the depth and skills of its managerial and supervisory personnel.

Running a business after marriage. Alumnae Advisory Center. 1963. 6p. 35c

Reprint from *Mademoiselle* describing the work of several business women.

Small business owners. Science Research Associates. 1966. 4p. 45c

Occupational brief describing work, training, qualifications, opportunities, and outlook.

Starting and managing a small business of your own. Small Business Administration. Supt. of Documents. 1962. 50p. 25c

Advice and questions to consider before establishing one's own business. Describes the common problems of launching small business operations and suggests specific steps to help those interested to arrive at sound decisions.

Union business agents. Science Research Associates. 1967. 4p. 45c

Occupational brief describing work, training, qualifications, opportunities, and outlook.

* Wanted: financial executive. Financial Executives Institute. 1968. 8p. Free

Describes the work of planning and controlling the financial operations of a business, training, salary, advancement, and how to get started. Includes case histories of several financial managers.

** Your future in your own business. Winter, Elmer. Richards Rosen Press. 1966. 187p. $4; library edition $3.78

Describes the risks and opportunities in starting one's own business and offers advice on how to finance a business, hire employees, and develop leadership qualities. Franchise business is discussed.

BUSINESS WORKER 160. and 164.

Business and commerce: earned degrees, by level, sex, and institution. One section of *Earned Degrees Conferred.*

Useful for judging the extent of a college's program in accounting, secretarial studies, hotel and restaurant administration, and general business and commerce.

** Career opportunities for marketing, business and office specialists. Ferguson Publishing Company. 1970. 300p. $11.95; $8.95 to schools and libraries.

Prepared for high school and two-year college students. For twenty-six occupations in this category, there is included educational requirements both in high school and after high school, job opportunities at entry level and advancement possibilities, working conditions, and immediate and future earning prospects.

BUSINESS WORKER–*Continued*

**Career opportunities for women in business. King, Alice Gore. Dutton and Company. 1963. 212p. $4.50

Survey of the opportunities in business from a woman's job-hunting perspective. Covers the training needed, the educational and personal attributes most helpful for the jobs, the kinds of advancement within each field, the salary range, and the areas in which the job opportunities are most prevalent.

Careers in business. Alpha Kappa Psi Fraternity. 1954. 23p. 10c

A series of articles written by alumni members on the various fields of business in which they are engaged.

Catalog. New Brunswick Secretarial, Accounting and Business Machines School. 1968. 12p. Free

An example of an inspirational recruiting bulletin, pointing out the advantages of training for business jobs.

* Get the right kind of education for a business career. Changing Times. 1967. 4p. 15c

Reprint advising young hopeful executives to major in business at college.

Preparing for your career in business: a college guide for junior and senior high school students. Council for Professional Education for Business. 1963. 23p. 25c

Information on preparation for college work leading to careers as business managers, administrators, or specialists such as accountants or financial advisers.

The world of business and how you fit in. Tri-State College. No date. 12p. Free

An example of a college recruiting leaflet describing opportunities and training.

See also Bookkeeper; Clerical worker; Programmer; Stenographer; Typist

BUTCHER **316.884**

Butcher. Guidance Centre. 1965. 4p. 35c postpaid

Definition, history and importance, nature of work, working conditions, qualifications, preparation, employment, advancement, outlook, remuneration, advantages, disadvantages, how to get started, and related occupations.

Butchers. Science Research Associates. 1968. 4p. 45c

Occupational brief describing nature of work, requirements, preparation, working conditions, earnings, and future outlook.

Finding out about butchers. Science Research Associates. 1967. 4p. 45c

Junior occupational brief containing concise facts about the job.

See also Meat cutter

BUYER 162.158

Buyer. California State Department of Employment. 1966. 5p. Single copy free

Occupational guide describing work, requirements, training, and outlook.

Buyer. Chronicle Guidance Publications. 1969. 4p. 35c

Occupational brief summarizing work performed, working conditions, personal qualifications, training requirements, opportunities, and employment outlook.

Buyer. Guidance Centre. 1967. 4p. 35c postpaid

Nature of work, qualifications, earnings, advantages, disadvantages, related occupations, and how to get started.

* Buyer (department store). Careers. 1968. 8p. 35c

Career brief describing duties, working conditions, training, personal qualifications, earnings, and outlook.

* Buyers. Science Research Associates. 1969. 4p. 45c

Occupational brief describing work, qualifications, training, earnings, advantages, disadvantages, and outlook. Selected references.

Finding out about store buyers. Science Research Associates. 1967. 4p. 45c

Junior occupational brief summarizing what the work requires and offers.

See also Merchandise manager; Retail manager

CABINETMAKER 660.280

Cabinetmaker. Careers. 1967. 2p. 20c

Career summary for desk-top file. Duties, qualifications, and outlook.

Cabinetmaker. California State Department of Employment. 1964. 3p. Single copy free

Occupational guide describing work, requirements, training, and outlook.

Cabinetmaker. Michigan Employment Security Commission. 1960. 2p. Single copy free

Job brief summarizing occupational data for use in Michigan.

Cabinetmaker and cabinetmaker apprentice. California State Department of Employment. 1968. 5p. Single copy free

Occupational guide describing work, requirements, training, and outlook.

Cabinetmaker (woodworking). Chronicle Guidance Publications. 1966. 4p. 35c

Occupational brief summarizing duties, working conditions, qualifications, training, earnings, and outlook.

Finding out about cabinetmakers. Science Research Associates. 1967. 4p. 45c

Junior occupational brief describing work and opportunities.

CAMP COUNSELOR 159.228

Camp counseling is channel number one. American Camping Association. 1959. 2p. 10c. Single copy free

A recruiting flier asserting that camp counseling is preparation for any job of working with people.

Camp counselor. California State Department of Employment. 1968. 4p. Single copy free

Job duties, working conditions, pay, hours, entrance requirements, promotion, training, and employment outlook.

* Camp counselor. Careers. 1967. 2p. 20c

Career summary for desk-top file. Duties, qualifications, and outlook.

Camp counselors. Science Research Associates. 1968. 4p. 45c

Occupational brief describing responsibilities, requirements, advancement, earnings, job opportunities, and outlook. Selected references.

**Careers in camping. American Camping Association. 1963. 8p. 10c. Single copy free

Brief statement of qualifications, training, and advantages of camping as a vocation.

CARPENTER 860.381

Carpenter. Guidance Centre. 1966. 4p. 35c postpaid

History and importance, conditions of work, qualifications, preparation, advancement opportunities, and how to get started.

Carpenter. Michigan Employment Security Commission. 1966. 2p. Single copy free

Job brief summarizing occupational data for use in Michigan.

Carpenter and carpenter apprentice. California State Department of Employment. 1964. 6p. Single copy free

Occupational guide describing work, requirements, training, and outlook.

* Carpenter, construction. Careers. 1967. 8p. 35c

Career brief describing duties, working conditions, personal qualifications, training, earnings, related careers, and outlook.

Carpenter (construction). Chronicle Guidance Publications. 1967. 4p. 35c

Occupational brief summarizing work performed, working conditions, personal qualifications, training requirements, opportunities, and employment outlook.

Carpenters. Science Research Associates. 1968. 4p. 45c

Occupational brief describing nature of work, preparation, qualifications, opportunities, advantages, disadvantages, and future outlook.

**Carpenters. One section of *Occupational Outlook Handbook*.

Nature of work, where employed, training, other qualifications, advancement, employment outlook, earnings, and working conditions.

**Employment outlook for carpenters, painters, paperhangers, glaziers. Bulletin No. 1650–70. Bureau of Labor Statistics, U.S. Department of Labor. Supt. of Documents. 1970. 20p. 20c
Reprint from the *Occupational Outlook Handbook.*

Finding out about carpenters. Science Research Associates. 1967. 4p. 45c
Junior occupational brief summarizing what the work requires and offers.

CARTOGRAPHER 017.218

Cartographer. Careers. 1969. 2p. 20c
Career summary for desk-top file. Duties, qualifications, and outlook.

**Cartographer. Chronicle Guidance Publications. 1969. 4p. 35c
Occupational brief summarizing work performed, qualifications, working conditions, training, earnings, where employed, and outlook.

Cartographer. Guidance Centre. 1968. 4p. 35c postpaid
Definition, history and importance, nature of work, working conditions, qualifications, preparation, employment, outlook, remuneration, advancement, and how to get started.

Cartographers. Science Research Associates. 1966. 4p. 45c
Occupational brief describing nature of work, requirements, getting started, advantages, disadvantages, and future outlook.

Finding out about cartographers. Science Research Associates. 1967. 4p. 45c
Junior occupational brief containing concise facts about the job.

CARTOONIST 144.081

Cartoonist. Careers. 1969. 8p. 35c
Career brief describing duties, working conditions, training, personal qualifications, earnings, advancement prospects, and outlook.

**Cartoonist. Chronicle Guidance Publications. 1969. 4p. 35c
Occupational brief summarizing work performed, working conditions, personal qualifications, training, related jobs, opportunities, outlook, and suggested activities.

* Cartoonists. Science Research Associates. 1969. 4p. 45c
Occupational brief describing nature of work, qualifications, training, earnings, opportunities, and future outlook.

Finding out about cartoonists. Science Research Associates. 1967. 4p. 45c
Junior occupational brief describing work and opportunities.

See also Artist; Commercial artist

CASE WORKER. *See* Social worker

CASHIER 211.468

Cashier. Careers. 1970. 2p. 20c
Career summary for desk-top file. Duties, qualifications, and outlook.

Cashier. California State Department of Employment. 1965. 3p. Single copy free
Occupational guide describing work, requirements, training, and outlook.

Cashier. Chronicle Guidance Publications. 1969. 4p. 35c
Occupational brief summarizing work performed, where employed, personal requirements, working conditions, earnings, and outlook.

* Cashiers. Science Research Associates. 1968. 4p. 45c
Occupational brief describing nature of work, training, qualifications, opportunities, advantages, disadvantages, and future outlook.

Cashiers. One section of *Occupational Outlook Handbook.*
Nature of work, where employed, training, qualifications, employment outlook, earnings, and working conditions.

Checkout cashiers. Michigan Employment Security Commission. 1965. 2p. Single copy free
Job brief summarizing occupational data for use in Michigan.

**Employment outlook for cashiers. Bulletin No. 1650–51. Bureau of Labor Statistics, U.S. Department of Labor. Supt. of Documents. 1970. 8p. 10c
Reprint from the *Occupational Outlook Handbook.*

Finding out about cashiers. Science Research Associates. 1967. 4p. 45c
Junior occupational brief summarizing what the work requires and offers.

CATERER 187.168

Caterer. Careers. 1967. 2p. 20c
Career summary for desk-top file. Duties, qualifications, and outlook.

**Caterers. Science Research Associates. 1966. 4p. 45c
Occupational brief describing work, training, qualifications, opportunities, and outlook.

Finding out about caterers. Science Research Associates. 1967. 4p. 45c
Junior occupational brief containing concise facts about the job.

CATTLEMAN 413.181

Cattle farmer. Careers. 1966. 2p. 20c
Career summary for desk-top file. Duties, qualifications, and outlook.

**Cattlemen. Science Research Associates. 1966. 4p. 45c
Occupational brief describing nature of work, qualifications, opportunities, advantages, disadvantages, and future outlook.

See also Animal husbandman; Cowpuncher

CEMENT MASON 852.884

Cement finisher. Careers. 1970. 2p. 20c

Career summary for desk-top file. Duties, qualifications, and outlook.

**Cement manufacturing workers. Science Research Associates. 1966. 4p. 45c

Occupational brief describing nature of work, requirements, getting started, earnings, advantages, disadvantages, and future outlook.

Cement mason. California State Department of Employment. 1968. 3p. Single copy free

Occupational guide describing work, requirements, training, and outlook.

Cement mason (cement and concrete finishers). Michigan Employment Security Commission. 1967. 2p. Single copy free

Job brief summarizing occupational data for use in Michigan.

Cement masons. Chronicle Guidance Publications. 1969. 4p. 35c

Occupational brief summarizing work performed, working conditions, where employed, opportunities for advancement, hours and earnings, employment outlook, and educational and training requirements.

* Cement masons. Science Research Associates. 1966. 4p. 45c

Occupational brief describing nature of work, qualifications, opportunities, advantages, disadvantages, and future outlook.

**Cement masons (cement and concrete finishers). One section of *Occupational Outlook Handbook.*

Nature of work, where employed, training, other qualifications, employment outlook, earnings, and working conditions.

Employment outlook for cement masons, lathers, plasterers. Bulletin No. 1650–71. Bureau of Labor Statistics, U.S. Department of Labor. Supt. of Documents. 1970. 20p. 20c

Reprint from the *Occupational Outlook Handbook.*

Finding out about cement masons. Science Research Associates. 1967. 4p. 45c

Junior occupational brief describing work and opportunities.

Job grading standards for mason. Civil Service Commission. Supt. of Documents. 1970. 5p. 10c

This job classification outlines duties, skill, and knowledge requirements, responsibility, physical effort, and working conditions which determine job grade levels in accordance with the U.S. Civil Service Commission standards.

Tile setter. Careers. 1970. 2p. 20c

Career summary for desk-top file. Duties, qualifications, and outlook.

CEMETERY MANAGER 187.168

Careers in memorial counseling. B'nai B'rith Vocational Service. 1969. 8p. 35c

Description of work, duties, opportunities, responsibilities, employment outlook, and rewards in this field.

CEMETERY MANAGER—*Continued*

Cemetery administration and management—a career opportunity for you. American Cemetery Association. 1960. 4p. Free

Discussion of opportunities, compensation, qualifications, advantages, and disadvantages.

CERAMIC ENGINEER 006.081

Ceramic engineer. California State Department of Employment. 1965. 6p. Single copy free

Occupational guide describing work, requirements, training, and outlook.

Ceramic engineer. Careers. 1968. 2p. 20c

Career summary for desk-top file. Duties, qualifications, and outlook.

* Ceramic engineer. Chronicle Guidance Publications. 1968. 4p. 35c

Occupational brief describing work performed, personal qualifications, training, and employment outlook. Includes list of thirteen accredited schools offering a degree in ceramic engineering.

The ceramic engineer—careers and opportunities. Chronicle Guidance Publications. 1969. 2p. 35c

Reprinted article from *American Ceramic Society Bulletin.*

* Ceramic engineers. Science Research Associates. 1968. 4p. 45c

Discusses work, areas of specialization, preparation, opportunities, and outlook.

Ceramic engineers. One section of *Occupational Outlook Handbook.*

Nature of work, where employed, and employment outlook.

Finding out about ceramic engineers. Science Research Associates. 1967. 4p. 45c

Junior occupational brief summarizing what the work requires and offers.

Institutions of ceramic engineering and ceramic art. Aluminum Company of America. 1968. 4p. Free

List of thirty-three schools coded to provide a guide to the programs and degrees offered.

** Opportunities in ceramic engineering. Scholes, Samuel Ray. Vocational Guidance Manuals. 1968. 88p. $1.95 paper; $3.75 library edition

Includes the growth and development of ceramics, description of various raw materials, ceramic industries, various kinds of work, qualifications, training, remuneration, where to seek employment, attributes necessary for success, and getting a job. Contains list of schools offering courses in ceramics.

Universities and colleges in the United States offering course in ceramic engineering or ceramic art. American Ceramic Society. 1968. 3p. Mimeographed. Free

List of 50 schools.

See also Engineer

CERAMIC INDUSTRY MANUFACTURING WORKER 77

* Ceramic industry manufacturing workers. Science Research Associates. 1966. 4p. 45c

Occupational brief describing nature of work, requirements, getting started and advancing, earnings, advantages, disadvantages, and future outlook.

Ceramics—today's technology, tomorrow's future. Aluminum Company of America. 1969. 20p. Free

Colored brochure depicting opportunities for skilled ceramic engineers in electronics, missiles, refractories, and in scores of industries.

**For career opportunities explore the wonder world of ceramics. American Ceramic Society. No date. 16p. 10c. Single copy free

Illustrated brochure describing opportunities in the aircraft industry, structural clay products, refractories, whiteware, glass, porcelain enamels, abrasives, cements, and electronics.

Pottery and porcelain ware industry workers. Chronicle Guidance Publications. 1968. 8p. 50c

Occupational brief summarizing importance, nature of industry, making of whiteware, work performed, working conditions, personal requirements, hours and earnings, outlook, and training.

* Structural clay products manufacturing workers. Science Research Associates. 1967. 4p. 45c

Occupational brief describing work of making brick, tiles, and other clay products. Includes requirements, earnings, getting started and advancing, advantages, disadvantages, and future outlook.

CERTIFIED PUBLIC ACCOUNTANT. *See* Public accountant

CHAIN STORE MANAGER. *See* Retail manager

CHAMBER OF COMMERCE MANAGER 187.118

Chamber of commerce manager. California State Department of Employment. 1965. 4p. Single copy free

Occupational guide describing work, requirements, training, and outlook.

* Consider a chamber of commerce career. American Chamber of Commerce Executives. No date. 12p. 10c. Free to counselors and librarians

Challenges of the career, qualifications, opportunities, earnings, related fields, advantages, disadvantages, and how to start.

CHAPLAIN. *See* Clergyman; Priest; Rabbi

CHAUFFEUR. *See* Driver

CHEF. *See* Cook and chef

CHEMICAL ENGINEER 008.081

Automation improves personal effectiveness while reducing drudgery. Chronicle Guidance Publications. 1967. 4p. 35c

Reprinted article from *Chemical and Engineering News* discusses automation's effects on employment, impact on chemical profession, in the laboratory, on computers and data processing. Also covers computer training in schools and industry.

Careers in marketing, pollution control, and other "new interest" fields. Chronicle Guidance Publications. 1969. 8p. 50c

Reprinted article from *Chemical Engineering* discusses the pollution control specialist; marketing careers; and the role of the chemical engineer in nuclear, aerospace, and ocean technology.

Chemical engineer. California State Department of Employment. 1965. 5p. Single copy free

Occupational guide describing work, requirements, training, and outlook.

Chemical engineer. Careers. 1970. 2p. 20c

Career summary for desk-top file. Duties, qualifications, and outlook.

Chemical engineer. Chronicle Guidance Publications. 1967. 4p. 35c

Occupational brief describing work performed, working conditions, personal qualifications, high school preparation, and employment outlook.

Chemical engineer. Guidance Centre. 1966. 4p. 35c postpaid

History and importance, qualifications, preparation, employment, advancement, earnings, advantages, disadvantages, and related occupations.

The chemical engineer in advertising. Chronicle Guidance Publications. 1968. 4p. 35c

Reprinted article from *Chemical Engineering* discusses opportunities in advertising for chemical engineers and salaries paid for such work.

Chemical engineers. Michigan Employment Security Commission. 1964. 2p. Single copy free

Job brief summarizing occupational data for use in Michigan.

* Chemical engineers. Science Research Associates. 1968. 4p. 45c

Occupational brief describing nature of work, qualifications, training, opportunities, advantages, disadvantages, and future outlook.

Chemical engineers. One section of *Occupational Outlook Handbook.*

Nature of work, where employed, and employment outlook.

Finding out about chemical engineers. Science Research Associates. 1967. 4p. 45c

Junior occupational brief containing concise facts about the job.

**Your future in chemical engineering. Feder, Raymond. Richards Rosen Press. Revised 1969. 155p. $4; library edition $3.78

Includes the importance and development of the work, duties, qualifications, preparation, rewards, opportunities, and related fields. Includes a list of accredited schools.

See also Chemist; Engineer; Scientist

CHEMICAL LAB TECHNICIAN 022.281

* A bright future for you as a chemical technician. Manufacturing Chemists' Association. 1969. 12p. Single copy free

Brochure explains the nature of work, preparation, and employment opportunities for a chemical technician.

Chemical laboratory technician. Careers. 1969. 2p. 20c

Career summary for desk-top file. Duties, qualifications, and outlook.

**Chemical laboratory technician. Chronicle Guidance Publications. 1969. 4p. 35c

Occupational brief summarizing work performed, working conditions, personal qualifications, training requirements, employment outlook, and methods of entering the job.

Chemical technicians. Chronicle Guidance Publications. 1966. 1p. 35c

Reprinted article from *American Vocational Journal* discusses the training and duties of chemical technicians.

* Chemical technicians. Science Research Associates. 1967. 4p. 45c

Occupational brief describing nature of work, qualities leading toward success, training, getting started, and outlook.

Finding out about chemical technicians. Science Research Associates. 1967. 4p. 45c

Junior occupational brief describing work and opportunities.

Is chemical technology the career for you? American Chemical Society. No date. 12p. 15c. Single copy free

Opportunity and training for the chemical technician.

CHEMIST 022.081

America's first woman chemist: Ellen Richards. Douty, E. M. Julian Messner. 1961. 191p. $3.50; library binding $3.34

Biography of a woman who overcame many barriers before her acceptance as the first woman student at Massachusetts Institute of Technology. Discusses her later pioneer work in nutrition.

Career opportunities. American Chemical Society. 1969. 120p. 25c. Single copy free

Published annually, an issue of *Chemical and Engineering News* contains a series of articles on trends affecting careers for chemists and chemical engineers. Includes a directory of some 750 organizations employing significant numbers of chemists, the number they now employ, the number they will employ in the coming year, and the broad categories of specialization for which they are seeking employees.

**Careers ahead in the chemical industry. Manufacturing Chemists' Association. 1969. 25p. 15c. Single copy free

A presentation of the numerous opportunities offered by chemical companies. Featured are the results of interviews with industry executives indicating the personal and professional qualifications expected of candidates for employment and the attractions that industry has to offer.

CHEMIST—*Continued*

**Careers and opportunities in chemistry. Pollack, Philip. Dutton and Company. 1960. 147p. $3.95

Included is information about educational requirements, qualifications, opportunities, and rates of pay in different types of chemical work. Given also is a list of colleges granting degrees in chemistry and chemical engineering which are approved by professional organizations. Illustrated.

* Careers in chemistry. Rochester Institute of Technology. 1965. 24p. Free

This illustrated bulletin gives information about various branches of the vocation, duties performed by persons employed, advantages, disadvantages, and requirements for initial employment and for promotions.

Chemist. California State Department of Employment. 1967. 5p. Single copy free

Occupational guide describing work, requirements, training, and outlook.

Chemist. Careers. 1969. 8p. 35c

Career brief describing duties, working conditions, training, personal qualifications, earnings, related careers, and outlook.

Chemist. Chronicle Guidance Publications. 1966. 4p. 35c

Occupational brief summarizing work performed, working conditions, qualifications, determination of aptitudes and interests, training, opportunities, outlook, and related jobs.

Chemist. Guidance Centre. 1969. 4p. 35c postpaid

Definition, history and importance, nature of work, working conditions, qualifications necessary for entry and success, preparation, employment, advancement, outlook, remuneration, advantages, disadvantages, how to get started toward the occupation, and related occupations.

* Chemistry and your career. American Chemical Society. 1967. 20p. 15c. Single copy free

Discussion of various areas of chemistry and chemical engineering by eminent men in these fields. Includes a question and answer section for high school students. Illustrated.

Chemistry project from start to finish. American Chemical Society. 1968. 20p. 15c. Single copy free

Explains how to select, prepare, execute, report, and exhibit a project. Includes instructions on how to use the library.

Chemists. Michigan Employment Security Commission. 1966. 2p. Single copy free

Job brief summarizing occupational data for use in Michigan.

* Chemists. Science Research Associates. 1968. 4p. 45c

Occupational brief describing nature of work, training, qualifications, opportunities, advantages, disadvantages, and future outlook.

**Chemists. One section of *Occupational Outlook Handbook.*

Nature of work, where employed, training and other qualifications, employment outlook, earnings, and working conditions.

Finding out about chemists. Science Research Associates. 1967. 4p. 45c

Junior occupational brief summarizing what the work requires and offers.

Frontiersman of the future. Manufacturing Chemists' Association. 1969. 16p. 6c. Single copy free

Explanation of nature of work, qualifications, and outlook for different types of jobs in chemistry.

Giant of the atom: Ernest Rutherford. McKown, Robin. Julian Messner. 1962. 192p. $3.50; library binding $3.34

Biography of the man who has a record of major discoveries concerning the atom and radioactivity, was knighted by the King of England, and won a Nobel prize in chemistry.

Great discoveries by young chemists. Kendall, James. Thomas Y. Crowell Company. 1954. 231p. $5.00

Describes the lives and struggles of some outstanding young chemists and their epoch-making achievements.

Industrial chemical industry occupations. Chronicle Guidance Publications. 1966. 4p. 35c

Occupational brief summarizing technical occupations, plant occupations, earnings, working conditions, and outlook.

Joseph Priestley, pioneer chemist. Marcus, R. B. Franklin Watts, Inc. 1961. 145p. $1.95

Biography of the man who is known as the "father of pneumatic chemistry," because of his pioneer work with gases.

List of institutions the committee deems to be qualified to offer professional training for chemists and chemical engineering. American Chemical Society. 1969. 10p. Single copy free

List of approved schools for training of chemists and chemical engineers, indicating the degrees offered at each.

Shall I study chemistry? American Chemical Society. 1968. 12p. Single copy free

Types of work, opportunities, salaries, personal characteristics, and training. Written for high school students.

**Your career in chemistry. Esterer, Arnulf K. Julian Messner. 1964. 192p. $3.95; library binding $3.64

Description of the various branches of chemistry and the anticipated growth in research and developmental activities expected to increase the employment of chemists. Includes information on necessary educational background, training, earnings, rewards, and employment outlook.

See also Chemical engineer; Scientist

CHIROPODIST. ***See*** **Podiatrist**

CHIROPRACTOR 079.108

**Chiropractic as a career. Belleau, Wilfrid. Park Publishing House. 1969. 25p. $1.00

Nature of work, training, qualifications, licensure, entering the field, conditions of work, income, opportunities, advantages, disadvantages, and recognition. Special section on opportunities for women. List of the 12 approved colleges for training.

Chiropractic guidance kit. Chiropractic Education Commission. 1970. Free to counselors

Packet of career materials in this field.

Chiropractor. Careers. 1969. 2p. 20c

Career summary for desk-top file. Duties, qualifications, and outlook.

Chiropractor. Chronicle Guidance Publications. 1969. 4p. 35c

Occupational brief summarizing work performed, working conditions, qualifications, determination of aptitudes and interests, training, advantages, outlook, and related jobs. List of approved chiropractic schools.

Chiropractor. Guidance Centre. 1969. 4p. 35c postpaid

Nature of work, qualifications, preparation, working conditions, advantages, disadvantages, how to get started, and related occupations.

Chiropractor. Michigan Employment Security Commission. 1958. 2p. Single copy free

Job brief summarizing occupational data for use in Michigan.

* Chiropractors. Science Research Associates. 1965. 4p. 45c

Occupational brief describing nature of work, training, qualifications, earnings, things to consider, and outlook. Selected references.

**Chiropractors. One section of *Occupational Outlook Handbook.*

Nature of work, where employed, training, other qualifications, employment outlook, earnings, and working conditions.

**Employment outlook for chiropractors. Bulletin No. 1650–13. Bureau of Labor Statistics, U.S. Department of Labor. Supt. of Documents. 1970. 6p. 10c

Reprint from the *Occupational Outlook Handbook.*

Guide to approved chiropractic colleges. International Chiropractors Association. 1966. 36p. Free

Description of scope of practice, requirements, opportunities, licensure qualifications, and future outlook. Includes a list of three colleges approved by the association.

**Opportunities in a chiropractic career. Produced with the cooperation of the American Chiropractic Association and the International Chiropractors Association. Vocational Guidance Manuals. 1967. 126p. $1.95 paper; library edition $3.75

A discussion of current developments in training and practice, and the future outlook. Information about educational preparation, licensure, and opportunities also included. List of the approved schools for training.

Your career as a doctor of chiropractic. Chiropractic Education Commission. 1968. 9p. Free

Points our career opportunities and outlook.

Your career as a doctor of chiropractic. International Chiropractors Association. No date. 12p. Free

Leaflet describing work, educational requirements, and opportunities.

CIRCUS PERFORMER 159.248

Acrobat (and aerialist). Chronicle Guidance Publications. 1967. 4p. 35c

Occupational brief summarizing work performed, qualifications, preparation, methods of entry and outlook.

Circus triumphant. Taylor, Reginald. Criterion Books, Inc. 1958. 251p. $3.50

Career fiction. Story of a boy and his father in their struggle to make their circus a success. Shows the adventure and difficulties involved.

The fabulous showman—the life and times of P. T. Barnum. Wallace, Irving. Knopf, Inc. 1959. 332p. $5.95

Biography of a noted circus owner.

The Ringlings: wizards of the circus. Harlow, Alvin. Julian Messner. 1951. 181p. Library binding $3.34

An account of the career of the Ringling brothers and the ups and downs of creating the spectacle of the circus.

Sawdust in his shoes. McGraw, Eloise Jarvis. Coward-McCann, Inc. 1950. 246p. $4.50

Career fiction. Story about a circus boy who becomes a star. For younger boys.

CITY MANAGER 188.118

Careers in city management. B'nai B'rith Vocational Service. 1969. 16p. 35c

This career brief summarizes the role and duties of the city manager, personal and educational requirements, training, opportunities, employment outlook, and remuneration.

Careers in municipal public relations. National League of Cities. 1967. 11p. $1

Nature of the work, need, possibilities, and outlook.

**Careers in public planning and administration. Cohn, Angelo. Henry Z. Walck, Inc. 1967. 112p. $4.50

One of the "Careers for Tomorrow" series, this includes description of duties, essential training, the potential for careers in public planning, financial expectations, and other compensation. A balanced account of advantages and disadvantages. The competitive aspects of the position are realistically presented. Illustrated.

CITY MANAGER—*Continued*

City manager. California State Department of Employment. 1965. 6p. Single copy free

Occupational guide describing work, requirements, training, and outlook.

City manager. Careers. 1970. 2p. 20c

Career summary for desk-top file. Duties, qualifications, and outlook.

City managers. Science Research Associates. 1969. 4p. 45c

Occupational brief describing the administration of local government, requirements, how to get started, advantages, disadvantages, and outlook. Selected references.

Finding out about city managers. Science Research Associates. 1967. 4p. 45c

Junior occupational brief describing work and opportunities.

CITY PLANNER. *See* Urban planner

CIVIL ENGINEER 005.081

Civil and highway technician. Chronicle Guidance Publications. 1969. 4p. 35c

Occupational brief summarizing the field of work, typical occupations, qualifications, training required, and training opportunities.

Civil engineer. California State Department of Employment. 1964. 8p. Single copy free

Occupational guide describing work, requirements, training, and outlook.

* Civil engineer. Careers. 1969. 8p. 35c

Career brief describing duties, working conditions, earnings, personal qualifications, training, suggested high school program, licensing, and outlook. Additional readings.

Civil engineer. Chronicle Guidance Publications. 1966. 4p. 35c

Occupational brief describing work performed, working conditions, personal qualifications, educational requirements, promotional opportunities, employment outlook, and licensing.

Civil engineering aide. California State Department of Employment. 1968. 3p. Single copy free

Occupational guide describing work, requirements, training, and outlook.

Civil engineers. Michigan Employment Security Commission. 1965. 2p. Single copy free

Job brief summarizing occupational data for use in Michigan.

Civil engineers. Science Research Associates. 1967. 4p. 45c

Occupational brief describing nature of work, qualifications, preparation, opportunities, advantages, disadvantages, and future outlook.

**Civil engineers. One section of *Occupational Outlook Handbook.*

Nature of work, where employed, and employment outlook.

Finding out about civil engineers. Science Research Associates. 1967. 4p. 45c

Junior occupational brief summarizing what the work requires and offers.

**Is civil engineering for you? American Society of Civil Engineers. 1967. 16p. Free

This booklet cites examples to show the wide-spread duties of civil engineers and offers encouragement to start early planning.

The land divided, the world united—the story of the Panama Canal. Rink, Paul. Julian Messner. 1963. 189p. $3.95; library binding $3.64

Among other things, this book portrays the many problems in a project of this kind.

The wonderful world of engineering. Jackson, David. Doubleday and Company. 1970. 96p. $3.95

Describes some of the great constructions of modern times to show the work and improved methods of civil engineering. For grades 5 to 8.

**Your future in civil engineering. American Society of Civil Engineers. 1965. 154p. Paper. Free

A description of functions, qualifications, financial requirements, educational preparation, career opportunities, professional status, financial rewards, procedures for obtaining employment, and history of the profession. Cites some notable biographies.

CIVIL SERVICE WORKER 001. through 999.99

Beginning professional careers with New York State. New York State Department of Civil Service. 1968. 5p. Free

Description of opportunities, requirements, and examination procedures.

Calling all majors for personnel, budget, administrative careers in Federal agencies. U.S. Civil Service Commission. 1969. 18p. Single copy free

Describes opportunities for high-caliber college graduates to enter professional-level jobs. Includes career "success stories." Outlines the benefits of Federal employment and explains how to apply through the Federal Service Entrance Examination.

Civil service jobs. Chronicle Guidance Publications. 1968. 4p. 35c

Occupational brief summarizing work performed, working day, how to apply, list of regional offices, examinations, kinds of appointments, and salaries.

The Civil Service retirement system. Civil Service Commission. Supt. of Documents. 1970. 6p. 10c

Brief information on when one can retire, how annuities are computed, minimum annuity for disability, what happens if one dies in service, how to provide for survivors on retirement, and other related information.

CIVIL SERVICE WORKER—*Continued*

**Federal career directory: a guide for college students. U.S. Civil Service Commission. Supt. of Documents. 1969. 87p. $1.25

Written to provide general guidance for the college student who aspires to a Federal public service career, this directory contains information on the method of filling jobs, student trainee programs, pay scales, and promotions. It also describes the work of the various agencies and the career opportunities in each.

The Federal career service . . . at your service: an introduction to the Federal personnel system. U.S. Civil Service Commission. Supt. of Documents. 1969. 24p. 30c

Includes regulations regarding recruiting, promotion, layoffs, pay, benefits, training, incentives, and the distribution of the Federal work force by agency and location.

Federal careers for women. U.S. Civil Service Commission. Supt. of Documents. 1967. 14p. 10c

Describes career opportunities for women in the Federal Government. Includes employment statistics for women.

Federal civil service workers. Science Research Associates. 1966. 4p. 45c

Occupational brief describing methods of entering Government service, training, earnings, advantages, and disadvantages. Selected references.

Federal white collar workers. Chronicle Guidance Publications. 1966. 4p. 35c

Occupational brief summarizing where employed, areas of employment, working conditions, applying for the job, kinds of appointments, and salaries.

Futures in the Federal Government. U.S. Civil Service Commission. Supt. of Documents. 1967. 32p. 20c

General information about Federal employment for college graduates. Describes the operation of the Federal Service Entrance Examination, which is the main gateway to career opportunities in the Federal Government for college-trained people. Describes career opportunities in individual Government agencies.

Key people: careers in education with your Federal Government. Government Printing Office. Supt. of Documents. 1969. 20p. 25c

Several Federal agencies that are major employers of educators are described in brief. The back cover is a postage paid tear-off card that can be mailed in for more detailed information.

Occupations of Federal blue-collar workers. U.S. Civil Service Commission. Supt. of Documents. 1968. 41p. 50c

A survey of full-time civilian employment in the Civil Service.

Occupations of Federal white-collar workers. U.S. Civil Service Commission. Supt. of Documents. 1968. 125p. $1.25

An occupational inventory of full-time Federal civilian white-collar employees by agency, grade, sex, and geographic area; with median grade and average salary for men and women within each occupation as of October 31, 1967.

Reemployment rights of Federal employees who perform duty in the Armed Forces. Civil Service Commission. Supt. of Documents. 1968. 7p. 5c

Up-to-date information about regulations.

Thinking about your first job? Remember Uncle Sam when it comes to choosing an employer. U.S. Civil Service Commission. 1968. 8p. Single copy free

A leaflet pointing out the advantages and opportunities of work for the Government.

**Working for the U.S.A.: applying for a civil service job, what the Government expects of Federal workers. U.S. Civil Service Commission. Supt. of Documents. 1969. 37p. 20c

Explanation of basis of rating, qualifications, opportunities for advancement, incentive awards, employee benefits, and salary scales.

**Your career in civil service. Liston, Robert A. Julian Messner. 1966. 223p. $3.95; library binding $3.64

This is a general guide to a wide variety of careers in the civil service. Includes the development of the civil service, qualifications, opportunities, and benefits. Separate chapters are devoted to the specific jobs available to the unskilled as well as the highly trained. Illustrated.

Your career in Federal civil service. DuPre, Flint O. Harper and Row. 1967. 243p. $5.95

Lists advantages and disadvantages of working for the Federal Government, training, salary, promotions, and retirement benefits, with information on specific jobs open and likely to employ young people. Stresses some opportunities for personally challenging activities.

See also Government service worker

CLEANING AND DYEING INDUSTRY WORKER. *See* Laundry industry worker

CLERGYMAN 120.108

Catholic priest: his training and ministry. Lothrop, Lee and Shepard. 1961. 127p. $4.95

Many photographs and simple text prepared for grades seven to ten.

Challenging careers in the church. McCabe, Joseph E. McGraw-Hill Book Company. 1966. 192p. $4.50

A discussion of broad opportunities, requirements, and returns.

The Christian ministry, a challenge. National Council of Churches. 1968. 16p. 30c

A motivational booklet directed to college and university students.

**The clergy. One chapter in *Occupational Outlook Handbook*.

Nature of work, where employed, training, other qualifications, and outlook for Protestant clergymen, Roman Catholic priests, and rabbis.

CLERGYMAN—*Continued*

The clergy and what they do. Spence, Hartzell. Franklin Watts, Inc. 1961. 195p. $3.95

Discussion of the necessary character traits and abilities, training, nature of work, related occupations in religious work, advancement, opportunities for women, and the challenge of the future. For grades 7 to 11.

Clergyman. Chronicle Guidance Publications. 1969. 4p. 35c

Occupational brief describing work performed, personal qualifications, remuneration, training, and employment outlook.

Clergyman. Guidance Centre. 1968. 4p. 35c postpaid

Nature of work, qualifications, preparation, working conditions, earnings, advantages, disadvantages, and related occupations.

Clergyman. Science Research Associates. 1966. 4p. 45c

Occupational brief describing nature of work, preparation, qualifications, opportunities, advantages, disadvantages, and future outlook.

Clergyman (protestant). Careers. 1968. 8p. 35c

Career brief describing duties, personal qualifications, training, salaries, how to enter, related jobs, and outlook. Includes list of accredited theological schools.

Directory of theological schools in the United States and Canada. American Association of Theological Schools. 1968. 148p. $1.70

Information concerning the accredited members of the Association.

**Employment outlook for clergymen. Bulletin No. 1650–29. Bureau of Labor Statistics, U.S. Department of Labor. Supt. of Documents. 1970. 12p. 15c

Reprint from the *Occupational Outlook Handbook*. Includes information about Protestant clergymen, Rabbis, and Roman Catholic priests.

The gospel ministry. Board of Christian Education, United Presbyterian Church. 1967. 4p. Free

Includes duties of the ordained minister, personal requirements, education, procedure for entering, need, opportunities for development, and disadvantages.

List of theological schools. American Association of Theological Schools. 1968. 4p. Free

List of schools which are accredited members.

**Minister. Coburn, John B. Macmillan Company. 1963. 205p. $4.95

The author discusses schooling, salaries, and the minister's average working day. Primarily for Protestants, though nonsectarian in spirit.

Preparing for the ministry. Kemp, Charles F. Bethany Press. 1959. 128p. $1.50

Answers to questions asked by young people who are considering the ministry.

Protestant clergymen. One section of *Occupational Outlook Handbook*.

Nature of work, training, qualifications, places of employment, and outlook.

Should I consider the ministry? National Council of Churches. No date. 14p. 20c

An illustrated booklet outlining many phases of the work for the college man or woman.

Statement on preseminary studies. American Association of Theological Schools. 1963. 4p. Free

Defines function of preseminary education and recommends course of study for college students who plan to become ministers.

When the minister is a woman. Gibson, Elsie. Holt, Rinehart and Winston, Inc. 1970. 174p. $4.95

An ordained Methodist minister who is also a wife of a minister produces a vocational profile from questionnaire information gathered from 270 ordained women in Protestant sects. She illustrates the difficulties, complexities, advantages, disadvantages, types of work, and the impact of training on status.

**Your future as a minister. Floyd, William. Richards Rosen Press. 1969. 160p. $4; library edition $3.78

Description of the life of a minister, training, advantages, and disadvantages.

See also Priest; Rabbi; Religious vocations worker

CLERICAL WORKER 219.388

Can I be an office worker? General Motors Corporation, Public Relations Staff. 1955. 32p. Free

Outlines various office positions and discusses duties, preparation, personal qualities, and chances for advancement. Includes stenography, bookkeeping, business machine operation, and general clerical work. Available in classroom sets.

A career in the modern office series. Gregg Division, McGraw-Hill Book Company. 1969. 4 booklets. $1.96 each

A series of four text-workbooks for use in a survey course exploring office occupations. Books in the series include: Opportunities in today's office, Making the most of yourself, Making the most of your skills, and Getting the right job.

Clerical airline jobs. Careers. 1968. 7p. 35c

Career brief describing duties and qualifications of the traffic agent, reservations agent, ticket agent, passenger agent, station manager, cargo agent, air freight agent, and personnel director.

Clerical and office work in the computer age. Chronicle Guidance Publications. 1967. 6p. 50c

Reprinted article from *Business Education Forum* discusses changing aspects and patterns of the work in the computer age.

**Clerical and related occupations. One section of *Occupational Outlook Handbook*.

Nature of clerical work, training, other qualifications, advancement, employment outlook, earnings, and working conditions. Specific information is given concerning secretary, stenographer, typist, bookkeeper, office machine operator, and electronic computer operator.

CLERICAL WORKER—*Continued*

Clerical occupations for women—today and tomorrow. Bulletin 289. Women's Bureau, U.S. Department of Labor. Supt. of Documents. 1964. 76p. 35c

Examines the trends in clerical jobs and discusses the expectations for the future. Surveys several occupations and considers the possible effects of automation on clerical work.

Clerk, general office. California State Department of Employment. 1964. 4p. Single copy free

Occupational guide describing work, requirements, training, and outlook.

Clerk-typist. California State Department of Employment. 1965. 5p. Single copy free

Duties, working conditions, wages, hours, finding the job, training, and employment outlook.

Correspondence clerk. Chronicle Guidance Publications. 1966. 4p. 35c

Occupational brief summarizing work performed, personal qualifications, earnings, methods of entry, advancement, related occupations, and outlook.

Correspondence clerks. Science Research Associates. 1969. 4p. 45c

Occupational brief describing work, training, qualifications, opportunities, and outlook.

Federal office assistant examination, stenographer; typist, clerk, and office machine operator; what it is, and how it is given. U.S. Civil Service Commission. Supt. of Documents. 1969. 60p. 60c

Information about experience, training requirements, and tests for filling a variety of office occupations. Brief statements about the nature of the work and opportunities in the major occupations.

Finding out about correspondence clerks. Science Research Associates. 1967. 4p. 45c

Junior occupational brief describing work and opportunities.

Finding out about office boys and messengers. Science Research Associates. 1967. 4p. 45c

Junior occupational brief containing concise facts about the job.

* General office clerk. Careers. 1969. 8p. 35c

Career brief describing duties, working conditions, training, personal qualifications, earnings, advancement prospects, and ways of measuring one's interest and ability.

General office clerk. Chronicle Guidance Publications. 1969. 4p. 35c

Occupational brief summarizing work performed, working conditions, qualifications, determination of aptitudes and interests, training, opportunities, outlook, methods of entry, and related jobs.

General office practice. Third edition. Gregg Division, McGraw-Hill Book Company. 1968. 544p. $5.96

Textbook for use in clerical or general office practice class. Includes suggestions for succeeding in a variety of clerical jobs.

Information concerning the clerical and clerical-technical positions in the Federal Bureau of Investigation. The Bureau. 1968. 1p. Free

Physical requirements, educational and job qualifications, working hours, and salaries. Positions include translator, fingerprint classifier, stenographer, typist, and clerk.

Jobs in clerical work. Science Research Associates. 1965. 32p. $1.15

Describes the variety of job prospects and opportunities within this field.

Marketing, business, and office specialists. Wiggs, Garland, ed. Ferguson Publishing Company. 1970. 393p. $11.95

Provides information about career opportunities for technicians in those areas which require only one or two years of college preparation. For each specialist there is given type of work, requirements, entry level jobs, advancement opportunities, earning potential, and future outlook.

Office clerk. Guidance Centre. 1969. 4p. 35c postpaid

Definition, history and importance of work, qualifications, employment and advancements, remuneration, advantages, disadvantages, how to get started, and related occupations.

**Opportunities in office occupations. Popham, Estelle D. Vocational Guidance Manuals. 1964. 110p. $1.95 paper; $3.75 library edition

Nature of work, qualifications, preparation, opportunities, and employment outlook.

Secretaries, stenographers, typists. Assignment, Washington, D.C., with the U.S. Department of State. U.S. Department of State. Publication Number RB-5. 1968. 14p. Free

Includes nature of the work, opportunities, qualifications, benefits, pay, and promotions.

**Your future as a temporary office worker. Winter, Elmer. Richards Rosen Press. 1968. 150p. $4; library edition $3.78

The president of a national organization supplying temporary office help explains the expanding opportunities created by modern business' demand for a more flexible work force. Gives advantages of temporary office and factory work.

See also Bookkeeper; Business worker; Stenographer; Typist

CLINICAL LABORATORY TECHNICIAN. *See* Laboratory technician; Medical technologist

CLOTHES DESIGNER 142.081

**Careers and opportunities in fashion. Brenner, Barbara. Dutton and Company. 1964. 191p. $3.95

The nature of work in designing, merchandising, advertising, illustrating, photographing, and modeling for the fashion industry is followed by brief information on qualifications, opportunities, and chances for advancement. Includes list of schools offering training.

CLOTHES DESIGNER—*Continued*

Clothes designer. Guidance Centre. 1968. 4p. 35 postpaid

Definition, nature of work, working conditions, qualifications, preparation, advancement, remuneration, advantages, disadvantages, how to get started, and related occupations.

Designers. Chronicle Guidance Publications. 1968. 4p. 35c

Occupational brief summarizing definition, work performed, working conditions, where employed, earnings, personal qualifications, education required, and outlook.

Dress designer. Careers. 1969. 2p. 20c

Career summary for desk-top file. Duties, qualifications, and outlook.

Fashion as a career. Heal, Edith. Julian Messner. 1966. 191p. $3.95; library binding $3.64

This is a general guide to careers in fashion with personal glimpses of many well-known designers, manufacturers, buyers, editors, columnists, models, and retailers. Includes a reading list and a directory of schools offering training in fashion and related fields. The final chapter presents ways to enter the fashion field.

Fashion designer. Chronicle Guidance Publications. 1966. 4p. 35c

Occupational brief containing nature of work, working conditions, personal qualifications, determination of aptitudes and interests, training, employment outlook, and methods of entry.

** Fashion designers. Science Research Associates. 1970. 4p. 45c

Occupational brief describing nature of work, qualifications, educational requirements, getting started, pros and cons, and future outlook.

Finding out about fashion designers. Science Research Associates. 1967. 4p. 45c

Junior occupational brief describing work and opportunities.

Flair for fashion. Ferm, Betty. Julian Messner. 1967. 192p. $3.50

Career fiction. Story set against the background of the fashion industry, showing nature of the work and problems.

Hey . . . look me over—an exciting career in the world of apparel. American Apparel Manufacturers Association. 1968. 16p. 20c

Explanation of the opportunities for training personnel for management available in some industry-related institutions.

No pattern for love. Williams, Beryl. Julian Messner. 1951. 178p. $3.50

Career fiction. The romance contains helpful hints to girls who are thinking of careers in fashion. The heroine is a student at a school for fashion design who explores several aspects of the fashion world before solving her career problems.

Women's clothing designer. California State Department of Employment. 1967. 5p. Single copy free

Occupational guide describing work, requirements, training, and outlook.

**Your future in fashion design. The Fashion Group. Richards Rosen Press. 1966. 159p. $4; library edition $3.78

Fifteen leading fashion specialists discuss several facets of the fashion world, including designing of clothing and accessories, fashion buying, advertising and publicity, fashion show and display, fashion reporting, and how to find a job in fashion.

See also Apparel industry worker

CLOTHING INDUSTRY WORKER. *See* Apparel industry worker; Clothes designer; Milliner

COAL INDUSTRY WORKER 939.281

Coal aid to higher education. National Coal Association. 1968. 12p. Free

Eligibility requirements for scholarship and work-study programs offered by various coal companies.

Coal miner. Careers. 1966. 2p. 20c

Career summary for desk-top file. Duties, qualifications, and outlook.

Coal miners. Science Research Associates. 1967. 4p. 45c

Occupational brief describing nature of work, qualifications, working conditions, opportunities, advantages, disadvantages, and future outlook.

**Engineering careers in the coal industry. National Coal Association. 1966. 15p. Free

Outlines responsibilities and opportunities in the coal industry and lists colleges which offer mining engineering.

See also Metallurgical engineer; Mining and quarrying industry worker; Mining engineer

COAST GUARDSMAN 368.999

**Bulletin of Information. U.S. Coast Guard Academy. 1969. 72p. Free

Description of the four-year curriculum leading to a B.S. degree and a commission in the Coast Guard. Includes scholastic and physical requirements for admission and procedures for application to take entrance examinations. Some sample questions and answers are suggested. Contains application forms. Fully illustrated.

The Coast Guard Academy. Engeman, Jack. Lothrop, Lee and Shepard Company. 1957. 128p. $4.95

Story showing the life of a cadet. Two hundred illustrations.

Coast guard in action. Bergaust, Erik and Foss, William. Putnam's Sons. 1962. 96p. 3.29

The history of the Coast Guard, the story of men who serve in it, and how they carry out their maritime and law enforcement duties. Written for ages 10 to 14.

Coast Guard officer. Careers. 1970. 2p. 20c

Career summary for desk-top file. Duties, qualifications, and outlook.

COAST GUARDSMAN—*Continued*

**Counselor's handbook. U.S. Coast Guard Academy. 1969-1970. 24p. Free to counselors

Handbook of information for advising students applying for appointment to the academy.

Current career booklets. U.S. Coast Guard. Five booklets. Free

Frequently revised materials are available from local recruiting offices or the above. Examples of present titles are: U.S. Coast Guard—a career service; Coast Guard history, and After boot camp.

Danger fighters: men and ships of the U.S. Coast Guard. Colby, C. B. Coward-McCann, Inc. 1953. 48p. Library binding $2.97

Photographs and brief text show how men protect life and property at sea and enforce applicable maritime, customs, immigration, and other laws. Written for grades 4 to 8.

Kendall of the Coast Guard. Wyckoff, James. Doubleday and Company. 1961. 142p. $3.50

Career fiction. Story of a boy's experiences on patrol in the North Atlantic reveals the nature of work, training, and gratifications of serving in the Coast Guard.

Let's go to the United States Coast Guard Academy. Butler, Roger. Putnam's Sons. 1964. 48p. Library edition $2.29

The cadets are seen in their daily activities as they prepare to be officers. For grades 3 to 6.

Rescue at sea. Waters, Capt. John M., Jr. Van Nostrand Reinhold Company. 1966. 264p. $5.95

Gives a picture of a dramatic and hazardous profession. Describes the Search and Rescue Division of the Coast Guard and the Air Forces' Air Rescue Service. By explaining many dangerous rescues, the author shows how radar and other technical equipment such as helicopters have saved lives.

Search and rescue at sea. Floherty, John J. Lippincott Company. 1963. 150p. $3.95

An account of the adventure, perils, and achievements of the Coast Guardsman. Stories about the service of weather ships, about hurricanes, abandoned ships, salvage, and rescues. Sixteen pages of photographs.

The United States Coast Guard—a career service. U.S. Coast Guard. 1961. 24p. Free

Illustrated booklet telling a young man what to expect as a member of the Coast Guard.

You have to go out! The story of the U.S. Coast Guard. Berry, Erick. David McKay Company. 1964. 192p. $4.50; library binding $4.19

Includes the background, history, and development of the U.S. Coast Guard.

See also Armed Forces

COIN-MACHINE OPERATOR 219.588

Coin-machine operator. California State Department of Employment. 1969. 4p. Single copy free

Occupational guide describing work, requirements, training, and outlook.

COLLECTOR. *See* Credit and collection manager; Fund raiser

COLLEGE ADMINISTRATOR 090.168 and 090.118

College administrators and advisers. Science Research Associates. 1967. 4p. 45c

Occupational brief describing work, training, qualifications, opportunities, and outlook.

College placement officers. One section of *Occupational Outlook Handbook.*

Nature of work, places of employment, qualifications, advancement, outlook, earnings, and working conditions.

Up the ivy ladder. Runnion, Norman. Doubleday and Company. 1969. 178p. $4.95

The author gives advice, with considerable satire, to the advanced student who aspires to the college presidency.

COLLEGE TEACHER 090.228

**Careers in college teaching. Friedberg, Robert M. and Hawes, Gene R. Henry Z. Walck, Inc. 1965. 100p. $4.50

This is a description of the activities of college teachers, including a day in the life of a typical instructor. Contains discussion of opportunities, trends, preparation, earnings, and other rewards.

**College and university teachers. One section of *Occupational Outlook Handbook.*

Nature of work, where employed, training, other qualifications, advancement, employment outlook, earnings, and working conditions.

College teacher. Careers. 1966. 8p. 35c

Career brief describing nature of work, training, advantages, disadvantages, earnings, and outlook.

* College teachers. Science Research Associates. 1966. 4p. 45c

Occupational brief describing nature of work, requirements, methods of securing appointment, earnings, advantages, disadvantages, and future outlook.

College teaching: perspectives and guidelines. Brown, James and Thornton, James. McGraw-Hill Book Company. 1963. 260p. $6.95

Part I emphasizes the background of higher education in the United States, the sociological and professional aspects of college teaching, and the goals of the curriculum of higher education in liberal arts colleges. Part II explores the practical aspects of teaching.

COLLEGE TEACHER—*Continued*

Faculty member (college or university). Chronicle Guidance Publications. 1969. 4p. 35c

Occupational brief summarizing work performed, personal qualifications, educational requirements, salaries, other benefits, and outlook.

Finding out about college teachers. Science Research Associates. 1967. 4p. 45c

Junior occupational brief summarizing what the work requires and offers.

The good life: college teaching. National Education Association. No date. 8p. 35 copies $1

This leaflet describes the kind of life that awaits a young man or woman who plans to teach in college.

Junior college teachers of science, engineering, and technology. National Science Foundation. Supt. of Documents. 1969. 89p. $1

Data on experience, employment characteristics, and educational backgrounds of 11,000 junior college teachers.

**Professor. Millett, Fred B. Macmillan Company. 1961. 189p. $3.95

Traces the span of a teaching career from preliminary studies in school and college, through graduate work, early teaching assignments, the importance of tenure, to full professorship and retirement.

Teaching in college. Alumnae Advisory Center. 1967. 6p. 35c

Reprint from *Mademoiselle* describing some experiences of several young women who have succeeded as college teachers.

University teacher. Guidance Centre. 1968. 4p. 35c postpaid

History and importance, nature of work, qualifications, working conditions, preparation, remuneration, advancement, outlook, related occupations, and how to get started.

* Your career as a college professor of business. Council for Professional Education for Business. Revised 1968. 10p. 10c

Prepared for individuals aspiring to be business teachers in colleges and universities. Includes educational requirements, preparation, satisfactions of academic life, and career development.

See also Teacher

COLUMNIST. *See* Journalist

COMEDIAN. *See* Actor and actress

COMMERCIAL ARTIST 141.081

**Careers and opportunities in commercial art. Biegeleisen, Jacob Israel. Dutton and Company. Revised 1963. 244p. $4.95

Information about the various careers that are related to art in industry such as book covers, caricatures and cartoons, show windows, sign painting, stage setting, and trademarks. A chapter on art in television is included.

Careers in graphic communications. Graphic Arts Industry, Inc. 1969. 14p. Single copy free

Four-color booklet describing the variety of career opportunities available in the industry. Gives sources of additional information.

Careers in illustration. Sound filmstrip with phonodisc and teacher's guide, for use with manual or automatic projector. Produced and distributed by Educational Dimensions Corporation. 1968. 77 fr. $15

Job opportunities and types of work a young art student can expect as a commercial illustrator. Also describes ways in which a beginner secures assignments in advertising agencies, publishing houses, industry, art studios, and free-lance work.

Commercial artist. California State Department of Employment. 1967. 5p. Single copy free

Duties, working conditions, pay, training, promotion, and employment prospects.

Commercial artist. Careers. 1969. 2p. 20c

Career summary for desk-top file. Duties, qualifications, and outlook.

Commercial artist. Guidance Centre. 1970. 4p. 35c postpaid

Definition, history and importance, working conditions, qualifications necessary for entry and success, preparation, employment and advancement, remuneration, advantages, disadvantages, and related occupations.

* Commercial artist. One section in *Occupational Outlook Handbook.*

Nature of work, where employed, training, other qualifications, advancement, employment outlook, earnings, and working conditions.

Commercial artists. Michigan Employment Security Commission. 1967. 2p. Single copy free

Job brief summarizing occupational data for use in Michigan.

Commercial artists. Science Research Associates. 1969. 4p. 45c

Occupational brief describing nature of work, training, qualifications, opportunities, advantages, disadvantages, and future outlook.

Fashion illustrator. Careers. 1970. 2p. 20c

Career summary for desk-top file. Duties, qualifications, and outlook.

Finding out about commercial artists. Science Research Associates. 1967. 4p. 45c

Junior occupational brief containing concise facts about the job.

Illustrating commercial artist. Chronicle Guidance Publications. 1966. 4p. 35c

Occupational brief summarizing work performed, working conditions, remuneration, qualifications, training, opportunities, methods of entry, and ways of developing talent while in high school.

Jobs in art. Science Research Associates. 1966. 32p. $1.15

Describes the variety of job prospects and opportunities within this field, especially for the artist, display worker, industrial designer, interior decorator, and photographer.

COMMERCIAL ARTIST—*Continued*

National scholarship program of the printing and publishing industry. Graphic Arts Industry, Inc. 1969. 16p. Free

Booklet describing the scholarship program available to qualified students interested in the graphic communications field.

**Opportunities in graphic arts carers. Ballinger, Raymond A. Vocational Guidance Manuals. 1968. 128p. $1.95 paper; library edition $3.75

Concise information on the craft of the graphic or commercial artist who works with the pictorial and written arts and the reproduction techniques. Includes the educational preparation, outlook, how to get started, and employment opportunities in industry and government. Names the schools and colleges accredited by the National Association of Schools of Art.

Technical schools, colleges and universities offering courses in graphic communications. Graphic Arts Industry, Inc. 1968. 3p. Free

List of schools offering either degree or certificate programs in graphic communications, with indication of type of program each school offers.

See also Artist

COMPARISON SHOPPER 296.388

Comparison shopper. Careers. 1966. 2p. 20c

Career summary for desk-top file. Duties, qualifications, and outlook.

Comparison shopper. Chronicle Guidance Publications. 1968. 4p. 35c

Occupational brief summarizing duties, personal qualifications, preparation, related occupations, and outlook.

Finding out about comparison shoppers. Science Research Associates. 1967. 4p. 45c

Junior occupational brief summarizing what the work requires and offers.

COMPOSITOR 650.582 and 973.381

Composing room occupations. California State Department of Employment. 1967. 6p. Single copy free

Occupational guide summarizing duties, employment prospects, earnings, requirements for entry, and suggestions for locating a job.

**Composing room occupations, printing. One section of *Occupational Outlook Handbook*.

Description of work of the hand compositor and typesetter, imposer, linotype operator, monotype keyboard operator, and phototypesetting operator. Also included is a discussion of training, other qualifications, employment outlook, earnings, and working conditions.

Compositor. Chronicle Guidance Publications. 1967. 4p. 35c

Occupational brief summarizing work performed, hours, earnings, requirements, training, and methods of entry.

Compositors and printing pressmen. Science Research Associates. 1966. 4p. 45c

Occupational brief describing various kinds of work, requirements, earnings, getting started and advancing, advantages, disadvantages, and future outlook.

Finding out about compositors. Science Research Associates. 1967. 4p. 45c

Junior occupational brief describing work and opportunities.

COMPUTER OPERATOR. ***See*** **Electronic computer operator; Programmer**

COMPUTER PROGRAMMER. ***See*** **Programmer**

CONDUCTOR, RAILROAD 198.160

Conductor (railroad). Chronicle Guidance Publications. 1968. 4p. 35c

Occupational brief summarizing work performed as passenger, pullman, road freight, and yard conductor; where employed, working conditions, earnings, personal qualifications, training required, and outlook.

**Conductors. One section of *Occupational Outlook Handbook.*

Nature of work, training, other qualifications, advancement, employment outlook, earnings, and working conditions.

Railroad conductor. Careers. 1966. 2p. 20c

Career summary for desk-top file. Duties, qualifications, and outlook.

CONFECTIONERY INDUSTRY WORKER 529.381

Confectionery industry workers. Chronicle Guidance Publications. 1968. 4p. 35c

Occupational brief summarizing work performed, outlook, working conditions, training requirements, personal qualifications, and earnings.

Confectionery industry workers. Science Research Associates. 1968. 4p. 45c

Occupational brief describing types of jobs, requirements, methods of getting started, earnings, advantages, disadvantages, and future outlook.

Finding out about candy makers. Science Research Associates. 1967. 4p. 45c

Junior occupational brief describing work and opportunities.

The retail manufacturing segment of the candy industry. Chronicle Guidance Publications. 1968. 4p. 35c

Reprinted article from Pennsylvania Manufacturing Confectioners' Association discusses the history of candymaking and current practices in manufacturing and retailing.

CONSERVATION SPECIALIST 379.168

* Careers for women in conservation. Leaflet 50. Women's Bureau, U.S. Department of Labor. Supt. of Documents. 1969. 8p. 10c

Brief sketch of nature of work, duties, qualifications, where employed, opportunities, and earnings. Illustrated.

**Careers in conservation; opportunities in natural resources. Clepper, Henry E., ed. Ronald Press. 1963. 141p. $3.75

Information about opportunities and training in soil conservation, wildlife management, fisheries, forestry, range management, watershed management, and parks and recreational development. Each chapter has been prepared by a specialist.

**Careers in natural resource conservation. Herbert, Fred W. Henry Z. Walck, Inc. 1965. 110p. $4.50

This book offers a detailed picture of the work of those who conserve and manage natural supply sources such as soil, water, forests, vegetation, and wildlife. Qualifications, preparation necessary, and outlook are described. The principal career areas include work of the soil scientist, agronomist, range conservationist, conservation forester, conservation biologist, conservation engineer, soil conservationist, and conservation aids and technicians. Reading list. Illustrated.

Careers in wildlife conservation. Madson, John and Kozicky, Edward. Olin Mathieson Chemical Corporation. 1964. 36p. 15c. Single copy free

Description of the work of the conservation officer.

Conservation officer. Chronicle Guidance Publications. 1968. 4p. 35c

Occupational brief summarizing importance of the job, nature of work, working conditions, personal qualifications, where employed, opportunities for advancement, hours and earnings, employment outlook, educational and training requirements, advantages, and disadvantages.

Conservation officer (Ontario). Guidance Centre. 1968. 4p. 35c postpaid

History and importance, nature of work, qualifications, working conditions, preparation, remuneration, outlook, related occupations, and how to get started.

**Employment outlook for conservation occupations. Bulletin No. 1650–31. Bureau of Labor Statistics, U.S. Department of Labor. Supt. of Documents. 1970. 16p. 15c

Reprint from the *Occupational Outlook Handbook*. Includes foresters, forestry aids, and range managers.

Exploring your future in the protective agencies. Sextant Systems, Inc. 1970. 96p. $8.95

One page is devoted to each of ninety-five jobs, describing the duties, requirements for entering, promotional outlook, and the pay and skill level.

Fellowships in conservation. National Wildlife Federation. 1968. 2p. Free

Description of program of student aid to doctoral candidates.

Fish and wildlife. Colby, C. B. Coward-McCann, Inc. 1955. 48p. $2.97

Illustrated with photographs portraying the work of the Fish and Wildlife Service. Written for grades 4 to 8.

**Nature's guardians: your career in conservation. Neal, Harry Edward. Julian Messner. 1963. 192p. Library binding $3.64

Includes explanation of what is expected in each general branch of the U.S. Fish and Wildlife Service, U.S. Forest Service, and the Soil Conservation Service, as well as similar posts with state and commercial institutions. A wide variety of careers described. Bibliography.

Unusual careers. Munzer, Martha E. Alfred A. Knopf, Inc. 1962. 160p. $3

The careers described are solar scientist, geologist, meterologists, oceanographer, ecologist, sanitary engineer, research chemist, and city and regional planner. This book emphasizes the opportunities in the conservation of natural resources.

**Wildlife. Harrison, C. William. Julian Messner. 1970. 192p. $3.95; library edition $3.64

Explains why ecology has become an important issue by showing how man's survival depends upon preservation of living things. Emphasizes the importance of wildlife conservation and the steps to be taken to save the natural resources.

**Your career in parks and recreation. McCall, Virginia and McCall, Joseph R. Julian Messner. 1970. 192p. $3.95; library binding $3.64

Describes the work of protecting and improving our natural preserves. Includes a list of over one hundred occupations for state park systems.

CONSTRUCTION INDUSTRY WORKER 869.

**Aim for a job in the building trades. Daly, Donald F. Richards Rosen Press. 1970. 158p. $4; library edition $3.78

Gives details of education, training, and experience requirements, as well as information on wage rates, fringe benefits, and opportunities for advancement. Includes a list of national unions for the building trades.

Building construction careers. Chronicle Guidance Publications. 1968. 4p. 35c

Occupational brief summarizing work performed in various jobs, working conditions, training, opportunities, and methods of entry.

Building inspector. California State Department of Employment. 1968. 2p. Single copy free

Occupational guide describing work, requirements, training, and outlook.

CONSTRUCTION INDUSTRY WORKER—*Continued*

**Building trades. One chapter of *Occupational Outlook Handbook.*

Nature of work, where employed, training, other qualifications, advancement, employment outlook, earnings, and working conditions for each of the following: carpenter, painter and paperhanger, plumber and pipefitter, bricklayer, operating engineer, electrician, rodman, plasterer, roofer, cement mason, sheet-metal worker, asbestos and insulating worker, glazier, marble setter, stonemason, and elevator constructor.

**Careers in the building trades. Kasper, Sydney. Henry Z. Walck, Inc. Revised 1969. 128p. $4.50

Following a general discussion of the opportunities and outlook for the building trades, specific information is given concerning seventeen occupations. For each the author discusses types of jobs, earnings, fringe benefits, apprentice programs, and special training, requirements, and skills.

Construction. One section of *Occupational Outlook Handbook.*

Estimated employment of each of eight occupational groups in 1968 in this industry and the employment outlook.

The construction industry. One chapter in Volume I of the *Encyclopedia of Careers and Vocational Guidance.*

The range of construction work, opportunities, apprentice training programs, and the future of the industry.

Exploring your future in construction. Sextant Systems, Inc. 1971. 96p. $8.95

One page is devoted to each of ninety-five jobs, summarizing duties, requirements for entering, promotional outlook, and pay and skill level. Accompanying the book is an organizational chart showing beginning jobs and those to which one may be promoted.

Finding out about molders. Science Research Associates. 1967. 4p. 45c

Junior occupational brief describing work and opportunities.

Jobs in building construction trades. Science Research Associates. 1966. 32p. $1.15

Describes the variety of job prospects and opportunities within this field.

Man against earth: the story of tunnels and tunnel builders. Murray, Don. J. B. Lippincott Company. 1961. 192p. $3.95

Includes description of modern technology and the men who work on tunnels. Railroad and highway tunnels, those through mountains and under rivers, tunnels called mines, and tunnel cities in the Arctic are included. Illustrated.

Molder. Chronicle Guidance Publications. 1969. 4p. 35c

Occupational brief summarizing work performed, working conditions, wages, training, opportunities, methods of entry, and outlook.

Moulder. Guidance Centre. 1967. 4p. 35c postpaid

Nature of work, qualifications, preparation, working conditions, advancement opportunities, earnings, advantages, disadvantages, and how to get started.

Starting and managing a small building business. Small Business Administration. Supt. of Documents. 1962. 102p. 35c

This volume is intended to help prospective builders and those just starting decide whether they can wisely establish themselves in this business. It provides them with some basic management practices which will help them avoid the pitfalls and contribute to success.

Student interviews point up industry problems. Chronicle Guidance Publications. 1969. 5p. 50c

Reprinted article from *Heating, Piping and Air Conditioning* discusses an on-the-job seminar with students concerning problems in the building industry.

CONSTRUCTION LABORER 860.887

Construction helpers and laborers. Careers. 1966. 8p. 35c

Career brief describing duties, personal requirements, training, earnings, related careers, and outlook.

Construction laborers. Chronicle Guidance Publications. 1966. 4p. 35c

Occupational brief summarizing work performed, working conditions, personal requirements, where employed, hours and earnings, educational and training requirements, and opportunities.

Construction laborers and hod carriers. One section of *Occupational Outlook Handbook.*

Nature of work, where employed, training and other qualifications, employment outlook, earnings, and working conditions.

**Employment outlook for construction laborers and hod carriers. Bulletin No. 1650–72. Bureau of Labor Statistics, U.S. Department of Labor. Supt. of Documents. 1970. 12p. 15c

Reprint from the *Occupational Outlook Handbook.*

Finding out about construction laborers. Science Research Associates. 1967. 4p. 45c

Junior occupational brief containing concise facts about the job.

Training construction and maintenance personnel. Chronicle Guidance Publications. 1966. 4p. 35c

Reprinted article from *Gas Age* discusses classroom and shop training courses to improve employee performance at Southern California Gas Company.

Union wages and hours, building trades. Bureau of Labor Statistics, U.S. Department of Labor. Supt. of Documents. 1970. 50p. 55c

Wage and benefit data for union members in sixty-eight cities. Shows wage and hour trends in the nation as a whole since 1907.

CONSTRUCTION MACHINERY OPERATOR 859.883

Construction machinery operator. California State Department of Employment. 1964. 4p. Single copy free

Occupational guide describing work, requirements, training, and outlook.

CONSTRUCTION MACHINERY OPERATOR—*Continued*

Construction machinery workers. Science Research Associates. 1969. 4p. 45c

Occupational brief describing nature of work, qualifications, training, getting a job, salaries, advantages, disadvantages, and future outlook.

Finding out about construction machinery operators. Science Research Associates. 1967. 4p. 45c

Junior occupational brief describing work and opportunities.

COOK AND CHEF 313.131 and 315.381

Chef-cook. Chronicle Guidance Publications. 1967. 4p. 35c

Occupational brief containing work performed, working conditions, personal requirements, training requirements, training opportunities, outlook, and suggested activities.

Chefs and cooks in fine restaurants. California State Department of Employment. 1967. 5p. Single copy free

Occupational guide summarizing duties, working conditions, employment prospects, earnings, training, requirements for entry, and suggestions for locating a job.

**Cook-chef as a career. Belleau, Wilfrid. Park Publishing House. 1969. 19p. $1

Importance and nature of the work, qualifications, training, working conditions, advancement, income, opportunities, advantages, disadvantages, and how to begin.

Cook, domestic. Careers. 1968. 2p. 20c

Career summary for desk-top file. Duties, qualifications, and outlook.

Cook or chef. Guidance Centre. 1968. 4p. 23c postpaid

History and importance, nature of work, qualifications, preparation, working conditions, earnings, advantages, disadvantages, how to get started, and related occupations.

**Cooks and chefs. Careers. 1969. 8p. 35c

Career brief describing duties, working conditions, training, earnings, and outlook.

**Cooks and chefs. Science Research Associates. 1966. 4p. 45c

Occupational brief describing many types of cooks, requirements, training, earnings and hours, how to enter, advantages, disadvantages, and future outlook.

**Cooks and chefs. One section of *Occupational Outlook Handbook.*

Nature of work of cooks and chefs in restaurants, where employed, training, other qualifications, advancement, employment outlook, earnings, and working conditions.

Dining car cooks. One section of *Occupational Outlook Handbook.*

Nature of work, training, other qualifications, advancement, employment outlook, earnings, and working conditions.

Domestic cook. California State Department of Employment. 1964. 2p. Single copy free

Occupational guide describing work, requirements, training, and outlook.

**Employment outlook for cooks and chefs, waiters and waitresses. Bulletin No. 1650–63. Bureau of Labor Statistics, U.S. Department of Labor. Supt. of Documents. 1970. 8p. 10c

Reprint from the *Occupational Outlook Handbook.*

Finding out about cooks and chefs. Science Research Associates. 1967. 4p. 45c

Junior occupational brief describing work and opportunities.

Finding out about short-order cooks. Science Research Associates. 1967. 4p. 45c

Junior occupational brief summarizing what the work requires and offers.

The making of a chef. Chronicle Guidance Publications. 1969. 2p. 35c

Reprinted article from *American Youth* discusses a New Orleans training course for chefs.

A most delicious career. Chronicle Guidance Publications. 1967. 4p. 35c

Reprinted article from *American Education* discusses a program for training cooks.

Prepare for a rewarding career in the culinary profession. American Culinary Federation. 1969. 6p. Free

Description of a work-study program.

Short order cook. California State Department of Employment. 1967. 4p. Single copy free

Occupational guide describing work, requirements, training, and outlook.

See also Caterer; Food technologist

COOPERATIVE EXTENSION SERVICE WORKER 096.128

Career exploration: a guide for extension workers. U.S. Department of Agriculture. Supt. of Documents. 1963. 19p. 15c

Explains how the county agent can interest youth and the community in career problems.

* Cooperative extension service workers. Science Research Associates. 1969. 4p. 45c

Occupational brief describing the work of the agricultural agent, the home demonstration agent, and the 4-H Club agent. Includes requirements, salaries, getting started, advantages, disadvantages, and future outlook.

Cooperative extension service workers. One section of *Occupational Outlook Handbook.*

Nature of work, training, other qualifications, employment outlook, earnings, and working conditions.

COOPERATIVE EXTENSION SERVICE WORKER–*Continued*

County agent. McDonnell, Virginia B. Julian Messner. 1968. 192p. $3.50

Career fiction. Experiences of a county agent in the remote wilderness of the Adirondack Mountains.

County agricultural agent. Careers. 1970. 2p. 20c

Career summary for desk-top file. Duties, qualifications, and outlook.

County agricultural agent. Chronicle Guidance Publications. 1968. 4p. 35c

Occupational brief summarizing work performed, working conditions, qualifications, training, opportunities, and outlook.

Extension home economics. American Home Economics Association. 1968. 4p. 10c

Stresses that home economics is an avenue to family stability, consumer competence, housing and home furnishings, family health, and community development.

Finding out about county extension agents. Science Research Associates. 1967. 4p. 45c

Junior occupational brief summarizing what the work requires and offers.

Home demonstration agent. Careers. 1970. 2p. 20c

Career summary for desk-top file. Duties, qualifications, and outlook.

COPY READER 132.288

Copy reader. California State Department of Employment. 1964. 4p. Single copy free

Occupational guide describing work, requirements, training, and outlook.

Editorial assistants. Science Research Associates. 1968. 4p. 45c

Junior occupational brief describing work, qualifications, outlook, and opportunities.

COPY WRITER 132.088

Advertising copy writer. Guidance Centre. 1968. 4p. 23c postpaid

Definition, history and importance, nature of work, qualifications necessary for entry and success, preparation, employment and advancement, remuneration, advantages, disadvantages, how to get started, and related occupations.

Advertising copywriter. Chronicle Guidance Publications. 1966. 4p. 35c

Occupational brief summarizing work performed, qualifications, preparation, working conditions, earnings, methods of entry, outlook, and high school background.

Advertising copywriters. Science Research Associates. 1965. 4p. 45c

Occupational brief describing work, training, qualifications, opportunities, and outlook.

Copy writer. Careers. 1969. 2p. 20c

Career summary for desk-top file. Duties, qualifications, and outlook.

Copywriter. California State Department of Employment. 1968. 6p. Single copy free

Description of the work of writing original advertising material, duties, working conditions, pay, hours, finding the job, promotion, and employment outlook.

Finding out about advertising copywriters. Science Research Associates. 1967. 4p. 45c

Junior occupational brief summarizing what the work requires and offers.

See also Advertising agent

COSMETOLOGIST 332.271

**Beauty as a career. Heal, Edith. Julian Messner. 1969. 192p. $3.95; library binding $3.64

Explains the necessary background for entering the field, discusses the basics of acquiring a license, and presents interviews with writers, publicists, and beauty editors. Contains a list of schools for training.

The beauty business. Alumnae Advisory Center. 1966. 8p. 35c

Reprint from *Mademoiselle* describing the industry and case histories of several women who have succeeded in these specialized fields.

Beauty operator. California State Department of Employment. 1967. 4p. Single copy free

Occupational guide describing work, requirements, training, and outlook.

Beauty operator. Chronicle Guidance Publications. 1969. 4p. 35c

Occupational brief summarizing work performed, employment conditions, qualifications, training, licensing, opportunities, outlook, and methods of entry.

Beauty operator. Michigan Employment Security Commission. 1965. 2p. Single copy free

Job brief summarizing occupational data for use in Michigan.

* Beauty operators. Science Research Associates. 1969. 4p. 45c

Occupational brief describing nature of work, requirements, getting started and advancing, earnings, advantages, disadvantages, related positions, and future outlook.

Cosmetologist. Careers. 1968. 8p. 35c

Career brief describing duties, working conditions, training, personal qualifications, earnings, and outlook.

**Cosmetologists. One section of *Occupational Outlook Handbook.*

Nature of work, where employed, training, other qualifications, advancement, employment outlook, earnings, and working conditions.

Cosmetology . . . a beautiful career. National Association of Cosmetology Schools. No date. 6p. 10c

Description of related jobs, preliminary requirements, qualifications, opportunities, and the training course.

COSMETOLOGIST—*Continued*

Cosmetology and hairdressing a look back . . . a focus on the present. National Career Center. 1970. 8p. 10c

An illustrated brochure describing modern trends, job training, and satisfactions in this work.

* Employment outlook for beauty operators. National Association of Cosmetology Schools. Not date. 6p. 10c

Nature of work, where employed, training, qualifications, employment outlook, earnings, and working conditions.

Facts about the beauty industry. National Association of Cosmetology Schools. No date. 4p. 10c

Questions and answers concerning the size, growth, and outlook.

Financial success is easily yours with a glamorous beauty career. National Association of Cosmetology Schools. No date. 6p. 10c

This booklet describes the beauty career, gives examples, and cites reasons for choosing this career.

Finding out about beauticians. Science Research Associates. 1967. 4p. 45c

Junior occupational brief summarizing what the work requires and offers.

Finding out about make-up artists. Science Research Associates. 1967. 4p. 45c

Junior occupational brief describing work and opportunities.

Hairdresser. Guidance Centre. 1968. 4p. 35c postpaid

Nature of work, qualifications, preparation, earnings, how to get started, and related occupations.

List of cosmetology schools located within your state. National Career Center. 1970. 1 page for each state. 10c

Names and locations of schools within each state.

Successful careers in beauty culture. National Association of Cosmetology Schools. No date. 32p. 35c

Stresses beauty culture as a growing field, desirable qualifications, types of jobs in a beauty shop, specializations, advancement, earnings, advantages, and limitations.

You can't tell about love. Olds, Helen Diehl. Julian Messner. 1950. 183p. $3.50

Career fiction. The romance contains helpful hints on entrance and progress in the beauty business.

** Your future in the beauty business. The Fashion Group. Richards Rosen Press. 1969. 159p. $4; library edition $3.78

Seventeen leaders of the beauty industry present their advice on careers in this field. Their viewpoints represent those who work in top management, product development, marketing, and advertising, as well as those engaged in such services as makeup and hairdressing. Includes discussion on the types of personalities likely to enjoy success.

COUNSELOR 045.108

**Counselors: school, rehabilitation, and employment. One section of *Occupational Outlook Handbook.*

Nature of work, where employed, training, other qualifications, advancement, employment outlook, earnings, and working conditions.

Employment counselors. One section of *Occupational Outlook Handbook.*

Nature of work, where employed, training, other qualifications, employment outlook, earnings, and working conditions.

**Employment outlook for counseling and placement occupations. Bulletin No. 1650–32. Bureau of Labor Statistics, U.S. Department of Labor. Supt. of Documents. 1970. 16p. 15c

Reprint from the *Occupational Outlook Handbook.* Includes school counselors, rehabilitation counselors, employment counselors, and college placement officers.

Financial aid for guidance and personnel graduate study, 1970-71. American Personnel and Guidance Association. 1970. 60p. $3

Information from 245 institutions in chart form.

Finding out about guidance counselors. Science Research Associates. 1967. 4p. 45c

Junior occupational brief containing concise facts about the job.

Frank Parsons: prophet, innovator, counselor. Davis, Howard V. Southern Illinois University Press. 1969. 163p. $5.85

In this first full-length biography of one of the pioneers in vocational guidance, the author examines Parsons' life and background, showing how these were related to his educational concerns.

Guidance counselor. Chronicle Guidance Publications. 1968. 4p. 35c

Occupational brief summarizing work performed, training, qualifications, earnings, opportunities, advantages, disadvantages, and outlook.

High school counselor. Careers. 1970. 2p. 20c

Career summary for desk-top file. Duties, qualifications, and outlook.

School counselor. California State Department of Employment. 1967. 5p. Single copy free

Occupational guide describing work, requirements, training, and outlook.

* School counselors. Science Research Associates. 1966. 4p. 45c

Occupational brief describing nature of work, training, qualifications, opportunities, advantages, disadvantages, and future outlook.

School counselors. One section of *Occupational Outlook Handbook.*

Nature of work, where employed, qualifications, earnings, and employment outlook.

**Your future as a guidance counselor. McDonough, Thomas. Richards Rosen Press. 1966. 160p. $4; library edition $3.78

Discussion of the work of a school guidance counselor and the types of problems he meets, together with the educational and personal requirements.

See also Personnel and employment manager; Rehabilitation counselor

COURT REPORTER 202.388

Court reporter. California State Department of Employment. 1964. 5p. Single copy free

Duties, working conditions, pay, hours, promotion, training, and employment outlook in California.

Court reporter. Careers. 1970. 8p. 35c

Career brief describing dutes, working conditions, training, qualifications, related careers, earnings, and outlook.

Court reporter. Chronicle Guidance Publications. 1968. 4p. 35c

Occupational brief describing work performed, where employed, working conditions, remuneration, personal qualifications, training, methods of entry, and employment outlook.

Court reporter. Guidance Centre. 1969. 4p. 35c postpaid

Nature of work, qualifications, preparation, advancement, outlook, remuneration, how to get started, and related occupations.

See also Stenographer

COWPUNCHER 413.884

Book of cowboys. Holling, C. Platt and Munk Company. 1962. 126p. $3.50

Prepared for grades three to five, this gives a picture of the work. In a series of connected stories, the author describes the life and work of cowboys in the West today.

Career opportunities in rangeland resource management. American Society of Range Management. 1969. 6p. Free

This describes the nature of the work, opportunities, and employment outlook. Includes a list of colleges offering degrees in range management.

The cowboy. Rennert, Vincent Paul. Crowell, Collier and Macmillan. 1966. 117p. $2.95; library edition $3.24

A straightforward factual history of cowboy customs, clothing, equipment, and duties, this is a good introduction to the cowboy and his world. The account also gives sidelights on the development of cattle raising. Illustrated with old prints and drawings. For grades 4 to 7.

Cowboy-artist: Charles M. Russell. Garst, Shannon. Julian Messner. 1960. 192p. $3.50; library binding $3.34

Riding herd, living among Indians in the Wild West, the author raced against time because a historical era was ending and his life's goal was to capture it on canvas and record it in bronze.

The cowboy in art. Ainsworth, Edward M. World Publishing Company. 1968. 242p. $15

Although this book features the cowboy as he has appeared in paintings and works of sculpture, it contains biographies and facts about cowboy life.

Cowpunchers—still around. Chronicle Guidance Publications. 1969. 4p. 50c

A reprint from *Occupational Outlook Quarterly* describing work on today's ranch.

Finding out about ranchers. Science Research Associates. 1967. 4p. 45c

Junior occupational brief describing work and opportunities.

Nat Love, Negro cowboy. Felton, Harold W. Dodd, Mead and Company. 1969. 93p. $3.25; library binding $2.99

The colorful story of a Negro from Tennessee who became a legendary cowpuncher, sharpshooter, and bronco rider. Written for grades 3 to 7.

What does a cowboy do? Hyde, Wayne. Dodd, Mead and Company. 1963. 64p. Library binding $2.99

Simple text and pictures portray calf roping, roundups, stampedes, and rodeo. Written for grades 3 to 7.

CREDIT AND COLLECTION MANAGER 168.168

Credit and collection manager. California State Department of Employment. 1967. 5p. Single copy free

Occupational guide describing work, requirements, training, and outlook.

Credit collectors. Science Research Associates. 1968. 4p. 45c

Occupational brief describing the role of the collector, related jobs, how and where to start, earnings, promotions, things to consider, and future outlook Selected references.

Credit manager. Chronicle Guidance Publications. 1968. 4p. 35c

Occupational brief describing work performed, training, personal qualifications, and employment outlook.

* Credit workers. Science Research Associates. 1968. 4p. 45c

Occupational brief describing nature of work, qualifications, educational requirements, getting started, earnings, advantages, disadvantages, and outlook.

Finding out about credit clerks. Science Research Associates. 1967. 4p. 45c

Junior occupational brief describing work and opportunities.

Finding out about credit collectors. Science Research Associates. 1967. 4p. 45c

Junior occupational brief summarizing what the work requires and offers.

**Your future in the credit field. Neifeld, M. R. Richards Rosen Press. Revised 1969. 160p. Library edition $3.78

Description of credit as applied to all business, qualifications, and outlook.

CRIMINOLOGIST 054.088

Criminologists. Science Research Associates. 1967. 4p. 45c

Occupational brief describing work, training, qualifications, opportunities, and outlook.

CRIMINOLOGIST–*Continued*

Educational preparation for a career in criminology. Fresno State College. 1968. 11p. Free

Statement of high school preparation, admission requirements to the program, and program planning.

Finding out about criminologists. Science Research Associates. 1967. 4p. 45c

Junior occupational brief describing work and opportunities.

CROP SCIENTIST. *See* **Agronomist**

CURATOR **102.118**

Curator. Chronicle Guidance Publications. 1967. 4p. 35c

Occupational brief summarizing kinds of museums, work performed, working conditions, educational requirements, hours and earnings, and outlook.

CUSTODIAN. *See* **Building custodian and janitor**

CUSTOMS AND IMMIGRATION INSPECTOR **168.168**

Border guard; the story of the United States Customs Service. Whitehead, Don. McGraw-Hill Book Company. 1963. 274p. $5.95

This account illustrates the ingenuity and courage of the agents who trap smugglers, thieves, saboteurs, and other lawbreakers.

Customs worker. Careers. 1968. 2p. 20c

Career summary for desk-top file. Duties, qualifications, and outlook.

* Customs workers. Science Research Associates. 1968. 4p. 45c

Occupational brief describing work, qualifications, training, opportunities, and outlook.

Finding out about customs inspectors. Science Research Associates. 1967. 4p. 45c

Junior occupational brief containing concise facts about the job.

Ports of entry, U.S.A. Fribourg, Marjorie. Little, Brown and Company. 1962. 256p. $4.50

Story of the episodes in the work of men and women in the U.S. Customs Bureau. Describes the nature of their work and the scope of our import and export trade.

See also Immigration inspector

DAIRY FARMER **411.181**

Dairy farmer. Careers. 1969. 2p. 20c

Career summary for desk-top file. Duties, qualifications, and outlook.

Dairy farmer. Chronicle Guidance Publications. 1967. 4p. 35c

Occupational brief summarizing work performed, qualifications, training, methods of entry, and outlook.

Dairy farmers. Science Research Associates. 1968. 4p. 45c
Occupational brief describing nature of work, training, qualifications, opportunities, advantages, disadvantages, and future outlook.

Finding out about dairy farmers. Science Research Associates. 1967. 4p. 45c
Junior occupational brief containing concise facts about the job.

DAIRY INDUSTRY WORKER 529.

Dairy industry jobs. Chronicle Guidance Publications. 1968. 4p. 35c
Occupational brief summarizing areas of work, kinds of jobs, working conditions, training, earnings, and outlook.

Dairy industry workers. Science Research Associates. 1966. 4p. 45c
Occupational brief describing nature of work, training, qualifications, opportunities, advantages, disadvantages, and future outlook.

Dairy processing equipment operator. Chronicle Guidance Publications. 1968. 4p. 35c
Occupational brief summarizing work performed, working conditions, personal requirements, training, and outlook.

Dairy technologists. Science Research Associates. 1966. 4p. 45c
Occupational brief describing nature of work, requirements, training, getting started, earnings, advantages, disadvantages, and future outlook.

Dairy technology. College of Agriculture, Ohio State University. 1968. 6p. Free
Qualifications, training needed, where employed, and a recommended sequence of required courses for a degree in dairy technology.

Finding out about dairy industry production workers. Science Research Associates. 1967. 4p. 45c
Junior occupational brief describing work and opportunities.

Finding out about dairy technologists. Science Research Associates. 1967. 4p. 45c
Junior occupational brief summarizing what the work requires and offers.

**Occupations and trends in the dairy products industry. U.S. Department of Labor. Supt. of Documents. 1970. 186p. 75c
Includes trends and the employment outlook.

Vocational image of a dairy science graduate. Chronicle Guidance Publications. 1968. 10p. 50c
Reprinted article from *Journal of Dairy Science* discusses conclusions gained from questionnaires from high school and dairy science graduates concerning personal preferences for work within the field.

DAIRY INDUSTRY WORKER—*Continued*

What industry wants for training in dairy manufacturing from the production and management standpoint. Chronicle Guidance Publications. 1969. 4p. 35c

Reprinted article from *Journal of Dairy Science* discusses educational changes, present leadership, type of men needed, human relations, knowledge of business, community interests, deficiencies, training needed, and social sciences.

DANCER 151.

Ballroom dance teachers. Science Research Associates. 1966. 4p. 45c

Occupational brief describing work, training, qualifications, opportunities, and outlook.

Careers in dance. Alumnae Advisory Center. 1966. 6p. 35c

Reprint from *Mademoiselle* describing a sampling of dance careers on the contemporary scene.

**Dance careers for men and women. American Association for Health, Physical Education, and Recreation. 1968. 6p. Single copy free

Description of careers and opportunities.

Dance directory. American Association for Health, Physical Education, and Recreation. 1969. 80p. $2

Directory of institutions offering professional preparation.

Dancer. Chronicle Guidance Publications. 1969. 4p. 35c

Occupational brief summarizing various fields of dancing, early training and preparation, earnings, and opportunities.

* Dancers. Careers. 1967. 8p. 35c

Career brief describing duties, working conditions, personal qualifications, training, places of employment, earnings, and outlook.

Dancers. Science Research Associates. 1966. 4p. 45c

Occupational brief describing opportunities, qualifications, education and training, earnings, advantages, disadvantages, and future outlook.

**Dancers. One section of *Occupational Outlook Handbook.*

Nature of work, where employed, training, other qualifications, employment outlook, earnings, and working conditions.

Dancers of the ballet. Atkinson, Margaret and Hillman, May. Alfred A. Knopf, Inc. 1955. 174p. $4.19

Biographical data, including training, career highlights, and personality of forty ballet dancers of today.

Finding out about ballroom dance teachers. Science Research Associates. 1967. 4p. 45c

Junior occupational brief containing concise facts about the job.

Finding out about dance teachers. Science Research Associates. 1967. 4p. 45c

Junior occupational brief containing concise facts about the job.

Finding out about dancers. Science Research Associates. 1967. 4p. 45c
Junior occupational brief containing concise facts about the job.

**Opportunities in a dancing career. Denis, Paul. Vocational Guidance Manuals. 1966. 119p. $1.95 paper; $3.75 library edition
Discussion of building a career in the popular fields of dancing, in ballet, in teaching of dancing, and in choreography. Advice to dancers is given by eight well-known dancers.

To a young dancer. De Mille, Agnes. Atlantic-Little, Brown. 1962. 175p. $4.95; paper $2.25
Description of the exaltation and training of the dancer, the discipline necessary, and the problems which a young choreographer must expect to meet.

Young dancer's career book. Woody, R. J. Dutton and Company. 1958. 185p. $3.50
Includes how to evaluate one's talent, education needed, job opportunities, salaries, and how to get a job. One section is devoted to dance therapy.

See also Motion picture industry worker; Television industry worker

DATA-PROCESSING MACHINE OPERATOR. ***See*** **Electronic computer operator**

DATA-PROCESSING MACHINE SERVICEMAN **828.281**

**Data-processing equipment servicemen. Brief section in *Occupational Outlook Handbook.*
Nature of work, where employed, and employment outlook.

Data processing equipment technician. California State Department of Employment. 1965. 4p. Single copy free
Occupational guide describing work, requirements, training, and outlook.

* Data-processing machine servicemen. Science Research Associates. 1968. 4p. 45c
Occupational brief describing nature of work, training, qualifications, opportunities, and outlook. Selected references.

Finding out about data processing machine servicemen. Science Research Associates. 1967. 4p. 45c
Junior occupational brief summarizing what the work requires and offers.

DATA-PROCESSING PROGRAMMER. ***See*** **Programmer**

DEMONSTRATOR **297.458**

Demonstrators. Science Research Associates. 1969. 4p. 45c
Occupational brief describing nature of work, training, qualifications, opportunities, and outlook. Selected references.

Finding out about demonstrators. Science Research Associates. 1967. 4p. 45c
Junior occupational brief containing concise facts about the job.

DENTAL ASSISTANT 079.378

Accredited dental assisting programs. American Dental Association. 1970. 7p. Free

List of schools arranged alphabetically by states.

* Dental assistant. Careers. 1969. 8p. 35c

Career brief describing duties, training, personal qualifications, earnings, how to enter, and outlook. Additional readings.

Dental assistant. Chronicle Guidance Publications. 1968. 4p. 35c

Occupational brief summarizing work performed, working conditions, personal qualifications, earnings, outlook, educational requirements, and certification.

Dental assistant. Guidance Centre. 1967. 4p. 35c postpaid

History and importance, nature of work, qualifications, preparation, earnings, how to get started, and related occupations.

Dental assistant. Pages 88-89 of *Health Careers Guidebook.*

Description of work, qualifications, and working conditions.

**Dental assistants. Science Research Associates. 1968. 4p. 45c

Occupational brief describing nature of work, training, qualifications, opportunities, advantages, disadvantages, and future outlook.

Dental assistants. One section of *Occupational Outlook Handbook.*

Nature of work, where employed, training, other qualifications, advancement, employment outlook, earnings, and working conditions.

Dentist's assistant. California State Department of Employment. 1967. 3p. Single copy free

Occupational guide describing work, requirements, training, and outlook.

The dentist's diplomat. Ritter Company. 1962. 40p. Free

A manual for dental assistants which includes the regular duties, description of a typical day's work, and suggestions for the assistant who would succeed. Illustrated.

Finding out about dental assistants. Science Research Associates. 1967. 4p. 45c

Junior occupational brief describing work and opportunities.

In the dentist's office—a guide for auxiliary dental personnel: hygienist, assistant, secretary. Morrison, G. Archanna. Lippincott Company. 1959. 280p. $8.00

Prepared as a reference for members of the dentist's staff, this book gives an idea of the nature of the work. Illustrated.

Organizing a dental assistant training program. Public Health Service, U.S. Department of Health, Education, and Welfare. Supt. of Documents. 1968. 43p. 35c. Free to school administrators and vocational educators

Summary of need for formal dental assistant training programs and guidelines for their establishment. Prepared for instructors and supervisors of a training program.

* Something new in white. Public Health Service, U.S. Department of Health, Education, and Welfare. 1967. 6p. Free

Illustrated brochure stating that today a fascinating career opportunity is opening up for the trained dental assistant. Describes nature of work, job satisfactions, advantages, training, and getting a job.

There's an action career ahead when you become a trained dental assistant. American Dental Association. No date. 6p. Free

Brief statement of attractive features of this work.

**The trained dental assistant—facts for counselors. Public Health Service, U.S. Department of Health, Education, and Welfare. Supt. of Documents. 1965. 7p. 15c

Describes background and importance of the dental assistant, nature of work, number employed, trends and outlook of demand, qualifications, licensing requirements, working conditions, earnings, and nonmonetary rewards.

Why employ a currently certified dental assistant? American Dental Association. No date. 6p. Free

Contains duties and qualifications.

DENTAL HYGIENIST 078.368

Accredited dental hygiene programs. American Dental Association. 1970. 7p. Free

Listed are the names and addresses of approved dental hygiene programs, new programs whose accreditation status is pending, and some proposed programs.

**Careers in dental hygiene. American Dental Hygienists Association. 1968. 6p. Free

Description of general duties and activities and the basic educational requirements.

Dental hygienist. California State Department of Employment. 1966. 3p. Single copy free

Duties, working conditions, pay, hours, promotion, training, and employment prospects.

* Dental hygienist. Careers. 1968. 8p. 35c

Career brief describing duties, personal qualifications, educational requirements, advantages, disadvantages, and outlook. List of colleges offering approved programs.

Dental hygienist. Chronicle Guidance Publications. 1969. 4p. 35c

Occupational brief summarizing work performed, income, qualifications, training, opportunities, outlook, methods of entry, and a list of schools.

The dental hygienist. Columbia University, Courses for Dental Hygienists. 1956. 8p. Free

Includes nature of work, educational preparation, professional education, scope of professional opportunities, and recommended preparatory courses to take in high school and college.

DENTAL HYGIENIST—*Continued*

Dental hygienist. Guidance Centre. 1967. 4p. 35c postpaid

History and importance, nature of work, qualifications, working conditions, preparation, remuneration, outlook, related occupations, and how to get started.

Dental hygienist. Michigan Employment Security Commission. 1967. 2p. Single copy free

Job brief summarizing occupational data for use in Michigan.

* Dental hygienists. Science Research Associates. 1968. 4p. 45c

Occupational brief describing nature of work, training, qualifications, opportunities, advantages, disadvantages, and future outlook.

**Dental hygienists. One section of *Occupational Outlook Handbook.*

Nature of work, where employed, training and other qualifications, employment outlook, earnings, and working conditions.

**Employment outlook for dental hygienists, dental assistants, dental laboratory technicians. Bulletin No. 1650–8. Bureau of Labor Statistics, U.S. Department of Labor. Supt. of Documents. 1970. 16p. 15c

Reprint from the *Occupational Outlook Handbook.*

Finding out about dental hygienists. Science Research Associates. 1967. 4p. 45c

Junior occupational brief summarizing what the work requires and offers.

Planning an education program for dental hygienists. Public Health Service, U.S. Department of Health, Education, and Welfare. Supt. of Documents. 1968. 55p. 60c. Free to school administrators and vocational educators

Summary of need for training programs in dental hygiene and guidelines for their establishment. Includes information on supply and demand of dental hygienists, staffing requirements, and costs. Gives an account of the evolution of a system of preventive dentistry known as dental hygiene.

**The registered dental hygienist—facts for counselors. Public Health Service, U.S. Department of Health, Education, and Welfare. Supt. of Documents. 1966. 8p. 15c

Describes background and importance of the dental hygienist, nature of work, number employed, trends and outlook of demand, qualifications, licensing requirements, working conditions, earnings, and nonmonetary rewards.

**Your future as a dental hygienist. Paige, Barbara. Richards Rosen Press. 1969. 160p. $4; library edition $3.78

Description of work, qualifications, training, opportunities, and outlook.

DENTAL LABORATORY TECHNICIAN 712.381

Approved dental laboratory technology programs. National Association of Certified Dental Laboratories. 1968. 1p. Free

Names and addresses of schools with length of course in each.

Dental laboratory technician. Chronicle Guidance Publications. 1968. 4p. 35c

Occupational brief containing definition, work performed, working conditions, personal requirements, opportunities, training requirements, training opportunities, certification, and outlook.

Dental laboratory technician. Pages 89-90 of *Health Careers Guidebook.*

Description of work, personal qualifications, education and training, and outlook.

**Dental laboratory technicians. Science Research Associates. 1969. 4p. 45c

Occupational brief describing nature of work, training, qualifications, opportunities, advantages, disadvantages, and future outlook.

**Dental laboratory technicians. One section of *Occupational Outlook Handbook.*

Nature of work, where employed, training, other qualifications, advancement, employment outlook, earnings, and working conditions.

Dental technician. Careers. 1966. 2p. 20c

Career summary for desk-top file. Duties, qualifications, and outlook.

Dental technician. California State Department of Employment. 1968. 5p. Single copy free

Occupational guide describing work, requirements, training, and outlook.

Dental technician. Guidance Centre. 1967. 4p. 35c postpaid

History and importance, nature of work, qualifications, working conditions, preparation, remuneration, outlook, related occupations, and how to get started.

Dental technician. Michigan Employment Security Commission. 1959. 2p. Single copy free

Job brief summarizing occupational data for use in Michigan.

Fact sheet. National Association of Certified Dental Laboratories. 1968. 1p. Free

Facts concerning need, salaries, and qualifications.

**Hands that think . . . a word about careers in modern dental laboratory technology. National Association of Certified Dental Laboratories. 1968. 6p. Free

Description of work, training, qualifications, earnings, benefits, and opportunities. Sources of information are included.

Planning an education program for dental laboratory technicians. Public Health Service, U.S. Department of Health, Education, and Welfare. Supt. of Documents. 1969. 50p. 60c. Free to school administrators and vocational educators

Summary of need for training programs and guidelines for their establishment. Includes information on supply and demand of dental laboratory technicians.

DENTIST 072.108

Accredited dental schools. American Dental Association. 1968. 5p. Free

List of dental schools which have been approved or provisionally approved. Revised list published annually.

**Admission requirements of American dental schools. American Association of Dental Schools. 1970. 150p. $4

Presents exact requirements for admission to each dental school in the United States and Canada. Useful to help in selecting a school of dentistry or in programming a preprofessional course of study to meet the requirements of the dental schools.

* Careers in dentistry. American Dental Association. 1966. 20p. 15c. Single copy free

Discussion of demand for dentists and dental care, income ranges, qualifications, admission requirements to dental schools, and ways of financing a dental education. List of fifty-three accredited dental schools.

Dental aptitude testing program. American Dental Association. Annually. 21p. Free

Information for applicants including an application to take the examination.

Dental internships in U.S. Public Health Service hospitals. Public Health Service, U.S. Department of Health, Education, and Welfare. 1967. 12p. Free

Explains the requirements for appointment, opportunities, and benefits.

Dentist. California State Department of Employment. 1964. 8p. Single copy free

Occupational guide describing work, requirements, training, and outlook.

* Dentist. Careers. 1968. 8p. 35c

Career brief describing duties, working conditions, training, personal qualifications, earnings, and outlook. List of accredited dental schools. Additional readings.

Dentist. Chronicle Guidance Publications. 1968. 4p. 35c

Occupational brief including work performed, working conditions, hours, earnings, requirements, opportunities, outlook, methods of entry, and licensing.

Dentist. Guidance Centre. 1967. 4p. 35c postpaid

History and importance, nature of work, qualifications, earnings, advantages, and disadvantages.

**Dentistry and allied services. Pages 84-8 of *Health Careers Guidebook*.

Personal qualifications, education, licensing, specialization, and future prospects.

**Dentistry as a career. Belleau, Wilfred. Park Publishing House. 1969. 27p. $1

History and importance of the work, nature of work, training, income, qualifications, licensure, entering the field, opportunities, advantages, and disadvantages. Includes a list of forty-seven dental schools with tuition and expenses.

Dentists. Science Research Associates. 1969. 4p. 45c

Occupational brief describing nature of work, training, qualifications, opportunities, advantages, disadvantages, and future outlook.

**Dentists. One section of *Occupational Outlook Handbook.*

Nature of work, where employed, training, other qualifications, advancement, employment outlook, earnings, and working conditions.

Educational qualifications of public health dentists. American Public Health Association. 1967. 10p. Single copy free

Approximate number employed, estimate of future needs, lines of promotional progress, opportunities, outlook, and training.

**Employment outlook for dentists. Bulletin No. 1650–7. Bureau of Labor Statistics, U.S. Department of Labor. Supt. of Documents. 1970. 12p. 15c

Reprint from the *Occupational Outlook Handbook.*

Financial aid for dental students. American Dental Association. No date. 10p. Free

Some suggested sources of aid from dental societies and others.

Finding out about dentists. Science Research Associates. 1967. 4p. 45c

Junior occupational brief containing concise facts about the job.

**Your future in dentistry. Vershell, Allen. Richards Rosen Press. 1969. 160p. $4; library edition $3.78

The author opens his office to the reader and shares his day as a dentist. He also presents the educational background and aptitudes necessary for a career in dentistry. Several chapters describe work in specialized fields such as oral surgery, orthodontia, periodontia, and oral pathology.

DEPARTMENT STORE WORKER 984.

**Careers in department store merchandising. Kaplan, Albert and de Mille, Margaret. Henry Z. Walck, Inc. 1962. 112p. $4.50

Describes especially the department store buyer who is responsible for the selection, purchase, and selling of one type of merchandise. Includes detailed description of a typical day's work, opportunities, and the present-day trend toward the suburban branch store. Reading list. Illustrated.

Department store occupations. Chronicle Guidance Publications. 1966. 4p. 35c

Occupational brief summarizing merchandising, buying jobs, publicity, earnings, hours, educational requirements, and employment requirements.

Department store receiving, delivering, and related occupations. Careers. 1970. 8p. 35c

Career brief describing duties, working conditions, training, related careers, earnings, and outlook.

Department store salespeople. Science Research Associates. 1966. 4p. 45c

Occupational brief describing nature of work, requirements, training, getting started, earnings, advantages, disadvantages, and future outlook.

DEPARTMENT STORE WORKER—*Continued*

Finding out about department store salespeople. Science Research Associates. 1967. 4p. 45c

Junior occupational brief containing concise facts about the job.

Kim fashions a career. Shaftner, Dorothy. Putnam's Sons. 1968. 190p. $3.75

Career fiction. A novel describing the fashion world. Kim learns about selling, buying, fashion coordination, daily department store routine, and the general workaday life.

See also Buyer; Retail manager; Retail salesperson

DETECTIVE 376.868

Crime scientists. McGrady, Mike. Lippincott Company. 1961. 160p. $4.25

True accounts of how criminals have been tracked down in the laboratory with scientific equipment. Describes the roles played by detectives, laboratory technicians, photographers, chemical analysts, biologists, and fingerprint technicians. Illustrated.

Detective (criminal investigator). Careers. 1966. 2p. 20c

Career summary for desk-top file. Duties, qualifications, and outlook.

**Detectives. Science Research Associates. 1968. 4p. 45c

Occupational brief describing nature of work, training, qualifications, opportunities, advantages, disadvantages, and future outlook.

Finding out about detectives. Science Research Associates. 1967. 4p. 45c

Junior occupational brief describing work and opportunities.

Nature of detective work. International Association of Chiefs of Police. No date. 2p. Free

Brief statement of duties and qualifications.

The Secret Service story. Dorman, Michael. Delacorte Press. 1967. 256p. $5

The book examines highlights of the history of the Secret Service, elaborating on two principal duties, presidential security and counterfeiting. The last part of the book concentrates on the death of President Kennedy and the Service.

What does a secret service agent do? Hyde, Wayne. Dodd, Mead and Company. 1962. 64p. Library binding $2.99

Simple text and pictures portray varied activities. Written for grades 3 to 7.

See also FBI agent; Police officer

DIESEL MECHANIC 625.281

Diesel engine tester. Chronicle Guidance Publications. 1966. 4p. 35c

Occupational brief summarizing work performed, working conditions, qualifications, training, earnings, related jobs, and outlook.

Diesel mechanic. California State Department of Employment. 1966. 5p. Single copy free

Occupational guide summarizing duties, working conditions, employment prospects, earnings, preparation, and suggestions for locating a job.

Diesel mechanic. Careers. 1969. 2p. 20c

Career summary for desk-top file. Duties, qualifications, and outlook.

Diesel mechanic. Chronicle Guidance Publications. 1969. 4p. 35c

Occupational brief summarizing work performed, working conditions, personal qualifications, training, wages, licensing, related jobs, and employment outlook.

Diesel mechanic. Guidance Centre. 1964. 4p. 35c postpaid

Definition, qualifications, preparation, employment, advancement, earnings, advantages, disadvantages, and how to get started.

* Diesel mechanics. Science Research Associates. 1967. 4p. 45c

Occupational brief describing nature of work, requirements, training, methods of entering, earnings, advantages, disadvantages, and future outlook.

Diesel mechanics. One section of *Occupational Outlook Handbook.*

Nature of work, where employed, training, other qualifications, advancement, employment outlook, earnings, and working conditions.

**Employment outlook for diesel mechanics and farm equipment mechanics. Bulletin No. 1650–84. Bureau of Labor Statistics, U.S. Department of Labor. Supt. of Documents. 1970. 12p. 10c

Reprint from the *Occupational Outlook Handbook.*

Finding out about diesel machanics. Science Research Associates. 1967. 4p. 45c

Junior occupational brief summarizing what the work requires and offers.

DIETITIAN 077.168

Academic requirements for active membership in the American Dietetic Association and entrance to approved dietetic internships. American Dietetic Association. 1967. 1p. Free

Includes required and recommended additional courses.

A dietetic internship. American Dietetic Association. 1968. 16p. 5c Single copy free

Answers to questions concerning advantages of internship, duties, requirements, and expenses. Contains brief description of work of a hospital intern, food service administration intern, and nutrition intern.

Dietetic internships approved by the American Dietetic Association. American Dietetic Association. 1962. 6p. Single copy free

List of institutions offering administrative, clinic, and hospital courses approved by the American Dietetic Association. Tabulated information includes name of institution, tuition fees, enrollment, and length of course.

DIETITIAN—*Continued*

**Dietetics as a profession. American Dietetic Association. 1966. 36p. 50c
Employment opportunities in twelve fields of activity, training, conditions of work, salaries, personal qualifications, and methods of securing positions. The Association's most complete description of the profession and the career possibilities. Illustrated. Reading list.

Dietitian. California State Department of Employment. 1967. 4p. Single copy free
Occupational guide describing work, requirements, training, and outlook.

* Dietitian. Careers. 1968. 8p. 35c
Career brief describing the work of the dietitian and nutritionist, training, personal qualifications, outlook, earnings, where employed, advantages, disadvantages, and opportunities.

Dietitian. Chronicle Guidance Publications. 1968. 4p. 35c
Occupational brief summarizing work performed, working conditions, hours, earnings, personal qualifications, training requirements, opportunities, and employment outlook.

Dietitian. Guidance Centre. 1969. 4p. 35c postpaid
History and importance, nature of work, qualifications, preparation, advancement, outlook, remuneration, advantages, disadvantages, how to get started, and related occupations.

Dietitian. Pages 93-5 of *Health Careers Guidebook.*
Description of work, opportunities, and prospects.

Dietitians. Science Research Associates. 1967. 4p. 45c
Occupational brief describing the dietitian at work, requirements, earnings, getting started, advantages, disadvantages, and future outlook.

**Dietitians. One section of *Occupational Outlook Handbook.*
Nature of work, where employed, training, other qualifications, advancement, employment outlook, earnings, and working conditions.

Dietitians in demand. American Dietetic Association. 1961. 8p. 5c. Single copy free
Illustrated leaflet showing dietitians at work in hospitals, food administration, community nutrition, and research.

Dietitians in the Veterans Administration. VA pamphlet 10-55. Veterans Administration Forms Depot. 1967. 4p. Free
Description of work, training program, qualifications, and benefits.

**Employment outlook for dietitians. Bulletin No. 1650–19. Bureau of Labor Statistics, U.S. Department of Labor. Supt. of Documents. 1970. 6p. 10c
Reprint from the *Occupational Outlook Handbook.*

Finding out about dietitians. Science Research Associates. 1967. 4p. 45c
Junior occupational brief containing concise facts about the job.

* Look ahead—the future is bright. American Dietetic Association. 1962. 12p. $2 per 100. Single copy free

Illustrated booklet pointing out the advantages and opportunities of dietetics.

**Your future as a dietitian. American Dietetic Association. Richards Rosen Press. Revised 1969. 160p. $4; library edition $3.78

Several dietitians have set down in separate chapters the requirements, talents, education, and interests which are necessary for their specialities. Includes list of schools which offer training.

See also Medical service and health service worker; Nutritionist

DIPLOMATIC SERVICE WORKER. *See* Foreign service worker

DISK JOCKEY 159.148

Disc jockey. California State Department of Employment. 1968. 3p. Single copy free

Description of the work of conducting a program of musical recordings, interspersed with comments and advertising material. Includes working conditions, training, salary, hours, promotion, and employment outlook.

Disk jockey. Chronicle Guidance Publications. 1968. 4p. 35c

Occupational brief describing nature of work, qualifications, working conditions, training required, and outlook.

Disk jockeys. Science Research Associates. 1965. 4p. 45c

Occupational brief describing work, qualifications, training, ways to get started, advantages, disadvantages, and outlook. Selected references.

Finding out about disk jockeys. Science Research Associates. 1967. 4p. 45c

Junior occupational brief summarizing what the work requires and offers.

DISPLAY WORKER 298.081

Display man. California State Department of Employment. 1967. 5p. Single copy free

Duties, pay, hours, training, promotion, and employment outlook.

Display man. Careers. 1970. 2p. 20c

Career summary for desk-top file. Duties, qualifications, and outlook.

Display man. Chronicle Guidance Publications. 1966. 4p. 35c

Occupational brief summarizing work performed, working conditions, wages, personal qualifications, training, opportunities, methods of entry, related jobs, outlook, and suggested activities.

Display man. Guidance Centre. 1969. 4p. 35c postpaid

Definition, history and importance, nature of work, preparation, qualifications, working conditions, employment, advancement, outlook, remuneration, and how to get started.

DISPLAY WORKER—*Continued*

* Display workers. Science Research Associates. 1970. 4p. 45c
  Occupational brief describing nature of work, training, qualifications, opportunities, advantages, disadvantages, and future outlook.

Finding out about display workers. Science Research Associates. 1967. 4p. 45c
  Junior occupational brief containing concise facts about the job.

Jobs in art. Science Research Associates. 1960. 32p. $1
  Describes the variety of work and opportunities for the display worker.

DIVER 899.281

Diver. Chronicle Guidance Publications. 1969. 4p. 35c
  Occupational brief summarizing work performed, working conditions, training requirements, personal qualifications, earnings, and outlook.

Diver. Guidance Centre. 1967. 4p. 35c postpaid
  Definition, requirements, earnings, how to get started, advantages, and disadvantages.

* Divers. Science Research Associates. 1966. 4p. 45c
  Occupational brief describing work, qualifications, earnings, things to consider, and outlook.

Finding out about divers. Science Research Associates. 1967. 4p. 45c
  Junior occupational brief describing work and opportunities.

Frogmen: training, equipment and operations of our Navy's underseas fighters. Colby, C. B. Coward-McCann, Inc. 1954. 48p. Library binding $2.97
  Photographs and brief text reveal the work and training of one of the Navy's newest units. Written for grades 4 to 8.

Salvage diver. Zachary, Ball. Holiday House. 1961. 220p. $3.50
  Career fiction. Story of two boys who are hired by a salvage master to search for sunken ships off the Florida Keys.

Skin-diving adventures. Floherty, John J. and McGrady, Mike. Lippincott Company. 1962. 160p. $3.75
  Accounts of the men and women who search beneath the sea for knowledge, sport, and excitement. Illustrated.

Submariner. Lent, Henry. Macmillan Company. 1962. 182p. $3
  Career fiction. Story of an eighteen-year-old boy and his shipmates during their tough eight-week training course at the U.S. Navy's submarine school. For ages 12 to 16.

Ten miles high, two miles deep. Honour, Alan. McGraw-Hill Book Company, Junior Book Division. 1957. 208p. $4.50
  True story of the twin scientists, Auguste and Jean Piccard, whose ascents into the stratosphere and descent beneath the ocean have revealed new findings in the world of science.

Underwater warriors. Berry, Erick. David McKay Company. 1967. 160p. $3.95; library binding $3.59

History and development of the Navy's Underwater Demolition Team. Includes chapters on current oceanographic studies.

What does a diver do? Hyde, Wayne. Dodd, Mead and Company. 1961. 62p. Library binding $2.99

Simple text and pictures portray the various tasks, training, and equipment. Written for grades 3 to 7.

See also Submarine officer

DOCTOR (MEDICAL). *See* Physician

DOMESTIC SERVICE WORKER 301.887

Domestic service occupations. Chronicle Guidance Publications. 1968. 4p. 35c

Occupational brief summarizing nature of work in various jobs, working conditions, earnings, and outlook.

Domestic service workers, general. California State Department of Employment. 1965. 6p. Single copy free

Occupational guide describing work, requirements, training, and outlook.

Household workers. Science Research Associates. 1970. 4p. 25c

Occupational brief describing nature of work, requirements, kinds of jobs, earnings, advantages, disadvantages, and future outlook.

DRAFTSMAN 017.

Aeronautical draftsman. Careers. 1968. 2p. 20c

Career summary for desk-top file. Duties, qualifications, and outlook.

**Aim for a job in drafting. DeLong, Fred. Richards Rosen Press. 1967. 159p. $4; library edition $3.78

Describes the opportunities in modern industry, what skills the draftsman needs, and how he gets his training.

Can I be a draftsman? General Motors Corporation. 1961. 16p. Free

Discussion of requirements, opportunities, and earnings.

Careers in graphic reproductions. Society of Reproduction Engineers. 1963. 6p. Free

Brief statement of duties and required skills.

The drafting and design program. Tri-State College. 1968. 6p. Free

An example of a college-recruiting leaflet describing training and opportunities.

Drafting as a career. American Institute for Design and Drafting, 1963. 8p. Free

Basic qualifications, preparation, advantages, opportunities for advancement, earnings, and recommended high school subjects.

DRAFTSMAN—*Continued*

Draftsman. California State Department of Employment. 1968. 4p. Single copy free

Occupational guide describing work, requirements, training, and outlook.

**Draftsman. Careers. 1968. 8p. 35c

Career brief describing duties, kinds of specialization, training, personal qualifications, outlook, earnings, and measuring one's interest and ability. Suggested readings.

Draftsman. Chronicle Guidance Publications. 1966. 4p. 35c

Occupational brief summarizing work performed, types of jobs, working conditions, qualifications, training, opportunities, outlook, and methods of entry.

Draftsman: architectural, electrical, marine, mechanical, structural. California State Department of Employment. 1965. 4p. Single copy free

Duties, working conditions, pay, finding the job, training, promotion, and employment prospects.

Draftsmen. Science Research Associates. 1967. 4p. 45c

Occupational brief describing different types of work, how to learn, paths toward advancement, salary possibilities, where draftsmen work, advantages, disadvantages, and future prospects.

**Draftsmen. One section of *Occupational Outlook Handbook*.

Nature of work, where employed, training, other qualifications, employment outlook, and earnings.

Electrical draftsman. Michigan Employment Security Commission. 1966. 2p. Single copy free

Job brief summarizing occupational data for use in Michigan.

Finding out about draftsmen. Science Research Associates. 1967. 4p. 45c

Junior occupational brief summarizing what the work requires and offers.

Machine draftsman. Guidance Centre. 1966. 4p. 35c postpaid

Nature of the work, qualifications, preparation, earnings, working conditions, employment outlook, advancement, and how to get started.

Mechanical draftsman. Careers. 1970. 2p. 20c

Career summary for desk-top file. Duties, qualifications, and outlook.

Mechanical draftsman. Chronicle Guidance Publications. 1967. 4p. 35c

Occupational brief summarizing work performed, working conditions, training, qualifications, where employed, earnings, related jobs, and outlook.

**Opportunities in a drafting career. Stern, Benjamin J. Vocational Guidance Manuals. 1967. 96p. $1.95 paper; library edition $3.75

Description of the draftsman's work, qualifications necessary, educational preparation, working conditions, how to get started, advancement possibilities, and outlook. There is a list of schools offering courses in drafting.

DRESS DESIGNER. *See* **Clothes designer**

DRESSMAKER 785.361

* Custom tailors and dressmakers. Science Research Associates. 1969. 4p. 45c

Occupational brief describing nature of work, training, qualifications, opportunities, advantages, disadvantages, and future outlook.

Drapery seamstress. California State Department of Employment. 1965. 3p. Single copy free

Occupational guide describing work, requirements, training, and outlook.

Dressmaker. Careers. 1967. 2p. 20c

Career summary for desk-top file. Duties, qualifications, and outlook.

Dressmaker. Chronicle Guidance Publications. 1969. 4p. 35c

Occupational brief summarizing work performed, where employed, wages, training, qualifications, advantages, disadvantages, related jobs, and outlook.

Finding out about dressmakers. Science Research Associates. 1967. 4p. 45c

Junior occupational brief containing concise facts about the job.

Seamstress. California State Department of Employment. 1964. 4p. Single copy free

Occupational guide describing work, requirements, training, and outlook.

See also Apparel industry worker; Clothes designer

DRIVER 905.883 and 913.883

Chauffeur. Chronicle Guidance Publications. 1969. 4p. 35c

Occupational brief summarizing work performed, hours and working conditions, earnings, personal requirements, high school preparation, how to get a job, advantages, disadvantages, and outlook.

Danny driver. Nicholas, Charles. Golden Press. 1968. 24p. 69c

A tall picture book, sixteen inches tall, prepared for nursery school and kindergarten children. Contains vivid color illustrations of typical activities of a driver of automobiles, explained in simple captions.

**Drivers, motor vehicle. Careers. 1970. 12p. 35c

Career brief describing duties, training requirements, earnings, places of employment, unionization, and outlook for each of the following: truck drivers, routemen, bus drivers, and taxi drivers.

**Driving occupations. One chapter of *Occupational Outlook Handbook.*

Nature of work, where employed, training, qualifications, employment outlook, earnings, and working conditions. Specific information is given for over-the-road truck driver, local truck driver, routeman, intercity bus driver, local transit bus driver, and taxi driver.

**Employment outlook for driving occupations. Bulletin No. 1650–94. Bureau of Labor Statistics, U.S. Department of Labor. Supt. of Documents. 1970. 20p. 20c

Reprint from the *Occupational Outlook Handbook.* Includes over-the-road truck drivers, local truck drivers, routemen, intercity bus drivers, local transit bus drivers, and taxi drivers.

DRIVER—*Continued*

Salesman driver. Chronicle Guidance Publications. 1969. 4p. 35c
Occupational brief summarizing work performed, working conditions, hours, earnings, personal qualifications, training requirements, opportunities, employment outlook, and entry into the job.

See also Bus driver; Truck driver

DRIVING INSTRUCTOR 099.228

Driving instructors. Science Research Associates. 1968. 4p. 45c
Occupational brief describing nature of work, training, qualifications, working conditions, earnings, and future outlook.

Finding out about driving instructors. Science Research Associates. 1967. 4p. 45c
Junior occupational brief describing work and opportunities.

DRUG MANUFACTURING WORKER 550.885

Drug manufacturing workers. Science Research Associates. 1966. 4p. 45c
Occupational brief describing some jobs in the industry, requirements, methods of getting started, earnings, advantages, disadvantages, and future outlook.

DRUGSTORE CLERK 289.458

Drugstore clerks. Science Research Associates. 1968. 4p. 45c
Occupational brief describing nature of work, training, qualifications, opportunities, advantages, disadvantages, and future outlook.

Finding out about drugstore clerks. Science Research Associates. 1967. 4p. 45c
Junior occupational brief summarizing what the work requires and offers.

DRY CLEANING INDUSTRY WORKER 362.782

Dry cleaner spotter. Michigan Employment Security Commission. 1963. 2p. Single copy free
Job brief summarizing occupational data for use in Michigan.

* Dry cleaning industry jobs. Careers. 1968. 8p. 35c
Career brief describing kinds of work, training, employment prospects, earnings, advancement prospects, and determination of aptitudes and interest. Suggested references.

Dry cleaning occupations. California State Department of Employment. 1968. 2p. Single copy free
Occupational guide describing work, requirements, training, and outlook.

Dry cleaning occupations. Chronicle Guidance Publications. 1967. 4p. 35c

Occupational brief summarizing work performed, working conditions, hours, wages, qualifications, training, opportunities, and outlook.

Finding out about dry cleaning workers. Science Research Associates. 1967. 4p. 45c

Junior occupational brief containing simplified information about nature of work, training, earnings, and opportunities.

Pressers. Michigan Employment Security Commission. 1963. 2p. Single copy free

Job brief summarizing occupational data for use in Michigan.

See also Laundry industry worker

ECOLOGIST 041.081

A career in ecology. Ecological Society of America. No date. 8p. Free

Describes the importance to society of taking action on the pollution of the environment, preparation for the work, opportunities, and salaries.

Careers "doing something" for the environment. Careers. 4p. 35c

Reprint from *Changing Times* describing university programs which provide foundations for a variety of approaches to environment control and restoration.

Ecological surveys from space. National Aeronautics and Space Administration. Supt. of Documents. 1970. 76p. $1.75

This monograph will suggest a few of the possible uses of surveys from spacecraft in seven important disciplines of natural science. Colored illustrations show examples such as detection of diseased areas in forests and shoals in harbors.

Ecology: new cause, new career. Guitar, Mary Anne. Alumnae Advisory Center. 1970. 6p. 35c

A reprint from Mademoiselle describing training at Yale School of Forestry and several women's experiences working on various environmental problems such as pollution, erosion, and conservation.

**Employment outlook for environmental scientists. Bulletin No. 1650–24. Bureau of Labor Statistics, U.S. Department of Labor. Supt. of Documents. 1970. 16p. 15c

Reprint from the *Occupational Outlook Handbook*. Includes information about geologists, geophysicists, meteorologists, and oceanographers.

Good training, good jobs: MDTA, water pollution control operator. Government Printing Office. Supt. of Documents. 1969. 8p. 10c

This leaflet introduces and discusses the need for an recruitment of water pollution control operators at the District of Columbia Water Pollution Control Plant. It describes the training for these positions provided under the Manpower Development and Training Act, whom to contact, and where to get further information.

ECOLOGIST—*Continued*

Plant agriculture; readings from *Scientific American*. W. H. Freeman & Co. 1970. 246p. $10. Paper $4.95

Selected articles dealing with the origins of agriculture, the physiology of plants, environmental requirements, the technology of production, and the world food problem. Basic information concerning future needs and outlook.

ECONOMIST 050.088

Agricultural economists. One section of *Occupational Outlook Handbook*.

Brief description of nature of work.

Economist. California State Department of Employment. 1967. 6p. Single copy free

Occupational guide describing work, requirements, training, and outlook.

**Economist. Careers. 1967. 8p. 35c

Career brief describing history and importance of this work, duties, working conditions, earnings, personal qualifications, measuring one's interest and ability, training requirements, promotional prospects, employment outlook, and where employed. Additional references.

Economist. Chronicle Guidance Publications. 1967. 4p. 35c

Occupational brief summarizing work performed, preparation, requirements, earnings, methods of entering, and job opportunities.

Economist. Guidance Centre. 1968. 4p. 35c postpaid

Definition, history and importance, nature of the work, outlook, qualifications, preparation, remuneration, advancement, and how to get started.

Economists. Science Research Associates. 1970. 4p. 45c

Occupational guide describing work, training, opportunities, and outlook.

**Economists. One section of *Occupational Outlook Handbook*.

Nature of work, where employed, training, other qualifications, earnings, and employment outlook.

Finding out about economists. Science Research Associates. 1967. 4p. 45c

Junior occupational brief containing brief facts about the job.

EDITOR AND EDITORIAL WRITER 132.

Book editors. Science Research Associates. 1969. 4p. 45c

Occupational brief describing nature of work, training, qualifications, opportunities, and outlook. Two illustrations. Selected references.

* Editors, general. Careers. 1966. 7p. 35c

Career brief describing duties, personal qualifications, training, related careers, earnings, how to enter, and outlook.

Finding out about book editors. Science Research Associates. 1967. 4p. 45c

Junior occupational brief containing concise facts about the job.

Finding out about editorial assistants. Science Research Associates. 1967. 4p. 45c

Junior occupational brief containing concise facts about the job.

Finding out about magazine editors. Science Research Associates. 1967. 4p. 45c

Junior occupational brief summarizing what the work requires and offers.

Finding out about newspaper editors. Science Research Associates. 1967. 4p. 45c

Junior occupational brief describing work and opportunities.

Magazine editorial workers. Science Research Associates. 1966. 4p. 45c

Occupational brief describing nature of work, training, qualifications, opportunities, advantages, and future outlook.

Newspaper editor. Careers. 1970. 2p. 20c

Career summary for desk-top file. Duties, qualifications, and outlook.

Newspaper editor. Chronicle Guidance Publications. 1969. 4p. 35c

Occupational brief summarizing work performed, working conditions, earnings, personal qualifications, how to determine interests and ability, training, methods of entry, opportunities, and outlook.

Newspaper editor. Guidance Centre. 1966. 4p. 35c postpaid

History and importance, nature of work, qualifications, working conditions, preparation, remuneration, advancement, outlook, related occupations, and how to get started.

* Newspaper editors. Science Research Associates. 1968. 4p. 45c

Occupational brief describing kinds of work, training, qualifications, opportunities, advantages, disadvantages, and future outlook.

See also Journalist; Reporter; Writer

ELECTRIC POWER INDUSTRY WORKER 952.

Careers in lighting. Illuminating Engineering Society. 1969. 4p. Single copy free

Brief description of work and opportunities. An attached reply card offers an expanded booklet.

Electric power in America. McCaig, Robert. Putnam's Sons. 1970. 160p. $3.94

One of the series on industries of America, this book describes the development of major power projects.

Electric power-plant occupations. Careers. 1966. 8p. 35c

Occupational brief describing duties, working conditions, training earnings, related careers, and outlook.

Electrical equipment (manufacturing) occupations. Chronicle Guidance Publications. 1969. 4p. 35c

Occupational brief summarizing work performed, number and where employed, working conditions, earnings, personal qualifications, training required, and outlook.

ELECTRIC POWER INDUSTRY WORKER—*Continued*

Electrical transmission occupations. Careers. 1967. 8p. 35c

Career brief describing duties, working conditions, personal qualifications, training, related jobs, unionization, and outlook.

**Employment outlook for the electric power industry. Bulletin No. 1650–118. Bureau of Labor Statistics, U.S. Department of Labor. Supt. of Documents. 1970. 16p. 15c

Reprint from the *Occupational Outlook Handbook.* Includes powerplant occupations, transmission and distribution occupations, and customer service occupations.

Exploring your future in the public utilities. Sextant Systems, Inc. 1971. 96p. $8.95

One page is devoted to each of ninety-five jobs, describing the duties, requirements for entering, promotional outlook, and the pay and skill level.

Finding out about power plant workers. Science Research Associates. 1967. 4p. 45c

Junior occupational brief describing work and opportunities.

The miracle of light and power. Leyson, B. W. Dutton and Company. 1955. 186p. $3.50

The last chapter of this account of the Consolidated Edison Company describes the various career opportunities, training, duties, benefits, and advantages. Illustrated.

**Occupations in the electric power industry. One chapter of *Occupational Outlook Handbook.*

Nature and location of the industry, kinds of work, employment outlook, earnings, and working conditions. Specific information is given concerning powerplant occupations, transmission and distribution occupations, and customer servicing occupations.

* Public utility workers. Science Research Associates. 1967. 4p. 45c

Occupational brief describing kinds of work, requirements, getting started, earnings, advantages, disadvantages, and future outlook.

Service representatives for utilities. Science Research Associates. 1966. 4p. 45c

Occupational brief describing work, training, qualifications, opportunities, and outlook.

Transmission and distribution occupations. One section of *Occupational Outlook Handbook.*

Nature of work, training, employment outlook, earnings, and working conditions.

ELECTRICAL APPLIANCE SERVICEMAN 827.281

Electrical appliance repairman. California State Department of Employment. 1968. 2p. Single copy free

Occupational guide describing work, requirements, training, and outlook.

Electrical appliance serviceman. Chronicle Guidance Publications. 1968. 4p. 35c

Occupational brief including history, work performed, working conditions, hours, wages, requirements, training, opportunities, and outlook.

Electrical engineering technician. Careers. 1967. 2p. 20c

Career summary for desk-top file. Duties, qualifications, and outlook.

Electrical household appliance serviceman. Careers. 1968. 8p. 35c

Occupational brief describing nature of work, qualifications, training, opportunities, and outlook.

Electrical-household appliance serviceman. Guidance Centre. 1970. 4p. 35c postpaid

Definition, history and importance, nature of work, qualifications, preparation, employment, advancement, remuneration, and how to get started.

Electrical repairman. Careers. 1969. 8p. 35c

Career brief describing duties, working conditions, qualifications, places of employment, earnings, and outlook.

Electrical repairman. Chronicle Guidance Publications. 1968. 4p. 35c

Occupational brief summarizing work performed, hours, earnings, training, and opportunities.

Electrical technician. Chronicle Guidance Publications. 1967. 4p. 35c

Occupational brief summarizing work performed, working conditions, requirements, earnings, training, and outlook.

Employment outlook for electric sign servicemen. Bulletin No. 1650–85. Bureau of Labor Statistics, U.S. Department of Labor. Supt. of Documents. 1970. 8p. 10c

Reprint from the *Occupational Outlook Handbook.*

ELECTRICAL ENGINEER 003.081

Electrical engineer. California State Department of Employment. 1964. 8p. Single copy free

Occupational guide describing work, requirements, training, and outlook.

Electrical engineer. Careers. 1970. 2p. 20c

Career summary for desk-top file. Duties, qualifications, and outlook.

Electrical engineer. Chronicle Guidance Publications. 1967. 4p. 35c

Occupational brief summarizing work performed, employment conditions, salaries, personal qualifications, aptitudes and interests, educational requirements, opportunities, and outlook.

Electrical engineers. Michigan Employment Security Commission. 1965. 2p. Single copy free

Job brief summarizing occupational data for use in Michigan.

* Electrical engineers. Science Research Associates. 1968. 4p. 45c

Occupational brief describing nature of work, qualifications, preparation, opportunities, advantages, disadvantages, and future outlook.

ELECTRICAL ENGINEER–*Continued*

**Electrical engineers. One section of *Occupational Outlook Handbook.*
Nature of work, where employed, employment outlook, and earnings.

Finding out about electrical engineers. Science Research Associates. 1967. 4p. 45c
Junior occupational brief describing work and opportunities.

Giants of electricity. Dunsheath, Percy. Crowell, Collier and Macmillan. 1967. 200p. $4.50
Biography of twelve scientists who advanced the knowledge of electricity. For grades 8 to 10.

**Opportunities in electrical and electronic engineering. Shackleton, S. Paul. Vocational Guidance Manuals. 1967. 128p. $1.95 paper; $3.75 library edition
Includes description of the branches of electrical engineering: power, communications, electronics, and control systems. Describes qualifications, education and training, requirements for state licenses, getting started, requisites for advancement, opportunities for employment, and related fields. List of schools offering accredited undergraduate engineering curricula.

Power engineering education. Chronicle Guidance Publications. 1969. 6p. 50c
Reprinted article from *Mechanical Engineering* discusses the scope of power engineering, communication from industry to student, attracting top students to the field, and advancement and compensation.

Powerplant occupations. One section of *Occupational Outlook Handbook.*
Description of the work of the boiler, turbine, auxiliary equipment, and switchboard operators in the electric power industry.

Wanted: Electric engineers. Chronicle Guidance Publications. 1967. 4p. 35c
Reprinted article from *Electronics* discusses why the shortage of workers in the field, the competition among employers for available engineers, salaries, and geographical opportunities.

**Your challenge in electrical engineering. Institute of Electrical and Electronics Engineers. 1966. 14p. Single copy free
Attractively illustrated brochure containing discussion of the growth of professional employment, the applications of electronics, requirements, outlook, and preparation. Included is a list of colleges offering training.

See also Atomic energy industry worker; Engineer; Scientist

ELECTRICAL LIGHT AND POWER UTILITY WORKER. *See* Electric Power Industry Worker

ELECTRICIAN 825.281

Career opportunities at General Electric. General Electric Company. 1968. 16p. Free
An introduction to the broad range of career opportunities.

Construction electrician. Careers. 1968. 2p. 20c

Career summary for desk-top file. Duties, qualifications, and outlook.

Construction electrician. Chronicle Guidance Publications. 1966. 4p. 35c

Occupational brief summarizing work performed by the construction electrician in installing electrical equipment in new or remodeled buildings. Includes description of working conditions, training, where employed, and outlook.

Electrician. Guidance Centre. 1968. 4p. 35c postpaid

Definition, nature of work, conditions of work, qualifications, preparation, earnings, how to get started, and related jobs.

Electrician (construction). California State Department of Employment. 1966. 3p. Single copy free

Occupational guide describing work, requirements, training, and outlook.

Electricians. Michigan Employment Security Commission. 1966. 2p. Single copy free

Job brief summarizing occupational data for use in Michigan.

* Electricians. Science Research Associates. 1968. 4p. 45c

Occupational brief describing nature of work, preparation, qualifications, opportunities, advantages, disadvantages, and future outlook.

Electricians (construction). One section of *Occupational Outlook Handbook.*

Nature of work, where employed, training, other qualifications, advancement, employment outlook, earnings, and working conditions.

** Employment outlook for electrician (construction). Bulletin No. 1650–73. Bureau of Labor Statistics, U.S. Department of Labor. Supt. of Documents. 1970. 12p. 15c

Reprint from the *Occupational Outlook Handbook.*

**Employment outlook for maintenance electricians, industrial machinery repairmen, and millwrights. Bulletin No. 1650–86. Bureau of Labor Statistics, U.S. Department of Labor. Supt. of Documents. 1970. 12p. 15c

Reprint from the *Occupational Outlook Handbook.*

Finding out about electricians. Science Research Associates. 1967. 4p. 45c

Junior occupational brief summarizing what the work requires and offers.

Maintenance electrician. California State Department of Employment. 1966. 3p. Single copy free

Occupational guide describing work, requirements, training, and outlook.

Maintenance electricians. Chronicle Guidance Publications. 1967. 4p. 35c

Occupational brief summarizing work performed, working conditions, where employed, earnings, education requirements, and outlook.

ELECTRICIAN—*Continued*

**Maintenance electricians. One section of *Occupational Outlook Handbook.*

Nature of work, where employed, training, other qualifications, advancement, employment outlook, earnings, and working conditions.

Make the right turn to an electrical career. Farm Electrification Company. 1965. 2p. Free

Provides information on training, educational requirements, and opportunities in research and development, engineering, marketing, and installing-servicing.

ELECTRONIC COMPUTER OPERATOR 213.138

Bright future careers with computers. Laskow, Robert and Feldzamen, A. N. Chilton Book Company. 1969. 217p. $5.50; paper $3.95

This book provides practical information on job qualifications and sources of training. It also points out the need for new workers. Suggesting an evaluation of skills suitable for careers in data processing, the authors incorporate some sample aptitude tests.

Careers, computers and you. National Better Business Bureau. 1970. 11p. 25c

Points to consider when investigating computer schools.

**Careers and opportunities in computer science. Carroll, John M. Dutton and Company. 1967. 191p. $3.95

Qualifications and job descriptions for work requiring college training include programming, system analysis, designing, manufacturing, and administration. Positions for high school graduates include managers of data processing, business-machine operators, and maintenance men for the equipment. Illustrated.

**Careers in computer programming. Barnett, Leo and Davis, Lou Ellen. Henry Z. Walck, Inc. 1967. 117p. $4.50

This is a survey of the responsibilities and opportunities for programmers and systems analysts. Information on how to prepare for and obtain jobs in this growing field includes where one might work, education, working conditions, advancement opportunities, and outlook.

**Careers in data processing. Englehardt, Stanley L. Lothrop, Lee and Shepard Company. 1969. 127p. $4.50; library edition $4.14

The descriptions cover jobs in designing, selling, and repairing as well as in programming and operating computers. Many facts about training, aptitudes, and salaries are included in the personal case histories of men and women working in the computer industry. Prepared for junior high and high school.

Computer education directory. Data Processing Horizons. 1970. 380p. $29.85

Reference material on data processing education has been condensed in this directory, designed to assist people entering this field. Includes occupational descriptions, schools and educational facilities for training, books and periodicals, associations involved in data processing, films, training aids, manufacturers, and computer characteristics.

Computer operator. California State Department of Employment. 1967. 4p. Single copy free

Job duties, working conditions, pay, hours, entrance requirements, promotion, training, and employment prospects in California.

Computer science: earned degrees, by level, sex, and institution. One section of *Earned Degrees Conferred.*

Useful for judging the extent of a college's program in each of the following specialties: computer science, data processing, and systems analysis.

Computers and data processing information sources: an annotated guide to the literature, associations and institutions concerned with input, throughput and output of data. Gale Research Company. 1969. 275p. $11.50

A comprehensive annotated bibliography.

Data processing explained. King, Alice Gore. Alumnae Advisory Center. 1968. 20p. $1

This explains where computers are used, what jobs are available, and what qualifications are needed.

Data-processing machine operators. Science Research Associates. 1968. 4p. 45c

Occupational brief describing nature of work, training, qualifications, opportunities, and outlook. Selected references.

* Electronic computer operating personnel. Careers. 1968. 8p. 35c

Career brief describing nature of work, duties of various operators, qualifications, training requirements, training opportunities, outlook, earnings, and advancement prospects.

** Electronic computer operating personnel. One section of *Occupational Outlook Handbook.*

Nature of work, where employed, training, other qualifications, advancement, employment outlook, earnings, and working conditions.

Electronic data processing manager. California State Department of Employment. 1966. 6p. Single copy free

Occupational guide describing work, requirements, training, and outlook.

Finding out about data processing machine operators. Science Research Associates. 1967. 4p. 45c

Junior occupational brief describing work and opportunities.

* A job with a future in computers. Cross, Wilbur. Grosset and Dunlap, Inc. 1969. 127p. Library edition $3.59

In explaining the career opportunities in the rapidly changing computer industry, the author describes the training required, the qualifications needed, and the future outlook. Job descriptions are presented for the basic positions in programming, computer operation, and other related occupations. Sources of additional information.

Jobs in electronic data processing. Science Research Associates. 1968. 48p. $1.15

Describes the variety of job prospects and opportunities within this field.

ELECTRONIC COMPUTER OPERATOR—*Continued*

New directions—career opportunities for computer specialists in the Federal government. U.S. Civil Service Commission. 1969. 16p. Single copy free

Describes the development of computer technology and the anticipated employment outlook. Contains franked tear-off card to be mailed to Federal job information centers.

Office machine operators. One section of *Occupational Outlook Handbook.*

Nature of work, places of employment, training, other qualifications, advancement, employment outlook, earnings, and working conditions.

* Your career in computers. Fischer, George. Meredith Press. 1968. 194p. $4.95

Description of the opportunities available to those who have a college education and fourteen different jobs for high school graduates. Includes qualifications and how to enter the computer field.

**Your future in the electronic computer field. Bibby, Dause. Richards Rosen Press. Revised 1969. 159p. Library edition $3.78

The author discusses job opportunities in many aspects of the electronic computer field: manufacturing, programming, and sales.

See also Programmer

ELECTRONICS ENGINEER 003.081

Acoustics and you. Acoustical Society of America. 1968. 20p. Single copy free

A description of specialized fields in acoustics, growth of the field, training, and occupational opportunities.

Electronics engineer. California State Department of Employment. 1965. 5p. Single copy free

Occupational guide describing work, requirements, training, and outlook.

Finding out about electronics engineers. Science Research Associates. 1967. 4p. 45c

Junior occupational brief containing concise facts about the job.

**Your future in electronic engineering. Levine, Sol. Richards Rosen Press. Revised 1969. 160p. $4; library edition $3.78

Includes the development and future outlook of electronics, opportunities, earnings, recommended high school subjects, application for college, and case histories of successful electronic engineers. List of accredited colleges.

See also Electrical engineer

ELECTRONICS MANUFACTURING INDUSTRY WORKER 72

Assemblers, electronics manufacturing. Careers. 1966. 8p. 35c

Career brief describing nature of work, training, working conditions, qualifications, earnings, and outlook.

Assemblers in the electronics industry. Science Research Associates. 1969. 4p. 45c

Occupational brief describing work, qualifications, training, opportunities, and outlook.

Career guidance in electronics. DeVry Institute of Technology. 1969. 64p. Free

Photographs and reprints showing current activities in television, radio, automation, space and missile electronics, industrial controls, communications, computers, and radar.

**Careers and opportunities in electronics. Carroll, John. Dutton and Company. 1963. 191p. $3.95

This book includes the personal qualifications needed, educational requirements, salary potentials, and employment outlook for many classifications in this field.

Electronics manufacturing industry workers. Chronicle Guidance Publications. 1967. 8p. 50c

Occupational brief summarizing various areas of work performed, working conditions, training requirements, personal qualifications, outlook, earnings, and method of entry.

**Electronics manufacturing occupations. One chapter of *Occupational Outlook Handbook.*

Nature of the industry, kinds of work, training, other qualifications, employment outlook, earnings, and working conditions.

Electronics pioneer: Lee De Forest. Levine, I. E. Julian Messner. 1964. 192p. $3.50; library binding $3.34

Biography of the famous inventor.

**Employment outlook for electronics manufacturing. Bulletin No. 1650–112. Bureau of Labor Statistics, U.S. Department of Labor. Supt. of Documents. 1970. 15p. 15c

Reprint from the *Occupational Outlook Handbook.*

Occupations in electronics manufacturing. One section in *Occupational Outlook Handbook.*

Nature and location of the industry, how electronics products are made, occupations in the industry, training, qualifications, employment outlook, earnings, and working conditions.

**Planning a career in electronics. Electronic Industries Association. 1966. 16p. 20c. Single copy free to counselors and librarians

Description of contributions made by principal scientific investigators in the field of electronics, the opportunities offered, and three plans for preparing for careers in electronics. Charts show educational requirements and growth of employment.

**Your career in electronics. Neal, Harry Edward. Julian Messner. 1963. 192p. $3.95

Challenging career opportunities in space exploration, industrial automation, medicine, and communications are described as part of the fascinating world of electronics.

ELECTRONICS MANUFACTURING INDUSTRY WORKER—*Continued*

Your future in microwave. Chronicle Guidance Publications. 1967. 4p. 35c

Reprinted article from *Radio-Electronics* discusses opportunities for technicians and engineers, and method of entry into the field of microwave.

ELECTRONICS TECHNICIAN 726.281

**Aim for a job as an electronic technician. Keefe, John. Richards Rosen Press. 1967. 146p. $4; library edition $3.78

Explanation of what the electronic technician does, what the available jobs are, and where he gets his training.

A career in IBM service puts the future in your hands. International Business Machines Corporation. No date. 12p. Free

This illustrated booklet describes the desirable features and nature of work of the customer engineer who diagnoses equipment problems and provides service.

Computer systems service technician (field engineer). California State Department of Employment. 1964. 4p. Single copy free

Occupational guide describing work, requirements, training, and outlook.

Data processing equipment technician. California State Department of Employment. 1967. 3p. Single copy free

Job duties, working conditions, wages, hours, entrance requirements, line of promotion, training, and employment outlook.

Electronic technician. Chronicle Guidance Publications. 1968. 4p. 35c

Occupational brief summarizing work performed, working conditions, qualifications, where employed, training, and outlook.

Electronic technician. Guidance Centre. 1969. 4p. 35c postpaid

History and importance, nature of work, qualifications, working conditions, preparation, remuneration, outlook, related occupations, and how to get started.

Electronic technicians. Science Research Associates. 1968. 4p. 45c

Occupational brief describing work, qualifications, training, earnings, advantages, disadvantages, and outlook. Selected references.

Electronic technologist. Guidance Centre. 1969. 35c postpaid

History and importance, nature of work, qualifications, working conditions, preparation, remuneration, outlook, related occupations, and how to get started.

Electronics technicans. Michigan Employment Security Commission. 1964. 2p. Single copy free

Job brief summarizing occupational data for use in Michigan.

Finding out about electronics technicians. Science Research Associates. 1967. 4p. 45c

Junior occupational brief containing concise facts about the job.

Industrial electronics technician. Careers. 1970. 2p. 20c
Career summary for desk-top file. Duties, qualifications, and outlook.

See also Instrumentation technician; Programmer

ELECTROPLATERS 500.380

Electroplater. California State Department of Employment. 1967. 3p. Single copy free
Occupational guide describing work, requirements, training, and outlook.

Electroplater. Chronicle Guidance Publications. 1966. 4p. 35c
Occupational brief summarizing definition, nature of work, where employed, earnings, personal qualifications, training, working conditions, and outlook.

Electroplaters. Careers. 1966. 7p. 35c
Career brief describing duties, working conditions, training, places of employment, earnings, unionization, and outlook.

Electroplaters. Science Research Associates. 1967. 4p. 45c
Occupational brief describing work, qualifications, points to ponder, and future outlook. Selected references.

**Electroplaters. One section of *Occupational Outlook Handbook.*
Nature of work, where employed, training, other qualifications, advancement, employment outlook, earnings, and working conditions.

Finding out about electroplaters. Science Research Associates. 1967. 4p. 45c
Junior occupational brief describing work and opportunities.

ELECTROTYPER AND STEREOTYPER 974.381

Electrotyper. Careers. 1967. 2p. 20c
Career summary for desk-top file. Duties, qualifications, and outlook.

Electrotypers and stereotypers. Chronicle Guidance Publications. 1967. 4p. 35c
Occupational brief summarizing work performed, process definition, working conditions, education required, advancement, hours, and earnings.

Electrotypers and stereotypers. One section of *Occupational Outlook Handbook.*
Nature of work, training and other qualifications, employment outlook, earnings, and working conditions.

ELEMENTARY SCHOOL TEACHER. *See* Teacher, Elementary school

ELEVATOR CONSTRUCTOR 825.381

**Elevator constructors. One section of *Occupational Outlook Handbook.*
Nature of work, where employed, training, other qualifications, employment outlook, earnings, and working conditions.

ELEVATOR CONSTRUCTOR—*Continued*

Employment outlook for elevator constructors, structural-ornamental and reinforcing-iron workers, riggers, machine movers. Bulletin No. 1650–74. Bureau of Labor Statistics, U.S. Department of Labor. Supt. of Documents. 1970. 12p. 15c

Reprint from the *Occupational Outlook Handbook.*

Finding out about elevator constructors. Science Research Associates. 1967. 4p. 45c

Junior occupational brief summarizing what the work requires and offers.

ELEVATOR OPERATOR 921.883

Elevator operator. Careers. 1970. 2p. 20c

Career summary for desk-top file. Duties, qualifications, and outlook.

Job grading standards for elevator elevator. Civil Service Commission. Supt. of Documents. 1969. 4p. 10c

This job classification outlines duties, skill and knowledge requirements, responsibility, physical effort, and working conditions which determine job grade levels in accordance with the U.S. Civil Service Commission standards.

EMBALMER. *See* Funeral director and embalmer

EMPLOYMENT INTERVIEWER 166.268

Employment counselor. California State Department of Employment. 1967. 3p. Single copy free

Occupational guide describing work, requirements, training, and outlook.

Employment interviewer. California State Department of Employment. 1966. 3p. Single copy free

Occupational guide describing work, requirements, training, and outlook.

Employment interviewer. Careers. 1968. 2p. 20c

Career summary for desk-top file. Duties, qualifications, and outlook.

* Employment service interviewers. Science Research Associates. 1967. 4p. 45c

Occupational brief describing nature of work, training, qualifications, opportunities, and outlook.

* Employment supervisor. Chronicle Guidance Publications. 1967. 4p. 35c

Occupational brief summarizing work performed, training, qualifications, earnings, and outlook.

Finding out about employment agency interviewers. Science Research Associates. 1967. 4p. 45c

Junior occupational brief containing concise facts about the job.

See also Personnel and employment manager

ENGINEER 001. through 015.

**Accredited curricula leading to first degrees in engineering in the United States. Engineers' Council for Professional Development. 1969. 20p. 25c

Reprint from the Council's annual report, made available February each year. Contains list of the engineering schools, arranged alphabetically, with indications of the accredited curricula such as civil, electrical, mechanical, and sanitary.

After high school, what? Does science or engineering offer a career for you? Engineers' Council for Professional Development. No date. 5p. 3c

Brief summary of nature of work, qualifications, and training. Explains how engineering differs from a career in science.

**Annual report. Engineers' Council for Professional Development. 1969. 86p. $1.50

Issued in January of each year, this contains reports from standing committees on accreditation, technology, professional recognition, and ethics. Contains list of accredited undergraduate curricula in each of the major branches of engineering.

Appointment to opportunity. General Motors Institute. 1968. 24p. Free

Illustrated brochure describing the cooperative plan and the engineering and industrial administration programs available to the students. Includes admission requirements and procedures.

Atomic Energy Commission special fellowships in nuclear science and engineering. Oak Ridge Associated Universities. 1968. 38p. Free

Description of the work, training, programs of study at the graduate level, and qualifications for fellowships.

The bridge to your success—engineering opportunities in the Bureau of Public Roads Highway Engineer Training Program. U.S. Department of Transportation, Federal Highway Administration. Supt. of Documents. 1968. 20p. 30c

Provides information for college students interested in highway or highway bridge engineering. Describes opportunities, training programs, and the various fields of activities.

Can I be a scientist or engineer? Let's find out. General Motors, Public Relations Staff. 1969. 24p. Free

Description of work in mathematics, chemistry, physics, and seven main branches of engineering, with typical jobs in each. Includes also opportunities and suggested high school preparation.

Careers and opportunities in engineering. Pollack, Philip and Alden, John. Dutton and Company. 1967. 224p. $4.95

This book answers the questions of what one can do in the numerous branches of this expanding profession and stresses as well the enthusiams, traits, and qualifications one must bring to this field. List of accredited institutions. Illustrated.

ENGINEER–*Continued*

* Careers in engineering. Wachs, Theodore. Henry Z. Walck, Inc. 1964. 102p. $4.50

In a survey of the increasing opportunities in engineering, the author describes the scope of the work, preparation, earnings, opportunities and functions of mechanical, electrical, civil, chemical, mining, and metallurgical engineers. He describes the engineer's role in applying research knowledge. Reading list. Illustrated.

Careers in engineering. Purdue University. 1965. 40p. 25c. Single copy free

Information about the different branches of engineering, the qualifications for a successful engineer, and his educational requirements. Special sections on courses to take in high school, difference between the engineer and technician, related careers, and the rewards of an engineer. Bibliography. Illustrated.

Careers in engineering–requirements, opportunities. Stewart, Lowell O. Iowa State University Press. 2nd edition, 1956. 105p. 50c

The work of the engineer is discussed under three headings: (1) the degree-granting departments such as agricultural, architectural, ceramic, chemical, civil, electrical, general, and mechanical engineering; (2) functional specialization such as design, development and experiment, construction and manufacturing, sales, commercial, application, service, and operations; (3) opportunities in specific industries such as automotive, radio, refrigeration and air conditioning, telephone, and aviation. Good discussions are included on who should study engineering and the factors determining success. Illustrated.

Definitions of occupational specialties in engineering. American Society of Mechanical Engineers. 1952. 112p. $3.50

This booklet was prepared for the Bureau of Naval Research to define and delineate the terms used for fields of specialization in nineteen branches of engineering. Clear exposition of duties, knowledge needed to work in the field, accessory techniques, and related activities are given for 266 specialties. Fairly technical information.

Demand for engineers. Engineers Joint Council. 1966. 96p. $4

Summary data on the engineering employment in industry and government, recruiting goals, required employment additions, turnover information, starting salaries, and growth in total employment. All data are broken down by industrial activity, such as chemical, petroleum, electrical machinery, electronics, and research, and by three levels of Government. Special sections are included on engineering technicians and physical scientists. Many tables and graphs.

**Do I have engineering aptitude? Johnson, A. Pemberton. Engineers' Council for Professional Development. Revised 1962. 8p. Fifty copies $2

A set of questions, answers, and interpretations of answers for use in self-analysis by young men and women considering careers in engineering. Distributed only in packages of fifty.

Education for engineers. Morgan, Arthur E. Antioch College. 1955. 44p. Free

Includes a discussion of the importance to the engineer of general education, fundamental courses, management courses, and cooperative work experience.

Educational programs and facilities in nuclear science and engineering. Oak Ridge Associated Universities. 1968. 101p. Free to counselors

Information about the degrees, courses, and facilities for nuclear education in 261 institutions.

**Employment outlook for engineers. Bulletin No. 1650–23. Bureau of Labor Statistics, U.S. Department of Labor. Supt. of Documents. 1970. 16p. 15c

Reprint from the *Occupational Outlook Handbook*. Provides information concerning the aerospace, agricultural, ceramic, civil, chemical, electrical, industrial, mechanical, metallurgical, and mining engineer.

Engineer, professional. Guidance Centre. 1966. 4p. 35c postpaid

Definition, history and importance, nature of work, qualifications necessary for entry and success, preparation, employment and advancement, remuneration, advantages, disadvantages, how to get started, and related occupations.

Engineer tax men. Internal Revenue Service. 1969. 14p. Free

Information about engineers in the Internal Revenue Service, the work they do and how they feel about it. Discussion of engineering issues in tax administration, job location, typical problems, scope of work, qualification standards, career aspects, and how to apply.

**Engineering. One chapter of *Occupational Outlook Handbook*.

Nature of work, where employed, training, qualifications, employment outlook, earnings, and sources of additional information. Specific information is also given for each of ten branches of engineering.

**Engineering, a career of opportunity. National Society of Professional Engineers. 1967. 15p. Free in limited quantities

Growth of the engineering profession, functions, fields of specialization, preparation, women in engineering, earnings, and future prospects. Bibliography.

Engineering–a challenge. Engineers' Council for Professional Development. 1967. 32p. 25c

Contains description of opportunities and requirements of engineering fields for young people.

Engineering and technician enrollments. Engineers Joint Council. 1968. 448p. $5

Detailed report giving national and state breakdowns by curriculum and type of school. A summary report also is available for $1.

Engineering as a career, 2nd edition. Smith, Ralph J. McGraw-Hill Book Company. 1962. 394p. $6.95; $4.95 paper

Designed to acquaint the beginning college student with the functions and branches of engineering, problem-solving, use of mathematical tools, and adjustment to college. Exercises and assignments are given at the end of each chapter.

ENGINEER—*Continued*

Engineering as a career today. Amstead, B. H. and McNutt, Wilbourn. Dodd, Mead and Company. 1967. 228p. $3.75

A look at the possibilities open to engineers in many fields—civil, mechanical, chemical, aeronautical, aerospace, and electrical. Includes the duties, training required, rewards, and opportunities.

Engineering careers in the coal industry. National Coal Association. 1968. 16p. Free

Description of the industry, opportunities, future outlook, and list of colleges offering courses useful to mining engineers.

Engineering is like this. Dodge, Bertha. Little, Brown and Company. 1963. 200p. $4.50

A look at great engineering feats demonstrates that they have been accomplished with human imagination and ingenuity. Written for ages 12 to 15.

Engineering packet. University of Missouri. 1968. 6 leaflets. Free

Example of recruiting leaflets describing work and training of the aerospace, chemical, civil, electrical, and mechanical engineer.

Engineering salaries—special industry reports. Engineers Joint Council. 1967. 8 reports. $25 each

Eight special reports covering the aerospace; chemical; consulting and construction; electrical and electronics; machinery and transportation; mining, metals and petroleum; research and development; and utilities industries in detail.

Engineers. Chronicle Guidance Publications. 1967. 8p. 50c

Occupational brief summarizing various areas of work, kinds of jobs, qualifications, determination of aptitudes and interest, educational requirements, opportunities, outlook, and related positions.

Engineers and engineering—some definitions. Newark College of Engineering. 1969. 20p. Free

Definition of engineering and some of the interdisciplinary specialties needed to build the world of tomorrow.

Engineers and scientists in the U.S. Air Force. U.S. Air Force Recruiting Service. 1967. 52p. Free

General information concerning opportunities for men and women with scientific or engineering degrees in the U.S. Air Force.

Engineers and what they do. Coy, Harold. Franklin Watts, Inc. 1961. 186p. $3.95

Description of the engineering specialties, places of employment, preparation, working conditions, earnings, and future outlook. Includes nuclear engineering and astronautics. Reading lists. For grades 7 to 11.

Engineers, general. Careers. 1970. 12p. 35c

Career brief describing fields of specialization, working conditions, training, places of employment, earnings, licensing, outlook, and measuring one's interest and ability. Additional readings.

Engineers in the Forest Service. U.S. Department of Agriculture. Miscellaneous Publication 1089. Supt. of Documents. 1968. 17p. 50c

Explains the functions of the Forest Service especially as they apply to engineering specialties. Describes the requirements and benefits.

Engineers' pay checks. Engineers Joint Council. 1967. 6p. $1

Reprint of an article comparing salaries and trends in engineering with other professions.

Engineers, the bridge to your success. Government Printing Office. Supt. of Documents. 1969. 20p. 45c

Prepared to provide information for college students interested in careers in highway or highway bridge engineering, this pamphlet presents information on the training program maintained by the Bureau of Public Roads, and on the Bureau's organization, operations, and history.

**Engineers unlimited: your career in engineering. Neal, Harry Edward. Julian Messner. Revised 1968. 192p. $3.95; library binding $3.64

Explanation of work in various divisions of engineering and subprofessional jobs which can lead to engineering, such as draftsman, engineering aide, and technician. Information on salaries, training, colleges, and scholarships.

**Guidance counselor kit. Engineers' Council for Professional Development. 1969. 15 brochures. $40

A collection of career information booklets published by the Engineers' Council. Compiled for counselor or library reference shelves.

Herbert Hoover, engineer, humanitarian, statesman. McGee, D. H. Dodd, Mead and Company. Revised 1965. 325p. $3.75

Biography revealing many fascinating events and achievements in the life of Herbert Hoover.

Jobs in engineering. Science Research Associates. 1965. 32p. $1.15

Describes the variety of job prospects and opportunities, especially for the aeronautical, ceramic, chemical, civil, electrical, mechanical, metallurgical, and sanitary engineer.

Listen to leaders in engineering. Love, A. and Childers, J. S. David McKay Company. 1964. 338p. $6.95

Discussion of expanding opportunities and career possibilities.

Manual for engineers serving as career advisors. Engineers' Council for Professional Development. 1968. 48p. 75c

A guide for engineers who are interested and active in working in guidance with young people. Contains charts and a basic reference list.

Modern American engineers. Yost, Edna. Lippincott Company. 1958. 182p. $3.95

Biographical sketches of twelve outstanding engineers representing mechanical, civil, electrical, mining, automotive, research, radio, and television branches of the field. Information covers early education, professional training, and special achievements.

ENGINEER—*Continued*

Need financial aid for college? Engineers' Council for Professional Development. No date. 8p. 3c

Advice to students to make college plans early and some suggestions concerning financial aid.

Opportunity: engineers. U.S. Department of the Navy, Naval Ship Systems Command. 1968. 32p. Free

Description of the work performed by naval architects, electronic and mechanical engineers in designing, building, and maintaining the ships of the United States Navy.

Professional income of engineers. Engineers Joint Council. 1967. 68p. $5

Seventh in a series of reports containing salary information on engineering graduates. Industrial categories, three levels of government, college teachers, technical institutes, and engineering societies are represented. Charts and tables show median, quartile, and decile figures for those with bachelor's, master's, and doctor's degrees.

Report of progress on engineering research. Government Printing Office. Supt. of Documents. 1970. 118p. $1.50

Gives an idea of kinds of work for which there may be manpower needs.

Salaries and income of engineering teachers. Engineers Joint Council. 1966. 40p. 35c

Detailed salary data and curves for engineering teachers, from a survey of over 9,000 faculty members.

Science and engineering careers in Government. U.S. Civil Service Commission. Supt. of Documents. 1968. 23p. 35c

Descriptions of beginning jobs and career opportunities in Federal science and engineering occupations.

Sources of engineering career information. Engineers' Council for Professional Development. 1969. 20p. Free

A bibliography of engineering career information, identified by field of specialty. Also contains a list of reference books and general guidance information.

U.S. Public Health Service engineers. Government Printing Office. Supt. of Documents. 1968. 10p. 10c

Includes information on the various programs, location of assignments, qualifications, and military service obligations for those interested in an engineering career with the Public Health Service.

Wanted: Women engineers and more chance for them. Society of Women Engineers. 1968. 10p. 6c

Discussion of more opportunities in product engineering.

Why not be an engineer? Leaflet 41. Women's Bureau, U.S. Department of Labor. Supt. of Documents. 1967. 8p. 5c

A report upon current trends and attitudes relating to women's prospects in engineering as a career. Presents some advantages that an engineering career offers to a woman. Lists sources of further information.

See also

Aeronautical engineer
Agricultural engineer
Ceramic engineer
Chemical engineer
Civil engineer
Electrical engineer
Electronics engineer
Highway engineer
Illuminating engineer
Industrial engineer
Locomotive engineer
Marine engineer
Mechanical engineer
Metallurgical engineer
Mining engineer
Operating engineer
Petroleum engineer
Radio and television engineer
Refrigerating engineer
Safety engineer
Sanitary engineer
Scientist
Urban planner

ENGINEERING TECHNICIAN 007.181

**Accredited curricula leading to degrees in engineering technology in the United States. Engineers' Council for Professional Development. 1969. 12p. 25c

Report from the Council's annual report, listing the institutions granting accredited degrees.

**Career opportunities for engineering technicians. Ferguson Publishing Company. 1970. 300p. $11.95; $8.95 to schools and libraries

Prepared for high school and two-year college students. For about twenty-five types of engineering technicians, there is included a description of work, the personal qualities required, educational requirements both in high school and after high school, job opportunities at entry level and advancement possibilities, working conditions, and immediate and future earning prospects.

Demand for engineers and engineering technicians. Engineers Joint Council. 1966. 96p. $4

A special section is included on employment data for engineering technicians.

**Engineering technician. American Society for Engineering Education. 1968. 21p. 50c

Topics include a description of the engineering technician, his role in society, opportunities, salaries, programs, qualifications, cost of education, and what to expect after graduation. Typical positions open to graduates and experienced technicians are described and sources of additional information are given.

Engineering technician. Careers. 1966. 2p. 20c

Career summary for desk-top file. Duties, qualifications, and outlook.

ENGINEERING TECHNICIAN—*Continued*

Engineering technicians. Brooking, Walter J., editor. Ferguson Publishing Company. 1969. 386p. $12; library edition $8.95

Information of interest to potential engineering technicians requiring only a two-year post high school course of study. Includes description of type of work, personal qualities, entry level jobs, advancement, working conditions, and benefits. A state-by-state list of schools offering engineering technician training is presented.

Engineering technicians. Science Research Associates. 1969. 4p. 45c

Occupational brief describing work, qualifications, training, earnings, and outlook. Selected references.

Engineering technologist. Guidance Centre. 1969. 4p. 35c postpaid

Definition, history and importance, nature of work, preparation, qualifications, outlook, remuneration, advancement, and how to get started.

Finding out about engineering technicians. Science Research Associates. 1967. 4p. 45c

Junior occupational brief describing work and opportunities.

Salaries of engineering technicians. Engineers Joint Council. 1966. 62p. $5

Salary curves and data tables from the original survey of engineering technician salaries, broken down by industry and technical institute graduation status.

Trends in engineering technician enrollments and graduates. Engineers Joint Council. 1967. 67p. $2

Analysis of trends and prospects in the education and supply of engineering technicians.

ENTOMOLOGIST 041.081

Entomologist. Careers. 1969. 2p. 20c

Career summary for desk-top file. Duties, qualifications, and outlook.

**Entomology—an exciting scientific career. Entomological Society of America. 1967. 20p. 25c. Single copy free

Description of nature of work, its service, employment prospects, training, and areas of research specialization. Illustrated.

EXECUTIVE HOUSEKEEPER. *See* Housekeeper and household workers

EXPLORER 102.

Exploring earth and space. Hyde, Margaret O. McGraw-Hill Book Company. 1970. 174p. $4.95; library edition $4.72

In this fifth edition chapters on pollution, earthquakes, weather satellites, and moon exploration are included. For grades 6 to 9.

The explorers: adventures in courage. Dolan, Edward, Jr. Reilly and Lee. 1970. 160p. $5.95

An account of the world's famous explorations and the men who undertook them.

Into the unknown: twentieth century explorers in action. Price, Bruce. Platt and Munk Company. 1968. 306p. $3.95

Interviews with ten explorers reveal the details of their lives and the history and results of their studies and activities.

Roald Amundsen: a saga of the Polar Seas. Kugelmass, J. Alvin. Julian Messner. 1955. 192p. Library binding $3.34

Biography of an Arctic explorer, giving experiences in exploring both the North Pole and the South Pole and navigating the Northwest Passage by sailing across the top of the world from ocean to ocean.

**Science explorer: Roy Chapman Andrews. Archer, Jules. Julian Messner. 1968. 192p. $3.50; library binding $3.34

Biography of the famous naturalist-explorer whose findings are on view in museums throughout the world.

EXPORT AND IMPORT WORKER 184.118

Careers in the export, import, and foreign operations field. Angel, Juvenal L. World Trade Academy Press. 1964. 28p. $1.25

Description of work, training, remuneration, and opportunities for several specialties in this field. Includes export manager, traffic manager, foreign market analyst, purchasing agent, and consular-export documents assistant.

Export and import workers. Science Research Associates. 1966. 4p. 45c

Occupational brief describing jobs in foreign trade, requirements, earnings, methods of entering, advantages, disadvantages, and future outlook.

How to get started in exporting—a $243 billion market. Crowell, Collier and Macmillan, Inc. 1970. 92p. $5.95; paper $1.95

Practical business information.

FACTORY WORKER 725.

**Assemblers. One section of *Occupational Outlook Handbook.*

Nature of work, where employed, employment outlook, earnings, and working conditions. Included with factory occupations not requiring specialized training.

Employment outlook for factory operatives. Bulletin No. 1650–95. Bureau of Labor Statistics, U.S. Department of Labor. Supt. of Documents. 1970. 16p. 15c

Reprint from the *Occupational Outlook Handbook.* Includes assemblers, electroplaters, inspectors, power truck operators, and production painters.

Finding out about factory assemblers. Science Research Associates. 1967. 4p. 45c

Junior occupational brief containing concise facts about the job.

FACTORY WORKER—*Continued*

Finding out about factory inspectors. Science Research Associates. 1967. 4p. 45c

Junior occupational brief describing work and opportunities.

FARM EQUIPMENT DEALER 624.381

Farm equipment dealers. Science Research Associates. 1969. 4p. 45c

Occupational brief describing nature of work, requirements, ways of getting started, earnings, advantages, disadvantages, and future outlook.

Finding out about farm equipment dealers. Science Research Associates. 1967. 4p. 45c

Junior occupational brief summarizing what the work requires and offers.

FARM MANAGER 429.131

Farm manager. Careers. 1967. 2p. 20c

Career summary for desk-top file. Duties, qualifications, and outlook.

Principles of farm management. Efferson, J. N. McGraw-Hill Book Company. 1953. 425p. $9.95

Presents the basic principles of farm management and the use of these principles in operation of a farm business.

Western stock ranching. Saunderson, Mont H. University of Minnesota Press. 1950. 262p. $5

Practical information on the economic problems of ranch management.

See also Animal husbandman; Cowpuncher

FARM SERVICE WORKER 421.887

Farm laborers. Science Research Associates. 1969. 4p. 45c

Occupational brief describing nature of work, opportunities, earnings, advantages, disadvantages, and future outlook.

Farm service jobs. One section of *Occupational Outlook Handbook.*

Brief description of work such as fruit spraying, well drilling, airplane dusting of crops, sheep shearing, fencing, and artificial breeding service.

FARMER, GENERAL 421.181

**Farmers. Careers. 1970. 8p. 35c

Career brief describing nature of work, types of farms, personal qualifications, advantages, disadvantages, earnings, and outlook.

The farmers of the future. Chronicle Guidance Publications. 1967. 4p. 35c

Reprinted article from *American Education* discusses farming and Future Farmers of America.

Finding out about farmers. Science Research Associates. 1967. 4p. 45c

Junior occupational brief containing concise facts about the job.

General farmer. Chronicle Guidance Publications. 1966. 4p. 35c
Occupational brief summarizing work performed, working conditions, hours, earnings, personal qualifications, training requirements, opportunities, and employment outlook.

General farmer. Guidance Centre. 1967. 4p. 35c postpaid
Nature of work, qualifications, getting started, earnings, advantages, disadvantages, and related occupations.

See also Agricultural specialist; Animal husbandman; Dairy farmer; Fruit grower; Poultryman

FASHION DESIGNER. ***See*** **Clothes designer**

FBI AGENT **375.168**

**Employment outlook for FBI special agents. Bulletin No. 1650–64. Bureau of Labor Statistics, U.S. Department of Labor. Supt. of Documents. 1970. 8p. 10c
Reprint from the *Occupational Outlook Handbook.*

FBI agents. Science Research Associates. 1968. 4p. 45c
Occupational brief describing work, training, opportunities, and outlook.

**FBI career opportunities. Federal Bureau of Investigation. 1968. 10p. Free
Statement of general qualifications, types of jobs, advantages, training, opportunities for advancement, and how to become an FBI agent. Positions include special agent, translator, fingerprint technician, radio maintenance technician, and laboratory positions. An insert provides salary rates.

* FBI: How the G-men use science as well as weapons to combat crime. Colby, Carroll. Coward-McCann, Inc. Revised edition 1970. 48p. Library edition $3.29
Photographs and brief text depict the work and training. This revised edition is updated to include information of FBI's new equipment and computer system. Written for grades 4 to 8.

F.B.I. special agent. Chronicle Guidance Publications. 1969. 4p. 35c
Occupational brief summarizing work performed, personal qualifications, training, earnings, where employed, methods of entry, and outlook.

FBI special agents. Careers. 1966. 8p. 35c
Career brief describing duties, working conditions, training, personal requirements, earnings, outlook, and ways of measuring one's interest and ability.

**FBI special agents. One section of *Occupational Outlook Handbook.*
Nature of work, where employed, training, other qualifications, advancement, employment outlook, earnings, and working conditions.

Finding out about FBI agents. Science Research Associates. 1967. 4p. 45c
Junior occupational brief describing work and opportunities.

FBI AGENT—*Continued*

Fingerprint classifier. Careers. 1968. 2p. 20c
Career summary for desk-top file. Duties, qualifications, and outlook.

How to become a fingerprint technician with the FBI. Federal Bureau of Investigation. 1967. 4p. Free
Brief statement of job qualifications, salary, and advancement.

Information concerning the position of special agent in the FBI. Federal Bureau of Investigation. 1968. 2p. Free
Brief statement of qualifications, training, salary, benefits, and addresses of field offices where applications may be sent.

**Our FBI, an inside story. Floherty, John J. Lippincott Company. 1951. 192p. $4.75
A book about the organization and activities of the Federal Bureau of Investigation. Includes history, training, and special work of the FBI men. Numerous reports of investigations made by special agents are included to show how they operate and what is required for the job. Illustrated.

Youth and the F.B.I. Floherty, John J. and McGrady, Mike. Lippincott Company. 1960. 160p. $4.95
A study of law enforcement and how the FBI deals with the problems of youth.

See also Detective; Police officer

FILE CLERK 206.388

File clerk. Chronicle Guidance Publications. 1967. 4p. 35c
Occupational brief describing duties, qualifications, training, hours, earnings, and future outlook.

File clerk. California State Department of Employment. 1966. 2p. Single copy free
Occupational guide describing work, requirements, training, and outlook.

File clerks. Science Research Associates. 1968. 4p. 45c
Occupational brief describing nature of work, training, qualifications, opportunities, and outlook.

Finding out about file clerks. Science Research Associates. 1967. 4p. 45c
Junior occupational brief containing concise facts about the job.

See also Clerical worker

FINANCE, INSURANCE, AND REAL ESTATE INDUSTRY WORKER 186.

Finance, insurance, and real estate. One section of *Occupational Outlook Handbook.*
Brief discussion of trends and outlook. Includes estimated employment in 1968, in this industry, of each of eight major occupational groups.

Occupations in banking. One section of *Occupational Outlook Handbook.*
Discussion of banks and their workers, places of employment, training, employment outlook, earnings, and working conditions.

FINANCIAL INSTITUTIONS INDUSTRY WORKER 212.368

Employment opportunities for college graduates for the position of financial analyst. U.S. Securities and Exchange Commission. 1962. 2p. Free
Information about the location of positions, duties to be performed, salaries, career opportunities, fringe benefits, training, recruitment policy, and civil service examination.

The new look in banking: careers for young women in finance. Paradis, Adrian. David McKay Company. 1961. 224p. $3.50
Description of enticing and varied career opportunities open to women in finance. Suggested readings.

**Opportunities in the securities business. Shulsky, Sam. Vocational Guidance Manuals. 1963. 128p. $1.95 paper; $3.75 library edition
Discussions of finance yesterday and today, requirements for entering the field, and how to get started. Description of brokerage, banking, investment banking, investment counseling, and related fields. Lists accredited colleges and universities giving degrees in business administration.

Opportunity ahead. Beneficial Management Corporation. No date. 16p. Free
Recruiting booklet describing opportunities in the field of finance. Includes a career quiz.

The small-loan business—saint or sinner? Beneficial Management Corporation. No date. 8p. Free
Includes a description of the duties and outlook.

Your future: careers in consumer finance. National Consumer Finance Association. Revised 1968. 24p. Free
Nature of work, qualifications, training, advantages, personal satisfactions, and potential rewards. Illustrated.

See also Bank worker; Securities salesman

FINGERPRINT EXAMINER 375.383

Fingerprint classifier. Careers. 1968. 2p. 35c
Career brief describing work and opportunities.

Fingerprint examiner. California State Department of Employment. 1965. 3p. Single copy free
Occupational guide describing work, requirements, training, and outlook.

How to become a fingerprint technician with the FBI. Federal Bureau of Investigation. 1967. 4p. Free
Description of the work and training.

FIRE FIGHTER 373.884

Careers in fire protection engineering. Society of Fire Protection Engineers. 1961. 6p. Free

Description on duties, opportunities, and training.

**Employment outlook for firefighters. Bulletin No. 1650–65. Bureau of Labor Statistics, U.S. Department of Labor. Supt. of Documents. 1970. 8p. 10c

Reprint from the *Occupational Outlook Handbook.*

Finding out about fire protection engineers. Science Research Associates. 1967. 4p. 45c

Junior occupational brief summarizing what the work requires and offers.

Finding out about firemen. Science Research Associates. 1967. 4p. 45c

Junior occupational brief containing concise facts about the job.

Fire fighter. Careers. 1969. 2p. 20c

Career summary for desk-top file. Duties, qualifications, and outlook.

Fire fighter. Guidance Centre. 1968. 4p. 35c postpaid

Nature of work, qualifications, preparation, working conditions, how to get started, earnings, advantages, and disadvantages.

Fire fighters. Science Research Associates. 1970. 4p. 45c

Occupational brief describing nature of work, training, qualifications, opportunities, advantages, disadvantages, and future outlook.

Fire fighters. One section of *Occupational Outlook Handbook.*

Nature of work, places of employment, training, qualifications, employment outlook, earnings, and working conditions.

Fire patrolman. Chronicle Guidance Publications. 1967. 4p. 35c

Reprinted article from *Industrial Bulletin* discusses the work performed by fire patrolmen.

Fire protection engineers. Science Research Associates. 1968. 4p. 45c

Occupational brief describing nature of work, requirements, training, places of employment, earnings, and future outlook.

Fireman. Chronicle Guidance Publications. 1968. 4p. 35c

Occupational brief summarizing work performed, working conditions, hours, earnings, personal qualifications, training requirements and opportunities, and employment outlook.

Fireman (city and suburban). California State Department of Employment. 1964. 5p. Single copy free

Occupational guide describing work, requirements, training, and outlook.

**Firemen. One section of *Occupational Outlook Handbook.*

Nature of work, where employed, training, other qualifications, advancement, employment outlook, earnings, and working conditions.

Firemen, stationary boiler. Michigan Employment Security Commission. 1960. 2p. Single copy free

Job brief summarizing occupational data for use in Michigan.

Forest fire fighters and what they do. Harrison, C. W. Franklin Watts, Inc. 1962. 143p. $3.95

An account of men who not only battle fire but also the conditions that encourage fire. For grades 7 to 11.

Forest fire! Judge, Frances. Alfred A. Knopf, Inc. 1962. 152p. $3.00

History of the fighting of forest fires in America.

Fred fireman. Kaufman, Joe. Golden Press. 1968. 24p. 69c

One of the series called "busy people" books. A tall picture book, sixteen inches tall, prepared for nursery school and kindergarten children. Contains vivid color illustrations of the uniforms, equipment, and some work-a-day activities, explained in simple caption texts.

Jeff White: forest fire fighter. Dietz, Lew. Little, Brown and Company. 1954. 210p. $3.95

Career fiction. Shows the work of the air forest patrol.

The smoke eaters. Archibald, Joseph. David McKay Company. 1965. 224p. $3.95

Career fiction. Includes information about the training of a fireman and the work of fire fighting and prevention. For grades 7 to 9.

**Smokejumpers and fire divers; firefighters of forests and harbors. Shannon, Terry and Payzant, Charles. Golden Gate Junior Books. 1969. 77p. $4.50; library edition $4.33

Photographs accompanied by brief explanatory text describe the function, responsibilities, and experiences of two special types of fire fighters. The first part of the book is devoted to paratroop units of the U.S. Forest Service who fight fires in inaccessible forest areas. The second part deals with scuba diving units who aid boat and ground firemen in fighting fires under wharves and piers. For grades 5 to 8.

A valiant career: make your career in the fire service. International Association of Fire Chiefs. 1963. 4p. Free

Description of requirements and rewards.

See also Forest ranger; Police officer

FIREARMS INDUSTRY WORKER 736.131

Firearms industry. Chronicle Guidance Publications. 1969. 4p. 35c

Occupational brief summarizing making of a firearm, work performed, opportunities, working conditions, earnings, and educational training requirements.

FIREMAN (BOILER). *See* Stationary fireman

FIREMAN (FIRE DEPARTMENT). *See* Fire fighter

FIREMAN, LOCOMOTIVE (RAILROAD) 910.383

**Locomotive fireman (helpers). One section of *Occupational Outlook Handbook.*

Nature of work, training, other qualifications, advancement, employment outlook, earnings, and working conditions.

FISH AND GAME WARDEN 379.168

Careers in wildlife conservation and management. Wildlife Management Institute. 1968. 6p. Free

Brief information on the work of the game warden.

Jeff White: young guide. Dietz, Lew. Little, Brown and Company. 1951. 213p. $3.75

Career fiction. Story of Maine game wardens during the hunting season, with accidents, lost hunters, tracking of deer, and a plea for conservation of wild life.

Jeff White, young trapper. Dietz, Lew. Little, Brown and Company. 1951. 191p. $3.75

Career fiction. This story is a sequel to *Jeff White, Young Woodsman* and contains information for a boy who is interested in becoming a trapper or game warden.

A nose for trouble. Kjelgaard, Jim. Holiday House. 1949. 250p. $3.95

Career fiction. An assistant game warden helps locate men who are violating game laws. For sixth or seventh grade boys.

Wilderness warden. James, Edward C. David McKay Company. 1955. 214p. $3.89

Career fiction. Conservation story of a young warden who endeavors to stop the illegal slaughter of animals in the Maine wilderness. For younger boys.

A wildlife conservation career for you. The Wildlife Society. 1968. 12p. 6c

Includes description of the protective work of the game warden.

See also Wildlife specialist

FISH CULTURIST 041.168

**Fisheries as a profession: a career guide for the field of fisheries science. American Fisheries Society. 1969 10p. Single copy free

Description of the work of fishery biologists, the education and training needed to become a fishery manager or fishery researcher, salaries and benefits, avenues of employment, and types of agencies that hire fishery specialists.

**Fisheries scientist (fish culturist). Chronicle Guidance Publications. 1968. 4p. 35c

Occupational brief summarizing work performed, where employed, working conditions, qualifications, training, earnings, and outlook.

Fishery science and related courses in North American colleges and universities. Sport Fishing Institute. 1969. 32p. 25c. Single copy free
A directory frequently revised.

The sea farmers. Waters, John F. Hastings House. 1970. 120p. $4.35
The problems, techniques, and importance of ocean farming are explored in this book which gives information about the areas, stages of growth in the farmed sea life, protection from predators, feeding, and methods of planting and harvesting. Among the farms discussed are those producing fish, lobster, shrimp, oysters, and clams.

FISHERMAN 43

Commercial fisherman. Careers. 1966. 2p. 20c
Career summary for desk-top file. Duties, qualifications, and outlook.

Finding out about fishermen. Science Research Associates. 1967. 4p. 45c
Junior occupational brief describing work and opportunities.

Fisherman. Chronicle Guidance Publications. 1967. 4p 35c
Occupational brief summarizing general information, work performed, personal qualifications, training, earnings, and outlook.

Fisherman. Guidance Centre. 1967. 4p. 35c postpaid
Definition, nature of work, qualifications, preparation, earnings, advancement opportunities, how to get started, advantages, disadvantages, and related occupations.

**Fishermen. Science Research Associates. 1969. 4p. 45c
Occupational brief describing nature of work, qualifications, opportunities, advantages, disadvantages, and future outlook.

FLIGHT ENGINEER 621.281

Finding out about flight engineers. Science Research Associates. 1967. 4p. 45c
Junior occupational brief summarizing what the work requires and offers.

**Flight engineer (second officer). Chronicle Guidance Publications. 1969. 4p. 35c
Occupational brief summarizing work performed, working conditions, personal requirements, certificate and education requirements, training requirements, where employed, hours and earnings, opportunities for advancement, employment outlook, company benefits, high school preparation, and post high school preparation.

Flight engineers. Science Research Associates. 1966. 4p. 45c
Occupational brief describing work, qualifications, working conditions, earnings, how to get started, and outlook. Selected references.

**Flight engineers. One section of *Occupational Outlook Handbook.*
Nature of work, qualifications, training, advancement, employment outlook, earnings, and working conditions.

FLIGHT ENGINEER—*Continued*

Flight officer. Careers. 1966. 8p. 35c
Career brief describing duties, working conditions, personal requirements, training, earnings, outlook, and ways of measuring one's interest and ability.

See also Aircraft mechanic

FLIGHT STEWARDESS. *See* Airplane stewardess

FLOOR COVERING INSTALLER 864.781

Employment outlook for floor covering installers. Bulletin No. 1650–75. Bureau of Labor Statistics, U.S. Department of Labor. Supt. of Documents. 1970. 12p. 15c
Reprint from the *Occupational Outlook Handbook.*

Floor covering installer. California State Department of Employment. 1968. 4p. Single copy free
Occupational guide describing work, requirements, training, and outlook.

Floor covering installers. Science Research Associates. 1969. 4p. 45c
Occupational brief describing work, training, qualifications, opportunities, and outlook.

**Floor covering installers. One section of *Occupational Outlook Handbook.*
Nature of work, where employed, training, other qualifications, advancement, employment outlook, earnings, and working conditions.

Floor layers and installers. Chronicle Guidance Publications. 1968. 4p. 35c
Occupational brief summarizing definition, history, work performed, working conditions, personal requirements, where employed, education and training requirements, licensure or registration, hours and earnings, opportunities for advancement, employment outlook, advantages, and disadvantages.

Floor mechanic, resilient. Careers. 1966. 2p. 20c
Career summary for desk-top file. Duties, qualifications, and outlook.

Your opportunity as a professional flooring craftsman. Armstrong Cork Company. 1968. 16p. Free
Points out the need for resilient floor mechanics, ways of learning the trade, advantages, and outlook.

FLORAL DESIGNER 142.081

Finding out about florists. Science Research Associates. 1967. 4p. 45c
Junior occupational brief containing concise facts about the job.

**Floral designer. Careers. 1970. 8p. 35c
Career brief describing duties, working conditions, training, personal qualifications, earnings, outlook, and ways of measuring one's interest and ability.

Floral designer. California State Department of Employment. 1968. 3p. Single copy free

Occupational guide describing work, requirements, training, and outlook.

Floral designer. Chronicle Guidance Publications. 1967. 4p. 35c

Occupational brief describing work performed, qualifications, training, hours, and opportunities. Includes list of ten schools of floral design.

Floral designing as a career. Rittners School. 1968. 5p. Free

Description of work, training, opportunities, and industry expansion.

Florist. Guidance Centre. 1961. 4p. 35c postpaid

Nature of work, qualifications, preparation, advancement, earnings, how to get started, and related occupations.

**Florists. Science Research Associates. 1966. 4p. 45c

Occupational brief describing the work of the grower, the wholesale florist, and the retail florist. Also includes requirements, training, getting started, earnings, advantages, disadvantages, and future outlook.

**Opportunities for you in the florist industry. Society of American Florists. 1969. 13p. 10c. Single copy free

Information concerning type of work, training, and future outlook for the grower, the wholesaler, the retailer, and teacher.

Starting and managing a retail flower shop. Small Business Administration. Supt. of Documents. 1970. 69p. 55c

Outlines the opportunities and problems that await a prospective owner-manager and suggests some methods of meeting them. Provides basic information about management and keeping up with developments in the field.

See also Horticulturist

FLORIST. *See* Floral designer; Horticulturist

FOOD CLERK 290.887

Finding out about grocery checkers. Science Research Associates. 1967. 4p. 45c

Junior occupational brief describing work and opportunities.

Finding out about produce clerks. Science Research Associates. 1967. 4p. 45c

Junior occupational brief summarizing what the work requires and offers.

Food clerk. California State Department of Employment. 1966. 3p. Single copy free

Occupational guide describing work, requirements, training, and outlook.

Food store checkers. Science Research Associates. 1967. 4p. 45c

Occupational brief describing nature of work, requirements, working conditions, training, advancement, earnings, and future outlook.

FOOD CLERK—*Continued*

Food store workers. Science Research Associates. 1966. 4p. 45c

Occupational brief describing nature of work, requirements, earnings, and future outlook.

Grocery checker. California Department of Employment. 1964. 4p. Free

Description of work, duties, employment prospects, earnings, working conditions, and how to find a job.

Grocery product salesman. California State Department of Employment. 1964. 6p. Single copy free

Occupational guide describing work, requirements, training, and outlook.

**Grocery products salesman. Careers. 1968. 2p. 20c

Career summary for desk-top file. Describes duties, working conditions, qualifications, training, working conditions, and outlook.

See also Retail manager

FOOD AND DRUG INSPECTOR 168.287

**Food and drug inspector. Careers. 1966. 2p. 20c

Career summary for desk-top file. Duties, qualifications, and outlook.

Food and drug protective services. Pages 117-122 of *Health Careers Guidebook.*

Information about qualifications, training, and opportunities for the food technologist and the Government food and drug inspector and analyst.

Fruitcake and arsenic. Hemphill, Josephine. Little, Brown and Company. 1962. 192p. $4.75

Story of the episodes in the work of members of the Food and Drug Administration. Describes the nature of their work and the importance of this agency.

FOOD FREEZING AND CANNING WORKER 529.

Canning and preserving industry. Chronicle Guidance Publications. 1968. 4p. 35c

Occupational brief summarizing work performed, jobs for unskilled and semiskilled labor, jobs for skilled and technical workers, opportunities, earnings, and working conditions.

Finding out about bottling plant workers. Science Research Associates. 1967. 4p. 45c

Junior occupational brief summarizing what the work requires and offers.

Finding out about frozen food processors. Science Research Associates. 1967. 4p. 45c

Junior occupational brief summarizing what the work requires and offers.

Food freezing and canning workers. Science Research Associates. 1969. 4p. 45c

Occupational brief describing nature of work, requirements, getting started, earnings, advantages, disadvantages, and future outlook.

**The food processing industry. One chapter in Volume I of the *Encyclopedia of Careers and Vocational Guidance.*
The growth of the industry, opportunities, and future outlook.

Maintenance mechanic (food processing). California State Department of Employment. 1964. 5p. Single copy free
Occupational guide describing work, requirements, training, and outlook.

See also Food preparation industry worker

FOOD PREPARATION INDUSTRY WORKER 319.138

Careers for youth in the food service industry. National Restaurant Association. 1969. 12p. Single copy free
Description of the industry and the nature of the available jobs, location of the work, duties, how to get started, and job satisfactions.

**Opportunities in food preparation and service. Rosenthal, Jacob and Folsom, Le Roi A. Vocational Guidance Manuals. 1969. 144p. $1.95 paper; library edition $3.75
Discussion of the nature of work, types of jobs available, qualifications, preparation, opportunities, rewards, and employment outlook.

Soft drink industry workers. Science Research Associates. 1966. 4p. 45c
Occupational brief describing nature of work, opportunities, advantages, disadvantages, and future outlook.

FOOD TECHNOLOGIST 041.081

* Careers in food services administration. Rochester Institute of Technology. 1961. 24p. Free
This illustrated bulletin gives information about the various branches of the vocation, duties performed by persons employed, advantages, disadvantages, and requirements for employment and for promotions.

Finding out about food technologists. Science Research Associates. 1967. 4p. 45c
Junior occupational brief containing brief facts about the job.

Food technologist. Chronicle Guidance Publications. 1968. 4p. 35c
Occupational brief summarizing definition, history, work performed, working conditions, educational requirements, personal requirements, methods of entry, earnings and hours, and employment outlook.

**Food technologists. Science Research Associates. 1969. 4p. 45c
Occupational brief describing nature of work, requirements, training, getting started and advancing, earnings, advantages, disadvantages, and future outlook.

**Your future in food technology. Brissey, George. Richards Rosen Press. 1966. 159p. $4; library edition $3.78
Discussion of requirements, training, and outlook for the application of food technology in the modern world.

FOOTBALL PLAYER. *See* **Athlete**

FOREIGN LANGUAGE WORKER. *See* **Linguist**

FOREIGN SERVICE WORKER 188.118

**A career in the foreign service of the United States. U.S. Department of State. Supt. of Documents. 1969. 24p. 50c

Includes qualifications for employment, opportunities, benefits, training, regulations, drawbacks, and rewards. Also gives information concerning the written, oral, and physical examinations.

**Careers and opportunities in international service. Krosney, Herbert and Krosney, Mary. Dutton and Company. 1965. 256p. $4.50

Prepared for those who would like to combine foreign travel and overseas living with unusual careers in international work. Gives accounts of opportunities with the U.S. Foreign Service, U.S. Information Service, Agency for International Development, the Peace Corps, United Nations, foreign missions, international business, and overseas airlines. Illustrated.

Careers in foreign service. Chronicle Guidance Publications. 1967. 4p. 35c

Reprinted article from *Occupational Outlook Quarterly* discusses the American image, assignments, preparation, salaries, and working conditions.

Finding out about foreign correspondents. Science Research Associates. 1967. 4p. 45c

Junior occupational brief summarizing what the work requires and offers.

Finding out about foreign service clerical workers. Science Research Associates. 1967. 4p. 45c

Junior occupational brief containing concise facts about the job.

Finding out about foreign service officers. Science Research Associates. 1967. 4p. 45c

Junior occupational brief describing work and opportunities.

Foreign service. Chronicle Guidance Publications. 1969. 4p. 35c

Occupational brief summarizing work performed, training, qualifications, salaries, and outlook.

Foreign service careers. Careers. 1970. 12p. 35c

Career brief describing the functions of the service, training, personal qualifications, advantages, disadvantages, salaries, and outlook. Additional readings.

The foreign service of the United States. Blancké, W. Wendell. Praeger Library of U.S. Government Departments and Agencies. 1969. 286p. $7.95

A career diplomat with twenty-eight years of experience describes the organization of the department, its activities, admission requirements, training, and promotion system. Includes a list of foreign service posts.

Foreign service secretary. Careers. 1970. 8p. 35c

Career brief describing duties, working conditions, personal qualifications, training, places of employment, earnings, outlook, and ways of measuring one's interest and ability. Additional readings.

Foreign service workers. Science Research Associates. 1968. 4p. 45c

Occupational brief describing the nature of the work of the career foreign service officer and the foreign service staff corps, advantages, disadvantages, and future outlook.

**Opportunities in foreign service. Harrigan, Lucille. Vocational Guidance Manuals. 1963. 126p. $1.95 paper; library edition $3.75

Detailed information on the requirements and methods of applying for openings in many areas of foreign service. Includes types of assignments, training, and salaries.

Sample questions from the foreign service officer examination. U.S. Department of State. Publication 7640. 1967. 88p. Free

Examples from each general type of question which has been asked in the last few years. Questions from general examinations and special examinations in history, government, and economics.

**Your career in foreign service. Neal, Harry Edward. Julian Messner. 1965. 192p. $3.95; library binding $3.64

This describes career opportunities in the Foreign Service, U.S. Information Agency, Central Intelligence Agency, Panama Canal Company, Foreign Agricultural Service, Agency for International Development, and the Peace Corps. Much of the information was obtained by interviews which are extensively quoted to describe positions ranging from diplomatic to clerical.

**Your future in international service. Calvert, Robert, Jr. Richards Rosen Press. 1969. 160p. $4; library edition $3.78

Description of opportunities for service abroad in international organizations, volunteer and government, religious and secular. Lists, addresses, and descriptions are given.

**Your future in the foreign service. Delaney, Robert. Richards Rosen Press. Revised 1969. 161p. $4; library edition $3.78

Information and advice concerning nature of work, basic trainings, salaries, other rewards, who can apply, requirements, and a listing of foreign service posts. Also included are examples from the oral and written examination.

FOREIGN TRADE WORKER. *See* Export and import worker

FOREMAN 559.132 and 869.131

**Employment outlook for foremen. Bulletin No. 1650–96. Bureau of Labor Statistics, U.S. Department of Labor. Supt. of Documents. 1970. 8p. 10c

Reprint from the *Occupational Outlook Handbook*.

Foremen. Science Research Associates. 1967. 4p. 45c

Occupational brief describing work, training, qualifications, opportunities, and outlook.

FOREMAN—*Continued*

Foremen. One section of *Occupational Outlook Handbook.*

Nature of the work of foremen who supervise and coordinate the activities of highly skilled, semiskilled, and unskilled blue-collar workers. Includes places of employment, earnings, outlook, and working conditions.

FOREST PRODUCTS INDUSTRIES WORKER 406.887

The demand and price situation for forest products. Government Printing Office. Supt. of Documents. 1970. 79p. 75c

A report covering the year 1969-70.

* Opportunities unlimited. National Forest Products Association. 1969. 18p. Free

Discussion of the major career areas of sales, research, and development. Includes a list of colleges having programs relating to careers in forest products.

FOREST RANGER 040.081

Forest firefighter. California State Department of Employment. 1964. 4p. Single copy free

Occupational guide describing work, requirements, training, and outlook.

Forest ranger. Floherty, John J. Lippincott Company. 1956. 143p. $4.50

Includes the rigorous training, varied duties, and hazardous adventures of the men who guard our timber from fire, disease, and crime. Illustrated.

**The forest rangers. Atwater, Montgomery. Macrae Smith Company. 1969. 190p. $4.95

Included are many episodes of fire fighting, dangerous rescue missions, and developments in forestry techniques. Some information is given about avalanche control and plant and animal conservation in national forests. For grades 7 to 10. Illustrated.

In your service—the work of Uncle Sam's forest rangers. U.S. Department of Agriculture. Agriculture Information Bulletin 136. Supt. of Documents. 1965. 24p. 20c

Illustrated folder describing the various kinds of work.

Range managers. One section of *Occupational Outlook Handbook.*

Nature of work, places of employment, qualifications, training, advancement, outlook, earnings, and working conditions.

Smoke over Sikanaska—my life as a forest ranger. Gowland, J. S. Ives Washburn, Inc. 1957. 224p. $3.50

Biographical account of the adventures of a forest ranger in the Canadian Rockies, where he battled fire, the elements, fur poachers, and many other hazards in the course of his patrol.

Tall timber; the work, machines and men of the United States Forest Service. Colby, Carroll B. Coward-McCann, Inc. 1955. 48p. $2.97; library binding $2.52 net

Includes description of typical events in the day of a forest ranger. Illustrated. Written for grades 4 to 8.

What does a forest ranger do? Hyde, Wayne. Dodd, Mead and Company. 1964. 64p. Library binding $2.99

Many photographs and simple text describe the work of men who guard and improve our national forests and parks. For grades 3 to 7.

See also Fire fighter; Park ranger

FORESTER 040.081

**Careers in forestry. U.S. Department of Agriculture. Miscellaneous Publication 249. Supt. of Documents. 1967. 22p. 20c

Character of forestry work; qualifications; opportunities in the Federal Government, states, community forests, private forestry, trade and conservation associations, and teaching. Also discussion of future outlook and opportunities for women.

Code of ethics. Society of American Foresters. 1951. 1p. Free

Included in a leaflet describing the purposes of the society.

Finding out about foresters. Science Research Associates. 1967. 4p. 45c

Junior occupational brief summarizing what the work requires and offers.

Forester. California State Department of Employment. 1966. 7p. Single copy free

Occupational guide describing work, requirements, training, and outlook.

**Forester. Careers. 1969. 8p. 35c

Career brief describing duties, working conditions, personal qualifications, places of employment, earnings, and outlook. List of accredited schools of forestry.

Forester. Chronicle Guidance Publications. 1967. 4p. 35c

Occupational brief summarizing work performed, working conditions, hours, earnings, personal qualifications, training requirements and opportunities, and employment outlook.

Forester. Guidance Centre. 1968. 4p. 35c postpaid

History and importance, nature of work, qualifications, preparation, advancement, outlook, remuneration, advantages, disadvantages, how to get started, and related occupations.

Forester. Michigan Employment Security Commission. 1960. 2p. Single copy free

Job brief summarizing occupational data for use in Michigan.

Foresters. Science Research Associates. 1967. 4p. 45c

Occupational brief describing nature of work, training, qualifications, opportunities, advantages, disadvantages, and future outlook.

FORESTER—*Continued*

**Foresters. One section of *Occupational Outlook Handbook.*

Nature of work, where employed, training and other qualifications, employment outlook, earnings, and working conditions.

Foresters and what they do. Perry, John. Franklin Watts, Inc. 1963. 192p. $3.95

Describes duties of the forestry service and the education and daily life of foresters. A brief history and career opportunities are included. For grades 7 to 11.

Forestry . . . a growth career. New York University College of Forestry. No date. 25p. Free

Describes work in forest management, research, utilization, and recreation.

Forestry—a growth career. State University of New York College of Forestry. 1968. 24p. Free

Describes the many professional fields of forestry, including resources management, forest biology, forest engineering, paper science, forest chemistry, wood products engineering, and landscape architecture.

Forestry aide. Chronicle Guidance Publications. 1968. 4p. 35c

Occupational brief summarizing work performed, working conditions, hours, earnings, where employed, personal requirements, education requirements, and methods of entry.

Forestry aids. One section of *Occupational Outlook Handbook.*

Nature of work, places of employment, training, advancement, outlook, earnings, and working conditions.

**Forestry as a profession. Society of American Foresters. 1965. 16p. 25c

Nature of forestry, types of employment, salaries, requirements, and training. List of colleges and universities offering instruction in forestry.

Forestry at Michigan State University. Michigan State University, Department of Forestry. 1969. 4p. Free

Recruiting bulletin describing entrance requirements, curricula, and employment opportunities.

Forestry: earned degrees, by level, sex, and institution. One section of *Earned Degrees Conferred.*

List of forty-six schools and the number of bachelor's, master's, and doctor's degrees conferred by each.

Forestry education in America today and tomorrow. Dana, S. T. and Johnson, E. W. Society of American Foresters. 1963. 402p. $5

Includes discussion of the scope of forestry, related fields, and current programs of professional training.

Forestry schools in the United States. U.S. Department of Agriculture. Supt. of Documents. 1970. 24p. 15c

Names and locations of schools offering training in forestry.

Gifford Pinchot: private and public forester. University of Illinois Press. 1970. 167p. $6.95

Biography of the man who made Pennsylvania's forest administration a model.

**A job with the Forest Service: a guide to nonprofessional employment. U.S. Department of Agriculture. Miscellaneous Publication 843. Supt. of Documents. 1970. 18p. 15c

Includes information about employment as forestry technician, forestry aid, forest and range fire control technician, engineering technician, and other skilled work.

* Opportunities in a forestry career. Demmon, E. L. Vocational Guidance Manuals. 1967. 128p. $1.95 paper; $3.75 library edition

History and importance of forestry developments, future outlook, fields of forestry work, requirements for entering, education, training, opportunities, and advancement. List of accredited schools of forestry.

School of Forestry bulletin. University of Missouri. 1969. 48p. Free

Example of a recruiting bulletin which describes fields of employment, undergraduate and graduate training, where work may be found, and examples of some typical jobs.

Schools of forestry accredited by the Society of American Foresters. The Society. 1968. 1p. Free

A directory of accredited schools of forestry.

So you want to be a forester? American Forestry Association. 1967. 20p. 25c

Description of work, qualifications, and training.

So you want to be a forester? State University of New York College of Forestry. 1968. 24p. Free

Describes types of work in forest management, research, and related conservation fields. Presents a list of thirty accredited and seventeen nonaccredited schools of forestry.

**Your future in forestry. Hanaburgh, David. Richards Rosen Press. Revised 1969. 160p. $4; library edition $3.78

Describes areas of specialization, places of employment, preparation, opportunities, advancement, satisfactions, and drawbacks. List of schools of forestry.

FORESTRY TECHNICIAN 441.384

Finding out about forestry technicians. Science Research Associates. 1967. 4p. 45c

Junior occupational brief containing concise facts about the job.

**Forest technician. Careers. 1968. 2p. 20c

Career summary for desk-top file. Duties, qualifications, and outlook.

FORESTRY TECHNICIAN—*Continued*

Forest technician training programs in the United States. Chronicle Guidance Publications. 1968. 4p. 35c

Reprinted article from *Journal of Forestry* discusses definition and role of forest technician, training programs, and list of schools offering training programs for forest technicians.

Forest technicians. Science Research Associates. 1969. 4p. 45c

Occupational brief describing nature of work, training, qualifications, opportunities, and outlook.

Forestry technician (Ontario). Guidance Centre. 1968. 4p. 35c postpaid

History and importance, nature of work, qualifications, preparation, advancement, outlook, remuneration, advantages, disadvantages, how to get started, and related occupations.

FORGE SHOP WORKER 612.

**The forging industry. One chapter in Volume I of the *Encyclopedia of Careers and Vocational Guidance.*

The scope of the industry, kinds of work, opportunities, and future outlook.

Forge shop occupations. California State Department of Employment. 1968. 3p. Single copy free

Occupational guide describing work, requirements, training, and outlook.

Forge shop occupations. Careers. 1967. 8p. 35c

Career brief describing work, training, working conditions, earnings, unionization, and outlook.

Forge shop occupations. Chronicle Guidance Publications. 1969. 4p. 35c

Occupational brief summarizing nature of work, various forging occupations, working conditions, hours and earnings, personal qualifications, where employed, education and training, and outlook.

FOUNDRY WORKER 518.

Coremakers. Careers. 1969. 8p. 35c

Career brief describing duties, working conditions, personal qualifications, training, earnings, and outlook.

Exploring your future in manufacturing (wage and shop jobs). Sextant Systems, Inc. 1969. 96p. $6.50

One page is devoted to fifteen foundry jobs, summarizing duties, requirements for entering, promotional outlook, and pay and skill level. Included are annealer, blacksmith, bench molder, core assembler, coremaker, crucible furnace melter, cupola charger, cupola operator, electric furnace melter, furnace tender, hammerman, machine molder, press operator trimmer, straightening press operator, and wheelabrator operator.

Finding out about foundry workers. Science Research Associates. 1967. 4p. 45c

Junior occupational brief containing simplified information about requirements, training, nature of work, earnings, and opportunities.

**The foundry industry. One chapter in Volume I of the *Encyclopedia of Careers and Vocational Guidance.*

History of the industry, kinds of work, opportunities, and future outlook.

Foundry occupations. Careers. 1970. 8p. 35c

Career brief describing work, training, working conditions, unionization, and ways of measuring your interest and ability.

Foundry occupations. Chronicle Guidance Publications. 1966. 8p. 50c

Occupational brief summarizing characteristics of foundries, working conditions, various jobs performed, training opportunities, earnings, and outlook.

The foundry of the future. Chronicle Guidance Publications. 1966. 4p. 35c

Reprinted article from *Foundry* discusses opinions on what a typical foundry might be like in the future.

Foundry workers. Science Research Associates. 1966. 4p. 45c

Occupational brief describing nature of work, requirements, how to enter foundry work, earnings, advantages, disadvantages, and future outlook. Includes work of the patternmaker, molder, coremaker, melter, and inspector.

Molder and coremaker (foundry). California State Department of Employment. 1968. 3p. Single copy free

Occupational guide summarizing duties, working conditions, employment prospects, earnings, training, requirements for entry, and suggestions for locating a job.

FOUR-H CLUB AGENT. *See* Group worker

FREE-LANCE WRITER. *See* Writer

FROZEN FOODS INDUSTRY WORKER. *See* Food freezing and canning worker

FRUIT GROWER 404.181

Blueberry mountain. Meader, Stephen W. Harcourt, Brace and World. 1941. 309p. $3.75

Career fiction. Story of two boys who decided to start a blueberry farm in the mountains of Pennsylvania. For younger readers.

Fruit farmer. Careers. 1968. 2p. 20c

Career summary for desk-up file. Duties, qualifications, and outlook.

Fruit grower. Guidance Centre. 1970. 4p. 35c postpaid

Definition, working conditions, qualifications necessary for entry and success, earnings, how to get started, and related occupations.

**Fruit growers. Science Research Associates. 1969. 4p. 45c

Occupational brief describing nature of work, preparation, opportunities, and future outlook.

FUND RAISER 293.358

Finding out about fund raisers. Science Research Associates. 1967. 4p. 45c

Junior occupational brief containing concise facts about the job.

* Fund raisers. Science Research Associates. 1969. 4p. 45c

Occupational brief describing nature of work, training, qualifications, opportunities, and outlook.

**Joint financing director (fund raiser). Chronicle Guidance Publications. 1969. 4p. 35c

Occupational brief summarizing work performed, where employed, requirements, earnings, methods of entry, advantages, disadvantages, and outlook.

FUNERAL DIRECTOR AND EMBALMER 187.168 and 388.381

Annual bulletins. Cincinnati College of Mortuary Science. 1969. 40p. Free

Informational publications including admission requirements, training, qualifications, opportunities, training programs, and the interne requirements of all fifty states.

Careers in memorial counseling. B'nai B'rith Vocational Service. 1969. 8p. 35c

Description of work, duties, requirements, opportunities, responsibilities, and rewards in this field.

Embalmer (mortician). California State Department of Employment. 1963. 5p. Single copy free

Occupational guide describing work, requirements, training, and outlook.

Finding out about funeral directors. Science Research Associates. 1967. 4p. 45c

Junior occupational brief describing work and opportunities.

Funeral director. Careers. 1968. 2p. 20c

Career summary for desk-top file. Duties, qualifications, and outlook.

Funeral director. Chronicle Guidance Publications. 1968. 4p. 35c

Occupational brief containing working conditions, personal qualifications, determination of aptitudes and interests, training requirements, training opportunities, outlook, and methods of entry.

Funeral director and embalmer. Guidance Centre. 1969. 4p. 35c postpaid

Nature of work, qualifications, preparation, outlook, remuneration, advantages, disadvantages, how to get started, and related occupations.

Funeral directors and embalmers. Science Research Associates. 1969. 4p. 45c

Occupational brief describing nature of work, personal qualifications, training, getting started and advancing, earnings, opportunities, advantages, disadvantages, and future outlook.

**Funeral service, a heritage, a challenge, a future. National Funeral Directors Association. Revised 1967. 20p. 35c

Historical background, functions of funeral service, typical duties of the embalmer-funeral director, opportunities, qualifications, cost of education, regulations for license, and list of twenty-one accredited schools and colleges of embalming and mortuary science.

**Funeral services as a career. Belleau, Wilfrid E. Park Publishing House. 1968. 26p. $1

History and importance of occupation, nature of work, training, entering the field, conditions of work, income, opportunities, advantages, disadvantages, and list of the twenty approved schools for training. Also included is a table giving licensing rules and regulations for funeral directors and embalmers in each of the states.

National scholarships for funeral service. American Board of Funeral Service Education, Committee on Scholarships. 1969. 6p. Free

Explanation of qualifications and how to apply for national scholarships.

**The vocation of funeral service. National Selected Morticians. 1968. 13p. Free

Discussion of historical background, responsibilities, remuneration, license requirements, and selection of a training school. Includes list of accredited mortuary schools.

FUR FARMER 419.181

Finding out about fur farmers. Science Research Associates. 1967. 4p. 45c

Junior occupational brief summarizing what the work requires and offers.

Fur farmers. Science Research Associates. 1970. 4p. 45c

Occupational brief describing nature of work, training, opportunities, advantages, disadvantages, and future outlook.

See also Animal husbandman

FUR INDUSTRY WORKER 783.

Finding out about furriers. Science Research Asociates. 1967. 4p. 45c

Junior occupational brief containing concise facts about the job.

Fur industry workers. Chronicle Guidance Publications. 1969. 4p. 35c

Occupational brief summarizing history, nature of the work, hours and earnings, employment outlook, working conditions, personal qualifications, and educational training preparation.

Fur industry workers. Science Research Associates. 1966. 4p. 45c

Occupational brief describing nature of work, training, qualifications, opportunities, advantages, disadvantages, and future outlook. Selected references.

Furrier. Careers. 1966. 2p. 20c

Career summary for desk-top file. Duties, qualifications, and outlook.

FUR INDUSTRY WORKER—*Continued*

Furrier. Guidance Centre. 1967. 4p. 35c postpaid

Definition, nature of work, qualifications, preparation, working conditions, advantages, disadvantages, how to get started and related occupations.

FURNITURE MANUFACTURING WORKER 783.

Finding out about furniture designers. Science Research Associates. 1967. 4p. 45c

Junior occupational brief containing concise facts about the job.

Furniture finisher. California State Department of Employment. 1968. 2p. Single copy free

Occupational guide describing work, requirements, training, and outlook.

Furniture (manufacturing) occupations. Chronicle Guidance Publications. 1966. 4p. 35c

Occupational brief summarizing industry and its products, work performed, earnings, and outlook.

Furniture manufacturing workers. Science Research Associates. 1966. 4p. 45c

Occupational brief describing nature of work, requirements, earnings, job prospects, advantages, disadvantages, and future outlook.

FURNITURE UPHOLSTERER 780.381

Automobile trimmers and installation men (automobile upholsterers). One section of *Occupational Outlook Handbook.*

Description of the work of replacing and repairing upholstery and other automobile fabrics, qualifications, employment outlook, earnings, and working conditions.

**Employment outlook for funiture upholsterers. Bulletin No. 1650–97. Bureau of Labor Statistics, U.S. Department of Labor. Supt. of Documents. 1970. 8p. 10c

Reprint from the *Occupational Outlook Handbook.*

Finding out about upholsterers. Science Research Associates. 1967. 4p. 45c

Junior occupational brief containing concise facts about the job.

Furniture upholsterer. California State Department of Employment. 1967. 3p. Single copy free

Occupational guide describing work, requirements, training, and outlook.

Furniture upholsterer. Careers. 1970. 8p. 35c

Career brief describing duties, working conditions, training, personal qualifications, earnings, outlook, and ways of measuring one's interest and ability.

Furniture upholsterers. One section of *Occupational Outlook Handbook.*

Nature of work, places of employment, training, qualifications, advancement, employment outlook, earnings, and working conditions.

Trade school helps ease trimmer shortage. Chronicle Guidance Publications. 1967. 2p. 35c

Reprinted article from *Auto Trim News* discusses training of auto trimmers.

Upholsterer (furniture). Chronicle Guidance Publications. 1969. 4p. 35c

Occupational brief summarizing work performed, training, working conditions, wages, personal requirements, and outlook.

Upholsterers. Michigan Employment Security Commission. 1960. 2p. Single copy free

Job brief summarizing occupational data for use in Michigan.

* Upholsterers. Science Research Associates. 1967. 4p. 45c

Occupational brief describing nature of work, requirements, how to enter, advancement, earnings and hours, advantages, disadvantages, and future outlook.

GAME WARDEN. ***See*** **Fish and game warden; Wildlife specialist**

GARDENER AND GROUNDS KEEPER **407.884**

Finding out about gardeners and grounds keepers. Science Research Associates. 1967. 4p. 45c

Junior occupational brief describing work and opportunities.

Groundsman-gardener. California Department of Employment. 1969. 3p. Single copy free

Description of work, duties, working conditions, requirements, wages, hours, promotion, and employment outlook.

See also Horticulturist

GAS PRODUCTION AND DISTRIBUTION WORKER. ***See*** **Petroleum production industry worker**

GENEALOGIST. ***See*** **Historian**

GENETICIST **041.081**

Geneticist. Careers. 1968. 2p. 20c

Career summary for desk-top file. Duties, qualifications, and outlook.

Geneticist. One section of *Occupational Outlook Handbook.*

Brief description of nature of work.

GEODESIST. ***See*** **Geophysicist**

GEOGRAPHER **059.088**

Finding out about geographers. Science Research Associates. 1967. 4p. 45c

Junior occupational brief summarizing what the work requires and offers.

GEOGRAPHER—*Continued*

Geographer. Careers. 1966. 2p. 20c

Career summary for desk-top file. Duties, qualifications, and outlook.

Geographer. Chronicle Guidance Publications. 1966. 4p. 35c

Occupational brief summarizing work performed, personal qualifications, training, opportunities, earnings, and outlook.

Geographer. Guidance Centre. 1967. 4p. 35c postpaid

History and importance, nature of work, qualifications, working conditions, preparation, remuneration, outlook, related occupations, and how to get started.

Geographers. Science Research Associates. 1967. 4p. 45c

Occupational brief describing nature of work, requirements, places of employment, earnings, and future outlook.

**Geographers. One section of *Occupational Outlook Handbook.*

Nature of work, where employed, training, other qualifications, employment outlook, earnings, and working conditions.

Geographers and what they do. Warntz, William. Franklin Watts, Inc. 1964. 160p. $3.95

A geographer writes of his profession, of the training necessary, the type of person best suited for this work, and some of the duties and satisfactions of geographers. For grades 7 to 11.

**Geography as a professional field. Association of American Geographers. 1968. 95p. Single copy free

Nature of work, opportunities, training, and outlook. Sixteen geographers describe the duties and outlook in their fields of specialization. Contains list of colleges with training programs in geography.

Geography: earned degrees, by level, sex, and institution. One section of *Earned Degrees Conferred.*

List of 165 schools and the number of bachelor's, master's and doctor's degrees conferred by each.

See also Scientist

GEOLOGIST 024.081

Directory of geoscience departments in the colleges and universities of the United States and Canada. American Geological Institute. 1968. 294p. $8.50

Detailed information on faculty, course offerings, degree requirements, and summer field camp programs of 380 degree-granting departments. Also provides geographic listing of 364 colleges offering some geology courses but no degree.

Environmental geology: conservation, land-use planning, and resource management. (Geoscience Series). Flawn, Peter T. Harper and Row. 1970. 313p. $13.95

Basic information on environmental geology and conservation.

Finding out about geologists. Science Research Associates. 1967. 4p. 45c
Junior occupational brief containing concise facts about the job.

From the eagle's wings. Swift, H. H. Morrow and Company. 1962. 287p. $4.95
Biography of John Muir, the geologist and nature lover, showing his intense dedication to his work.

Frontier scientist: Clarence King. Young, Bob and Young, Jan. Julian Messner. 1968. 192p. $3.50; library binding $3.34
Biography of a capable mountaineer who became the first director of the U.S. Geological Survey and organized its work.

The future of petroleum geologists. Chronicle Guidance Publications. 1969. 4p. 35c
Reprinted article from *American Association of Petroleum Geologists Bulletin* discusses the history, present, and future of the occupation.

Geological engineering. Colorado School of Mines. No date. 6p. Free
Description of the work, prospects, training, and requirements for admission for study.

Geologist. California State Department of Employment. 1966. 6p. Single copy free
Occupational guide describing work, requirements, training, and outlook.

Geologist. Careers. 1968. 2p. 20c
Career summary for desk-top file. Duties, qualifications, and outlook.

Geologist. Chronicle Guidance Publications. 1967. 8p. 50c
Occupational brief summarizing work performed, fields of specialization, working conditions, qualifications, training, salaries, opportunities, where employed, and outlook.

Geologist. Guidance Centre. 1969. 4p. 35c postpaid
Definition, history and importance, nature of work, working conditions, qualifications, preparation, employment and advancement, remuneration, advantages, disadvantages, how to get started, related occupations, outlook, and further information.

Geologist. Michigan Employment Security Commission. 1958. 2p. Single copy free
Job brief summarizing occupational data for use in Michigan.

* Geologists. Science Research Associates. 1967. 4p. 45c
Occupational brief describing nature of work, requirements, preparation, earnings, and future outlook.

**Geologists. One section of *Occupational Outlook Handbook*.
Nature of work, where employed, training and other qualifications, employment outlook, earnings, and working conditions.

**Geology: science and profession. American Geological Institute. Revised 1967. 28p. 35c
Illustrates the kind of work geologists do and discusses educational requirements and employment opportunities.

GEOLOGIST—*Continued*

Our earth: geology and geologists. Place, Marian. Putnam's Sons. 1961. 192p. $3.64

Story of man's discoveries in geology and their eventual effects, including why geology's possibilities make it a career worth considering. Written for ages 10 to 14.

Paleontologist. Careers. 1968. 2p. 20c

Career summary for desk-top file. Duties, qualifications, and outlook.

**The sphere of the geological scientist. Roy, Chalmer J. American Geological Institute. 1965. 30p. 40c

The author aims to reveal earth science as a way of life which offers challenge and fascination to intellectually alert and competent students. Describes the major career opportunities, personal qualifications, educational requirements, and outlook.

U.S. geological survey, 1970. U.S. Geological Survey. 1970. 12p. Free

A brief description of the work of the agency and its four operating divisions for mapping, field research, water investigation, and conservation.

**Your future in geology. Weitz, Joseph. Richards Rosen Press. 1966. 160p. $4; library edition $3.78

The advantages of a career in the outdoors are presented together with the requirements and education needed.

See also Scientist

GEOPHYSICIST 024.081

Careers in exploration geophysics. Society of Exploration Geophysicists. 1963. 8p. Free

Illustrated brochure describing what to expect in the field of geophysical exploration.

Deep sea, high mountain. Roberts, Elliott. Little, Brown and Company. 1961. 288p. $4.75

Story of the episodes in the work of members of the United States Coast and Geodetic Survey. Describes the nature of their work and the importance of this agency.

Geophysical engineering. Colorado School of Mines. No date. 6p. Free

Description of the work, prospects, training, and requirements for admission for study.

Geophysicist. Careers. 1970. 8p. 35c

Career brief describing duties, working conditions, training, personal qualifications, earnings, and outlook.

Geophysicist. Chronicle Guidance Publications. 1967. 4p. 35c

Occupational brief summarizing work performed, working conditions, qualifications, determination of aptitudes and interests, training, opportunities, outlook, and related jobs.

Geophysicist. Guidance Centre. 1968. 4p. 35c postpaid

History and importance, nature of work, qualifications, working conditions, preparation, remuneration, outlook, and how to get started.

**Geophysicist. One section of *Occupational Outlook Handbook*.

Nature of work, where employed, training and other qualifications, employment outlook, earnings, and working conditions.

* Geophysicists. Science Research Associates. 1968. 4p. 45c

Occupational brief describing nature of work, training, qualifications, opportunities, and outlook.

Information concerning geophysics. American Geophysical Union. 1969. 10p. Free

Defines and describes geophysics as a whole and the ten specialties: geodesy, seismology, meteorology, geomagnetism, oceanography, volcanology, hydrology, tectonophysics, planetology, and solar-terrestrial relationships.

Information for high school students and vocational guidance counselors concerning the broad field of geophysics. Chronicle Guidance Publications. 1968. 7p. 50c

Reprinted article from *American Geophysical Union* discusses geodesy; seismology; meteorology; geomagnetism and aeronomy; oceanography; volcanology, geochemistry, and petrology; hydrology; tectonophysics; and planetary sciences.

See also Scientist

GIFT SHOP OWNER AND MANAGER 185.168

Finding out about gift shop owners and managers. Science Research Associates. 1967. 4p. 45c

Junior occupational brief describing work and opportunities.

Gift shop owners and managers. Science Research Associates. 1966. 4p. 45c

Occupational brief describing nature of work, requirements, getting started, income possibilities, advantages, disadvantages, and future outlook.

GIRL SCOUTS PROFESSIONAL WORKER 159.228

Girl Scout professional workers. Careers. 1968. 2p. 20c

Career summary for desk-top file. Duties, qualifications, and outlook.

**A job, a future, and you. Girl Scouts of the United States of America. 1967. 16p. Free

An illustrated brochure pointing out the need for trained workers for the variety of executive and specialist jobs in Girl Scouting. Includes qualifications, benefits, and rewards.

The job duties and responsibilities of the Girl Scout professional worker. Girl Scouts of the United States of America. 1968. 2p. Free

Brief description of jobs with local units and work on the national staff.

Jobs in Girl Scout camps. Girl Scouts of the United States of America. 1965. 6p. Free

List of positions with brief statement of duties.

Look into the career of your life. Girl Scouts of the United States of America. 1967. 8p. Free

Illustrated brochure pointing out that a Girl Scout executive's work is varied, stimulating, and fun.

Someone like you. Girl Scouts of the United States of America. 1968. 6p. Free

A brief flier announcing a sound film aimed to recruit qualified personnel. The film rental is $5 first day; $2.50 each day thereafter.

GLASS MANUFACTURING WORKER 772.

Finding out about glass blowers. Science Research Associates. 1967. 4p. 45c

Junior occupational brief summarizing what the work requires and offers.

Glass manufacturing workers. Science Research Associates. 1966. 4p. 45c

Occupational brief describing nature of work, requirements, methods of getting started, wages, advantages, disadvantages, and future outlook.

GLAZIER 865.781 and .131

Finding out about glaziers. Science Research Associates. 1967. 4p. 45c

Junior occupational brief containing concise facts about the job.

Glazier. Careers. 1966. 2p. 20c

Career summary for desk-top file. Duties, qualifications, and outlook.

Glazier. Chronicle Guidance Publications. 1966. 4p. 35c

Occupational brief summarizing nature of work, where employed, hours and earnings, personal qualifications, training, working conditions, and outlook.

Glazier. Michigan Employment Security Commission. 1962. 2p. Single copy free

Job brief summarizing occupational data for use in Michigan.

Glazier (construction). California State Department of Employment. 1965. 4p. Single copy free

Occupational guide describing work, requirements, training, and outlook.

Glaziers. Science Research Associates. 1965. 4p. 45c

Occupational brief describing work, training, qualifications, opportunities, and outlook.

Glaziers. One section of *Occupational Outlook Handbook*.

Nature of work, where employed, training and other qualifications, employment outlook, earnings, and working conditions.

GOVERNMENT SERVICE WORKER 001. through 999.99

Adventures in public service; the careers of eight honored men in the United States Government. Simons, Howard. Vanguard Press. 1964. 272p. $3.95

Biographical sketches of eight men who are serving the Federal Government in important positions and have received the Rockefeller Public Service Award for their achievements.

Annual report of Federal civilian employment in the United States by geopraphic area, December 31, 1970. U.S. Civil Service Commission. Supt. of Documents. 1970. 180p. $1.50

A useful annual report.

Career fields in the U.S. Department of Commerce. Government Printing Office. Supt. of Documents. 1968. 100p. 70c

Prepared for those wishing to explore opportunities in the Commerce Department, which engages almost one thousand college-trained people annually. For over one hundred positions there is given the duties, in what agency the job may be found, and available training programs connected with that work.

Careers for college graduates in New York state government. New York State Department of Civil Service. 1968. 16p. Free to counselors, librarians, ard college faculty members

Description of kinds of work and opportunities in various fields of work, such as public administration internships, conservation, economics, social work, statistics, biology, health services, and bank examining.

**Careers in government. Sullivan, Mary B. Henry Z. Walck, Inc. 1964. 128p. $4.50

This book concentrates on the Federal Government's extensive and diverse opportunities both in large, well-known departments and in smaller, more recently created sections such as the Federal Aviation Agency and the Bureau of Outdoor Recreation. The functions and jobs in various departments are explained.

Careers in the United States Department of the Interior. Government Printing Office. Supt. of Documents. 1970. 71p. 50c

Description of the functions of the department and its employment and career opportunities. Includes the entrance requirements, benefits, promotion plans, and wages.

**Civilian employment in Federal Government. One chapter of *Occupational Outlook Handbook.*

Employment trends and outlook in work in Federal, state, and local governments; post office occupations; and armed forces.

The department of justice. Huston, Luther A. Frederick Praeger, Inc. 1967. 256p. $5.95

Describes the origins of the department, its functions, and many of the men and incidents associated with it. Includes a concise statement on jobs available in the department.

GOVERNMENT SERVICE WORKER—*Continued*

Employment outlook for government (except post office) Federal civilian employment. Bulletin No. 1650–127. Bureau of Labor Statistics, U.S. Department of Labor. Supt. of Documents. 1970. 12p. 15c

Reprint from the *Occupational Outlook Handbook*. Includes state and local governments, and the armed forces.

Federal civilian government. One section of *Occupational Outlook Handbook*.

Discussion of kinds of jobs, earnings, advancement, working conditions, employment trends, and outlook.

Go government. U.S. Civil Service Commission. 1968. 28p. Single copy free

Gives the college graduate an overview of opportunities available with the Federal civil service and explains how to apply. Includes a franked tear-off card to be mailed to Federal job information centers.

Government occupations. One section of *Occupational Outlook Handbook*.

Discusses opportunities for civilian employment in the major divisions of Federal, state, and local government.

Government services: an urgent need for talent. Chronicle Guidance Publications. 1967. 4p. 35c

Reprinted article from *Occupational Outlook Quarterly* discusses career opportunities in government, employment trends for blue-collar and white-collar workers, opportunities for the handicapped and retarded, work-study arrangements, entering government employment, and pay.

A guide to professional careers. Duckat, Walter. Julian Messner. 1970. 288p. $5.95; library binding $5.64

An overview of careers for the college bound student, including requirements, training, duties, salaries, and future outlook. Also contains a list of jobs with the Federal Government for various college majors.

The highest dream. Whitney, Phyllis. David McKay Company. 1956. 256p. $4.19

Career fiction. The United Nations as seen by a college graduate whose job as guide leads to romance and a career.

**Occupations in government. One chapter of *Occupational Outlook Handbook*.

Includes civilian employment in Federal, state, and local government; post office occupations; and career fields for military personnel.

**Our Federal government: how it works; an introduction to the United States government. Acheson, Patricia C. Dodd, Mead and Company. 1969. 210p. $4.50

This book had been revised to take into account the many recent changes in the Government, for example the addition of the Department of Housing and Urban Development, Economic Development Administration, and the Federal Water Pollution Control Administration.

Patent agent. Guidance Centre. 1967. 4p. 23c postpaid

Definition, history and importance, nature of work, preparation, qualifications, employment, advancement, outlook, remuneration, and how to get started.

Paths of diplomacy; America's Secretaries of State. Heller, Deane and Heller, David. Lippincott Company. 1967. 192p. $3.95

Anecdotal career sketches of twenty Secretaries of State from Thomas Jefferson to Dean Rusk, describing each man's major achievements during his term of office.

* Professional careers in the Federal Government. Careers. 1967. 8p. 35c

Career brief describing a number of professional careers, how jobs are filled, earnings, and outlook.

** Six against crime: treasury agencies in action. Neal, Harry Edward. Julian Messner. 1959. 192p. $3.95; library binding $3.64

Description of the law enforcement agencies of the U.S. Treasury Department and their efficiency and accomplishments. Includes a chapter on the training of a Treasury agent. Photographs.

State and local governments. One section of *Occupational Outlook Handbook.*

Discussion of kinds of jobs, employment trends, earnings, working conditions, and outlook.

State and local governments burgeoning need for manpower. Chronicle Guidance Publications. 1968. 7p. 50c

Reprinted article from *Occupational Outlook Quarterly* discusses manpower needs and ways in which technology affects occupations.

The United States Department of Labor; a story of workers, unions, and the economy. Terrell, John Upton. Meredith Press. 1968. 122p. 3.95

Description of the operations, responsibilities, and activities of the Labor Department and its numerous subdivisions. The author traces the growth and development of the Labor Department from its formation in 1913 to the present.

The United States Department of the Treasury; a story of dollars, customs, and secret agents. Terrell, John Upton. Duell, Sloan and Pearce. 1963. 116p. $3.50

Discussion of the duties carried out by the Bureau of Customs, Bureau of Engraving and Printing, Bureau of the Mint, Secret Service, Coast Guard, Bureau of Narcotics, and Internal Revenue Service.

Visual history of the United Nations, year by year. Sterling Publishing Company. 1966. 64p. $2.50

Arranged by year, this book gives the major accomplishments of the United Nations. Includes a short biography and picture of each secretary-general.

What does a congressman do? Lavine, David. Dodd, Mead and Company. 1965. 64p. $3.25; library binding $2.99

Simple text and pictures portray various duties. Written for grades 3 to 7.

GOVERNMENT SERVICE WORKER—*Continued*

What does a senator do? Lavine, David. Dodd, Mead and Company. 1967. 64p. $3.25; library binding $2.99

With an introduction by Senator Robert F. Kennedy, simple text and pictures portray the role and activities of senators in the Government. Prepared for grades 3 to 7.

What your congressman does. Klapper, Ivan. Sterling Publishing Company. 1968. 128p. $3.95

Following the legislators through a typical day, the author discusses their duties and powers and the many services rendered.

What your U.S. senator does. Klapper, Ivan. Sterling Publishing Company. 1967. 128p. $3.95

A behind-the-scenes look at how a senator works, his duties and powers.

Your Department of State. Government Printing Office. Supt. of Documents. 1967. 16p. 15c

Information on how the department operates and a brief statement of the foreign policy.

**Your future in the Federal Government. Gould, Stephen. Richards Rosen Press. Revised 1969. 157p. $4; library edition $3.78

The author explains the civil service programs and discusses overseas job opportunities as well as the multiplicity of Government positions in local communities in the United States.

See also Civil Service worker; Foreign service worker

GROCERY STORE WORKER. *See* Food clerk; Retail manager

GROUNDS KEEPER. *See* Horticulturist

GROUP WORKER 195.108

Career clubs. Boys' Clubs of America. 1963. 24p. $1

A handbook for conducting special interest groups for the exploration of occupations, employment, and education.

**Career opportunities for community service and related specialists. Ferguson Publishing Company. 1970. 300p. $11.95; $8.95 to schools and libraries

Prepared for high school and two-year college students. For twenty occupations in this category, there is included the educational requirements both in high school and after high school, job opportunities at entry level and advancement possibilities, working conditions, and immediate and future earning prospects.

For a job in a growing field and an opportunity to serve others. American Heart Association. 1962. 6p. Single copy free from local Heart Associations.

Leaflet presenting descriptions of work as field representative, program consultant or director, chapter executive, and information and education specialist.

Highlighting your future: a professional career in Boys' Club work. Boys' Clubs of America. 1968. 8p. Free

Types of positions, basic characteristics needed, qualifications, salaries, and opportunities.

How to be a Boys' Club group leader. Boys' Clubs of America. 1968. 24p. $1

Information on organizing group clubs and conducting programs.

Looking for a career? Camp Fire Girls, Inc. 1969. 6p. Free

Brief description of work as field director, district director, camp director, and executive director.

My sixty years with rural youth. Erickson, T. A. University of Minnesota Press. 1956. 162p. $2.75

Biography of a pioneer leader in the 4-H club movement for boys and girls. Illustrated.

**Professional leadership in Boys' Clubs. Boys' Clubs of America. 1959. 26p. 50c

This booklet sets forth the desirable qualifications for full-time positions in a boys' club. Duties and educational and experience qualifications are given for the following: executive director, assistant executive director, program director, physical director, swimming director, group club supervisor, director of social program, and membership secretary.

**Those who care—how you can help people through group work. Baker, Laura Nelson. Little, Brown and Company. 1964. 260p. $4.75

An account of social group work designed to interest young readers in entering the field. Includes a list of professional schools of social work which offer group work courses.

See also Boy Scouts professional worker; Girl Scouts professional worker; Jewish center worker; Social worker; YMCA professional worker; YWCA professional worker

GUARD, WATCHMAN AND ALARM SYSTEM WORKER 372.868

Finding out about guards and watchmen. Science Research Associates. 1967. 4p. 45c

Junior occupational brief summarizing what the work requires and offers.

Guard. California State Department of Employment. 1966. 5p. Single copy free

Description of work, pay, hours, how to find work, and employment outlook in California.

GUARD, WATCHMAN AND ALARM SYSTEM WORKER—*Continued*

Guard (watchman). Careers. 1968. 2p. 20c

Career summary for desk-top file. Duties, qualifications, and outlook.

Guards, watchmen, and alarm investigators. Chronicle Guidance Publications. 1968. 4p. 35c

Occupational brief summarizing definition, history and importance, work performed, working conditions, physical demands, hours and earnings, employment outlook, education, and training.

**Guards, watchmen, and alarm system workers. Science Research Associates. 1966. 4p. 45c

Occupational brief describing nature of work, qualifications, training, earnings, and outlook. Selected references.

GUIDANCE AND PERSONNEL WORKER. ***See*** **Counselor; Personnel and employment manager; Rehabilitation counselor**

GUNSMITH **632.281**

Gunsmith. California State Department of Employment. 1965. 4p. Single copy free

Job duties, working conditions, pay, hours, entrance requirements, promotion, training, and employment outlook in California.

Gunsmith. Careers. 1967. 2p. 20c

Career summary for desk-top file. Duties, qualifications, and outlook.

Gunsmith. Chronicle Guidance Publications. 1967. 4p. 35c

Occupational brief summarizing definition, work performed, working conditions, training, qualifications, outlook, and earnings.

HEALTH EDUCATOR. ***See*** **Physical education teacher**

HEALTH PHYSICIST **079.021**

Health physicist. California State Department of Employment. 1965. 4p. Single copy free

Occupational guide describing work, requirements, training, and outlook.

Health physicist. Careers. 1969. 8p. 35c

Career brief describing work, training, personal qualifications, working conditions, related careers, earnings, outlook, and ways of measuring one's interest and ability.

Health physicist. Chronicle Guidance Publications. 1968. 4p. 35c

Occupational brief summarizing work performed, where employed, qualifications, training, working conditions, earnings, and outlook.

Health physics technician. Chronicle Guidance Publications. 1968. 4p. 35c

Occupational brief summarizing work performed, working conditions, qualifications, training, earnings, and outlook.

HEALTH SERVICE WORKER. *See* **Medical service and health service worker**

HEARING THERAPIST. *See* **Speech pathologist and audiologist**

HEAT TREATER **504.782**

Heat treater. California State Department of Employment. 1968. 4p. Single copy free

Occupational guide describing work, requirements, training, and outlook.

Heat treater. Chronicle Guidance Publications. 1966. 4p. 35c

Occupational brief summarizing work performed, working conditions, qualifications, earnings, unionization, and outlook.

HELICOPTER PILOT **196.283**

Finding out about helicopter pilots. Science Research Associates. 1967. 4p. 45c

Junior occupational brief containing concise facts about the job.

Helicopter pilots. Science Research Associates. 1965. 4p. 45c

Occupational brief describing work, qualifications, training, earnings, ups and downs, and outlook.

HERPETOLOGIST **041.081**

**Career opportunities for the herpetologist. U.S. National Museum. 1963. 4p. Single copy free

Brochure containing information about the preparation, opportunities, and required training.

Raymond L. Ditmars: his exciting career with reptiles, animals, and insects. Wood, Laura N. Julian Messner. 1944. 256p. Library binding $3.64

Entertaining biography of the man whose boyhood hobby of snake collecting developed into a career of scientist and curator of reptiles and mammals of the New York Zoological Park. Illustrated.

Snakes: the keeper and the kept. Kauffeld, Carl F. Doubleday and Company. 1969. 248p. $5.95

Contains instructions for amateurs who are interested in keeping snakes as pets, informing them of the basic requirements and of the problems that arise and how to deal with them.

HIGHWAY ENGINEER **005.081**

**Careers in road building. American Road Builders' Association. 1969. 8p. Free

Information concerning the road construction industry and opportunities in it.

HIGHWAY ENGINEER—*Continued*

Highway engineer. Careers. 1969. 2p. 20c

Career summary for desk-top file. Duties, qualifications, and outlook.

Highway engineer. Chronicle Guidance Publications. 1967. 4p. 35c

Occupational brief summarizing work performed, working conditions, educational and personal requirements, where employed, hours and earnings, and outlook.

Highway engineers. Science Research Associates. 1967. 4p. 45c

Occupational brief describing work, training, qualifications, opportunities, and outlook.

New opportunities for training highway technicians. Chronicle Guidance Publications. 1966. 2p. 35c

Reprinted article from *American Vocational Journal* discusses types of training, visual aids in training, need for training, vocational education, and cooperative programs as they relate to the highway technician.

HISTORIAN 052.088

Finding out about historians. Science Research Associates. 1967. 4p. 45c

Junior occupational brief describing work and opportunities.

Genealogy as pastime and profession. Jacobus, Donald Lines. Genealogical Publishing Company. 1968. 120p. $7.50

An explanation of the principles of genealogical research by a professional scientific genealogist.

Historian. Careers. 1968. 8p. 35c

Career brief describing duties, working conditions, personal qualifications, training, places of employment, related careers, earnings, and outlook.

Historian. Chronicle Guidance Publications. 1969. 4p. 35c

Occupational brief summarizing work performed, where employed, earnings, educational qualifications, and outlook.

Historians. Science Research Associates. 1966. 4p. 45c

Occupational brief describing work, training, qualifications, opportunities, and outlook.

**Historians. One section of *Occupational Outlook Handbook*.

Nature of work, where employed, training, other qualifications, and employment outlook.

**History as a career: to undergraduates choosing a profession. American Historical Association. 1964. 21p. 8c. Single copy free

Designed to help the undergraduate decide whether he wants to make college history teaching a career. Describes what it requires and what it offers. Includes brief discussion of the work of historians who are not college teachers.

**In the steps of the great American museum collector, Carl Ethan Akeley. Clark, James L. Lippincott Company. 1968. 128p. $3.95

Description of the life work of a specimen collector for natural history museums, giving information about the necessary requirements for that career.

HOME APPLIANCE SERVICEMAN 827.281

Finding out about home appliance servicemen. Science Research Associates. 1967. 4p. 45c

Junior occupational brief summarizing what the work requires and offers.

**Home appliance servicemen. Science Research Associates. 1967. 4p. 45c

Occupational brief describing work, training, qualifications, opportunities, earnings, and outlook.

HOME ECONOMIST 096.128

Careers in home economics. Changing Times. 1962. 3p. 15c

Reprint containing discussion of preparation, earnings, and opportunities.

Colleges and universities offering undergraduate majors in home economics. American Home Economics. 1967. 32p. 25c

Tabulated information about 400 colleges, including the majors in home economics offered in each.

**Employment outlook for home economists. Bulletin No. 1650–33. Bureau of Labor Statistics, U.S. Department of Labor. Supt. of Documents. 1970. 8p. 10c

Reprint from the *Occupational Outlook Handbook.*

Exciting careers for home economists. Spencer, Lila. Julian Messner. 1967. 191p. $3.95; library binding $3.64

This book explores the opportunities for trained home economists in a wide variety of specialized areas. Many case histories of successful persons are intertwined with advice on preparing for this field. List of colleges offering majors or degrees in home economics.

Extension home economist. Chronicle Guidance Publications. 1968. 4p. 35c

Occupational brief summarizing work performed, working conditions, qualifications, training, earnings, opportunities, where employed and outlook.

Finding out about home economists. Science Research Associates. 1967. 4p. 45c

Junior occupational brief containing concise facts about the job.

**Futures for home economists. Humphreyville, Theresa. Prentice-Hall, Inc. 1963. 334p. $8.50

Description of careers open to home economists with bachelor's degrees in schools, social group work, test kitchen research, retailing, journalism, and cooperative extension service.

Graduate opportunities for home economists. American Home Economics Association. 1968. 16p. 25c

Listing of graduate assistantships, fellowships, and scholarships available to home economists in colleges and universities in the United States.

Home advisor. California State Department of Employment. 1964. 3p. Single copy free

Occupational guide describing work, requirements, training, and outlook.

HOME ECONOMIST—*Continued*

* Home economics as a profession. Tate, Mildred T. McGraw-Hill Book Company. 1961. 432p. $6.95

Presents a comprehensive view of the many professions and vocations open to home economists. Includes the education and training necessary as preparation.

**Home economics career packet. American Home Economics Association. 1969. 10 booklets. $2

Attractive folder containing ten assorted career booklets available from the association.

Home economics careers for you. American Home Economics Association. 1964. 6p. Minimum order of 200 copies $2

Pictures of eight different careers useful for high school career days or recruitment programs.

Home economics careers in health and welfare. American Home Economics Association. 1965. 10p. 25c

Booklet describing the home economist's role in community health and welfare organizations. Outlines basic requirements, education, major duties, and career opportunities.

Home economics: earned degrees, by level, sex, and institution. One section of *Earned Degrees Conferred.*

Useful for judging the extent of a college's program in general home economics, child development, clothing textiles, foods and nutrition, and institution management.

**Home economics has a career for you in textiles and clothing. American Home Economics Association. 1966. 20p. 25c

Discussion of the basic requirements, major duties, qualifications, employment opportunities, salaries, and related work. Includes information about careers in fashion, teaching, research, extension, and communications. Reading list.

Home economics in colleges and universities. Department of Home Economics, National Education Association. 1968. 56p. $1.50

List of about 400 colleges offering a degree in home economics and their majors.

Home economics in institutions granting bachelors' or higher degrees. American Home Economics Association. 1966. 51p. 50c

Selected tables from the biennial survey of the U.S. Office of Education. Data on degree-granting institutions, undergraduate enrollments, number of degrees granted, and major areas.

Home economics related occupations. Kupsinel, Penelope E. Interstate Printers and Publishers. 1967. 180p. $3.50

Written for the student who is preparing for a cooperative work-study program and training for entry-level positions. Includes qualifications for work in food and nutrition, textiles, clothing, household management, and adult and child care.

Home economist. Chronicle Guidance Publications. 1966. 4p. 35c

Occupational brief summarizing work performed, working conditions, hours, earnings, personal requirements, training requirements, opportunities, and employment outlook.

Home economist. Guidance Centre. 1967. 4p. 35c postpaid

Nature of work, qualifications, preparation, outlook, advancement, earnings, how to get started, and related occupations.

Home economist in business. California State Department of Employment. 1967. 4p. Single copy free

Occupational guide describing work, requirements, training, and outlook.

* Home economists. Careers. 1970. 8p. 35c.

Career brief describing duties, working conditions, training, personal qualifications, places of employment, earnings, outlook, and ways of measuring your interest and ability.

Home economists. Science Research Associates. 1969. 4p. 45c

Occupational brief describing nature of work, qualifications, preparation, opportunities, advantages, disadvantages, and future outlook.

**Home economists. One section of *Occupational Outlook Handbook.*

Nature of work, where employed, related fields of work, training, other qualifications, advancement, employment outlook, earnings and working conditions.

Jobs in professional home economics. Science Research Associates. 1965. 48p. $1.15

Describes the variety of job prospects and opportunities within this field.

Meet the young home economist. American Home Economics Association. 1963. 12p. 25c

Portfolio of picture pages describing the home economist in communications, education, research, fashion, interior design, community service, and food careers.

Unfold your future in home economics. American Home Economics Association. 1965. 10p. 5c. Single copy free

Illustrated folder depicting the career areas in home economics.

What does home economics teaching offer you? Department of Home Economics, National Education Association. 1968. 8p. Single copy free

Stresses the advantages and rewards of this field of work.

**The wonderful world of home economics. American Home Economics Association. 1967. 8 leaflets. 15c

Set of eight colorful leaflets describing career opportunities and college preparation in the home economics areas of art, family economics, family relations, food and nutrition, education, housing, institution administration, and textiles and clothing. Leaflets may be ordered individually for $2 per 100.

HOME ECONOMIST—*Continued*

**Your future as a home economist. Paris, Jeanne. Richards Rosen Press. Revised 1969. 160p. $4; library edition $3.78

Description of the numerous fields open to a graduate with a degree in home economics. Includes the type of studies to expect and a list of schools offering such degrees.

HORTICULTURIST 040.081

Arborist. Guidance Centre. 1967. 4p. 23c postpaid

Definition, history and importance, qualifications, preparation, remuneration, outlook, and how to get started.

**Careers in horticultural sciences. Dowdell, Dorothy and Dowdell, Joseph. Julian Messner. 1969. 222p. $3.95; library binding $3.64

This book gives information on the education, training, and financial rewards for work in the branches of agriculture dealing with the cultivation and utilization of vegetables, fruits, flowers, and ornamental plants. Included are four lists of colleges offering courses in horticultural science, landscape architecture, floral design, and floriculture.

Finding out about horticulturists. Science Research Associates. 1967. 4p. 45c

Junior occupational brief describing work and opportunities.

* Gardeners and grounds keepers. Science Research Associates. 1967. 4p. 45c

Occupational brief describing work, training, qualifications, opportunities, and outlook.

Greenhouse worker. Careers. 1968. 2p. 20c

Career summary for desk-top file. Duties, qualifications, and outlook.

**Horticulture, a rewarding career. American Society for Horticultural Science. 1968. 10p. $4.50 per 100. Single copy free

Illustrated brochure describing opportunities in work with shrubs, lawns, fruit, vegetables, and flowers.

Horticulturist. Careers. 1970. 2p. 20c

Career summary for desk-top file. Duties, qualifications, and training.

Horticulturist. Chronicle Guidance Publications. 1968. 4p. 35c

Occupational brief summarizing work performed, working conditions, qualifications, training, earnings, advantages, disadvantages, and outlook.

Horticulturist. Guidance Centre. 1966. 4p. 35c postpaid

History and importance, nature of work, qualifications, working conditions, preparation, remuneration, outlook, and how to get started.

Horticulturists. Science Research Associates. 1966. 4p. 45c

Occupational brief describing work, training, qualifications, opportunities, and outlook.

Ornamental horticulturist. California State Department of Employment. 1965. 4p. Single copy free

Occupational guide describing work, requirements, training, and outlook.

The plant hunters. Coats, Alice M. McGraw-Hill Company. 1970. 400p. $10.95

This is an account of the botanical and horticultural explorations of many pioneer plant collectors in their search for hardy and unusual varieties. Includes a bibliography, an index of collectors, and a plant index.

Viticulturist. California State Department of Employment. 1964. 5p. Single copy free

Occupational guide describing work, requirements, training, and outlook.

See also Floral designer; Landscape architect; Nurseryman and landscape gardener; Tree expert

HOSPITAL ADMINISTRATOR 187.118

**Administration of health services. Pages 54-76 of *Health Careers Guidebook.*

Description of work, qualifications, training, and future outlook. Also includes information concerning administrative specialties in public health administration and voluntary health agencies.

**Aim for a job in a hospital. Kirk, W. R. Richards Rosen Press. 1968. 156p. $4; library edition $3.78; edition in large type $5.97

Discussion of the various jobs available in the hospital from ambulance drivers to nurses aides and dietetic assistants.

Employment outlook for hospital administrators. Bulletin No. 1650–20. Bureau of Labor Statistics, U.S. Department of Labor. Supt. of Documents. 1970. 8p. 10c

Reprint from the *Occupational Outlook Handbook.*

Exploring your future in hospitals. Sextant Systems, Inc. 1971. 96p. $8.95

One page is devoted to each of ninety-five jobs, describing the duties, requirements for entering, promotional outlook, and the pay and skill level.

Finding out about hospital administrators. Science Research Associates. 1967. 4p. 45c

Junior occupational brief summarizing what the work requires and offers.

* Hospital administration as a career. American College of Hospital Administrators. 1968. 8p. Single copy free

Description of the profession of hospital administration, including responsibilities, training, and opportunities. Also includes a list of universities offering graduate programs in hospital administration.

Hospital administrator. Association of University Programs in Hospital Administration. 1969. 4p. Free

A concise statement of the scope, preparation, opportunity, and challenge of the hospital administrator. Includes a list of twenty-four accredited graduate programs in hospital administration.

HOSPITAL ADMINISTRATOR—*Continued*

Hospital administrator. California State Department of Employment. 1966. 6p. Single copy free

Occupational guide describing work, requirements, training, and outlook.

Hospital administrator. Careers. 1966. 8p. 35c

Career brief describing duties, working conditions, training, personal requirements, advantages, disadvantages, earnings, and outlook. Additional readings.

Hospital administrator. Chronicle Guidance Publications. 1968. 4p. 35c

Occupational brief summarizing work performed, working conditions, personal qualifications, training, opportunities, and outlook.

Hospital administrator. Guidance Centre. 1969. 4p. 35c postpaid

History and importance, nature of work, qualifications, preparation, employment, advancement, remuneration, outlook, and how to get started.

**Hospital administrators. Science Research Associates. 1967. 4p. 45c

Occupational brief describing work, requirements, training, getting started, earnings, advantages, disadvantages, and future outlook.

**Hospital administrators. One section of *Occupational Outlook Handbook.*

Nature of work, where employed, training, other qualifications, advancement, employment outlook, earnings, and working conditions.

Hospital public relations officer. American Hospital Association. 1968. 4p. Single copy free

Description of the nature of work, requirements, importance of the work, preparation, and employment outlook.

Your career opportunities in hospitals. Charles Pfizer and Company. 1968. 36p. Free

Illustrated brochure describing qualifications, training, specialization, opportunities, licensure, where necessary, and what to plan for in high school.

**Your future in hospital administration. Kirk, Weir Richard. Richards Rosen Press. Revised 1969. 160p. 160p. $4; library edition $3.78

Describes the work of a physician from an institutional and administrative point of view.

See also Medical service and health service worker

HOSPITAL ATTENDANT 079.368 and 355.687

Finding out about hospital attendants. Science Research Associates. 1967. 4p. 45c

Junior occupational brief containing concise facts about the job.

Hospital attendants. Michigan Employment Security Commission. 1967. 2p. Single copy free

Job brief summarizing occupational data for use in Michigan.

Hospital attendants. Science Research Associates. 1967. 4p. 45c

Occupational brief describing nature of work, requirements, getting started, earnings, advantages, disadvantages, and future outlook.

Hospital attendants. One section of *Occupational Outlook Handbook.*

Nature of work, where employed, training, other qualifications, advancement, employment outlook, earnings, and working conditions.

HOSTESS. *See* Airplane stewardess

HOTEL INDUSTRY WORKER 31 and 32

**Aim for a job in restaurants and food service. Westbrook, James. Richards Rosen Press. 1969. 191p. $4; library edition $3.78

A general survey of jobs in food service from bus boy to manager, stressing the possibility of on-the-job progress. Includes training, earnings, and outlook.

Bus boys. Science Research Associates. 1969. 4p. 45c

Occupational brief describing work, qualifications, opportunities, and outlook.

Careers for youth in the food service industry. National Restaurant Association. 1968. 5p. Free

Scope of the restaurant industry; entry, intermediate, and management positions; and training. For high school students.

Careers for youth kit. National Restaurant Asociation. 1968. Selected pamphlets. Free to counselors

Includes file folder, student brochures, and order card.

**Careers in hotels and restaurants. Lattin, Gerald W. Henry Z. Walck, Inc. 1967. 128p. $4.50

Analyzes the functions of each department in a hotel and each service in a restaurant. Many suggestions for both entry and advancement in hotels, motels, motor hotels, and restaurants. Helpful information is provided on the training needed, promotional pathways, salaries, working conditions, and opportunities in related industries.

Directory of schools and colleges offering courses for the training of managers, supervisors, and workers in hotels, restaurants, and institutions. Council on Hotel, Restaurant, and Institutional Education. 1968. 32p. 25c

List of schools arranged geographically.

Doormen. Science Research Associates. 1966. 4p. 45c

Occupational brief describing work, training, qualifications, opportunities, and outlook.

**Employment outlook for hotels. Bulletin No. 1650–126. Bureau of Labor Statistics, U.S. Department of Labor. Supt. of Documents. 1970. 12p. 15c

Reprint from the *Occupational Outlook Handbook.* Includes bellmen and bell captains, front office clerks, housekeepers and assistants, managers and assistants.

HOTEL INDUSTRY WORKER—*Continued*

Exploring your future in hotels and restaurants. Sextant Systems, Inc., 1971. 96p. $8.95

One page is devoted to each of ninety-five jobs, describing the duties, requirements for entering, promotional outlook, and the pay and skill level.

Finding out about doormen. Science Research Associates. 1967. 4p. 45c

Junior occupational brief summarizing what the work requires and offers.

Finding out about hotel and motel room clerks. Science Research Associates. 1967. 4p. 45c

Junior occupational brief describing work and opportunities.

Finding out about hotel bellmen. Science Research Associates. 1967. 4p. 45c

Junior occupational brief summarizing what the work requires and offers.

Finding out about hotel maids. Science Research Associates. 1967. 4p. 45c

Junior occupational brief containing concise facts about the job.

Front office clerks (hotel). One section of *Occupational Outlook Handbook.*

Nature of work, training, other qualifications, advancement, and employment outlook.

Hotel and motel clerk. Chronicle Guidance Publications. 1969. 4p. 35c

Occupational brief containing history, work performed, working conditions, requirements, opportunities, outlook, and methods of entry.

Hotel and motel workers. Science Research Associates. 1970. 4p. 45c

Occupational brief describing nature of work, training, qualifications, opportunities, advantages, disadvantages, and future outlook.

Hotel clerk. Guidance Centre. 1968. 4p. 35c postpaid

Nature of work, qualifications, preparation, working conditions, earnings, advantages, disadvantages, and how to get started.

The hotel-motel industry. One chapter in Volume I of the *Encyclopedia of Careers and Vocational Guidance.*

Entrance requirements, kinds of work, employment outlook, and rewards.

**Hotel-motel maid as a career. Belleau, Wilfrid. Park Publishing House. 1969. 11p. $1

Nature of the work, qualifications, training, working conditions, income, advancement, employment outlook, and how to begin.

**Hotel occupations. One section of *Ocupational Outlook Handbook.*

Nature of business, kinds of work, employment outlook, earnings and working conditions, and sources of additional information. Specific information is given concerning bellman, front-office clerk, hotel housekeeper, hotel manager, and assistants.

Opportunities in the hotel and motel industry. Henkin, Shepard. Vocational Guidance Manuals. 1967. 112p. $1.95 paper; $3.75 library edition

Includes the future of the industry, remuneration, personal requirements, educational preparation, opportunities, how to start, and description of various jobs. List of schools offering courses in hotel training.

* Restaurant hostess. Careers. 1969. 8p. 35c

Career brief describing duties, working conditions, training, personal qualifications, earnings, and outlook.

Room clerk. California State Department of Employment. 1968. 3p. Single copy free

Occupational guide describing work, requirements, training, and outlook.

Room clerk. Careers. 1968. 8p. 35c

Career brief describing duties, working conditions, training, personal qualifications, earnings, and outlook.

Scholarships in hotel and restaurant schools. Council on Hotel, Restaurant, and Institutional Education. 1969. 20p. 25c

Lists sources of aid that are open for students preparing for a career in the mass housing and feeding field.

Vocational guidance manual for the food service industry. National Restaurant Association. No date. 16p. Free to counselors

Description of the restaurant industry, types of positions available, and preparation. Included in the *Careers for Youth Kit.*

**Your career in the hotel-motel industry. American Hotel and Motel Association. 1966. 16p. Free

Description of the work of the various divisions of the hotel-motel and the training necessary for each. Includes list of scholarships.

See also Cook; Food preparation industry worker; Food technologist

HOTEL MANAGER 320.137

**Careers in hotel management. McDonnell, Virginia B. Julian Messner. 1971. 192p. $4.50; library edition $4.92

This book stresses the expanding opportunities in hotel, resort, and motor hotel management because of the growth of tourism. Includes functions and responsibilities of various managers, preparation, promotional possibilities, and outlook. A directory of training schools is arranged by state.

Finding out about hotel managers. Science Research Associates. 1967. 4p. 45c

Junior occupational brief describing work and opportunities.

Hotel manager. California State Department of Employment. 1964. 4p. Single copy free

Duties, working conditions, pay, hours, entrance requirements, training, promotion, and employment outlook.

HOTEL MANAGER—*Continued*

**Hotel manager. Careers. 1970. 8p. 35c

Career brief describing duties, working conditions, personal qualifications, advantages, disadvantages, earnings, advancement prospects, and outlook. Additional readings.

Hotel manager. Chronicle Guidance Publications. 1969. 4p. 35c

Occupational brief summarizing nature of the work, working conditions, hours and earnings, personal qualifications, education, training, and outlook.

Hotel manager. Guidance Centre. 1970. 4p. 35c

History and importance of the work, qualifications, preparation, employment outlook, advancement, earnings, related occupations, and how to get started.

Hotel managers. Science Research Associates. 1969. 4p. 45c

Occupational brief describing nature of work, training, qualifications, opportunities, and outlook.

**Hotel managers and assistants. One section of *Occupational Outlook Handbook.*

Nature of work, where employed, training, other qualifications, employment outlook, earnings, and working conditions.

Modern hotel and motel management. Lattin, Gerald W. Freeman and Company. 2nd edition. 1968. 230p. $4.50

Career opportunities are described and duties of many of the staff are given in the explanation of organization and functions of the various departments.

Starting and managing a small motel. Small Business Administration. Supt. of Documents. 1963. 70p. 30c

This booklet describes the advantages and disadvantages of entering this particular business, the risks involved, the personal characteristics that will contribute to success, and some management practices.

**Your future in hotel management. Sonnabend, Roger. Richards Rosen Press. Revised 1969. 160p. $4; library edition $3.78; edition in large type $5.97

Description of varied kinds of work, training, qualifications, and opportunities. Includes list of schools which offer courses and degrees in hotel management.

HOUSEKEEPER AND HOUSEHOLD WORKERS 30 and 321.

Employment outlook for private household workers. Bulletin No. 1650–67. Bureau of Labor Statistics, U.S. Department of Labor. Supt. of Documents. 1970. 8p. 10c

Reprint from the *Occupational Outlook Handbook.*

Executive housekeeper. Careers. 1969. 2p. 20c

Career summary for desk-top file. Duties, qualifications, and outlook.

Executive housekeeper. Chronicle Guidance Publications. 1969. 4p. 35c
Occupational brief summarizing nature of work, working conditions, personal qualifications, education and training, hours, earnings, and outlook.

* Executive housekeepers. Science Research Associates. 1967. 4p. 45c
Occupational brief describing nature of work, training, qualifications, opportunities, and outlook. Selected references.

Finding out about executive housekeepers. Science Research Associates. 1967. 4p. 45c
Junior occupational brief summarizing what the work requires and offers.

Finding out about household workers. Science Research Associates. 1967. 4p. 45c
Junior occupational brief summarizing what the work requires and offers.

Housekeepers and assistants (hotel). One section of *Occupational Outlook Handbook.*
Nature of work, training, other qualifications, and employment outlook.

**Household workers. Science Research Associates. 1969. 4p. 45c
Occupational brief describing nature of work, personal qualifications, opportunities, advantages, disadvantages, and future outlook.

In choosing a career—consider executive housekeeping. National Executive Housekeepers Association. 1967. 4p. Free
Brochure describing the nature of work, requirements, and compensation.

Kitchen helper. California State Department of Employment. 1968. 4p. Single copy free
Occupational guide describing work, requirements, training, and outlook.

HUNTING AND FISHING GUIDE. *See* Wildlife specialist

ICE CREAM MANUFACTURING WORKER 313.781

**Ice cream manufacturing workers. Science Research Associates. 1967. 4p. 45c
Occupational brief describing types of work, requirements, methods of getting started, earnings, advantages, disadvantages, and future outlook.

ICE PILOT 197.133

Ice pilot: Bob Bartlett. Sarnoff, Paul. Julian Messner. 1966. 192p. $3.50; library binding $3.34
Biography of a man who traveled by sail, sled, and foot over 100,000 miles of Polar ice desert, beginning with Perry's expedition to the North Pole in 1894.

ICHTHYOLOGIST. *See* Herpetologist; Zoologist

ILLUMINATING ENGINEER 003.081

Careers in lighting. Illuminating Engineering Society. 1969. 8p. Single copy free

Description of the following specialists: lighting designer, luminaire designer, lighting researcher, market analyst, sales engineer, and promotion expert.

Light bulb checker. One unit in *Finding Your Job* series, published by Finney Company. Not available separately.

Description of work, opportunities, and employment outlook.

ILLUSTRATING COMMERCIAL ARTIST. *See* Commercial artist; Medical and scientific illustrator

ILLUSTRATOR 141.081

Illustrator; draftsman; poster and display artist. Pages 128-130 of *Health Careers Guidebook*.

Brief statement of qualifications and opportunities.

Illustrator, technical. Chronicle Guidance Publications. 1968. 4p. 35c

Occupational brief summarizing nature of work, working conditions, earnings and hours, personal qualifications, education and training, and outlook.

Technical illustrator (technical artist). California State Department of Employment. 1965. 3p. Single copy free

Occupational guide describing work, requirements, training, and outlook.

IMMIGRATION INSPECTOR 168.168

**A career with the immigration and naturalization service. Immigration and Naturalization Service. Annually. 12p. Free

Includes answers to the questions most frequently asked about immigration patrol inspection positions in the U.S. Border Patrol. Examination and job requirements are listed.

Immigration inspector. Careers. 1967. 2p. 20c

Career summary for desk-top file. Duties, qualifications, and outlook.

Immigration officer. Guidance Centre. 1967. 4p. 35c postpaid

Definition, history and importance, nature of work, outlook, preparation, qualifications, advancement, remuneration, and how to get started.

Immigration patrol inspector. California State Department of Employment. 1963. 4p. Free

Occupational guide describing job duties, employment outlook, working conditions, earnings, entrance requirements, and training.

See also Customs and immigration inspector

IMPORTER. *See* Export and import worker

INDUSTRIAL ARTS TEACHER 091.228

A career in teaching industrial arts. American Industrial Arts Association. 1968. 8p. 20c

Written to interest young people in teaching careers.

Directory of colleges and universities offering degrees in industrial arts. American Industrial Arts Association. 1968. 4p. Single copy free

Information includes whether undergraduate, graduate, or other degrees are offered.

Manual arts therapists in the Veterans Administration. VA pamphlet 10-64. Veterans Administration Forms Depot. 1968. 4p. Free

Description of work, training program, qualifications, and benefits.

INDUSTRIAL CHEMIST 558.885

**Employment outlook for the industrial chemical industry. Bulletin No. 1650–113. Bureau of Labor Statistics, U.S. Department of Labor. Supt. of Documents. 1970. 12p. 15c

Reprint from the *Occupational Outlook Handbook.*

Industrial chemical manufacturing workers. Science Research Associates. 1967. 4p. 45c

Occupational brief describing kinds of work, requirements, training, getting started and advancing, earnings, advantages, disadvantages, and future outlook.

**Occupations in the industrial chemical industry. One chapter of *Occupational Outlook Handbook.*

Nature of the industry, kinds of work, training, other qualifications, advancement, employment outlook, earnings, and working conditions.

INDUSTRIAL DESIGNER 142.081

**Aim for a job in graphic design. Fujita, Neil. Richards Rosen Press. 1968. 146p. $4; library edition $3.78

Description of the work, qualifications, salary range, and outlook. Some biographies of successful designers are provided.

Automobile-body designer. Careers. 1967. 2p. 20c

Career summary for desk-top file. Duties, qualifications, and outlook.

Careers in industrial design. Chronicle Guidance Publications. 1968. 8p. 50c

Reprinted article from *Industrial Designers Society of America* contains material from roundtable discussion attended by students and a representative of the Industrial Designers Society of America answering students' questions concerning the field of work.

Careers in industrial design. Industrial Designers Society of America. 1966. 11p. 25c

Description of work, qualifications, training, and outlook.

INDUSTRIAL DESIGNER—*Continued*

Finding out about industrial designers. Science Research Associates. 1967. 4p. 45c

Junior occupational brief summarizing what the work requires and offers.

Finding out about stage designers. Science Research Associates. 1967. 4p. 45c

Junior occupational brief describing work and opportunities.

* Industrial designer. Careers. 1970. 8p. 35c

Career brief describing duties, working conditions, training, personal qualifications, advancement prospects, earnings, and outlook.

Industrial designer. Chronicle Guidance Publications. 1966. 4p. 35c

Occupational brief summarizing work performed, working conditions, wages, personal qualifications, training, opportunities, and outlook.

Industrial designer. Guidance Centre. 1968. 4p. 35c postpaid

Nature of work, history and importance, qualifications, preparation, employment, advancement, remuneration, working conditions, how to get started, and related occupations.

Industrial designers. Science Research Associates. 1969. 4p. 45c

Occupational brief describing nature of work, qualifications, preparation, opportunities, advantages, disadvantages, and future outlook.

**Industrial designers. One section of *Occupational Outlook Handbook.*

Nature of work, where employed, training, other qualifications, advancement, employment outlook, earnings, and working conditions.

**Opportunities in industrial design. Pulos, Arthur J. Vocational Guidance Manuals. 1969. 160p. $1.95; library edition $3.75

Discussion of the nature of work, types of jobs available, educational preparation, qualifications, opportunities, rewards, and employment outlook. Suggestions are also given for secondary school preparation and choosing a school of art for training.

What executives should know about industrial designers. Chronicle Guidance Publications. 1968. 4p. 35c

Reprinted article from *Think Magazine* discusses practice of industrial design, educational preparation necessary, and styled obsolescence.

See also Commercial artist

INDUSTRIAL ENGINEER 012.188

Finding out about industrial engineers. Science Research Associates. 1967. 4p. 45c

Junior occupational brief containing concise facts about the job.

Industrial engineer. California State Department of Employment. 1965. 5p. Single copy free

Occupational guide describing work, requirements, training, and outlook.

Industrial engineer. Careers. 1966. 2p. 20c
Career summary for desk-top file. Duties, qualifications, and outlook.

Industrial engineer. Chronicle Guidance Publications. 1968. 4p. 35c
Occupational brief summarizing work performed, earnings, outlook, personal qualifications, educational requirements, and licensing.

Industrial engineer. Guidance Centre. 1969. 4p. 35c postpaid
History and importance, nature of work, qualifications, preparation, advancement, outlook, remuneration, and how to get started.

Industrial engineering technicians. Chronicle Guidance Publications. 1969. 8p. 50c
Occupational brief summarizing work performed, qualifications, training, opportunities, salaries, location of work, and outlook.

Industrial engineering . . . the profession with a future. American Institute of Industrial Engineers. 1967. 16p. Single copy free
Explanation of the activities of the industrial engineer, opportunities, preparation, earnings, employment outlook, and advancement.

* Industrial engineers. Science Research Associates. 1968. 4p. 45c
Occupational brief describing areas of specialization, requirements, getting started and advancing, earnings, and future outlook.

Industrial engineers. Brief section in *Occupational Outlook Handbook.*
Nature of work, where employed, and employment outlook.

See also Engineer; Scientist

INDUSTRIAL HYGIENIST 079.188

Finding out about industrial hygienists. Science Research Associates. 1967. 4p. 45c
Junior occupational brief describing work and opportunities.

Industrial hygienist. American Industrial Hygiene Association. 1966. 4p. Free
Description of work, requirements, employment outlook, and working conditions.

Industrial hygienist. Pages 106-8 of *Health Careers Guidebook.*
Personal qualifications, training, opportunities, and prospects.

* Industrial hygienists. Science Research Associates. 1966. 4p. 45c
Occupational brief describing nature of work, requirements, training, getting started, earnings, advantages, disadvantages, and future outlook. Selected references.

See also Dental hygienist

INDUSTRIAL MACHINERY REPAIRMAN 638.281

Finding out about industrial machinery repairmen. Science Research Associates. 1967. 4p. 45c
Junior occupational brief summarizing what the work requires and offers.

INDUSTRIAL MACHINERY REPAIRMAN—*Continued*

Finding out about industrial technicians. Science Research Associates. 1967. 4p. 45c

Junior occupational brief describing work and opportunities.

Industrial machinery mechanic. Chronicle Guidance Publications. 1968. 4p. 35c

Occupational brief summarizing work performed, working conditions, personal requirements, where employed, opportunities for advancement, hours and earnings, educational and training requirements, and employment outlook.

Industrial machinery repairmen. Science Research Associates. 1967. 4p. 45c

Occupational brief describing work, training, opportunities, and outlook.

**Industrial machinery repairmen. One section of *Occupational Outlook Handbook*.

Nature of work, where employed, training, other qualifications, employment outlook, earnings, and working conditions.

INSPECTOR 736.

Factory inspectors. Science Research Associates. 1968. 4p. 45c

Occupational brief describing nature of work, training, working conditions, opportunities, and outlook.

Federal Government inspectors and examiners. Science Research Associates. 1967. 4p. 45c

Occupational brief describing work, training, qualifications, opportunities, and outlook.

**Inspectors (manufacturing). One section of *Occupational Outlook Handbook*.

Nature of work, where employed, training, employment outlook, earnings, and working conditions.

INSTRUMENT MAKER 600.280

Finding out about instrument makers. Science Research Associates. 1967. 4p. 45c

Junior occupational brief summarizing what the work requires and offers.

Instrument maker. Chronicle Guidance Publications. 1969. 4p. 35c

Occupational brief summarizing work performed, training, qualifications, and outlook.

* Instrument makers. Science Research Associates. 1969. 4p. 45c

Occupational brief describing work, qualifications, training, advantages, disadvantages, and outlook.

**Instrument makers. One section of *Occupational Outlook Handbook*.

Nature of work, where employed, training, other qualifications, advancement, employment outlook, earnings, and working conditions.

Model maker. Careers. 1968. 2p. 20c
Career summary for desk-top file. Duties, qualifications, and outlook.

**Musical instrument manufacturing workers. Science Research Associates. 1967. 4p. 45c
Occupational brief describing nature of work, requirements, getting started, earnings, advantages, disadvantages, and future outlook.

INSTRUMENT REPAIRMAN 710.281

**Employment outlook for instrument repairmen. Bulletin No. 1650–87. Bureau of Labor Statistics, U.S. Department of Labor. Supt. of Documents. 1970. 8p. 10c
Reprint from the *Occupational Outlook Handbook.*

Finding out about instrument repairmen. Science Research Associates. 1967. 4p. 45c
Junior occupational brief containing concise facts about the job.

Instrument repairman. Chronicle Guidance Publications. 1969. 4p. 35c
Occupational brief summarizing work performed, working conditions, qualifications, training, earnings, where employed, and methods of entry.

Instrument repairmen. Careers. 1970. 8p. 35c
Career brief describing duties, working conditions, personal qualifications, places of employment, advancement prospects, earnings, and outlook.

Instrument repairmen. Science Research Associates. 1970. 4p. 25c
Occupational brief describing working conditions, requirements, training, earnings, and future outlook.

**Instrument repairmen. One section of *Occupational Outlook Handbook.*
Nature of work, where employed, training, employment outlook, earnings, and working conditions.

Instrument serviceman. California State Department of Employment. 1965. 4p. Single copy free
Occupational guide describing work, requirements, training, and outlook.

Instrument technologist. Guidance Centre. 1968. 4p. postpaid
Definition, history and importance, nature of work, preparation, qualifications, employment, advancement, remuneration, and how to get started.

INSTRUMENTAL MUSICIAN 152.048

Examination papers for associateship with solutions. American Guild of Organists. 1969. 6p. $1
Also available from the same source are examination papers for fellowship and choir master, with solutions.

Finding out about instrumentalists in classical music. Science Research Associates. 1967. 4p. 45c
Junior occupational brief describing work and opportunities.

INSTRUMENTAL MUSICIAN—*Continued*

Finding out about instrumentalists in popular music. Science Research Associates. 1967. 4p. 45c

Junior occupational brief describing work and opportunities.

Finding out about orchestra conductors. Science Research Associates. 1967. 4p. 45c

Junior occupational brief containing concise facts about the job.

Instrumental musician. Careers. 1970. 2p. 20c

Career summary for desk-top file. Duties, qualifications, and outlook.

Musician, instrumental. California State Department of Employment. 1968. 4p. Single copy free

Description of work, duties, working conditions, employment outlook, training requirements, and how to find work in California.

Musician, instrumental. Chronicle Guidance Publications. 1969. 4p. 35c

Occupational brief summarizing work performed, working conditions, earnings, personal qualifications, training requirements, opportunities, and employment outlook.

The unashamed accompanist. Moore, Gerald. Macmillan Company. 1945. 84p. $3.50

Encourages amateur pianists to take up accompanying for their careers and suggests preparation and qualifications. Most useful, however, as advice to the beginning accompanist. Out of print but available in many libraries.

Well-tempered accompanist. Bos, Coenraad Valentyn. Theodore Presser Company. 1950. 162p. $2.50

Autobiography of a piano accompanist telling of his experiences over fifty years with the famous singers he accompanies.

See also Music teacher; Musician

INSTRUMENTATION TECHNICIAN 003.281

Instrumentation technician. Careers. 1970. 2p. 20c

Career summary for desk-top file. Duties, qualifications, and outlook.

Instrumentation technician. One section of *Occupational Outlook Handbook.*

Brief description of work and employment outlook.

See also Electronics technician; Programmer

INSURANCE INDUSTRY WORKER 250.

Beginning jobs in the insurance industry. California State Department of Employment. 1967. 4p. Single copy free

Occupational guide describing work, requirements, training, and outlook.

Careers in insurance. Insurance Information Institute. 1968. 16p. Free

Description of positions in property and liability insurance such as agent, field representative, actuary, underwriter, adjuster, and loss prevention engineer. Illustrated.

Claims adjuster (insurance). California State Department of Employment. 1966. 5p. Single copy free

Occupational guide describing work, requirements, training, and outlook.

Employment outlook for insurance agents and brokers. Bulletin No. 1650–57. Bureau of Labor Statistics, U.S. Department of Labor. Supt. of Documents. 1970. 8p. 10c

Reprint from the *Occupational Outlook Handbook.*

Employment outlook for the insurance business. Bulletin No. 1650–125. Bureau of Labor Statistics, U.S. Department of Labor. Supt. of Documents. 1970. 8p. 15c

Reprint from the *Occupational Outlook Handbook.*

Exploring your future in insurance. Sextant Systems, Inc. 1971. 96p. $8.95

One page is devoted to each of ninety-five jobs, describing the duties, requirements for entering, promotional outlook, and the pay and skill level.

Finding out about insurance adjusters. Science Research Associates. 1967. 4p. 45c

Junior occupational brief summarizing what the work requires and offers.

Finding out about insurance agents. Science Research Associates. 1967. 4p. 45c

Junior occupational brief containing concise facts about the job.

Finding out about insurance clerks. Science Research Associates. 1967. 4p. 45c

Junior occupational brief describing work and opportunities.

General insurance agent. Guidance Centre. 1967. 4p. 35c postpaid

History and importance, nature of work, qualifications, working conditions, preparation, remuneration, outlook, related occupations, and how to get started.

A great career—for those who measure up. Fidelity Mutual Life Insurance Company. 1965. 18p. Free

In question and answer form, information is given about training, ways to advance, and opportunities.

Insurance adjuster. Guidance Centre. 1966. 4p. 35c postpaid

Nature of work, qualifications, advancement, outlook, remuneration, advantages, disadvantages, how to get started, and related occupations.

Insurance adjusters. Science Research Associates. 1968. 4p. 45c

Occupational brief describing nature of work, qualifications, getting started and advancing, earnings, advantages, disadvantages, and future outlook.

INSURANCE INDUSTRY WORKER—*Continued*

Insurance agent. Michigan Employment Security Commission. 1961. 2p. Single copy free

Job brief summarizing occupational data for use in Michigan.

Insurance agents. Science Research Associates. 1966. 4p. 45c

Occupational brief describing nature of work, requirements, education and training, earnings, how to get a job, advantages, disadvantages, and future outlook.

Insurance agents and brokers. One section of *Occupational Outlook Handbook.*

Nature of work, where employed, training, other qualifications, advancement, employment outlook, earnings, and working conditions.

Insurance industry careers. Chronicle Guidance Publications. 1967. 4p. 35c

Occupational brief summarizing definition, nature of work, working conditions, hours and wages, education and training requirements, and outlook.

It's up to you—a guide to a career in life and health insurance. Institute of Life Insurance. 1968. 36p. Free to guidance counselors in quantities up to 25

This is a type of workbook giving the student an opportunity to answer questions about his school work, interests, and personal preferences. Information is included about the insurance business and opportunities.

Life insurance agent. Careers. 1968. 8p. 35c

Career brief describing duties, working conditions, personal qualifications, advantages, disadvantages, advancement prospects, earnings, and outlook.

Life insurance agent. Chronicle Guidance Publications. 1969. 4p. 35c

Occupational brief summarizing work performed, where employed, personal requirements, training, earnings, methods of entry, and outlook.

Life insurance agent. Guidance Centre. 1966. 4p. 35c postpaid

Nature of work, qualifications, preparation needed for entry and success, employment and advancement, earnings, how to get started, and related occupations.

The life insurance career. Life Insurance Agency Management Association. 1962. 20p. Free

This booklet stresses insurance as a social and economic force and points out the advantages of insurance as a career.

Life underwriting as a career. Connecticut Mutual Life Insurance Company. 1967. 15p. Single copy free

Description of work, responsibilities, opportunities, rewards, challenges, and difficulties.

**Occupations in the insurance business. One chapter in *Occupational Outlook Handbook.*

Nature of the business, kinds of jobs, where employed, training, other qualifications, advancement, employment outlook, earnings, and working conditions.

**Opportunities in life insurance selling. Rosler, Lee. Vocational Guidance Manuals. 1965. 112p. $1.95 paper; library edition $3.75

Starting with the importance of life insurance and what it takes to be a successful agent, the author presents details of educational preparation, training opportunities, compensation, how to get started, management opportunities, and professional aspects. A week in the life of an agent is described hour by hour.

Property and liability insurance agent. Careers. 1966. 2p. 20c

Career summary for desk-top file. Duties, qualifications, and outlook.

Property and liability insurance agents and brokers. One section of *Occupational Outlook Handbook.*

Nature of work, where employed, training, and qualifications.

Underwriter (insurance). California State Department of Employment. 1966. 4p. Single copy free

Occupational guide describing work, requirements, training, and outlook.

See also Real estate salesman

INTERIOR DESIGNER AND DECORATOR 142.051

Apprentices—interior designers. Chronicle Guidance Publications. 1968. 2p. 35c

Reprinted article from *Interiors* discusses supply of and demand for interior designers.

A critical study of interior design education. Interior Design Educators Council. 1968. 134p. $3. Free to schools, colleges, and professional societies

For the use of interior design educators interested in curriculum improvement.

Directory of Institutions offering interior design education. Interior Design Educators Council. 1968. 29p. $2. Free to schools, colleges, and professional societies

A complete survey of schools in the United States and Canada.

Finding out about interior designers. Science Research Associates. 1967. 4p. 45c

Junior occupational brief summarizing what the work requires and offers.

Interior decoration. Alumnae Advisory Center. 1963. 6p. 35c

Reprint from *Mademoiselle* describing the work of several successful women in this field.

Interior designer. California State Department of Employment. 1968. 6p. Single copy free

Occupational guide describing work, requirements, training, and outlook.

* Interior designer. Careers. 1968. 8p. 35c

Career brief describing duties, where employed, personal qualifications, training requirements, training opportunities, measuring one's interest and ability, opportunities for men, employment outlook, and related jobs. Suggested references.

INTERIOR DESIGNER AND DECORATOR—*Continued*

Interior designer. Chronicle Guidance Publications. 1967. 4p. 35c

Occupational brief containing history, work performed, working conditions, personal requirements, training requirements, outlook, where employed, and methods of entry.

Interior designer. Guidance Centre. 1968. 4p. 35c postpaid

History and importance, working conditions, qualifications necessary for entry and success, preparation, employment and advancement, advantages, disadvantages, how to enter this field, and related occupations.

* Interior designers and decorators. Science Research Associates. 1969. 4p. 46c

Occupational brief describing nature of work, training, qualifications, preparation, opportunities, advantages, disadvantages, and future outlook.

** Interior designers and decorators. One section of *Occupational Outlook Handbook*.

Nature of work, where employed, training, other qualifications, advancement, employment outlook, earnings, and working conditions.

** Opportunities in interior design and decoration. Ball, Victoria. Vocational Guidance Manuals. 1963. 126p. $1.95 paper; library edition $3.75

Includes discussion of the development of the work, future outlook, qualifications, preparation, opportunities, how to get started, and related fields.

Scene designers. Science Research Associates. 1967. 4p. 45c

Occupational brief describing work, training, qualifications, opportunities, and outlook.

Schools offering courses in interior design and decoration. One section of the *American Art Directory*.

List of schools in the United States, Canada, and Latin America with information concerning courses and costs.

Student career guide. National Society of Interior Designers. 1968. 6p. Free

Leaflet describing job duties, working conditions, employment prospects, job advancement, and compensation.

Three professionals look at interior design. Chronicle Guidance Publications. 1966. 2p. 35c

Reprinted article from *Practical Forecast for Home Economics* discusses interior decorating in the home.

Your career in interior design. Doyle, Robert V. Julian Messner. 1969. 192p. $3.95; library binding $3.64

Describes the work and opportunities of many specialists and several kinds of employment that can lead to a career in the home-furnishings and interior-designing field. Explains work in motion pictures and television, in home furnishing stores, and as consultant and teacher. Includes preparation for this work and a list of recommended schools, colleges, and art institutes.

**Your future in interior design. Greer, Michael. Richards Rosen Press. Revised 1969. 157p. $4; library edition $3.78

Stresses the training and knowledge required for skill in participating in this creative field.

INTERNAL REVENUE AGENT 188.168

**A career and a sense of purpose. Internal Revenue Service. 1969. 24p. Free

General introduction to opportunities available nationwide for college graduates with majors in a variety of fields. Information on qualification standards, training, promotion opportunities, and how to apply. Describes seven major positions: internal revenue agent, revenue officer, estate tax attorney, special intelligence agent, tax technician, internal auditor, and alcohol and tobacco tax inspector.

**Careers in taxation. Internal Revenue Service. 1968. 13p. Free

Information about jobs in the tax field, employment outlook, location of jobs, personal qualifications, educational requirements, earnings, advancement, advantages, and disadvantages. Selected references.

Engineer tax man. Internal Revenue Service. 1969. 14p. Free

Information about engineers in the Internal Revenue Service, the work they do and how they feel about it. Discussion of engineering issues in tax administration, job location, typical problems, scope of work, qualification standards, career aspects, and how to apply.

* Internal revenue agent. Careers. 1966. 8p. 35c

Career brief describing duties, working conditions, training, personal qualifications, advantages, disadvantages, advancement prospects, earnings, and outlook.

Internal revenue agent. Internal Revenue Service. 1969. 16p. Free

Information on the professional career of the agent who examines and audits the accounting books and records of individuals, fiduciaries, and corporations to determine their correct Federal tax liabilities. Describes qualification requirements, promotion opportunities, job location, training, and how to apply.

Internal revenue agents. Science Research Associates. 1967. 4p. 45c

Occupational brief describing nature of work, training, qualifications, opportunities, and outlook.

Internal revenue officer. Internal Revenue Service. 1969. 16p. Free

Explains the work of the officer who has the responsibility for collecting unpaid taxes and helping people to understand and meet their tax obligations. Describes qualification requirements, training, promotion opportunities, job locations, and how to apply.

Tax technician. Internal Revenue Service. 1969. 16p. Free

Explains the duties of the tax technician who works specifically in solving a variety of Federal income tax questions not involving professional accounting issues. Describes qualification standards, training, promotion opportunities, and how to apply for the position.

INTERNAL REVENUE AGENT—*Continued*

Treasury enforcement agent. U.S. Treasury Department. Distributed by Internal Revenue Service. 1969. 20p. Free

Information on positions available for men as a treasury enforcement agent: customs agents and port investigators, alcohol and tobacco tax special investigators, internal security inspectors, secret service special agent, and others responsible for curtailment of illicit distilleries, counterfeiting, tax fraud, prevention and detection of smuggling, and the protection of the President and his family.

INTERPRETER AND TRANSLATOR. *See* Linguist

INVENTOR 693.281

Fathers of industries. Fanning, Leonard. Lippincott Company. 1962. 256p. $4.75

Twenty-four biographies of inventors whose discoveries led to the huge industries of today. Includes accomplishments of men whose inventive genius helped to develop air conditioning, airplane, aluminum, automobile, machine tool, paper, petroleum, radio, rubber, steel, and textile industries. Illustrated.

From spinning wheel to space craft. Neal, Harry E. Julian Messner. 1964. 192p. Library binding $3.64

Story of modern man's startling inventions and discoveries that have changed standards of living throughout the world. Includes accounts of many inventors who overcame handicaps to bring their discoveries into existence.

Inventive wizard: George Westinghouse. Levine, I. E. Julian Messner. 1962. 192p. $3.50; library binding $3.34

Biography of the inventor whose air brakes and signal devices changed the railroad industry and whose work on transmitting electricity at low cost brought power and light to millions.

Inventors in industry. Radford, Ruby. Julian Messner. 1969. 96p. $3.95; library binding $3.64

The author shows how many inventors left their mark on industry through trial-and-error experiments, obstacles, failures, and persistent effort. For ages 8 to 12.

Men who pioneered inventions. Poole, Lynn and Poole, Gray. Dodd, Mead and Company. 1969. 176p. $4

Chapter-length biographies of the thirteen men who have played a major role in determining our present way of life. Inventions such as the automobile, sewing machine, and the computer are included.

Modern Americans in science and technology. Yost, Edna. Dodd, Mead and Company. 1962. 175p. $3.50

Thirteen short biographies of engineers, inventors, and scientists.

The telescope. Neal, Harry Edward. Julian Messner. 1958. 192p. Library binding $3.64

Includes description of different scientific careers in the brief biographies of the men who invented various parts of the telescope. Sixteen pages of illustration.

IRON AND STEEL INDUSTRY WORKER 50

**Aim for a job in the iron and steel industry. Sullivan, John W. W. Richards Rosen Press. 1967. 185p. $4; library edition $3.78

Consists of job descriptions of sixty jobs "for which high school graduates may become eligible within two months after they begin employment." Includes discussion of requirements, wages, opportunities, and outlook.

Andrew Carnegie. Harlow, Alvin. Julian Messner. 1953. 192p. $3.50; library binding $3.34

Biography of an immigrant boy who became one of America's leading industrialists, founded a vast steel empire, and used his wealth to endow libraries and other institutions.

Employment outlook for the iron and steel industry. Bulletin No. 1650–114. Bureau of Labor Statistics, U.S. Department of Labor. Supt. of Documents. 1970. 15p. 15c

Reprint from the *Occupational Outlook Handbook.*

Finding out about structural-iron workers. Science Research Associates. 1967. 4p. 45c

Junior occupational brief describing work and opportunities.

Iron and steel workers. Science Research Associates. 1966. 4p. 45c

Occupational brief describing some kinds of work, requirements, training, earnings, getting started, advantages, disadvantages, and future outlook.

Ironworker (structural). Guidance Centre. 1968. 4p. 35c postpaid

Definition, history and importance, nature of work, working conditions, qualifications, preparation, outlook, remuneration, advancement, and how to get started.

**A job with a future in the steel industry. Davis, Robert O. Grosset and Dunlop, Inc. 1969. 127p. $3.59

This is a survey of jobs in the steel industry, emphasizing those which do not require a high school diploma. After describing jobs related to the handling of raw materials such as work at the ore mines, coke plants, blast furnaces, and rolling mills, the author covers supporting services including maintenance and office work. He includes wage rates, paths for advancemet, and employment outlook.

**Occupations in the iron and steel industry. One section of *Occupational Outlook Handbook.*

Description of jobs in the industry, training, other qualifications, advancement, employment outlook, earnings, and working conditions.

IRON AND STEEL INDUSTRY WORKER–*Continued*

Opportunities in steel. American Iron and Steel Institute. 1967. 96p. Single copy free to counselors or librarians

Potential jobs in the steel industry are given for people with high school training, with technical institute courses, and with college preparation. Includes list of sources of information about job opportunities in steel.

Structural iron workers. Science Research Associates. 1966. 4p. 45c

Occupational brief describing work, training, earnings, some things to consider, and outlook. Selected references.

**Structural-, ornamental-, and reinforcing-iron (rodmen) workers, riggers, and machine movers. One section of *Occupational Outlook Handbook.*

Nature of work, where employed, training, other qualifications, employment outlook, earnings, and working conditions.

Structural-, ornamental-, and reinforcing-iron workers. Careers. 1966. 8p. 25c

Career brief describing duties, working conditions, training, places of employment, earnings, and outlook.

Structural steel worker. Chronicle Guidance Publications. 1969. 4p. 35c

Occupational brief summarizing nature of work, working conditions, hours and earnings, personal qualifications, where employed, education, training, and outlook.

Wage trends in the iron and steel industry. American Iron and Steel Institute. 1968. 4p. Free

Shows the average hourly employment costs of production workers and hourly earnings comparisons with other industries.

INVESTMENT COUNSELOR. *See* Securities salesman

JANITOR. *See* Building custodian

JEWELER AND JEWELER REPAIRMAN 700.281 and .381

**Employment outlook for jewelers and jewelry repairmen and watch repairmen. Bulletin No. 1650–88. Bureau of Labor Statistics, U.S. Department of Labor. Supt. of Documents. 1970. 12p. 15c

Reprint from the *Occupational Outlook Handbook.*

Finding out about jewelers. Science Research Associates. 1967. 4p. 45c

Junior occupational brief describing work and opportunities.

* Jeweler. Careers. 1968. 8p. 35c

Career brief describing duties, working conditions, personal requirements, training, earnings, and outlook.

Jeweler. Chronicle Guidance Publications. 1967. 4p. 35c

Occupational brief containing definitions, work performed, working conditions, personal requirements, determination of aptitudes and interests, training requirements, training opportunities, outlook, where employed, and suggested activities.

* Jewelers. Science Research Associates. 1967. 4p. 45c

Occupational brief describing the jewelry trades, requirements, training, getting started and advancing, advantages, disadvantages, and future outlook. Selected references.

**Jewelers and jewelry repairmen. One section of *Occupational Outlook Handbook*.

Nature of work, where employed, training, other qualifications, employment outlook, earnings, and working conditions.

Jeweller. Guidance Centre. 1966. 4p. 23c postpaid

Definition, working conditions, qualifications, preparation, advancement, outlook, remuneration, how to get started, and related occupations.

See also Watchmaker

JEWISH CENTER WORKER 195.108

Career in health and physical education in the Jewish community center. National Jewish Welfare Board. 1962. 15p. Free

Description of the health and physical education program and placement of qualified personnel. A separate publication describes a work-scholarship program for health and physical education personnel.

Careers in Jewish education. B'nai B'rith Vocational Service. 1968. 15p. 35c

Opportunities in the specialized field of Jewish education, preparation, opportunities, and advantages.

Careers in social group work in Jewish agencies. B'nai B'rith Vocational Service. 1969. 16p. 35c

Description of the nature of work and duties of social group workers in various work settings. Also included are qualifications, advancement, employment outlook, and salaries.

Careers in synagogue and temple administration. B'nai B'rith Vocational Service. 1969. 11p. 35c

A description of this relatively new profession in terms of duties, personal requirements, training, earnings, and opportunities. Sources of additional information are included.

Careers in the cantorate. B'nai B'rith Vocational Service. 1969. 12p. 35c

Description of career opportunities, responsibilities, vocal ability, qualifications, and employment outlook.

Careers in vocational service in Jewish agencies. B'nai B'rith Vocational Service. 1969. 19p. 35c

Discussion of nature of work, fields of specialization, Jewish aspects of guidance, requirements, opportunities and employment outlook. Includes a directory of Jewish-sponsored agencies.

JEWISH CENTER WORKER—*Continued*

Scholarships, fellowships, and work-study plans for graduate social work education for individuals interested in Jewish community center work as a career. National Jewish Welfare Board. 1963. 8p. Free

Annual listing of plans which help a potential social work student to prepare for work in a Jewish community center.

Your career opportunity in the Jewish community center. National Jewish Welfare Board. 1962. 12p. Free

Nature of work, qualifications, and practices.

Your opportunity for a professional career in Jewish communal service. B'nai B'rith Vocational Service. 1968. 10p. 35c

This booklet discusses opportunities for professional workers in areas of Jewish communal service; for example, rabbis, cantors, educators, counselors, journalists, and librarians.

JOB ANALYST 166.088

Job analyst. Careers. 1967. 2p. 20c

Career summary for desk-top file. Duties, qualifications, and outlook.

Job analyst. Chronicle Guidance Publications. 1969. 4p. 35c

Occupational brief describing nature of work, qualifications, working conditions, opportunities for promotion, and outlook.

Job analyst (wage and salary administration). California State Department of Employment. 1966. 4p. Single copy free

Occupational guide describing work, requirements, training, and outlook.

JOURNALIST 132.268 and 139.288

Accredited programs in journalism. American Council on Education for Journalism. 1968. 24p. Free

List of institutions of higher learning accredited by the American Council on Education for Journalism and holding membership in the American Association of Schools and Departments of Journalism. Also lists the schools offering accredited sequences or curricula, such as advertising, radio journalism, news-editorial, etc., with description of accrediting standards, policies, and procedures.

**Careers and opportunities in journalism. Freeman, Ira H. and Freeman, Beatrice O. Dutton and Company. 1966. 237p. $4.95

A survey of kinds of work on newspapers, wire services, magazines, trade publications, house organs, radio and television. Includes satisfactions, disadvantages, requirements, and opportunities. Illustrated. Good reading list.

Careers in daily newspapers, weekly newspapers, and wire services. Quill and Scroll Foundation. 1965. 40p. 60c

Includes the nature of work, abilities required, rewards, and opportunities in these media.

Careers in magazines and books. Wolseley, Roland E. Quill and Scroll Foundation. 1965. 15p. 35c

Types of positions, opportunities, and outlook for career journalists.

Directory issue. Journalism Educator. 1968. 48p. $3.

Bulletin of the American Society of Journalism School Administrators containing list of 159 schools and departments offering majors or degrees in journalism. Name of journalism unit is followed by year in which established, association affiliations, student organizations, facilities, and degrees offered.

**Do you belong in journalism? Gemmill, Henry and Kilgore, Bernard. Appleton-Century-Crofts. 1959. 92p. $3

Eighteen leading newspaper editors give the advice they would give to an interested young man or woman who was considering newspaper work. Carefully considered counsel. The final chapters sum up the requirements: "The first requirement is a college diploma . . . one should like people, reading, travel, and new experience." Illustrated.

Employment report on journalism graduates. Newspaper Fund, Inc. 1968. 26p. Free

An annual survey which reported on the number of journalism graduates in the classes of 1968, average beginning salary, and the communications media in which they went to work. Updated annually.

English and journalism: earned degrees, by level, sex, and institution. One section of *Earned Degrees Conferred.*

Useful for judging the extent of a college's program in journalism and in English and literature.

Fighting journalist: Horace Greeley. Archer, Jules. Julian Messner. 1966. 192p. $3.50; library binding $3.34

Biography of a pioneering newspaperman and ardent crusader of the nineteenth century. Greeley is shown as charting a new course for journalism and becoming a force in political and social life.

Get that story—journalism, its lore and thrills. Floherty, John J. Lippincott Company. 1964. 192p. $4.75

A résumé of the origin and early history of newspapers is followed by an account of reporting, editing, printing, and distribution of a large metropolitan daily. Chapters are included on the work of country newspapers, newspaper photography, and stories of reporters' luck and achievement in journalism.

Getting started in photojournalism. Payne, Lee. Chilton Book Company. 1967. 128p. $4.95

Includes a discussion of where to find opportunities in photojournalism, qualifications needed, and how to get started. Illustrated.

Headliners: famous American journalists. Forsee, Aylesa. Macrae Smith Company. 1967. 192p. $3.75

Profiles of six famous journalists.

JOURNALIST—*Continued*

I wanted to write. Roberts, Kenneth Lewis. Doubleday and Company. 1949. 471p. $5.95

An author describes his experiences as a roving reporter and his ambition to become a successful writer.

Information on the road to a career in journalism. Newspaper Fund, Inc. 1969. 10 leaflets. Free

A career kit of information. Updated annually.

Introduction to mass communications. Emery, Edwin; Ault, Philip H.; and Agee, Warren K. Dodd, Mead and Company. 1965. 434p. $6.95

An analysis of the mass media with a discussion of job opportunities, qualifications, and salaries.

Jobs in journalism. Changing Times. 1959. 3p. 15c

Reprint discussing opportunities in newspaper work and related careers.

Joseph Pulitzer: front page pioneer. Noble, Iris. Julian Messner. 1957. 192p. $3.50; library binding $3.34

Biography of a reporter and newspaper owner, containing considerable inspiring material.

Journalism scholarship guide. Newspaper Fund, Inc. 1969. 68p. Free

A listing of scholarships, fellowships, assistantships, and loans at 140 universities. Also included is a listing of scholarships offered by newspapers and by chapters of the major professional societies: Sigma Delta Chi (men), and Theta Sigma Phi (women). A final section on general university scholarships is included. Updated annually.

Journalism's new era. Chronicle Guidance Publications. 1967. 7p. 50c

Reprinted article from *The Quill* discusses opportunities, personal requirements, and salaries for beginning journalists.

**Journalist. Brucker, Herbert. Macmillan Company. 1962. 211p. $3.95

The author draws upon his experience as a journalist and editor to provide a picture of education and necessary preparation, the different kinds of work available, and the excitement of an average day at a newspaper office.

* Journalist. Careers. 1967. 8p. 35c

Career brief describing the work of news gathering and writing, working conditions, training, requirements, personal qualifications, employment prospects, advantages, disadvantages, earnings, promotional prospects, measuring one's interest and ability, and suggested high school subjects.

One hundred books for new journalists. Journalism Educator. 1968. 16p. Free

Includes many biographies and anecdotal accounts.

**Opportunities in journalism careers. Barry, John M. Vocational Guidance Manuals. 1967. 136p. $1.95 paper; $3.75 library edition

Discussion of the newspaper industry, the challenge of the future, intangible rewards, outlook for jobs, training, educational preparations, related fields, and classifications of editorial work. List of schools and departments of journalism.

Printer's devil to publisher; Adolph S. Ochs of the New York Times. Faber, Doris. Julian Messner. 1963. 192p. $3.50; library binding $3.34

Biography of the man who worked his way up from delivery boy to control of one of the world's greatest newspapers.

Report on the interns, 1960-69. The Newspaper Fund. 1969. 10p. Free

A ten-year report on former Newspaper Fund intern scholarship winners and where they are working. Salary information is also included.

What it takes to become a foreign correspondent. The Newspaper Fund. 1968. 6p. Free

Some suggested approaches and a reading list of books on the work of foreign correspondents.

**Your career in journalism. Stein, M. L. Julian Messner. 1965. 192p. $3.95; library binding $3.64

Beginning with the preparation and abilities needed to enter a career in journalism, a former newspaperman describes a typical assignment and discusses the various types of work and media. Also reviews the challenges, rewards, and future trends of communicating news and ideas to the public. Reading list.

Your future in daily newspapers. American Newspaper Publishers Association Foundation. 1968. 31p. 35c. Single copy free

Describes opportunities in various phases of newspaper work such as editorial, business, and production. Attempts to answer questions that young people have about daily newspapers: What are the advantages and disadvantages? Is newspaper work hard to get into? Where is the newspaper business going?

**Your future in journalism. Schaleben, Arville. Richards Rosen Press. Revised 1969. 158p. $4; library edition $3.78

Describes the work of the editor, news reporter, and some of the specialists such as the photographer and picture editor. Includes also a discussion of requirements, opportunities, salaries, and a self-evaluation test. List of accredited schools.

See also Editor; Reporter; Writer

KEY PUNCH OPERATOR 213.582

Finding out about keypunch operators. Science Research Associates. 1967. 4p. 45c

Junior occupational brief containing concise facts about the job.

Key punch operator. California State Department of Employment. 1966. 3p. Single copy free

Occupational guide describing work, requirements, training, and outlook.

Key-punch operator. Michigan Employment Security Commission. 1963. 2p. Single copy free

Job brief summarizing occupational data for use in Michigan.

KEY PUNCH OPERATOR—*Continued*

Key punch operators. Science Research Associates. 1968. 4p. 45c
Occupational brief describing nature of work, training, qualifications, opportunities, advantages, disadvantages, and future outlook.

KINDERGARTEN AND NURSERY SCHOOL TEACHER 092.228

Finding out about kindergarten and nursery school teachers. Science Research Associates. 1967. 4p. 45c
Junior occupational brief describing work and opportunities.

**Kindergarten and elementary school teachers. One section of *Occupational Outlook Handbook.*
Nature of work, where employed, training, other qualifications, advancement, employment outlook, earnings, and working conditions.

Kindergarten and nursery school teacher. Chronicle Guidance Publications. 1968. 4p. 35c
Occupational brief summarizing work performed, personal qualifications, educational requirements, earnings, and outlook.

**Kindergarten and nursery school teachers. Science Research Associates. 1966. 4p. 45c
Occupational brief describing nature of work, requirements, training, getting started, earnings, advantages, disadvantages, and future outlook.

Kindergarten teacher. Careers. 1966. 2p. 20c
Career summary for desk-top file. Duties, qualifications, and outlook.

* Nursery school teacher. Careers. 1969. 2p. 20c
Career summary for desk-top file. Duties, qualifications, and outlook.

Nursery-school teacher. Guidance Centre. 1968. 4p. 35c postpaid
Definition, history and importance, nature of work, working conditions, qualifications, preparation, employment and advancement, remuneration, advantages, disadvantages, how to get started, and related occupations.

See also Teacher

LABOR-RELATIONS SPECIALIST 169.118

Finding out about industrial relations workers. Science Research Associates. 1967. 4p. 45c
Junior occupational brief containing concise facts about the job.

Industrial and labor relations director. Careers. 1969. 2p. 20c
Career summary for desk-top file. Duties, qualifications, and outlook.

**Industrial and labor relations workers. Science Research Associates. 1970. 4p. 45c
Occupational brief describing nature of work, training, qualifications, opportunities, advantages, disadvantages, and future outlook.

Industrial development coordinator. California State Department of Employment. 1965. 4p. Single copy free

Occupational guide describing work, requirements, training, and outlook.

Labor relations man (in industry). California State Department of Employment. 1964. 6p. Single copy free

Job duties, working conditions, pay, hours, entrance requirements, promotion, training, and employment outlook.

Labor's advocate, Eugene V. Debs. Noble, Iris. Julian Messner. 1966. 192p. $3.50; library binding $3.34

Biography of a union organizer of the first railroad union who sought to advance the cause of the laboring man.

Woman at work, the autobiography of Mary Anderson as told to Mary N. Winslow. Anderson, Mary. University of Minnesota Press. 1951. 266p. $3.50

Account of her experiences as head of the Women's Bureau of the U.S. Department of Labor for twenty-five years and other work as a labor leader. Illustrated.

See also Personnel and employment manager

LABORATORY TECHNICIAN 078.128

**Basic sciences in the health field. Pages 76-84 of *Health Careers Guidebook.*

Discussion of some of the interlocking specialties, exploring new health frontiers, getting a start in science, outlook for careers in science, a list of science specialists, and a description of work in laboratory administration and maintenance.

A career as a laboratory technician. Chronicle Guidance Publications. 1968. 4p. 35c

Reprinted article by permission of Armstrong Cork Company discusses specific character traits of a good technician.

Educational and experience qualifications of public health laboratory workers. American Public Health Association. 1967. 9p. Single copy free

Includes qualifications for various grades of laboratory workers.

For an age of science: a laboratory career. Ohio Department of Health. No date. 6p. Free

Description of work and qualifications of public health bacteriologist, public health chemist, clinical laboratory technician, and scientific research worker.

Laboratory assistant (laboratory technician). California State Department of Employment. 1966. 3p. Single copy free

Occupational guide describing work, requirements, training, and outlook.

Laboratory tester. Chronicle Guidance Publications. 1968. 4p. 35c

Occupational brief summarizing work performed with chemicals, animals, plants, and soil. Includes also training, qualifications, opportunities, and outlook.

LABORATORY TECHNICIAN—*Continued*

Positions of laboratory aid in the laboratory of the Federal Bureau of Investigation. The Bureau. 1968. 1p. Free

Brief statement of nature of work and qualifications.

Schools for the training of certified laboratory assistants. American Society of Medical Technologists. 1967. 3p. Free

Name and location of 148 approved schools.

Technical positions for applicants in the laboratory of the FBI. Federal Bureau of Investigation. 1968. 3p. Free

Describes job characteristics and qualifications.

See also Medical technologist

LANDSCAPE ARCHITECT 019.081

**Employment outlook for landscape architects. Bulletin No. 1650–34. Bureau of Labor Statistics, U.S. Department of Labor. Supt. of Documents. 1970. 8p. 10c

Reprint from the *Occupational Outlook Handbook.*

Have you ever thought of being a landscape nurseryman? National Landscape Nurserymen's Association. 1962. 4p. $3 per 100. Single copy free upon receipt of self-addressed stamped envelope

Brief description of duties, qualifications, training, and employment opportunities.

Jobs in outdoor work. Science Research Associates. 1964. 48p. $1

Describes the variety of job prospects and opportunities in outdoor work, especially for the wildlife manager, treeman, oceanographer, forester, geologist, archaeologist, landscape nurseryman, and surveyor.

Landscape architect. California State Department of Employment. 1965. 6p. Single copy free

Occupational guide describing work, requirements, training, and outlook.

Landscape architect. Careers. 1968. 2p. 20c

Career summary for desk-top file. Describes duties, qualifications, training, working conditions, outlook, and ways of measuring one's interest and ability.

Landscape architect. Chronicle Guidance Publications. 1967. 4p. 35c

Occupational brief summarizing work performed, working conditions, requirements, training, where employed, methods of entry, and outlook.

Landscape architect. Guidance Centre. 1967. 4p. 35c postpaid

History and importance, nature of work, qualifications, working conditions, preparation, remuneration, advancement, outlook, related occupations, and how to get started.

The landscape architect and land planning. American Society of Landscape Architects. 1962. 4p. 10c. Free to counselors or librarians

Illustrated folder describing the character and scope of the work, opportunities, and compensation.

* Landscape architects. Science Research Associates. 1966. 4p. 45c
Occupational brief describing nature of work, requirements, methods of getting started, earnings, opportunities, advantages, disadvantages, and future outlook.

**Landscape architects. One section of *Occupational Outlook Handbook.*
Nature of work, where employed, training, other qualifications, advancement, employment outlook, earnings, and working conditions.

**Landscape architecture, a professional career in land planning. American Society of Landscape Architects. 1970. 8p. 6c. Single copy free
Illustrated brochure describing need, training, duties, and opportunities.

Landscape maintenance superintendent (park superintendent, superintendent of gardeners, supervising greenskeeper, head groundsman). California State Department of Employment. 1966. 6p. Single copy free
Occupational guide describing work, requirements, training, and outlook.

List of accredited schools in landscape architecture. American Society of Landscape Architects. 1962. 1p. Free
List of sixteen accredited schools and the degrees conferred on completion of their professional curricula in landscape architecture.

List of accredited schools in landscape architecture. Chronicle Guidance Publications. 1967. 1p. 35c
Reprinted by permission of the American Society of Landscape Architects.

**Your future in landscape architecture. Frazier, John and Julin, Richard. Richards Rosen Press. 1967. 124p. $4; library edition. $3.78
Description of varied kinds of work, training, qualifications, and opportunities.

See also Architect; Horticulturist; Nurseryman and landscape gardener

LATHER 842.781

Lather. One section of *Occupational Outlook Handbook.*
Nature of work, where employed, training and other qualifications, employment outlook, earnings, and working conditions.

Lathers. Careers. 1966. 8p. 35c
Career brief describing duties, working conditions, training, earnings, and outlook. Additional readings.

Lathers. Chronicle Guidance Publications. 1968. 4p. 35c
Occupational brief summarizing work performed, working conditions, where employed, personal requirements, education and training requirements, hours and earnings, and outlook.

Lathers. Science Research Associates. 1969. 4p. 45c
Occupational brief describing work, qualifications, opportunities, and outlook.

LAUNDRY INDUSTRY WORKER 361.

* Cleaning and dyeing workers. Science Research Associates. 1967. 4p. 45c
Occupational brief describing nature of work, conditions of work, opportunities, advantages, disadvantages, and future outlook.

Education at NID. National Institute of Drycleaning. No date. 31p. Free
School catalog describing resident and correspondence courses offered by the institute.

Dry cleaner spotter. Careers. 1966. 2p. 20c
Career summary for desk-top file. Duties, qualifications, and outlook.

Finding out about laundry workers. Science Research Associates. 1967. 4p. 45c
Junior occupational brief summarizing what the work requires and offers.

Laundry industry workers. Chronicle Guidance Publications. 1967. 4p. 35c
Occupational brief summarizing nature of work, where employed, working conditions and hours, personal requirements, training, earnings, and outlook.

Laundry workers. California State Department of Employment. 1968. 2p. Single copy free
Occupational guide describing work, requirements, training, and outlook.

* Laundry workers. Science Research Associates. 1967. 4p. 45c
Occupational brief describing types of work, requirements, getting started and advancing, earnings, pros and cons, and future outlook.

Presser, women's garments. Careers. 1967. 2p. 20c
Career summary for desk-top file. Duties, qualifications, and outlook.

Shirt presser. Careers. 1968. 2p. 20c
Career summary for desk-top file. Duties, qualifications, and outlook.

LAWYER 110.108

The bramble bush. Llewellyn, K. N. Oceana Publications. Revised 1960. 160p. $5.50
A former professor of law discusses factors involved in choosing and pursuing a legal career, beginning with the training required and following through to the responsibilities a practicing attorney must assume.

**Careers in law. American Bar Association. 1968. 30p. 25c. Ten per cent reduction on bulk orders of 100 or more
Discussion of the lawyer's role in society, legal and prelegal education, and statistics of the profession. Contains reading list.

Careers in the law. Changing Times. 1960. 4p. 15c
Report on prospects, pay, and preparation for the legal profession.

**Careers in the legal profession. Sarnoff, Paul. Julian Messner. 1970. 192p. $3.95; library binding $3.64

Information on qualifications required in the varied fields of law, advice on state bar examinations, and the young lawyer's first professional steps. Discussion of the work of trial lawyers and corporation lawyers and a sampling of legal specialties ranging from admiralty law to civil rights cases. A list of law schools for training, with comparative enrollments.

Clarence Darrow: defense attorney. Noble, Iris. Julian Messner. 1958. 192p. $3.50; library binding $3.34

Biography of a man known as a fighter for social progress and a defender of unpopular causes.

Court in session. Lieberman, Jethro K. Sterling Publishing Company. 1966. 112p. 3.95

Describing two cases in full as orientation, the author explains the role of state and Federal courts and court activities.

Employment opportunities for attorneys. U.S. Securities and Exchange Commission. 1962. 4p. Free

Information about the location of positions, duties to be performed, recruitment policy, salaries, career opportunities, fringe benefits, and examinations.

**Employment outlook for lawyers. Bulletin No. 1650–35. Bureau of Labor Statistics, U.S. Department of Labor. Supt. of Documents. 1970. 8p. 10c

Reprint from the *Occupational Outlook Handbook.*

Estate tax attorney. Internal Revenue Service. 1968. 16p. Free

Describes the duties of the estate tax attorney who examines Federal tax returns and determines value, ownership of interest, and taxability of estate. Information on qualifications, training, promotion opportunities, job locations, and how to apply.

Felix Frankfurter. Baker, Liva. Coward-McCann, Inc. 1969. 376p. $8.95

A biography of a lawyer and Supreme Court judge identified with many liberal causes. Describes many aspects of his legal career.

Finding out about lawyers. Science Research Associates. 1967. 4p. 45c

Junior occupational brief containing concise facts about the job.

I, the lawyer. Kutner, Luis. Dodd, Mead and Company. 1966. 239p. $3.50

A Chicago lawyer of international fame offers advice to young people who are considering law as a career.

Judges. Science Research Associates. 1967. 4p. 45c

Occupational brief describing work, training, qualifications, opportunities, and outlook.

Law: earned degrees, by level, sex, and institution. One section of *Earned Degrees Conferred.*

List of 135 schools and the number of bachelor's, master's, and doctor's degrees conferred by each.

LAWYER–*Continued*

* Lawyer. Careers. 1968. 8p. 35c

Career brief describing history, duties, working conditions, training requirements, personal qualifications, employment prospects, advancement prospects, earnings, related careers, measuring one's interest and ability, and suggested high school program.

Lawyer. California State Department of Employment. 1968. 4p. Single copy free

Occupational guide describing work, requirements, training, and outlook.

Lawyer. Chronicle Guidance Publications. 1969. 4p. 35c

Occupational brief summarizing work performed, working conditions, earnings, personal qualifications, training requirements, opportunities, and employment outlook.

Lawyer. Guidance Centre. 1968. 4p. 35c postpaid

History and importance of the profession, nature of work, qualifications, preparation, advancement opportunities, earnings, how to get started, and related occupations.

**Lawyer; opportunities for careers in the legal profession. Smith, Talbot. Macmillan Company. 1961. 201p. $3.50

Discussion of the various kinds of specialization open to the young lawyer, the necessary characteristics to achieve success, and the future outlook. Written by a justice of the Supreme Court of Michigan.

Lawyers. Michigan Employment Security Commission. 1967. 2p. Single copy free

Job brief summarizing occupational data for use in Michigan.

* Lawyers. Science Research Associates. 1969. 4p. 45c

Occupational brief describing nature of work, training, qualifications, opportunities, advantages, disadvantages, and future outlook.

**Lawyers. One section of *Occupational Outlook Handbook.*

Nature of work, where employed, training, other qualifications, advancement, employment outlook, earnings, and working conditions.

Lawyers and what they do. Ernst, Morris and Schwarts, Alan. Franklin Watts, Inc. 1965. 140p. $3.95

A description of what lawyers do in various fields such as business law, criminal law, real estate law, and tax law. For grades 7 to 11.

Lawyers in industry. Fisch, Edith L. Oceana Publications. 1956. 225p. $6

Biographies of the outstanding lawyer leaders who have contributed to the growth of the eleven major American industries: iron and steel, mining and metals, oil and petroleum, chemicals, public utilities, railroads, aeronautics, food and beverages, banking, insurance, and mass media.

Lawyers in the Federal Government in public practice. Civil Service Commission. Supt. of Documents. 1970. 20p. 20c

A recent report of lawyers under Civil Service who serve the public.

Legal careers in the Federal Government. U.S. Civil Service Commission. 1967. 13p. Single copy free

Describes Federal career opportunities open to lawyers and persons with a legal background. Also lists principal employers of attorneys and provides information on salaries, qualifications, and application procedures.

**Opportunities in a law career. Elliott, Shelden D. Vocational Guidance Manuals. 1969. 128p. $1.95 paper; $3.75 library edition

Nature of work, qualifications, preparation, opportunities, and employment outlook. Includes list of approved law schools.

The profession of law. American Bar Association. 1969. 4p. $2.50 per hundred. Single copy free

A concise statement describing what lawyers do, personal characteristics necessary, legal education, economics of the profession, and how to obtain further information.

So you want to be a lawyer! A vocational guidance manual. Redden, Kenneth R. Bobbs-Merrill Company. 1953. 139p. $3.25

Discussion of what law is like and what lawyers do, what it takes to be a lawyer, what to study to become a lawyer, how to become a lawyer, number and distribution of lawyers, women lawyers, income, and outlook. Average net income of lawyers is given by years, age, number of years in practice, and type of practice.

Tax law specialist. Internal Revenue Service. 1969. 16p. Free

Information about tax law specialist positions located in the national office of Internal Revenue Service. Describes qualification standards, training, advancement opportunities, and how to apply for the position.

What lawyers really do: six lawyers talk about their life and work. Asbell, Bernard. Peter Wyden, Inc. 1970. 114p. $3.95

Six young lawyers, engaged in different phases of the law, discuss what they do and what they like and dislike about their work. As they relate typical cases, they discuss the difficulties of getting started in the legal profession and the problems and rewards they have encountered.

Women in law. Alumnae Advisory Center. 1965. 8p. 35c

Reprint from *Mademoiselle* giving experiences of young women who entered law schools and are progressing in that field.

LAY-OUT MAN (MACHINE TOOLS) 600.381

Layout man (machine shop). Chronicle Guidance Publications. 1966. 4p. 35c

Occupational brief summarizing work performed, working conditions, training requirements, earnings, hours, and outlook.

Layout men (machine tools). One section of *Occupational Outlook Handbook.*

Nature of work, where employed, training, other qualifications, and employment outlook.

LAY-OUT MAN (PRINTING) 141.081

Lay-out man (printing). Careers. 1967. 2p. 20c

Career summary for desk-top file. Duties, qualifications, and outlook.

LEATHER MANUFACTURING INDUSTRY WORKER 58

Leather manufacturing industry. Chronicle Guidance Publications. 1968. 4p. 35c

Occupational brief summarizing nature of work, working conditions, personal qualifications, training, hours, earnings, opportunities for advancement, and employment outlook.

* Leather manufacturing workers. Science Research Associates. 1966. 4p. 45c

Occupational brief describing types of work, requirements, methods of getting started, wages, advantages, disadvantages, and future outlook.

LEGAL SECRETARY 201.368

Finding out about legal secretaries. Science Research Associates. 1967. 4p. 45c

Junior occupational brief describing work and opportunities.

* Legal secretaries. Science Research Associates. 1966. 4p. 45c

Occupational brief describing work, qualifications, training, earnings, things to consider, related jobs, and outlook. Selected references.

Legal secretary. Careers. 1970. 2p. 20c

Career summary for desk-top file. Duties, qualifications, and outlook.

Legal secretary. California State Department of Employment. 1964. 4p. Single copy free

Job duties, working conditions, pay, hours, training, promotion, and employment outlook.

**So you want to be a legal secretary. National Association of Legal Secretaries. 1967. 12p. 6c

Description of the work, places of employment, preparation, qualifications, and how to apply for the position.

Toby: law stenographer. Bloom, Pauline. Julian Messner. 1959. 192p. $3.50

Career fiction. Working for a law firm as stenographer, Toby makes mistakes in the first few weeks, but enthusiasm and adaptability help her meet the tests of a difficult job.

LIBRARIAN 100.168

Accredited graduate library schools. American Library Association. 1970. 2p. Free

Names and selected characteristics of accredited library schools. Revised semi-annually.

Behind the scenes at the library. Busby, Edith. Dodd, Mead and Company. 1960. 64p. Library binding $2.99

Simple text and pictures portray some of the interesting fields of library work. Written for grades 3 to 7.

Bright particular star. Garthwaite, Marion. Julian Messner. 1958. 192p. $3.50

Career fiction. Includes description of training in a graduate library school and work as a children's librarian.

A career in hospital and institution librarianship. American Library Association. No date. 6p. $2.25 per 100. Single copy free

Curriculum guide intended to answer questions often asked about preparation for careers as hospital and special librarians.

* The career of the academic librarian. American Library Association. 1969. 176p. $4.50

A study of the social origins, educational attainments, vocational experience, and personality characteristics of a group of 707 American academic librarians. Also indicates talents and traits that tend to be in short and long supply in academic librarianship. Objectives of the study are to assist individual librarians in planning their careers and to provide guidance in recruiting and training librarians.

**Careers in libraries—information packet. American Library Association. 1969. 12 booklets. $3

Includes single copies of current career materials, except those addressed to librarians.

Challenging careers in the library world. Oakes, Vanya. Julian Messner. 1970. 189p. $3.95; library edition $3.64

This book describes the technological and social challenges facing libraries, the educational preparation, opportunities, outlook, and some non-professional positions in many libraries.

Children's librarian. Careers. 1968. 2p. 20c

Career summary for desk-top file. Duties, qualifications, and outlook.

The children's librarian . . . challenge to creativity. American Library Association. 1966. 8p. $4 per 100. Single copy free

Brief statement of requirements and training.

The crying need for librarians. Changing Times. 1964. 2p. 15c

Facts on training, earnings, and opportunities.

Data sheets on special librarianship. Special Libraries Association. 1962. 24 titles. Single copy free

One page is devoted to special librarianship in each of several fields including: advertising and public relations, biological sciences, business and finance, fine and applied arts, gas and petroleum industry, insurance, publishing and newspapers, and science and technology.

**Employment outlook for librarians and library technicians. Bulletin No. 1650–36. Bureau of Labor Statistics, U.S. Department of Labor. Supt. of Documents. 1970. 12p. 15c

Reprint from the *Occupational Outlook Handbook*.

LIBRARIAN—*Continued*

Financial assistance for library education, academic year 1970-1971. American Library Association. 1970. 56p. 50c

Includes awards from state library agencies, national and state library associations, groups of school librarians, library schools, and some regional organizations. For each there is given the granting body, type of assistance, amount, academic and other requirements, and deadline for application. Booklet also contains names of the forty-four accredited graduate library schools.

Finding out about children's librarians. Science Research Associates. 1967. 4p. 45c

Junior occupational brief containing concise facts about the job.

Finding out about librarians. Science Research Associates. 1967. 4p. 45c

Junior occupational brief containing concise facts about the job.

Finding out about music librarians. Science Research Associates. 1967. 4p. 45c

Junior occupational brief describing work and opportunities.

Finding out about special librarians. Science Research Associates. 1967. 4p. 45c

Junior occupational brief summarizing what the work requires and offers.

* Future unlimited—what you need to be a librarian. American Library Association. 1963. 12p. $4 per 100. Single copy free

Discussion of undergraduate preparation, requirements for admission to a graduate library school, and general qualifications.

Jinny Williams: library assistant. Temkin, Sara A. and Hovell, Lucy A. Julian Messner. 1962. 192p. $3.50

Career fiction. The book suggests that those for whom college is impossible may find rewarding work as a library assistant. The clerical duties, cataloging, mending, sorting, assisting where needed, and volunteering where useful won deserved promotion.

Librarian. California State Department of Employment 1966. 8p. Single copy free

Occupational guide describing work, requirements, training, and outlook.

* Librarian. Careers. 1968. 8p. 35c

Career brief describing duties, working conditions, personal qualifications, advantages, disadvantages, training, earnings, and outlook. List of accredited library schools.

Librarian. Chronicle Guidance Publications. 1969. 4p. 35c

Occupational brief summarizing work performed, working conditions, earnings, personal qualifications, training requirements, opportunities, and employment outlook.

Librarian. Guidance Centre. 1970. 4p. 35c postpaid

Definition, qualifications, preparation, working conditions, remuneration, advantages, disadvantages, and related occupations.

Librarian. Michigan Employment Security Commission. 1967. 2p. Single copy free

Job brief summarizing occupational data for use in Michigan.

Librarian, high school. Careers. 1967. 2p. 20c

Career summary for desk-top file. Duties, qualifications, and outlook.

The librarian in the hospital. American Library Association. 1964. 8p. 25 copies for $1.25. Single copy free

Description of work and opportunities.

The librarian speaking; interviews with university librarians. Lyle, Guy R. University of Georgia Press. 1970. 206p. $3.75

Interviews in which sixteen American libraries answer questions about trends in the world of the university library, the changing role of academic librarians, and other pertinent issues. Brief career sketches of each librarian are included.

Librarian (special). Guidance Centre. 1966. 4p. 35c postpaid

History and importance, preparation, qualifications, outlook, remuneration, advancement, advantages, disadvantages, and how to get started.

Librarian with wings. Thum, Marcella. Dodd, Mead and Company 1967. 207p. $3.50

Career fiction. Story depicting experiences of a young Special Services librarian stationed at a United States Air Base in South Korea.

**Librarians. One section of *Occupational Outlook Handbook.*

Nature of work, where employed, training, other qualifications, advancement, employment outlook, earnings, and working conditions.

Librarians in the Veterans Administration hospitals. VA pamphlet 10-61. Veterans Administration Forms Depot. 1967. 4p. Free

Description of work, training programs, qualifications, and benefits.

Librarians wanted: careers in library service. Paradis, Adrian. David McKay Company. 1959. 288p. $4.50

Opportunities in library work, including numerous special libraries such as legal, newspaper, hospital, etc. Complete list of library science schools.

Library assistant. California State Department of Employment. 1966. 5p. Single copy free

Occupational guide describing work, requirements, training, and outlook.

Library assistant. Careers. 1968. 2p. 20c

Career summary for desk-top file. Describes duties, working conditions, training, qualifications, outlook, working conditions, and related careers.

**Library careers. Logsdon, Richard and Logsdon, Irene. Henry Z. Walck, Inc. 1963. 111p. $4.50

This book describes the scope of librarianship, the preparation, requirements, rewards, and the outlook for future developments in libraries. Includes a list of accredited library schools and a good reading list.

Library careers—a bibliography for guidance counselors. American Library Association. 1967. 8p. 25 copies for 75c. Single copy free

List of vocational materials and films.

LIBRARIAN—*Continued*

Library science: earned degrees, by level, sex, and institution. One section of *Earned Degrees Conferred.*

List of ninety-eight schools and the number of bachelor's, master's, and doctor's degrees conferred by each in library science.

Library technicians. One section of *Occupational Outlook Handbook.*

Description of work of library technicians, sometimes called library assistants, who perform reader and technical services that include furnishing information on library services, facilities, and rules. Includes employment outlook, salaries, and training.

The lively career of a school librarian. American Library Association. 1964. 12p. $4 per 100. Single copy free

Description of nature of work, training, satisfactions, need, and how to begin.

Meet the future. Meyer, Edith Patterson. Little, Brown and Company. 1964. 278p. $4.75

A description of the importance of libraries to the future and the nature and extent of library work in the present. Describes the various categories of work in libraries and the need for interested trained personnel. List of library schools.

Metropolitan libraries. American Library Association. 1969. 64p. $1.75

An examination of the concept of the public library as an agent of urban change. A contribution to an understanding of the role of the library in today's society.

Music librarian. Careers. 1968. 2p. 20c

Career summary for desk-top file. Duties, qualifications, and outlook.

Nancy runs the bookmobile. Johnson, Enid. Julian Messner. 1956. 192p. $3.50

Career fiction. Experiences of a girl working temporarily with a bookmobile, without library training, followed by her university training for a library science degree and ultimate success. Shows the satisfactions of bringing the right child and the right book together.

The public librarian. American Library Association. 1965. 12p. $4 per 100. Single copy free

Description of opportunities, varied work, necessary education, and how to get started.

Public librarians. Science Research Associates. 1968. 4p. 45c

Occupational brief describing nature of work, training, qualifications, opportunities, advantages, disadvantages, and future outlook.

Recruiting librarians : a bibliography for librarian recruiters. American Library Association. 1966. 4p. $2.25 per 100. Single copy free

Prepared for practicing librarians.

A recruitment primer. Ricking, Myrl. American Library Association, Office of Recruitment. 1960. 15p. Single copy free

Written for practicing librarians. Description of various approaches to interest young people to prepare for library work.

Rich the treasure; public library service to children. Long, Harriet G. American Library Association. 1953. 88p. $2

Traces the early beginnings of children's librarianship and the role of the librarian as a guiding influence on the child's reading and cultural development.

Special librarian. Careers. 1970. 8p. 35c

Career brief describing duties, working conditions, personal qualifications, opportunities, earnings, advancement prospects, and outlook.

Special librarian. Chronicle Guidance Publications. 1969. 4p. 35c

Occupational brief summarizing work performed, working conditions, earnings, qualifications, training, opportunities, and outlook.

* Special librarians. Science Research Associates. 1966. 4p. 45c

Occupational brief describing nature of work, requirements, earnings, advantages, disadvantages, and future outlook.

Thousands of librarians needed. American Library Association. 1969. 1p. $2.25 per 100. Single copy free to librarians

Two-color 5″ by 9″ recruitment card.

What does a librarian do? Busby, Edith. Dodd, Mead and Company. 1963. 64p. Library binding $2.99

Varied activities from story hours, bookmobiles, and card catalogs to radio programs, exhibits, books for the blind, and libraries overseas are described. Written for grades 3 to 7.

With a high heart. De Leeuw, Adele L. Macmillan Company. 1964. 207p. $3.74

Career fiction. Experiences in a rural library, revealing difficulties as well as advantages and rewards. A job in a county library develops into the management of a bookmobile circuit.

**Your future as a librarian. Clarke, Joan Dorn. Richards Rosen Press. Revised 1969. 160p. $4; library edition $3.78

Stresses the opportunities in various aspects of library work and the necessary training and education.

LIFE SCIENTIST 04

Careers in aerospace medicine and life sciences. Aerospace Medicine Association. 1969. 11p. Free

Explains the role played in aerospace medicine by physicians, biologists, physiologists, psychologists, physicists, engineers, chemists, mathematicians, and technicians. Includes brief information about training opportunities.

**Employment outlook for life science occupations. Bulletin No. 1650–25. Bureau of Labor Statistics, U.S. Department of Labor. Supt. of Documents. 1970. 12p. 15c

Reprint from the *Occupational Outlook Handbook*. Includes career information about botanists, zoologists, microbiologists, and biochemists.

See also Agricultural specialist, Biochemist, Biologist, Botanist, Microbiologist, Zoologist

LINEMAN AND CABLE SPLICER 822.381

Cable splicer. California State Department of Employment. 1965. 5p. Single copy free

Occupational guide describing work, requirements, training, and outlook.

Finding out about linemen. Science Research Associates. 1967. 4p. 45c

Junior occupational brief summarizing what the work requires and offers.

Lineman. California State Department of Employment. 1965. 5p. Single copy free

Occupational guide describing work, requirements, training, and outlook.

Lineman. Guidance Centre. 1966. 4p. 35c postpaid

History and importance, nature of work, qualifications, working conditions, preparation, remuneration, advancement, outlook, related occupations, and how to get started.

Lineman (light, heat, and power). Chronicle Guidance Publications. 1969. 4p. 35c

Occupational brief summarizing work performed, working conditions, hours, earnings, personal qualifications, training requirements, opportunities, and employment outlook.

Linemen and cable splicers. Science Research Associates. 1968. 4p. 45c

Occupational brief describing work, training, wage rates, and job prospects.

**Linemen and cable splicers. One section of *Occupational Outlook Handbook.*

Nature of work, training, other qualifications, advancement, employment outlook, earnings, and working conditions.

Telephone lineman and cable splicers. Careers. 1969. 8p. 35c

Career brief describing duties, working conditions, training requirements, personal qualifications, earnings, advancement prospects, and outlook.

LINGUIST 137.268 and 137.288

* Bilingual secretary. Careers. 1968. 8p. 35c

Career brief describing duties, working conditions, training, qualifications, places of employment, earnings, and outlook.

Careers in translating and interpreting. Angel, Juvenal. World Trade Academy Press. 1962. 28p. $1.25

Includes information about each of several specialties utilizing these skills.

**Careers with foreign languages. Cohn, Angelo. Henry Z. Walck, Inc. 1963. 110p. $4.50

This book describes the many opportunities, educational requirements, benefits, drawbacks, and the advantage in almost any pursuit of having language skills. Stresses the need for linguists in business, government, teaching, churches, and social agencies.

Finding out about translators and interpreters. Science Research Associates. 1967. 4p. 45c

Junior occupational brief summarizing what the work requires and offers.

Foreign languages and literature: earned degrees, by level, sex, and institution. One section of *Earned Degrees Conferred.*

Useful for judging the extent of a college's program in each of the languages.

Information kit. American Translators Association. 1969. 8p. Single copy free

Folders describing objectives and activities of the association.

Interpreter. Careers. 1968. 2p. 20c

Career summary for desk-top file. Duties, qualifications, and outlook.

Interpreter. Chronicle Guidance Publications. 1967. 4p. 35c

Occupational brief containing definition, work performed, personal requirements, determination of aptitudes and interests, training requirements, outlook, where employed, and methods of entry.

**Opportunities in foreign languages. Heubener, Theodore. Vocational Guidance Manuals. 1964. 144p. $1.95 paper; library binding $3.75

Discussion of opportunities in various vocations, in government positions, and as a teacher of languages. Personal qualifications, training, and methods of securing employment also are included.

Translators and interpreters. California State Department of Employment. 1966. 7p. Single copy free

Occupational guide describing work, requirements, training, and outlook.

Translators and interpreters. Science Research Associates. 1970. 4p. 45c

Occupational brief describing jobs in business, government, teaching, and miscellaneous agencies.

**Vocational opportunities for foreign language students. Kettlekamp, Gilbert C. Modern Language Association. 1967. 26p. 75c

Discussion of opportunities and qualifications in business and industry, civil service, teaching, and twelve other vocations in which competence in a foreign language may be a specific requirement for employment.

**Your future in translating and interpreting. Hendry, J. M. Richards Rosen Press. 1969. 128p. $4; library edition $3.78

Description of training, qualifications, and opportunities. Also, a variety of jobs related to translation work are described and helpful information is presented concerning on-the-job training, finding a position, and fringe benefits. Appendix lists schools offering courses in linguistics.

LINOTYPE OPERATOR 650.582

Linotype operator. Careers. 1969. 8p. 35c

Career brief describing duties, working conditions, training, personal qualifications, places of employment, how to enter, earnings, and outlook. Additional readings.

Linotyping, the trade with a future. New York Mergenthaler Linotype School. 1962. 12p. Free

A recruiting brochure including nature of work, its importance, advantages, qualifications, and training.

LINOTYPE OPERATOR—*Continued*

Questions and answers about a linotype course. New York Mergenthaler Linotype School. 1963. 2p. Free

Information about the training, qualifications, and future outlook.

See also Printing industry worker

LITERARY AGENT 191.118

Agents (literary, theatrical, art gallery). Alumnae Advisory Center. 1969. 6p. 35c

Reprint from *Mademoiselle* describing the work of a number of young women agents who are assisting writers, painters, and performers.

Finding out about literary agents. Science Research Associates. 1967. 4p. 45c

Junior occupational brief containing concise facts about the job.

**Literary agents. Science Research Associates. 1969. 4p. 45c

Occupational brief describing nature of work, training, qualifications, opportunities, advantages, disadvantages, and future outlook.

LOCKSMITH 709.281

Locksmith and locksmith apprentice. California State Department of Employment. 1965. 4p. Single copy free

Occupational guide describing work, requirements, training, and outlook.

LOCOMOTIVE ENGINEER (RAILROAD) 910.383

Finding out about locomotive engineers. Science Research Associates. 1967. 4p. 45c

Junior occupational brief summarizing what the work requires and offers.

Locomotive engineer. Careers. 1966. 2p. 20c

Career summary for desk-top file. Duties, qualifications, and outlook.

Locomotive engineer. Chronicle Guidance Publications. 1968. 4p. 35c

Occupational brief describing work, qualifications, earnings, and outlook.

Locomotive engineer (railroad). One section of *Occupational Outlook Handbook.*

Nature of work, training, other qualifications, advancement, employment outlook, earnings, and working conditions.

**Locomotive engineers. One section of *Occupational Outlook Handbook.*

Nature of work, training, other qualifications, advancement, employment outlook, earnings, and working conditions.

Locomotive engineman. Guidance Centre. 1966. 4p. 35c postpaid

Definition, history and importance, nature of work, qualifications necessary for entry and success, preparation, employment and advancement, earnings, advantages, disadvantages, how to get started, related occupations, working conditions, and outlook.

LONGSHOREMAN 911.883

Finding out about longshoremen. Science Research Associates. 1967. 4p. 45c

Junior occupational brief containing brief facts about the job.

Longshoremen and stevedores. Science Research Associates. 1969. 4p. 45c

Occupational brief describing duties, requirements, wages, getting started, advancing, advantages, disadvantages, and future outlook.

LUMBER INDUSTRY WORKER 940.884

Faller (logger, lumberjack). Careers. 1961. 2p. 15c

Career summary for desk-top file. Duties, qualifications, and outlook.

Finding out about lumberjacks. Science Research Associates. 1967. 4p. 45c

Junior occupational brief summarizing what the work requires and offers.

Gifts from the forest. Wall, Gertrude Wallace. Charles Scribner's Sons. 1952. 96p. $3.31

Photographs and brief explanatory text describe the work involved in converting timber into lumber. For grades 5 to 8.

The logging industry. Chronicle Guidance Publications. 1968. 4p. 35c

Occupational brief summarizing work performed, personal requirements, opportunities for advancement, employment outlook, and educational training requirements.

**Lumbermen. Science Research Associates. 1970. 4p. 45c

Occupational brief describing nature of work, requirements, getting a job, earnings, advantages, disadvantages, and future outlook. Includes working in the logging camp, in the sawmill, and moving the timber.

MACHINE TOOL OPERATOR 609.885

Finding out about machine tool operators. Science Research Associates. 1967. 4p. 45c

Junior occupational brief containing concise facts about the job.

Machine tool operator (all-round). Chronicle Guidance Publications. 1968. 4p. 35c

Occupational brief summarizing work performed, working conditions, training, earnings, where employed, related jobs, and outlook.

Machine tool operators. California State Department of Employment. 1964. 4p. Single copy free

Occupational guide describing work, requirements, training, and outlook.

Machine tool operators. Careers. 1968. 8p. 35c

Career brief describing duties, working conditions, training, personal qualifications, advancement prospects, earnings, unionization, and outlook.

MACHINE TOOL OPERATOR—*Continued*

Machine tool operators. Michigan Employment Security Commission. 1964. 2p. Single copy free

Job brief summarizing occupational data for use in Michigan.

**Machine tool operators. One section of *Occupational Outlook Handbook.*

Nature of work, where employed, training, other qualifications, advancement, employment outlook, earnings, and working conditions.

MACHINIST 600.280

**All-round machinists. One section of *Occupational Outlook Handbook.*

Nature of work, where employed, training, other qualifications, advancement, employment outlook, earnings, and working conditions.

**Employment outlook for machining occupations. Bulletin No. 1650–98. Bureau of Labor Statistics, U.S. Department of Labor. Supt. of Documents. 1970. 12p. 15c

Reprint from the *Occupational Outlook Handbook.* Includes all-round machinists, machine tool operators, tool and die makers, instrument makers, setup men, and layout men.

Finding out about crane operators. Science Research Associates. 1967. 4p. 45c

Junior occupational brief containing concise facts about the job.

Finding out about machinists. Science Research Associates. 1967. 4p. 45c

Junior occupational brief describing work and opportunities.

Machine shop inspectors. California State Department of Employment. 1968. 4p. Single copy free

Occupational guide describing work, requirements, training, and outlook.

Machinery repairman, industrial. Careers. 1968. 8p. 35c

Career brief describing duties, working conditions, training, personal qualifications, where employed, earnings, and outlook.

**Machining occupations. One section of *Occupational Outlook Handbook.*

Nature of work, training, other qualifications, advancement, employment outlook, earnings, and working conditions. Information is given concerning all-round machinist, machine tool operator, tool and die maker, instrument maker, setup man, and layout man.

* Machinist. Careers. 1970. 8p. 35c

Career brief describing duties, working conditions, training, personal qualifications, advancement prospects, places of employment, earnings, and outlook.

Machinist. Chronicle Guidance Publications. 1967. 6p. 35c

Occupational brief containing definition, work performed, working conditions, personal requirements, training requirements, where employed, job outlook, related jobs, and suggested activities.

Machinist. Guidance Centre. 1966. 4p. 35c postpaid

Nature of work, qualifications, preparation, working conditions, advancement, outlook, earnings, advantages, disadvantages, how to get started, and related occupations.

Machinist and machinist apprentice. California State Department of Employment. 1964. 5p. Single copy free

Occupational guide describing work, requirements, training, and outlook.

Machinists. Science Research Associates. 1968. 4p. 45c

Occupational brief describing nature of work, preparation, qualifications, opportunities, advantages, disadvantages, and future outlook.

Marine mechanics and repairmen. Chronicle Guidance Publications. 1969. 4p. 35c

Occupational brief summarizing work performed, working conditions, training requirements, personal qualifications, methods of entry, advancement, employment outlook, and earnings.

**Opportunities in machine shop trades. Stern, Benjamin J. Vocational Guidance Manuals. 1965. 112p. $1.95 paper; $3.75 library edition

Historical sketch, current needs and future outlook, requirements for success, wages, analysis of machine shop occupations, training, getting started, the machinist's progress, and possibilities in related fields. Contains lists of state apprenticeship agencies and field and regional offices of the Bureau of Apprenticeship, U.S. Department of Labor.

Setup man (machine shop). Chronicle Guidance Publications. 1966. 4p. 35c

Occupational brief summarizing work performed, working conditions, hours and earnings, education and training requirements, and outlook.

**Setup men (machine tools). One section of *Occupational Outlook Handbook.*

Nature of work, where employed, training, other qualifications, and employment outlook.

See also Skilled trades worker

MAIL CARRIER 233.388

Finding out about letter carriers. Science Research Associates. 1967. 4p. 45c

Junior occupational brief summarizing what the work requires and offers.

Finding out about mailing service workers. Science Research Associates. 1967. 4p. 45c

Junior occupational brief describing work and opportunities.

Letter carrier. Careers. 1970. 2p. 20c

Career summary for desk-top file. Duties, qualifications, and outlook.

Letter carrier. Guidance Centre. 1970. 4p. 35c postpaid

Nature of work, qualifications, working conditions, preparation, earnings, advantages, disadvantages, how to get started, and related occupations.

Mail carrier. California State Department of Employment. 1966. 4p. Single copy free

Occupational guide describing work, requirements, training, and outlook.

MAIL CARRIER—*Continued*

Mail carrier. Michigan Employment Security Commission. 1964. 2p. Single copy free

Job brief summarizing occupational data for use in Michigan.

Mail carriers. Science Research Associates. 1969. 4p. 45c

Occupational brief describing work, training, qualifications, opportunities, and outlook.

**Mail carriers. One section of *Occupational Outlook Handbook*.

Nature of work, qualifications, training, advancement, employment outlook, earnings, and working conditions.

Rural mail carrier. Careers. 1967. 2p. 20c

Career summary for desk-top file. Duties, qualifications, and outlook.

MANAGEMENT ENGINEER. ***See*** **Industrial engineer**

MANAGER, CATERER. ***See*** **Caterer**

MANAGER, RETAIL STORE. ***See*** **Retail manager**

MANUFACTURER **50 and 183.**

Exploring your future in manufacturing—salaried jobs. Sextant Systems, Inc. 1968. 96p. $8.95

One page is devoted to each of ninety-five jobs, describing the duties, requirements for entering, promotional outlook, and the pay and skill level.

Exploring your future in manufacturing—wages. Sextant Systems, Inc. 1970. 96p. $8.95

One page is devoted to each of ninety-five jobs, presenting the duties, requirements for entering, promotional outlook, and the pay and skill level.

Manufacturing. One section of *Occupational Outlook Handbook*.

Includes estimated employment in manufacturing for 1968 in each of eight major occupational groups.

MANUFACTURERS' SALESMAN **289.158**

Finding out about manufacturers' representatives. Science Research Associates. 1967. 4p. 45c

Junior occupational brief summarizing what the work requires and offers.

Manufacturer's representative. Careers. 1966. 8p. 35c

Career brief describing duties, working conditions, training, personal requirements, places of employment, earnings, and outlook.

**Manufacturers' salesmen. One section of *Occupational Outlook Handbook*.

Nature of work, where employed, training, employment outlook, earnings, and working conditions.

Salesman, manufacturer's. Chronicle Guidance Publications. 1966. 4p. 35c

Occupational brief summarizing work performed, working conditions, training requirements, personal qualifications, earnings, and outlook.

Salesmen—manufacturers' and wholesalers'. Science Research Associates. 1966. 4p. 45c

Occupational brief describing duties, requirements, getting started and advancing, earnings, advantages, disadvantages, and future outlook.

MAP MAKER. *See* Cartographer

MARBLE SETTER 861.381

Marble setters, tile layers and terrazzo workers. Chronicle Guidance Publications. 1968. 4p. 35c

Occupational brief summarizing work performed, working conditions, personal requirements, earnings, training requirements, and advancement.

Marble setters, tile setters and terrazzo workers. Careers. 1967. 8p. 35c

Career brief describing duties, working conditions, training, personal qualifications, earnings, advancement prospects, and outlook.

Marble setters, tile setters, and terrazzo workers. One section of *Occupational Outlook Handbook.*

Nature of work, where employed, training, other qualifications, advancement, outlook, earnings, and working conditions.

MARINA WORKER 342.867

Marina workers. Science Research Associates. 1965. 4p. 45c

Occupational brief describing work, training, qualifications, opportunities, and outlook.

MARINE 378.

**Current career booklets. U.S. Marine Corps. Six booklets. Free

Frequently revised materials are available from local recruiting offices or the above. Examples of present titles are: *The marine aviator, Occupational opportunities,* and *Be a leader of men.*

Leatherneck. Colby, C. B. Coward-McCann, Inc. 1957. 48p. $2.97

Includes description of the training of a U.S. Marine and the methods of combat used. Written for grades 4 to 8.

The Marine Corps. Hammond, Cleon. Viking Press. Revised 1962. 192p. $3.19

Details of regulations and opportunities. For grades 7 to 10.

Marine corps as a career. Chronicle Guidance Publications. 1966. 4p. 35c

Occupational brief summarizing history, importance, work performed, working conditions, training requirements, earnings, and personal qualifications.

MARINE—*Continued*

**Occupational opportunities. U.S. Marine Corps. 1966. 46p. Free
A guide to the military occupational specialties and schools.

What is a marine? U.S. Marine Corps. 1968. 32p. Free
An illustrated color brochure explaining requirements and traditions.

**Your future in the Marine Corps. Fraser, Angus M. Richards Rosen Press. 1969. 176p. $4; library edition $3.78
Description of the physical, mental, and educational requirements for entrance, officer training, professional schooling, and details of specialties. The spirit and enthusiasm of the marines are depicted in the account.

See also Armed Forces

MARINE ENGINEER 014.081

Marine engineer. Chronicle Guidance Publications. 1968. 4p. 35c
Occupational brief summarizing history and importance, work performed, hours and earnings, working conditions, education, scholarships, and where employed.

Marine engineer. Guidance Centre. 1966. 4p. 35c postpaid
Definition, history and importance, nature of work, qualifications, working conditions, preparation, remuneration, advancement, outlook, related occupations, and how to get started.

MARKET RESEARCH WORKER 050.088

Finding out about market research interviewers. Science Research Associates. 1967. 4p. 45c
Junior occupational brief containing concise facts about the job.

Market-research analyst. California State Department of Employment. 1966. 6p. Single copy free
Job duties, working conditions, pay, hours, entrance requirements, promotion, training, and employment prospects in California.

**Market research workers. One section of *Occupational Outlook Handbook*.
Nature of work, where employed, training, other qualifications, employment outlook, earnings, and working conditions.

Marketing careers in the jet air age. Chronicle Guidance Publications. 1968. 4p. 35c
Reprinted article from *The Distributor* discusses airline services and salaries paid various personnel in airline marketing and service occupations.

**Marketing research workers. Chronicle Guidance Publications. 1969. 4p. 35c
Occupational brief summarizing work performed, working conditions, personal requirements, where employed, opportunities, outlook, and educational requirements.

Marketing research workers. Science Research Associates. 1966. 4p. 45c
Occupational brief describing nature of wo ', requirements, methods of getting started, earnings, advantages, disadvantages, and future outlook.

Marketing researchers. Careers. 1966. 2p. 20c
Career summary for desk-top file. Duties, qualifications, and outlook.

**Opportunities in market research. Platten, John H. Vocational Guidance Manuals. 1966. 118p. $1.95 paper; $3.75 library edition
Includes consumer and opinion research. Description of market research, educational preparation, training while in other jobs, analysis of jobs in market research, organizing your job-hunting, the path to advancement, and types of research. List of colleges which offer courses in marketing and allied subjects.

See also Economist

MASON. *See* Cement mason

MATERIAL HANDLING COORDINATOR 221.168

Material handling engineer. Careers. 1966. 2p. 20c
Career summary for desk-top file. Duties, qualifications, and outlook.

Material handling engineer. Chronicle Guidance Publications. 1968. 4p. 35c
Occupational brief summarizing work performed, working conditions, qualifications, where employed, and outlook.

Rigger. Careers. 1967. 2p. 20c
Career summary of the work of moving heavy objects such as structural steel, heavy machinery and equipment, oil drilling equipment, bulk steel, and ship sections.

Warehouse workers. Science Research Associates. 1967. 4p. 45c
Occupational brief describing nature of work, requirements, getting started and advancing, wages, advantages, disadvantages, and future outlook.

Warehouseman. Careers. 1967. 2p. 20c
Career summary for desk-top file. Duties, qualifications, and outlook.

MATHEMATICIAN 020.088

Assistantships and fellowships in mathematics. American Mathematical Society. 1968. 96p. 50c
Special issue of the notices available in January of each year.

**Employment outlook for mathematicians and related occupations. Bulletin No. 1650–37. Bureau of Labor Statistics, U.S. Department of Labor. Supt. of Documents. 1970. 12p. 15c
Reprint from the *Occupational Outlook Handbook*. Includes mathematicians, statisticians, and actuaries.

MATHEMATICIAN—*Continued*

Finding employment in the mathematical sciences. American Mathematical Society. 1968. 13p. Free

Written for the trained mathematician who is entering the professional field, this booklet explains the role of the mathematician in teaching, academic and industrial research, computing, and in government. It also contains information on seeking and applying for a position.

Finding out about mathematicians. Science Research Associates. 1967. 4p. 45c

Junior occupational brief describing work and opportunities.

Guidebook to departments in the mathematical sciences. Mathematical Association of America. 1968. 88p. 50c

Provides in summary form information about the location, size, staff, library facilities, course offerings, and special features of departments of mathematical sciences in four-year colleges in the United States and Canada.

Jobs in mathematics. Science Research Associates. 1965. 32p. $1.15

Describes the variety of job prospects and opportunities within the field of mathematics.

Mathematical subjects: earned degrees, by level, sex, and institution. One section of *Earned Degrees Conferred.*

Useful for judging the extent of a college's program in mathematics and in statistics.

Mathematical technician. Chronicle Guidance Publications. 1966. 4p. 35c

Occupational brief summarizing work performed, working conditions, earnings, qualifications, training requirements, and outlook.

* Mathematician. Careers. 1968. 8p. 35c

Career brief describing duties, working conditions, personal qualifications, training, outlook, earnings, where employed, related jobs, and measuring one's interest and ability. Suggested references.

Mathematician. Chronicle Guidance Publications. 1967. 4p. 35c

Occupational brief summarizing: work performed in teaching, industry, and government; employment conditions; qualifications; training; opportunities; where employed; and outlook.

Mathematician. Guidance Centre. 1969. 4p. 35 postpaid

History and importance, definition, qualifications, preparation, employment, remuneration, outlook, and how to get started.

Mathematician. Michigan Employment Security Commission. 1960. 2p. Single copy free

Job brief summarizing occupational data for use in Michigan.

* Mathematicians. Science Research Associates. 1966. 4p. 45c

Occupational brief describing nature of work, training, qualifications, opportunities, advantages, disadvantages, and future outlook.

**Mathematicians. One section of *Occupational Outlook Handbook.*

Nature of work, where employed, training, other qualifications, employment outlook, earnings, and working conditions.

**Mathematics teaching as a career. National Council of Teachers of Mathematics. Revised 1968. 8p. Single copy free

Discussion of the demand for teachers of mathematics, preparation, salaries, responsibilities, satisfactions, and benefits.

Niels Henrik Abel, mathematician extraordinary. Oystein, Ore. University of Minnesota Press. 1957. 277p. $5.75

Biography of a Norwegian scientist who made notable contributions to mathematics.

**Opportunities in mathematics. Gehman, Harry M. Vocational Guidance Manuals. 1964. 88p. $1.95 paper; library binding $3.75

Discussion of the nature of work and opportunities for the mathematician in industry, government, high school and college teaching, and research. Also some information about work as a statistician, actuary, and electronic computer programmer.

**Professional opportunities in mathematics. Mathematical Association of America. 1967. 32p. 25c

Includes discussion of opportunities in teaching, mathematical and applied statistics, industry, government, and in the actuarial profession. Contains a section on the employment of mathematicians in nonacademic organizations.

Professional training in mathematics. Ficken, F. A. and MacDuffee, C. C. American Mathematical Society. 1965. 40p. 25c

Analysis of current trends in education for the profession.

Why not be a mathematician ? Leaflet 45. Women's Bureau, U.S. Department of Labor. Supt. of Documents. 1968. 8p. 10c

Sketches briefly the present and future supply and demand, preparation, personal characteristics needed, methods of obtaining employment, and advancement. Prepared to encourage high school girls to investigate the field of mathematics.

You will like geometry. Museum of Science and Industry. 1962. 12p. 41c

Guide book published as an adjunct to the Illinois Institute of Technology's permanent geometry exhibit at the museum.

See also Actuary; Scientist; Statistician

MEAT CUTTER 316.781

**Employment outlook for meat cutters. Bulletin No. 1650–99. Bureau of Labor Statistics, U.S. Department of Labor. Supt. of Documents. 1970. 8p. 10c

Reprint from the *Occupational Outlook Handbook.*

Meat cutter. Chronicle Guidance Publications. 1969. 4p. 35c

Occupational brief summarizing work performed, working conditions, personal qualifications, training requirements, opportunities, employment outlook, and methods of entry.

MEAT CUTTER—*Continued*

Meat cutter. Michigan Employment Security Commission. 1962. 2p. Single copy free

Job brief summarizing occupational data for use in Michigan.

Meat cutters. One section of *Occupational Outlook Handbook.*

Nature of work, places of employment, qualifications, employment outlook, earnings, and working conditions.

* Meat cutter-butcher. Careers. 1969. 8p. 35c

Career brief describing duties, working conditions, training, earnings, unionization, and outlook.

Meat cutter-jobber and meat-cutter-jobber apprentice. California State Department of Employment. 1965. 6p. Single copy free

Occupational guide describing work, requirements, training, and outlook.

MEAT PACKING INDUSTRY WORKER 525.

Career opportunities in the meat packing industry. American Meat Institute. 1968. 12p. Single copy free

A representative listing of job titles and job descriptions, and the academic requirements for each.

Eight ways to learn about meat industry operations. American Meat Institute. No date. 6p. Free

Announcement of eight home-study courses.

Meat packing industry. Chronicle Guidance Publications. 1966. 4p. 35c

Occupational brief summarizing work performed, working conditions, hours, earnings, personal requirements, training requirements, opportunities, outlook, and where employed.

Meat-packing workers. Science Research Associates. 1967. 4p. 45c

Occupational brief describing work, getting started and advancing, wages, things to consider, and future outlook.

Occupations in meat packing. California State Department of Employment. 1967. 5p. Single copy free

Occupational guide describing work, requirements, training, and outlook.

Opportunities for you for rewarding careers in the meat industry. American Meat Institute. No date. 12p. Single copy free

Opportunities for those who are trained in agriculture, business, science, engineering, or communications. Includes a list of job titles for college graduates with diverse majors.

MECHANIC AND REPAIRMAN 620. and 637.

** Appliance servicemen. One section of *Occupational Outlook Handbook.*

Nature of work, where employed, training, other qualifications, advancement, employment outlook, earnings, and working conditions.

Camera repairman. California State Department of Employment. 1969. 5p. Single copy free

Occupational guide describing work, requirements, training, and outlook.

Camera repairman. Careers. 1968. 2p. 20c

Career summary for desk-top file. Duties, qualifications, and outlook.

Electric sign serviceman. One section of *Occupational Outlook Handbook.*

Nature of work, places of employment, qualifications, advancement, outlook, earnings, and working conditions.

**Employment outlook for appliance servicemen. Bulletin No. 1650–81. Bureau of Labor Statistics, U.S. Department of Labor. Supt. of Documents. 1970. 8p. 10c

Reprint from the *Occupational Outlook Handbook.*

Farm equipment mechanic. Careers. 1968. 2p. 20c

Career summary for desk-top file. Duties, qualifications, and outlook.

Farm equipment mechanic. Chronicle Guidance Publications. 1967. 4p. 35c

Occupational brief summarizing work performed, where employed, working conditions, methods of entry, promotion, and outlook.

Farm equipment mechanics. One section of *Occupational Outlook Handbook.*

Nature of work, places of employment, qualifications, outlook, earnings, and working conditions.

Finding out about musical instrument repairmen. Science Research Associates. 1967. 4p. 45c

Junior occupational brief containing concise facts about the job.

Mechanical technologist. Guidance Centre. 1967. 4p. 35c postpaid

Definition, history and importance, nature of work, preparation, qualifications, employment, remuneration, advancement, and how to get started.

Mechanics and repairmen. Chronicle Guidance Publications. 1968. 4p. 35c

Occupational brief describing the work of various kinds of repairmen, qualifications, training, and apprenticeship.

**Mechanics and repairmen. One chapter of *Occupational Outlook Handbook.*

Nature of work, where employed, training, other qualifications, employment outlook, earnings, and working conditions for each of the following: air conditioning and refrigeration mechanic, appliance serviceman, automobile mechanic, business machine serviceman, diesel mechanic, industrial machinery repairman, instrument repairman, jewelry repairman, maintenance electrician, millwright, watch repairman, and television and radio serviceman.

Tire vulcanizer. California State Department of Employment. 1964. 4p. Single copy free

Occupational guide describing work, requirements, training, and outlook.

MECHANIC AND REPAIRMAN—*Continued*

Truck mechanics and bus mechanics. One section of *Occupational Outlook Handbook.*

Nature of work, places of employment, training, advancement, employment outlook, earnings, and working conditions.

See also Technician

MECHANICAL ENGINEER 007.081

Careers in mechanical engineering. Aluminum Company of America. No date. 12p. Free

A recruiting brochure describing nature of work and personnel policies.

Definitions of occupational specialties in engineering. American Society of Mechanical Engineers. 1952. 114p. $3.50

Definitions of about five hundred engineering fields of specialization and the knowledge required to work in each field.

Finding out about mechanical engineers. Science Research Associates. 1967. 4p. 45c

Junior occupational brief summarizing what the work requires and offers.

Jobs in mechanical work. Science Research Associates. 1963. 48p. $1.15

Describes the variety of job prospects and opportunities within this field, especially for the auto mechanic, airplane mechanic, machinist, millwright, office machine serviceman, radio and television serviceman, stationary engineer, and tool and die maker.

Mechanical engineer. California State Department of Employment. 1968. 7p. Single copy free

Occupational guide describing work, requirements, training, and outlook.

Mechanical engineer. Careers. 1966. 2p. 20c

Career summary for desk-top file. Duties, qualifications, and outlook.

Mechanical engineer. Chronicle Guidance Publications. 1969. 4p. 35c.

Occupational brief summarizing work performed, engineering functions, earnings, personal qualifications, outlook, and educational requirements.

Mechanical engineering technician. Careers. 1966. 2p. 20c

Career summary for desk-top file. Duties, qualifications, and outlook.

Mechanical engineers. Michigan Employment Security Commission. 1958. 2p. Single copy free

Job brief summarizing occupational data for use in Michigan.

* Mechanical engineers. Science Research Associates. 1967. 4p. 45c

Occupational brief describing nature of work, qualifications, preparation, opportunities, advantages, disadvantages, and future outlook.

** Mechanical engineers. One section of *Occupational Outlook Handbook.*

Nature of work, where employed, and employment outlook.

Mechanical technician. Chronicle Guidance Publications. 1968. 4p. 35c
Occupational brief summarizing work performed, training, outlook, opportunities, and certification.

See also Aeronautical engineer; Air-conditioning, refrigeration, and heating mechanic; Engineer

MEDICAL AND SCIENTIFIC ILLUSTRATOR 141.081

Finding out about medical illustrators. Science Research Associates. 1967. 4p. 45c
Junior occupational brief describing work and opportunities.

Histology technician. Careers. 1969. 2p. 20c
Career summary for desk-top file. Duties, qualifications, and outlook.

Medical artist (illustrator). Careers. 1966. 2p. 20c
Career summary for desk-top file. Duties, qualifications, and outlook.

**Medical illustration. Association of Medical Illustrators. 1966. 7p. Single copy free
Includes description of nature of work, desirable qualifications of applicants, entrance requirements, and training. List of seven teaching departments of medical illustration in medical schools.

Medical illustrator. Pages 129-131 of *Health Careers Guidebook.*
Description of work, qualifications, training, and prospects.

**Medical illustrators. Science Research Associates. 1969. 4p. 45c
Occupational brief describing nature of work, personal qualifications, training, methods of entrance, earnings, advantages, disadvantages, and future outlook.

Technical illustrator. Careers. 1967. 2p. 20c
Career summary for desk-top file. Duties, qualifications, and outlook.

See also Commercial artist

MEDICAL ASSISTANT 079.368

Finding out about medical assistants. Science Research Associates. 1967. 4p. 45c
Junior occupational brief containing concise facts about the job.

Medical assistant. Chronicle Guidance Publications. 1966. 4p. 35c
Occupational brief summarizing work performed, working conditions, qualifications, determination of interest and ability, training, opportunities, outlook, and methods of entry.

Medical assistant. Michigan Employment Security Commission. 1960. 2p. Single copy free
Job brief summarizing occupational data for use in Michigan.

Medical assistants. Science Research Associates. 1965. 4p. 45c
Occupational brief describing work, qualifications, training, earnings, things to consider, related jobs, and outlook. Selected references.

MEDICAL ASSISTANT—*Continued*

Medical office assistant. Careers. 1968. 2p. 20c

Career summary for desk-top file. Duties, qualifications, and outlook.

Plan your career as a medical assistant. American Association of Medical Assistants. No date. 4p. Single copy free

Information concerning the nature of work, qualifications, training, favorable aspects, rewards, and how to enter the field.

**Your future in medical assisting. Chernok, Norma. Richards Rosen Press. 1966. 128p. $4; library edition $3.78

Career opportunities as well as the educational requirements are presented. Includes list of colleges offering this new curriculum.

MEDICAL LABORATORY ASSISTANT 078.381

Jobs for medical laboratory assistants. Chronicle Guidance Publications. 1967. 4p. 35c

Reprinted article from *Occupational Outlook Quarterly* discusses nature of work, where employed, training required, opportunities, earnings, and working conditions in the field.

Medical laboratory assistant—a suggested guide for a training program. Vocational and Technical Education Division, U.S. Office of Education. Supt. of Documents. 1966. 115p. 60c

Prepared for instructors and supervisors of a training program.

Medical laboratory assistants. Science Research Associates. 1966. 4p. 45c

Occupational brief describing work, training, qualifications, opportunities, and outlook.

MEDICAL LABORATORY WORKER 078.128

A career in a medical laboratory. Registry of Medical Technologists. 1967. 16p. Free

Information about the work and training of the pathologist, medical technologist, cytotechnologist, and laboratory assistant.

**Careers in the medical laboratory. Registry of Medical Technologists. 1968. 4p. Free

Discussion of duties, employment outlook, scholastic requirements, and opportunities for registered medical technologists, certified laboratory assistants, and cytotechnologists. Also contains an explanation of the difference between the requirements for registration and those of several registries which are not under medical auspices.

**Employment outlook for medical laboratory workers. Bulletin No. 1650–16. Bureau of Labor Statistics, U.S. Department of Labor. Supt. of Documents. 1970. 8p. 10c

Reprint from the *Occupational Outlook Handbook*.

Medical laboratory careers with a future. Registry of Medical Technologists. 1967. 2p. Free

A flyer-poster in color describing the work and training of the pathologist, cytotechnologist, histologic technician, registered medical technologist, and the certified laboratory assistant.

Medical laboratory technologist. Guidance Centre. 1969. 4p. 35c postpaid

Nature of the work, qualifications, preparation, working conditions, advancement, employment outlook, earnings, and how to get started.

Medical laboratory workers. One section of *Occupational Outlook Handbook.*

Nature of work, places of employment, training, other qualifications, outlook, earnings, and working conditions.

**What kind of career could I have in a medical laboratory? American Society of Medical Technologists. 1968. 16p. Single copy free

Illustrated folder describing the work, opportunity, need, and training required.

MEDICAL LIBRARIAN 100.168

Medical librarian. Careers. 1969. 2p. 20c

Career summary for desk-top file. Duties, qualifications, and outlook.

Medical librarian. Pages 140-42 of *Health Careers Guidebook.*

Nature of work, training, opportunities for employment, and status and standards.

* Medical librarians. Science Research Associates. 1968. 4p. 45c

Occupational brief describing nature of work, requirements, training, getting started, earnings, advantages, disadvantages, and future outlook.

**Medical library careers. Medical Library Association. 1968. 8p. Single copy free

Discussion of the variety and extent of medical libraries, functions of a medical librarian, preparation, job opportunities, and salaries.

MEDICAL RECORD LIBRARIAN 100.388

Accredited schools for medical record librarians. Council on Medical Education of the American Medical Association. 1967. 2p. Free

Names and locations of twenty-seven schools.

**Employment outlook for medical record librarians. Bulletin No. 1650–18. Bureau of Labor Statistics, U.S. Department of Labor. Supt. of Documents. 1970. 6p. 10c

Reprint from the *Occupational Outlook Handbook.*

Finding out about medical record librarians. Science Research Associates. 1967. 4p. 45c

Junior occupational brief summarizing what the work requires and offers.

MEDICAL RECORD LIBRARIAN—*Continued*

Medical office services. Pages 160-61 of *Health Careers Guidebook.*
Nature of work, personal qualifications, training, and prospects for the medical secretary and assistant.

Medical record librarian. California State Department of Employment. 1968. 4p. Single copy free
Occupational guide describing work, requirements, training, and outlook.

* Medical record librarian. Careers. 1970. 8p. 35c
Career brief describing duties, working conditions, training, personal qualifications, registration requirements, places of employment, earnings, and outlook.

Medical record librarian. Chronicle Guidance Publications. 1969. 4p. 35c
Occupational brief summarizing work performed, working conditions, earnings, personal qualifications, training requirements, opportunities, employment and a list of approved schools.

Medical record librarian. Guidance Centre. 1967. 35c postpaid
Definition, history and importance, nature of work, qualifications, working conditions, preparation, remuneration, advancement, outlook, related occupations, and how to get started.

Medical-record librarian. Michigan Employment Security Commission. 1960. 2p. Single copy free
Job brief summarizing occupational data for use in Michigan.

* Medical record librarians. Science Research Associates. 1966. 4p. 45c
Occupational brief describing nature of work, personal qualifications, training, opportunities, earnings, advantages, and future outlook.

** Medical record librarians. One section of *Occupational Outlook Handbook.*
Nature of work, where employed, training, other qualifications, advancement, employment outlook, earnings, and working conditions.

Medical record technician. Page 160 of *Health Careers Guidebook.*
Brief statement of training and qualifications.

MEDICAL SECRETARY 201.368

Medical secretary. Chronicle Guidance Publications. 1969. 4p. 35c
Occupational brief summarizing work performed, working conditions, qualifications, determination of aptitudes and interests, training, opportunities, and outlook.

Medical secretary. Guidance Centre. 1967. 4p. 35c postpaid
Definition, history and importance, nature of work, preparation, qualifications, employment, advancement, outlook, remuneration, and how to get started.

Medical secretary and medical assistant. California State Department of Employment. 1968. 4p. Single copy free

Occupational guide describing work, requirements, training, and outlook.

Your career as a medical secretary. United Business Schools Association. 1968. 6p. Free

Description of work, training, advantages, and opportunities.

MEDICAL SERVICE AND HEALTH SERVICE WORKER

07 and 079.

**Because you like people . . . choose a career in mental health. National Association for Mental Health. 1965. 16p. $3.95 per 100

Provides general information about the mental health field and specific details about seven mental health jobs: psychiatric aide, recreational therapist, occupational therapist, psychiatric nurse, psychiatric social worker, clinical psychologist, and psychiatrist.

Career opportunities: health technicians. Kinsinger, Robert E., ed. Ferguson Publishing Company. 1970. 386p. $11.95

Information about twenty-five major career areas in the health field. Includes a geographical listing of 1,890 educational institutions offering programs for health technicians.

The career you want. National Tuberculosis and Respiratory Disease Association. 1967. 8p. Free

Brochure describes the nature of the work with local or state branches, job opportunities, working conditions, advancement, and future prospects.

Careers in psychiatry. National Commission on Mental Health Manpower. Macmillan Company. 1968. 192p. $4.95

Prepared with the assistance of the American Psychiatric Association, this describes the work, qualifications, and types of practice.

Careers that count. American Hospital Association. 1967. 8p. Single copy free

The brochure lists a number of career opportunities in hospitals and gives addresses of professional organizations to contact for further information.

**Counselors' kit: mental health careers. National Association for Mental Health. 1968. 12 booklets. $1

A kit of materials to introduce mental health occupations and provide information about seven basic fields of work.

**Disease detectives: your career in medical research. Neal, Harry E. Julian Messner. Revised 1968. 192p. $3.95; library binding $3.64

Information on nature of work, qualifications, and preparation of a wide variety of research workers. Includes bacteriologist, biochemist, medical artist, pharmacist, physiologist, psychiatrist, and radiation specialist.

Education for the allied health professions and services. Public Health Service, U.S. Department of Health, Education, and Welfare. Publication Number 1600. Supt. of Documents. 1967. 61p. 45c

Summary and recommendations of health manpower supply and needs and the education and training for the allied health occupations.

MEDICAL SERVICE AND HEALTH SERVICE WORKER—*Continued*

Educational qualifications and functions of public health educators. American Public Health Association. 1957. 8p. Single copy free

Scope of work, functions, and educational requirements.

Four medical jobs. Alumnae Advisory Center. 1963. 6p. 35c

Encouragement to girls who are interested in health work, but not an M.D., to follow their bent as a biologist, psychiatric nurse, medical technologist, or medical secretary. Case histories of young women who have succeeded in these specialized fields.

Good jobs in the health fields. Changing Times. 1966. 3p. 15c

Some information about promising careers which do not require a college degree.

**Hands that help—careers for medical workers. Dodge, Bertha. Little, Brown and Company. 1967. 247p. $4.75

A description and history of the various careers allied to the medical profession, including medical technologists, certified laboratory assistants, X-ray technologists, anesthetists, inhalation therapists, and medical record librarians. Includes a list of the professional societies.

Health careers. Careers. 1968. 8p. 35c

Career brief describing the need for semiprofessional health workers, employment prospects, related careers, and training opportunities. A table presents the number of men and women employed in each of fifteen health careers, normal yearly earnings, and length of training beyond high school.

**Health careers guidebook. Bureau of Employment Security, U.S. Department of Labor. Supt. of Documents. 1965. 204p. $1.75

The first forty pages consist of a preview of health careers, a greeting to future members of the health teams, some cautions, and a health careers calendar showing the time that is required for education or special training for 102 health occupations. These sections are followed by health career briefings, containing information about qualifications, training, and future prospects for thirty-two health career opportunities.

Health careers series. American Hospital Association. 1967. 6 leaflets. $2.75 per 100. Single copy free

Information leaflets on hospital occupations: hospital admitting officer, hospital engineer, hospital purchasing agent, supportive nursing personnel, electrocardiograph technician, electroencephalograph technician, and hospital public relations officer.

Health careers—where the action is. Public Health Service, U.S. Department of Health, Education, and Welfare. 1967. 6p. Free

Leaflet listing types of health careers by the level of education needed.

The health manpower gap: A high hurdle. Chronicle Guidance Publications. 1968. 6p. 50c

A reprinted article from *Occupational Outlook Quarterly* discusses shortage of trained manpower in various health occupations.

Health manpower perspective: 1967. Public Health Service, U.S. Department of Health, Education, and Welfare. Publication Number 1667. Supt. of Documents. 1967. 81p. 55c

Reports on current and prospective supply and demand for health manpower. Prepared for those who are responsible for education in the health professions and in the organization of health services.

Health manpower source book—hospital house staffs. Public Health Service, U.S. Department of Health, Education, and Welfare. Publication Number 263, Section 13. Supt. of Documents. 1961. 42p. 30c

Data on the numbers, distribution, and characteristics of personnel. Includes information on training, age, sex, employment status, and income level.

Health manpower source book—industry and occupation data. Public Health Service, U.S. Department of Health, Education, and Welfare. Publication Number 263, Section 17. Supt. of Documents. 1964. 104p. 55c

Presents basic data on the health services industry and on eighteen occupations as reported in the 1960 Census of Population.

Health manpower source book—manpower in the 1960's. Public Health Service, U.S. Department of Health, Education, and Welfare. Supt. of Documents. 1964. 67p. 40c

Basic data concerning physicians, dentists, and professional nurses.

Health manpower source book, Section 21, allied health manpower. U.S. Department of Health, Education, and Welfare. Supt. of Documents. 1970. 107p. $1.25

A report covering 1950-80.

Health professions: earned degrees, by level, sex, and institution. One section of *Earned Degrees Conferred.*

Useful for judging the extent of a college's program in each of the following specialties: chiropody or podiatry, dental hygiene, hospital administration, medical technology, medicine, nursing, occupational therapy, optometry, osteopathy, pharmacy, physical therapy, public health, radiologic technology, veterinary medicine, and the clinical sciences.

**Health service occupations. One chapter of *Occupational Outlook Handbook.*

Outlook summary for medical and other health service occupations. Specific information concerning each of the foremost services. Fifteen illustrations.

Health technicians; career opportunities for technicians and specialists. Kinsinger, Robert, ed. Ferguson Publishing Company. 1970. 366p. $11.95

Includes description of twenty-five specific career areas in the health services. For each there is a summary of type of work, qualifications, entry level jobs, advancement opportunities, working conditions, and earnings.

MEDICAL SERVICE AND HEALTH SERVICE WORKER—*Continued*

**Horizons unlimited. American Medical Association. Revised annually. 134p. Free to counselors and librarians

Opportunities, preparation, and rewards are presented for eight major fields allied to medicine. Lists of sources of added information conclude each unit.

**Hospital health services. Roth, Claire Jaret and Weiner, Lillian. I. Z. Walck, Inc. 1964. 117p. $4.50

Career possibilities are explored for members of the health team, including the hospital administrator, dietitian, occupational therapist, physical therapist, medical technologist, medical record librarian and technician, and rediologic technologist. Training, qualifications, earnings, and opportunities are discussed. Lists schools and sources of information. Illustrated.

Jobs in health. Science Research Associates. 1965. 32p. $1.15

Describes the variety of job prospects and opportunities within this field.

**The life you save: your career in health. Burke, Betsy and Paradis, Adrian. David McKay Company. 1962. 256p. $3.95

A practical book about the rewarding opportunities in the health field, pointing up the great need for nurses, aides, therapists and other dedicated people in areas related to health. Suggested readings at the end of each chapter.

Lifesaving jobs where you earn as you learn. Chronicle Guidance Publications. 1968. 80p. 50c

Reprinted article from *Today's Health* discusses operating room technicians, various therapist aides, X-ray technicians, nurses aides, ward clerks, EEG technicians, LPN's, medical-record technicians, medical secretaries, and dental assistants.

Marvels of medical engineering. Carlisle, Norman and Carlisle, Jon. Sterling Publishing Company. 1966. 152p. $3.95

Includes explanation of new medical devices and processes. Illustrated.

Professional schools in the health field. American Hospital Association. 1968. 24p. Single copy free

List of dental, medical, and paramedical schools in the United States and Canada. Revised annually.

Psychiatric aide. Careers. 1966. 2p. 20c

Career summary for desk-top file. Duties, qualifications, and outlook.

Susan, hospital aide. Colver, Alice Ross. Dodd, Mead and Company. 1964. 256p. $3.50

Career fiction. Story of a college undergraduate who spent a summer working in a New York City hospital.

Today's hospital . . . career center for America's youth. American Hospital Association. 1963. 8p. Free

A recruiting leaflet pointing out the variety of opportunities and the need for specially trained people in hospital services.

Vicky Barnes, junior hospital volunteer—the story of a candy striper. Colver, Alice Ross. Dodd, Mead and Company. 1966. 171p. $3.50

Career fiction. Story of experiences and satisfactions as a hospital volunteer. Written for grades 7 to 10.

Where to get health career information. National Health Council. 1968. 2p. Free

Alphabetical list of national agencies which publish and distribute free on request single copies of career information on health service occupations.

See also Hospital administrator; Medical technologist; Physician

MEDICAL SOCIAL WORKER 195.108

Educational qualifications of medical social workers in public health programs. American Public Health Association. 1962. 8p. Single copy free

Scope of the work, duties performed, types of positions, educational preparation, and qualifications.

Finding out about medical social workers. Science Research Associates. 1967. 4p. 45c

Junior occupational brief describing work and opportunities.

Medical social worker. Careers. 1969. 2p. 20c

Career summary for desk-top file. Duties, qualifications, and outlook.

MEDICAL TECHNOLOGIST 078.381

Accredited schools of medical technology. Council on Medical Education of the American Medical Association. 1967. 21p. Free

Name and locations of 783 schools, arranged by states.

Answers to your questions about an exciting career in medical technology. American Medical Technologists. 1968. 6p. Single copy free

Explanation of medical technology, places of employment, how to become a registered technologist, outlook, and the difference between the technologist and the technician.

Approved schools of cytotechnology. Council on Medical Education of the American Medical Association. 1967. 2p. Free

List of 100 schools arranged by states.

**Are you dreaming of a career in medical science? Be a medical technologist. American Society of Medical Technologists. 1968. 6 leaflets. 25c. Single copy free to counselors and librarians.

Folder containing career information.

**Career opportunities for health technicians. Ferguson Publishing Company. 1970. 300p. $11.95; $8.95 to schools and libraries

Prepared for high school and two-year college students. For twenty-five occupations in this category, there is included the educational requirements both in high school and after high school, job opportunities at entry level and advancement possibilities, working conditions, and immediate and future earning prospects.

MEDICAL TECHNOLOGIST—*Continued*

College undergraduate scholarships and loans in medical technology and cytotechnology. Registry of Medical Technologists. 1968. 6p. Free

Names and addresses of the state chairmen of the various state societies of medical technologists. Also presents a list of sources of information about scholarships.

Finding out about medical technologists. Science Research Associates. 1967. 4p. 45c

Junior occupational brief summarizing what the work requires and offers.

The human cell and the cytotechnologist. Registry of Medical Technologist. 1966. 6p. Free

Describes nature of the work and scholastic requirements.

**Medical technicians. One section of *Occupational Outlook Handbook.*

Nature of work, where employed, training, other qualifications, advancement, employment outlook, earnings, and working conditions.

* Medical technologist. Careers. 1967. 7p. 35c

Career brief describing duties, working conditions, training, personal qualifications, places of employment, earnings, and outlook. Additional readings.

Medical technologist. Chronicle Guidance Publications. 1966. 4p. 35c

Occupational brief summarizing nature of work, working conditions, qualifications, training, opportunities, and outlook.

Medical technologists. Michigan Employment Security Commission. 1966. 2p. Single copy free

Job brief summarizing occupational data for use in Michigan.

* Medical technologists. Science Research Associates. 1970. 4p. 45c

Occupational brief describing nature of work, qualifications, opportunities, advantages, disadvantages, and future outlook.

Medical technology. Pages 164-7 of *Health Careers Guidebook.*

Nature of work, qualifications, and prospects for the medical technologist, cytological technologist, and the blood bank technologist.

Opportunities unlimited—your career ladder in medical technology. American Medical Technologists. 1969. 6p. Single copy free

Describes openings in the new areas of medicine, medical research, and health careers. Predicts unlimited challenges.

Renee Manley: Medical technologist. Chronicle Guidance Publications. 1967. 4p. 35c

Reprinted article from *Today's Health* discusses training experiences in preparation for work in the field of medical technology.

Wanted: medical technologists. Ogg, Elizabeth. Public Affairs Committee. 1969. 20p. 25c

A summary of work in a community hospital laboratory reveals the many specialized areas of opportunities.

What is a medical technologist? Upjohn Company. 1966. 4p. Free
Illustrated brochure describing work, training, and opportunities.

Why not be a medical technologist? Leaflet 44. Women's Bureau, U.S. Department of Labor. Supt. of Documents. 1968. 8p. 10c
Brief sketch of nature of work, duties, qualifications, advantages, and earnings. Illustrated.

**Your future in medical technology. Paul, Grace. Richards Rosen Press. Revised 1969. 156p. $4; library edition $3.78
Emphasizes that medical technology is an important contributor to the health of the nation and offers opportunities for service, investigation, and many rewards besides financial ones.

See also Laboratory technician; Medical service worker

MERCHANDISE MANAGER. *See* Buyer; Retail manager

MERCHANT MARINE 197.133 and 197.168

Carrying cargo. Boardman, Gwenn R. Thomas Nelson and Sons. 1968. 192p. $3.95; library edition $3.70
A descriptive account of an around-the-world voyage aboard a modern cargo liner. The author explains the ship's routine at sea and in port, including the crew duties.

**Employment outlook for merchant marine occupations. Bulletin No. 1650–119. Bureau of Labor Statistics, U.S. Department of Labor. Supt. of Documents. 1970. 12p. 15c
Reprint from the *Occupational Outlook Handbook*. Includes licensed merchant marine officers and unlicensed merchant seamen.

Finding out about merchant marine officers. Science Research Associates. 1967. 4p. 45c
Junior occupational brief containing concise facts about the job.

Finding out about merchant seamen. Science Research Associates. 1967. 4p. 45c
Junior occupational brief describing work and opportunities.

**Licensed merchant marine officers. One section of *Occupational Outlook Handbook*.
Nature of work, training, qualifications, advancement, employment outlook, earnings, and working conditions.

Maritime College catalog. State University of New York Maritime College. 1968. 144p. Free
Statement of program, admission requirements, and explanation of curricula offered: marine transportation and management, marine engineering, nuclear science, meteorology, oceanography, and naval architecture. Illustrated.

Merchant marine: earned degrees, by level, sex, and institution. One section of *Earned Degrees Conferred*.
List of five academies and the number of degrees conferred by each.

MERCHANT MARINE—*Continued*

Merchant marine occupations. Chronicle Guidance Publications. 1966. 4p. 35c

Occupational brief summarizing fields of work; deck, engineering, purser's, and steward's departments; wages; hours; working conditions; and outlook.

Merchant marine occupations. One section of *Occupational Outlook Handbook.*

Nature and location of the industry, training, qualifications, advancement, employment outlook, earnings, and working conditions.

Merchant seamen. Science Research Associates. 1969. 4p. 45c

Occupational brief describing nature of work, training, qualifications, opportunities, advantages, disadvantages, and future outlook.

Ocean challenge: the new U.S. merchant marine. Carse, Robert. Norton and Company. 1967. 104p. $3.25; library edition $3.03

An account of modern ship transportation, including description of the jet skimmers and the atom-powered and jet-propelled ships. For grades 7 to 9.

Unlicensed merchant seaman. One section of *Occupational Outlook Handbook.*

Nature of the work, training, qualifications, outlook, earnings, and working conditions.

**Your future in the merchant marine. McLintock, Adm. Gordon. Richards Rosen Press. 1968. 160p. $4; library edition $3.78

Life at the Merchant Marine Academy is described. Requirements for entrance, and academic and physical programs are discussed.

MESSENGER 230.878

Messengers. Chronicle Guidance Publications. 1967. 4p. 35c

Occupational brief describing work, qualifications, earnings, and outlook.

Messengers and clerks. Assignment, Washington, D.C., with the U.S. Department of State. U.S. Department of State. Publication Number RB-2. 1968. 6p. Free

Gives the qualifications for employment, benefits, kinds of work, and pay.

Messengers and office boys. Science Research Associates. 1969. 4p. 45c

Occupational brief describing nature of work, training, qualifications, opportunities, advantages, and future outlook.

METALLURGICAL ENGINEER 011.081

**A career in metallurgy will extend your reach. American Society for Metals. 1966. 28p. 25c. Single copy free

Brochure explaining qualifications, preparation, opportunities, and future outlook.

**Careers in metallurgy and metallurgical engineering. Metallurgical Society. 1968. 10p. Single copy free

Description of the profession, service, rewards, training, and qualifications. Includes list of forty-two schools with curricula in metallurgical engineering accredited by the Engineers Council for Professional Development.

Finding out about metallurgical engineers. Science Research Associates. 1967. 4p. 45c

Junior occupational brief summarizing what the work requires and offers.

Metal mining workers. Science Research Associates. 1967. 4p. 45c

Occupational brief describing types of work, requirements, methods of getting started, advantages, disadvantages, and future outlook.

Metallurgical engineer. Chronicle Guidance Publications. 1968. 4p. 35c

Occupational brief describing work, qualifications, training, earnings, outlook, and a list of accredited schools.

Metallurgical engineering. Colorado School of Mines. No date. 6p. Free

Description of the work, prospects, training, and requirements for admission to the School of Mines.

* Metallurgical engineers. Science Research Associates. 1969. 4p. 45c

Occupational brief describing nature of work, requirements, methods of getting started and advancing, earnings, advantages, disadvantages, and future outlook.

Metallurgical engineers. One section of *Occupational Outlook Handbook.*

Nature of work, where employed, and employment outlook.

Metallurgist. Careers. 1966. 2p. 20c

Career summary for desk-top file. Duties, qualifications, and outlook.

Metallurgist. Guidance Centre. 1968. 4p. 35c postpaid

Definition, history and importance, nature of work, qualifications, preparation, advancement, outlook, remuneration, how to get started, and related occupations.

Nonferrous metals industry workers. Science Research Associates. 1967. 4p. 45c

Occupational brief describing nature of work, qualifications, opportunities, advantages, disadvantages, and future outlook.

Penetrating new frontiers with minerals engineers, geologists, and metallurgists. American Institute of Mining, Metallurgical, and Petroleum Engineers. 1968. 16p. Single copy free

Discussion of work, need, demand, and training.

Physical metallurgist (metallurgical engineer). California State Department of Employment. 1965. 5p. Single copy free

Occupational guide describing work, requirements, training, and outlook.

Structural metal workers. Michigan Employment Security Commission. 1958. 2p. Single copy free

Job brief summarizing occupational data for use in Michigan.

METALLURGICAL ENGINEER—*Continued*

**Your future in the metal castings industry. American Foundrymen's Society. 1965. 16p. Free to counselors

Brochure describes the work, job titles, salaries, opportunities, and geographic distribution of industry employees.

METEOROLOGIST 025.088

The activities of universities. American Meteorological Society. 1967. 32p. Single copy free

Brief accounts of meteorological education in each of thirty-four institutions which offer degrees in this field.

A century of weather service: a history of the birth and growth of the National Weather Service. Hughes, Patrick. Gordon and Breach. 1970. 212p. 10; paper $5

An account of the development of our nation's weather services from 1870 to 1970. Illustrated.

**The challenge of meteorology. American Meteorological Society. Revised 1966. 16p. Single copy free

Description of work, requirements, earnings, employment opportunities, and preparation.

Curricula in the atmospheric sciences in the colleges and universities. American Meteorological Society. 1968. 204p. $3

Report of academic programs in fifty-three colleges, including course titles, types of degrees granted, numbers of degrees granted, and description of special facilities.

Finding out about meteorologists. Science Research Associates. 1967. 4p. 45c

Junior occupational brief containing concise facts about the job.

Meteorological technician. Chronicle Guidance Publications. 1967. 4p. 35c

Occupational brief summarizing where employed, work performed, specializations, working conditions, earnings, personal and training requirements, and outlook.

Meteorological technician. Guidance Centre. 1965. 4p. 35c postpaid

Definition, history and importance, nature of work, qualifications, working conditions, preparation, remuneration, advancement, outlook, related occupations, and how to get started.

Meteorologist. California State Department of Employment. 1965. 6p. Single copy free

Job duties, working conditions, salaries, hours, finding the job, promotion, training, and employment outlook.

Meteorologist. Careers. 1970. 2p. 20c

Career summary for desk-top file. Duties, qualifications, and outlook.

Meteorologist. Chronicle Guidance Publications. 1966. 8p. 50c

Occupational brief summarizing work performed, working conditions, qualifications, training, and employment outlook.

Meteorologist. Guidance Centre. 1970. 4p. 35c postpaid

Definition, history, importance, nature of work, qualifications, preparation, working conditions, how to get started, opportunities for advancement, advantages, disadvantages, and related occupations.

Meteorologists. Science Research Associates. 1967. 4p. 45c

Occupational brief describing nature of work, requirements, training, working conditions, how to get started, and future outlook.

**Meteorologists. One section of *Occupational Outlook Handbook.*

Nature of work, where employed, training, other qualifications, employment outlook, earnings, and working conditions.

Skywatchers: the U.S. Weather Bureau in action. Bixby, William. David McKay Company. 1962. 192p. $4.50

Stories of individuals at work at their far-flung posts and how their information helps people in many walks of life. Points up the need for trained meteorologists and the steps the Government takes to increase the supply.

Tiros: weather eye in space. Jakes, John. Julian Messner. 1966. 192p. $3.95; library binding $3.64

Describes the program to increase the reliability of worldwide weather forecasting known as Tiros—Television Infra-red Observation Satellite. Illustrated.

The weather changers. Halacy, D. S., Jr. Harper and Row. 1968. 280p. $5.95

An account of man's attempts to control the weather, from witchcraft to the sophisticated modern methods.

**Your future in meteorology. Berry, Frederick and Frank, Sidney. Richards Rosen Press. Revised 1969. 155p. $4; library edition $3.78

The authors pinpoint salient facts concerning the applications and appeal of meteorological research and development. Includes description of activities of the U.S. Weather Bureau and the opportunities in the Navy and Air Force weather services. List of schools offering specialized training.

METERMAN AND METER READER 239.588

Finding out about meter readers. Science Research Associates. 1967. 4p. 45c

Junior occupational brief describing work and opportunities.

Metermen and meter readers. Brief description in *Occupational Outlook Handbook.*

Nature of work and employment outlook.

Meter reader. California State Department of Employment. 1966. 3p. Single copy free

Occupational guide describing work, requirements, training, and outlook.

MICROBIOLOGIST 041.081

Bacteriologist. Guidance Centre. 1965. 4p. 35c postpaid
History and importance, nature of work, qualifications, preparation, outlook, remuneration, how to get started, and related occupations.

A career in mycology. Mycological Society of America. 1965. 8p. Single copy free
Nature of work and opportunities in this field which is similar to microbiology.

Finding out about microbiologists. Science Research Associates. 1967. 4p. 45c
Junior occupational brief summarizing what the work requires and offers.

List of college and university departments offering degree programs in microbiology. American Society for Microbiology. 1968. 8p. 25c
Revised annually.

Men against death. De Kruif, Paul. Harcourt, Brace and World. 1936. 363p. $4.50
Biographies of scientists who made discoveries in the field of medicine.

Microbiologist. Careers. 1966. 2p. 20c
Career summary for desk-top file. Duties, qualifications, and outlook.

Microbiologist. Chronicle Guidance Publications. 1966. 4p. 35c
Occupational brief summarizing work performed, working conditions, earnings, personal qualifications, ways of determining interest and ability, training, opportunities, related occupations, and outlook.

Microbiologist (bacteriologist). California State Department of Employment. 1965. 5p. Single copy free
Occupational guide describing work, requirements, training, and outlook.

* Microbiologists. Science Research Associates. 1968. 4p. 45c
Occupational brief describing nature of work, requirements, preparation, getting started, advancing, earnings, and outlook.

** Microbiology in your future. American Society for Microbiology. 1969. 20p. 15c. Single copy free
Attractively illustrated brochure describing scope of microbiology, areas of work, recommended high school program of studies, college preparation, salaries, and employment outlook. Fields of specialization include medical, agricultural, industrial, public health, marine, geobiology, and space.

Robert Koch, father of bacteriology. Knight, D. C. Franklin Watts, Inc. 1961. 165p. $1.95
Biography of the man who first perfected the pure techniques of cultivating and studying bacteria and first isolated the tubercle bacillus, the cause of tuberculosis.

MILITARY SERVICEMAN. *See* Armed Forces

MILLINER 784.281

Finding out about milliners. Science Research Associates. 1967. 4p. 45c
Junior occupational brief containing concise facts about the job.

Hat and millinery workers. Science Research Associates. 1967. 4p. 45c
Occupational brief describing kinds of work, qualifications, educational requirements, getting started and advancing, earnings, advantages, disadvantages, and future outlook.

Milliner. Chronicle Guidance Publications. 1968. 4p. 35c
Occupational brief summarizing work performed, working conditions, qualifications, and outlook.

See also Clothing industry worker

MILLMAN (WOODWORKING). *See* Wood technologist

MILLWRIGHT 638.281

Finding out about millwrights. Science Research Associates. 1967. 4p. 45c
Junior occupational brief describing work and opportunities.

Millwright. California State Department of Employment. 1965. 5p. Single copy free
Occupational guide summarizing duties, working conditions, employment prospects, earnings, training, requirements for entry, and suggestions for locating a job.

**Millwright. Careers. 1969. 8p. 35c
Career brief describing duties, working conditions, training, places of employment, earnings, unionization, and outlook.

Millwright. Chronicle Guidance Publications. 1969. 4p. 35c
Occupational brief summarizing work performed, working conditions, hours, earnings, personal qualifications, training requirements, opportunities, and employment outlook.

Millwright. Michigan Employment Security Commission. 1967. 2p. Single copy free
Job brief summarizing occupational data for use in Michigan.

Millwrights. Science Research Associates. 1969. 4p. 45c
Occupational brief describing nature of work, requirements, training, getting started, earnings, advantages, disadvantages, and future outlook.

**Millwrights. One section of *Occupational Outlook Handbook*.
Nature of work, where employed, training, other qualifications, employment outlook, earnings, and working conditions.

MINING AND QUARRYING INDUSTRY WORKER

850.781 and 930.

College viewbook. Colorado School of Mines. 1968. 32p. Free

An example of an illustrated college bulletin containing explanations of the fields of mineral engineering offered: geological, geophysical, metallurgical, mining, petroleum, and petroleum refining.

Finding out about miners. Science Research Associates. 1967. 4p. 45c

Junior occupational brief describing work and opportunities.

Miner. Chronicle Guidance Publications. 1968. 4p. 35c

Occupational brief summarizing work, requirements, advantages, disadvantages, trends, and outlook.

Miner (metal). Guidance Centre. 1966. 4p. 35c postpaid

Definition, history and importance, nature of work, qualifications, preparation, working conditions, earnings, how to get started, advantages, and disadvantages, employment, advancement, outlook, and importance.

Mining. One section of *Occupational Outlook Handbook.*

Brief description of occupations in the industry and the employment outlook.

Penetrating new frontiers with minerals engineers, geologists and metallurgists. American Institute of Mining, Metallurgical, and Petroleum Engineers. 1968. 16p. Single copy free

Discussion of careers in exploration, production, beneficiation, management, and systems engineering. Includes a list of thirty universities offering training.

Research in the earth and mineral sciences. College of Earth and Mineral Sciences. 1967. 45p. Free

Reports of a sampling of research indicating the type of graduate training offered.

See also Coal industry worker

MINING ENGINEER

010.081

Finding out about mining engineers. Science Research Associates. 1967. 4p. 45c

Junior occupational brief summarizing what the work requires and offers.

Mining and metallurgy. University of Missouri. 1968. 5 leaflets. Free

Example of recruiting leaflets describing work and training of the mining, metallurgical, petroleum, nuclear, and ceramic engineer.

Mining and quarrying industry. Chronicle Guidance Publications. 1968. 4p. 35c

Occupational brief summarizing scope, work performed, working conditions, educational training requirements, personal requirements, mining as a growth industry, earnings and hours, unionization, and mineral producing areas of the United States.

Mining engineer. Careers. 1970. 2p. 20c
Career summary for desk-top file. Duties, qualifications, and outlook.

Mining engineer. Chronicle Guidance Publications. 1968. 40p. 35c
Occupational brief summarizing mineral industry team, work performed, working conditions, personal requirements, outlook, salary, and training required.

Mining engineering. Colorado School of Mines. No date. 6p. Free
Description of the work, prospects, training, and requirements for admission for study.

Mining engineers. Science Research Associates. 1967. 4p. 45c
Occupational brief describing nature of work, duties, places of employment, training, earnings, and future outlook.

**Mining engineers. One section of *Occupational Outlook Handbook.*
Nature of work, where employed, and employment outlook.

**Penetrating new frontiers with minerals engineers, geologists, mining engineers, and metallurgists. Society of Mining Engineers. 1967. 16p. Free
Discussion of possibilities, opportunities, and outlook.

Take a look at Tech. New Mexico Institute of Mining and Technology. 1969. 8p. Free
A recruiting brochure which includes brief descriptions of nature of work and opportunities. Includes mining, metallurgical, and petroleum engineering; physics, geology, geophysics; mathematics, chemistry; and computer science.

See also Engineer; Petroleum engineer

MINISTER. *See* Clergyman

MISSILEMAN 002.081

Countdown; rockets and missiles for national defense. Colby, Carroll B. Coward-McCann, Inc. 1970. 48p. $3.29
This revised edition concentrates on the new and important rockets and missiles presently in the national defense arsenal. For grades 6 to 9.

Rocketmen and what they do. Coombs, Charles. Franklin Watts, Inc. 1962. 184p. $3.95
Description of work, personal qualifications, specialized training, outlook, and rewards. For grades 7 to 11.

Rockets, missiles and space. Pizer, Vernon. Lippincott Company. 1962. 160p. $3.95
Explanations of how rockets, missiles, and space vehicles work and a history of man's efforts to conquer space. Illustrated.

See also Aerospace industry worker; Air Force airman; Airplane pilot; Astronaut

MODEL 297.868 and 961.868

Beth Hilton: model. Wyndham, Lee. Julian Messner. 1961. 192p. $3.50

Career fiction. Because Beth is tall and gawky, she enrolls in a charm school, becomes interested in modeling, and learns the realistic side of a competitive field that requires effort and dedication.

* A career in modeling. Fraser, Helen. Barbizon School of Modeling. 1968. 31p. $1

A recruiting booklet which includes a description of photographic and fashion modeling, types of models used, requirements, employment opportunities, and the training program.

**Employment outlook for models. Bulletin No. 1650–38. Bureau of Labor Statistics, U.S. Department of Labor. Supt. of Documents. 1970. 8p. 10c

Reprint from the *Occupational Outlook Handbook.*

Finding out about models. Science Research Associates. 1967. 4p. 45c

Junior occupational brief containing concise facts about the job.

Model. California State Department of Employment. 1964. 5p. Single copy free

Occupational guide describing work, requirements, training, and outlook.

Model. Careers. 1969. 8p. 35c

Career brief describing duties, working conditions, training, personal qualifications, advantages, disadvantages, earnings, and outlook. Additional readings.

Model. Chronicle Guidance Publications. 1969. 4p. 35c

Occupational brief summarizing work performed, working conditions, hours, earnings, personal qualifications, training requirements, opportunities, employment outlook, and entry into the job.

Model. Guidance Centre. 1969. 4p. 35c postpaid

Nature of work, qualifications, preparation, working conditions, employment, outlook, remuneration, and how to get started.

**Modeling and other glamour careers. Jones, Candy. Harper and Row. 1969. 227p. $5.95

The author suggests various ways to get started and gives specific information on physical and personal qualifications. She answers many questions from aspiring models, describes a typical day for a New York photographic model, and touches on other careers such as company goodwill ambassadress, guide, receptionist, and traveling hostess. Several chapters are devoted to information gathered from fifteen cities outside New York.

Modeling careers—glamour and hard work. Chronicle Guidance Publications. 1968. 4p. 35c

Reprinted article from *Occupational Outlook Quarterly* discusses fashion models, retail store models, photographic models, entry into the field, physical characteristics, and earnings.

Models. Michigan Employment Security Commission. 1960. 2p. Single copy free

Job brief summarizing occupational data for use in Michigan.

* Models. Science Research Associates. 1966. 4p. 45c

Occupational brief describing kinds of modeling, qualifications, training, methods of getting started, earnings, advantages, disadvantages, and future outlook.

Models. One section of *Occupational Outlook Handbook.*

Nature of work, places of employment, training, other qualifications, advancement, employment outlook, earnings, and working conditions.

**Your future in modeling. MacGil, Gillis. Richards Rosen Press. Revised 1969. 160p. $4; library edition $3.78

The founder of a fashion model agency describes qualifications, opportunities, and the varied kinds of work.

MORTICIAN. *See* Funeral director

MOTEL MANAGER. *See* Hotel manager

MOTION PICTURE INDUSTRY WORKER 187.168

Careers in motion picture production. Eastman Kodak Company. 1969. 16p. Single copy free

Brief discussion of possibilities offered by Hollywood, television, business and industry, education, government, religion, medicine and film teaching. Includes a list of colleges that have film study programs.

Film editor. California State Department of Employment. 1966. 5p. Single copy free

Occupational guide describing work, requirements, training, and outlook.

Film editors. Science Research Associates. 1969. 4p. 45c

Occupational brief describing nature of work, training, qualifications, opportunities, and outlook.

Finding out about film editors. Science Research Associates. 1967. 4p. 45c

Junior occupational brief describing work and opportunities.

Making movies: student films to features. Colman, Hila. World Publishing Company. 1969. 191p. $4.95; library edition $4.61

A survey of career opportunities in the film industry. The author interviews many individuals from director, editor, and producer to make-up artist and hair stylist on their background and duties.

Motion picture producers and directors. Science Research Associates. 1965. 4p. 45c

Occupational brief describing nature of work, training, qualifications, opportunities, advantages, disadvantages, and future outlook. Selected references.

MOTION PICTURE INDUSTRY WORKER—*Continued*

**Your career in film making. Gordon, George N. and Falk, Irving A. Julian Messner. 1969. 224p. $3.95; library binding $3.64

Contains interviews with leading figures in many phases of contemporary films such as the giant spectacular, the sixty-second commercial, the documentary, and the underground film. Includes a list of colleges offering courses in film making.

MOTION-PICTURE PROJECTIONIST 960.382

**Employment outlook for motion picture projectionists. Bulletin No. 1650–100. Bureau of Labor Statistics, U.S. Department of Labor. Supt. of Documents. 1970. 8p. 10c

Reprint from the *Occupational Outlook Handbook.*

Finding out about motion-picture projectionists. Science Research Associates. 1967. 4p. 45c

Junior occupational brief containing simplified information about requirements, training, earnings, and opportunities.

Motion picture projectionist. Chronicle Guidance Publications. 1969. 4p. 35c

Occupational brief summarizing work performed, working conditions, hours, earnings, personal qualifications, training requirements, opportunities, employment outlook, and entry into the job.

Motion-picture projectionist. Michigan Employment Security Commmission. 1967. 2p. Single copy free

Job brief summarizing occupational data for use in Michigan.

**Motion picture projectionists. Science Research Associates. 1969. 4p. 45c

Occupational brief describing nature of work, training, qualifications, opportunities, advantages, disadvantages, and future outlook.

Motion picture projectionists. One section of *Occupational Outlook Handbook.*

Nature of work, places of employment, training, qualifications, employment outlook, earnings, and working conditions.

Moving picture projectionist. Careers. 1969. 2p. 20c

Career summary for desk-top file. Duties, qualifications, and outlook.

MOTOR VEHICLE AND EQUIPMENT MANUFACTURING WORKER 806.887

**Automobile manufacturing workers. Science Research Associates. 1969. 4p. 45c

Occupational brief describing various kinds of work, requirements, earnings, and future outlook.

Automotive draftsmen. Michigan Employment Security Commission. 1965. 2p. Single copy free

Job brief summarizing occupational data for use in Michigan.

Birth of a giant: the men and incidents that gave America the motor car. Crabb, Alexander Richard. Chilton Book Company. 1969. 467p. $9.50

Anecdotal account of the major developments and personal contributions of leading persons associated with the emergence of the automobile industry.

Can I make the production team? Let's find out. General Motors, Public Relations Staff. 1969. 17p. Single copy free

Discussion of opportunities in production work and jobs on the assembly line. Includes educational and personal qualifications desired and ways of obtaining a job.

**Employment outlook for motor vehicle and equipment manufacturing. Bulletin No. 1650–115. Bureau of Labor Statistics, U.S. Department of Labor. Supt. of Documents. 1970. 15p. 15c

Reprint from the *Occupational Outlook Handbook.*

Finding out about automobile manufacturing workers. Science Research Associates. 1967. 4p. 45c

Junior occupational brief describing work and opportunities.

Model makers in auto industry. Michigan Employment Security Commission. 1958. 2p. Single copy free

Job brief summarizing occupational data for use in Michigan.

Motor vehicle and equipment manufacturing occupations. One section of *Occupational Outlook Handbook.*

Nature and location of the industry, how motor vehicles are made, occupations in the industry, employment outlook, earnings, and working conditions.

**Motor vehicle manufacturing occupations. One section of *Occupational Outlook Handbook.*

Nature of work, where employed, training, other qualifications, advancement, employment outlook, earnings, and working conditions.

Question—what does it take to make your car? Automobile Manufacturers Association. 1967. 52p. Single copy free to teachers and librarians

Booklet, copiously illustrated, showing the various processes of transforming raw materials into the components of an automobile. Good material to illustrate the interdependence of workers.

MOTOR VEHICLE TRANSPORTATION WORKER 90 and 91

Directory of transportation education in U.S. colleges and universities. American Trucking Associations. 1968. 24p. Free

A listing by state of about 600 colleges indicating the courses and degrees offered in transportation, traffic management, and related subjects.

Exploring your future in motor transportation. Sextant Systems, Inc., 1970. 96p. $8.95

One page is devoted to each of ninety-five jobs, describing the duties, requirements for entering, promotional outlook, and the pay and skill level.

Opportunities in the trucking industry. American Trucking Associations. 1968. 6p. Free

Includes discussion of work in sales, traffic, operations, truck driving, maintenance engineering, and public relations.

MOTOR VEHICLE TRANSPORTATION WORKER—*Continued*

Truck transportation. One chapter in Volume I in the *Encyclopedia of Careers and Vocational Guidance.*

Kinds of work, the predicted growth of the industry, and employment outlook.

Unlimited opportunities in America's fastest growing industry—motor transportation. Tri-State College. No date. 6p. Free

An example of a college recruiting leaflet describing training and opportunities.

**Your future in the automotive industry. Taylor, Dawson. Richards Rosen Press. Revised 1969. 160p. $4; library edition $3.78

Various aspects of the automobile industry from manufacture to sales and maintenance are presented.

**Your future in the trucking industry. Eskow, Gerald. Richards Rosen Press. Revised 1969. 160p. $2.95; library edition $2.79

Description of the various jobs including business administration, traffic control, engineering, and personnel management.

See also Transportation agent; Truck driver

MUSEUM WORKER 102.118

* Behind these doors: science museum makers. Facklam, Margery. Rand McNally and Company. 1968. 143p. $4.50

Explanation of opportunities for employment and educational requirements. Describes how special exhibits are created from the start of the field trip where materials are gathered until the finished display in the museum.

Finding out about museum curators. Science Research Associates. 1967. 4p. 45c

Junior occupational brief containing concise facts about the job.

In the steps of the great American museum collector, Carl Ethan Akeley. Clark, James L. Evans and Company. 1968. 127p. $3.95

Biography revealing the work of tracking down specimens and preserving them for display in the American Museum of Natural History. For grades 6 to 10.

Museum jobs. Alumnae Advisory Center. 1966. 6p. 35c

Reprint from *Mademoiselle* describing the work of several young women who have succeeded in this kind of a career.

**Museum workers. Science Research Associates. 1970. 4p. 45c

Occupational brief describing nature of work, requirements, getting started, rewards, and future outlook.

Treasures by the millions: the story of the Smithsonian Institution. Neal, Harry Edward. Julian Messner. 1961. 192p. $3.95; library binding $3.64

The author leads the reader on a tour through the various departments of the Smithsonian Institution, describing the activities of the curators and other museum experts.

**Your future in museums. Burns, William A. Richards Rosen Press. 1967. 140p. $4; library edition $3.78

An account of the jobs and challenges of working in a museum, especially in curatorial positions. Includes list of institutions offering training programs in various museum fields.

MUSIC TEACHER 152.028

**A career in music education. Music Educators National Conference. Revised 1965. 24p. 50c

Information for high school students interested in teaching music. Includes qualifications, training, and opportunities. Good list of references.

Finding out about instrumental music teachers. Science Research Associates. 1967. 4p. 45c

Junior occupational brief containing concise facts about the job.

Instrumental music teachers. Science Research Associates. 1966. 4p. 45c

Occupational brief describing work, training, qualifications, opportunities, and outlook.

The market for music teachers. Reimer, Bennett. Music Educators National Conference. 1963. 20p. 50c

Brochure which examines the picture of supply and demand in the field of music. Facts are given about different "market places" for the music teacher.

Music teacher. Careers. 1969. 2p. 20c

Career summary for desk-top file. Duties, qualifications, and outlook.

Music teacher. Chronicle Guidance Publications. 1966. 4p. 35c

Occupational brief summarizing work performed, hours, working conditions, outlook, qualifications, training requirements, opportunities, and earnings.

**Musicians and music teachers. One section of *Occupational Outlook Handbook.*

Nature of work, where employed, training, other qualifications, employment outlook, earnings, and working conditions.

See also Instrumental musician; Musician; Singer

MUSICAL INSTRUMENT MAKER. *See* Instrument maker

MUSICIAN 152.

Associates and fellowship examination requirements. American Guild of Organists. 1969. 2p. Free

Includes description of the tests at the organ and paper work tests. Another statement is available for the choir master examinations requirements.

A career in music education. Music Educators National Conference. 1965. 22p. 50c

Explanation of the many careers in music education in addition to classroom teaching.

MUSICIAN—*Continued*

**Careers and opportunities in music. Rich, Alan. Dutton and Company. 1964. 224p. $4.50

Includes the opportunities and qualifications needed for the solo performer, the ensemble musician, the operatic specialist, the composer, teacher, and music critic.

**Careers in music. Ward, John Owen. Henry Z. Walck, Inc. 1968. 128p. $4.50

A survey of opportunities in the field of music, including both the discouraging difficulties and the satisfying rewards. In addition to work with classical music, the author discusses church music, popular music, broadcasting, working in the recording industry, concert managing, and working as a music librarian. Good reading list.

Careers in music. Berklee School of Music. 1968. 8p. Free

Information on qualifications, training, rewards, and opportunities.

Careers in music. Changing Times. 1962. 3p. 15c

Reprint describing jobs, satisfactions, and opportunities.

**Careers in music. Music Educators National Conference. Revised 1968. 4p. 10c

Brochure prepared for music educators and counselors calling attention to opportunities. The inside is a chart containing career information on teacher, music therapist, instrumentalist, vocalist, church musician, composer, conductor, tuner-technician, and music librarian.

Composers. Science Research Associates. 1967. 4p. 45c

Occupational brief describing work, training, qualifications, opportunities, and outlook.

Famous modern conductors. Ewen, David. Dodd, Mead and Company. 1967. 159p. $3.50

Contains brief sketches of twelve living conductors "who dominate the musical scene of our times." Includes information about the life and achievements of each conductor.

Finding out about band leaders. Science Research Associates. 1967. 4p. 45c

Junior occupational brief describing work and opportunities.

Finding out about composers and arrangers. Science Research Associates. 1967. 4p. 45c

Junior occupational brief containing concise facts about the job.

Leonard Bernstein. Ewen, David. Chilton Book Company. Revised 1967. 180p. $4.25

A biography of one of the world's foremost symphony conductors and composers which shows not only his accolades and triumphs but also the frustrations and despair that preceded his success.

The music hunter, the autobiography of a career. Boulton, Laura Theresa. Doubleday and Company. 1969. 513p. $8.95

An account of a musician's search for traditional and liturgical music of primitive peoples living in remote areas of the world. The author describes her experiences in twenty-eight expeditions to capture and preserve the local folk music. Will appeal to readers interested in musicology.

Music therapist. Careers. 1970. 2p. 20c

Career summary for desk-top file. Duties, qualifications, and outlook.

Music therapy as a career. National Association for Music Therapy. 1969. 4p. Free

Discussion of the basic preparation needed and a list of accredited institutions offering degrees in music therapy.

Musician. Guidance Centre. 1967. 4p. 35c postpaid

Nature of work, qualifications, preparation, working conditions, remuneration, advantages, disadvantages, how to get started, and related occupations.

Musicians. Chronicle Guidance Publications. 1968. 4p. 35c

Occupational brief summarizing work performed, qualifications, training, opportunities, earnings, and outlook.

Musicians, general. Careers. 1967. 8p. 35c

Career brief describing duties, working conditions, training, personal qualifications, earnings, and outlook. Additional readings.

Nonperforming jobs in music. Alumnae Advisory Center. 1965. 6p. 35c

Reprint from *Mademoiselle* describing case histories of several young women who have succeeded in jobs such as concert manager, lyricist, museum assistant, editor, programmer, therapist, or music director.

**Opportunities in music careers. Spaeth, Sigmund. Vocational Guidance Manuals. 1966. 128p. $1.95 paper; $3.75 library edition

Discussion of individual fields of performance, and qualifications and opportunities in vocal music, conducting, composing and arranging, and teaching. Also opportunities for musical amateurs, music criticism, lecturing, research, selling, and management. A section presents excerpts from experts giving well-considered opinions as to opportunities in music.

Performing musicians. Science Research Associates. 1966. 4p. 45c

Occupational brief describing nature of work, requirements, earnings, getting started, advantages, disadvantages, and future outlook. Selected references.

Post-baccalaureate grants and awards in music. Music Educators National Conference. 1969. 40p. $1

A listing of sources of assistance for the mature musician including awards, commissions, fellowships, and scholarships.

**Your future in music. Curtis, Robert. Richards Rosen Press. Revised 1969. 160p. $4; library edition $3.78

Includes discussion of many job opportunities in the field of music that are not generally known to the student.

See also Instrumental musician; Music teacher; Singer

MUSICIAN, INSTRUMENTAL. *See* **Instrumental musician**

NUCLEAR ENGINEER **015.081**

Finding out about nuclear engineers. Science Research Associates. 1967. 4p. 45c

Junior occupational brief summarizing what the work requires and offers.

Nuclear engineer. California State Department of Employment. 1964. 6p. Single copy free

Occupational guide describing work, requirements, training, and outlook.

Nuclear engineer. Chronicle Guidance Publications. 1969. 4p. 35c

Occupational brief summarizing nature of the work, working conditions, location of work, educational requirements, hours and earnings, opportunities for advancement, and employment outlook.

Nuclear engineers. Science Research Associates. 1969. 4p. 45c

Occupational brief describing uses of atomic energy, types of workers, qualifications, earnings, and outlook. Selected references.

Nuclear technician. California State Department of Employment. 1964. 5p. Single copy free

Occupational guide describing work, requirements, training, and outlook.

NUCLEAR PHYSICIST. *See* **Atomic energy industry worker; Physicist**

NURSE, PROFESSIONAL **075.378**

Aerospace nurse. McDonnell, Virginia B. Julian Messner. 1966. 192p. $3.50

Career fiction. Story ends with a member of the Air Force Nursing Corps undergoing training to administer medical aid to the astronauts. This is one of the series of "career romances for young moderns."

American women of nursing. Yost, Edna. Lippincott Company. 1965. 224p. $3.95

Biographies of ten nurses who were outstanding in their special fields: pediatrics, physiotherapy, public health, nursing education, and visiting nursing.

America's first trained nurse: Linda Richards. Baker, Rachel. Julian Messner. 1959. Library binding $3.34

Biography of a nurse who helped to revolutionize hospital care.

Arlene Perry, orthopedics nurse. McLeod, Ruth. Julian Messner. 1966. 192p. $3.50

Career fiction. Story of a nurse who displays considerable courage and an unusual capacity for supervision at a time of crisis. This is one of the series of "career romances for young moderns."

Arrow book of nurses. Elting, Mary. Scholastic Book Services. 1963. 64p. 35c paper

How nurses are trained and the challenging jobs open to them. This title is available to only schools, through the Scholastic Book Services.

Associate degree education for nursing. Committee on Careers, National League for Nursing. 1968. 15p. 25c

A description of associate degree nursing education, with a list of state approved and accredited programs in nursing education leading to the associate degree.

Catholic institutions offering programs in nursing. Conference of Catholic Schools of Nursing. 1968. 6p. Mimeographed. Free

Lists of schools of nursing located in Catholic institutions.

College education: key to a professional career in nursing. Committee on Careers, National League for Nursing. 1967. 15p. 25c

Information about collegiate education for beginning students, with a list of accredited degree programs.

Do you want to be a nurse? Committee on Careers, National League for Nursing. 1966. 24p. 15c

Illustrated booklet describing preparation and opportunities.

Education for nursing the diploma way. Committee on Careers, National League for Nursing. 1967. 15p. 25c

Information about the hospital diploma program, including a directory of accredited programs.

Educational opportunities and financial assistance for nursing students. Army Opportunities, U.S. Army Recruiting Command. 1968. 8p. Free

Describes the requirements and benefits of the diploma, degree, and registered nurse sections. Includes opportunities upon completion of the program.

**Employment outlook for registered nurses, licensed practical nurses, hospital attendants. Bulletin No. 1650–9. Bureau of Labor Statistics, U.S. Department of Labor. Supt. of Documents. 1970. 12p. 15c

Reprint from the *Occupational Outlook Handbook.*

Finding out about registered professional nurses. Science Research Associates. 1967. 4p. 45c

Junior occupational brief describing work and opportunities.

The first book of nurses. Kay, Eleanor. Franklin Watts, Inc. 1968. 56p. $2.65; library edition $1.98

In this revised edition a factual, concise text and numerous photographs provide a brief view of present-day nursing. For grades 5 to 8.

Frontier nurse: Mary Breckinridge. Wilkie, Katharine and Moseley, Elizabeth. Julian Messner. 1969. 192p. $3.50; library binding $3.34

Biography of a nurse dedicated to fighting infant mortality in the Kentucky mountains and who established the Frontier Nursing Service.

Get with it, Joan. Roberts, Mary. Ives Washburn, Inc. 1961. 176p. $2.95

Career fiction. Includes the story of the training of a nurse at a large New York hospital. For grades 7 to 9.

NURSE, PROFESSIONAL—*Continued*

Health manpower source book—nursing personnel. Public Health Service, U.S. Department of Health, Education, and Welfare. Supt. of Documents. 1969. 144p. $1.50

Considerable data on the number, distribution, and characteristics of nursing personnel. Trends are reported by states. Useful for those planning new health programs.

Heroic nurses. McKown, Robin. Putnam's Sons. 1966. 320p. $3.64

Twelve biographies of heroic nurses.

Holly Andrews: nurse in Alaska. Roberts, Suzanne. Julian Messner. 1967. 190p. $3.50

Career fiction. Story includes description of the routine life and work of nurses in a remote town in Alaska with a large Eskimo settlement. This is one of the series of "career romances for young moderns."

The hospital school of nursing. American Hospital Association. 1967. 12p. Single copy free

Explanation of the educational program offered by the hospital school of nursing.

Judy George: student nurse. Stone, Patti. Julian Messner. 1966. 192p. $3.50

Career fiction. Story of a student nurse's senior year of training.

Licensed vocational nurse. California State Department of Employment. 1967. 4p. Single copy free

Occupational guide describing work, requirements, training, and outlook.

* The life you save—your career in health. Burke, Betsy and Paradis, Adrian. David McKay Company. 1962. 256p. $3.95

Discussion of the job opportunities in the health field, details of the work in these positions, and necessary training.

Man nurse. Careers. 1969. 2p. 20c

Career summary for desk-top file. Duties, qualifications, and outlook.

Man nurse. Chronicle Guidance Publications. 1966. 8p. 50c

Occupational brief summarizing work performed, working conditions, qualifications, training, earnings, opportunities, where employed, licensing, and outlook.

Masters education: route to opportunities in modern nursing. Committee on Careers, National League for Nursing. 1967. 15p. 35c

Information about master's degree preparation in nursing, factors to be considered in choosing a school, and a list of colleges offering accredited master's programs.

** Modern nursing. Ducas, Dorothy. Henry Z. Walck, Inc. 1962. 111p. $4.50

Emphasizes the larger scope of present nursing duties, the place of the nurse in hospitals and related institutions, and the many new opportunities offered by the recent growth of nursing specialties. Reading list. Illustrated.

Navy nurse. McCall, Virginia. Julian Messner. 1968. 191p. $3.50. Library binding $3.34

Career fiction. A story blending adventure and romance with some information about a specialized area of nursing.

Nina Grant: pediatric nurse. Stone, Patti. Julian Messner. 1960. 192p. $3.50

Career fiction. Nina's sympathy interfered with her efficiency, but when an epidemic struck testing her courage and nursing skill, she proved herself the good nurse she longed to be.

**Nurse. Lewis, Edith Patton. Macmillan Company. 1962. 178p. $3.50

The author describes the qualities desirable in the successful nurse and the opportunities and fields of practice open to her.

Nurse. Guidance Centre. 1969. 4p. 35c postpaid

History and importance, nature of work, qualifications, preparation, advancement, outlook, remuneration, advantages, disadvantages, how to get started, and related occupations.

Nurse: husband, father, humanitarian, specialist. Committee on Careers, National League for Nursing. 1967. 12p. 25c

Picture folder depicting opportunities and preparation for careers in professional nursing for men.

Nurse in Vietnam. Dean, Nell M. Julian Messner. 1969. 192p. $3.50. Library binding $3.34

Career fiction. A story of a young girl's courage under dangerous wartime conditions.

Nurse, professional (hospitals and related institutions). California State Department of Employment. 1964. 4p. Single copy free

Occupational guide describing work, requirements, training, and outlook.

Nurse, professional (industrial and office). California State Department of Employment. 1968. 6p. Single copy free

Job duties, working conditions, employment outlook, wages, hours, entrance requirements, lines of promotion, and training.

Nurse, registered. Careers. 1970. 8p. 35c

Career brief describing duties, working conditions, training, personal qualifications, licensing, earnings, advancement prospects, outlook, and ways of measuring one's interest and ability.

Nurse scholarship programs. Public Health Service, U.S. Department of Health, Education, and Welfare. 1969. 4 pamphlets. Free

Several pamphlets revised annually to describe student loans, traineeship programs, scholarships, and other nursing educational opportunities.

Nurse Training Act of 1964. Public Health Service, U.S. Department of Health, Education, and Welfare. Publication 1740. Supt. of Documents. 1967. 78p. 55c

A program review report on the enlargement and improvement of nursing education programs. The tables include a percentage distribution of registered nurses in various fields of employment by educational preparation. For administrators.

NURSE, PROFESSIONAL—*Continued*

Nurses—a position for you as a nursing consultant. American National Red Cross. 1968. 1p. Free

Description of qualifications and jobs available for nurses in the Red Cross.

Nurses and what they do. Kay, Eleanor. Franklin Watts, Inc. 1968. 144p. $3.95

What a nursing student may expect, whatever phase of nursing she might choose—surgical, pediatrics, shipboard nursing, research, etc. Discusses the new attitudes toward educating nurses and the three available nursing education programs. For grades 7 to 11.

Nursing and related services for patients. Pages 170-79 of *Health Careers Guidebook.*

Qualifications, opportunities, and prospects for the professional nurse, practical nurse, nursing aide, orderlies, inhalation therapist, and the ward clerk.

Nursing careers in mental health. Public Health Service, U.S. Department of Health, Education, and Welfare. Publication Number 1051. Supt. of Documents. 1969. 15p. 30c

Tells of opportunities in the area of psychiatric-mental health nursing programs supported by the National Institute of Mental Health. Includes information about opportunities in community health centers, Public Health Service, Armed Forces, Veterans Administration, and in research.

Occupational health nurse. California State Department of Employment. 1968. 4p. Single copy free

Occupational guide describing work, requirements, training, and outlook.

**Opportunities in nursing careers. Weiss, M. Olga. Vocational Guidance Manuals. 1964. 128p. $1.95 paper; library edition $3.75

This is a realistic look at the career picture in professional and practical nursing. Written by an experienced nurse, this presents a frank discussion of the educational preparation, duties, outlook, opportunities, avenues of advancement, and employment prospects.

Orientation to nursing. Chamberlain, Edith M. McGraw-Hill Book Company. 1962. 196p. $4.95

Orients the student not only to the nursing education program that lies ahead but to nursing itself, providing the new student with skills and techniques for her personal and professional development and adjustment to nursing.

**Penny Marsh, R.N., director of nurses. Deming, Dorothy. Dodd, Mead and Company. 1960. 320p. $3

Career fiction. Interwoven in this story of a nurse's successes and failures is a picture of preparation for nursing and other career information. The Penny Marsh series is distinguished because the stories, written by a registered nurse, center around the romance of nursing rather than on personal anecdotes about the heroines.

Professional nurse. Chronicle Guidance Publications. 1968. 4p. 35c
Occupational brief summarizing work performed, working conditions, personal qualifications, training requirements, earnings, opportunities, and employment outlook.

**Professional nurse as a career. Belleau, Wilfrid. Park Publishing House. 1969. 24p. $1
Importance and nature of the work, qualifications, licensure, training, entrance requirements, expenses, conditions of work, income, opportunities, men in nursing, employment outlook, and how to begin.

Professional nursing—trends, responsibilities, and relationships. Spalding, Eugenia Kennedy. Lippincott Company. 1965. 684p. $8.75
A discussion of major trends and problems affecting nursing. One section is devoted to choosing, preparing and succeeding in a field of nursing. Seventy-five illustrations.

Psychiatric nurse. Careers. 1966. 2p. 20c
Career summary for desk-top file. Duties, qualifications, and outlook.

Registered nurse. Michigan Employment Security Commission. 1967. 2p. Single copy free
Job brief summarizing occupational data for use in Michigan.

The registered nurse in the psychiatric setting. National Association for Mental Health. 1968. 4p. 10c
Duties, training, earnings, and future outlook. Selected references.

Registered nurses. Science Research Associates. 1968. 4p. 45c
Occupational brief describing nature of work, training, qualifications, opportunities, advantages, and future outlook.

**Registered nurses. One section of *Occupational Outlook Handbook.*
Nature of work, where employed, training, other qualifications, advancement, employment outlook, and earnings.

Scholarships and loans for beginning education in nursing. Committee on Careers, National League for Nursing. 1969. 6p. 15c
Folder pointing out sources of aid for those beginning their training in nursing.

Scholarships, fellowships, educational grants, and loans for registered nurses. Committee on Careers, National League for Nursing. 1967. 6p. 10c
For graduate nurses.

Sources of scholarships and loans for beginning education in nursing. Committee on Careers, National League for Nursing. 1967. 6p. 10c
For students entering schools of nursing.

**The story of nursing. Dodge, Bertha. Little, Brown and Company. 1965. 244p. $4.50

NURSE, PROFESSIONAL—*Continued*

A revised edition of the book that describes the history and current aspects of the nursing profession. Part one tells about the heritage of the profession through persons like Florence Nightingale and those who followed her. Part two describes the opportunities in private, hospital, and public health nursing. A six-page bibliography.

Student nurse: her life in pictures. Engeman, Jack. Lothrop, Lee and Shepard Company. 1958. 128p. $4.95

More than 250 photographs, with informative text and captions, show activities of a student nurse from orientation week to graduation.

There's a star in your future—Veterans Administration nursing service. VA pamphlet 10-30. Veterans Administration Forms Depot. 1963. 12p. Free

Illustrated brochure describing opportunities, qualifications, and benefits.

Trudy Wells, R.N., pediatric nurse. Deming, Dorothy. Dodd, Mead and Company. 1957. 244p. $3.25

Career fiction written by an R.N. Story of the experiences of a supervising nurse for an infirmary in a modern children's home of 150 girls and boys.

What it's like to be a nurse. Changing Times. 1964. 3p. 15c

Reprint containing discussion of preparation, satisfactions, and opportunities.

Winds of fate. Strachan, Margaret. Ives Washburn, Inc. 1968. 192p. $3.95; library binding $3.59

Career fiction. A story that does not minimize the difficulties but brings out the compensations of a career as a nurse.

**Your career in nursing. Searight, Mary. Julian Messner. 1970. 192p. $3.95; library edition $3.64

This book describes the scope of modern nursing, sets down the academic training and personal qualities required, and gives case histories of many successful nurses.

**Your future in nursing. McDonnell, Virginia. Richards Rosen Press. Revised 1969. 157p. $4; library edition $3.79

Various areas of nursing are presented with the preparation and qualifications necessary for entrance into this field.

See also Practical nurse; Public health nurse

NURSE AID 355.878

Candy stripers. Wyndham, Lee. Julian Messner. 1958. 192p. $3.50; library binding $3.34

Career fiction. As a junior volunteer aide in a medical center, wearing a pink-striped uniform, Bonnie realized that her work could lead to other careers in the field of science.

**Nurse aid as a career. Belleau, Wilfrid. Park Publishing House. 1969. 13p. $1

History and importance of the work, qualifications, training, conditions of work, income, advancement, employment outlook, and how to begin.

Nurse aid (hospital orderly). California State Department of Employment. 1968. 3p. Single copy free

Occupational guide describing work, requirements, training, and outlook.

Nurse aide. Careers. 1970. 2p. 20c

Career summary for desk-top file. Duties, qualifications, and outlook.

Nursing assistant. Guidance Centre. 1967. 4p. 35c postpaid

Definition, history and importance, nature of work, working conditions, qualifications necessary for entry and success, preparation, employment and advancement, remuneration, advantages, disadvantages, how to get started toward the occupation, and related occupations.

The psychiatric aide. National Association for Mental Health. 1968. 4p. 10c

Nature of work, training, earnings, and future outlook.

NURSE ANESTHETIST 075.378

Anesthesia, a special type of nursing. American Association of Nurse Anesthetists. 1968. 8p. Free

A booklet designed for nurses describing the work, outlook, and requirements for becoming a certified registered nurse anesthetist.

Anesthesia, an art, a science. American Association of Nurse Anesthetists. 1968. 16p. Free

An illustrated booklet prepared for use with a film strip available from the same source.

**Anesthetists. Science Research Associates. 1966. 4p. 45c

Occupational brief describing nature of work, training, qualifications, opportunities, advantages, disadvantages, and future outlook.

Approved schools for nurse anesthetists. American Association of Nurse Anesthetists. 1969. 8p. Free

List designed for nurses, arranged alphabetically by states. Revised semi-annually.

Approved schools of inhalation therapy. Council on Medical Education of the American Medical Association. 1967. 1p. Free

List of thirty-one schools.

Considering a career in inhalation therapy? American Association for Inhalation Therapy. 1970. 16p. 15c

Nature of work, education requirements, training, and names of professional organizations serving specialists in this area.

Finding out about anesthetists. Science Research Associates. 1967. 4p. 45c

Junior occupational brief describing work and opportunities.

NURSE ANESTHETIST—*Continued*

Inhalation therapists. Science Research Associates. 1966. 4p. 45c
Occupational brief describing work, training, qualifications, opportunities, and outlook.

* Nurse anesthetist. Careers. 1969. 2p. 20c
Career summary for desk-top file. Duties, qualifications, and outlook.

**Nurse anesthetist career. American Association of Nurse Anesthetists. 1968. 8p. Free
Kind of work, where services are used, what to study in high school, professional training, and advantages.

NURSERY SCHOOL TEACHER. *See* Kindergarten and nursery school teacher

NURSERYMAN AND LANDSCAPE GARDENER

406.168 and 407.181

**Career opportunities in the nursery business. American Association of Nurserymen. 1965. 6p. $3 per 100. Single copy free upon receipt of self-addressed stamped envelope.
Description of nursery work, career opportunities, and training.

Finding out about nurserymen. Science Research Associates. 1967. 4p. 45c
Junior occupational brief containing concise facts about the job.

Nurseryman. Careers. 1969. 2p. 20c
Career summary for desk-top file. Duties, qualifications, and outlook.

Nurseryman. Chronicle Guidance Publications. 1969. 4p. 35c
Occupational brief summarizing work performed, working conditions, earnings, personal qualifications, training requirements, opportunities, and employment outlook.

Nurserymen and landscapers. Science Research Associates. 1969. 4p. 45c
Occupational brief describing nature of work, qualifications, training, earnings, methods of getting started, advantages, disadvantages, and future outlook. Selected references.

**Your future in the nursery industry. Pinney, John. Richards Rosen Press. 1967. 160p. $4; library edition $3.78
An account of the pleasures and problems of this industry, including opportunities for organizing one's own business. Contains description of specific job specialties such as plant propagator, storage foreman, plant breeder, and researcher. Brief biographies of ten successful nurserymen offer encouragement to young men with little formal education.

See also Horticulturist

NUTRITIONIST 077.128

Career opportunities in nutrition. American Institute of Nutrition. 1963. 4p. Free

Brief description of the growing opportunities in this field.

Careers in nutrition. American Institute of Nutrition. 1968. 4p. Free

Brochure contains discussion of the need for research workers in the field of nutrition and the educational preparation.

Careers in the U. S. Public Health Service: nutritionist . . . dietitian. Public Health Service, U.S. Department of Health, Education, and Welfare. Publication Number 1721. 1967. 20p. Free

Description of the kinds of activities and positions available and qualifications for appointment to both the Commissioned Corps and the Civil Service systems.

Do you know them? Dietitians and nutritionists. American Dietetic Association. 1968. 4p. 75c per 100. Single copy free

Description of nature of work and where employed.

Educational qualifications of nutritionists in health agencies. American Public Health Association. 1962. 6p. Single copy free

Scope of work, duties, educational qualifications, and experience recommended for each of three types of work: staff nutritionist, nutritionist consultant, and director of nutrition service in a health agency.

Nutritionist. Careers. 1968. 2p. 20c

Career summary for desk-top file. Duties, qualifications, and outlook.

**Nutritionist. Pages 95-8 of *Health Careers Guidebook.*

Description of work, training, opportunities, and prospects.

See also Dietitian

OCCUPATIONAL THERAPIST 079.128

Before you enter an occupational therapy course. American Occupational Therapy Association. 1968. 1p. 25 copies for 75c. Single copy free

A check list of admission requirements for the high school student, beginning college student, and the college graduate.

Careers in the U.S. Public Health Service: occupational therapist. U.S. Public Health Service, U.S. Department of Health, Education, and Welfare. Publication Number 1668. 1967. 20p. Free

Describes the assignment possibilities and the qualification requirements.

Colleges and universities offering courses in occupational therapy. American Occupational Therapy Association. 1969. 12p. 15c. Single copy free. 25 copies for $3

For each of the schools accredited by the Council on Medical Education and the American Occupational Therapy Association there is given the name and address of director, amount of tuition, type of course, entrance requirements, length of course, and month classes start.

OCCUPATIONAL THERAPIST—*Continued*

Colleges and universities offering approved courses in occupational therapy. Council on Medical Education of the American Medical Association. 1967. 2p. Free

Name and location of thirty-one schools.

**Employment outlook for occupational therapists and physical therapists. Bulletin No. 1650–14. Bureau of Labor Statistics, U.S. Department of Labor. Supt. of Documents. 1970. 8p. 10c

Reprint from the *Occupational Outlook Handbook.*

Finding out about occupational therapists. Science Research Associates. 1967. 4p. 45c

Junior occupational brief describing work and opportunities.

Man wanted in occupational therapy. American Occupational Therapy Association. 1968. 4p. 25 copies for 75c. Single copy free

Flyer for male recruitment.

Occupational therapist. California State Department of Employment. 1964. 4p. Single copy free

Occupational guide describing work, requirements, training, and outlook.

* Occupational therapist. Careers. 1968. 8p. 35c

Career brief describing duties, working conditions, salaries, personal qualifications, training requirements, list of accredited schools, outlook, opportunities for men, related jobs, measuring one's interest and ability, and suggested high school program.

Occupational therapist. Chronicle Guidance Publications. 1969. 4p. 35c

Occupational brief summarizing work performed, working conditions, earnings, personal qualifications, training requirements, opportunities, and employment outlook.

Occupational therapist. Guidance Centre. 1969. 4p. 35c postpaid

History and importance of growth of the profession, nature of work, qualifications, preparation, outlook, earnings, advantages, disadvantages, how to get started, and related occupations.

Occupational therapist. Michigan Employment Security Commission. 1963. 2p. Single copy free

Job brief summarizing occupational data for use in Michigan.

The occupational therapist. National Association for Mental Health. 1968. 4p. 10c

Describes duties of the occupational therapist in the mental health field, training, earnings, and future outlook. Selected references.

Occupational therapists. Science Research Associates. 1968. 4p. 45c

Occupational brief describing nature of work, personal qualifications, educational requirements, getting started, earnings, advantages, disadvantages, and future outlook.

**Occupational therapists. One section of *Occupational Outlook Handbook*.
Nature of work, where employed, training, other qualifications, advancement, employment outlook, earnings, and working conditions.

Occupational therapists in the Veterans Administration. VA pamphlet 10-58. Veterans Administration Forms Depot. 1968. 4p. Free
Description of work, training program, qualifications, and benefits.

* Occupational therapy. Pages 180-84 of *Health Careers Guidebook*.
Nature of work, types of therapy, personal qualifications, opportunities, and educational requirements. Also information is given about the homemaking counselor.

Occupational therapy assistant. Chronicle Guidance Publications. 1968. 4p. 35c
Occupational brief summarizing definition, work performed, working conditions, salary, personal qualifications, training requirements, and outlook.

**Occupational therapy handbook. American Occupational Therapy Association. 1968. 15p. 25c. 25 copies for $4.75
Facts about the number of occupational therapists, the projected need, education, salaries, and where to look for financial help.

Occupational therapy—publications and other materials. American Occupational Therapy Association. 1969. 19p. Free
A listing of professional literature and other materials available from the association. Prices are given for items for which there is a charge and they are subject to change without notice.

Opportunities in occupational therapy. Franciscus, Marie Louise and Abbott, Marguerite. Vocational Guidance Manuals. 1968. 128p. $1.95 paper; $3.75 library binding
Description of occupational therapy, tools of the profession, scope of the field, development and growth, requirements to enter the profession, job descriptions, personal expectations and limitations, present trends and future outlook, related fields, and professional organizations. Also included is a list of schools offering courses in occupational therapy.

**Where to look for financial help. American Occupational Therapy Association. 1969. 2p. 25 copies for $4.75. Single copy free
Lists sources of scholarships for professional education in occupational therapy, funds available for higher education, organizations with local chapters or member agencies awarding funds for general education, sources of loans, and a reference list of further sources of information.

**Your future in occupational therapy. Shuff, Frances. Richards Rosen Press. Revised 1969. 160p. $4; library edition $3.78
Description of the work, training, qualifications, and opportunities. Includes list of schools offering training.

See also Medical service worker; Physical therapist

OCEANOGRAPHER 024.081 and 041.081

**Agricultural, forestry, and oceanographic technicians: career opportunities for technicians and specialists. Sidney, Howard, editor. Ferguson Publishing Company. 1969. 344p. $8.95

Twenty-nine contributors describe career opportunities for technicians in animal science, plant science, ornamental horticulture, forest and conservation, oceanography, and off-farm employment.

Explorers of the deep; pioneers of oceanography. Cox, Donald W. Hammond Incorporated. 1968. 93p. $3.50. Library edition $3.39

Capsule information on eighteen oceanographers who have contributed in various ways to man's knowledge of the sea and its resources.

Exploring the ocean world; a history of oceanography. Idyll, C. P., ed. Crowell, Collier, and Macmillan, Inc. 1970. 280p. $14.95

A collection of articles dealing with marine geology, biology, physics, and chemistry and their application to the extraction of food and minerals from the sea. Both old and new methods of studying the ocean and developing its potential use are described.

Finding out about oceanographers. Science Research Associates. 1967. 4p. 45c

Junior occupational brief summarizing what the work requires and offers.

The new world of the oceans; men and oceanography. Behrman, Daniel. Little, Brown and Company. 1969. 436p. $10

The author takes the reader on a tour of the major oceanographic institutes and discusses the areas of research, the scientists currently working in the field, and the many diversified projects.

Ocean harvest: the future of oceanography. Vogel, Helen and Caruso, Mary. Alfred A. Knopf, Inc. 1961. 147p. $3.29

Focuses attention on the fact that only one per cent of mankind's food comes from the sea and that scientists are needed to take more interest in the potential food and minerals from the ocean.

Oceanographer. Careers. 1966. 2p. 20c

Career summary for desk-top file. Duties, qualifications, and outlook.

Oceanographer. Chronicle Guidance Publications. 1969. 4p. 35c

Occupational brief summarizing work performed, working conditions, qualifications, training, opportunities, where employed, and outlook.

Oceanographer. Guidance Centre. 1969. 4p. 35c postpaid

History and importance, nature of work, qualifications, working conditions, preparation, remuneration, advancement, outlook, related occupations, and how to get started.

**Oceanographers. Science Research Associates. 1968. 4p. 45c

Occupational brief describing nature of work, requirements, training, methods of entering, advantages, disadvantages, and future outlook.

**Oceanographers. One section of *Occupational Outlook Handbook.*

Nature of work, where employed, training, other qualifications, advancement, employment outlook, earnings, and working conditions.

Pioneer oceanographer. Alexander Agassiz. Williams, Beryl and Epstein, Samuel. Julian Messner. 1963. 192p. $3.50

Biography of the man whose work contributed to marine zoological information and techniques.

Riches of the sea—the new science of oceanology. Carlisle, Norman. Sterling Publishing Company. 1967. 136p. $3.95

An illustrated book describing the advances in this science.

Seawatchers—oceanographers in action. Bixby, William. David McKay Company. 1967. 224p. $4.25

An account of sea research and man's exploration of the sea.

Training and careers in marine science. International Oceanographic Foundation. 1969. 14p. Single copy free

Discussion of branches of marine science, career opportunities in different specialties, educational preparation, and remuneration. Includes list of colleges offering courses in marine science or marine science technology.

Undersea frontiers. Soule, Gardner. Rand McNally and Company. 1968. 253p. $6.95

Interviewing the men who develop and pilot the deep-diving submarines, the author forecasts their use in submarine rescues and in locating underwater mineral deposits.

University curricula in marine sciences. Committee on Marine Research, Education, and Facilities. 1969. 120p. Free to counselors

Description of courses offered in the marine sciences in several American colleges. Aimed to present information about existing training in the application of science to the study of the sea.

What does an oceanographer do? Waters, John Forrest. Dodd, Mead and Company. 1970. 64p. 3.50; library edition $3.23

Description of the four main areas of oceanography—chemical, physical, biological, and geological. Photographs and simple text feature equipment for pollution measurement, the study of sea life, and weather prediction. For grades 4 to 6.

World beneath the sea. Dugan, James. National Geographic Society 1967. 204p. $4.50

Beautifully illustrated in color, this is an account of the exploration of inner space and undersea research.

**Your career in oceanology. Boyd, Waldo T. Julian Messner. 1968. 221p. $3.95; library edition $3.64

This is a general survey of a wide variety of activities aimed at exploring and developing the oceans. Explains the U.S. Government and Navy programs and other industrial experiments. Includes lists of universities offering programs in oceanology, professional organizations interested, Government offices conducting activities, representative companies engaged in oceanics, and recommended reading.

OCEANOGRAPHER—*Continued*

**Your future in oceanography. Gaber, Norman H. Richards Rosen Press. 1967. 143p. $4; library edition $3.78

Covers qualifications, salaries, academic preparation, future potential, and interests required to find a place in this profession. Brief biographies are given. Includes list of colleges offering degree programs in oceanography.

What does an oceanographer do? Waters, John Forrest. Dodd, Mead and Company. 1970. 64p. $3.50; library edition $3.23

Work in the four main areas of oceanography—chemical, physical, biological, and geological—is the subject of this concisely written book featuring many photographs. Considerable space is devoted to the types of equipment developed to collect data for such scientific projects as pollution measurement, the study of sea life, and weather prediction. For grades 4 to 7.

See also Scientist

OFFICE-MACHINE OPERATOR 207.782

Calculating-machine operator. California State Department Employment. 1966. 4p. Single copy free

Occupational guide describing work, requirements, training, and outlook.

Duplicating machine operator. California State Department of Employment. 1964. 3p. Single copy free

Occupational guide describing work, requirements, training, and outlook.

Duplicating machine operators. Science Research Associates. 1969. 4p. 45c

Occupational brief describing work, training, qualifications, opportunities, and outlook.

Finding out about office machine operators. Science Research Associates. 1967. 4p. 45c

Junior occupational brief describing work and opportunities.

Mailing machine operator. Careers. 1966. 2p. 20c

Career summary for desk-top file. Duties, qualifications, and outlook.

Office-machine operator. Careers. 1970. 2p. 20c

Career summary for desk-top file. Duties, qualifications, and outlook.

* Office-machine operator. Chronicle Guidance Publications. 1967. 4p. 35c

Occupational brief summarizing work performed, working conditions, hours, earnings, personal qualifications, training requirements and opportunities, and employment outlook.

Office machine operator. Guidance Centre. 1966. 4p. 35c postpaid

History and importance, nature of work, qualifications, working conditions, preparation, remuneration, advancement, outlook, related occupations, and how to get started.

**Office machine operators. One section of *Occupational Outlook Handbook*.

Nature of work, where employed, training, other qualifications, advancement, employment outlook, earnings, and working conditions.

OFFICE-MACHINE SERVICEMAN 633.281

**Business machine servicemen. One section of *Occupational Outlook Handbook.*

Nature of work, where employed, qualifications, training, advantages, employment outlook, earnings, and working conditions. Brief information about the servicemen who repair the typewriter, adding machine, calculating machine, cash register, bookkeeping machine, dictating machine, duplicating machine, and data-processing equipment.

**Employment outlook for business machine servicemen. Bulletin No. 1650–83. Bureau of Labor Statistics, U.S. Department of Labor. Supt. of Documents. 1970. 12p. 15c

Reprint from the *Occupational Outlook Handbook.*

Finding out about office machine servicemen. Science Research Associates. 1967. 4p. 45c

Junior occupational brief summarizing requirements, training, earnings, and opportunities.

Job grading standards for office appliance repairer. Civil Service Commission. Supt. of Documents. 1970. 6p. 10c

This job classification outlines duties, skill, and knowledge requirements, responsibility, physical effort, and working conditions which determine job grade levels in accordance with the U.S. Civil Service Commission standards.

Office machine serviceman. California State Department of Employment. 1965. 4p. Single copy free

Occupational guide describing work, requirements, training, and outlook.

**Office machine serviceman. Careers. 1968. 8p. 35c

Career brief describing duties, working conditions, training, training opportunities, personal qualifications, earnings, advancement prospects, and outlook.

Office-machine serviceman. Chronicle Guidance Publications. 1967. 4p. 35c

Occupational brief summarizing work performed, working conditions, earnings, hours, personal qualifications, training requirements and opportunities, employment outlook, and entry into the job.

Office machine serviceman. Guidance Centre. 1968. 4p. 35c postpaid

History and importance, nature of work, preparation, employment, qualifications, advancement, remuneration, outlook, and how to get started.

* Office machine servicemen. Science Research Associates. 1967. 4p. 45c

Occupational brief describing duties, qualifications, training, earnings, getting started and advancing, advantages, disadvantages, and future outlook.

OFFICE MANAGER 169.168

Finding out about office managers. Science Research Associates. 1967. 4p. 45c

Junior occupational brief containing concise facts about the job.

OFFICE MANAGER—*Continued*

Manager, administrative (office) services. California State Department of Employment. 1968. 4p. Single copy free
Occupational guide describing work, requirements, training, and outlook.

Office manager. Careers. 1967. 8p. 35c
Career brief describing duties, personal qualifications, working conditions, training, earnings, advancement prospects, and outlook. Additional readings.

Office managers. Science Research Associates. 1969. 4p. 45c
Occupational brief describing work, qualifications, training, opportunities, and outlook.

OFFSET LITHOGRAPHER AND PRESSMAN 651.782

Finding out about offset lithographers. Science Research Associates. 1967. 4p. 45c
Junior occupational brief describing work and opportunities.

Offset lithographers. Science Research Associates. 1969. 4p. 45c
Occupational brief describing jobs, qualifications, earnings, things to consider and outlook. Selected references.

Offset pressman. Careers. 1968. 8p. 35c
Career brief describing duties, working conditions, training, earnings, advancement prospects, places of employment, and outlook.

OIL BURNER INSTALLATION AND SERVICE MAN 862.281

Oil burner mechanic. Job description in *Occupational Outlook Handbook*.
Brief statement of nature of the work.

Oil-burner serviceman. Guidance Centre. 1966. 4p. 35c postpaid
Nature of work, qualifications, definition, history and importance, preparation needed, employment, advancement, outlook, remuneration, advantages, disadvantages, and how to get started.

OPERATING ENGINEER (CONSTRUCTION) 850.782

**Employment outlook for operating engineers (construction). Bulletin No. 1650–76. Bureau of Labor Statistics, U.S. Department of Labor. Supt. of Documents. 1970. 12p. 15c
Reprint from the *Occupational Outlook Handbook*.

Operating engineer. California State Department of Employment. 1964. 4p. Single copy free
Occupational guide describing work, requirements, training, and outlook.

Operating engineer (heavy equipment operator). Chronicle Guidance Publications. 1969. 4p. 35c
Occupational brief summarizing work performed, earnings, and outlook.

**Operating engineers (construction machinery operators). Careers. 1970. 8p. 35c

Career brief describing duties, working conditions, training, personal qualifications, places of employment, earnings, and outlook. Additional readings.

**Operating engineers (construction machinery operators). One section of *Occupational Outlook Handbook.*

Nature of work, where employed, training, other qualifications, advancement, employment outlook, earnings, and working conditions.

See also Engineer

OPHTHALMOLOGIST 070.108

Ophthalmologist. Careers. 1968. 2p. 20c

Career summary for desk-top file. Duties, qualifications, and outlook.

* Ophthalmologists. Science Research Associates. 1970. 4p. 45c

Occupational brief describing nature of work, requirements, methods of entrance, related occupations, advantages, disadvantages, and future outlook.

OPTICIAN 713.381

**Dispensing opticians and optical mechanics. One section of *Occupational Outlook Handbook.*

Nature of work, where employed, training, other qualifications, advancement, and employment outlook.

**Employment outlook for dispensing opticians and optical mechanics. Bulletin No. 1650–93. Bureau of Labor Statistics, U.S. Department of Labor. Supt. of Documents. 1970. 8p. 10c

Reprint from the *Occupational Outlook Handbook.*

Finding out about optical mechanics. Science Research Associates. 1967. 4p. 45c

Junior occupational brief containing concise facts about the job.

Finding out about opticians. Science Research Associates. 1967. 4p. 45c

Junior occupational brief describing work and opportunities.

Optician. California State Department of Employment. 1965. 5p. Single copy free

Occupational guide describing work, requirements, training, and outlook.

* Optician. Careers. 1968. 8p. 35c

Career brief describing duties, working conditions, training, earnings, advancement opportunities and outlook.

Optician. Chronicle Guidance Publications. 1968. 4p. 35c

Occupational brief summarizing work performed, working conditions, personal qualifications, training, opportunities, and outlook.

Optician. Guidance Centre. 1968. 4p. 35c postpaid

Definition, history and importance, nature of work, preparation, qualifications, employment, advancement, outlook, remuneration, and how to get started.

OPTICIAN—*Continued*

Optician. Pages 231-3 of *Health Careers Guidebook.*
Nature of work, aptitudes, training, and outlook.

Opticianry: a world of infinite career opportunities. American Board of Opticianry. 1966. 16p. Free
Discussion of what the work of an ophthalmic dispenser is, training, opportunities, and methods of earning while learning.

* Opticians. Science Research Associates. 1970. 4p. 45c
Occupational brief describing nature of work, requirements, training, entrance and advancement, earnings, opportunities, related occupations, advantages, disadvantages, and future outlook.

Your career in optics. Optical Society of America. 1964. 24p. Single copy free
Illustrated booklet describing typical activities in optical physics, astronomy, and optical engineering.

**Your future as an optician. Hirschhorn, Hans. Richards Rosen Press. 1970. 159p. $4; library edition $3.78
This book contains brief historical data, detailed summary of an optician's work, and a thorough survey of qualifications. The author also describes licensing requirements, opportunities, training, apprentice programs, and the technical aspects of dispensing prescription lenses.

OPTOMETRIST 079.108

Careers in optometry. B'nai B'rith Vocational Service. 1968. 15p. 35c
Description of the work, educational preparation, specialties, opportunities, and rewards. Includes a list of the ten accredited schools for training.

**Employment outlook for optometrists. Bulletin No. 1650–10. Bureau of Labor Statistics, U.S. Department of Labor. Supt. of Documents. 1970. 8p. 10c
Reprint from the *Occupational Outlook Handbook.*

Finding out about optometrists. Science Research Associates. 1967. 4p. 45c
Junior occupational brief summarizing what the work requires and offers.

Fundamentals for the optometric assistant. Bates, Steven S. Chilton Book Company. 1970. 263p. $9.50
Details and business procedures included in the duties of the optometric assistant give an idea of the nature of the work.

**Monograph on optometry. American Optometric Association. 1968. 30p. Single copy free
Discussion of nature of work, qualifications, training, and place in society. Includes the requirements for admission to the schools and colleges of optometry.

* Opportunities in an optometry career. Kitchell, Frank M. Vocational Guidance Manuals. 1967. 93p. $1.95 paper; $3.75 library edition

Discussion of the history and importance of the work, qualifications, earnings, and outlook. The training required to be an optometrist, optician, or an optical engineer is given.

The optometric profession. Hirsch, Monroe and Wick, Ralph. Chilton Book Company. 1968. 359p. $8.50

Includes discussions of the history and development of this profession, prospects for the future, and the economic and social status of the optometrist.

Optometrist. Careers. 1968. 2p. 20c

Career summary for desk-top file. Duties, qualifications, and outlook.

Optometrist. Chronicle Guidance Publications. 1967. 4p. 35c

Occupational brief summarizing work performed, working conditions, earnings, personal qualifications, training requirements, opportunities, employment outlook, and a list of accredited schools.

Optometrist. Guidance Centre. 1968. 4p. 35c postpaid

Definition, history and importance, nature of work, qualifications, preparation, outlook, remuneration, advantages, disadvantages, how to get started, and related occupations.

Optometrist. Michigan Employment Security Commission. 1966. 2p. Single copy free

Job brief summarizing occupational data for use in Michigan.

Optometrist. Pages 233-5 of *Health Careers Guidebook.*

Nature of work, aptitudes, training, licensing, and how to get started.

Optometrists. Science Research Associates. 1968. 4p. 45c

Occupational brief describing nature of work, training, qualifications, opportunities, advantages, disadvantages, and future outlook.

** Optometrists. One section of *Occupational Outlook Handbook.*

Nature of work, where employed, training, other qualifications, advancement, employment outlook, earnings, and working conditions.

** Optometry—a career with vision. American Optometric Association. 1968. 32p. Single copy free

Illustrated booklet describes the need, services, and the cost of training. One table includes the number of optometrists and the ratio to the population in each of the states. Also presents a list of colleges of optometry with their basic entrance requirements.

Optometry seeks bright young men and women who are looking for a rewarding, exciting professional career. American Optometric Association. 1960. 6p. Free

A self-mailing folder with coupon to request further information. Brief discussion of opportunities and a list of schools for training.

A profession that counts for your son and daughter. American Optometric Association. No date. 6p. Free

A self-mailing folder describing qualifications and basic requirements.

OPTOMETRIST—*Continued*

Scholarships in optometry. American Optometric Association. 1968. 30p. Free

An annual listing of the scholarships and loan funds available from optometric colleges, state associations, and other allied organizations.

What is an optometrist? American Optometric Association. 1968. 8p. Free

Describes the educational background and service rendered by the optometrist.

Why not be an optometrist? Leaflet 42. Women's Bureau, U.S. Department of Labor. Supt. of Documents. 1968. 8p. 10c

Brief sketch of the nature of work, duties, advantages, training, and beginning income. Illustrated.

**Your future in optometry. Gregg, James R. Richards Rosen Press. Revised 1969. 160p. $4; library edition $3.78

Describes the functions of optometrists, preparation, specialized training, licensure, employment opportunities, qualifications for success, and future outlook. Includes a list of schools of optometry.

ORTHOPTIST 079.378

Orthoptist. Careers. 1970. 2p. 20c

Career summary for desk-top file giving duties, qualifications, and outlook. Explanation that an orthoptist usually functions as an assistant to an opthalmologist.

Orthoptist. Chronicle Guidance Publications. 1966. 4p. 35c

Occupational brief describing nature of the work, working conditions, personal qualifications, training requirements, outlook, methods of entry, and certification. Also included is a list of training centers.

Orthoptist. Page 235 of *Health Careers Guidebook*.

Brief statement of nature of work and training for the highly specialized job in the field of eye improvement, that of helping people overcome the handicap of crossed eyes.

A profession in orthoptics. American Orthoptic Council. No date. 6p. Free

Description of work, qualifications, prospects, earnings, training, and costs. List of centers offering training.

ORTHOTIST AND ORTHOPEDIC TECHNICIAN. *See* Prosthetist-orthotist

OSTEOPATHIC PHYSICIAN 071.108

Doctor of osteopathy. Pages 187-9 of *Health Careers Guidebook*.

Nature of work, training requirements, licensure, and outlook.

**Opportunities in osteopathic medicine. Mills, Lawrence W. Vocational Guidance Manuals. 1964. 112p. $1.95 paper; library edition $3.75

This contains many factual suggestions to the preosteopathic student concerning professional training and state licensure. One table gives the number of osteopathic certified specialists. Advantages and disadvantages are presented.

Osteopathic physician. Careers. 1969. 8p. 35c

Career brief describing duties, working conditions, training, personal qualifications, advantages, disadvantages, earnings, advancement prospects, and outlook.

Osteopathic physician. Chronicle Guidance Publications. 1968. 4p. 35c

Occupational brief summarizing work performed, working conditions, earnings, personal qualifications, training requirements, opportunities, and employment outlook.

Osteopathic physician. Guidance Centre. 1968. 4p. 35c postpaid

Nature of work, qualifications, preparation, outlook, remuneration, advantages, disadvantages, how to get started, and related occupations.

Osteopatic physician. Michigan Employment Security Commission. 1963. 2p. Single copy free

Job brief summarizing occupational data for use in Michigan.

**The osteopathic physician and surgeon. Belleau, Wilfrid. Park Publishing House. 1969. 27p. $1

Nature of work, training, qualifications, licensure, entering the field, conditions of work, a typical day's work, income, opportunities, advantages, disadvantages, and salaries. Geographical distribution and ratio of osteopathic physicians to population in each of the states. Discussion of opportunities for women. Bibliography.

Osteopathic physicians. Science Research Associates. 1966. 4p. 45c

Occupational brief describing nature of work, personal qualifications, training, licensing, earnings, how to get started, advantages, disadvantages, and future outlook.

**Osteopathic physicians. One section of *Occupational Outlook Handbook*.

Nature of work, where employed, training, other qualifications, employment outlook, earnings, and working conditions.

The osteopathic profession. American Osteopathic Association. No date. 8p. Free

Description of work, license requirements, and admission requirements to the five approved osteopathic colleges.

**The osteopathic profession and its colleges. Mills, Lawrence. American Osteopathic Association. 1963. 36p. Free

Growth of osteopathy, qualifications, preprofessional requirements, professional training, and distribution of osteopathic physicians in each of the states. Information concerning each of the five colleges approved by the American Osteopathic Association. Good bibliography.

PACKAGING ENGINEER 019.187

Finding out about packers and wrappers. Science Research Associates. 1967. 4p. 45c

Junior occupational brief describing work and opportunities.

**Package manufacturing workers. Science Research Associates. 1967. 4p. 45c

Occupational brief describing nature of work, requirements, wages, advantages, disadvantages, and future outlook.

* Packaging engineer. Careers. 1965. 2p. 20c

Career summary for desk-top file. Duties, qualifications, and outlook.

**The packaging field. One chapter in Volume I in the *Encyclopedia of Careers and Vocational Guidance*.

Growth of the industry, qualifications, employment opportunities, and rewards.

Preservation and packaging specialist. California State Department of Employment. 1965. 4p. Single copy free

Occupational guide describing work, requirements, training, and outlook.

PAINTER AND PAPERHANGER 841.781

Automobile painter. One section of *Occupational Outlook Handbook*.

Description of the work of painters who make old and damaged motor vehicles look like new. Includes training, employment outlook, earnings, and working conditions.

The coatings industry—creative challenges in management and science. Paint Industry Education Bureau. 1967. 18p. 50c

Describes the coatings industry in the areas of production engineering, laboratory work, and management. Stresses the growth potential and typical advancement opportunities.

Construction painter. Careers. 1969. 8p. 35c

Career brief describing duties, working conditions, training, personal qualifications, places of employment, earnings, and outlook.

Finding out about painters and paperhangers. Science Research Associates. 1967. 4p. 45c

Junior occupational brief summarizing what the work requires and offers.

Finding out about production painters. Science Research Associates. 1967. 4p. 45c

Junior occupational brief containing concise facts about the job.

Job grading standards for painter. Civil Service Commission. Supt. of Documents. 1970. 6p. 10c

This job classification outlines duties, skill and knowledge requirements, responsibility, physical effort, and working conditions which determine job grade levels in accordance with the U.S. Civil Service Commission standards.

Paint, varnish and lacquer industry. Chronicle Guidance Publications. 1968. 4p. 35c

Occupational brief summarizing nature of work, training requirements, personal qualifications, earnings, and outlook.

Paint, varnish, and lacquer industry workers. Science Research Associates. 1967. 4p. 45c

Occupational brief describing kinds of work, requirements, getting started, earnings, advantages, disadvantages, and future outlook.

Painter. California State Department of Employment. 1967. 3p. Single copy free

Occupational guide describing work, requirements, training, and outlook.

Painter. Guidance Centre. 1967. 4p. 35c postpaid

Nature of work, qualifications, preparation, earnings, advancement opportunities, how to get started, advantages, disadvantages, and related occupations.

Painter (construction). Chronicle Guidance Publications. 1966. 4p. 35c

Occupational brief summarizing work performed, training, qualifications, wages, opportunities, and outlook.

Painters and paperhangers. Science Research Associates. 1968. 4p. 45c

Occupational brief describing nature of work, training, requirements, earnings, getting started and advancing, advantages, disadvantages, and future outlook.

**Painters and paperhangers. One section of *Occupational Outlook Handbook.*

Nature of work, where employed, training, other qualifications, advancement, employment outlook, earnings, and working conditions.

Painters, decorators and paperhangers. Brotherhood of Painters, Decorators and Paperhangers of America. 1960. 4p. Free

Occupational brief describing nature of work, advantages of learning a trade, opportunities, qualifications, apprenticeship requirements, advancement, and employment outlook.

Paperhanger. Careers. 1968. 2p. 20c

Career summary for desk-top file. Duties, qualifications, and outlook.

Paperhanger (wall covering applicator). Chronicle Guidance Publications. 1967. 4p. 35c

Occupational brief summarizing work performed, working conditions, hours, earnings, personal qualifications, training requirements, opportunities, and employment outlook.

**Production painters. One section of *Occupational Outlook Handbook.*

Description of painting metal or wood products in factories, where employed, training, employment outlook, earnings, and working conditions.

Spray painter, production. Careers. 1967. 2p. 20c

Career summary for desk-top file. Duties, qualifications, and outlook.

PALEONTOLOGIST. ***See* Geologist**

PAPER INDUSTRY WORKER 53

After college, what? Pulp and Paper Foundation, Inc. 1968. 16p. Free

Attractively illustrated booklet sponsored by the Pulp and Paper Foundations at the University of Maine, Miami University, North Carolina State University, Syracuse University, University of Washington, and Western Michigan University.

Challenge and opportunity in the fibre box industry. Fibre Box Association. 1968. 16p. Free

Illustrated booklet pointing out the career opportunities.

**Employment outlook for the paper and allied products industries. Bulletin No. 1650–116. Bureau of Labor Statistics, U.S. Department of Labor. Supt. of Documents. 1970. 12p. 15c

Reprint from the *Occupational Outlook Handbook.*

Finding out about papermaking production workers. Science Research Associates. 1967. 4p. 45c

Junior occupational brief containing concise facts about the job.

How paper came to America. American Paper Institute. 2 by 3 feet. $10 per 100. Single copy free to teachers.

Wall chart illustrating the history of paper and how it is made.

How you can get a scholarship toward a college degree and a future. Syracuse Pulp and Paper Foundation. 1968. 8p. Free in limited quantities

Includes qualifications for the aid.

The new world of paper. Eberle, Irmengarde. Dodd, Mead and Company. 1969. 79p. $3.25; library edition $2.99

This book gives essential information on the successive stages in paper manufacture, stressing advances in logging and reforestation, and stressing the many uses of paper and the industry's continuing innovations in developing new forms of paper.

**Occupations in the paper and paper products industry. One section of *Occupational Outlook Handbook.*

Nature and location of the industry, kinds of jobs, training, other qualifications, and working conditions.

**Paper industry workers. Science Research Associates. 1969. 4p. 45c

Occupational brief describing kinds of work, requirements, getting started and advancing, earnings, advantages, disadvantages, and future outlook.

Paper products (manufacturing) occupations. Chronicle Guidance Publications. 1966. 4p. 35c

Occupational brief summarizing nature and location of industry, how paper is made, occupations in industry, training, earnings, working conditions, and outlook.

Prepare for career opportunities in pulp and paper. Chronicle Guidance Publications. 1968. 7p. 50c

Reprinted article from *American Paper Industry* discusses schools and specific degree programs in pulp and paper fields.

**Pulp and paper, a rewarding career. Syracuse Pulp and Paper Foundation. 1965. 10p. Free in limited quantities

Description of the industry, opportunities, training, and some available financial student aids.

Pulpwood production. Bromley, W. S. Interstate Printers and Publishers. 1969. 259p. $3.95

Affirms a challenging future for the pulpwood industry. Describes opportunities, general requirements, and fields of possible employment.

PAPERHANGER *See* Painter and paperhanger

PARACHUTIST 159.348

Bailout: the story of parachuting and skydiving. Dwiggins, Don. Crowell, Collier and Macmillan, Inc. 1969. 196p. $4.50

The author traces the development of parachuting. He highlights the personalities who made landmark steps, discusses rival claims to fame, and describes the techniques used in sport, military, and space exploration. Includes many human interest biographical sketches.

The complete book of sky sports. Emrich, Linn. Macmillan Company. 1970. 208p. $7.95; paper $2.95

The owner and operator of a flying school extols the pleasures in a practical guide to parachuting, soaring, flying gyrocopters, ballooning, and flying power planes. Detailed instructions for each sport include training and costs.

The space age sport: sky diving. Darby, Ray. Julian Messner. 1964. 192p. $3.95

Includes information about the parachutist.

What does a parachutist do? Hyde, Wayne. Dodd, Mead and Company. 1960. 64p. $3.25; library binding $2.99

An account of the thrills and dangers encountered, the vigorous training, the exciting first descent, and work done with the aid of parachutes. Illustrated. Written for grades 4 to 7.

PARK RANGER 169.168

Park ranger. California State Department of Employment. 1966. 5p. Single copy free

Occupational guide describing work, requirements, training, and outlook.

Park ranger. Chronicle Guidance Publications. 1966. 4p. 35c

Occupational brief summarizing work performed, working conditions, personal qualifications, training, opportunities, related jobs, and outlook.

PARK RANGER—*Continued*

Park rangers; the work, thrills and equipment of the National Park Rangers. Colby, Caroll Burleigh. Coward-McCann, Inc. 1955. 48p. $2.50. Library binding $2.97

Describes what life is like for a ranger in a national park where he must serve as guide, surveyor, policeman, fire fighter, and rescuer of wildlife. For younger readers, grades 4 to 8.

Sledge patrol. Howarth, David. Macmillan Company. 1957. 239p. $5.50

Story of the wartime assignment of seven hunters to patrol a stretch of coast and to protect Greenland's weather stations from German invasion. A true story of one of the Allied victories. Out of print but available in many libraries.

See also Forest ranger; Forester

PARKING-LOT ATTENDANT **915.878**

Automobile parking attendant. Careers. 1969. 2p. 20c

Career summary for desk-top file. Duties, qualifications, and outlook.

Finding out about parking attendants. Science Research Associates. 1967. 4p. 45c

Junior occupational brief describing work and opportunities.

Parking attendants. Science Research Associates. 1969. 4p. 45c

Occupational brief describing work, qualifications, opportunities, and outlook.

PAROLE OFFICER. ***See*** **Probation and parole worker**

PASTOR. ***See*** **Clergyman**

PATHOLOGIST **070.081**

Clinical pathologist. Careers. 1970. 2p. 20c

Career summary for desk-top file. Duties, qualifications, and outlook.

Pathologists. Science Research Associates. 1966. 4p. 45c

Occupational brief describing work, training, qualifications, opportunities, and outlook.

PATROLMAN **375.268**

Patrolman and policewoman. Chronicle Guidance Publications. 1969. 4p. 35c

Occupational brief summarizing work performed, employment conditions, training, opportunities, and employment outlook.

State highway patrolman. Chronicle Guidance Publications. 1969. 4p. 35c

Occupational brief summarizing work performed, working conditions, qualifications, training, entering this career, employment outlook, opportunities for advancement, and earnings.

State highway patrolman (trooper). Careers. 1968. 2p. 20c

Career summary for desk-top file. Duties, qualifications, and outlook.

State traffic officer (California highway patrolman). California State Department of Employment. 1966. 4p. Single copy free

Duties of the job, working conditions, wages, hours, entrance requirements, promotion, training, and employment outlook.

See also Armed Forces; Police officer

PATTERNMAKER 661.281

Finding out about patternmakers. Science Research Associates. 1967. 4p. 45c

Junior occupational brief containing concise facts about the job.

Metal patternmaker. Careers. 1968. 2p. 20c

Career summary for desk-top file. Duties, qualifications, and outlook.

**Patternmaker. Chronicle Guidance Publications. 1968. 4p. 35c

Occupational brief summarizing work performed, working conditions, where employed, requirements, training, methods of entry, and outlook.

Patternmaker. Guidance Centre. 1968. 4p. 35c postpaid

Definition, history and importance, nature of work, qualifications, preparation, advancement opportunities, advantages, disadvantages, how to get started, and related occupations.

Patternmaker (foundry). California State Department of Employment. 1968. 2p. Single copy free

Occupational guide summarizing duties, working conditions, employment prospects, earnings, training, requirements for entry, and suggestions for locating a job.

* Patternmakers. Science Research Associates. 1969. 4p. 45c

Occupational brief describing nature of work, training, qualifications, opportunities, and outlook.

PEACE CORPS VOLUNTEER 001. through 999.

Assignment: Latin America—a story of the Peace Corps. Wiley, Karia. David McKay Company. 1968. 256p. $4.50

Story of a girl talented in handicrafts who serves with the Peace Corps in Latin America helping a group of village weavers start a community project for making and marketing straw products.

**The complete Peace Corps guide. Hoopes, Roy. Dial Press, Inc. 1968. 211p. $4.95

This fourth edition contains an introduction by Jack H. Vaughn and R. Sargent Shriver and a revised chapter on the future plans.

PEACE CORPS VOLUNTEER–*Continued*

Opportunities in the Federal civil service for returning Peace Corps Volunteers. U.S. Civil Service Commission. 1969. 6p. Single copy free

Describes the special opportunities available to former Peace Corps volunteers for obtaining other Federal employment.

The Peace Corps experience. Potter, Clarkson N. Crown Publishers. 1968. 310p. $6.95

Text written by corpsmen describes all stages in initial training through field experience to completion of service. Over 350 photographs illustrate the many activities of the Peace Corps.

**Peace Corps factbook. Peace Corps. Revised frequently. Free

Illustrated booklet explaining application procedures, requirements, training, pay, and examples of services being rendered.

**Skill brochures. Peace Corps. Revised frequently. Free

Recruiting booklets explaining the nature of the work in which volunteers are engaged. Available for fields of health, teaching, agriculture, and community development.

U.S. Peace Corps: the challenge of good will. Whittlesey, Susan. Coward-McCann, Inc. 1963. 128p. $2.80

A book to challenge young people to find a career with the Peace Corps.

What does a Peace Corps volunteer do? Lavine, David and Mandelbaum, Ira. Dodd, Mead and Company. 1964. 64p. $3.25; library binding $2.99

Simple text and pictures portray various activities. Prepared for grades 3 to 7. Introduction by Sargent Shriver, former director of the Peace Corps.

PEDIATRICIAN. ***See*** **Physician**

PERFORMING ARTIST **150. through 152.**

**Employment outlook for the performing arts occupations. Bulletin No. 1650–39. Bureau of Labor Statistics, U.S. Department of Labor. Supt. of Documents. 1970. 16p. 15c

Reprint from the *Occupational Outlook Handbook.* Includes actors and actresses, dancers, musicians and music teachers, singers and singing teachers.

**Grants and aid to individuals in the arts. Washington International Arts Letter. 1970. 75p. $8.95 paper

Contains listings of professional awards and information about colleges and professional schools of the arts, including music and writing. Approximately 1,300 sources are listed, but only amounts over $1,000 are included. Marginal symbols indicate the arts involved.

Jobs in the performing arts. Science Research Associates. 1966. 32p. $1.15

Describes the variety of job prospects and opportunities for actor, dancer, singer, dramatic arts teacher, and instrumental musician.

**The performing arts. One chapter of *Occupational Outlook Handbook.*

Nature of work, where employed, training, employment outlook, earnings, and working conditions for each of the following: musicians and music teachers, singers and singing teachers, actors and actresses, and dancers.

See also Artist

PERSONAL SERVICE WORKER 301. and 306.

Checkroom, locker room, and rest room attendant. California State Department of Employment. 1967. 3p. Single copy free

Occupational guide describing work, requirements, training, and outlook.

Love's golden circle. Hager, Alice Rogers. Julian Messner. 1962. 192p. $3.50

Career fiction. Lisa becomes a "grandma sitter" for the elderly to earn money for college and decides to major in social service.

One golden summer. Noble, Iris. Julian Messner. 1959. 192p. $3.50

Career fiction. Story of a girl's first job away from home as a maid at a sophisticated summer camp.

Private household workers. One section of *Occupational Outlook Handbook.*

Nature of work, places of employment, training, other qualifications, employment outlook, earnings, and working conditions.

Summer resort jobs. Alumnae Advisory Center. 1969. 6p. 35c

Reprint from *Mademoiselle* giving examples of several kinds of summer jobs at summer resorts.

See also Barber; Cosmetologist; Domestic service worker

PERSONNEL AND EMPLOYMENT MANAGER 166.118

The business healers. Higdon, Hal. Random House. 1969. 320p. $6.95

A popularized work about management consultants and how they operate. Includes material about careers and fees in the field.

**Careers in personnel administration. Splaver, Sarah. Henry Z. Walck, Inc. 1962. 107p. $4.50

Description of the work; opportunities in industry, schools, and labor unions; preparation; responsibilities of various positions; personal qualities needed; and the satisfactions and disadvantages of the field.

**Careers in personnel and industrial relations. American Society for Personnel Administration. 1969. 4p. Free

Discussion of the duties and responsibilities of the personnel worker, educational and training requirements, salaries, and outlook for the future.

**Opportunities in personnel management. Mack, David. Vocational Guidance Manuals. 1969. 128p. $1.95 paper; library edition $3.75

Discussion of the nature of work, types of jobs available, educational preparation, qualifications, opportunities, rewards, and employment outlook.

PERSONNEL AND EMPLOYMENT MANAGER—*Continued*

Personnel administration occupations. Careers. 1970. 8p. 35c

Career brief describing duties, working conditions, training, personal requirements, earnings, advancement prospects, and outlook.

The personnel director's handbook. Scheer, Wilbert E. Dartnell Corporation. 1969. 960p. $21.50

Covers many aspects of personnel work, giving information about nature of work.

The personnel job in a changing world. Blood, Jerome W. American Management Association. 1964. 368p. $9

Forty authorities discuss present practices and view the future of personnel management.

Personnel manager. California State Department of Employment. 1967. 4p. Single copy free

Duties, working conditions, wages, entrance requirements, promotion, training, and employment outlook.

Time-and-motion study technician or engineer. Careers. 1967. 8p. 35c

Career brief describing duties, working conditions, training, personal qualifications, earnings, advancement prospects, and outlook.

Your career in public personnel administration. Public Personnel Association. 1963. 13p. Single copy free

Description of work, functions, training, opportunities, earnings, and advantages.

**Your future in personnel work. Pond, John. Richards Rosen Press. Revised 1969. 159p. $4; library edition $3.78; edition in large type $5.97

Various areas of personnel work are described with the qualifications necessary.

See also Counselor; Rehabilitation counselor

PERSONNEL WORKER 166.088 and 169.118

**Employment outlook for personnel workers. Bulletin No. 1650–4. Bureau of Labor Statistics, U.S. Department of Labor. Supt. of Documents. 1970. 8p. 10c

Reprint from the *Occupational Outlook Handbook.*

Finding out about personnel workers. Science Research Associates. 1967. 4p. 45c

Junior occupational brief describing work and opportunities.

Personnel supervisor. Chronicle Guidance Publications. 1968. 4p. 35c

Occupational brief summarizing duties, qualifications, training, salary, and outlook.

Personnel worker. Guidance Centre. 1968. 4p. 35c postpaid

Definition, history and importance, preparation, qualifications, employment, advancement, outlook, remuneration, advantages, disadvantages, and how to get started.

Personnel workers. Michigan Employment Security Commission. 1966. 2p. Single copy free

Job brief summarizing occupational data for use in Michigan.

Personnel workers. Science Research Associates. 1970. 4p. 45c

Occupational brief describing work in labor relations, in a personnel department, and in industrial personnel. Includes requirements, getting started, salaries, advantages, disadvantages, and future outlook.

**Personnel workers. One section of *Occupational Outlook Handbook.*

Nature of work, where employed, training, other qualifications, advancement, employment outlook, earnings, and working conditions.

Why not be a personnel specialist? Leaflet 48. Women's Bureau, U.S. Department of Labor. Supt. of Documents. 1968. 8p. 10c

Brief sketch of nature of work, duties, opportunities, qualifications, and earnings. Illustrated.

See also Counselor; Personnel and employment manager; Rehabilitation counselor

PEST CONTROL OPERATOR 389.884

Finding out about pest control operators. Science Research Associates. 1967. 4p. 45c

Junior occupational brief summarizing what the work requires and offers.

Pest control operators. Science Research Associates. 1965. 4p. 45c

Occupational brief describing work, training, qualifications, opportunities, and outlook.

Pest control serviceman. California State Department of Employment. 1965. 5p. Single copy free

Occupational guide describing work, requirements, training, and outlook.

PETROLEUM ENGINEER 010.081

**Careers in petroleum engineering. Society of Petroleum Engineers. 1968. 18p. Single copy free

Discussion of the work in exploration, drilling, production, transportation, refining, and marketing. Includes growth, trends, high school preparation, compensation, and benefits. Presents list of twenty-seven colleges offering degrees in petroleum engineering.

Finding out about petroleum engineers. Science Research Associates. 1967. 4p. 45c

Junior occupational brief containing concise facts about the job.

Going places in oil. American Petroleum Institute. 1968. 23p. Free

Cites examples of career opportunities in the oil industry for young people.

Petroleum engineer. Careers. 1966. 2p. 20c

Career summary for desk-top file. Duties, qualifications, and outlook.

PETROLEUM ENGINEER—*Continued*

Petroleum engineer. Chronicle Guidance Publications. 1968. 4p. 35c
Occupational brief summarizing work performed, working conditions, qualifications, training, earnings, and outlook.

Petroleum engineering. Colorado School of Mines. No date. 6p. Free
Description of the work, prospects, training, and requirements for admission for study.

Petroleum engineering schools in the United States. Society of Petroleum Engineers. 1967. 56p. $3
A directory of schools for training petroleum engineers.

**Petroleum engineers. Science Research Associates. 1969. 4p. 45c
Occupational brief describing nature of work, requirements, training, methods of getting started, earnings, advantages, disadvantages, and future outlook.

PETROLEUM PRODUCTION INDUSTRY WORKER 54

**Employment outlook for petroleum and natural gas production and processing. Bulletin No. 1650–107. Bureau of Statistics, U.S. Department of Labor. Supt. of Documents. 1970. 12p. 15c
Reprint from the *Occupational Outlook Handbook*. Also includes petroleum refining.

Flowing gold; the romance of oil. Floherty, John J. Lippincott Company. 1957. 224p. $3.95
Description of the oil industry with dramatic glimpses behind the scenes. Includes history, exploration, refineries, laboratories where new products are developed, and distribution by pipe lines and tank ships. Illustrated.

Gas production and distribution occupations. Chronicle Guidance Publications. 1969. 4p. 35c
Occupational brief summarizing work performed, working conditions, training, earnings, opportunities, and outlook.

**A job with a future in the petroleum industry. Drotning, Philip T. and Mayes, James. Grosset and Dunlap, Inc. 1969. 128p. $3.59
An overview of the jobs in the petroleum industry, including exploration, production, refining, marketing, research, administration, and service management. Contains useful lists of companies presently hiring young people and offering programs to earn while learning.

* Men, money, and oil: the story of an industry. Fanning, Leonard. World Publishing Company. 1966. 192p. $4.50
One of the few accounts on the high school level covering the history of the petroleum industry. For grades 7 to 10.

Oil driller. Guidance Centre. 1966. 4p. 35c postpaid
History and importance, nature of work, qualifications, working conditions, preparation, remuneration, advancement, outlook, related occupations, and how to get started.

Oilmen and what they do. Harrison, William. Franklin Watts, Inc. 1965. 160p. $3.95

This book describes possible careers in the oil industry, showing that searching for oil is a frustrating but fascinating business for both wildcatters and big industry. Includes sources of more information. For grades 7 to 11.

**Petroleum and natural gas production and refining occupations. One chapter of *Occupational Outlook Handbook*.

Nature and location of the industry, training, earnings, and employment outlook in petroleum production and in petroleum refining.

Petroleum exploration and production workers. Science Research Associates. 1970. 4p. 45c

Occupational brief describing nature of work, requirements, training, earnings, methods of getting started, advantages, disadvantages, and future outlook.

Petroleum products occupations (production occupations). Careers. 1966. 8p. 35c

Career brief describing duties, working conditions, training, earnings, and outlook. Additional readings.

* Petroleum refinery workers. Science Research Associates. 1967. 4p. 45c

Occupational brief describing duties, requirements, training, methods of getting started, earnings, advantages, disadvantages, and future outlook.

Petroleum-refining engineering. Colorado School of Mines. No date. 6p. Free

Description of the work, prospects, training, and requirements for admission for study.

Petroleum refining occupations. Careers. 1967. 8p. 35c

Career brief describing duties, working conditions, training, personal qualifications, earnings, and outlook.

Prospector. Guidance Centre. 1965. 4p. 35c postpaid

Nature of work, qualifications, preparation, working conditions, outlook, advantages, disadvantages, how to get started, and related occupations.

Your unlimited opportunities in the liquified petroleum gas industry. National LP-Gas Association. 1968. 8p. Free

Description of job opportunities and training at Southern Technical Institute.

PHARMACEUTICAL SALES REPRESENTATIVE 266.158

A medical representative with Burroughs Wellcome and Company. Burroughs Wellcome and Company. 1968. 4p. Free

Duties, qualifications, training, earnings, and advancement.

Pharmaceutical sales representative (pharmaceutical detail man-drug salesman). California State Department of California. 1968. 4p. Single copy free

Occupational guide describing work, requirements, training, and outlook.

PHARMACIST **074.081**

Accredited colleges of pharmacy. American Council on Pharmaceutical Education. 1969. 10p. Single copy free

List of accredited colleges of pharmacy in the United States. Revised annually.

Careers in the U.S. Public Health Service: pharmacist. Public Health Service, U.S. Department of Health, Education, and Welfare. Publication Number 1648. 1967. 18p. Free

Describes the assignment possibilities and the qualification requirements.

**Employment outlook for pharmacists. Bulletin No. 1650–11. Bureau of Labor Statistics, U.S. Department of Labor. Supt. of Documents. 1970. 8p. 10c

Reprint from the *Occupational Outlook Handbook.*

Finding out about pharmacists. Science Research Associates. 1967. 4p. 45c

Junior occupational brief describing work and opportunities.

Health manpower source book—pharmacists. Public Health Service, U.S. Department of Health, Education, and Welfare. Publication Number 263. Supt. of Documents. 1963. 66p. 40c

Presents basic data on the numbers, location, and characteristics of pharmacists in the United States. The appendix contains statistics on undergraduate enrollments and graduates of the United States schools of pharmacy.

**Opportunities in pharmacy careers. Gable, Fred B. Vocational Guidance Manuals. Revised 1969. 144p. $3.75; paper $1.95

Includes educational requirements, cost of education, financial assistance available, duties, rewards, and the various areas of employment. Also contains a list of accredited schools of pharmacy.

Orientation to pharmacy. Burlage, Henry; Lee, Charles; and Rising, L. Wait. McGraw-Hill Book Company. 1959. 306p. $7.95

A guide for beginning pharmacy students, this book contains a discussion of the professional aspects, requirements, and opportunities of the pharmacist.

Pharmacist. California State Department of Employment. 1965. 5p. Single copy free

Occupational guide describing work, requirements, training, and outlook.

Pharmacist. Careers. 1968. 8p. 35c

Career brief describing duties, working conditions, earnings, personal qualifications, licensure, opportunities, and outlook. List of accredited colleges of pharmacy.

Pharmacist. Chronicle Guidance Publications. 1967. 4p. 35c

Occupational brief summarizing work performed, working conditions, hours, earnings, personal qualifications, training requirements, opportunities, employment outlook, and a list of accredited pharmacy schools.

Pharmacist. Guidance Centre. 1967. 4p. 35c postpaid

Definition, nature of work, qualifications, working conditions, remuneration, outlook, advantages, disadvantages, how to get started, and related occupations.

Pharmacist. Michigan Employment Security Commission. 1958. 2p. Single copy free

Job brief summarizing occupational data for use in Michigan.

* Pharmacists. Science Research Associates. 1969. 4p. 45c

Occupational brief describing nature of work, requirements, salaries, getting started, advantages, disadvantages, and future outlook.

**Pharmacists. One section of *Occupational Outlook Handbook.*

Nature of work, where employed, training, other qualifications, advancement, employment outlook, earnings, and working conditions.

Pharmacists in the Veterans Administration. VA pamphlet 10-62. Veterans Administration Forms Depot. 1968. 4p. Free

Description of work, training program, qualifications, and benefits.

**Pharmacy. Pages 189-195 of *Health Careers Guidebook.*

Personal qualifications, education, licensing and registration, opportunities, and prospects. Also a discussion of retail pharmacy and hospital pharmacy.

* Pharmacy—the profession of unlimited opportunity for young men and women. National Association of Chain Drug Stores. 1969. 6p. Single copy free. $4 per hundred copies

Brief statement of the outlook, opportunities, earnings, and qualifications for pharmacy, the bridge between scientific knowledge and health. Included is a list of colleges which offer training in pharmacy.

**See your future in pharmacy. American Pharmaceutical Association. 1968. 16p. Free

Nature of the work, personal qualifications, education, opportunities, and prospects. Included is a list of the accredited colleges of pharmacy.

**Shall I study pharmacy? American Pharmaceutical Association. 1968. 32p. 35c

Discussion of nature of work, earnings, conditions of work, advancement, specialized fields, training, and prospects. Includes list of seventy-four accredited colleges of pharmacy. Illustrated.

There is a future for you in pharmacy. National Association of Retail Druggists. 1968. 12p. Free

Illustrated booklet describing typical job opportunities for men and women. Also lists accredited colleges of pharmacy.

What is a pharmacist? Upjohn Company. 1966. 6p. Free

Illustrated brochure describing work, training, advantages, and opportunities.

What it's like to be a pharmacist. Changing Times. 1965. 3p. 15c

Reprint describing the work, pay, and opportunities.

PHARMACIST—*Continued*

Why not be a pharmacist? Leaflet 43. Women's Bureau, U.S. Department of Labor. Supt. of Documents. 1968. 8p. 10c

Brief sketch of nature of work, qualifications, opportunities, earnings, and advantages. Illustrated.

Your career opportunities in pharmacy. Charles Pfizer and Company. 1969. 27p. Free

Illustrated brochure describing qualifications, training, specialization, opportunities, licensure, and what to plan for in high school. Includes list of pharmaceutical schools.

**Your future in pharmacy. Kraemer, James. Richards Rosen Press. Revised 1969. 160p. $4; library edition $3.78

Stresses the various aspects of work in this field in addition to retail pharmacy, preparation, and opportunities. Includes list of schools offering training.

PHARMACOLOGIST 041.081

Pharmacologist. Careers. 1968. 4p. 20c

Career summary for desk-top file. Duties, qualifications, and outlook.

Pharmacologist. Chronicle Guidance Publications. 1969. 4p. 35c

Occupational brief summarizing work performed, qualifications, training, earnings, opportunities, and outlook.

Pharmacologists. Science Research Associates. 1966. 4p. 45c

Occupational brief describing nature of work, preparation, qualifications, opportunities, advantages, disadvantages, and future outlook.

This is the profession of pharmacology. American Society for Pharmacology and Experimental Therapeutics, Inc. 1970. 20p. Free

History and development of the work, future outlook, educational requirements, working conditions, and rewards. Also contains a brief discussion of areas of specialization.

PHOTOENGRAVER 971.381

Finding out about photoengravers. Science Research Associates. 1967. 4p. 45c

Junior occupational brief summarizing what the work requires and offers.

Photoengraver. Chronicle Guidance Publications. 1967. 4p. 35c

Occupational brief summarizing work performed, working conditions, qualifications, training, opportunities, outlook, and methods of entry.

Photoengraver. Guidance Centre. 1968. 4p. 35c postpaid

History and importance, nature of work, qualifications, working conditions, preparation, remuneration, advancement, outlook, related occupations, and how to get started.

Photoengraver (relief printing). Careers. 1970. 2p. 20c

Career summary for desk-top file. Duties, qualifications, and outlook.

Photoengravers. Science Research Associates. 1968. 4p. 45c
Occupational brief describing nature of work, preparation, qualifications, opportunities, advantages, disadvantages, and future outlook.

**Photoengravers. One section of *Occupational Outlook Handbook.*
Nature of work, where employed, training, other qualifications, employment outlook, earnings, and working conditions.

PHOTOGRAPHER 143.062

* Careers in photography. Rochester Institute of Technology. 1965. 28p. Free
This career bulletin gives information about the various branches of the vocation, duties performed by persons employed, advantages, disadvantages, and requirements for initial employment and for promotions.

Commercial and industrial photographers. Science Research Associates. 1968. 4p. 45c
Occupational brief describing nature of work, preparation, qualifications, opportunities, advantages, disadvantages, and future outlook.

Commercial photographer. Careers. 1968. 2p. 20c
Career summary for desk-top file. Duties, qualifications, and outlook.

Dark room technician. California State Department of Employment. 1965. 3p. Single copy free
Occupational guide describing work, requirements, training, and outlook.

Developer. Careers. 1968. 2p. 20c
Career summary for desk-top file. Duties, qualifications, and outlook.

**Employment outlook for photographers and photographic laboratory occupations. Bulletin No. 1650–40. Bureau of Labor Statistics, U.S. Department of Labor. Supt. of Documents. 1970. 12p. 15c
Reprint from the *Occupational Outlook Handbook.*

Famous photographers: excellence in professional photography as seen through the lives and works of five masters. Forsee, Aylesa. Macrae Smith Company. 1968. 224p. $4.95
Biographies of five contemporary photographers.

Finding out about commercial photographers. Science Research Associates. 1967. 4p. 45c
Junior occupational brief describing work and opportunities.

Finding out about news cameramen. Science Research Associates. 1967. 4p. 45c
Junior occupational brief describing work and opportunities.

Finding out about news photographers. Science Research Associates. 1967. 4p. 45c
Junior occupational brief containing concise facts about the job.

PHOTOGRAPHER–*Continued*

Finding out about photographic equipment manufacturing workers. Science Research Associates. 1967. 4p. 45c

Junior occupational brief containing concise facts about the job.

Finding out about photographic laboratory technicians. Science Research Associates. 1967. 4p. 45c

Junior occupational brief describing work and opportunities.

Finding out about portrait photographers. Science Research Associates. 1967. 4p. 45c

Junior occupational brief summarizing what the work requires and offers.

Katie and her camera. Hobart, Lois. Julian Messner. 1955. 192p. $3.50

Career fiction. A story that combines career interest in photography with light romance.

* Opportunities in photography careers. Johnson, Bervin M. Vocational Guidance Manuals. 1969. 144p. $1.95 paper; $3.75 library edition

Contents: The new photographer, photography grows up, learning photography, getting started, occupations in photography, organizations and honors, related fields, and places where career photography is taught.

Photographer. California State Department of Employment. 1964. 4p. Single copy free

Occupational guide describing work, requirements, training, and outlook.

Photographer. Careers. 1966. 8p. 35c

Career brief describing duties, working conditions, training, personal requirements, earnings, advancement opportunities, and outlook. Additional readings.

Photographer. Chronicle Guidance Publications. 1966. 4p. 35c

Occupational brief summarizing work performed, working conditions, earnings, determination of aptitudes and interests, opportunities, and outlook.

Photographer. Guidance Centre. 1968. 4p. 35c postpaid

Nature of work, qualifications, preparation, employment, advancement, working conditions, remuneration, and how to get started.

** Photographers. One section of *Occupational Outlook Handbook*.

Nature of work, where employed, training, other qualifications, advancement, employment outlook, earnings, and working conditions.

Photographic laboratory occupations. One section of *Occupational Outlook Handbook*.

Nature of work, places of employment, training, other qualifications, advancement, employment outlook, earnings, and working conditions.

Photographic manufacturing workers. Science Research Associates. 1966. 4p. 45c

Occupational brief describing nature of the work, requirements, getting started and advancing, earnings, advantages, disadvantages, and future outlook.

Photography as a career. Chronicle Guidance Publications. 1967. 4p. 35c
Reprinted article from *Professional Photographers of America, Inc.* discusses opportunities in various fields of photography, salaries, and preparation for a photographic career.

Photography as a career. Professional Photographers of America. 1959. 4p. Free
Description of the various kinds of photography, preparation, professional background needed, and list of schools offering instruction in photography.

Photography on the plant. Chronicle Guidance Publications. 1969. 6p. 35c
Reprinted article from *Better Living* discusses photography in industry.

Photolithographer. Chronicle Guidance Publications. 1966. 4p. 35c
Occupational brief summarizing work performed, working conditions, training, qualifications, earnings, advantages, disadvantages, where employed, and methods of entry.

Portrait photographer. Michigan Employment Security Commission. 1960. 2p. Single copy free
Job brief summarizing occupational data for use in Michigan.

Press photographers. Science Research Associates. 1969. 4p. 45c
Occupational brief describing work, training, qualifications, opportunities, and outlook.

Survey of photographic instruction. Eastman Kodak Company. 1968. 25p. Free
An analysis of the instruction in photography offered above the secondary school level. The responses were from teachers of photography in 2,200 schools.

What does a photographer do? Mergendahl, T. E. and Ramsdell, Sheldon. Dodd, Mead and Company. 1965. 64p. $3.25; library binding $2.99
Simple text and pictures portray activities in a variety of fields. Written for grades 3 to 7.

PHYSICAL EDUCATION TEACHER 153.228

Careers in physical education for girls. American Association for Health, Physical Education, and Recreation. 1964. 16p. 10c
Kinds of work, opportunities, employment outlook, and working conditions.

Directory of professional preparation institutions. American Association for Health, Physical Education, and Recreation. 1966. 16p. 50c
Includes names and locations.

Finding out about physical education teachers. Science Research Associates. 1967. 4p. 45c
Junior occupational brief summarizing what the work requires and offers.

Health education. American Association for Health, Physical Education, and Recreation. 1968. 8p. Single copy free
Discussion of the need for health educators, opportunities, and outlook.

PHYSICAL EDUCATION TEACHER—*Continued*

Health education. Pages 122-128 of *Health Careers Guidebook.*

Information about qualifications, training, and opportunities in public health education, school health education, and health information ond communications.

**Physical education and coaching—boys. American Association for Health, Physical Education, and Recreation. 1968. 6p. Single copy free

Kinds of opportunities, outlook, advantages, and training.

Physical education instructor. Chronicle Guidance Publications. 1966. 4p. 35c

Occupational brief describing work performed, working conditions, training requirements, promotional opportunities, employment outlook, and where employed.

* Physical education teacher. Careers. 1966. 8p. 35c

Career brief describing the importance of the work, duties, working conditions, training, personal requirements, earnings, advancement prospects, and outlook. Additional readings.

Physical education teachers. Science Research Associates. 1970. 4p. 45c

Occupational brief describing kinds of work, requirements, earnings, getting started, advantages, disadvantages, and future outlook. Two illustrations.

Physical educator. Guidance Centre. 1967. 4p. 35c postpaid

History and importance, nature of work, qualifications, working conditions, preparation, remuneration, advancement, outlook, related occupations, and how to get started.

Professional preparation in health education, physical education, and recreation education. American Association for Health, Physical Education, and Recreation. 1962. 176p. $2

Full discussion of recommended training.

See also Athlete; Athletic coach; Baseball player; Dancer

PHYSICAL SCIENTIST 021., 022., and 023.

Demand for engineers and engineering technicians. Engineers Joint Council. 1966. 96p. $4

A special section is included on employment data for physical scientists.

**Employment outlook for physical scientists. Bulletin No. 1650–26. Bureau of Labor Statistics, U.S. Department of Labor. Supt. of Documents. 1970. 12p. 15c

Reprint from the *Occupational Outlook Handbook.* Includes information about chemists, physicists, and astronomers.

**Physical sciences. One section of *Occupational Outlook Handbook.*

Summary of trends and outlook in natural sciences. Specific information is given for each of the major branches: chemistry, astronomy, and physics.

Physical sciences: earned degrees, by level, sex, and institution. One section of *Earned Degrees Conferred.*

Useful for judging the extent of a college's program in each of the following specialties: astronomy, chemistry, metallurgy, meteorology, physics, general physical science, geology, geophysics, and oceanography.

The physical sciences: report of the National Science Board submitted to the Congress, 1970. Government Printing Office. Supt. of Documents. 1970. 62p. 50c

Recounts the accomplishments of the physical sciences for the last two decades and discusses the challenges that lie ahead.

See also Scientist

PHYSICAL THERAPIST 079.378

Accredited schools of physical therapy. Council on Medical Education. 1967. 2p. Free

Name and location of forty-six schools.

Career facts. American Physical Therapy Association. 1967. 2p. 80c per 100. Single copy free

Brief statement of preparation, opportunities, rewards, and disadvantages.

Careers in the U.S. Public Health Service: physical therapist. Public Health Service, U.S. Department of Health, Education, and Welfare. Publication Number 1648. 1967. 20p. Free

Describes the assignment possibilities and the qualification requirements.

Educational and experience qualifications of physical therapists in public health agencies. American Public Health Association. 1966. 6p. Single copy free

General scope of the field, duties, types of positions, educational preparation, and qualifications for different types of positions.

Educational programs leading to professional qualification in physical therapy. American Physical Therapy Association. 1968. 2p. $2.15 per 100. Single copy free

List of forty-eight accredited programs arranged alphabetically by states.

Educational qualifications of physical therapists in public health agencies. Chronicle Guidance Publications. 1966. 4p. 35c

Reprinted article from *American Journal of Public Health* discusses general scope of the field, functions, education, specific knowledge, skills, and experience by positions in the field.

Finding out about physical therapists. Science Research Associates. 1967. 4p. 45c

Junior occupational brief containing concise facts about the job.

Laurie: physical therapist. Hobart, Lois. Julian Messner. 1957. 192p. $3.50

Career fiction. Laurie encounters daily challenges as she helps patients.

PHYSICAL THERAPIST—*Continued*

Janet Moore, physical therapist. Colver, Alice Ross. Dodd, Mead and Company. 1965. 205p. $3.25

Career fiction. Experiences of a physical therapist in a hospital, showing nature of work and satisfactions.

**Opportunities in physical therapy. Krumhansl, Bernice. Vocational Guidance Manuals. 1968. 124p. $1.95 paper; library edition $3.75

This panoramic view of physical therapy includes the nature of the work, educational and professional requirements, the rewards and the demands, advancement possibilities, outlook, and related fields. List of approved schools for training.

Physical therapist. California State Department of Employment. 1968. 3p. Single copy free

Occupational guide describing work, requirements, training, and outlook.

Physical therapist. Careers. 1970. 8p. 35c

Career brief describing duties, working conditions, training, personal qualifications, earnings, advancement prospects, and outlook.

Physical therapist. Chronicle Guidance Publications. 1966. 4p. 35c

Occupational brief summarizing work performed, working conditions, qualifications, training, opportunities, and outlook.

Physical therapist. Guidance Centre. 1967. 4p. 35c postpaid

Working conditions, preparation, opportunities for advancement, earnings, advantages, disadvantages, how to get started, and related occupations.

Physical therapist in the Veterans Administration. VA pamphlet 10-59. Veterans Administration Forms Depot. 1968. 4p. Free

Description of work, training program, qualifications, and benefits.

* Physical therapists. Science Research Associates. 1966. 4p. 45c

Occupational brief describing nature of work, requirements, college courses, getting started, salaries, working hours, advantages, disadvantages, and future outlook.

**Physical therapists. One section of *Occupational Outlook Handbook*.

Nature of work, where employed, training, other qualifications, employment outlook, and earnings.

Physical therapy. Pages 195-7 of *Health Careers Guidebook*.

Nature of work, qualifications, education, opportunities, and salary.

**Physical therapy—the career for you. American Physical Therapy Association. 1969. 8p. Single copy free

Illustrated folder describing nature of work, qualifications, preparation, training, and opportunities.

Sources of financial assistance for physical therapy students. American Physical Therapy Association. 1968. 8p. 2.90 per 100. Single copy free

A representative sampling of scholarships and loans.

* Your career in physical therapy. Darby, Patricia and Darby, Ray. Julian Messner. 1969. 192p. $3.95; library binding $3.64

Discusses educational requirements, necessary skills and abilities, and the personal satisfactions, challenges, and reward for those specializing in this field. Lists accredited schools for training.

PHYSICIAN 070.108

Careers in anatomy. American Association of Anatomists. 1963. 2p. $30 per 100. Single copy free

Information concerning nature of work, training, and opportunities.

Doctor Betty. Wells, Helen. Julian Messner. 1969. 192p. $3.50; library binding $3.34

Career fiction. Story of a dedicated young woman with a modern problem of combining marriage with a career. Depicts medical training in both classroom and hospital, as well as an intern and resident physician.

Doctor: his education and training. Engeman, Jack. Lothrop, Lee and Shepard Company. 1964. 152p. $4.95

More than 250 photographs and informative text present the day-to-day life of a medical student from the start of his studies until he is a practicing physician. For grades 7 to 11.

Doctor of medicine. California State Department of Employment. 1966. 6p. Single copy free

Occupational guide describing work, requirements, training, and outlook.

The doctor who dared: William Osler. Nobel, Iris. Julian Messner. 1959. 192p. Library binding $3.34

An inspirational biography with insight into the medical profession.

The Doctors Mayo. Clapesattle, Helen. University of Minnesota Press. 1941. Second edition, condensed. 426p. $8.50; $2.25 paper.

Biography of the Mayo brothers and the Mayo Clinic. Illustrated.

The Doctors Warren of Boston: first family of surgery. Houghton Mifflin Company. 1968. 369p. $7.95

Biography of the doctors who were instrumental in founding the Harvard Medical School and Massachusetts General Hospital.

**Employment outlook for physicians and osteopathic physicians. Bulletin No. 1650–6. Bureau of Labor Statistics, U.S. Department of Labor. Supt. of Documents. 1970. 8p. 10c

Reprint from the *Occupational Outlook Handbook*.

Famous men of medicine. Chandler, Caroline. Dodd, Mead and Company. 1950. 140p. $3.50

Biographies of men and women whose works represent the milestones in medical progress from antiquity until the present time.

Finding out about physicians. Science Research Associates. 1967. 4p. 45c

Junior occupational brief describing work and opportunities.

PHYSICIAN—*Continued*

The first woman doctor. Baker, Rachel. Scholastic Book Services. 1961. 192p. 50c paper

Paperback edition of biography of Elizabeth Blackwell. This title is available to schools, only, through the Scholastic Book Services.

The great doctors. Silverberg, Robert. Scholastic Book Services. 1966. 288p. 50c paper

Biographies of men who risked their lives and fortunes to improve medicine. This title is available to schools, only, through the Scholastic Book Services.

Health manpower source book—medical specialists. Public Health Service, U.S. Department of Health, Education, and Welfare. Publication Number 263, Section 14. Supt. of Documents. 1962. 234p. $1.25

This source book presents basic data on the numbers, distribution, and characteristics of physicians engaged in medical specialties. Information on physicians by type of practice and by type of specialty is shown for selected years, 1931-1962. For each of twenty-six specialties there are given findings on certification, age, sex, state location, and medical school from which graduated.

Health manpower source book—physician's age, type of practice, and location. Public Health Service, U.S. Department of Health, Education, and Welfare. Supt. of Documents. 1960. 199p. 55c

Basic data on age and type of practice of physicians according to their location by region, state, and county. The numbers and location of osteopathic physicians, dentists, and veterinarians are included. Provides background information for persons concerned with the provision of health services.

**Horizons unlimited. American Medical Association. Revised annually. 134p. Free to counselors and librarians

The first half of the paperback provides insight into career pursuits in medicine; the second half in allied fields. Good reading lists.

How medical students finance their education. Public Health Service, U.S. Department of Health, Education, and Welfare. Publication Number 1336. Supt. of Documents. 1965. 110p. 45c

Results of a questionnaire survey of medical and osteopathic students, 1963-64.

Intern or internist? American Society of Internal Medicine. 1964. 6p. Free

Differentiates between hospital apprenticeship and the work of the specialist in internal medicine.

Jungle doctors. McGrady, Mike. Lippincott Company. 1962. 128p. $3.95

Short biographies of the heroic men and women who take medical help to people in distant lands. Illustrated.

**Listen to leaders in medicine. Love, Albert and Childers, J. S., eds. Tupper and Love, Inc. 1963. 340p. $4.75

Seventeen medical authorities tell their personal experiences and offer advice concerning the opportunities open to young doctors.

Mayo; the story of my family and my career. Mayo, Charles W. Doubleday and Company. 1968. 351p. $6.95

Autobiography of the late Dr. Mayo covers the history of his distinguished family, the growth of the Mayo Clinic, and his own life story.

The Mayos: pioneers in medicine. Regli, Adolph. Julian Messner. 1942. 256p. $3.95; library binding $3.64

Biography recommended for boys considering the medical field as a career.

Medical education loan guarantee program. American Medical Association. 1970. 6p. Free

Explanation of the loan program for medical students, interns, and residents.

**Medical professions. Pages 149-58 of *Health Careers Guidebook*.

Qualifications, training, licensing, advantages, and disadvantages of a career as a physician. Also included is a list of twenty recognized fields of medical specialization.

**Medical school admission requirements: U.S.A. and Canada. Association of American Medical Colleges. 1969-70. 320p. $4

Focusing on the medical school admission process, this handbook contains two-page descriptive entries for every medical school in the United States and Canada. School entries detail entrance requirements, selection factors, financial aid programs, application-acceptance timetables, expenses, and applicant statistics for the 106 American and 16 Canadian medical schools. Supplementary data are presented on premedical planning, choosing a medical school, opportunities for degrees in the basic medical sciences, and career planning for high school students. Revised annually.

Medicine as a career for women. American Medical Women's Association. 1968. 16p. 50c

This pamphlet stresses what a medical career offers women, the qualities needed, and the educational preparation. It also contains discussion of financial planning and the combining of marriage with the career.

Medicine can be for you. American Medical Women's Association. 1968. 8p. Single copy free

Illustrated brochure describing the different fields of medical training, education requirements, and financial aid.

Medicine in action today and tomorrow. Hyde, Margaret. McGraw-Hill Book Company, Junior Book Division. Revised 1964. 144p. $4.25

Presents opportunities in 150 areas of medicine or allied fields and cites the need for more workers. Charts furnish information concerning educational requirements and length of training needed for the various careers.

PHYSICIAN—*Continued*

New opportunities for Negroes in medicine. National Medical Fellowships. 1969. 36p. Free

An illustrated brochure.

**The opportunities and rewards of medicine can be yours. American Medical Association. 1965. 8p. Free

This booklet answers many of the questions which students ask when exploring the challenges, demands, and opportunities of a career in medicine. Includes suggested high school preparation, desirable qualities, and basic costs of medical study.

Pediatricians. Science Research Associates. 1966. 4p. 45c

Occupational brief describing work, training, qualifications, opportunities, and outlook.

* Physician. Careers. 1969. 8p. 35c

Career brief describing duties, working conditions, training, personal qualifications, earnings, outlook, and ways of measuring one's interest and ability.

Physician. Guidance Centre. 1966. 4p. 35c postpaid

History and growth of the profession, working conditions, qualifications, preparation, remuneration, advantages, disadvantages, how to get started, and related occupations.

Physician (general practitioner). Chronicle Guidance Publications. 1969. 4p. 35c

Occupational brief summarizing work performed, working conditions, earnings, personal qualifications, training requirements, opportunities, and employment outlook.

**Physician: healer and scientist. Atchley, Dana W. Macmillan Company. 1961. 129p. $3.50

Discussion of the varieties of specialization, premedical education, medical school training, internship, residency, recompense, and responsibilities of the physician. Lists of medical colleges included.

Physicians. Michigan Employment Security Commission. 1958. 2p. Single copy free

Job brief summarizing occupational data for use in Michigan.

Physicians. Science Research Associates. 1969. 4p. 45c

Occupational brief describing nature of work, qualifications needed, training requirements, entering, earnings, advantages, disadvantages, and future outlook.

**Physicians. One section of *Occupational Outlook Handbook*.

Nature of work, where employed, training, other qualifications, employment outlook, earnings, and working conditions.

Physicians in the Department of Medicine and Surgery, Veterans Administration. VA pamphlet 10-35. Veterans Administration Forms Depot. 1968. 16p. Free

Description of opportunities, training program, qualifications, and benefits.

Physicians for a growing America. Public Health Service, U.S. Department of Health, Education, and Welfare. Publication Number 709. Supt. of Documents. 1959. 95p. 60c

Recommendations aimed to safeguard and improve the quality of medical education and to bring about the needed substantial increase in the number of physicians. Good statistical tables.

Pioneer in blood plasma: Dr. Charles R. Drew. Lichello, Robert. Julian Messner. 1968. 192p. $3.50; library binding $3.34

Biography of a Negro who overcame prejudice to win professional recognition through his research in blood plasma. Records his direction of a vast war-time medical effort in World War II which saved countless lives.

The Sherlock Holmes of medicine: Dr. Joseph Goldberger. Buchman, Dian Dincin. Julian Messner. 1969. 192p. $3.50; library binding $3.34

A doctor's triumph as a scientific detective came with his discovery of the cause and cure for pellagra. A biography showing the overcoming of many obstacles in one's career.

So you want to be a doctor. Changing Times. 1960. 4p. 15c

Reprint surveying prospects, opportunities, training, and preparation for a medical career.

Story behind great medical discoveries. Montgomery, Elizabeth R. Dodd, Mead and Company. 1945. 247p. $3.50

Biographies, of individuals who made medical discoveries such as penicillin, radium, insulin, vaccination, and sulfonamides. Illustrated.

The woman doctor; her career in modern medicine. Beshiri, Patricia H. Cowles Book Company. 1969. 240p. $5.95

Contains information on medical school admission requirements, financial aid available, areas of specialization, and opportunities for study and practice in foreign countries. Discussing women's tendency to leave the profession after marriage, the author stresses the types of positions women doctors can hold without neglecting their families.

The woman M.D. Alumnae Advisory Center. 1963. 6p. 35c

Reprint from *Mademoiselle* containing case histories of some successful women physicians.

The young medics. Woody, Regina J. Julian Messner. 1968. 187p. $3.50

Career fiction. One of the series of "career romances for young moderns" about a girl convinced that there is a place for women in medicine.

**Your career in medicine. Bleich, Alan Ralph. Julian Messner. 1964. 191p. $3.95; library binding $3.64

A physician explains the duties in such fields as surgery, psychiatry, general practice, radiology, and pediatrics. His appraisal of the time and cost of medical training compared with the possible income provides a realistic survey of the profession. A list of approved medical colleges is included.

PHYSICIAN—*Continued*

Your career opportunities in medicine. Charles Pfizer and Company. 1967. 32p. Free

Illustrated brochure describing qualifications, training, specialization, opportunities, licensure, and what to plan for in high school. Includes list of medical schools.

**Your future as a physician. Kalb, S. William. Richards Rosen Press. Revised 1969. 158p. $4; library edition $3.78

The book contains a discussion of desirable personal qualifications, required high school courses, cost of a medical education, training, internship, license eligibility, and future outlook. Includes a list of approved medical schools and a suggested reading list.

See also Chiropractor; Medical service worker; Ophthalmologist; Optometrist; Osteopathic physician; Pathologist; Podiatrist; Veterinarian

PHYSICIAN'S ASSISTANT. ***See*** **Medical assistant; Medical secretary**

PHYSICIST **023.081**

Atomic Energy Commission special fellowships in health physics. Oak Ridge Associated Universities. 1968. 19p. Free

Description of the work, training, programs of study at the graduate level, and qualifications for fellowships.

**Careers and opportunities in physics. Pollack, Philip. Dutton and Company. 1961. 1959p. $3.95

Some chapter headings are: Physics designs the modern world, Electronics, Atomic energy, Optical engineering, Aeronautical research, Power production, Meteorology, and Physics invades other fields. Includes lists of schools and qualifications for a career in physics.

**Careers in physics. Smith, Alpheus W. and Hole, Winston L. Long's College Book Company. Revised 1960. 310p. $5.95

Discussion of the nature and scope of physics, the opportunities it offers for service to mankind and for a satisfying way of life, and the variety of activities in which physicists may engage. Describes the fields of specialization in fundamental and applied physics as well as interdisciplinary fields of specialization. Includes list of research laboratories having major programs in physics. Selected references.

Enrico Fermi, physicist. Segre, Emilo. University of Chicago Press. 1970. 276p. $6.95

Advanced high school physics student will find this biography an interesting history of nuclear physics as well as a portrait of a scientist at work.

Finding out about physicists. Science Research Associates. 1967. 4p. 45c

Junior occupational brief describing work and opportunities.

Graduate programs in physics and astronomy. American Institute of Physics. 1968. 464p. $5

A handbook for advisers of prospective doctoral and master's degree students, this provides comparative information on programs in 284 institutions of higher education.

List of colleges and universities offering physics majors. American Institute of Physics. 1962. 4p. Free

List of 695 schools, arranged alphabetically by states, with symbols indicating those offering bachelor's, master's, and doctorate degrees.

Michael Faraday: from errand boy to master physicist. Sootin, Harry. Julian Messner. 1954. 192p. Library binding $3.34

Biography of the scientist whose experiments led to the development of the dynamo and the electric motor.

Physicist. California State Department of Employment. 1966. 6p. Single copy free

Occupational guide describing work, requirements, training, and outlook.

* Physicist. Careers. 1968. 8p. 35c

Career brief describing duties, major branches, working conditions, training requirements, personal qualifications, employment prospects, earnings, related careers, measuring one's interest and ability, and suggested high school program.

Physicist. Chronicle Guidance Publications. 1967. 4p. 35c

Occupational brief summarizing work performed, working conditions, qualifications, training, salaries, opportunities, outlook, methods of entry, and suggested activities.

Physicist. Guidance Centre. 1970. 4p. 35c postpaid

History and importance of the work, qualifications necessary for entry and success, preparation, outlook, remuneration, advantages, disadvantages, and related occupations.

Physicist. Michigan Employment Security Commission. 1963. 2p. Single copy free

Job brief summarizing occupational data for use in Michigan.

* Physicists. Science Research Associates. 1967. 4p. 45c

Occupational brief describing nature of work, requirements, earnings, where physicists work, advantages, disadvantages, and future outlook.

** Physicists. One section of *Occupational Outlook Handbook.*

Nature of work, where employed, training and other qualifications, employment outlook, earnings and working conditions.

** Physics as a career. American Institute of Physics. 1965. 24p. Free

Includes nature of work, training, and opportunities in industry, in teaching, and in the Federal Government. Explains opportunities in such newer specializations as nuclear physics, solid-state physics, and the electronics and communications areas of applied physics.

PHYSICIST—*Continued*

Rewarding careers for women in physics. American Institute of Physics. 1962. 20p. Free

Includes discussion of opportunities that are offered to women and the problems they face in becoming physicists. Descriptions of biophysics, astrophysics, and communications suggest areas of work. Includes a distribution of salary by type of employer and level of education.

Why should you study physics in high school? American Institute of Physics. 1962. 16p. Free

Case histories showing that physics is a help in many careers.

The world of cryogenics; the story of heatlessness. Boyd, Waldo T. Putnam's Sons. 1969. 191p. $3.64

A survey of scientific research into the effects and production of the ultracold. The author explains the physics of extremely low temperatures and some of the contributions cryogenics has made in biology, surgery, rocketry, electronics, physics, and metallurgy. For the reader with a background knowledge of physics.

**Your future in physics. Bell, Raymond. Richards Rosen Press. 1967. 138p. $4; library edition $3.78

Description of the varied opportunities, qualifications, and outlook.

See also Atomic energy industry worker; Scientist

PHYSICS TECHNICIAN **023.**

Finding out about physics technicians. Science Research Associates. 1967. 4p. 45c

Junior occupational brief summarizing what the work requires and offers.

Physicist technician. Careers. 1968. 2p. 20c

Career summary for desk-top file. Duties, qualifications, and outlook.

Physics technicians. Science Research Associates. 1967. 4p. 45c

Occupational brief describing nature of work, training, qualifications, opportunities, and outlook. Selected references.

PHYSIOLOGIST **041.081**

**Consider physiology. American Physiological Society. 1967. 14p. Free

An illustrated brochure describing nature of work, the specialization within the profession, places of employment, training, opportunities, rewards, and outlook.

PIANO TUNER **730.281**

Finding out about piano tuners. Science Research Associates. 1967. 4p. 45c

Junior occupational brief containing concise facts about the job.

Piano tuner. Chronicle Guidance Publications. 1967. 4p. 35c

Occupational brief summarizing where employed, work performed, earnings, personal requirements, and outlook.

Piano tuner. Michigan Employment Security Commission. 1960. 2p. Single copy free

Job brief summarizing occupational data for use in Michigan.

Piano tuner or technician. Guidance Centre. 1968. 4p. 35c postpaid

Nature of work, preparation, qualifications, employment, outlook, advancement, remuneration, and how to get started.

PICTURE FRAME MAKER 739.884

Picture frame maker. California State Department of Employment. 1964. 3p. Single copy free

Occupational guide describing work, requirements, training, and outlook.

PIPE FITTER. *See* Plumber and pipefitter

PLANT PATHOLOGIST 041.081

Careers in plant pathology. American *Phytopathological* Society. 1965. 16p. Free

Description of fields of work, preparation, getting started, and rewards.

Plant pathologist. California State Department of Employment. 1966. 5p. Single copy free

Occupational guide describing work, requirements, training, and outlook.

* Plant pathologist. Careers. 1969. 2p. 20c

Career summary for desk-top file. Duties, qualifications, and outlook.

** Plant physiology as a career. American Society of Plant Physiologists. 1969. 8p. $7 per hundred. Single copy free

Nature of work, places of employment, earnings, training, and outlook.

Plant scientist. California State Department of Employment. 1966. 6p. Single copy free

Description of several specialties in this field, entrance requirements, salaries, preparation, and employment outlook in California.

Plant scientists and what they do. Harlan, Jack. Franklin Watts, Inc. 1964. 186p. $3.95

An introduction to the many worlds of the plant scientist, such as breeding and improving plants, experimenting with crops and soils, and understanding the relationship between plants and their environments.

PLASTERER 842.781

Finding out about plasterers. Science Research Associates. 1967. 4p. 45c

Junior occupational brief containing some concise facts about the job and listing ways of finding out about the nature of the work. Includes suggestions for reading and a list of other occupational briefs on related topics.

PLASTERER—*Continued*

Job grading standards for plasterer. Civil Service Commission. Supt. of Documents. 1970. 3p. 10c

This job classification outlines duties, skill, and knowledge requirements, responsibility, physical effort, and working conditions which determine job grade levels in accordance with the U.S. Civil Service Commission standards.

Plasterer. California State Department of Employment. 1967. 3p. Single copy free

Occupational guide describing work, requirements, training, and outlook.

Plasterer. Careers. 1969. 2p. 20c

Career summary for desk-top file. Duties, qualifications, and outlook.

Plasterer. Chronicle Guidance Publications. 1969. 4p. 35c

Occupational brief summarizing work performed, working conditions, hours, earnings, personal qualifications, training requirements, opportunities, and employment outlook.

Plasterer. Guidance Centre. 1970. 4p. 35c postpaid

History and nature of work, conditions of work, preparation, qualifications, advancement, advantages, disadvantages, how to get started, and related occupations.

* Plasterers. Science Research Associates. 1968. 4p. 45c

Occupational brief describing nature of work, training, wages, getting started and advancing, advantages, disadvantages, and future outlook.

* Plasterers. One section of *Occupational Outlook Handbook.*

Nature of work, where employed, training, other qualifications, advancement, employment outlook, earnings, and working conditions.

* Plastering. National Plastering Industry's Joint Apprenticeship Trust Fund. 1969. 31p. Single copy free

Apprenticeship, work duties, salary, benefits, and advancement. Includes list of local plastering unions in the United States.

PLASTICS INDUSTRY WORKER 55

Engineering education in plastics. Society of Plastics Engineers. 1967. 12p. Free

Description of specialized training desirable for an engineering career in the plastics industry, including two introductory courses to supply broad coverage of the field and four more highly specialized courses.

** Opportunities in plastics. Dearle, Denis A. Vocational Guidance Manuals. 1963. 128p. $1.95 paper; $3.75 library edition

Includes a history of plastic materials, description of the plastics industry and jobs in its various branches, qualifications, outlook for jobs, the future of the industry, getting started, and wage rates and salaries. Contains lists of plastic material manufacturers, custom molders and extruders, and colleges offering plastics study.

Plastic products (manufacturing) workers. Chronicle Guidance Publications. 1966. 4p. 35c

Occupational brief summarizing plastics industry, occupations in field, training, earnings, working conditions, and outlook.

Plastics as an eningeering career. Society of Plastics Engineers. 1966. 8p. Free

History and development of the plastics industry, training, opportunities, and outlook.

* Plastics industry workers. Science Research Associates. 1967. 4p. 45c

Occupational brief describing kinds of work, requirements, training, getting started, earnings, advantages, disadvantages, and future outlook.

Plastics products manufacturing occupations. California State Department of Employment. 1964. 7p. Single copy free

Occupational guide describing work, requirements, training, and outlook.

The story of the plastics industry. Society of the Plastics Industry. 1969. 40p. Free

Includes a list of colleges offering instruction in plastics.

PLAYWRIGHT 131.088

* Playwright. Careers. 1968. 2p. 20c

Career summary for desk-top file. Duties, qualifications, and outlook.

* Playwrights. Science Research Associates. 1967. 4p. 45c

Occupational brief describing the work, training, getting started, rewards, and outlook. Selected references.

See also Writer

PLUMBER AND PIPEFITTER 862.381

**Aim for a job in the pipe trades. Daly, Donald F. Richards Rosen Press. 1969. 160p. $4; library edition $3.78

Discussion of the opportunities in the many industries that use the services of an expert in the pipe trades: plumber, pipefitter, steamfitter, automatic-sprinkler fitter, lead burner, coppersmith, welder, and refrigeration and air-conditioning fitter.

Employment outlook for plumbers and pipefitters. Bulletin No. 1650–77. Bureau of Labor Statistics, U.S. Department of Labor. Supt. of Documents. 1970. 12p. 15c

Reprint from the *Occupational Outlook Handbook.*

Finding out about pipefitters. Science Research Associates. 1967. 4p. 45c

Junior occupational brief containing some concise facts about the job and listing ways of finding out about the nature of the work.

Finding out about plumbers. Science Research Associates. 1967. 4p. 45c

Junior occupational brief containing concise facts about the job.

PLUMBER AND PIPEFITTER—*Continued*

Job grading standards for pipefitter. Civil Service Commission. Supt. of Documents. 1969. 3p. 10c

These job classifications outline duties, skill, and knowledge requirements, responsibility, physical effort, and working conditions which determine job grade levels in accordance with the U.S. Civil Service Commission standards.

Pipefitter and steamfitter. Chronicle Guidance Publications. 1969. 4p. 35c

Occupational brief describing nature of work, qualifications, working conditions, training, and outlook.

Plumber. Guidance Centre. 1966. 4p. 35c postpaid

Nature of work, qualifications, working conditions, outlook, earnings, advantages, disadvantages and related occupations.

Plumber and plumber apprentice. California State Department of Employment. 1965. 5p. Single copy free

Nature of apprenticeship, duties, working conditions, wages, hours, entrance requirements, promotion, training, and employment outlook in California.

Plumber (construction). Chronicle Guidance Publications. 1967. 4p. 35c

Occupational brief containing history, work performed, working conditions, personal requirements, training requirements, training opportunities, outlook, where employed, methods of entry, and suggested activities.

* Plumbers and pipefitters. Science Research Associates. 1969. 4p. 45c

Occupational brief describing nature of work, requirements, training, earnings, advantages, disadvantages, and future outlook.

** Plumbers and pipefitters. One section of *Occupational Outlook Handbook.*

Nature of work, where employed, training, other qualifications, advancement, employment outlook, earnings, and working conditions.

Plumbers and pipefitters (construction). Careers. 1969. 8p. 35c

Career brief describing duties, working conditions, training, personal qualifications, earnings, unionization, and outlook. Additional readings.

Your future in plumbing, heating, and cooling. National Association of Plumbing-Heating-Cooling Contractors. 1966. 12p. 25c

Discussion of opportunities and employment outlook.

PODIATRIST 079.108

Employment outlook for podiatrists. Bulletin No. 1650–12. Bureau of Labor Statistics, U.S. Department of Labor. Supt. of Documents. 1970. 6p. 10c

Reprint from the *Occupational Outlook Handbook.*

Finding out about podiatrists. Science Research Associates. 1967. 4p. 45c

Junior occupational brief describing work and opportunities.

Podiatrist. California State Department of Employment. 1964. 6p. Single copy free

Nature of work, duties, working conditions, income, hours, entrance requirements, promotion, training, and employment outlook in California.

Podiatrist. Chronicle Guidance Publications. 1969. 4p. 35c

Occupational brief summarizing work performed, working conditions, personal qualifications, training requirements, opportunities, employment outlook, and suggested activities.

Podiatrist (chiropodist). Careers. 1968. 2p. 20c

Career summary for desk-top file. Describes duties, working conditions, qualifications, training, and outlook.

Podiatrist (chiropodist). Guidance Centre. 1969. 4p. 35c postpaid

History and importance, nature of work, qualifications, working conditions, preparation, remuneration, advancement, outlook, related occupations, and how to get started.

Podiatrists. Science Research Associates. 1967. 4p. 45c

Occupational brief describing nature of work, training, qualifications, opportunities, advantages, disadvantages, and future outlook. Two illustrations. Selected references.

**Podiatrists. One section of *Occupational Outlook Handbook.*

Nature of work, where employed, training, other qualifications, advancement, employment outlook, earnings, and working conditions.

**Podiatry (chiropody) as a career. Belleau, Wilfrid. Park Publishing House. 1969. 27p. $1

Nature of work, types of practice, training, qualifications, licensure, entering the field, conditions of work, a typical day's work, income, opportunities, and disadvantages. Discussion of opportunities for women. Geographical distribution and ratio of chiropodists to population by states and large cities. Bibliography.

**Students, consider a career in podiatry. American Podiatry Association. 1969. 6p. Single copy free

Points out the manpower needs in podiatry and describes the educational requirements, opportunities, and outlook. Lists the five accredited colleges for training.

What's a podiatrist? Chronicle Guidance Publications. 1967. 1p. 35c

Reprinted article from *Boot and Shoe Recorder* discusses what the modern podiatrist is and does, how and where he serves—and how his activities relate to shoes and shoe business.

POLICE OFFICER 375.268

Behind the silver shield. Floherty, John J. Lippincott Company. Revised 1957. 208p. $4.50

Description of work of police officer, detective, and patrolman. Includes qualifications, training, and advancement. Sixteen illustrations.

POLICE OFFICER–*Continued*

**Careers in the protective services. Chamberlin, Jo Hubbard. Henry Z. Walck, Inc. 1963. 100p. $4.50

Presenting a view of this growing career field, this book describes the range of work in the various services, the qualifications, and training required. The field includes police and detectives; fire fighters; guards, watchmen, and doorkeepers; the investigative agents of the Treasury, the Department of Justice, and other Government agencies; and county sheriffs, marshals, constables, and bailiffs.

Colleges offering training for policemen. International Association of Chiefs of Police. 1962. 5p. Free

List of eighty colleges with indications of departments offering training, degrees and majors in law enforcement, corrections, or criminalistics.

**Employment outlook for police officers and state police officers. Bulletin No. 1650–66. Bureau of Labor Statistics, U.S. Department of Labor. Supt. of Documents. 1970. 12p. 15c

Reprint from the *Occupational Outlook Handbook*.

Exploring your future in protective agencies. Sextant Systems, Inc. 1970. 96p. $8.95

One page is devoted to each of ninety-five jobs, summarizing duties, requirements for entering, promotional outlook, and pay and skill level. Accompanying the book is an organizational chart showing beginning jobs and those to which one may be promoted.

Finding out about policemen. Science Research Associates. 1967. 4p. 45c

Junior occupational brief summarizing what the work requires and offers.

Finding out about policewomen. Science Research Associates. 1967. 4p. 45c

Junior occupational brief containing concise facts about the job.

Law enforcement; an introduction to the police role in the community. Adams, Thomas Francis. Prentice-Hall, Inc. 1968. 256p. $6.95

Career information is included with a discussion of the history, organization, primary functions, and ethics of police work.

The mounties–the story of the Royal Canadian mounted police. McDonald, Jo. Sterling Publishing Company. 1966. 112p. $3.95

Well illustrated with both historic and modern pictures.

Peter Policeman. Pineo, Craig. Golden Press. 1968. 24p. 69c

A tall picture book, sixteen inches tall, prepared for nursery school and kindergarten children. Contains vivid color illustrations of the uniforms and equipment and some work-a-day activities, explained in simple captions.

Police. Science Research Associates. 1969. 4p. 45c

Occupational brief describing nature of work, training, qualifications, opportunities, advantages, disadvantages, and future outlook.

Police science programs of universities, colleges, junior colleges in the United States. Chronicle Guidance Publications. 1967. 12p. 50c

Reprinted article from *The Police Chief* listing police science programs by states.

**Police officers. One section of *Occupational Outlook Handbook*.

Nature of work, where employed, training, other qualifications, advancement, employment outlook, earnings, and working conditions.

* Policeman. Careers. 1969. 2p. 20c

Career summary for desk-top file. Duties, qualifications, and outlook.

The policeman; an inside look at his role in a modern society. Arm, Walter. Dutton and Company. 1969. 120p. $4.95

Of special interest to those considering a career in law enforcement.

Policeman and deputy sheriff. California State Department of Employment. 1968. 5p. Single copy free

Occupational guide describing work, requirements, training, and outlook.

Policeman (municipal). Guidance Centre. 1967. 4p. 35c postpaid

History and importance, nature of work, qualifications, working conditions, preparation, remuneration, advancement, outlook, related occupations, and how to get started.

Policeman-policewoman. International Association of Chiefs of Police. No date. 4p. Free

Statement of duties and responsibilities, employment conditions, requirements, education needed, personal attributes, and residency requirements.

Policeman (Provincial police). Guidance Centre. 1967. 4p. 35c postpaid

History and importance, nature of work, qualifications for entry and success, working conditions, preparation, earnings, advancement, outlook, related occupations, and how to get started.

Policeman (Royal Canadian Mounted Police). Guidance Centre. 1967. 4p. 35c postpaid

Nature of work, qualifications, preparation, opportunities for advancement, employment, outlook, how to get started, advantages, and disadvantages.

Policewoman. Science Research Associates. 1966. 4p. 45c

Occupational brief describing work, qualifications, training, earnings, advancement, and outlook. Selected references.

Policewoman; a young woman's initiation into the realities of justice. Uhnak, Dorothy. Simon and Schuster, Inc. 1964. 251p. $4.50

Includes typical episodes based on ten years of experience with the New York City Transit Police Department. Describes police work as a social service and pays respect to dedicated officers.

Policewoman (municipal). Guidance Centre. 1969. 4p. 35c postpaid

Definition, history and importance, preparation, qualifications, employment, advancement, outlook, remuneration, and how to get started.

POLICE OFFICER–*Continued*

Psychological assessment of patrolman qualifications in relation to field performance. Government Printing Office. Supt. of Documents. 1969. 246p. $2

Predictors for overall performance of patrolmen, an analysis of the working environment, and description of the psychological test batteries given to applicants.

Requirements for a police career. Chronicle Guidance Publications. 1968. 4p. 35c

Reprinted article from *International Association of Chiefs of Police, Inc.* discusses personal and educational requirements, nature of work, duties and responsibilities, and working conditions.

Requirements for a police career. International Association of Chiefs of Police. No date. 2p. Free

A statement of the recruiting standards of age, physical condition, educational attainment, personal attributes, and residency requirements.

State police officers. One section of *Occupational Outlook Handbook.*

Nature of work, places of employment, training, qualifications, advancement, employment outlook, earnings, and working conditions.

State policeman: guardian of the highways. Chronicle Guidance Publications. 1967. 3p. 35c

Reprinted article from *Occupational Outlook Quarterly* discusses nature of work, where employed, qualifications, training, outlook, earnings, and working conditions.

Young scientist and the police department. Barr, George. McGraw-Hill Book Company. 1967. 160p. $3.75; library edition $3.26

In discussing the well-trained policeman, the author explains the role of modern science in detection, collecting evidence, and law enforcement. For grades 5 to 7.

**Your career in law enforcement. Liston, Robert A. Julian Messner. 1965. 190p. $3.95; library binding $3.64

Information about qualifications for many fields of law enforcement, including the work of the FBI, Treasury Department agents, and the police. Also contains information about training, salaries, and opportunities for advancement. Includes a list of college courses or degrees in law enforcement and police science. Illustrated.

**Your future in law enforcement. Gammage, Allen. Richards Rosen Press. Revised 1969. 159p. $4; library edition $3.78

Police work is described as not only an exciting career but one that challenges those who want to make tomorrow's world a better one.

See also Detective; FBI agent; Patrolman

POLITICAL SCIENTIST 051.088

Finding out about political scientists. Science Research Associates. 1967. 4p. 45c

Junior occupational brief describing work and opportunities.

**Political scientist. Careers. 1967. 8p. 35c

Career brief describing history, work performed, working conditions, salaries, personal qualifications, determination of aptitudes and interest, training requirements, promotional opportunities, outlook, and possibilities for women. Additional references.

Political scientist. Chronicle Guidance Publications. 1969. 4p. 35c

Occupational brief summarizing work performed, requirements, training, opportunities, where employed, and outlook.

Political scientists. Science Research Associates. 1965. 4p. 45c

Occupational brief describing work, training, qualifications, opportunities, and outlook.

**Political scientists. One section of *Occupational Outlook Handbook*.

Nature of work, where employed, training, other qualifications, and employment outlook.

Jobs in politics. Alumnae Advisory Center. 1964. 8p. 35c

Reprint from *Mademoiselle* containing case histories of several successful women in politics.

See also Politician

POLITICIAN 051.088

Battlefield president: Dwight D. Eisenhower. Archer, Jules. Julian Messner. 1967. 192p. $3.50; library binding $3.34

Biography from early boyhood through the White House years.

Boys' life of John F. Kennedy. Lee, Bruce. Sterling Publishing Company. 1964. 192p. $3.95

Teen-agers enjoy this reportorial account and the thirty-two pages of photographs.

Diary of democracy: the story of political parties in America. Neal, Harry Edward. Julian Messner. 1962. 192p. $3.95; library binding $3.64

Account of the rise and fall of political parties in terms of important persons, issues, and events in American political history. Has relevance for those interested in seeking political office.

Dwight D. Eisenhower; a guage of greatness. Morin, Relman. Simon and Schuster, Inc. 1969. 256p. $4.95

An informative biography which measures greatness by the possession of vision, integrity, understanding, courage, depth of character, and the ability to communicate. Illustrated.

Few are chosen: American women in political life today. Lamson, Peggy. Houghton Mifflin Company. 1968. 256p. $5.95

Biography of ten politically successful women, including Margaret Chase Smith, Esther Peterson, and Francis Bolton.

POLITICIAN—*Continued*

I know a mayor. Williams, Barbara. Putnam's Sons. 1967. 47p. $2.29

A simple factual account of city government as explained to young children when visiting city hall. For grades 1 to 3.

John F. Kennedy. Killy, Regina. Follett Publishing Company. 1969. 157p. $1.95; library edition $2.97

One of the Library of American Heroes series, this is a simply written biography of Kennedy, tracing his political career from his campaign for Congress in 1945 to his death. Sympathetic but objective in treatment, the account gives a well-balanced view of his ideas. For grades 5 to 8.

The many worlds of Herbert Hoover. Terzian, James P. Julian Messner. 1966. 192p. $3.50; library binding $3.34

Biography of a former president who rose through his own talents to preeminence as an engineer, humanitarian, and public servant. His experiences are rich in inspiration and the triumph over adversity.

Paths of diplomacy: America's secretaries of state. Heller, Deane and Heller, David. Lippincott Company. 1967. 192p. $3.95

A chapter on each of twenty Secretaries of State, up to and including Dean Rusk, provides personal anecdotes and a description of the increase of the Secretary's responsibilities.

* Political workers. Science Research Associates. 1970. 4p. 45c

Occupational brief describing nature of work, methods of getting started, requirements, advantages, disadvantages, and future outlook.

The second man: the changing role of the vice presidency. Dorman, Michael. Delacorte Press. 1968. 305p. $4.95

A narrative about the men and events that have molded the office and the problems connected with it. The book ranges through the term of Hubert Humphrey.

See how they run: the making of a congressman. Allyn, Paul and Greene, Joseph, pseuds. Chilton Book Company. 1964. 176p. $4.50

Dramatization of a candidate's campaign gives an idea of the work of a politician during an election.

The senator from Maine: Margaret Chase Smith. Thomas Y. Crowell Company. 1969. 136p. $3.95

One of the few biographies of a woman politician.

Spokesman for the free world: Adlai E. Stevenson. Levine, I. E. Julian Messner. 1967. 192p. $3.50; library binding $3.34

Biography showing how Stevenson exemplified fine traditions of public service.

What does a senator do? Lavine, David. Dodd, Mead and Company. 1967. 64p. $3; library edition $2.79

Description of the social and political aspects of a United States senator's career. Illustrated. For grades 4 to 6.

Winning your campaign: a nuts-and-bolts guide to political victory. Parkinson, Hank. Prentice-Hall, Inc. 1970. 207p. $6.95

Practical advice for candidates, including many specific examples, concerning topics such as opening moves, publicity, advertising, fund raising, and scheduling.

Women of the 90th Congress. Women's Bureau, U.S. Department of Labor. Supt. of Documents. 1967. 32p. 25c

Biographical sketches of the twelve women of the 90th Congress of the United States, of whom one is in the Senate and eleven are in the House of Representatives.

World citizen: Woodrow Wilson. Archer, Jules. Julian Messner. 1967. 192p. $3.50; library binding $3.34

Biography of the 28th president of the United States, showing a career blending achievement and frustration.

You and your senator. Harike, Vance. Coward, McCann and Geoghegan, Inc. 1970. 251p. $6.95

A United States senator describes his busy life and the importance of the Senate in American government. Includes some short biographies of prominent members of the 91st Congress. Some typical schedules show the scope and quantity of senatorial duties.

Young John Kennedy. Schoor, Gene. Harcourt, Brace and World. 1963. 253p. $3.95

Biography from boyhood to his election, including excerpts from letters and journals. Illustrated. Written for grades 6 to 10.

See also Political scientist

PORT DIRECTOR (HARBOR MANAGER) 375.168

Port director (harbor manager). California State Department of Employment. 1965. 3p. Single copy free

Occupational guide describing work, requirements, training, and outlook.

POSTAL CLERK 232.368

America's silent investigations. Denniston, Elinore. Dodd, Mead and Company. 1964. 160p. $3.75

The little-known story of the postal inspectors and their work in protecting the mails. The history of the service is included as well as the selection and training of candidates for postal inspector positions.

Behind the scenes at the post office. Lewis, Alfred. Dodd, Mead and Company. 1965. 64p. $3.25; library binding $2.99

Simple text and pictures portray various activities of the postal service. Written for grades 3 to 7.

POSTAL CLERK—*Continued*

**Employment outlook for post office occupations. Bulletin No. 1650–128. Bureau of Labor Statistics, U.S. Department of Labor. Supt. of Documents. 1970. 12p. 15c

Reprint from the *Occupational Outlook Handbook*. Includes mail carriers and postal clerks.

Finding out about mailing service workers. Science Research Associates. 1967. 4p. 45c

Junior occupational brief containing concise facts about the job.

Finding out about postal clerks. Science Research Associates. 1967. 4p. 45c

Junior occupational brief containing concise facts about the job.

Post office clerk. California State Department of Employment. 1966. 4p. Single copy free

Occupational guide describing work, requirements, training, and outlook.

Post-office clerks. Michigan Employment Security Commission. 1963. 2p. Single copy free

Job brief summarizing occupational data for use in Michigan.

**Post office occupations. One section of *Occupational Outlook Handbook*.

Occupations in the postal service, employment outlook, earnings, and working conditions. Specific information is given concerning mail carrier and postal clerk.

Postal clerk. Careers. 1968. 2p. 20c

Career summary for desk-top file. Duties, qualifications, and outlook.

Postal clerks. Science Research Associates. 1967. 4p. 45c

Occupational brief describing nature of work, training, qualifications, opportunities, advantages, disadvantages, and future outlook.

**Postal clerks. One section of *Occupational Outlook Handbook*.

Nature of work, qualifications, training, advancement, employment outlook, earnings, and working conditions.

Postal employees. Chronicle Guidance Publications. 1969. 8p. 50c

Occupational brief describing various jobs, hours, earnings, requirements, opportunities, advantages, disadvantages, and outlook.

Prepare yourself for the postal examination, mail handler, distribution clerk, mail carrier. U.S. Civil Service Commission. Supt. of Documents. 1969. 129p. $1.25

The booklet shows how to apply for the test and discusses the types of questions asked. Good study material.

A short history of the mail service. Scheele, Carl H. Smithsonian Institution Press. Supt. of Documents. 1970. 250p. $6.95

A review of the U.S. postal service from Colonial times to the present. Covers types of service, the variety of carriers, developments in postal processing, kinds of equipment, and acts of government.

POULTRYMAN 412.181

Find your career in the poultry industry. Interstate Printers and Publishers. No date. 47p. 25c

Discussion of personnel needed, preparation, opportunities, and nature of work in various branches of poultry husbandry.

Finding out about poultrymen. Science Research Associates. 1967. 4p. 45c

Junior occupational brief containing concise facts about the job.

Poultry farm hand. California State Department of Employment. 1965. 4p. Single copy free

Occupational guide describing work, requirements, training, and outlook.

Poultry farmer. Careers. 1970. 2p. 20c

Career summary for desk-top file. Duties, qualifications, and outlook.

Poultryman. Chronicle Guidance Publications. 1968. 4p. 35c

Occupational brief summarizing work performed, requirements, earnings, and outlook.

Poultryman. Guidance Centre. 1966. 4p. 35c postpaid

Working conditions, employment outlook, advancement, earnings, and how to get started.

* Poultrymen. Science Research Associates. 1968. 4p. 45c

Occupational brief describing nature of work, preparation, opportunities, advantages, disadvantages, and future outlook.

POWER TRUCK OPERATOR 892.883 and 922.883

Finding out about power truck drivers. Science Research Associates. 1967. 4p. 45c

Junior occupational brief summarizing what the work requires and offers.

Finding out about power truck operators. Science Research Associates. 1967. 4p. 45c

Junior occupational brief containing brief facts about the job.

Industrial truck operator. Careers. 1967. 2p. 20c

Career summary for desk-top file. Duties, qualifications, and outlook.

Power truck operators. Science Research Associates. 1970. 4p. 45c

Occupational brief describing work, qualifications, opportunities, and outlook.

**Power truck operators. One section of *Occupational Outlook Handbook*.

Nature of work, where employed, training, employment outlook, earnings, and working conditions.

PRACTICAL NURSE (LICENSED) 079.378

**Career opportunities as a licensed practical nurse. National Association for Practical Nurse Education and Service. 1968. 52p. Single copy free to counselors

Discussion of opportunities and training. Includes list of state-approved schools of practical nursing.

PRACTICAL NURSE (LICENSED)—*Continued*

Career opportunities as a licensed practical nurse. National Association for Practical Nurse Education and Service. No date. 2p. Free

Information on duties, qualifications, preparation, opportunities, and salaries. Foreword of longer publication described above.

Catholic institutions offering practical nursing programs. Conference of Catholic Schools of Nursing. 1968. 2p. Free

List of forty-eight schools located in Catholic institutions.

Directory of state-approved schools and programs of practical nursing. National Association for Practical Nurse Education and Service. 1969. 4p. Free

Frequently-revised list.

Finding out about licensed practical nurses. Science Research Associates. 1967. 4p. 45c

Junior occupational brief describing work and opportunities.

Guides for developing curricula for the education of practical nurses. Vocational and Technical Education Division, U.S. Office of Education. Supt. of Documents. 1959. 165p. 60c

Prepared for instructors and supervisors of training courses. Includes the role of the practical nurse, qualifications, and training.

Let's be practical about a nursing career. Committee on Careers, National League for Nursing. 1967. 40p. 25c

Describes how to become a licensed practical nurse. Lists all state-approved schools of practical nursing, together with prenursing academic requirements for licensure in each state and admission policies of individual schools on men, married students, and nonwhite students. Published annually.

Licensed practical nurse. Chronicle Guidance Publications. 1966. 4p. 35c

Occupational brief summarizing work performed, employment conditions, earnings, qualifications, determination of aptitudes and interest, training requirements, opportunities, outlook, and opportunities for men.

**Licensed practical nurse as a career. Belleau, Wilfrid. Park Publishing House. 1969. 16p. $1

Importance and nature of the work, qualifications, training, licensure, expenses, conditions of work, income, advancement, where employed, employment outlook, and how to begin.

LPN: The gentle people. Chronicle Guidance Publications. 1966. 4p. 35c

Reprinted article from *American Education* discusses licensed practical nurses and stresses the shortage of trained nurses.

* Licensed practical nurses. Science Research Associates. 1969. 4p. 45c

Occupational brief describing nature of work, requirements, training, getting started, salaries, advantages, disadvantages, and future outlook.

Licensed practical nurses. One section of *Occupational Handbook.*
Nature of work, where employed, training, other qualifications, employment outlook, and earnings.

Practical nurse. Careers. 1970. 8p. 35c
Career brief describing duties, working conditions, training, personal qualifications, places of employment, earnings, and advancement prospects.

Practical nurse. Michigan Employment Security Commission. 1960. 2p. Single copy free
Job brief summarizing occupational data for use in Michigan.

Practical nursing in the Veterans Administration. VA pamphlet 10-52. Veterans Administration Forms Depot. 1969. 12p. Free
Description of work, training program, qualifications, and benefits.

**Practically speaking for a nursing career. National Federation of Licensed Practical Nurses. 1968. 6p. Single copy free. 100 copies $5
Explanation of functions, educational requirements, licensing procedures, and average earnings.

Programs preparing for practical nursing. Committee on Careers, National League for Nursing. 1967. 38p. 15c
Description of programs, qualifications for admission, and academic requirements for licensure. Lists the state-approved schools.

Statement concerning the practical nurse in industry. American Association of Industrial Nurses. 1968. 1p. 10c
Description of the practical nurse's position, working under the supervision of a registered professional nurse.

PRESSMAN 651.782

Commercial pressman. California State Department of Employment. 1968. 3p. Single copy free
Occupational guide describing work, requirements, training, and outlook.

Cylinder press man. Chronicle Guidance Publications. 1969. 4p. 35c
Occupational brief summarizing definition, work performed, working conditions, hours, earnings, personal qualifications, training requirements, opportunities, and outlook.

Exploring your future in graphic arts and publishing. Sextant Systems, Inc. 1971. 96p. $8.95
One page is devoted to each of ninety-five jobs, presenting the duties, requirements for entering, promotional outlook, and the pay and skill level. An organizational chart for the industry also is available.

Finding out about printing pressmen. Science Research Associates. 1967. 4p. 45c
Junior occupational brief containing concise facts about the job.

Offset pressman. Chronicle Guidance Publications. 1967. 4p. 35c
Occupational brief containing definition, work performed, working conditions, training requirements, training opportunities, and outlook.

**Printing pressmen and assistants. One section of *Occupational Outlook Handbook.*

Nature of work, training, other qualifications, employment outlook, earnings, and working conditions.

PRIEST **120.108**

The Catholic priest: his training and ministry. Engeman, Jack. Lothrop, Lee and Shepard Company. 1961. 128p. $4.95

More than 250 photographs, with informative text and captions, describe the training for the priesthood and the way of life in a Catholic seminary.

Priest. Chronicle Guidance Publications. 1966. 4p. 35c

Occupational brief summarizing work performed, training required, where employed, qualifications, salaries, hours, and outlook.

**Roman Catholic priests. One section of *Occupational Outlook Handbook.*

Nature of work, where employed, training, other qualifications, advancement, employment outlook, earnings, and working conditions.

See also Clergyman; Religious vocations worker

PRINCIPAL, SCHOOL. ***See*** **School administrator**

PRINTING (GRAPHIC ARTS) INDUSTRY WORKER **650.**

The art and science of book publishing. Bailey, Herbert S. Harper and Row. 1970. 216p. $7.95

Several chapters survey the dominant characteristics of a publishing house and outline the functions of the various departments. Serves as an introduction to the procedures and management techniques of book publishing.

Bowker lectures on book publishing. R. R. Bowker Company. 1957. 389p. $5

Seventeen lectures on various phases of book publishing. One chapter by Edward Weeks traces his publishing career from first reader to editor-in-chief.

Careers in graphic communications. Graphic Arts Industry, Education Council. 1969. 16p. Single copy free

Discussion of the varied career opportunities in the publishing or graphic arts industry, asserting that this is one of the fastest growing industries.

* Careers in printing. Rochester Institute of Technology. 1965. 28p. Free

This illustrated bulletin gives information about various branches of the vocation, duties performed by persons employed, advantages, disadvantages, and requirements for initial employment and for promotions.

**Employment outlook for printing occupations. Bulletin No. 1650–101. Bureau of Labor Statistics, U.S. Department of Labor. Supt. of Documents. 1970. 20p. 20c

Reprint from the *Occupational Outlook Handbook.*

Exploring your future in graphic arts and publishing. Sextant Systems, Inc. 1971. 96p. $8.95

One page is devoted to each of ninety-five jobs, presenting the duties, requirements for entering, promotional outlook, and the pay and skill level. Includes an organizational chart showing beginning jobs and those to which one may be promoted.

In the next ten years—40,000 new jobs in printing. Printing Industries Technical Institute. 1969. 24p. Free

Opportunities and employment outlook.

Information communication occupations; a suggested curriculum guide. U.S. Office of Education. Supt. of Documents. 1970. 148p. $1.50

Suggested courses of study, tests, and teaching materials for conducting specialized training programs in this field of graphic communications.

Jobs in book publishing. Alumnae Advisory Center. 1965. 10p. 35c

Reprint from *Mademoiselle* describing typical jobs, how to begin, and case histories of several women who succeedd in the publishing business.

Jobs in publishing. Science Research Associates. 1966. 32p. $1.15

Describes the variety of job prospects and opportunities within this field.

Jobs in the printing trade. Careers. 1970. 8p. 35c

Career brief describing nature of work, working conditions, training, personal qualifications, earnings, and outlook.

Literary market place; the business directory of American book publishing. R. R. Bowker Company. 1970. 851p. $10

The thirtieth annual revision of this directory gives information about book publishers and provides lists of literary agents, book manufacturers, book wholesalers, and many services connected with communications industries.

**Lithographic (offset) occupations. One section of *Occupational Outlook Handbook*.

Nature of work, training and other qualifications, employment outlook, earnings, working conditions, and sources of additional information. Describes the main groups of lithographic workers: cameramen, artists and letterers, platemakers, strippers, and pressmen.

Printer. Guidance Centre. 1968. 4p. 35c postpaid

Nature of work, qualifications, working conditions, opportunities for advancement, wages, how to get started, advantages, and disadvantages.

Printing and publishing industry. Chronicle Guidance Publications. 1968. 4p. 35c

Occupational brief summarizing work performed, working conditions, training requirements, earnings, and outlook.

**Printing (graphic arts) occupations. One chapter of *Occupational Outlook Handbook*.

Discussion of nature and location of the industry, kinds of jobs, training, other qualifications, employment outlook, earnings, and working conditions. Specific information is given for each of the following: composing room occupations, photoengraver, electrotyper, printing pressman, lithographer, and bookbinder.

PRINTING (GRAPHIC ARTS) INDUSTRY WORKER—*Continued*

The printing industry. One chapter in Volume I of the *Encyclopedia of Careers and Vocational Guidance.*

Kinds of work, trends, and the future of the industry.

**So you want to get into book publishing—the jobs, the pay, and how to start. Melcher, Daniel. R. R. Bowker Company. Revised 1967. 16p. 25c

Advice about preparation, getting facts about book publishing, opportunities, job hunting, getting ahead on the job, and description of editorial and noneditorial work. List of books for further reading.

Technical schools, colleges, and universities offering courses in graphic communications. Graphic Arts Industry. 1968. 15p. Free

The directory, listing two hundred schools according to state, includes information on the types of programs offered by each school and the type of degree or certificate awarded by the institution.

Union wages and hours, printing industry. Bureau of Labor Statistics, U.S. Department of Labor. Supt. of Documents. 1970. 65p. 65c

Wage and benefit data for union members in sixty-eight cities. Shows wage and hour trends in the nation as a whole since 1907.

Your career in printing. Printing Industries of Metropolitan New York, Inc. 1957. 26p. $1

Illustrated booklet describing nature of work, qualifications, and opportunities in the printing industry. Excellent pictures of people at work and excellent typography.

**Your future in printing. Reinfeld, George, Jr. Richards Rosen Press. Revised 1969. 159p. $4; library edition $3.78

A descriptive view of various career opportunities in the printing industry.

See also Compositor

PROBATION AND PAROLE WORKER 195.108

Careers in the criminal justice system. National Council on Crime and Delinquency. 1969. 7p. Free

Employment opportunities, qualifications, preparation, and rewards are presented for police work, probation and parole work, and institutional counseling.

Correctional officer. California State Department of Employment. 1965. 4p. Single copy free

Occupational guide describing work, requirements, training, and outlook.

Finding out about criminologists. Science Research Associates. 1967. 4p. 45c

Junior occupational brief describing work and opportunities.

Finding out about probation officers. Science Research Associates. 1967. 4p. 45c

Junior occupational brief describing work and opportunities.

Parole (and probation) officer. Chronicle Guidance Publications. 1968. 4p. 35c

Occupational brief describing work performed, working conditions, remuneration, personal qualifications, training required, and employment outlook.

* Probation and parole workers. Science Research Associates. 1965. 4p. 45c

Occupational brief describing work, qualifications, how to get started, things to consider, and outlook. Selected references.

Probation officer. Careers. 1970. 2p. 20c

Career summary for desk-top file. Duties, qualifications, and outlook.

Probation officer. Guidance Centre. 1967. 4p. 35c postpaid

Definition, history and importance, nature of work, preparation, qualifications, employment, advancement, outlook, remuneration, and how to get started.

Probation officer and parole agent. California State Department of Employment. 1965. 8p. Single copy free

Duties, working conditions, wages, hours, entrance requirements, promotion, training, and employment outlook in California.

Training for juvenile probation officers. Children's Bureau, Social and Rehabilitation Service. Supt. of Documents. 1966. 78p. 30c

A report of a workship concerned with the necessity for providing adequate training for the people who work with delinquent youth. One section is a discussion of the role of the probation officer and another summarizes the knowledge, skills, and attitudes necessary for effective performance.

PROGRAMMER 020.188

Bright future careers with computers. Laskow, Robert and Feldzamen, A. N. Chilton Book Company. 1969. 250p. $5.50; paper $3.95

The authors discuss the promising careers existing in data processing, the training, salary ranges, the availability of financial assistance, and preparation for aptitude tests and job interviews.

Computer programmer. Guidance Centre. 1970. 4p. 35c postpaid

Definition, history and importance, nature of work, preparation, qualifications, employment, advancement, outlook, remuneration, and how to get started.

Computer programming—a new profession for you. Electronic Computer Programming Institute. 1961. 16p. Free

Explanation of the development of office automation, the nature of work of the programmers to utilize the electronic data processing equipment, requirements, and training.

PROGRAMMER—*Continued*

Data processing explained. King, Alice Gore. Alumnae Advisory Center. 1968. 21p. $1

This booklet explains how data processing works, where computers are used, what the jobs are, duties of each, qualifications, education, and training.

**Employment outlook for programers, systems analysts, electronic computer operating personnel. Bulletin No. 1650–41. Bureau of Labor Statistics, U.S. Department of Labor. Supt. of Documents. 1970. 12p. 15c

Reprint from the *Occupational Outlook Handbook.*

Finding out about part-time programmers. Science Research Associates. 1967. 4p. 45c

Junior occupational brief summarizing what the work requires and offers.

Finding out about programmers. Science Research Associates. 1967. 4p. 45c

Junior occupational brief containing concise facts about the job.

Jobs in computer programming. Alumnae Advisory Center. 1967. 4p. 35c

Reprint from *Mademoiselle* describing the work in general followed by the training and qualifications needed. Case histories are included of several young women who are working in this field.

Programmer. Careers. 1967. 8p. 35c

Occupational brief describing nature of work, qualifications, training, opportunities, and outlook.

Programmer. California State Department of Employment. 1965. 7p. Single copy free

Occupational guide describing work, requirements, training, and outlook.

Programmer. Chronicle Guidance Publications. 1969. 4p. 35c

Occupational brief summarizing work performed, personal qualifications, training, where employed, promotional opportunities, and outlook.

Programmers. Science Research Associates. 1968. 4p. 45c

Occupational brief describing nature of work, training, qualifications, opportunities, and outlook. Selected references.

**Programers. One section of *Occupational Outlook Handbook.*

Nature of work of preparing the step-by-step directions for the electronic computer, where employed, training, other qualifications, advancement, employment outlook, earnings, and working conditions.

**Your career in computer programming. Seligsohn, I. J. Julian Messner. 1967. 222p. $3.95; library binding $3.64

Considerable insight is given into this rapidly expanding profession. The author discusses the type of young person best suited for this work, the nature of the work, possibilities for future outlook, material rewards, and personal satisfactions. Enlivened by many case histories. Illustrated.

**Your future in computer programming. Davis, Sidney. Richards Rosen Press. 1969. 143p. $4; library edition $3.78

Discussion of the nature of work, requisites, training, and advancement opportunities. Describes the kinds of companies which need computer programmers.

See also Electronic computer operator

PROOFREADER 209.688

Finding out about proofreaders. Science Research Associates. 1967. 4p. 45c

Junior occupational brief containing concise facts about the job.

Proofreader. Careers. 1968. 2p. 20c

Career summary for desk-top file. Duties, qualifications, and outlook.

Proofreader. Guidance Centre. 1967. 4p. 35c postpaid

Nature of work, qualifications, preparation, working conditions, advancement, outlook, earnings, and related occupations.

Proofreaders. Science Research Associates. 1966. 4p. 45c

Occupational brief describing work, training, qualifications, opportunities, and outlook.

PROSTHETIST-ORTHOTIST 078.368

Orthopedic and prosthetic appliance making. Pages 184-5 of *Health Careers Guidebook.*

Personal qualifications, training, opportunities, and prospects for the prosthetist and orthotist.

Orthotist. Careers. 1967. 2p. 20c

Career summary for desk-top file. Duties, qualifications, and outlook.

Professional preparation in prosthetics and orthotics. New York Uiversity, School of Education. 1969. 6p. Free

Growing need, requirements, and training for the prosthetist in work with the design, fabrication, and fitting of artificial limbs, and for the orthotist in work with braces.

Prosthetist. California State Department of Employment. 1964. 6p. Single copy free

Occupational guide describing work, requirements, training, and outlook.

Prosthetist-orthotist (orthopedic appliance and limb technician). Careers. 1966. 2p. 20c

Career summary for desk-top file. Duties, qualifications, and outlook.

Traineeship assistance for undergraduate study in prosthetics and orthotics. New York University, School of Education. 1969. 6p. Free

Admission and eligibility requirements. Explains that the orthopedic and prosthetic appliance maker provides and fits artificial limbs, while the orthotist makes and fits orthopedic braces.

PROSTHETIST-ORTHOTIST—*Continued*

What everyone should know about orthotics and orthotists. American Orthotic and Prosthetic Association. 1964. 15p. Single copy free

Brochure explaining the duties, qualifications, preparation, training, opportunities, and prospects of orthotics.

What everyone should know about prosthetics and prosthetists. American Orthotic and Prosthetic Association. 1965. 15p. Single copy free

Brochure explaining the nature of the work, training, opportunities, and employment outlook.

PSYCHIATRIC SOCIAL WORKER 195.108

Finding out about psychiatric social workers. Science Research Associates. 1967. 4p. 45c

Junior occupational brief summarizing what the work requires and offers.

Health manpower source book—medical and psychiatric social workers. Public Health Service, U.S. Department of Health, Education, and Welfare. Publication Number 263, Section 12. Supt. of Documents. 1961. 71p. 40c

Data on the numbers, distribution, and characteristics of personnel. Includes information on training, age, sex, employment status, and income level.

Psychiatric social worker. Careers. 1970. 2p. 20c

Career summary for desk-top file. Duties, qualifications, and outlook.

Psychiatric social worker. Pages 209-11 of *Health Careers Guidebook*.

Nature of work, training, opportunities, personal qualifications, and salaries.

Psychiatric social workers. Science Research Associates. 1968. 4p. 45c

Occupational brief describing nature of work, qualifications, training, earnings, advantages, disadvantages, and future outlook.

Psychiatric technician trainee. California State Department of Employment. 1967. 4p. Single copy free

Occupational guide describing work, requirements, training, and outlook.

PSYCHIATRIST 070.108

**Careers in psychiatry. Macmillan Company. 1968. 192p. $4.95

Produced under the auspices of the National Commission on Mental Health Manpower, this presents the opportunities as members of a modern psychiatric team. Career information is summarized for the work of the psychiatrist, recreational therapist, rehabilitation counselor, clinical psychologist, psychiatric nurse, and psychiatric aide.

Careers in psychiatry in the U.S. Public Health Service. Public Health Service, U.S. Department of Health, Education, and Welfare. Publication Number 1199. Supt. of Documents. 1968. 25p. 25c

Describes the National Institute of Mental Health's career development program for psychiatrists.

Finding out about psychiatrists. Science Research Associates. 1967. 4p. 45c

Junior occupational brief containing concise facts about the job.

**Opportunities in a psychiatry career. Davidson, Henry A. Vocational Guidance Manuals. 1964. 144p. $1.95 paper; library edition $3.75

Written by a practicing psychiatrist, this contains a discussion of duties, training, internship, licensure, and how to enter private practice. The rewards and drawbacks are pointed out as well as the personal qualities needed.

Psychiatric aid. Chronicle Guidance Publications. 1969. 4p. 35c

Occupational brief summarizing work performed, working conditions, wages, personal qualifications, education, and outlook.

Psychiatrist. Careers. 1968. 2p. 20c

Career summary for desk-top file. Duties, qualifications, and outlook.

Psychiatrist. Chronicle Guidance Publications. 1969. 4p. 35c

Occupational brief summarizing work performed, types of practice, educational requirements, personal qualifications, earnings, and outlook.

Psychiatrist. Guidance Centre. 1967. 4p. 35c postpaid

Definition, history and importance of the work, preparation, qualifications, employment outlook, advancement, remuneration, advantages, disadvantages, related occupations, and how to get started.

* The psychiatrist. National Association for Mental Health. 1967. 4p. 10c

What the psychiatrist does, professional training, earnings, and future outlook. Selected references.

* Psychiatrists. Science Research Associates. 1967. 4p. 45c

Occupational brief describing nature of work, training, earnings, and future outlook.

**What is a psychiatrist? American Psychiatric Association. 1968. 12p. Single copy free

Description of nature of work, essential personality traits, types of practice, earnings, and professional development.

PSYCHOLOGIST 045.088

Careers in psychology. B'nai B'rith Vocational Service. 1968. 15p. 35c

Description of career opportunities and specialties within the field of psychology. Requirements, certification, and employment outlook are discussed.

Clinical psychologist. Careers. 1966. 2p. 20c

Career summary for desk-top file. Duties, qualifications, and outlook.

Clinical psychologist. Michigan Employment Security Commission. 1952. 2p. Single copy free

Job brief summarizing occupational data for use in Michigan.

The clinical psychologist. National Association for Mental Health. 1967. 4p. 10c

Duties, training, earnings, and future outlook. Selected references.

PSYCHOLOGIST—*Continued*

Educational psychologist. Careers. 1966. 2p. 20c
Career summary for desk-top file. Duties, qualifications, and outlook.

Employment outlook for psychologists. Bulletin No. 1650–42. Bureau of Labor Statistics, U.S. Department of Labor. Supt. of Documents. 1970. 8p. 10c
Reprint from the *Occupational Outlook Handbook.*

Finding out about clinical psychologists. Science Research Associates. 1967. 4p. 45c
Junior occupational brief containing concise facts about the job.

Finding out about experimental psychologists. Science Research Associates. 1967. 4p. 45c
Junior occupational brief containing concise facts about the job.

Jobs in psychology. Science Research Associates. 1962. 43p. $1.15
Describes the variety of job prospects and opportunities within this field. Each area is introduced through a case study approach of a psychologist engaged in the work of that area.

**Opportunities in psychology careers. Super, Donald E. Vocational Guidance Manuals. 1968. 110p. $1.95 paper; $3.75 library edition
Nature of the psychologist's work in each of the special branches, status and employment prospects, education and training, tangible and intangible rewards, advantages and disadvantages, and how to get started and get ahead.

Psychologist. California State Department of Employment. 1965. 5p. Single copy free
Occupational guide describing work, requirements, training, and outlook.

Psychologist. Chronicle Guidance Publications. 1967. 4p. 35c
Occupational brief summarizing work performed, working conditions, qualifications, training, and outlook.

Psychologist. Guidance Centre. 1966. 4p. 35c postpaid
Definition, history and importance, preparation, qualifications, working conditions, employment, advancement, outlook, remuneration, and how to get started.

Psychologist, school. Careers. 1968. 2p. 20c
Career summary for desk-top file. Duties, qualifications, and outlook.

Psychologists. Science Research Associates. 1966. 4p. 45c
Occupational brief describing nature of work, requirements, earnings, getting started, advantages, disadvantages, and future outlook.

**Psychologists. One section of *Occupational Outlook Handbook.*
Nature of work, where employed, training and other qualifications, employment outlook, earnings, and working conditions.

**Psychologists in mental health. Federal Security Administration. Supt. of Documents. 1969. 31p. 45c

An analysis compiled by the National Science Foundation of the characteristics, employment status, and kinds of work of psychologists with particular reference to their work in mental health.

Psychologists in the Veterans Administration. VA pamphlet 10-57. Veterans Administration Forms Depot. 1968. 4p. Free

Description of work, training program, qualifications, and benefits.

Psychology. Pages 200-4 of *Health Careers Guidebook.*

Brief discussion of the clinical psychologist, counseling psychologist, social psychologist, and the psychometrist.

Psychology: earned degrees, by level, sex, and institution. One section of *Earned Degrees Conferred.*

List of 553 schools and the number of bachelor's, master's, and doctor's degrees conferred by each in psychology.

School psychologist. Chronicle Guidance Publications. 1968. 4p. 35c

Occupational brief summarizing duties, qualifications, preparation, methods of entering, advancement, and outlook.

**Your future in school psychology. Gelinas, Paul and Gelinas, Robert. Richards Rosen Press. 1968. 160p. $4; library edition $3.78

Description of typical cases to illustrate the varied kinds of work, requirements, training, and outlook.

PUBLIC ACCOUNTANT 160.188

Accounting orientation test for high school pupils. American Institute of Certified Public Accountants. 1968. 2p. Free

For counselors. Brief description of the testing program and directions for ordering.

**Career as a CPA. American Institute of Certified Public Accountants. 1968. 32p. Single copy free

Describes the profession of accounting, the nature of the work, and preparation. Contains list of college programs in accounting and addresses of state boards of accountancy.

Certified public accountant. California State Department of Employment. 1965. 6p. Single copy free

Occupational guide describing work, requirements, training, and outlook.

Certified public accountants. Science Research Associates. 1966. 4p. 45c

Occupational brief describing work, training, qualifications, opportunities, and outlook.

The making of a CPA. American Institute of Certified Public Accountants. 1968. 20p. 25c

A photographic description, with accompanying text, of one young man's early years in public accounting.

PUBLIC ACCOUNTANT—*Continued*

Men of account. American Institute of Certified Public Accountants. 1968. 6p. Free

A flier describing a 16 mm. sound film designed to show the work of the CPA. Distributed on free loan by Association Films, Inc.

**Public accounting as a career for you. National Society of Public Accountants. 1969. 6p. Single copy free

Brief statement of requirements, duties, advancement, rewards, advantages, disadvantages, and professional status.

See also Accountant; Bookkeeper

PUBLIC ADMINISTRATION WORKER. *See* Government service worker

PUBLIC HEALTH NURSE 075.128

Careers in the Public Health Service—nurse. Public Health Service, U.S. Department of Health, Education, and Welfare. Publication Number 1609. 1967. 8p. Free

Presents various nursing assignments, rewards, career development possibilities, and application information. For graduate nurses.

Educational qualifications of public health nurses. American Public Health Association. 1962. 5p. Single copy free

Scope of work, functions, and educational qualifications.

Elaine Forrest: visiting nurse. Hobart, Lois. Julian Messner. 1959. 192p. $3.50

Career fiction. The story shows that public health nursing duties and responsibilities include a warm, sympathetic approach to patients.

Finding out about public health nurses. Science Research Associates. 1967. 4p. 45c

Junior occupational brief describing work and opportunities.

Functions and qualifications for an occupational health nurse in a one-nurse service. American Nurses' Association, Division on Community Health Nursing Practice. 1968. 10p. Single copy free

Written for the trained nurse, this booklet sets forth the functions and qualifications of a service provided by the management of a company or organization to deal with the health of its employees.

The industrial nurse. American Association of Industrial Nurses. 1960. 4p. 10c

Who the industrial nurse is and the duties that she performs. For student nurses.

Nurses in public health. Government Printing Office. Supt. of Documents. 1969. 78p. 75c

Presents a census of nurses employed in public health. The statistical and narrative data cover registered and licensed practical nurses employed in national state, local, official and non-official agencies.

Nurses in public health. Public Health Service, U.S. Department of Health, Education, and Welfare. Publication Number 785. Supt. of Documents. 1967. 54p. 40c

Presents the number, educational preparation, and other characteristics of nurses employed for public health work in the United States, Puerto Rico, the Virgin Islands, and Guam.

The occupational health nurse goes to college. American Association of Industrial Nurses. 1966. 12p. 50c

What the nurse needs for entry into a baccalaureate degree program and what opportunities are available.

The occupational health nurse—her role in America's health. American Association of Industrial Nurses. 1968. 8p. 25c

Contains brief summary of duties.

Public health nurse. California State Department of Employment. 1968. 4p. Single copy free

Occupational guide describing work, requirements, training, and outlook.

Public health nurse. Careers. 1968. 2p. 20c

Career summary for desk-top file. Duties, qualifications, and outlook.

Public health nurses. Science Research Associates. 1967. 4p. 45c

Occupational brief describing work, training, qualifications, opportunities, and outlook.

Recommended job responsibilities. American Association of Industrial Nurses. 1962. 7 reprints. 50c

Duties of a consultant, administrator of a health service, administrator of nursing services, charge nurse, staff nurse, supervisor, and junior supervisor.

Recommended qualifications of an industrial nurse. American Association of Industrial Nurses. 1962. 4p. 40c

Personal qualifications and the preparation needed for all levels in occupational health nursing.

With the world at your doorstep, have you considered a career in occupational health nursing? American Association of Industrial Nurses. 1969. 3p. Single copy free

Description of the nature of the work, discussion of the purpose of an occupational health nursing service, and recommended preparation.

See also Nurse, Professional; Practical nurse

PUBLIC HEALTH NUTRITIONIST. ***See*** **Nutritionist**

PUBLIC HEALTH SANITARIAN. *See* **Sanitarian**

PUBLIC HEALTH SERVICE OFFICER **187.118**

Careers in the U.S. Public Health Service. Public Health Service, U.S. Department of Health, Education, and Welfare. Publication Number 1567. Supt. of Documents. 1967. 7p. 25c

Sketches the career opportunities, eligibility requirements, advancement programs, and benefits of the Civil Service and Commissioned Corps employment systems.

Educational qualifications of directors of survey, planning, and licensing programs for hospital and other health facilities. American Public Health Association. 1964. 5p. Single copy free

Scope of the field, duties, personal requirements, and training.

Educational qualifications of medical administrators of specialized health programs. American Public Health Association. 1968. 5p. Single copy free

Scope of the field, duties, and training.

Educational qualifications of physician-directors of official health agencies. American Public Health Association. 1969. 5p. Single copy free

General scope of the field, responsibilities, future outlook, and basic education and experience needed.

Public health inspector. Guidance Centre. 1968. 4p. 35c postpaid

History and importance, nature of work, qualifications, working conditions, preparation, earnings, advancement, outlook, and how to get started.

Public Health Service: grants and awards. Govt. Printing Office. Supt. of Documents. 1970. 557p. $2.50

Part II includes training, training grants, traineeship awards, fellowship awards, and research career program awards.

You can work in the health services. Dietz, Betty. John Day Company. 1968. 98p. $2.45 paper

Describes work in the food and drug protective services, the city sanitation workers, environmental health workers, and the food, maintenance and housekeeping services in hospitals.

PUBLIC RELATIONS WORKER **165.068**

Angela in public relations. Brown, Mary L. T. Dodd, Mead and Company. 1964. 243p. $3.25

Career fiction. Story of a college junior who takes a summer job in public relations. Written for grades 7 to 10.

Careers in public relations. Heath, Harry E. Quill and Scroll Foundation. 1965. 15p. 35c

Discussion of the role of public relations, types of positions, opportunities, and outlook.

Colleges offering public relations courses. Public Relations Society of America. 1967. 19p. Free

List of 6 institutions offering a master's degree and 6 offering bachelor's degree in public relations; 39 colleges offering special sequences in public relations; 51 colleges offering two or more courses; and 81 offering one course in the subject.

Consider a career in public relations or in editing. Chronicle Guidance Publications. 1968. 6p. 50c

Reprinted article from *Chemical Engineering* discusses job descriptions, together with hints on how to break into these interesting and well-paid fields.

Finding out about public relations workers. Science Research Associates. 1967. 4p. 45c

Junior occupational brief containing concise facts about the job.

For immediate release. Paradis, Adrian. David McKay Company. 1955. 209p. $3

Discussion of public relations in business, government, social agencies, education, entertainment, and publishing.

Jobs in public relations—the art of persuasion. Alumnae Advisory Center. 1968. 6p. 35c

Reprint from *Mademoiselle* describing the work and experiences of several young women who are successful in public relations work.

An occupational guide to public relations. Public Relations Society of America. 1969. 24p. Free

This booklet describes the role of public relations, qualifications, preparation, employment opportunities, kinds of organizations using public relations, salaries, how to get started, advantages, and drawbacks. Suggested readings.

* Opportunities in public relations. Henkin, Shepard. Vocational Guidance Manuals. 1964. 144p. $1.95 paper; $3.75 library edition

Description of public relations, educational preparation, chances for success, general returns, personal attributes, how to get started, and fields of public relations and publicity such as political, government, social agencies, hotels and institutions, house organ, industrial, entertainment, and public relations for personalities. List of colleges offering courses in public relations.

A profile of university graduates in public relations practice. Chronicle Guidance Publications. 1967. 2p. 35c

Reprinted article from *Public Relations Journal* discusses type of work done in public relations, background for work, salaries, and reasons for entering occupation.

Public relations man. California State Department of Employment. 1967. 6p. Single copy free

Occupational guide describing work, requirements, training, and outlook.

**Public relations man. Careers. 1967. 8p. 35c

Career brief describing duties, media used, training requirements, training opportunities, personal qualifications, employment prospects, earnings, promotional prospects, where employed, related careers, measuring one's interest and ability, and suggested high school courses. Additional references.

PUBLIC RELATIONS WORKER—*Continued*

Public relations man. Chronicle Guidance Publications. 1969. 4p. 35c

Occupational brief summarizing work performed, where employed, personal qualifications, training, earnings, and outlook.

Public relations secretary. Careers. 1969. 2p. 20c

Career summary for desk-top file. Duties, qualifications, training, and outlook.

* Public relations workers. Science Research Associates. 1970. 4p. 45c

Occupational brief describing nature of work, requirements, how to get started, incomes, advantages, disadvantages, and future outlook.

**Public relations workers. One section of *Occupational Outlook Handbook.*

Nature of wok, where employed, training, other qualifications, advancement, employment outlook, earnings, and working conditions.

Why not be a public relations worker? Leaflet 47. Women's Bureau, U.S. Department of Labor. Supt. of Documents. 1968. 8p. 10c

Brief sketch of nature of work, duties, where employed, opportunities, qualifications, earnings, and how to get started. Illustrated.

**Your career in public relations. Donohue, Jody. Julian Messner. 1967. 192p. $3.95; library binding $3.64

This book presents a discussion of public relations for corporations, nonprofit concerns, government departments, agencies, and trade associations. It explains the varying nature of the work involving such media as newspapers, magazines, radio, and television. It offers advice on how to obtain the desirable training and how to break into the field. Includes list of colleges offering courses and degrees in public relations.

**Your future in public relations. Bernays, Edward L. Richards Rosen Press. Revised 1969. 158p. $4; library edition $3.78

A picture of public relations as a rapidly expanding field offering a wide variety of opportunity in the complex area of communications.

PULP AND PAPER INDUSTRY WORKER. *See* Paper industry worker

PURCHASING AGENT 162.158

Finding out about purchasing agents. Science Research Associates. 1967. 4p. 45c

Junior occupational brief describing work and opportunities.

Purchasing agent. California State Department of Employment. 1963. 5p. Single copy free

Occupational guide describing work, requirements, training, and outlook.

* Purchasing agent. Careers. 1970. 8p. 35c

Career brief describing duties, working conditions, training, personal qualifications, earnings, advancement prospects, and outlook.

Purchasing agent. Chronicle Guidance Publications. 1967. 4p. 35c

Occupational brief summarizing work performed, working conditions, qualifications, training, earnings, opportunities, and outlook.

Purchasing agent. Guidance Centre. 1968. 4p. 35c postpaid

Definition, history and importance, nature of work, preparation, qualifications, employment, advancement, outlook, remuneration, and how to get started.

* Purchasing agents. Science Research Associates. 1968. 4p. 45c

Occupational brief describing nature of work, requirements, training, earnings, getting started, advantages, disadvantages, and future outlook.

**Purchasing agents. One section of *Occupational Outlook Handbook.*

Nature of work, where employed, training, other qualifications, advancement, employment outlook, earnings, and working conditions.

Purchasing as a career. National Association of Purchasing Management. 1965. 26p. 50c

Description of the purchasing function and its importance, types of positions, types of training, compensation, and opportunities for qualified college graduates.

When a salesman turns P.A. Chronicle Guidance Publications. 1966. 4p. 35c

Reprinted article from *Purchasing Magazine* discusses the position of a purchasing agent who formerly was a salesman.

**Your career in purchasing management. National Association of Purchasing Management. 1969. 8p. Single copy free

Leaflet describing work, advantages, preparation, opportunities, employment outlook, and intangible rewards.

RABBI 120.108

Careers in the rabbinate. B'nai B'rith Vocational Service. 1969. 15p. 35c

Duties, responsibilities, rewards, and challenges of this career are analyzed. Sources of information, including addresses of major rabbinical seminaries, are listed.

Rabbi. Chronicle Guidance Publications. 1967. 4p. 35c

Occupational brief summarizing work performed, working conditions, personal requirements, earnings, educational requirements, and outlook.

Rabbis. One section of *Occupational Outlook Handbook.*

Nature of work, places of employment, training, other qualifications, outlook, and sources of further information.

What makes a reform rabbi? Hebrew Union College and Jewish Institute of Religion. 1959. 16p. Free

Illustrated brochure describing responsibilities and training of a rabbi.

Would you be a rabbi? Hebrew Union College and Jewish Institute of Religion. 1968. 8p. Free

Brochure dealing with questions students ask about rabbinic school.

RABBI—*Continued*

**Your future as a rabbi: a calling that counts. Gottschalk, Alfred. Richards Rosen Press. 1967. 128p. $4; library edition $3.78

The book treats all branches of the rabbinate, orthodox, conservative, and reform. Contains basic considerations involved in the choice of this career and information about the necessary education and training.

RADIO AND TELEVISION ANNOUNCER 159.148

Announcers' qualifications. National Broadcasting Company, Department of Information. 1963. 3p. Mimeographed. Free

Personal requisites, education, duties, experience, and opportunities for advancement.

Finding out about radio and television announcers. Science Research Associates. 1967. 4p. 45c

Junior occupational brief summarizing what the work requires and offers.

Radio and television announcer. California State Department of Employment. 1965. 7p. Single copy free

Occupational guide describing work, requirements, training, and outlook.

Radio and television announcer. Chronicle Guidance Publications. 1967. 4p. 35c

Occupational brief including work performed, working conditions, personal requirements, educational requirements, outlook, and methods of entry.

Radio and TV announcer. Michigan Employment Security Commission. 1958. 2p. Single copy free

Job brief summarizing occupational data for use in Michigan.

**Radio and television announcers. Careers. 1967. 8p. 35c

Career brief describing duties, working conditions, training requirements, personal qualifications, employment prospects, advantages, disadvantages, earnings, advancement prospects, how to enter, measuring one's interest and ability, and suggested high school program.

Radio and television announcers. Science Research Associates. 1965. 4p. 45c

Occupational brief describing nature of work, training, qualifications, opportunities, disadvantages, and future outlook.

* Radio and television announcers. One section of *Occupational Outlook Handbook*.

Nature of work, training, other qualifications, advancement, employment outlook, earnings, and working conditions.

RADIO AND TELEVISION BROADCASTING INDUSTRY WORKER 96 and 159, 148 and 963.168

Behind the scenes in television. Cooke, David C. Dodd, Mead and Company. Revised 1967. 64p. Library binding $2.99

Simple text and pictures portray various activities in television production. Written for grades 3 to 7.

**Careers in broadcasting. Lerch, John, editor. Appleton-Century-Crofts. 1962. 113p. $3.95

Twenty-six of radio and television's leading performers give advice on the career opportunities in broadcasting. A penetrating inside view is given concerning what radio and television offer and what they demand. The reader will also find reasoned advice from executives in the industry. Illustrated.

**Careers in radio. National Association of Broadcasters. 1967. 20p. 35c. Single copy free

Discussion of the miracle of communication, preparation, special traits required, typical jobs, getting started, and opportunities for women.

Careers in radio and television. Brown, Donald E. Quill and Scroll Foundation. 1965. 16p. 35c

Nature of work, qualifications, and opportunities in journalism in the broadcasting area. Good reading list.

Employment outlook for radio and television broadcasting industry. Bulletin No. 1650–120. Bureau of Labor Statistics, U.S. Department of Labor. Supt. of Documents. 1970. 16p. 15c

Reprint from the *Occupational Outlook Handbook*. Includes radio and television announcers and broadcast technicians.

Marconi: pioneer of radio. Coe, Douglas, pseud. Julian Messner. 1943. 256p. $3.95. Library binding $3.64

Biography which includes the story of the development of wireless telegraphy.

**Radio and television broadcasting occupations. One chapter of *Occupational Outlook Handbook*.

Nature and location of the industry, kinds of jobs, training, other qualifications, advancement, employment outlook, earnings, and working conditions. Specific information is given concerning the announcer and broadcast technician.

Radio and TV production occupations. Chronicle Guidance Publications. 1969. 4p. 35c

Occupational brief summarizing work performed, working conditions, hours, earnings, training needed, personal qualifications, and outlook.

Radio and television program director. Chronicle Guidance Publications. 1967. 4p. 35c

Occupational brief summarizing duties, number of workers, qualifications, preparation, methods of entry, and working conditions.

**Your future in television. Deutscher, J. Noel. Richards Rosen Press. Revised 1969. 158p. $4; library edition $3.78

This book presents the problems and opportunities in the broad field of television.

RADIO AND TELEVISION ENGINEER AND TECHNICIAN 003.187 and 720.281

Broadcast technician. Careers. 1970. 2p. 20c

Career summary for desk-top file. Duties, qualifications, and outlook.

RADIO AND TELEVISION ENGINEER AND TECHNICIAN—*Continued*

Broadcast technicians. One section of *Occupational Outlook Handbook.*

Description of the work of the technicians who set up, operate, and maintain the electronic equipment used to record or transmit radio and television programs. Also includes training, qualifications, and employment outlook.

**Employment outlook for television and radio service technicians. Bulletin No. 1650–89. Bureau of Labor Statistics, U.S. Department of Labor. Supt. of Documents. 1970. 8p. 10c

Reprint from the *Occupational Outlook Handbook.*

Finding out about special effects technicians. Science Research Associates. 1967. 4p. 45c

Junior occupational brief describing work and opportunities.

Ground radio operators and teletypists. One section of *Occupational Outlook Handbook.*

Description of work of transmitting messages between ground station and flight personnel, where employed, training, and employment outlook.

Radio and TV broadcasting technicians. Michigan Employment Security Commission. 1959. 2p. Single copy free

Job brief summarizing occupational data for use in Michigan.

Radio and TV engineer and radio and TV broadcasting technicians. Chronicle Guidance Publications. 1967. 4p. 35c

Occupational brief summarizing work performed, working conditions, hours, earnings, license requirements, training, and outlook.

Radio and television service technician. Guidance Centre. 1967. 4p. 35c postpaid

Work performed, qualifications, advancement opportunities, employment outlook, remuneration, and how to get started.

* Radio-TV servicemen. Science Research Associates. 1970. 4p. 45c

Occupational brief describing nature of work, qualifications, training, getting started, earnings, advantages, disadvantages, and future outlook.

Television and radio service technicians. One section of *Occupational Outlook Handbook.*

Description of work of the technicians who use their knowledge of electrical and electronic parts and circuits to install and repair a growing number of electronic products. Also includes training, qualifications, earnings, and outlook.

RADIO AND TELEVISION TIME SALESMAN 253.358

Finding out about radio-TV time salesmen. Science Research Associates. 1967. 4p. 45c

Junior occupational brief describing work and opportunities.

Radio and television broadcast-time salesman. Careers. 1967. 2p. 20c
Career summary for desk-top file. Duties, qualifications, and outlook.

Radio-TV time salesmen. Science Research Associates. 1967. 4p. 45c
Occupational brief describing nature of work, growth of the media, requirements, earnings, and future outlook.

RADIO REPAIRMAN. ***See*** **Television and radio service technician**

RADIOLOGIC TECHNOLOGIST 078.368

The American registry of radiologic technologists. American Registry of Radiologic Technologists. 1969. 12p. Free
Description of training, registration procedures, and services of the registry.

Approved schools of X-ray technology. Council on Medical Education of the American Medical Association. 1967. 18p. Free
Tabulated information about 1073 approved schools.

**Careers in X-ray technology. American Society of Radiologic Technologists. 1968. 6p. Free
Description of duties, qualifications, opportunities, types of employment, advantages, disadvantages, earnings, and employment outlook.

Discoverer of X Ray: Wilhelm Conrad Röntgen. Esterer, Arnulf K. Julian Messner. 1968. 192p. $3.50; library binding $3.34
Biography of a Nobel prize winner who discovered the short wave ray which has proved an invaluable servant in medicine, laboratory research, industry, art, and astronomy.

Educational qualifications of radiological personnel in the field of public health. American Public Health Association. 1967. 5p. Single copy free
General scope of the work, personal qualities, and training.

**Employment outlook for radiologic technologists. Bulletin No. 1650–17. Bureau of Labor Statistics, U.S. Department of Labor. Supt. of Documents. 1970. 6p. 10c
Reprint from the *Occupational Outlook Handbook.*

Finding out about x-ray technicians. Science Research Associates. 1967. 4p. 45c
Junior occupational brief summarizing what the work requires and offers.

Radiation monitor. Careers. 1967. 2p. 20c
Career summary for desk-top file. Duties, qualifications, and outlook.

Radiographer. California State Department of Employment. 1966. 5p. Single copy free
Occupational guide describing work, requirements, training, and outlook.

Radiographer. Careers. 1967. 2p. 20c
Career summary for desk-top file. Duties, qualifications, and outlook.

RADIOLOGIC TECHNOLOGIST—*Continued*

Radiologic technologist. Careers. 1968. 8p. 35c

Career brief describing duties, working conditions, personal qualifications, training, places of employment, earnings, and outlook.

Radiologic technologist. Chronicle Guidance Publications. 1966. 4p. 35c

Occupational brief summarizing work performed, working conditions, qualifications, training, opportunities, and related jobs.

Radiologic technologist. Michigan Employment Security Commission. 1967. 2p. Single copy free

Job brief summarizing occupational data for use in Michigan.

Radiologic technologist. Pages 204-7 of *Health Careers Guidebook.*

Personal qualifications, training, status and standards, getting started, advancement, and future prospects.

Radiologic technologists. Science Research Associates. 1967. 4p. 45c

Occupational brief describing nature of work, training, preparation, qualifications, opportunities, advantages, disadvantages, and future outlook.

**Radiologic technologists. One section of *Occupational Outlook Handbook.*

Nature of work, where employed, training, other qualifications, advancement, employment outlook, earnings, and working conditions.

Radiologists. Science Research Associates. 1966. 4p. 45c

Occupational brief describing work, training, qualifications, opportunities, and outlook.

X-ray technician. Guidance Centre. 1968. 4p. 35c postpaid

Nature of work, qualifications, preparation, earnings, advantages, disadvantages, how to get started and related occupations.

X-ray technologist, medical. California State Department of Employment. 1968. 5p. Single copy free

Occupational guide describing work, requirements, training, and outlook.

**Your future in radiologic technology. Spirko, Sister Christina. Richards Rosen Press. 1966. 160p. $4; library edition $3.78

Directed to the student investigating a career in X-ray technology. One chapter describes application in industry.

RAILROAD BRAKEMAN 910.364

Brakeman (railroad transportation). Chronicle Guidance Publications. 1968. 4p. 35c

Occupational brief summarizing work performed, working conditions, requirements, training, methods of entry, outlook, and earnings.

Brakemen. One section of *Occupational Outlook Handbook.*

Nature of work, employment outlook, earnings, and working conditions.

Railroad brakeman. Careers. 1967. 2p. 20c

Career summary for desk-top file. Duties, qualifications, and outlook.

Railroad brakeman. Science Research Associates. 1969. 4p. 45c
Occupational brief describing work, qualifications, training, opportunities, and outlook.

Railway brakeman. Guidance Centre. 1966. 4p. 35c postpaid
Nature of work of train, and yard brakeman, working conditions, qualifications, outlook, earnings, advantages, disadvantages, and related occupations.

RAILROAD CONDUCTOR. *See* Conductor, Railroad

RAILROAD INDUSTRY WORKER 910.

**Bridge and building workers. One section of *Occupational Outlook Handbook.*
Nature of work, training, other qualifications, advancement, earnings, and working conditions. Pertains to the work of constructing, maintaining, and repairing structures owned by the railroads.

Employment outlook for railroads. Bulletin No. 1650–121. Bureau of Labor Statistics, U.S. Department of Labor. Supt. of Documents. 1970. 20p. 20c
Reprint from the *Occupational Outlook Handbook.* Includes locomotive engineers, locomotive firemen, conductors, brakemen, telegraphers, telephoners, towermen, station clerks, shop trades, signal department workers, track workers, and bridge and building workers.

Finding out about railroad freight conductors. Science Research Associates. 1967. 4p. 45c
Junior occupational brief summarizing what the work requires and offers.

Finding out about railroad passenger conductors. Science Research Associates. 1967. 4p. 45c
Junior occupational brief containing concise facts about the job.

The human side of railroading. Association of American Railroads. 1967. 16p. Free
A discussion of the railroad organization, payroll, opportunities in the railway field, and how to seek employment. Illustrated.

Operating railroad workers. Science Research Associates. 1966. 4p. 45c
Occupational brief describing kinds of work, requirements, how to enter and advance, earnings, and future outlook.

Quiz on railroads and railroading. Association of American Railroads. 1966. 64p. Free
Contains two hundred questions and answers on many phases of railroading.

Railroad clerks. One section of *Occupational Outlook Handbook.*
Nature of work, training, other qualifications, advancement, employment outlook, earnings, and working conditions.

RAILROAD INDUSTRY WORKER—*Continued*

Railroad conductor. Guidance Centre. 1966. 4p. 35c postpaid

Nature of work, history and importance, working conditions, qualifications necessary for entry and success, preparation needed, employment and advancement, remuneration, advantages, disadvantages, how to get started, and related occupations.

**Railroad occupations. One chapter of *Occupational Outlook Handbook.*

Nature and location of the industry, kinds of jobs, training, other qualifications, advancement, employment outlook, earnings, and working conditions. Specific information is given concerning locomotive engineer, fireman, conductor, brakeman, telegrapher, station agents, signal department workers, and track workers.

Railroad shop craftsman. California State Department of Employment. 1968. 3p. Single copy free

Occupational guide describing work, requirements, training, and outlook.

Railroad track workers. Science Research Associates. 1969. 4p. 45c

Occupational brief describing nature of work, training, qualifications, opportunities, and outlook.

Railroad transportation industry. Chronicle Guidance Publications. 1967. 4p. 35c

Occupational brief summarizing work performed in various areas of the industry, and earnings.

Railroads in action. Association of American Railroads. 1967. 48p. Free

Subtitle: A picture book of the American railroads. About sixty photographs with explanatory captions showing many workers in action.

**Shop trades (railroad). One section of *Occupational Outlook Handbook.*

Nature of work in building, maintaining, and repairing railroads cars and locomotives. Also included is description of training, other qualifications, advancement, employment outlook, earnings, and working conditions.

**Signal department workers (railroad). One section of *Occupational Outlook Handbook.*

Nature of work, training, other qualifications, advancement, employment outlook, earnings, and working conditions.

**Station agents. One section of *Occupational Outlook Handbook.*

Nature of work, training, other qualifications, employment outlook, earnings, and working conditions.

Track workers (railroad). One section of *Occupational Outlook Handbook.*

Nature of work, training, other qualifications, advancement, employment outlook, earnings, and working conditions.

Workin' on the railroad; reminiscences from the age of steam. Reinhardt, Richard. American West Publishing Company. 1970. 318p. $8.95

To record railroad history from the point of view of the railroad workers, the author uses memoirs, diaries, local histories, and magazine articles. Anecdotes and folklore are included about conductors, surveyors, brakemen, engineers, telegraphers, and section gangs.

You and Santa Fe. Atchison, Topeka and Santa Fe Railway Company. 1968. 16p. Free

Importance of the railway in the unification and growth of the nation, specific job opportunities, and benefits.

REAL ESTATE APPRAISER 191.287

Finding out about real estate appraisers. Science Research Associates. 1967. 4p. 45c

Junior occupational brief containing concise facts about the job.

Real estate appraiser. California State Department of Employment. 1968. 5p. Single copy free

Occupational guide describing work, requirements, training, and outlook.

Real estate appraiser. Careers. 1967. 2p. 20c

Career summary for desk-top file. Duties, qualifications, and outlook.

Real estate appraisers. Science Research Associates. 1965. 4p. 45c

Occupational brief describing work, training, qualifications, opportunities, and outlook.

REAL ESTATE SALESMAN AND BROKER 250.358

Employment outlook for real estate salesmen and brokers. Bulletin No. 1650–59. Bureau of Labor Statistics, U.S. Department of Labor. Supt. of Documents. 1970. 8p. 10c

Reprint from the *Occupational Outlook Handbook.*

Finding out about real estate agents. Science Research Associates. 1967. 4p. 45c

Junior occupational brief summarizing what the work requires and offers.

Preparing for the real estate business. Chronicle Guidance Publications. 1967. 4p. 35c

Reprinted article from *National Association of Real Estate Boards* discusses the broad scope of the real estate business—its rewards and the principal fields of real estate activity.

Real estate: a career with a bright future. Davis, John G. National Association of Real Estate Boards. 1962. 5p. Single copy free

Reprint describing nature of work, opportunities, and outlook.

Real estate agent. Guidance Centre. 1970. 4p. 35c postpaid

Nature of work, qualifications, earnings, advancement opportunities, advantages, disadvantages, how to get started, and related occupations.

**Real estate agents. Science Research Associates. 1967. 4p. 45c

Occupational brief describing real estate specialties, requirements, training, methods of getting started, earnings, advantages, disadvantages, and future outlook.

Real estate salesman. California State Department of Employment. 1966. 4p. Single copy free

Occupational guide describing work, requirements, training, and outlook.

REAL ESTATE SALESMAN AND BROKER—*Continued*

* Real estate salesman. Careers. 1969. 2p. 20c
  Career summary for desk-top file. Duties, qualifications, and outlook.

Real estate salesman. Chronicle Guidance Publications. 1967. 4p. 35c
  Occupational brief including work performed, working conditions, hours, earnings, personal requirements, training, opportunities, outlook, methods of entry, related jobs, and suggested activities.

Real estate salesman. Michigan Employment Security Commission. 1960. 2p. Single copy free
  Job brief summarizing occupational data for use in Michigan.

**Real estate salesmen and brokers. One section of *Occupational Outlook Handbook.*
  Nature of work, where employed, training, employment outlook, earnings, and working conditions.

**Your future in real estate. Durst, Seymour and Stern, Walter. Richards Rosen Press. Revised 1969. 159p. $4; library edition $3.78
  The author describe the requirements, opportunities, and methods of entering the field. Information is given about residential brokerage, commercial brokerage, realty management, building, realty finance, and other related opportunities.

RECEPTIONIST 237.368

* Employment outlook for receptionists. Bulletin No. 1650–52. Bureau of Labor Statistics, U.S. Department of Labor. Supt. of Documents. 1970. 8p. 10c
  Reprint from the *Occupational Outlook Handbook.*

Finding out about receptionists. Science Research Associates. 1967. 4p. 45c
  Junior occupational brief describing work and opportunities.

Receptionist. California State Department of Employment. 1968. 2p. Single copy free
  Duties, preparation, how to start, promotion, and employment prospects.

Receptionist. Careers. 1968. 2p. 20c
  Career summary for desk-top file. Duties, qualifications, and outlook.

Receptionist. Chronicle Guidance Publications. 1966. 4p. 35c
  Occupational brief summarizing work performed, working conditions, hours, earnings, personal qualifications, training requirements, opportunities, employment outlook, and entry into the job.

Receptionists. One section of *Occupational Outlook Handbook.*
  Nature of work, places of employment, earnings, working conditions, and employment outlook.

Receptionists. Science Research Associates. 1969. 4p. 45c

Occupational brief describing nature of work, training, qualifications, opportunities, advantages, disadvantages, and future outlook.

See also Airplane hostess

RECORD INDUSTRY WORKER 194.282

Record company jobs. Watt, Robin. Alumnae Advisory Center. 1968. 4p. 35c

Examples of jobs held by female college graduates are described, with suggestions for entering this field.

**Your future in the high fidelity industry. Newman, Bernard. Richards Rosen Press. 1966. 160p. $4; library edition $3.78

The wide variety of opportunities that exist in this field are discussed, together with the training and skills needed. Two final chapters give pointers on obtaining a job in this field. Includes list of colleges offering courses in electrical engineering.

RECORDS MANAGER 206.388

Records management. Benedon, William. Prentice-Hall, Inc. 1969. 272p. $19.95

A thorough treatment of managing records and forms by a career records manager. Includes the justifying, organizing, managing and maintaining a records center.

Records management: earned degrees, by level, sex, and institution. One section of *Earned Degrees Conferred.*

Useful for judging the extent of a college's program in this specialty.

RECREATION WORKER 079.128 and 195.228

Colleges and universities reporting major curricula in recreation and parks. National Recreation and Park Association. 1968. 20p. Single copy free

List of schools indicating the curriculum specialization and whether graduate or undergraduate degrees are offered.

Employment outlook for recreation workers. Bulletin No. 1650–43. Bureau of Labor Statistics, U.S. Department of Labor. Supt. of Documents. 1970. 8p. 10c

Reprint from the *Occupational Outlook Handbook.*

Exploring your future in recreation, parks, and youth services. Sextant Systems, Inc. 1971. 96p. $8.95

One page is devoted to each of ninety-five jobs, summarizing duties, requirements for entering, promotional outlook, and pay and skill level. Includes an organizational chart showing the beginning jobs and those to which one may be promoted.

Finding out about recreation workers. Science Research Associates. 1967. 4p. 45c

Junior occupational brief summarizing what the work requires and offers.

RECREATION WORKER—*Continued*

A future for you . . . recreation. American National Red Cross. 1969. 12p. Free

Description of positions and qualifications for women recreation workers and recreation supervisors assigned to Red Cross programs in military hospitals.

The future is yours—a career in recreation leadership. National Recreation and Park Association. 1968. 6p. $3 per 100. Single copy free

Types of leadership positions, professional preparation, qualifications, and demand.

Group-recreation worker. California State Department of Employment. 1964. 4p. Single copy free

Occupational guide describing work, requirements, training, and outlook.

**Opportunities in recreation and outdoor education. Nash, Jay B. Vocational Guidance Manuals. 1963. 112p. $1.95 paper; library binding $3.75

Includes discussion of opportunities, qualifications, personal satisfaction, historical background, future outlook, and pathways to advancement. List of institutions offering professional training.

Recreation. One chapter in Volume I in the *Encyclopedia of Careers and Vocational Guidance*.

Discussion of the need for recreational programs and their diversity. A table gives the number of people involved in various recreational activities and in organized recreational pursuits.

* Recreation director. Careers. 1967. 8p. 35c

Career brief describing duties, working conditions, training requirements, lists of colleges offering major curriculums in recreation, personal qualifications, employment prospects, earnings, where employed, measuring one's interest and ability, and suggested high school program.

Recreation director. Guidance Centre. 1966. 4p. 35c postpaid

History and importance, nature of work, qualifications for entry and success, working conditions, preparation, earnings, advancement, outlook, related occupations, and how to get started.

Recreation facility attendant. Chronicle Guidance Publications. 1969. 4p. 35c

Occupational brief summarizing work performed, where employed, salary, personal qualifications, and outlook.

Recreation leader. California State Department of Employment. 1968. 5p. Single copy free

Occupational guide describing work, requirements, training, and outlook.

Recreation leader (director). Chronicle Guidance Publications. 1967. 4p. 35c

Occupational brief summarizing work performed, working conditions, hours, earnings, personal qualifications, training requirements, opportunities, employment outlook, and entry into the job.

Recreation leadership with the ill and the handicapped. National Recreation and Park Association. 1968. 10p. Single copy free

Brief description of the expanding field of therapeutic recreation specialist.

Recreation therapist. Careers. 1966. 2p. 20c

Career summary for desk-top file. Duties, qualifications, and outlook.

* Recreation workers. Science Research Associates. 1968. 4p. 45c

Occupational brief describing nature of work in youth-serving organizations, community recreation, hospital recreation, armed services, and industrial recreation. Also includes requirements, getting started, salaries, advantages, disadvantages, and future outlook.

Recreation workers. One section of *Occupational Outlook Handbook.*

Nature of work, places of employment, training, qualifications, employment outlook, earnings, advancement, and working conditions.

The recreational therapist. National Association for Mental Health. 1967. 4p. 10c

Describes the duties of the recreational therapist in the mental health field, training, earnings, and future outlook. Selected references.

**Your career in parks and recreation. McCall, Virginia and McCall, Joseph. Julian Messner. 1970. 190p. $3.95; library edition $3.64

Stressing the need to preserve natural and historic sites, the supervisor of a Sierra Nevada park discusses careers in outdoor recreation. The book includes a wide range of positions both in government and private organizations and contains specific information on qualifications, educational requirements, personal attributes, salary ranges, and fringe benefits.

RED CROSS WORKER 195.108

Careers at military installations. American National Red Cross. 1968. 6p. Free

Information about qualifications and work as an assistant field director in the Red Cross program of service at military installations.

Careers in first aid, small craft, and water safety programs. American National Red Cross. 1968. 1p. Free

Description of qualifications and jobs available in Red Cross programs.

**Employment opportunities. American National Red Cross. 1969. 6p. Free

Mimeographed sheet giving spectrum of entry positions for professional workers.

A worthwhile experience for you. American National Red Cross. 1966. 12p. Free

Description of positions and qualifications for women recreation workers assigned to the Red Cross clubmobile program in Vietnam and Korea.

REFRIGERATION ENGINEER. *See* Air-conditioning and refrigeration engineer

REFRIGERATION MECHANIC. *See* **Air-conditioning, refrigeration, and heating mechanic**

REHABILITATION COUNSELOR 045.108

Career and traineeship information for graduate study in rehabilitation counseling. Rehabilitation Services Administration. 1968. 9p. Free

Discussion of careers and employment opportunities followed by information about available traineeships.

A career with a challenge—vocational rehabilitation counseling of blind persons. Wood, Maxine. American Foundation for the Blind. 1959. 23p. Free

A discussion of the need for vocational rehabilitation counselors, their role, duties, and satisfactions.

Careers in rehabilitation: helping the helping professions. National Easter Seal Society for Crippled Children and Adults. 1967. 6p. Single copy free

Brief statement concerning need and opportunities in this field.

Finding out about vocational rehabilitation counselors. Science Research Associates. 1967. 4p. 45c

Junior occupational brief containing concise facts about the job.

How will you choose to help others? National Rehabilitation Counseling Association. 1968. 6p. Single copy free

Discusses growing job openings and training in rehabilitation of the mentally retarded.

**An introduction to the professional career opportunities in rehabilitation. National Easter Seal Society for Crippled Children and Adults. 1968. 28p. 25c

Description of rehabilitation and the work of specialists such as physical therapist, occupational therapist, speech pathologist, audiologist, rehabilitation counselor, medical social worker, recreation therapist, rehabilitation nurse, psychologist, and special education teacher.

List of colleges offering rehabilitation traineeships. Vocational Rehabilitation Services Administration. 1968. 2p. Free

List of schools that have received grants to provide traineeships on a graduate level.

The most important thing in the world. National Easter Seal Society for Crippled Children and Adults. 1968. 24p. 25c

An introduction to the professional career opportunities in rehabilitation, such as physical therapist, speech pathologist, and the recreation therapist.

The rehabilitation counselor. Ogg, Elizabeth. Public Affairs Committee, Inc. 1970. 28p. 25c

Describes the work of the rehabilitation counselor with the physically disabled, the emotionally handicapped, the mentally retarded, and those unemployed or underemployed because of alcoholism, drug addiction, a prison record, too little education, or poverty. Includes preparation, advantages, and widening horizons in this field.

Rehabilitation counselor. California State Department of Employment. 1967. 4p. Single copy free

Occupational guide describing work, requirements, training, and outlook.

Rehabilitation counselor. Careers. 1968. 2p. 20c

Career summary for desk-top file. Duties, qualifications, and outlook.

Rehabilitation counselor. Chronicle Guidance Publications. 1969. 4p. 35c

Occupational brief summarizing work performed, qualifications, where employed, educational requirements, training opportunities, earnings, working conditions, and outlook.

The rehabilitation counselor. National Association for Mental Health. 1968. 4p. 10c

Describes the duties of the rehabilitation counselor in the mental health field. Also discusses training, earnings, and future outlook. Selected sources for more information.

**Rehabilitation counselor. One section of *Occupational Outlook Handbook.*

Nature of work, where employed, training, other qualifications, employment outlook, earnings, and working conditions.

Rehabilitation counselors. Science Research Associates. 1969. 4p. 45c

Occupational briefs describing nature of work, requirements, getting started, earnings, advantages, disadvantages, and future outlook.

**The roles and functions of the rehabilitation counselor. American Rehabilitation Counselors Association. Order from American Personnel and Guidance Association. 1969. 168p. $1.50

A special issue of the *Rehabilitation Counseling Bulletin,* providing information about the work and traits of rehabilitation counselors in state agencies and rehabilitation facilities. Includes functions performed in various settings.

Vocational rehabilitation counseling. Pages 236-9 of *Health Careers Guidebook.*

Duties, qualifications, and a description of a traineeship program.

Vocational rehabilitation training grants. Rehabilitation Services Administration. 1967. 29p. Free

Information concerning the training grant program of the Rehabilitation Services Administration.

REHABILITATION OFFICER. *See* Rehabilitation counselor

RELIGIOUS VOCATIONS WORKER 120.108

Become a director or minister of Christian education. National Council of Churches, Division of Christian Education. No date. 6p. 5c

Discusses the need for persons in the field, the requirements of the job, and the rewards of the work.

Called to Mission. Board of Missions of The United Methodist Church. 1962. 6p. Free

Demands of and qualifications for missionary service.

RELIGIOUS VOCATIONS WORKER—*Continued*

Christian education director. Careers. 1968. 2p. 20c

Career summary for desk-top file. Duties, qualifications, and outlook.

Church occupation packet. United Methodist Church. 1969. 20 leaflets. 50c

Leaflets on specific church occupations. Some contain discussions on selecting a college, planning a career, and investigating Church-related occupations.

Church occupations and voluntary service. United Methodist Church. 1969. 64p. 20c

Annual directory of church-related occupations and voluntary service opportunities, with explanation of qualifications and training required for each. Contains sections on summer service projects, selective service law, and United Methodist student loan and scholarship funds.

Church worker (woman). Guidance Centre. 1968. 4p. 23c postpaid

Definition, history and importance, nature of the work, qualifications, preparation, employment, outlook, remuneration, advancement, and how to get started.

College majors and careers in the church. National Council of Churches. No date. 3p. 20c

Listing of major fields of study in college and their relation to possible church occupations.

Journey into mission. Williams, Philip. Friendship Press. 1957. 190p. $1

This is the diary of a young missionary who spent five years in Japan. It reveals opportunities and problems a Christian missionary faces in lands abroad.

Men and women overseas. Board of Missions of The United Methodist Church. 1962. 6p. Free

Description of career missionary service and the qualifications.

Packet of career materials. Lutheran Church in America Vocational Services. 1969. Five leaflets. Free

Discussions of the continuing need and expanding opportunities in church occupations for both men and women.

Protestant church occupations. National Council of Churches. 1968. 12p. 30c

An information booklet prepared for those who counsel college and university students.

Religion as an occupation: a study in the sociology of professions. Fichter, Joseph H. University of Notre Dame Press. 1961. 295p. $3.95 paper

Material presented in a course in sociology of vocations at Notre Dame. Includes discussion of selection of candidates, their professional training and education, the roles they perform, and problems they meet during their careers.

Religion: earned degrees, by level, sex, and institution. One section of *Earned Degrees Conferred.*

Useful for judging the extent of a college's program in religion, theology, and religious education.

Religious education director. Chronicle Guidance Publications. 1967. 4p. 35c

Occupational brief summarizing work performed, training, qualifications, advancement, earnings, and outlook.

Religious Sister, Religious Brother. Chronicle Guidance Publications. 1966. 4p. 35c

Occupational brief summarizing work performed, training requirements, personal qualifications, hours and earnings, and outlook.

Religious vocations. Science Research Associates. 1966. 4p. 45c

Occupational brief describing nature of work, training, qualifications, opportunities, advantages, disadvantages, and future outlook.

Vocation and church careers kit. National Council of Churches. 1966. 4 booklets. $1

File folder containing four career pamphlets.

**Vocation and Protestant religious occupations. Nelson, John Oliver. Vocational Guidance Manuals. 1963. 160p. $1.95 paper; library binding $3.75

Describes opportunities in church vocations, the pastorate, the church's world mission, Christian education, chaplaincies, campus work, church music, social work, and interchurch work. Also discusses preparation in high school and college, choosing a seminary, and how to begin.

Your calling as a Brother. Cashin, Brother Edward. Richards Rosen Press. 1966. 159p. $4; library edition $3.78

The history, founding, and place of Brothers in the church. Various orders and their functions are discussed.

Your calling as a nun. Maureen, Sister Mary. Richards Rosen Press. 1967. 128p. $4; library edition $3.78

What it means to have this calling and what kind of life to expect.

Your faith and your life. Million, Elmer. Friendship Press. 1960. 80p. $1

Presentation of a variety of church occupations.

See also Clergyman; Priest; Rabbi

REPAIR MECHANIC. *See* Technician

REPORTER 132.268

Finding out about newspaper reporters. Science Research Associates. 1967. 4p. 45c

Junior occupational brief describing work and opportunities.

REPORTER–*Continued*

The making of the President 1960. White, T. H. Atheneum Publishers. 1961. 400p. $6.95

Reporting on the workings of American politics, this book gives insight into political reporting.

Nellie Bly: first woman reporter. Noble, Iris. Julian Messner. 1956. 192p. $3.50. Library binding $3.34

Biography of a reporter who pioneered the way for today's newspaperwomen in exposing crime and corruption.

Newspaper reporter. Careers. 1970. 2p. 30c

Career summary for desk-top file. Duties, qualifications, and outlook.

**Newspaper reporters. One section of *Occupational Outlook Handbook.*

Nature of work, where employed, training, other qualifications, advancement, employment outlook, earnings, and working conditions.

Reporter. California State Department of Employment. 1968. 5p. Single copy free

Duties, working conditions, finding the work, pay, hours, training, promotion, and employment outlook.

Reporter. Chronicle Guidance Publications. 1969. 4p. 35c

Occupational brief summarizing work performed, working conditions, qualifications, training, earnings, opportunities, methods of entry, related jobs, and outlook.

Reporter. Guidance Centre. 1967. 4p. 35c postpaid

History and importance, nature of work, qualifications, working conditions, preparation, remuneration, advancement, outlook, related occupations, and how to get started.

Reporter. Michigan Employment Security Commission. 1959. 2p. Single copy free

Job brief summarizing occupational data for use in Michigan.

* Reporters. Science Research Associates. 1967. 4p. 45c

Occupational brief describing nature of work, requirements, earnings, and future outlook.

Reporters at war. Fleming, Alice. Cowles and Company. 1970. 134p. $3.95

Through biographical sketches of ten frontline correspondents from the time of the Crimean War to the present, the author shows what it means to be a reporter covering a war and stresses the qualities needed by a good war correspondent.

Reporting jobs. Alumnae Advisory Center. 1968. 8p. 35c

Reprint from *Mademoiselle* describing case histories of several young women who have succeeded as feature writer, news editor, or reporter.

**Your future as a shorthand reporter. Van Allen, Edward. Richards Rosen Press. 1969. 140p. 4; library edition $3.78

Explanation of the work, qualifications, and training.

See also Editor; Journalist; Writer

RESEARCH WORKER 109.288

**Careers in research science. Wachs, Theodore, Jr. Henry Z. Walck, Inc. 1961. 96p. $4.50

Describes scientific research in each of the major divisions of physical science: physics, chemistry, mathematics, and astronomy. Contains discussion of work in government, universities, and industry with the advantages and disadvantages of each. Reading list. Illustrated.

Decision for research. American Heart Association. 1962. 12p. Single copy free from local Heart Associations

Booklet for high school and college students describing research opportunities and steps to be taken by students interested in research careers. Illustrated.

**Disease detectives: your career in medical research. Neal, Harry Edward. Julian Messner. Revised 1968. 192p. $3.95; library binding $3.64

Scientists at work in modern medical research laboratories.

Finding out about medical researchers. Science Research Associates. 1967. 4p. 45c

Junior occupational brief containing concise facts about the job.

Manpower for medical research requirements and resources, 1965-1970. Public Health Service, U.S. Department of Health, Education, and Welfare. Publication Number 1001. Supt. of Documents. 1963. 72p. 55c

Describes the growth of medical research and the outlook for the future. Emphasizes the manpower requirements to meet the future growth of medical research.

The nurse in research—an approach to professional excellence. Public Health Service, U.S. Department of Health, Education, and Welfare. Publication Number 1275. 1968. 17p. Free

Beautifully illustrated in color, this booklet describes the assignment possibilities and the qualification requirements for research work at the Clinical Center of the National Institutes of Health.

Operations research analysts. Science Research Associates. 1967. 4p. 45c

Occupational brief describing work, training, qualifications, opportunities, and outlook.

Questions and answers on agricultural research in the U.S. Department of Agriculture and the state agricultural experiment stations. U.S. Department of Agriculture. Agriculture Information Bulletin 224. Supt. of Documents. 1963. 28p. 25c

Describes the functions of the several research divisions.

Research activities in Atomic Energy Commission laboratories. Oak Ridge Associated Universities. 1968. 92p. Free

Summarizes typical research activities.

Title examiner. Careers. 1968. 2p. 20c

Career summary for desk-top file. Duties, qualifications, and outlook.

See also Scientist

RESTAURANT INDUSTRY WORKER 31 and 32

**Aim for a job in restaurants and food service. Westbrook, James. Richards Rosen Press. 1969. 191p. $4; library edition $3.78

A description of the jobs in hotels, restaurants, motels, and food service organizations. Includes information about nature of work, earnings, and how to get started.

Countergirl. California State Department of Employment. 1966. 4p. Single copy free

Occupational guide describing work, requirements, training, and outlook.

Counterman (lunchroom or coffee shop). California State Department of Employment. 1968. 2p. Single copy free

Occupational guide describing work, requirements, training, and outlook.

**Employment outlook for restaurants. Bulletin No. 1650–123. Bureau of Labor Statistics, U.S. Department of Labor. Supt. of Documents. 1970. 8p. 10c

Reprint from the *Occupational Outlook Handbook.*

The restaurant business. One chapter in Volume I of the *Encyclopedia of Careers and Vocational Guidance.*

Opportunities in different types of restaurant work, trends, and future outlook.

Restaurant industry. One section of *Occupational Outlook Handbook.*

Nature and location of the industry, employment outlook, earnings, and working conditions.

RESTAURANT MANAGER 187.168

Finding out about restaurant managers. Science Research Associates. 1967. 4p. 45c

Junior occupational brief containing concise facts about the job.

Food service supervisor. Careers. 1970. 2p. 20c

Career summary for desk-top file. Duties, qualifications, and outlook.

Restaurant manager. Careers. 1966. 2p. 20c

Career summary for desk-top file. Duties, qualifications, and outlook.

Restaurant manager. Chronicle Guidance Publications. 1966. 4p. 35c

Occupational brief summarizing work performed, where employed, requirements, training, methods of entry, advantages, disadvantages and outlook.

Restaurant managers. Science Research Associates. 1970. 4p. 45c

Occupational brief describing nature of work, training, qualifications, opportunities, and outlook.

Starting and managing a small restaurant. Small Business Administration. Supt. of Documents. 1964. 116p. 45c

Published to help prospective restaurant owners decide whether they have the basic qualifications, financing, and experience for success.

See also Hotel manager

RETAIL MANAGER 185. and 260.

**Careers and opportunities in retailing. Wilinsky, Harriet. Dutton and Company. 1970. 251p. $5.95

Information concerning department stores, chain stores, discount stores, and specialty stores. The kinds of work, qualifications, preparation, and outlook are described for merchandising, publicity, operations, finance, and personnel work. Includes list of professional schools. Practical advice is also given on owning a retail store.

Careers in retailing. American Collegiate Retailing Association. 1968. 1p. Free

A fact sheet giving brief information.

* Careers in retailing. Rochester Institute of Technology. 1963. 24p. Free

This career bulletin gives information about the various branches of the vocation, duties performed by persons employed, advantages, disadvantages, and requirements for initial employment and for promotions.

Defining the manager's job. American Management Association. 1958. 447p. $9

Description of functions and responsibilities, based on a survey of 140 companies.

Employee earnings and hours in retail trade. Bureau of Labor Statistics. Supt. of Documents. 1968. 86p. $1

Presents estimates of employment, average hourly earnings, and weekly hours of work of nonsupervisory employees in retail trade.

Exploring your future in merchandising. Sextant Systems, Inc. 1970. 96p. $8.95

One page is devoted to each of ninety-five jobs, describing the duties, requirements for entering, promotional outlook, and the pay and skill level.

Finding out about store managers. Science Research Associates. 1967. 4p. 45c

Junior occupational brief containing concise facts about the job.

Membership roster. American Collegiate Retailing Association. 1969. 2p. Free

Includes names and locations of twenty-nine degree-granting institutions offering a major in retailing.

Retail store manager (general merchandise and apparel stores). California State Department of Employment. 1966. 6p. Single copy free

Occupational guide describing work, requirements, training, and outlook.

Starting and managing a retail flower shop. Small Business Administration. Supt. of Documents. 1970. 121p. 55c

Suggestions for efficient management of a flower shop.

Starting and managing a small retail camera shop. Small Business Administration. Supt. of Documents. 1969. 69p. 40c

Outlines the opportunities and problems that await a prospective photographic retail manager and suggests some methods of meeting them. Provides basic information about management and keeping up with developments in the field.

RETAIL MANAGER—*Continued*

**Your future in retailing. Scott, George. Richards Rosen Press. Revised 1969. 160p. $4; library edition $3.78

Presents the field of retailing from the specialty shop to the store as rich in opportunity and interest.

Your opportunities in retailing. National Retail Merchants Association. 1962. 22p. 25c

Description of positions available to graduates of a specialized retailing program. Education, salary, outlook, and opportunities are discussed.

See also Department store worker; Salesperson; Super market manager

RETAIL SALESPERSON 260. through 298.877

Career opportunities in food retailing. National Association of Retail Grocers of the United States. 1966. 16p. Free

Description of opportunities and employment outlook.

**Employment outlook for retail trade salesworkers, wholesale trade salesworkers, manufacturer's salesmen. Bulletin No. 1650–58. Bureau of Labor Statistics, U.S. Department of Labor. Supt. of Documents. 1970. 12p. 15c

Reprint from the *Occupational Outlook Handbook.*

Looking for a career? National Association of Food Chains. 1963. 6p. Free

Information about challenges and opportunities in this work.

Retail clothing salespeople. Science Research Associates. 1967. 4p. 45c

Occupational brief describing nature of work, requirements, preparation, working conditions, earnings, and future outlook.

Retail salespeople. Science Research Associates. 1969. 4p. 45c

Occupational brief describing nature of work, requirements, getting started and advancing, earnings, advantages, disadvantages, and future outlook. Selected references.

Retail trade sales workers. One section of *Occupational Outlook Handbook.*

Nature of work, where employed, training, other qualifications, advancement, employment outlook, earnings, and working conditions.

ROOFER 866.381

Employment outlook for roofers and sheet-metal workers. Bulletin No. 1650–78. Bureau of Labor Statistics, U.S. Department of Labor. Supt. of Documents. 1970. 12p. 15c

Reprint from the *Occupational Outlook Handbook.*

Finding out about roofers. Science Research Associates. 1967. 4p. 45c

Junior occupational brief describing work and opportunities.

Roofer. Careers. 1970. 2p. 20c
Career summary for desk-top file. Duties, qualifications, and outlook.

Roofer. Chronicle Guidance Publications. 1967. 4p. 35c
Occupational brief summarizing nature of work, where employed, earnings, personal qualifications, training, working conditions, and outlook.

Roofers. Science Research Associates. 1966. 4p. 45c
Occupational brief describing work, qualifications, working conditions, earnings, and outlook.

**Roofers. One section of *Occupational Outlook Handbook.*
Nature of work, where employed, training, other qualifications, advancement, employment outlook, earnings, and working conditions.

ROUTEMAN 292.358

* Delivery route salesmen. Science Research Associates. 1967. 4p. 45c
Occupational brief describing work, qualifications, earnings, things to consider, and outlook. Selected references.

Finding out about routemen. Science Research Associates. 1967. 4p. 45c
Junior occupational brief summarizing what the work requires and offers.

Route salesman. Careers. 1968. 2p. 20c
Career summary for desk-top file. Duties, qualifications, and outlook.

Routeman. California State Department of Employment. 1964. 4p. Single copy free
Duties, pay, hours, promotion, training, and employment prospects in California.

**Routemen. One section of *Occupational Outlook Handbook.*
Nature of work, where employed, qualifications, earnings, employment outlook, and working conditions.

RUBBER INDUSTRY WORKER 55

Finding out about rubber products workers. Science Research Associates. 1967. 4p. 45c
Junior occupational brief containing concise facts about the job.

Rubber goods (manufacturing) occupations. Chronicle Guidance Publications. 1969. 4p. 35c
Occupational brief summarizing need and importance, work performed, where employed, working conditions, salary, personal qualifications, training required, and outlook.

**Rubber industry workers. Science Research Associates. 1967. 4p. 45c
Occupational brief describing kinds of work, requirements, training, earnings, advantages, disadvantages, and future outlook.

SAFETY ENGINEER 012.081

Careers in fire protection engineering. Illinois Institute of Technology. 1964. 6p. Free

Description of work, opportunities, salaries, and training. The sequence of college courses required to earn a degree in fire protection and safety engineering is listed for eight semesters.

Finding out about safety engineers. Science Research Associates. 1967. 4p. 45c

Junior occupational brief describing work and opportunities.

Safety engineer. Careers. 1966. 2p. 20c

Career summary for desk-top file. Duties, qualifications, and outlook.

Safety engineer. Pages 112-13 of *Health Careers Guidebook.*

Personal qualifications, training, opportunities, and prospects.

* Safety engineers. Science Research Associates. 1966. 4p. 45c

Occupational brief describing work, qualifications, how to get started, and outlook.

SAILOR 378.

Annapolis today. United States Naval Institute. 1963. 329p. $6

The preface to this sixth edition states that the text has been revised, additional chapters included, and a new selection of photographs used. Includes description of customs, traditions, and way of life at the Naval Academy. A final chapter on how to become a midshipman gives general eligibility requirements.

Captain Charlie. Dugan, William. Golden Press. 1968. 24p. 69c

A tall picture book, sixteen inches tall, prepared for nursery school and kindergarten children. Contains vivid color illustrations of typical activities of a ship captain and his crew, explained in simple captions.

Go, Navy, go. Archibald, Joseph. Macrae Smith Company. 1956. 192p. $3.75

Fictional account of an Annapolis cadet who learns to participate in football and other activities with true Navy spirit.

Midshipman Plowright. Pole, James T. Dodd, Mead and Company. 1969. 272p. $4.50

This novel tells of a midshipman attending Annapolis during the Naval Academy's first year and his later adventures in the Mexican War. Written for grades 7 to 10.

The Naval Reserve Officers Training Corps. U.S. Department of the Navy. Revised annually. 20p. Free

Opportunities offered, obligations involved, eligibility requirements, and the selection procedures of the NROTC program. Includes names and locations of the colleges which are recognized as training centers. Information concerning the test which all applicants are required to take, including physical requirements and the physical defects for which they may be disqualified. Deadline dates and the list of documents required for interviews.

The navy. Robertson, Keith. Viking Press. Revised 1962. 192p. $3
Details of regulations and opportunities. For grades 7 to 10.

Navy career opportunities. Careers. 1966. 8p. 35c
Career brief describing opportunities and requirements for enlistment.

**Navy career planner. U.S. Department of the Navy. 1968. 166p. Free to counselors and librarians
This handbook contains seventy-two vocational information briefs containing information about related civilian jobs. This book also includes the Navy's "stay in school" policy for schools, with information on education, classification, enlistment requirements, promotions, pay and retirement, a school subject index for educational guidance, career pattern, and suggestions for use. The briefs may be obtained separately. Each of the briefs describes the nature of work, duties, work assignment, qualifications, preparation, training given, related civilian jobs, and emergency service ratings. Suitable for boys and girls. Generously illustrated.

Our space age navy. Colby, Carroll B. Coward-McCann, Inc. 1962. 48p. $2.50; library edition $2.97
Illustrated with many photographs of carriers, aircraft, submarines, and missiles. Written for ages 8 to 12.

Wings for the fleet. U.S. Department of the Navy. 1968. 52p. Free
A booklet, amply illustrated, describing in story form the development of a naval aviator. The story conveys the general atmosphere of the life of an aviation student and is supported throughout with interesting factual material.

See also Armed Forces; Submarine officer

SALESMAN, GENERAL 289.358

Bookshop and bookstore sales clerks. Science Research Associates. 1966. 4p. 45c
Occupational brief describing nature of work, requirements, getting started, income, advantages, disadvantages, and future outlook. Selected references.

Careers in industrial marketing. Aluminum Company of America. No date. 8p. Free
A recruiting brochure describing work and opportunities.

Direct selling and the direct-to-consumer salespeople. National Association of Direct Selling Companies. No date. 4p. Free
Discussion of the nature of work, requirements, earnings, and the career opportunities offered in the growing industry.

Drugstore salesperson. Careers. 1967. 2p. 20c
Career summary for desk-top file. Duties, qualifications, and outlook.

Finding out about bookstore clerks. Science Research Associates. 1967. 4p. 45c
Junior occupational brief describing work and opportunities.

Finding out about clothing store salespeople. Science Research Associates. 1967. 4p. 45c
Junior occupational brief describing work and opportunities.

SALESMAN, GENERAL—*Continued*

Finding out about house-to-house salespeople. Science Research Associates. 1967. 4p. 45c

Junior occupational brief describing work and opportunities.

Finding out about music store clerks. Science Research Associates. 1967. 4p. 45c

Junior occupational brief summarizing what the work requires and offers.

Finding out about newstand vendors. Science Research Associates. 1967. 4p. 45c

Junior occupational brief describing work and opportunities.

Finding out about salesmen. Science Research Associates. 1967. 4p. 45c

Junior occupational brief summarizing what the work requires and offers.

General salesman (retail and wholesale trade). Chronicle Guidance Publications. 1967. 4p. 35c

Occupational brief explaining the differences and similarities between the work of the wholesale, retail, and the manufacturer's salesmen. Also description of qualifications, working conditions, earnings, methods of entry, opportunities, and outlook.

House-to-house salesman. Careers. 1969. 8p. 35c

Career brief describing work performed, personal qualifications, training, working conditions, earnings, and outlook.

House-to-house salespeople. Science Research Associates. 1967. 4p. 45c

Occupational brief describing the nature of work, requirements, entering the field and advancing, earnings, advantages, disadvantages, and future outlook.

House-to-house salesperson. Chronicle Guidance Publications. 1969. 4p. 35c

Occupational brief summarizing work performed, working conditions, earnings, personal qualifications, ways of determining interest and ability, training, opportunities, methods of entry, and outlook.

Jobs in selling. Science Research Associates. 1965. 32p. $1.15

Describes the variety of job prospects and opportunities within the field, especially for the selling of automobiles, travel, real estate, insurance, or merchandise in department stores.

Newstand vendors. Science Research Associates. 1966. 4p. 45c

Occupational brief describing work, training, qualifications, opportunities, and outlook.

**Opportunities in sales careers. Haas, Kenneth B. Vocational Guidance Manuals. 1968. 126p. $1.95 paper; $3.75 library edition

This manual explains the meaning and scope of salesmanship, describes the various kinds of selling, suggests a pathway for advancement, summarizes opportunities and rewards, and tells what is required of a person who wants to be a success in the selling field.

Opportunities in selling. Council on Opportunities in Selling, Inc. 1968. 24p. Single copy free

Addressed to college students this booklet suggests courses for prospective sales-minded individuals to follow. Also contains information on careers in sales and sales management.

Sales careers—what you should know about them. Sales and Marketing Executives-International. 1967. 20p. Single copy free

Written for college students, this booklet explains how major fields of study relate to careers in sales and marketing management.

Sales clerk. Chronicle Guidance Publications. 1966. 4p. 35c

Occupational brief describing work performed, working conditions, personal qualifications, determination of aptitudes and interests, training requirements, promotional opportunities, and employment outlook.

Sales clerk, variety store. California State Department of Employment. 1964. 5p. Single copy free

Occupational guide describing work, requirements, training, and outlook.

Sales manager, marketing. Careers. 1966. 2p. 20c

Career summary for desk-top file. Duties, qualifications, and outlook.

**Sales occupations. One chapter of *Occupational Outlook Handbook.*

Nature of work, where employed, training, other qualifications, advancement, employment outlook, earnings, and working conditions for each of the following: salesmen and saleswomen in retail stores, salesmen in wholesale trade, manufacturers' salesmen, life insurance agents, property and casualty insurance agents and brokers, real estate salesmen and brokers, and securities salesmen.

Sales promotion manager, retail. Careers. 1968. 20c

Career summary for desk-top file. Duties, qualifications, and outlook.

Salesman. Guidance Centre. 1966. 4p. 35c postpaid

History and importance, nature of work, qualifications, preparation, advancement, outlook, remuneration, advantages, disadvantages, how to get started, and related occupations.

The salesman: ambassador of progress. Sales and Marketing Executives-International. 1968. 16p. Single copy free

Prepared for high school audiences, this is a discussion of opportunities for promotion, advantages, requirements, and the challenges in the field of selling.

Salesman, building materials and supplies. California State Department of Employment. 1965. 3p. Single copy free

Occupational guide describing work, requirements, training, and outlook.

Salesperson. Careers. 1970. 2p. 20c

Career summary for desk-top file. Duties, qualifications, and outlook.

Salesperson, cosmetics. California State Department of Employment. 1965. 6p. Single copy free

Occupational guide describing work, requirements, training, and outlook.

SALESMAN, GENERAL—*Continued*

Salesperson, hardware. California State Department of Employment. 1966. 4p. Single copy free

Occupational guide describing work, requirements, training, and outlook.

Salesperson, home furnishings. California State Department of Employment. 1965. 5p. Single copy free

Occupational guide describing work, requirements, training, and outlook.

Salesperson (wearing apparel). California State Department of Employment. 1964. 4p. Single copy free

Occupational guide describing work, requirements, training, and outlook.

Scientific apparatus salesman. Careers. 1969. 2p. 20c

Career summary for desk-top file. Duties, qualifications, and outlook.

* Selling as a career. Changing Times. 1962. 3p. 15c

Reprint discussing the preparation and future of a career in sales.

The service of the direct seller in today's market place. National Association of Direct Selling Companies. No date. 8p. Free

A recruiting brochure describing nature of work and advantages.

Variety store salesclerks. Science Research Associates. 1966. 4p. 45c

Occupational brief describing jobs for young women, jobs for young men, requirements, training, getting started and advancing, earnings, advantages, disadvantages, and future outlook.

Wholesale trade salesman. Chronicle Guidance Publications. 1969. 4p. 35c

Occupational brief summarizing work performed, qualifications, training, where employed, earnings, and outlook.

**Your career in selling. Liston, Robert A. Julian Messner. 1967. 192p. Library binding $3.64

The areas of retail, wholesale, brokerage, insurance, and industrial selling are discussed, as well as qualifications, education, salaries paid, and opportunities for advancement. Enlivened with case histories and underscoring its positive values, this gives a picture of a future of potential and promise.

**Your future in direct selling. Goodrich, Foster. Richards Rosen Press. Revised 1969. 158p. $4; library edition $3.78. Edition in large type $5.97

Describes the qualifications, training programs, and the increase in direct selling with the suburban trend.

Your job in distribution. Beaumont, John A. and Langan, Kay. Gregg Division, McGraw-Hill Book Company. 1968. 336p. $5.12

Text for use in a survey course describing specific fields in distribution and how to go about getting a job.

See also Automobile salesman; Department store worker; Retail manager

SALESMAN, MANUFACTURERS' AND WHOLESALERS'. *See* **Manufacturers' salesman**

SANITARIAN **079.118**

Educational and other qualifications of public health sanitarians. American Public Health Association. 1957. 8p. Single copy free

General scope of the work, functions, and educational requirements.

**Employment outlook for sanitarians. Bulletin No. 1650–21. Bureau of Labor Statistics, U.S. Department of Labor. Supt. of Documents. 1970. 8p. 10c

Reprint from the *Occupational Outlook Handbook.*

Environmental health services. Pages 104-117 of *Health Careers Guidebook.*

Information about qualifications, training, and opportunities for the sanitary engineer and the sanitarian.

Finding out about public health sanitarians. Science Research Associates. 1967. 4p. 45c

Junior occupational brief summarizing what the work requires and offers.

**Health manpower source book—sanitarians. Public Health Service, U.S. Department of Health, Education, and Welfare. Publication Number 263. Supt. of Documents. 1963. 52p. 35c

Basic data on the employment, salaries, education, location, and characteristics of sanitarians. Many statistical summaries.

The professional sanitarian. National Association of Sanitarians. No date. 16p. Single copy free

Description of the job requirements, need, advancement, and employment outlook.

* Public health sanitarians. Science Research Associates. 1968. 4p. 45c

Occupational brief describing nature of work, training, qualifications, opportunities, advantages, disadvantages, and future outlook. Selected references.

Sanitarian. California State Department of Employment. 1968. 4p. Single copy free

Occupational guide describing work, requirements, training, and outlook.

Sanitarian. Chronicle Guidance Publications. 1967. 4p. 35c

Occupational brief summarizing work performed, where employed, hours and earnings, educational requirements, list of schools, personal qualifications, and outlook.

Sanitarians. One section of *Occupational Outlook Handbook.*

Nature of work, places of employment, training, other qualifications, outlook, earnings, and working conditions.

SANITARY ENGINEER 005.081

Finding out about sanitary engineers. Science Research Associates. 1967. 4p. 45c

Junior occupational brief containing concise facts about the job.

Sanitary engineer. Careers. 1970. 2p. 20c

Career summary for desk-top file. Duties, qualifications, and outlook.

**Sanitary engineers. Science Research Associates. 1968. 4p. 45c

Occupational brief describing nature of work, duties, requirements, training, earnings, advantages, disadvantages, and future outlook.

SAWMILL WORKER 667. and 669.

Finding out about sawmill workers. Science Research Associates. 1967. 4p. 45c

Junior occupational brief describing work and opportunities.

Sawmill occupations. Chronicle Guidance Publications. 1969. 4p. 35c

Occupational brief summarizing definition, history, work performed, personal qualifications, training requirements, opportunities for advancement, working conditions, earnings, and employment outlook.

SCHOOL ADMINISTRATOR 091.118

Dean of women. Careers. 1967. 2p. 20c

Career summary for desk-top file. Duties, qualifications, and outlook.

Finding out about school principals. Science Research Associates. 1967. 4p. 45c

Junior occupational brief summarizing what the work requires and offers.

**The principalship—job specifications and salary considerations for the 70's. National Association of Secondary School Principals. 1970. 68p. $2

These guidelines contain an updated job description, performance criteria, and criteria for designing salary structures. The appendix contains selected data on administrative salaries.

School principal. Chronicle Guidance Publications. 1968. 4p. 35c

Occupational brief summarizing duties, requirements, entrance, advancement, and outlook.

School superintendents. Science Research Associates. 1966. 4p. 45c

Occupational brief describing work, qualifications, training, earnings, advantages, disadvantages, and outlook. Selected references.

Supervisory and administrative management occupations: a suggested curriculum guide. U.S. Office of Education. Supt. of Documents. 1970. 208p. $2

Suggested courses of study, texts, teaching materials, and other information helpful to those involved in administering vocational education programs in supervision and administration.

SCIENTIST 02, 04, and 07

American science manpower. Government Printing Office. Supt. of Documents. 1970. 277p. $2

Report of the National Register of Scientific and Technical Personnel.

**Can I be a scientist or engineer? Let's find out. General Motors, Public Relations Staff. 1961. 24p. Free

Description of work in mathematics, chemistry, physics, and seven main branches of engineering, with typical jobs in each. Includes also opportunities and suggested high school preparation.

A career for you as a science teacher. National Science Teachers Association. 1966. 24p. 25c

Booklet discusses the rewards and challenges of science teaching, the preparation required, and the advantages of such a career.

**Careers and opportunities in science. Pollack, Philip. Dutton and Company. 1960. 194p. $4.95

Revised edition providing information about work in chemistry, physics, atomic power production, geology, biology, conservation, and medical research. For each special field the author discusses the ever-growing opportunities, the personal and educational qualifications, working conditions, prospects for advancement, and further rewards. This book communicates to the reader a sense of the creative excitement that a career in science has to offer, while at the same time imparting the requirements of hard work and adequate training.

Challengers of the unknown. Brewer, Fred. Four Winds Press. 1966. 128p. $2.95; library binding $3.27

Thirteen scientists probe the mysteries of earth and space.

The creative scientist—his training and his role. U.S. Atomic Energy Commission, Division of Technical Information. 1964. 12p. Free

Reprint of an address to open a National Science Fair, stressing that research utilizes many talents.

Dr. George Washington Carver: scientist. Graham, Shirley and Lipscomb, George. Julian Messner. 1944. 248p. $3.95; library binding $3.64

Biography of the Negro scientist whose research and experiments helped to change agriculture in the South.

Edison at work: the Thomas A. Edison laboratory at West Orange, N.J. Hutchings, David. Hastings House. 1969. 94p. $4.95; library edition $3.69

A study of Edison's technical achievements, especially in his laboratory, which is now a museum. For grades 6 to 9.

**Employment of scientists and engineers in the United States, 1950-66. National Science Foundation. Supt. of Documents. 1968. 55p. 70c

Presents the findings of an employment study including many sectors of the economy by each major scientific occupational group.

SCIENTIST—*Continued*

Eternal quest: the story of the great naturalists. Adams, Alexander B. Putnam's Sons. 1969. 509p. $10.95

The author portrays the lives and works of many scientists and naturalists, revealing their unique contributions to developments in botany, zoology, geology, astronomy, and physics.

George Washington Carver: an American biography. Holt, Rackham. Doubleday and Company. 1963. 360p. $4.95

Biography of the Negro scientist.

Incredible man of science: Irving Langmuir. Westervelt, Virginia V. Julian Messner. 1968. 192p. $3.50; library binding $3.34

Biography of the pioneer researcher of the atom. A Nobel prize winner for his studies in surface chemistry, Langmuir produced breakthroughs in electronic technology, useful in the two world wars.

International science youth program. Science Clubs of America. 1969. 4p. Free

Brief descriptions of science service activities to encourage science talent.

Jobs in science. Science Research Associates. 1963. 48p. $1.15

Describes the variety of job prospects and opportunities within this field, especially for the agronomist, astronomer, chemist, meteorologist, biologist, and physicist.

Keys to careers in science and technology. National Science Teachers Association. 1967. 56p. $1

Bibliography of booklets and inexpensive materials for career guidance in thirty-one fields of science. List of names and addresses of professional scientific organizations.

**Listen to leaders in science. Love, A. and Childers, J. S. David McKay Company. 1964. 278p. $5.50

Eighteen essays written by recognized leaders with particlar emphasis on career possibilities.

Madame Curie, a biography. Curie, Eve. Doubleday and Company. 1949. 393p. $5.95

Biography which unmistakably points out the value of effort and persistence.

Marie Curie. McKown, Robin. Coward-McCann, Inc. 1959. 128p. $3.49

This biography conveys the spirit of perseverance and devotion to science of the woman who discovered radium. Written for ages 10 to 14.

Marie Curie, discoverer of radium. Henry, Joanne Landers. Macmillan Company. 1966. 44p. $2.95; library edition $3.24

This book shows the value of perseverance and devotion to science as well as some insight into the methods of the research scientist. For grades 4 to 7.

The microscope. Harrison, C. William. Julian Messner. 1965. 190p. $3.95; library binding $3.64

Describes the history and development of the microscope, covering the people involved and what they did.

National survey of compensation, scientists and engineers in research and development. Govt. Printing Office. Supt. of Documents. 1970. 269p. $2.50

Presents the results of a survey on the compensation paid to scientific and engineering personnel engaged in research and development in the United States.

Nine roads to tomorrow. Halacy, D. S., Jr. Macrae Smith Company. 1965. 176p. $3.95

Cites the rapid growth of development of the laser, electric computer, communications satellite, solar battery, and ground effect machines.

PhD. scientists and engineers in private industry. U.S. Department of Labor. Supt. of Documents. 1970. 20p. 30c

Results of a survey of manpower 1968-1980.

Picture book of today's scientists. Gourlay, Walter E. Sterling Publishing Company. 1962. 64p. $1.10 paper

This book presents the discoveries and brief biographies of twenty-eight leading modern scientists.

A program for basic research in the physical sciences. Alfred P. Sloan Foundation. 1968. 16p. Free

Description of program which provides grants to selected young scientists for basic research. Candidates do not apply but are nominated by department chairmen or other scientists.

**Salaries and selected characteristics of U.S. scientists. National Science Foundation. Supt. of Documents. 1969. 8p. 10c

A report on the numbers and median salaries of scientists in the major science fields, by highest degree attained, type of employer, and primary work activity. Also includes the numbers of scientists reporting some Federal support of their work, by field of science and Government programs.

Science activities handbook. Science Clubs of America. 1968. 64p. $1. Free to sponsors of science clubs.

Ideas to help sponsors with science club programs and other science youth activities. Good reference lists on scholarships and careers.

Science and technology in the world of the future. Bronwell, Arthur, ed. Wiley and Sons, Inc. 1970. 394p. $11.95

An analysis of possible use of science and technology in the years to come. Among topics treated are interplanetary space travel, the exploration of the oceans, hypersonic air transportation, and the use of lasers, computers, and other advanced mechanisms.

Science for society: a bibliography. American Association for the Advancement of Science. 1970. 42p. Distributed free to high schools

The purpose of this compilation of references is to encourage serious thought and increase knowledge of problems of population, food, pollution, race, aggression, and the quality of life.

SCIENTIST—*Continued*

Science: man and change. U.S. Atomic Energy Commission, Division of Technical Information. 1968. 107p. Free

A collection of speeches including a discussion of how to become a scientist and the proliferation of the peaceful atom.

Science packet. University of Missouri. 1968. 5 leaflets. Free

Example of recruiting leaflets describing work and training of the earth scientist, geophysicist, chemist, geophysicist, and mathematician.

Science projects handbook. Science Clubs of America. 1965. 254p. 55c

Includes a discussion on how to become a scientist. Describes a variety of successful projects done by winners in the Science Talent Search and the National Science Fair.

Scientific careers in the Agricultural Research Service. U.S. Dept. of Agriculture. Supt. of Documents. 1969. 37p. 55c

Opportunities and some facts regarding employment.

**Scientist. Morison, Robert S. Macmillan Company. 1964. 200p. $4.95

The author draws upon his experience as a physician to provide a picture of education and necessary preparation, the various opportunities, and the excitement of achievements in modern science.

Scientists and engineers in the Federal personnel system. U.S. Civil Service Commission. Supt. of Documents. 1968. 23p. 35c

Information on position classification, selection of staff, and the pay system. Also describes the methods of training for excellence, recognizing achievement, and encouraging a creative environment.

Scientists who changed the world. Poole, Lynn and Poole, Gray. Dodd, Mead and Company. 1960. 164p. $3.50

Biographies of seventeen pioneers who have opened up new frontiers in their various fields of science.

Scientists who work with astronauts. Poole, Lynn and Poole, Gray. Dodd, Mead and Company. 1964. 192p. $3.50

Biographies of key men and women in twelve areas of science that are essential to the success of the space program.

She lived for science: Irene Joliot-Curie. McKown, Robin. Julian Messner. 1961. 192p. $3.50; library binding $3.34

Biography of the oldest daughter of the noted Marie and Pierre Curie, who with her husband discovered artificial radioactivity and won a Nobel prize in chemistry. For grades 7 to 11.

Sources of career information in scientific fields. Manufacturing Chemists' Association. 1969. 28p. Single copy free

List of free and inexpensive materials about careers in major scientific fields.

The story of Madame Curie. Thorne, Alice. Scholastic Book Services. 1961. 160p. 50c paper

Paperback edition of biography of the scientist. This title is available to schools only, through the Scholastic Book Services.

Support of full-time graduate students in the sciences, fall 1967. National Science Foundation. Supt. of Documents. 1969. 157p. $1.25

These charts and statistical data provide information about major support sources and other means of support for graduate students. Enrollment figures for the various fields of science are also given.

Twelve pioneers of science. Sootin, Harry. Vanguard Press. 1960. 254p. $3.50

Inspiring biographies of twelve scientists from various countries, each a pioneer in his field. All of them persisted through years of failure and disappointment but continued to explore frontier areas of human knowledge such as radioactivity, chlorine, electric battery, barometric pressure, potassium, and electromagnetic waves.

* Unusual careers. Munzer, Martha A. Alfred A. Knopf, Inc. 1962. 142p. $3

Opportunities in careers necessary to conserve the country's natural resources, especially the city and regional planner, ecologist, geologist, meteorologist, oceanographer, research chemist, sanitary engineer, and solar scientist.

Women of modern science. Yost, Edna. Dodd, Mead and Company. 1959. 176p. $3.50

Biographies of eleven women who have made contributions to research in the science to which they were dedicated.

See also Engineer; Research worker

SECRETARY 201.368

Applied secretarial practice. Sixth edition. Gregg, John Robert; Fries, Albert; Rowe, Margaret; and Travis, Dorothy. Gregg Division, McGraw-Hill Book Company. 1968. 528p. $5.96

Textbook for use with classes in secretarial practice. Includes skills and personal qualities needed, duties, finding a job, and how to succeed on the job.

Certified professional secretary. National Secretaries Association. 1968. 6p. Single copy free

Membership qualifications and benefits of the certification.

College secretarial procedures. Third edition. Place, Irene and Hicks, Charles. Gregg Publishing Division, McGraw-Hill Book Company. 1964. 536p. $6.75

This college textbook includes discussion of many secretarial duties.

Complete secretary's handbook. Doris, Lillian and Miller, Besse May. Prentice-Hall, Inc. 1970. 528p. $6.95

Suggestions on procedures for handling office routines and related responsibilities.

Confidential secretary. Carr, Harriett H. Macmillan Company. 1958. 212p. $2.95

Career fiction. As confidential secretary to a business executive, Joyce finds excitement in her job and in the nation's capital. Written for ages 12 to 16.

SECRETARY—*Continued*

An exciting business career awaits you. National Career Center. 1970. 8p. 10c

An example of an illustrated brochure describing executive and specialized secretaries.

Executive secretary. Careers. 1970. 8p. 35c

Career brief describing duties, working conditions, personal qualifications, training, earnings, places of employment, opportunities for men, outlook, and ways of measuring one's interest and ability.

The executive secretary: patterns for success. Ingoldsby, Patricia and Focarino, Joseph. Doubleday and Company. 1969. 336p. $5.95

A useful guide for the aspiring secretary, revealing the nature and demands of the work. Intended for secretaries in the $10,000 bracket. Included in each chapter is a wide range of do's and don'ts to assist a secretary to become a competent well-paid executive secretary. An appendix lists sources of commonly needed information.

Finding out about secretaries. Science Research Associates. 1967. 4p. 45c

Junior occupational brief containing concise facts about the job.

Foreign service secretaries. Assignment, worldwide with the U.S. Department of State. U.S. Department of State. Publication Number RB-4. 1968. 16p. Free

Includes qualifications for employment, nature of work, training, benefits, and opportunities.

The girl with the halo. Underwood Corporation. 1962. 24p. 50c

A cross section of opinion from executives throughout the country on what is needed to become an ideal secretary. Also contains "Twenty tips for tiptop typing."

The high-paid secretary. Becker, Esther R. and Rollason, Peggy N. Prentice-Hall, Inc. 1967. 233p. $5.95

This is a book on secretarial practice which goes beyond the intent of enhancing the secretary's earning power.

Male secretary. Careers. 1968. 8p. 35c

Career brief describing duties, working conditions, training, personal qualifications, employment prospects, and earnings.

Male secretary. Chronicle Guidance Publications. 1969. 4p. 35c

Occupational brief summarizing work performed, working conditions, personal requirements, training, opportunities, and outlook.

My life on the caviar circuit. Chronicle Guidance Publications. 1969. 2p. 35c

Reprinted article from *Today's Secretary* discusses a secretary's experiences working for a publishing company.

**Secretarial careers. Anderson, Ruth I. Henry Z. Walck, Inc. 1961. 106p. $3.75

Presentation of the responsibilities, opportunities, qualifications, and personality and temperament factors to be considered. Includes discussion of specialized secretarial work such as legal, medical, foreign service, bilingual positions, public stenography, social secretary, and civil service. Reading list. Illustrated.

Secretarial futures. Bryant College. 1969. 36p. Single copy free

Booklet discussing the value of a college education for a secretary, good grooming, and qualities that lead to promotion.

Secretarial jobs. Alumnae Advisory Center. 1967. 6p. 35c

Reprint from *Mademoiselle* describing the positions of several new-style secretaries. Also contains considerable sensible advice.

Secretaries and stenographers. Science Research Associates. 1968. 4p. 45c

Occupational brief describing nature of work, qualifications, preparation, opportunities, advantages, disadvantages, and future outlook.

**Secretary. Careers. 1968. 8p. 35c

Career brief summarizing duties, working conditions, training requirements, personal qualifications, employment prospects, earnings, related careers, measuring one's interest and ability, and suggested high school program. Additional references.

Secretary. Chronicle Guidance Publications. 1966. 4p. 35c

Occupational brief summarizing work performed, working conditions, qualifications, training, opportunities, and outlook.

Secretary. Guidance Centre. 1970. 4p. 35c postpaid

Definition, qualifications, preparation, advancement, outlook, remuneration, advantages, disadvantages, how to get started, and related occupations.

Secretary. Michigan Employment Security Commission. 1967. 2p. Single copy free

Job brief summarizing occupational data for use in Michigan.

The secretary at work. Strony, Madeline and Greenaway, M. Emily. Gregg Publishing Division, McGraw-Hill Company. 1958. 224p. $3.00

A textbook for secretarial office practice classes that shows the importance of personality and proper work habits for success in secretarial work. Emphasizes proper grooming and public relations as well as skills. Illustrated with case histories.

Secretary (clerical). California State Department of Employment. 1966. 5p. Single copy free

Occupational guide describing work, requirements, training, and outlook.

The secretary's handbook; a manual of correct usage. Taintor, Sarah, Monro, Kate, and Shertzer, M. Macmillan Company. 1969. 530p. $6.95

This is the ninth revised edition of this reference book. Suggests secretarial procedures, especially for the writing of letters and other business forms.

SECRETARY—*Continued*

Standard handbook for secretaries. Hutchinson, Lois. McGraw-Hill Book Company. 1969. 638p. $7.95

This is a useful reference book which reveals the nature of the work, responsibilities, opportunities, and varied duties.

Stephanie Lane: editorial secretary. Haughey, Betty E. Julian Messner. 1967. 192p. $3.50; library binding $3.34

Career fiction. Story of an editorial secretary who wins promotion to the position of assistant editor, showing nature of the work and problems.

Strictly for secretaries. Whitcomb, Helen and Whitcomb, John. McGraw-Hill Book Company. Revised 1965. 167p. $3.95

A reference book for secretaries including discussion of the most effective way to apply for the position one wants and preparation for the top secretarial position.

The successful secretary. Royal Typewriter Company. 1968. 32p. Single copy free

This is a condensed secretarial handbook which includes the personal qualities of a good secretary and brief hints for transcription and correct telephone techniques.

Technical secretary. Careers. 1969. 2p. 20c

Career summary for desk-top file. Duties, qualifications, and outlook.

White collar girl. Hall, Marjory. Funk and Wagnalls Company. 1959. 248p. $2.95

Career fiction. Experiences of a girl in secretarial school and her first year of work.

Your career as a secretary. United Business Schools Association. 1968. 24p. Free

Includes description of various specialties such as court reporter, executive secretary, and engineering-scientific secretary.

**Your future as a secretary. Noyes, Nell Braly. Richards Rosen Press. Revised 1969. 158p. $4; library edition $3.78

An experienced secretary describes various positions open to a skilled secretary and the qualifications needed.

See also Legal secretary; Medical secretary; Stenographer

SECURITIES SALESMAN 251.258

Bond trader. Guidance Centre. 1968. 4p. 35c postpaid

Definition, nature of work, qualifications, advancement, earnings, working conditions, advantages, disadvantages, and how to get started.

Employment opportunities for college graduates for the position of trainee investigator. U.S. Securities and Exchange Commission. 1962. 2p. Free

Information about the location of positions, duties to be performed, salaries, career opportunities, fringe benefits, training, recruitment policy, and civil service examination.

**Employment outlook for securities salesman. Bulletin No. 1650–60. Bureau of Labor Statistics, U.S. Department of Labor. Supt. of Documents. 1970. 8p. 10c

Reprint from the *Occupational Outlook Handbook.*

Employment outlook for securities salesmen. Chronicle Guidance Publications. 1968. 4p. 35c

Reprinted article from *Occupational Outlook Quarterly* discusses nature of work, where employed, training, advancement, outlook, earnings, and working conditions.

Financial analyst. California State Department of Employment. 1966. 3p. Single copy free

Duties, working conditions, pay, hours, entrance requirements, training, and employment prospects.

Finding out about securities salesmen. Science Research Associates. 1967. 4p. 45c

Junior occupational brief describing work and opportunities.

**Opportunities in the securities business. Shulsky, Sam. Vocational Guidance Manuals. 1963. 126p. $1.95 paper; library edition $3.75

Description of the world of finance, requirements for entering, personal attributes, how to get started, and opportunities in brokerage, investment banking, investment counseling, and mutual funds.

Securities broker. California State Department of Employment. 1967. 4p. Single copy free

Occupational guide describing work, requirements, training, and outlook.

* Securities salesman. Careers. 1968. 2p. 20c

Career summary for desk-top file. Duties, qualifications, and outlook.

Securities salesmen. Science Research Associates. 1966. 4p. 45c

Occupational brief describing nature of work, requirements, methods of entering and advancing, earnings, advantages, disadvantages, and future outlook.

Securities salesmen. One section of *Occupational Outlook Handbook.*

Nature of work, where employed, outlook, and working conditions.

Security officer. California State Department of Employment. 1965. 5p. Single copy free

Occupational guide describing work, requirements, training, and outlook.

SECURITIES SALESMAN—*Continued*

**Wall Street careers. Sarnoff, Paul. Julian Messner. 1968. 189p. $3.95; library edition $3.64

Considerable vocational information for young people who are interested in the buying and selling of investment securities. An appendix gives the duties, compensation, training, and education for each of fifteen Wall Street jobs in member firms. Illustrated.

See also Financial institutions industry worker

SERVICE-STATION ATTENDANT. *See* Automobile-service-station attendant

SEWAGE-PLANT OPERATOR 955.782

**Employment outlook for waste water treatment plant operators. Bulletin No. 1650–104. Bureau of Labor Statistics, U.S. Department of Labor. Supt. of Documents. 1970. 8p. 10c

Reprint from the *Occupational Outlook Handbook.*

Waste water treatment plant operators (sewage plant operator). One section of *Occupational Outlook Handbook.*

Nature of work, places of employment, training, qualifications, advancement, earnings, and working conditions.

Water treatment plant operator. California State Department of Employment. 1968. 2p. Single copy free

Occupational guide describing work, requirements, training, and outlook.

SEWING MACHINE OPERATOR 786.782

Drapery seamstress. Careers. 1967. 2p. 20c

Career summary for desk-top file. Duties, qualifications, and outlook.

Finding out about sewing machine operators. Science Research Associates. 1967. 4p. 45c

Junior occupational brief describing work and opportunities.

Sewing machine operator. California State Department of Employment. 1966. 3p. Single copy free

Occupational guide describing work, requirements, training, and outlook.

Sewing-machine operator. Careers. 1966. 8p. 35c

Career brief describing duties, working conditions, training, personal qualifications, earnings, advancement opportunities, and outlook.

Sewing machine operators. Science Research Associates. 1970. 4p. 45c

Occupational brief describing nature of work, training, qualifications, opportunities, and outlook.

SHEEP HERDER 413.887

Sheep herder. California State Department of Employment. 1966. 4p. Single copy free

Nature of work, duties, working conditions, employment outlook, wages, hours, training requirements, and how to find employment.

Sheep: life on the South Dakota range. Gilfillan, Archer B. University of Minnesota Press. 1957. 272p. $4

One of the few books on sheepherding.

SHEET-METAL WORKER 804.281

Finding out about sheet-metal workers. Science Research Associates. 1967. 4p. 45c

Junior occupational brief containing some concise facts about the job and listing ways of finding out about the nature of the work.

Job grading standards for sheet metal mechanic. Civil Service Commission. Supt. of Documents. 1969. 7p. 10c

This job classification outlines duties, skill, and knowledge requirements, responsibility, physical effort, and working conditions which determine job grade levels in accordance with the U.S. Civil Service Commission standards.

Sheet metal worker. Careers. 1969. 2p. 20c

Career summary for desk-top file. Duties, qualifications, and outlook.

**Sheet metal worker. Chronicle Guidance Publications. 1967. 4p. 35c

Occupational brief summarizing work performed, where employed, qualifications, training, earnings, advancement, and outlook.

Sheet metal worker. Guidance Centre. 1967. 4p. 35c postpaid

Definition, history and importance of the work, qualifications, preparation, earnings, working conditions, how to get started, advantages, and disadvantages.

Sheet metal worker, aircraft. California State Department of Employment. 1964. 2p. Single copy free

Occupational guide describing work, requirements, training, and outlook.

Sheet metal worker (sheet metal worker apprentice). California State Department of Employment. 1965. 5p. Single copy free

Occupational guide describing work, requirements, training, and outlook.

Sheet metal workers. Michigan Employment Security Commission. 1962. 2p. Single copy free

Job brief summarizing occupational data for use in Michigan.

* Sheet metal workers. Science Research Associates. 1966. 4p. 45c

Occupational brief describing nature of work, requirements, apprenticeship training, paths of advancement, earnings, advantages, disadvantages, and future outlook.

**Sheet-metal workers. One section of *Occupational Outlook Handbook*.

Nature of work, where employed, training, other qualifications, advancement, employment outlook, earnings, and working conditions.

SHIP CAPTAIN AND OFFICER 197.

Finding out about ship pilots. Science Research Associates. 1967. 4p. 45c

Junior occupational brief describing work and opportunities.

Ships captains and officers. Chronicle Guidance Publications. 1966. 4p. 35c

Occupational brief summarizing duties, number employed, qualifications, preparation, formal maritime training, earnings, conditions of work, and methods of entering.

SHIPBUILDER 80

Finding out about ship designers. Science Research Associates. 1967. 4p. 45c

Junior occupational brief containing concise facts about the job.

Ship and boat building industry. Chronicle Guidance Publications. 1967. 8p. 50c

Occupational brief summarizing nature and location of industry, how ships and boats are built, occupations in industry, working conditions, personal requirements, hours and earnings, education, and training opportunities.

Ship designers. Science Research Associates. 1968. 4p. 45c

Occupational brief describing work, training, qualifications, opportunities, and outlook.

Shipbuilders. Science Research Associates. 1967. 4p. 45c

Occupational brief describing various kinds of work, qualifications, training, earnings, advantages, disadvantages, and future outlook.

SHIPPING AND RECEIVING CLERK 222.138

**Employment outlook for shipping and receiving clerks. Bulletin No. 1650–53. Bureau of Labor Statistics, U.S. Department of Labor. Supt. of Documents. 1970. 8p. 10c

Reprint from the *Occupational Outlook Handbook.*

Finding out about shipping clerks. Science Research Associates. 1967. 4p. 45c

Junior occupational brief summarizing what the work requires and offers.

Shipping and receiving clerk. California State Department of Employment. 1968. 2p. Single copy free

Duties, pay, hours, finding the job, training, promotion, and employment prospects.

Shipping and receiving clerks. Chronicle Guidance Publications. 1968. 4p. 35c

Occupational brief describing nature of work, qualifications, working conditions, and opportunities for promotion.

**Shipping and receiving clerks. One section of *Occupational Outlook Handbook*.

Nature of work, where employed, training, other qualifications, advancement, employment outlook, earnings, and working conditions.

* Shipping clerks. Science Research Associates. 1970. 4p. 45c

Occupational brief describing nature of work, training, qualifications, opportunities, and outlook.

SHOE MANUFACTURING WORKER 788.

Finding out about shoe salesmen. Science Research Associates. 1967. 4p. 45c

Junior occupational brief describing work and opportunities.

Shoe manufacturing industry. Chronicle Guidance Publications. 1968. 4p. 35c

Occupational brief summarizing trends and outlook, automation and hand operations, work performed, working conditions, training required, personal qualifications, earnings, and advancement opportunities.

Shoe manufacturing workers. Science Research Associates. 1967. 4p. 45c

Occupational brief describing nature of work, requirements, earnings, getting started, advantages, disadvantages, and future outlook.

SHOE REPAIRMAN 365.381

**Employment outlook for shoe repairman. Bulletin No. 1650–102. Bureau of Labor Statistics, U.S. Department of Labor. Supt. of Documents. 1970. 8p. 10c

Reprint from the *Occupational Outlook Handbook*.

Finding out about shoe repairmen. Science Research Associates. 1967. 4p. 45c

Junior occupational brief containing some concise facts about the job and listing ways of finding out about the nature of the work. Includes suggestions for reading.

Shoe repairman. California State Department of Employment. 1964. 3p. Single copy free

Occupational guide describing work, requirements, training, and outlook.

**Shoe repairman. Careers. 1968. 8p. 35c

Career brief describing duties, working conditions, training, personal qualifications, earnings, and outlook.

Shoe repairman. Chronicle Guidance Publications. 1969. 4p. 35c

Occupational brief summarizing work performed, working conditions, hours, earnings, personal qualifications, training requirements, opportunities, employment outlook, and entry into the job.

Shoe repairman. Guidance Centre. 1966. 4p. 35c postpaid

Nature of work, qualifications, working conditions, outlook, earnings, advantages, disadvantages, and related occupations.

SHOE REPAIRMAN—*Continued*

Shoe repairman. Michigan Employment Security Commission. 1965. 2p. Single copy free

Job brief summarizing occupational data for use in Michigan.

**Shoe repairmen. Science Research Associates. 1967. 4p. 45c

Occupational brief describing nature of work, requirements, getting started, earnings, advantages, disadvantages, and future outlook.

Shoe repairmen. One section of *Occupational Outlook Handbook.*

Nature of work, places of employment, training, qualifications, employment outlook, earnings, and working conditions.

Starting and managing a small shoe service shop. Small Business Administration. Supt. of Documents. 1968. 86p. 45c

Outlines the problems and opportunities that await a prospective shop owner and suggests some techniques for meeting them. Provides basic information about management and keeping up with developments in the field.

SHORTHAND REPORTER 202.388

* Employment opportunities for shorthand reporters. Chronicle Guidance Publications. 1967. 3p. 35c

Reprinted article from *Occupational Outlook Quarterly* discusses work performed, where employed, qualifications, outlook, and earnings.

Finding out about shorthand reporters. Science Research Associates. 1967. 4p. 45c

Junior occupational brief containing concise facts about the job.

Shorthand reporters. Science Research Associates. 1968. 4p. 45c

Occupational brief describing nature of work, requirements, preparation, getting started, earnings, advantages, disadvantages, and future outlook.

Shorthand reporting as a career. National Shorthand Reporters Association. 1968. 16p. 25c

Information about the work, qualifications, and opportunities. Includes names of the state shorthand association secretaries.

**Your future as a shorthand reporter. Van Allen, Edward J. Richards Rosen Press. 1969. 140p. $4; library edition $3.78

Essential information on training, qualifications, and remuneration is accompanied by accounts of court cases illustrating the nature of the shorthand reporter's job. Emphasizes the growing demand in both free-lance work and in government employment. Appended are a table of official salaries by state and lists of shorthand reporting schools for training.

SIGN WRITER (HAND) 970.081

Sign painter. California State Department of Employment. 1965. 5p. Single copy free

Occupational guide describing work, requirements, training, and outlook.

**Sign writer (hand). Chronicle Guidance Publications. 1968. 4p. 35c
Occupational brief summarizing work performed, number employed, qualifications, preparation, conditions of work, earnings, and methods of entering.

SINGER AND SINGING TEACHER 152.

Awards for singers. Central Opera Service. 1969. 16p. 50c
A list, arranged alphabetically by states, of colleges and other organizations that offer scholarships, competitions, grants, and awards to singers. Also includes special opportunities for young professional singers.

Finding out about opera and concert singers. Science Research Associates. 1967. 4p. 45c
Junior occupational brief summarizing what the work requires and offers.

Finding out about singers in popular music. Science Research Associates. 1967. 4p. 45c
Junior occupational brief summarizing what the work requires and offers.

Finding out about singing teachers. Science Research Associates. 1967. 4p. 45c
Junior occupational brief containing concise facts about the job.

Singers. Science Research Associates. 1966. 4p. 45c
Occupational brief describing work, qualifications, training, earnings, getting started, and things to consider. Selected references.

**Singers and singing teachers. One section of *Occupational Outlook Handbook.*
Nature of work, where employed, training, other qualifications, employment outlook, earnings, and working conditions.

Vocalists. Chronicle Guidance Publications. 1968. 4p. 35c
Occupational brief summarizing work performed, working conditions, earnings, education and training, personal qualifications, and outlook.

See also Musician; Music teacher

SKI INSTRUCTOR 153.228

Ski instructor. California State Department of Employment. 1965. 3p. Single copy free
Occupational guide describing work, requirements, training, and outlook.

Ski instructor. One unit in the *Occupational Guidance* series published by Finney Company. Not available separately.
Description of work, opportunities, and outlook.

SKILLED TRADES WORKER 62, 63, and 86

Blue-collar workers in the Federal service. Careers. 1970. 4p. 35c
Career brief describing duties, working conditions, training, earnings, qualifications, and opportunities.

SKILLED TRADES WORKER—*Continued*

Can I be a craftsman? Let's find out. General Motors, Public Relations Staff. 1961. 24p. Free

Description of work of machinist, die maker, tool maker, pattern maker, sheet metal worker, millwright, machine repairman, and electrician. Includes a check list for self-inventory of interests and abilities and explanation of the apprentice program.

Good jobs waiting for men who learn a trade. Changing times. 1966. 3p. 15c

For each of seventeen trades, tabular information is given concerning training, qualifications, pay, and opportunities.

Job qualification system for trades and labor occupations. Government Printing Office. Supt. of Documents. 1969. 83p. $1

This publication tells how to identify the basic skills, knowledge, and abilities needed to be able to do the work in Federal trades and labor jobs and how to determine the extent to which applicants' qualifications match the job requirements.

Opportunities in trades and crafts with the Federal Government. U.S. Civil Service Commission. 1964. 8p. Single copy free

Describes opportunities for skilled and semiskilled workers and explains how to locate and apply for jobs.

The shortage of skilled and technical workers. Franke, Walter and Sobel, Irvin. D. C. Heath and Company. 1970. 352p. $15

Evaluation of labor market adjustments to shortages of workers such as medical technologists and tool and die makers.

**Skilled trades and other manual occupations. One section of *Occupational Outlook Handbook.*

Nature of work, training, qualifications, employment trends, and outlook.

Skilled trades for girls. Chronicle Guidance Publications. 1968. 7p. 50c

Reprinted article from *Occupational Outlook Quarterly* reports that in some crafts the employment of women has increased recently at a faster rate than that of men.

Trade and industrial training: earned degrees, by level, sex, and institution. One section of *Earned Degrees Conferred.*

List of seventy-four colleges and number of bachelor's degrees conferred by each in trade and industrial training.

SOCIAL SCIENTIST 05

Applied social sciences: earned degrees, by level, sex, and institution. One section of *Earned Degrees Conferred.*

Useful for judging the extent of a college's program in each of the following specialties: agricultural economics, foreign service programs, industrial relations, public administration, and social work.

Careers in the social sciences. Changing Times. 1960. 4p. 15c

Report on career opportunities in the social sciences.

**Employment outlook for social scientists. Bulletin No. 1650–44. Bureau of Labor Statistics, U.S. Department of Labor. Supt. of Documents. 1970. 16p. 15c

Reprint from the *Occupational Outlook Handbook.* Includes anthropologists, economists, geographers, historians, political scientists, and sociologists.

My several lives; memoirs of a social inventor. Conant, James B. Harper and Row. 1969. 701p. $12.50

The memoirs include activities in science, weapons development, pedagogy, statecraft, and diplomacy. Sixteen pages of illustrations.

**Social sciences. One chapter of *Occupational Outlook Handbook.*

Nature of work, where employed, training, other qualifications, and employment outlook for each of the following: economists, historians, political scientists, sociologists, anthropologists, and geographers.

Social sciences: earned degrees, by level, sex, and institution. One section of *Earned Degrees Conferred.*

Useful for judging the extent of a college's program in each of the following specialties: anthropology, basic social sciences, economics, history, international relations, political sciences, and sociology.

See also Scientist

SOCIAL WORKER 195.108

Annotated listing of audio-visual materials. National Commission for Social Work Careers. 1967. 13p. 25c. Single copy free

Useful for a range of recruiting activities to careers in social welfare.

Better human relations—the challenge of social work. Freeman, Lucy. Public Affairs Pamphlet. 1967. 28p. 25c

Describes the many ways of helping people and the unlimited opportunities.

The career that makes a difference! American Public Welfare Association. 1968. 4p. 5c

Brief statement of need, opportunities, nature of work, and advantages.

**Careers in social service. Gay, Kathlyn. Julian Messner. 1969. 192p. $3.95; library binding $3.64

This book shows the vast scope of social service under the authority of Federal, state or local government, church institutions, and private foundations. It covers the preparation, special skills, and qualifications needed. Lists of colleges offering graduate and undergraduate training.

**Careers in social work. Koestler, Frances. Henry Z. Walck, Inc. 1963. 128p. $4.50

Description of the main fields of social work, qualifications and training needed, and how to get a foretaste of the work. The rewards and drawbacks are candidly discussed.

SOCIAL WORKER–*Continued*

Careers in social work. Changing Times. 1961. 3p. 15c
Facts on training, pay, and opportunities in social work.

**Counselor's kit for vocational guidance counselors and social workers. National Commission for Social Work Careers. 1968. 20 booklets. $2.50
Career items that would cost $3.15 if purchased individually. Three additional kits are available at a cost of one dollar each for high school students, college students, and college graduates.

**Employment outlook for social workers. Bulletin No. 1650–45. Bureau of Labor Statistics, U.S. Department of Labor. Supt. of Documents. 1970. 8p. 10c
Reprint from the *Occupational Outlook Handbook.*

A family social work career. Family Service Association of America. 1968. 6p. Single copy free
Brochure describing how some people became social workers.

Finding out about social workers. Science Research Associates. 1967. 4p. 45c
Junior occupational brief describing work and opportunities.

A future for you . . . in social work. American National Red Cross. 1969. 12p. Free
Description of positions and qualifications for social workers and case aides assigned to Red Cross programs in military hospitals.

Graduate professional schools of social work. Council of Social Work Education. 1968. 12p. Single copy free
Names and addresses of accredited schools in United States and Canada.

Jane Addams: pioneer for social justice; a biography. Meigs, Cornelia Lynde. Little, Brown and Company. 1970. 274p. $5.95
A biography devoted to the social worker's forty years at Hull House, her efforts to awaken the public to socioeconomic injustices of the day, and her attempts to legalize reform programs.

Jobs in social work. Science Research Associates. 1968. 48p. $1.15
Describes the variety of job prospects and opportunities within this field.

Medical social worker. Pages 207-9 of *Health Careers Guidebook.*
Nature of work, training, personal qualifications, and prospects.

1968 facts about social work manpower supply and demand. National Commission for Social Work Careers. 1968. 4p. 5c
Employment forecast, factors influencing demand, expanding social work education, and progress in the profession.

**Opportunities in social work. Anderson, Joseph P. Vocational Guidance Manuals. Revised 1963. 128p. $1.95 paper; $3.75 library edition

Historical background and growth of social work, supply and demand, employment conditions, personal qualifications, educational preparation, typical jobs, how to get started, member schools of American Association of Schools of Social Work, organizations, and national social welfare agencies. Also, a chapter is included on scholarships, fellowships, and other student aids.

Salaries and working conditions of social welfare manpower in 1960. National Social Welfare Assembly. 1960. 130p. $1.75

This study provides current information and statistics on the education, salaries, and working conditions of personnel in welfare, health, rehabilitation, and recreation settings in voluntary and government agencies. Prepared to assist government and voluntary agencies to evaluate personnel standards and working conditions.

School social worker. Chronicle Guidance Publications. 1967. 4p. 35c

Occupational brief summarizing nature of work, where employed, earnings, personal qualifications, training required, and outlook.

Services in public assistance—the role of the caseworker. Foster, Helen B. Bureau of Public Assistance, U.S. Department of Health, Education, and Welfare. Report Number 30. Supt. of Documents. 1967. 34p. 20c

Includes the nature and the components of the basic job of the public assistance worker.

Social welfare as a career—a bibliography. National Assembly for Social Policy and Development. 1968. 11p. 25c

A bibliography of printed materials on the various fields of social welfare.

* Social work as a profession. National Commission for Social Work Careers. Revised 1966. 40p. 25c

Description of nature of the work, talents and preparation required, opportunities for employment, and rewards.

Social work opportunities abroad. National Assembly for Social Policy and Development. 1968. 6p. 15c

Information circular about employment and study abroad.

Social worker. California State Department of Employment. 1967. 6p. Single copy free

Occupational guide describing work, requirements, training, and outlook.

Social worker. Chronicle Guidance Publications. 1969. 4p. 35c

Occupational brief summarizing work performed, working conditions, hours, earnings, personal qualifications, training requirements, opportunities, employment outlook, and entry into the job.

Social worker. Guidance Centre. 1970. 4p. 35c postpaid

History and importance, nature of work, qualifications, preparation, opportunities for advancement, remuneration, advantages, disadvantages, and related occupations.

The social worker in mental health. National Association for Mental Health. 1968. 4p. 10c

Duties, training, earnings, and future outlook. Selected references.

SOCIAL WORKER–*Continued*

Social workers. Careers. 1968. 8p. 35c

Career brief describing work performed, training, personal qualifications, earnings, advancement prospects, and outlook.

Social workers. Michigan Employment Security Commission. 1960. 2p. Single copy free

Job brief summarizing occupational data for use in Michigan.

* Social workers. Science Research Associates. 1968. 4p. 45c

Occupational brief describing several kinds of social work, requirements, earnings, advantages, disadvantages, and future outlook.

** Social workers. One section of *Occupational Outlook Handbook*.

Nature of work, where employed, training, other qualifications, advancement, employment outlook, earnings, and working conditions.

Social workers in the Veterans Administration. VA pamphlet 10-56. Veterans Administration Forms Depot. 1968. 4p. Free

Description of work, training program, qualifications, and benefits.

To candidates for graduate professional social work education. National Commission for Social Work Careers. 1968. 11p. 10c

Information about selecting a school, application procedures, programs of study, and financial aid.

Touch . . . exciting . . . rewarding . . . a family social work career. Family Service Association of America. 1968. 8p. 15c

Brief profiles of several people who became family social workers. Prepared for use at the college level.

Toward a better world–the growth and challenge of social service. Paradis, Adrian. David McKay Company. 1966. 224p. $3.95

Exploration of the positions the profession of social service offers with discussion of current education requirements.

The truth about family social work. Family Service Association of America. 1968. 12p. 15c

Prepared for use at the high school and college level, this brochure describes the work of family service.

Try a career-testing job–apply for a summer work experience in social work. National Commission for Social Work Careers. 1969. 4p. 10c. Single copy free

Introduces the idea of summer career testing opportunities and suggests job resources.

Twenty questions and answers about social work. National Commission on Social Work Careers. 1968. 16p. 10c

The most frequently asked questions about social work careers are factually answered.

**Your future in social work. Beck, Bertram. Richards Rosen Press. Revised 1969. 158p. $4; library edition $3.78

Describes the necessary education and preparation, qualifications, outlook, and work in family counseling, psychiatric clinics, and institutions.

See also Group worker; Psychiatric social worker

SOCIOLOGIST 054.088

**A career in sociology. American Sociological Association. 1968. 16p. Free

Description of training and kinds of work in which sociologists are employed.

Finding out about sociologists. Science Research Associates. 1967. 4p. 45c

Junior occupational brief summarizing what the work requires and offers.

Sociologist. Careers. 1970. 7p. 35c

Career brief describing duties, working conditions, training, personal qualifications, earnings, advancement prospects, and outlook.

Sociologist. Chronicle Guidance Publications. 1969. 4p. 35c

Occupational brief summarizing work performed, field of specialization, educational requirements, training opportunities, personal qualifications, earnings, and outlook.

Sociologist. Guidance Centre. 1967. 4p. 35c postpaid

Definition, history and importance, nature of work, preparation, qualifications, employment, advancement, outlook, remuneration, and how to get started.

Sociologists. Science Research Associates. 1966. 4p. 45c

Occupational brief describing work, training, qualifications, opportunities, and outlook.

**Sociologists. One section of *Occupational Outlook Handbook*.

Nature of work, where employed, training, other qualifications, and employment outlook.

SOIL CONSERVATIONIST AND SCIENTIST 040.081

**Careers in conservation. Soil Conservation Society of America. 1961. 12p. 4c. Single copy free

Discussion of kinds of work, places of employment, training, and opportunities. Illustrated.

Careers in soil conservation service. U.S. Department of Agriculture. Miscellaneous Publication Number 717. Supt. of Documents. 1967. 12p. 10c

Illustrated folder describing nature of work in twelve branches of the soil conservation service, qualifications, and how to apply for a Federal job.

SOIL CONSERVATIONIST AND SCIENTIST—*Continued*

An engineering career for you in Soil Conservation Service. U.S. Dept. of Agriculture. Miscellaneous Publication Number 715. Supt. of Documents. 1965. 12p. 10c

An illustrated folder describing the types of work, opportunities, and employment facts such as work locations, training, benefits, and how to apply.

Finding out about soil conservationists. Science Research Associates. 1967. 4p. 45c

Junior occupational brief containing concise facts about the job.

The Soil Conservation Service. Simms, Harper D. Praeger, Inc. 1970. 264p. $8.50

A detailed description of the agency by a man who spent thirty-two years working in it, finally as director of information.

Soil conservationist. Careers. 1966. 2p. 20c

Career summary for desk-top file. Duties, qualifications, and outlook.

Soil conservationist. Chronicle Guidance Publications. 1968. 4p. 35c

Occupational brief summarizing work performed, working conditions, qualifications, training, earnings, opportunities, and outlook.

**Soil conservationists. One section of *Occupational Outlook Handbook*.

Nature of work, where employed, training, advancement, employment outlook, and earnings.

Soil savers. Colby, C. B. Coward-McCann, Inc. 1957. 48p. $2.97

Describes the work of the Soil Conservation Service of the U.S. Department of Agriculture. Describes jobs in crop rotation, contour plowing, strip cropping, and restricted grazing. Written for grades 4 to 8. Fifty illustrations.

A soil science career for you in Soil Conservation Service. U.S. Department of Agriculture. Supt. of Documents. 1969. 8p. 15c

Description of jobs and information on how to apply, work locations, training, advancement, and employment benefits.

Soil scientist. Chronicle Guidance Publications. 1968. 4p. 35c

Occupational brief summarizing work performed, employment conditions, earnings, qualifications, training requirements, and outlook.

* Soil scientists. Science Research Associates. 1968. 4p. 45c

Occupational brief describing nature of work, training, qualifications, opportunities, and outlook.

Soil scientists. One section of *Occupational Outlook Handbook*.

Nature of work, places of employment, training, other qualifications, advancement, employment outlook, earnings, and working conditions.

Students . . . start your career in Soil Conservation Service before you graduate. U.S. Department of Agriculture. Miscellaneous Publication Number 714. Supt. of Documents. 1966. 4p. 5c

An illustrated folder describing the work of a student trainee, qualifications, training, and how to apply.

See also Agricultural specialist. Agronomist

SOIL SCIENTIST. ***See*** **Soil conservationist and scientist**

SOLDIER **378.**

The army. Daugherty, Charles M. Viking Press. Revised 1962. 192p. $3

Detailed regulations and opportunities. For grades 7 to 10.

Army careers (non-commissioned). Careers. 1966. 8p. 35c

Career brief describing ten career specialty areas.

**Army opportunities—U.S. Army handbook for counselors and students. Army Opportunities, U.S. Army Recruiting Command. 1966. 43p. Free

A handbook to provide guidance to young adults who are making career decisions, this is a comprehensive reference handbook explaining job training opportunities in the Army. Includes thumbnail sketches of Army job fields.

Current career booklets. Army Opportunities, U.S. Army Recruiting Command. 10 booklets. Free

Frequently revised materials are available from local recruiting offices or the above. Examples of present titles are: *The secret of getting ahead; Education in leadership; A new life, a new world;* and *U.S. Army opportunities.*

A guidance handbook for counselors. Army Opportunities, U.S. Army Recruiting Command. 1966. 24p. Free to counselors

Guide for counselors to assist students and parents with military obligation problems. Contains information about enlistment, the draft, and deferments. Explains Army programs, commission opportunities, and the new "G. I. Bill."

Let's go to West Point. Hamilton, Lee David. Putnam's Sons, Inc. 1962. 48p. $2.29

The reader is taken on a tour through the U.S. Military Academy and views cadets in their barracks, in classes, in the gym, and on parade. For younger boys.

The secret of getting ahead. Army Opportunities, U.S. Army Recruiting Command. 1966. 38p. Free

Illustrated booklet explains the advantages of voluntary enlistment, emphasizes the technical school and vocational training opportunities in the Army, and describes the Graduate Specialist Program which offers the high school graduate his choice of over one hundred technical school courses.

U.S. army opportunities. U.S. Army Recruiting Command. 1966. 52p. Free to counselors and librarians

A comprehensive reference handbook explaining job training opportunities in the Army. Includes occupational briefs and pertinent information.

West Point: cadets, training, and equipment. Colby, C. B. Coward-McCann, Inc. 1963. 48p. Library edition $2.97

Photographs and brief text depict life at West Point. Written for grades 4 to 8.

SOLDIER–*Continued*

West Point; the life of a cadet. Engeman, Jack. Lathrop, Lee and Shepard Company. Revised 1967. 151p. $4.95

Photographs and brief text depicting life at West Point from plebe year through graduation.

What does a U.N. soldier do? Pierson, Sherleigh. Dodd, Mead and Company. 1965. 64p. $3.25; library edition $2.99

Simple text and pictures portray various activities in an international army. Prepared for grades 3 to 7.

**Your future in the army. Walmsley, Harold. Richards Rosen Press. Revised 1969. 159p. $4; library edition $3.78

Information and advice concerning life in the army, attitudes necessary for success, factors to consider, dividends of an army career, disadvantages, and preparation.

See also Armed Forces

SPEECH PATHOLOGIST AND AUDIOLOGIST 079.108

Audiologist. Careers. 1966. 8p. 35c

Career brief describing duties, working conditions, training, places of employment, earnings, and outlook. List of sixty-five colleges offering programs in audiology and speech pathology.

Audiologists and speech pathologists in the Veterans Administration. VA pamphlet 10-69. Veterans Administration Forms Depot. 1967. 4p. Free

Description of work, training program, qualifications, and benefits.

Beth Donnis: speech therapist. Gay, Kathlyn. Julian Messner. 1968. 190p. $3.50

Career fiction. One of the series of "career romances for young moderns" about the life and hopes of a girl in her first position in this specialized teaching area.

A career in speech pathology and audiology. American Speech and Hearing Association. 1968. 6p. Free

Brief description of work and preparation.

College and university programs in speech pathology and audiology. American Speech and Hearing Association. 1968. 22p. Free

Three lists total 265 colleges. One list names the doctoral programs, one the master's degree programs, and a third the schools that offer training only at the undergraduate level.

**Employment outlook for speech pathologists and audiologists. Bulletin No. 1650–15. Bureau of Labor Statistics, U.S. Department of Labor. Supt. of Documents. 1970. 8p. 10c

Reprint from the *Occupational Outlook Handbook*.

Finding out about speech and hearing clinicians. Science Research Associates. 1967. 4p. 45c

Junior occupational brief containing concise facts about the job.

Hearing clinician. Careers. 1966. 8p. 35c

Career brief describing duties, working conditions, training, personal qualifications, certification, places of employment, earnings, and outlook.

The immediate gift. Pont, Clarice. David McKay Company. 1961. 224p. $3.25

Career fiction. Story of a dedicated young teacher at work in her chosen field of speech therapy.

Opportunities in speech pathology. Newman, Parley W. Vocational Guidance Manuals. 1968. 112p. $1.95 paper; library edition $3.75

A director of a speech and hearing clinic explains what a speech pathologist does to help people with the problems of talking and being understood. The rewards and demands of the profession, salaries, educational preparation, how to enter the field, and future outlook are discussed. A list of schools offering graduate courses and training programs is appended.

Speech and hearing therapists. Science Research Associates. 1966. 4p. 45c

Occupational brief describing nature of work, duties, qualifications, training, where employed, earnings, advantages, disadvantages, and future outlook.

Speech clinician. Careers. 1970. 8p. 35c

Career brief describing duties, working conditions, training, personal qualifications, earnings, advancement prospects, and outlook.

Speech pathologist and audiologist. Guidance Centre. 1970. 4p. 35c postpaid

History and importance of the work, qualifications, preparation, employment, advancement, remuneration, how to get started, and related occupations.

Speech pathologist (and audiologist). Chronicle Guidance Publications. 1968. 4p. 35c

Occupational brief summarizing work performed, where employed, qualifications, training, and outlook.

Speech pathologist and audiologist. Pages 223-6 of *Health Careers Guidebook.*

Nature of work, where therapists work, personal qualifications, training, certification, opportunities, and prospects.

Speech pathologists and audiologists. One section of *Occupational Outlook Handbook.*

Nature of work, where employed, training and other qualifications, earnings, working conditions, and outlook.

**Speech pathology and audiology. American Speech and Hearing Association. 1968. 24p. Free

Illustrated booklet describing current trends, places of employment, duties, working conditions, advantages, and training.

See also Physical therapist

SPORTS ANNOUNCER. ***See*** **Radio and television announcer**

STATION AGENT. ***See*** **Railroad worker**

STATIONARY ENGINEER 950.782

**Employment outlook for stationary engineers, stationary firemen (boiler). Bulletin No. 1650–103. Bureau of Labor Statistics, U.S. Department of Labor. Supt. of Documents. 1970. 8p. 10c

Reprint from the *Occupational Outlook Handbook.*

Finding out about stationary engineers. Science Research Associates. 1967. 4p. 45c

Junior occupational brief summarizing what the work requires and offers.

Stationary engineer. California State Department of Employment. 1965. 5p. Single copy free

Occupational guide describing work, requirements, training, and outlook.

Stationary engineer. Careers. 1966. 8p. 35c

Career brief describing duties, working conditions, training, personal requirements, earnings, advancement, related careers, and outlook.

Stationary engineer. Chronicle Guidance Publications. 1968. 4p. 35c

Occupational brief summarizing work performed, wages, working conditions, qualifications, preparation, types of employment, and outlook.

Stationary engineer. Michigan Employment Security Commission. 1960. 2p. Single copy free

Job brief summarizing occupational data for use in Michigan.

**Stationary engineers. Science Research Associates. 1967. 4p. 45c

Occupational brief describing the work of the stationary fireman and the stationary engineer. Includes requirements, methods of getting started, earnings, advantages, disadvantages, and future outlook.

**Stationary engineers. One section of *Occupational Outlook Handbook.*

Nature of work, where employed, training, employment outlook, earnings, and working conditions.

STATIONARY FIREMAN (BOILER) 951.885

**Stationary fireman (boiler). One section of *Occupational Outlook Handbook.*

Nature of work, where employed, training, employment outlook, earnings, and working conditions.

STATISTICIAN 020.188

Bureau of the Census, fact finder for the nation. Bureau of the Census. Supt. of Documents. 1970. 62p. $1.25

Information on the organization and operation of a large statistical agency. This is also of interest to the college student who is considering employment at the Bureau.

A career for you in agricultural statistics. U.S. Department of Agriculture. Office of Management Services, Division of Personnel. 1963. 4p. Free

Explanation of opportunities available through the student trainee program of the Federal Service Entrance Examinations.

A career in statistics with the National Center for Health Statistics. Public Health Service, U.S. Department of Health, Education, and Welfare. Publication Number 1034. 1965. 22p. Free

Gives information on qualifications, salary, benefits, and the role that statisticians play in the Center.

**Careers in statistics. American Statistical Association. Revised 1966. 24p. Single copy free

Important concepts of statistics, where statistics may be applied, duties, qualifications, preparation, outlook, and rewards. Included is a list of eighty-six colleges awarding degrees in statistics.

Economists and statisticians. Internal Revenue Service. 1968. 12p. Free

Information on positions in the national office of Internal Revenue Service as economist or statistician. Assignments are directly related to tax administration. Describes duties, qualification standards, training, promotion opportunities, and how to apply for a position.

The educational qualifications of public health statisticians. American Public Health Association. 1963. 9p. Single copy free

Finding out about statisticians. Science Research Associates. 1967. 4p. 45c

Junior occupational brief containing concise facts about the job.

Health statistics. Pages 136-8 of *Health Careers Guidebook*.

Information about qualifications, training, and opportunities for the public health statistician and the statistical clerk.

Statistical clerk. Chronicle Guidance Publications. 1967. 4p. 35c

Occupational brief summarizing work performed, where employed, qualifications, preparation, related jobs, methods of entry, and outlook.

* Statistical workers. Science Research Associates. 1967. 4p. 45c

Occupational brief describing the importance of statistics, nature of work, requirements, earnings, methods of getting started, advantages, disadvantages, and future outlook.

Statistician. California State Department of Employment. 1964. 6p. Free

Job duties, working conditions, salaries, hours, entrance requirements, promotion, training, and employment outlook.

Statistician. Careers. 1969. 2p. 20c

Career summary for desk-top file. Duties, qualifications, and outlook.

Statistician. Chronicle Guidance Publications. 1968. 4p. 35c

Occupational brief summarizing work performed, earnings, personal qualifications, training, opportunities, where employed, related positions, and employment outlook.

STATISTICIAN—*Continued*

Statistician. Guidance Centre. 1966. 4p. 35c postpaid
Definition, history and importance, nature of work, preparation, qualifications, working conditions, employment, outlook, remuneration, and how to get started.

**Statisticians. One section of *Occupational Outlook Handbook.*
Nature of work, where employed, training, other qualifications, advancement, employment outlook, earnings, and working conditions.

See also Actuary; Mathematician

STEEL INDUSTRY WORKER. ***See*** **Iron and steel industry worker**

STENOGRAPHER **202.388**

**Employment outlook for stenographers and secretaries, typists. Bulletin No. 1650–54. Bureau of Labor Statistics, U.S. Department of Labor. Supt. of Documents. 1970. 8p. 10c
Reprint from the *Occupational Outlook Handbook.*

Stenographer. California State Department of Employment. 1965. 5p. Single copy free
Occupational guide describing work, requirements, training, and outlook.

Stenographer. Careers. 1968. 2p. 20c
Career summary for desk-top file. Duties, qualifications, and outlook.

Stenographer. Chronicle Guidance Publications. 1968. 4p. 35c
Occupational brief summarizing work performed, working conditions, earnings, personal qualifications, training requirements, opportunities, and employment outlook.

Stenographer. Guidance Centre. 1967. 4p. 35c postpaid
Nature of work, qualifications, preparation, earnings, advancement opportunities, how to get started, advantages, and disadvantages.

Stenographer. Michigan Employment Security Commission. 1967. 2p. Single copy free
Job brief summarizing occupational data for use in Michigan.

Stenographers—a job for you overseas. American National Red Cross. 1968. 1p. Free
Description of qualifications for stenographers assigned to Red Cross offices in the Far East.

Stenographers and secretaries. One section of *Occupational Outlook Handbook.*
Nature of work, where employed, training, other qualifications, employment outlook, earnings, and working conditions.

Stenotypist. Careers. 1966. 8p. 35c

Career brief describing duties, working conditions, training, personal qualifications, employment prospects, earnings, how to enter, and advancement prospects.

See also Court reporter; Legal secretary; Medical secretary; Secretary

STOCK BROKER. ***See*** **Securities salesman**

STOCK CLERK **223.387**

Finding out about stock clerks. Science Research Associates. 1967. 4p. 45c

Junior occupational brief describing work and opportunities.

Stock clerk. California State Department of Employment. 1964. 2p. Single copy free

Occupational guide describing work, requirements, training, and outlook.

Stock clerk. Careers. 1970. 2p. 20c

Career summary for desk-top file. Duties, qualifications, and outlook.

Stock clerk. Chronicle Guidance Publications. 1966. 4p. 35c

Occupational brief summarizing work performed, working conditions, hours, earnings, personal qualifications, training requirements, opportunities, employment outlook, and entry into the job.

**Stock clerks. Science Research Associates. 1970. 4p. 45c

Occupational brief describing work, qualifications, opportunities, and outlook.

STONEMASON **861.181 and 861.781**

Stonemason. Chronicle Guidance Publications. 1968. 4p. 35c

Occupational brief summarizing work performed, where employed, wages and hours, qualifications, training, opportunities, and outlook.

**Stonemasons. One section of *Occupational Outlook Handbook.*

Nature of work, where employed, training, other qualifications, employment outlook, earnings, and working conditions.

SUBMARINE OFFICER **899.281**

Nuclear submarine skippers and what they do. Steele, George and Gimpel, H. J. Franklin Watts, Inc. 1962. 140p. $3.95

Description of typical background of a submarine captain, personal requirements, physical and mental qualifications, specialized training, nature of work, and the role and exploits of a nuclear submarine. For grades 7 to 11.

SUPER MARKET MANAGER **185. and 260.**

Super market manager. Careers. 1968. 8p. 35c

Career brief describing duties, working conditions, training, personal qualifications, earnings, advancement prospects, and outlook. Additional readings.

SUPER MARKET MANAGER—*Continued*

Supermarket manager. Chronicle Guidance Publications. 1966. 4p. 35c
Occupational brief summarizing duties, working conditions, personal qualifications, training requirements, opportunities, earnings, and outlook.

See also Retail manager

SURGEON 070.101

Cancer, cocaine and courage: the story of Dr. William Halsted. Beckhard, Arthur J. and Crane, William D. Julian Messner. 1960. 192p. $3.50; library binding $3.34
Biography of a surgeon who unwittingly became a drug addict, overcame the habit, and went on to perform miracles of surgery.

* Finding out about surgeons. Science Research Associates. 1967. 4p. 45c
Junior occupational brief summarizing what the work requires and offers.

First woman ambulance surgeon: Emily Barringer. Noble, Iris. Julian Messner. 1962. 192p. $3:50; library binding $3.34
Biography of the first woman who was allowed to intern in a hospital, illustrating the courage and talent to enter a profession reserved for men.

See also Physician

SURVEYOR 018.188

**Careers in surveying and mapping. American Congress on Surveying and Mapping. 1969. 32p. Single copy free
This gives the nature of work, requirements, earnings, and outlook for the major activities in surveying and mapping. Covers cartography, photogrammetric surveying, aeronautical and nautical charting, satellite geodesy, and topographic and oceanographic mapping.

**Employment outlook for surveyors. Bulletin No. 1650–46. Bureau of Statistics, U.S. Department of Labor. Supt. of Documents. 1970. 8p. 10c
Reprint from the *Occupational Outlook Handbook.*

Finding out about surveyors. Science Research Associates. 1967. 4p. 45c
Junior occupational brief containing concise facts about the job.

The land surveyor of the future. Chronicle Guidance Publications. 1967. 4p. 35c
Reprinted article from *Surveying and Mapping* discusses the past, present, and future of the occupation.

Rod and chainman. California State Department of Employment. 1964. 4p. Single copy free
Occupational guide describing work, requirements, training, and outlook.

Rodman and chainman (surveying). Careers. 1968. 2p. 20c
Career summary for desk-top file. Duties, qualifications, and outlook.

Status of the surveying profession in the USA. Chronicle Guidance Publications. 1967. 7p. 50c

Reprinted article from *Surveying and Mapping* discusses the evolution of the occupation in the United States to its current professional status.

Surveyor. California State Department of Employment. 1964. 5p. Single copy free

Occupational guide describing work, requirements, training, and outlook.

Surveyor. Careers. 1968. 2p. 20c

Career summary for desk-top file. Duties, qualifications, and outlook.

* Surveyor. Chronicle Guidance Publications. 1969. 4p. 35c

Occupational brief summarizing work performed, working conditions, qualifications, training, licensing, earnings, and outlook.

Surveyor. Guidance Centre. 1966. 4p. 35c postpaid

Definition, history and importance, working conditions, qualifications, preparation, employment and advancement, earnings, advantages, disadvantages, how to get started, and related occupations.

Surveyor. Michigan Employment Security Commission. 1958. 2p. Single copy free

Job brief summarizing occupational data for use in Michigan.

* Surveyors. Science Research Associates. 1968. 4p. 45c

Occupational brief describing nature of work, requirements, training, earnings, and future outlook.

**Surveyors. One section of *Occupational Outlook Handbook*.

Nature of work, where employed, training, other qualifications, advancement, employment outlook, earnings, and working conditions.

SWIMMING-POOL SERVICEMAN 891.884

Swimming pool service technician. California State Department of Employment. 1968. 3p. Single copy free

Job duties, working conditions, pay, hours, entrance requirements, promotion, training, and employment outlook in California.

Swimming pool service technician. Careers. 1967. 2p. 20c

Career summary for desk-top file. Duties, qualifications, and outlook.

SYSTEMS ANALYST 012.168 and 033.187

Finding out about systems analysts. Science Research Associates. 1967. 4p. 45c

Junior occupational brief summarizing what the work requires and offers.

Systems analyst. Careers. 1970. 2p. 20c

Career summary for desk-top file. Duties, qualifications, and outlook.

Systems analysts. Science Research Associates. 1970. 4p. 45c

Occupational brief describing nature of work, training, qualifications, opportunities, and outlook. Selected references.

SYSTEMS ANALYST—*Continued*

Systems analysts. One section of *Occupational Outlook Handbook.*
Nature of work, places of employment, training, qualifications, employment outlook, earnings, and working conditions.

Systems engineers. Science Research Associates. 1967. 4p. 45c
Occupational brief describing work, training, qualifications, opportunities, and outlook.

TABULATING-MACHINE OPERATOR 213.782

Tabulating-machine operator. California State Department of Employment. 1968. 2p. Single copy free
Occupational guide describing work, requirements, training, and outlook.

Tabulating machine operator. Chronicle Guidance Publications. 1970. 4p. 35c
Occupational brief summarizing work performed, training, qualifications, opportunities, and outlook.

Tabulating-machine operator. Michigan Employment Security Commission. 1963. 2p. Single copy free
Job brief summarizing occupational data for use in Michigan.

TAILOR 785.261

Custom tailors and dressmakers. Science Research Associates. 1969. 4p. 45c
Occupational brief describing work, requirements, opportunities, earnings, things to consider, and outlook.

Finding out about tailors. Science Research Associates. 1967. 4p. 45c
Junior occupational brief containing concise facts about the job.

Tailor. Chronicle Guidance Publications. 1967. 4p. 35c
Occupational brief summarizing work performed, employment conditions, qualifications, training, opportunities, outlook, and methods of entry.

Tailor. Guidance Centre. 1967. 4p. 35c postpaid
Nature of work, qualifications, preparation, working conditions, employment, advancement, outlook, remuneration, advantages, and disadvantages.

Tailor, men's garments. California State Department of Employment. 1964. 3p. Single copy free
Occupational guide describing work, requirements, training, and outlook.

* Tailors. Careers. 1970. 8p. 35c
Career brief describing duties, working conditions, training, personal qualifications, earnings, unionization, and outlook.

Tailors. Michigan Employment Security Commission. 1960. 2p. Single copy free
Job brief summarizing occupational data for use in Michigan.

TAPE LIBRARIAN 223.387

Tape librarians. Science Research Associates. 1970. 4p. 45c

Occupational brief describing nature of work, training, qualifications, opportunities, and outlook. Selected references.

TAXI DRIVER 913.363

Finding out about taxi drivers. Science Research Associates. 1967. 4p. 45c

Junior occupational brief describing work and opportunities.

Taxi driver. Careers. 1970. 2p. 20c

Career summary for desk-top file. Duties, qualifications, and outlook.

**Taxi driver. Chronicle Guidance Publications. 1969. 4p. 35c

Occupational brief summarizing work performed, working conditions, hours, wages, personal requirements, training, licensing, and outlook.

Taxi driver. Guidance Centre. 1966. 4p. 35c postpaid

History and importance, nature of work, qualifications, preparation, outlook, remuneration, advantages, disadvantages, and how to get started.

**Taxi drivers. One section of *Occupational Outlook Handbook*.

Nature of work, where employed, qualifications, training, employment outlook, earnings, and working conditions.

* Taxicab drivers. Science Research Associates. 1966. 4p. 45c

Occupational brief describing nature of work, requirements, earnings, getting started, advantages, disadvantages, and future outlook.

TAXIDERMIST 199.281

Big game hunter: Carl Akeley. Sutton, Felix. Julian Messner. 1960. 192p; library binding $3.34

Biography of a pioneer taxidermist who created many natural history exhibits for the Chicago Natural History Museum.

Taxidermist. California State Department of Employment. 1967. 4p. Single copy free

Occupational guide describing work, requirements, training, and outlook.

Taxidermist. Michigan Employment Security Commission. 1957. 2p. Single copy free

Job brief summarizing occupational data for use in Michigan.

TEACHER 091.228

Born to teach. Burt, Olive. Julian Messner. 1967. 192p. $3.50; library binding $3.34

Career fiction. Experiences of a beginning teacher in a one-room rural school in Utah.

TEACHER—*Continued*

Buenos días, teacher. MacLeod, Ruth. Julian Messner. 1970. 192p. $3.50; library binding $3.34

Career fiction. Set against the background of racial conflicts and urban problems, a teacher's first job was in a rundown area of a large city where more than half of her third grade class were Mexican, many of whom spoke no English.

**Careers and opportunities in teaching. Biegeleisen, J. I. Dutton and Company. 1969. 255p. $4.95

Description of the diversified careers in education, the preparation, opportunities for professional growth, and many practical considerations. Includes a self-administering aptitude test and a list of accredited teachers' colleges in the United States.

Careers in education. Wynn, Richard. McGraw-Hill Book Company. 1960. 307p. $6.50

An introduction to careers in the field of education, this book is a discussion of some of the contemporary forces and issues affecting teaching. Also it describes the satisfactions and frustrations of teaching as a profession.

**Careers in education. National Commission on Teacher Education and Professional Standards. 1968. 35p. 35c

Provides general information about a wide variety of education and education-related careers. Aimed at able young people considering a teaching career. Includes discussion of preparation, costs, employment outlook, and estimated earnings. Sources of information.

Careers in teaching and education. B'nai B'rith Vocational Service. 1970. 40p. $1.25

Essential nature of the teacher's work, personal qualities needed, benefits, rewards, opportunities, and employment outlook. Also suggests ways to explore teaching and obtain practical experience before entering the field.

Classroom teacher salary schedules, 1967-68, districts having 6,000 or more pupils. National Education Association. 1968. 161p. $3

A tabulation of minimum and maximum salaries and annual increments for 557 of the largest urban school districts and 178 suburban districts. Also states the professional growth required for the maximum salary.

Economic status of teachers in 1967-68. National Education Association. 1968. 56p. $1.25

Annual report including certification and average salaries. Salaries are compared with earnings of other professional workers.

Education: earned degrees, by level, sex, and institution. One section of *Earned Degrees Conferred.*

Useful for judging the extent of a college's program in the specialized teaching fields, such as business education, speech correction, health education, and teaching of exceptional children.

The education of American teachers. Conant, James B. McGraw-Hill Book Company. 1963. 275p. $5

Contains many recommendations for changes in the preparation of teachers.

The education professions: a report on the people who serve our schools and colleges. Government Printing Office. Supt. of Documents. 1969. 377p. $2.75

Includes such topics as supply and demand, preparation, recruitment, utilization, support services, and teachers of special groups. One chapter contains a discussion of support personnel related to pupil personnel services.

Employment opportunities in teaching. Katcher, Barbara M. L. Arco Publishing Company. 1967. 97p. $5; paper $3

Techniques of securing employment are followed by teaching opportunities, requirements, and rewards in public schools, colleges, and in teaching abroad.

**Employment outlook for teachers. Bulletin No. 1650–47. Bureau of Labor Statistics, U.S. Department of Labor. Supt. of Documents. 1970. 16p. 15c

Reprint from the *Occupational Outlook Handbook*. Includes kindergarten and elementary school teachers, secondary school teachers, and college and university teachers.

The extra-special room. Hill, Margaret. Little, Brown and Company. 1962. 312p. $3.75

Career fiction. A story of a teacher's career. Written for junior high school girls.

Fair is the morning. Erdman, Loula Grace. David McKay Company. 1945. 186p. $3.95

Career fiction. Story of a rural school teacher and her experiences in making the school the center of community activities and in meeting problems in health, soil conservation, and social needs.

Find a career in education. Smith, Frances. Putnam's Sons. 1960. 160p. $3.50

Describes work in the elementary schools, junior and senior high schools, and colleges. Includes preparation, salaries, outlook, advantages, and disadvantages. Written for ages 11 to 15.

Finding and training new teachers. Chronicle Guidance Publications. 1969. 8p. 50c

Reprinted article from *Industrial Arts and Vocational Education* discusses the accreditation of undergraduate programs in industrial arts, trade teachers recruitment and training, and the need for industrial arts teachers.

Finding out about teachers. Science Research Associates. 1967. 4p. 45c

Junior occupational brief summarizing what the work requires and offers.

FTA: Join the action. Future Teachers of America. 1967. 6p. Free

Description of Future Teachers of America programs.

Future teachers of America. Future Teachers of America. 1968. 8p. Free

A leaflet about teaching and exploring teaching through membership in the Future Teachers of America.

High school teachers. Science Research Associates. 1968. 4p. 45c

Occupational brief describing work, training, qualifications, opportunities, and outlook.

TEACHER—*Continued*

Industrial arts teacher. Chronicle Guidance Publications. 1967. 4p. 35c

Occupational brief summarizing where employed, work performed, working conditions, hours and wages, training requirements, and outlook.

Introduction to teaching. Peters, Herman J. and others. Macmillan Company. 1963. 389p. $7.25

Prepared as a college text to help the student evaluate the qualifications for a teaching career by introducing him to the requirements and rewards of teaching.

Invitation to teaching. Association for Childhood Education International. Revised 1967. 6p. 6c

Includes the satisfaction of teaching and questions to consider in testing one's interest.

Jobs in education. Science Research Associates. 1968. 48p. $1.15

Describes the variety of job prospects and opportunities within this field.

Jobs in the education field. Changing Times. 1959. 3p. 15c

Reprint discussing demand, pay, prestige, and benefits of careers in the education field.

Kathie: the new teacher. Rosenheim, Lucile G. Julian Messner. 1949. 195p. $3.50

Career fiction. A romance that tells of Kathie's first year of teaching.

A manual on certification requirements for school personnel in the United States. National Commission on Teacher Education and Professional Standards. 1967. 268p. $5

Contains specific requirements for all certificates in the fifty states and territories, a listing of all institutions approved for the preparation of teachers, and current trends in certification practices. Also includes information about teaching positions in the Overseas Dependents Schools and a list of teacher placement agencies in the respective states.

* Opportunities in teaching careers. Fine, Benjamin. Vocational Guidance Manuals. 1963. 160p. $1.95 paper; $3.75 library edition

The teaching profession today, need, outlook, satisfactions, what the educators think, the Indiana survey, personal attributes necessary for success, the changing role of the teaching profession, types of teachers, educational preparation, finding your job, salaries, paths to advancement, rural versus urban teaching, advantages, disadvantages, related fields, and educational associations.

Rankings of the states, 1969. National Education Association. 1969. 71p. $1.25

Research report showing rankings of the states by population, enrollment, number of teachers, educational attainment, and financial resources. Contains seventy-four tables.

Really, Miss Hillsboro! Hill, Margaret. Little, Brown and Company. 1960. 256p. $3.75

Career fiction. Story of a young teacher of the fifth grade.

Requirements for certification: teachers, counselors, librarians, administrators for elementary schools, secondary schools, junior colleges. Woellner, Elizabeth H. and Wood, Maude Aurilla. University of Chicago Press. 35th edition. 1970. 223p. $7.85

An annual revision brings up to date the requirements for certification in each of the states.

Salaries paid and salary practices in universities, colleges, and junior colleges, 1967-68. National Education Association. 1968. 92p. $1.50

The seventh report in this biennial series.

* School teaching as a career. Boylan, James R. Henry Z. Walck, Inc. 1962. 100p. $4.50

Discussion of preparation, opportunities, personal factors to be considered, and satisfactions. Illustrated.

**Secondary school teachers. One section of *Occupational Outlook Handbook.*

Nature of work, where employed, training, other qualifications, advancement, employment outlook, earnings, and working conditions.

Teacher. Careers. 1966-1968. 2p. 20c each

Career summaries for various subject areas:

Business teacher, high school	Foreign language teacher
Elementary art teacher	Social studies teacher
English teacher	Industrial arts teacher
High school art teacher	Teacher of handicapped children
Homemaking teacher	Teacher of the deaf and hard of hearing
Science teacher	

The teacher and the law. National Education Association. 1959. 92p. $1

Summarizes the general legal status of the public school teacher as defined by state law and court decisions; includes admission to the profession, tenure, salaries, privileges, rights, and immunities.

Teacher (elementary and secondary). Guidance Centre. 1969. 4p. 23c postpaid

Nature of work, qualifications, preparation, advancement, outlook, remuneration, advantages, disadvantages, how to get started, and related occupations.

Teacher, public school. Careers. 1968. 8p. 35c

Career brief describing duties, advantages, disadvantages, earnings, advancement prospects, and outlook.

Teacher (secondary school). Chronicle Guidance Publications. 1969. 4p. 35c

Occupational brief summarizing work performed, working conditions, personal qualifications, training requirements, earnings, opportunities, and employment outlook.

Teacher supply and demand in public schools. National Education Association. 1968. 88p. $1.75

This annual study focuses upon the continuance of the national shortage of teachers.

TEACHER—*Continued*

Teachers. Michigan Employment Security Commission. 1960. 2p. Single copy free

Job brief summarizing occupational data for use in Michigan.

**Teaching. One chapter of *Occupational Outlook Handbook.*

Nature of work, training, other qualifications, employment outlook, advancement, earnings, and working conditions for each of the following: kindergarten and elementary school teachers, secondary school teachers, and college and university teachers.

**Teaching career fact book. National Education Association. 1966. 56p. $1

Among the subjects covered are teacher supply and demand, teacher preparation, certification requirements, current salaries, conditions of work, professional responsibilities, and a list of colleges and universities accredited by the National Council for the Accreditation of Teacher Education. Good bibliography.

Tomboy teacher. Betts, Miriam P. Julian Messner. 1961. 192p. $3.50

Career fiction. Shedding her tomboy ways, Nancy becomes a dedicated young teacher who tries to bring modern methods into an antiquated school system.

Vocational training instructor. Chronicle Guidance Publications. 1968. 4p. 35c

Occupational brief summarizing work performed, educational requirements, personal qualifications, working conditions, earnings, and outlook.

What every teacher should know about New Jersey school law. New Jersey Education Association. 1968. 8p. Free

An example of a brochure available from many state education associations pertaining to contract, salary, certification, sick leave, retirement plans, life insurance, liability, and pupil behavior.

Your career in teaching. Dowdell, Dorothy and Dowdell, Joseph. Julian Messner. 1967. 191p. $3.95; library binding $3.64

Emphasis is on the advantages that teaching offers young people of promise. Case histories focus on the scope of opportunities and the striking innovations taking place in some schools throughout the country. Reading lists.

Your certification for teaching in New Jersey. New Jersey Education Association. 1968. 6p. Free

An example of a brochure available from many state education associations explaining the procedures to get proper certification for teaching in the state.

See also College teacher; Kindergarten and nursery school teacher; Teacher, Elementary school

TEACHER, ELEMENTARY SCHOOL 092.228

Elementary school teachers. Science Research Associates. 1968. 4p. 45c

Occupational brief describing work, training, qualifications, opportunities, and outlook.

Elementary teacher. Careers. 1969. 2p. 20c

Career summary for desk-top file. Duties, qualifications, and outlook.

Elementary teacher. Chronicle Guidance Publications. 1969. 4p. 35c

Occupational brief summarizing work performed, personal requirements, opportunities, salaries, methods of entry, advantages, disadvantages, and outlook.

Teacher, elementary (public schools). California State Department of Employment. 1964. 5p. Single copy free

Occupational guide describing work, requirements, training, and outlook.

**Your future in elementary school teaching. Shodkley, Robert. Richards Rosen Press. Revised 1969. 159p. $4; library edition $3.78; edition in in large type $5.97

Describes the need for well-trained and inspiring teachers, qualifications, and outlook.

TEACHER, EXCEPTIONAL CHILDREN 094.228

Finding out about teachers of exceptional children. Science Research Associates. 1967. 4p. 45c

Junior occupational brief containing concise facts about the job.

Teacher of exceptional children. Chronicle Guidance Publications. 1966. 4p. 35c

Occupational brief describing work performed, personal qualifications, training requirements, working conditions, earnings, and outlook.

Teachers of exceptional children. Science Research Associates. 1966. 4p. 45c

Occupational brief describing nature of work, personal qualifications, training, earnings, pros and cons, and future outlook.

TEACHER AID 09

Aides to teachers and children. Association for Childhood Education International. Bulletin No. 24-A. 1968. 64p. $1.50

A number of papers on the nature of work and preparation for the work as teacher aides.

Teacher aide. Chronicle Guidance Publications. 1969. 4p. 35c

Occupational brief summarizing work performed, physical and personal requirements, training requirements, where employed, hours and earnings, opportunities, outlook, and certification.

Teacher aides to the rescue. Wright, Betty Atwell. John Day Company. 1969. 208p. $4.95

The emphasis is on planning for the effective use of teacher assistants, but the case studies give an idea of the nature of the work.

TEACHER AID—*Continued*

The use of auxiliary personnel. New Jersey Education Association. 1968. 6p. Free

Points out the responsibilities of teacher aides. Gives job description, training, assignment, how to evaluate, and steps to gain full professional status.

What is the teacher aide's role? Chronicle Guidance Publications. 1968. 2p. 35c

Reprinted article from *Minnesota Journal of Education* discusses duties of aides and their certification.

TECHNICAL WRITER. ***See*** **Writer**

TECHNICIAN **.002 through .029**

**Aim for a job in appliance service. Keefe, John. Richards Rosen Press. 1969. 160p. $4; library edition $3.78

Discussion of the training necessary to be an appliance service man, opportunities, earnings, and outlook. Emphasizes the growing demand for repairmen. Also contains advice on applying for a job, on work habits and attitudes for beginners, and on the pitfalls and advantages of owning one's own business. Includes a list of appliance repair training schools, by states.

Air-cooled and marine engine repairman. Guidance Centre. 1968. 4p. 23c postpaid

Definition, history and importance, nature of the work, qualifications, preparation, remuneration, outlook, and how to get started.

Automatic bowling machine mechanics. Chronicle Guidance Publications. 1968. 4p. 35c

Occupational brief summarizing nature of work, working conditions, training requirements, personal qualifications, outlook, hours, and earnings.

Beyond tomorrow. Halacy, D. S., Jr. Macrae Smith Company. 1965. 176p. $3.95

The author reports on the research being done and discusses future possibilities of science and technology in nine areas: man-powered flying machines, mental telepathy, wireless power transmission, electric rocket ships, utilization of the moon, man's living under water, salt water conversion, artificial parts for the human body, and artificial cultivation of meat and vegetables.

Can I be a technician? Let's find out. General Motors Corporation, Public Relations Staff. 1961. 20p. Free

Description of nature of work, preparation, opportunities, and typical course of study in a technical institute.

**Careers for women as technicians. Bulletin 282. Women's Bureau, U.S. Department of Labor. Supt. of Documents. 1961. 28p. 20c

This booklet presents the specializations of technicians as an emerging occupational field. It describes the basic requirements and characteristics of technicians, training, earnings, possibilities for advancement, outlook, and obstacles to women's employment.

The critical need for trained technicians. Chronicle Guidance Publications. 1969. 3p. 35c

Reprinted article from *Technical Education News* discusses the supply and demand for technicians.

Electroencephalographic technician. Michigan Employment Security Commission. 1967. 2p. Single copy free

Job brief summarizing occupational data for use in Michigan.

**Employment outlook for technicians, engineering and science, draftsmen. Bulletin No. 1650–27. Bureau of Labor Statistics, U.S. Department of Labor. Supt. of Documents. 1970. 16p. 15c

Reprint from the *Occupational Outlook Handbook.* Includes aeronautical, chemical, civil engineering, electronics, and air-conditioning, heating, and refrigeration technology.

The engineering technician. American Society for Engineering Education. Available from Engineers' Council for Professional Development. 1968. 21p. 50c

Thirteen fields of engineering technology are described. Includes educational requirements, job opportunities, salaries, and outlook.

**Engineering technicians. Brooking, Walter J., ed. Ferguson Publishing Company. 1969. 386p. $12; library edition $8.95

Twenty-three types of technicians are described as to nature of work, qualifications, and outlook.

Household appliance repairman. California State Department of Employment. 1965. 5p. Single copy free

Occupational guide describing work, requirements, training, and outlook.

Jobs in technical work. Science Research Associates. 1965. 32p. $1.15

Describes the variety of job prospects and opportunities within this field, especially for the air conditioning technician, draftsman, cartographer, instrument technician, electronics technician, medical technologist, and X-ray technician.

Lasers; tools of modern technology. Brown, Ronald. Doubleday and Company. 1968. 192p. $2.45

A scientific report on the structure and use of a new instrument and source of light which derives its name from the initials of Light Amplification by Stimulated Emission of Radiation.

Lens grinder. California State Department of Employment. 1965. 4p. Single copy free

Occupational guide describing work, requirements, training, and outlook.

A million and a half technicians needed by 1975. Chronicle Guidance Publications. 1967. 4p. 35c

Reprinted article from *Occupational Outlook Quarterly,* discusses education, demand, supply, specialties, and opportunities for technicians.

Outboard motor and small engine repairman. California State Department of Employment. 1967. 3p. Single copy free

Occupational guide describing work, requirements, training, and outlook.

TECHNICIAN—*Continued*

The technician and tomorrow. General Electric Company. 1968. 12p. Free

Defines the work of a technician in his role as the "action man" who teams with the scientist and engineer in fields ranging from aerospace to medicine. Motivates the student who cannot continue in a four-year college to take other alternatives such as technical school or junior college. Illustrated.

Technician education yearbook 1969-70. Prakken Publications, Inc. 1969. 274p. $10

This fourth edition of the yearbook contains information of various phases of technician education—industrial, health-related, business-related, and agricultural. Includes directory of 1,211 institutions offering technician training, list of professional organizations concerned with technician education, and selected references.

Technicians. Chronicle Guidance Publications. 1967. 4p. 35c

Occupational brief summarizing work performed in a variety of classifications, working conditions, training, qualifications, earnings, opportunities, and outlook.

Technicians, physical science and engineering. Careers. 1967. 8p. 35c

Career brief describing the growing importance of technicians, duties, working conditions, training, earnings, and outlook. Additional readings.

Training and technology program activities. Oak Ridge Associated Universities. 1968. 15p. Free

Ways utilized for the training of vocational-technical workers.

Typewriter serviceman. Chronicle Guidance Publications. 1969. 4p. 35c

Occupational brief summarizing nature of work, where employed, hours and working conditions, personal requirements, earnings, training requirements, opportunities, and outlook.

See also Laboratory technician; Mechanic and repairman; Medical technologist

TELEGRAPH OPERATOR 236.588

Finding out about telegraph operators. Science Research Associates. 1967. 4p. 45c

Junior occupational brief containing some concise facts about the job and listing ways of finding out about the nature of the work.

**Telegraphers, telephoners, and towermen (railroad). One section of *Occupational Outlook Handbook.*

Nature of work, training, other qualifications, advancement, employment outlook, earnings, and working conditions.

See also Telephone operator

TELEPHONE AND PBX INSTALLER AND REPAIRMAN 822.381

Finding out about telephone installers. Science Research Associates. 1967. 4p. 45c

Junior occupational brief containing concise facts about the job.

Telephone and PBX installers and repairmen. One section of *Occupational Outlook Handbook.*

Nature of work, training, other qualifications, advancement, employment outlook, earnings, and working conditions.

Telephone installer. Careers. 1970. 2p. 20c

Career summary for desk-top file. Duties, qualifications, and outlook.

Telephone installers. Science Research Associates. 1968. 4p. 45c

Occupational brief describing nature of work, training, qualifications, opportunities, and outlook. Selected references.

Telephone technician. Guidance Centre. 1966. 4p. 35c postpaid

Definition, history and importance, conditions, qualifications, preparation, advancement opportunities, earnings, and how to get started.

TELEPHONE INDUSTRY WORKER 235. and 822.381

Central office craftsmen. One section of *Occupational Outlook Handbook.*

Nature of work, training, other qualifications, advancement, employment outlook, earnings, and working conditions.

Central office equipment installers. One section of *Occupational Outlook Handbook.*

Nature of work, training, other qualifications, advancement, employment outlook, earnings, and working conditions.

Employment outlook for the telephone industry. Bulletin No. 1650–122. Bureau of Labor Statistics, U.S. Department of Labor. Supt. of Documents. 1970. 12p. 15c

Reprint from the *Occupational Outlook Handbook.* Includes central office craftsmen, central office equipment installers, linemen and cable splicers, telephone and PBX installers and repairmen.

Finding out about service representatives for telephone companies. Science Research Associates. 1967. 4p. 45c

Junior occupational brief summarizing what the work requires and offers.

Telephone answering service operator. California State Department of Employment. 1968. 3p. Single copy free

Job duties, working conditions, pay, hours, entrance requirements, promotion, and employment outlook.

**Telephone industry occupations. One chapter of *Occupational Outlook Handbook.*

Nature and location of the industry, kinds of work, employment outlook, earnings, and working conditions. Specific information is given for central office craftsmen, linemen, cable splicers, telephone and PBX installers and repairmen.

TELEPHONE INDUSTRY WORKER—*Continued*

Telephone service representative. California State Department of Employment. 1964. 2p. Single copy free

Occupational guide describing work, requirements, training, and outlook.

TELEPHONE OPERATOR 235.862

Employment outlook for telephone operators. Bulletin No. 1650–55. Bureau of Labor Statistics, U.S. Department of Labor. Supt. of Documents. 1970. 8p. 10c

Reprint from the *Occupational Outlook Handbook.*

Finding out about switchboard operators. Science Research Associates. 1967. 4p. 45c

Junior occupational brief describing work and opportunities.

Finding out about telephone operators. Science Research Associates. 1967. 4p. 45c

Junior occupational brief containing some concise facts about the job and listing ways of finding out about the nature of the work. Includes suggestions for reading and a list of other occupational briefs on related topics.

PBX operator. Careers. 1967. 2p. 20c

Career summary for desk-top file. Duties, qualifications, and outlook.

Private switchboard operators. Science Research Associates. 1969. 4p. 45c

Occupational brief describing nature of work, training, qualifications, training opportunities, and outlook. Two illustrations. Selected references.

Telephone operator. California State Department of Employment. 1966. 3p. Single copy free

Occupational guide describing work, requirements, training, and outlook.

Telephone operator. Careers. 1969. 2p. 20c

Career summary for desk-top file. Duties, qualifications, and outlook.

Telephone operator. Guidance Centre. 1966. 4p. 35c postpaid

Definition, importance of work, qualifications, preparation, earnings, how to get started, advantages, disadvantages, working conditions, employment, advancement, and outlook.

Telephone operator (central office). Chronicle Guidance Publications. 1966. 4p. 35c

Occupational brief summarizing work performed, employment conditions, qualifications, determination of aptitudes and interests, opportunities, outlook, methods of entry, and related jobs.

Telephone operators. Michigan Employment Security Commission. 1957. 2p. Single copy free

Job brief summarizing occupational data for use in Michigan.

* Telephone operators. Science Research Associates. 1968. 4p. 45c

Occupational brief describing nature of work, qualifications, preparation, opportunities, advantages, disadvantages, and future outlook.

**Telephone operators. One section of *Occupational Outlook Handbook.*
Nature of work, training, other qualifications, advancement, employment outlook, earnings, and working conditions.

TELETYPE OPERATOR 203.588

Ground radio operators and teletypists. One section of *Occupational Outlook Handbook.*
Nature of work, training, other qualifications, advancement, employment outlook, earnings, and working conditions.

Teletype operators. Science Research Associates. 1969. 4p. 45c
Occupational brief describing work, training, qualifications, opportunities, and outlook.

Teletypewriter operator. California State Department of Employment. 1967. 4p. Single copy free
Occupational guide describing work, requirements, training, and outlook.

Teletypewriter operator. Careers. 1966. 2p. 20c
Career summary for desk-top file. Duties, qualifications, and outlook.

TELEVISION AND RADIO SERVICE TECHNICIAN 720.281

Finding out about radio and television servicemen. Science Research Associates. 1967. 4p. 45c
Junior occupational brief containing concise facts about the job.

Job qualification of position of radio maintenance technician in the FBI. Federal Bureau of Investigation. 1968. 1p. Free
Description of work and qualifications.

Radio and television repairman. Careers. 1967. 2p. 20c
Career summary for desk-top file. Duties, qualifications, and outlook.

Radio and television serviceman. California State Department of Employment. 1965. 5p. Single copy free
Duties, working conditions, how to find work, pay, hours, training, and employment prospects.

Radio and TV servicemen. Michigan Employment Security Commission. 1957. 2p. Single copy free
Job brief summarizing occupational data for use in Michigan.

Radio and television technician. Careers. 1970. 2p. 20c
Career summary for desk-top file. Duties, qualifications, and outlook.

**Television and radio service technicians. One section of *Occupational Outlook Handbook.*
Nature of work, where employed, training, other qualifications, advancement, employment outlook, earnings, and working conditions.

TELEVISION AND RADIO SERVICE TECHNICIAN—*Continued*

Television service and repairman. Chronicle Guidance Publications. 1967. 4p. 35c

Occupational brief summarizing work performed, where employed, qualifications, training, and employment outlook.

The two-way radio technician. Chronicle Guidance Publications. 1966. 2p. 35c

Reprinted article from *Radio-Electronics* discusses mobile radio services, training, entering the field, equipment necessary, and outlook.

See also Radio and television engineer and technician

TELEVISION ANNOUNCER. *See* Radio and television announcer

TELEVISION INDUSTRY WORKER 963.

**Careers in television. National Association of Broadcasters. 1967. 20p. 35c. Single copy free

Discussion of the future of television, finding a job, special traits desirable, typical jobs, training, and opportunities for women.

Job opportunities in television. National Broadcasting Company, Department of Information. 1963. 5p. Mimeographed. Free

Description of duties and qualifications for eleven jobs in programming, eleven in technical operation, five in administration and sales, and one in research and development.

Jobs in children's entertainment. Alumnae Advisory Center. 1968. 6p. 35c

Reprint from *Mademoiselle* describing the work of several young women who have succeeded in children's theatre and other forms of entertainment.

Television directors. Careers. 1967. 8p. 35c

Career brief describing duties, working conditions, training, personal qualifications, earnings, related careers, and outlook. Additional readings.

Television installation man. California State Department of Employment. 1965. 5p. Single copy free

Occupational guide summarizing duties, working conditions, employment prospects, earnings, training, requirements for entry, and suggestions for locating a job.

Television production jobs. Kevles, Barbara. Alumnae Advisory Center. 1969. 7p. 35c

Brief accounts of female college graduates, many of whom started as secretaries. A glimpse of the varied opportunities in this field.

Television production jobs. Alumnae Advisory Center. 1969. 6p. 35c

Reprint from *Mademoiselle* describing the work of a dozen young women who have infiltrated television program production.

TV girl Friday. Milne, Ruth. Little, Brown and Company. 1957. 248p. $3.75

Career fiction. Story of a girl with her heart set on a career in front of the cameras who overcame her disappointment and discovered interesting work behind the scenes.

What happens at a television station. Shay, Arthur. Reilly and Lee Books. 1969. 31p. $3.50

The author takes readers behind the scenes in television studios to give them some understanding of the workers, their jobs and equipment. Prepared for grades 2 to 5.

**Your career in TV and radio. Gordon, George N. and Falk, Irving A. Julian Messner. 1966. 221p. $3.95; library binding $3.64

Qualifications and opportunities are presented for many occupations such as director, playwright, researcher, announcer, and engineer. Includes many personal career anecdotes of people important in their areas of broadcasting. Includes list of colleges offering degrees in television and radio and a list of scholarships available to broadcasting students.

See also Radio and television broadcasting industry worker

TELLER. ***See*** **Bank Teller**

TERRAZZO WORKERS. ***See*** **Marble setter**

TEXTILE INDUSTRY WORKER 68

**Aim for a job in the textile industry. Cone, Sydney. Richards Rosen Press. 1969. 146p. $4; library edition $3.78

Description of the kinds of work involved in making natural and synthetic fabrics. Also outlines the education and training needed, opportunities, and outlook.

Career opportunities for you in the fabulous world of fabrics. Textile Distributors Association. 1970. 10p. Free

Discussion of the role of the converter in the manufacture and distribution of textiles, with details concerning job opportunities.

Fabric designer. Careers. 1969. 2p. 20c

Career summary for desk-top file. Duties, qualifications, and outlook.

Finding out about textile finishers and dyers. Science Research Associates. 1967. 4p. 45c

Junior occupational brief summarizing what the work requires and offers.

**Home economics has a career for you in textiles and clothing. American Home Economics Association. 1966. 20p. 25c

Discussion of the basic requirements, major duties, qualifications, employment opportunities, salaries, and related work. Includes information about careers in fashion, teaching, research, extension, and communications. Reading list.

TEXTILE INDUSTRY WORKER—*Continued*

* Opportunities in the textile industry. Barnhardt, Robert A. Vocational Guidance Manuals. 1966. 128p. $1.95 paper; library edition $3.75

A discussion of the importance and future of the textile industry is followed by the educational preparation, special education, the types of jobs available, and related industries.

Textile industry workers. Science Research Associates. 1967. 4p. 45c

Occupational brief describing work with cotton, woolen, and synthetic fibers. Also includes requirements, earnings, methods of getting started, advantages, disadvantages, and a look ahead.

Textile (manufacturing) occupations. Chronicle Guidance Publications. 1969. 4p. 35c

Occupational brief summarizing work performed, where employed, working conditions, salary, qualifications, training required, and outlook.

Textile technologist. Guidance Centre. 1970. 4p. 35c postpaid

Definition, history and importance, nature of work, working conditions, qualifications, preparation, employment, advancement, outlook, remuneration, and how to get started.

**Your career in textiles: an industry, a science, an art. American Textile Manufacturers Institute. Revised 1968. 18p. 30c. Single copy free

Attractive brochure, illustrated in color, presenting the varied career opportunities in each of three areas of textiles. The outlook is described in the industry for those with marketing, manufacturing, and management abilities; in science for those with engineering, science, and research skills; and in art for those with artistic and creative talents. Includes list of colleges offering degrees in this specialty.

Your executive career in textiles. Philadelphia College of Textiles and Science. 1968. 6p. Free

Description of work, opportunities, and outlook.

THEATER MANAGER 187.168

Finding out about theater managers. Science Research Associates. 1967. 4p. 45c

Junior occupational brief containing concise facts about the job.

Theater manager. Careers. 1968. 2p. 20c

Career summary for desk-top file. Duties, qualifications, and outlook.

**Theater manager. Chronicle Guidance Publications. 1969. 4p. 35c

Occupational brief summarizing work performed, personal and educational requirements, earnings, and outlook.

Theatre manager. Guidance Centre. 1970. 4p. 35c postpaid

History and importance, nature of work, qualifications, working conditions, preparation, remuneration, advancement, outlook, related occupations, and how to get started.

**Theater managers. Science Research Associates. 1969. 4p. 45c

Occupational brief describing nature of work, duties, requirements, getting started, earnings and hours, advantages, disadvantages, and future outlook.

TICKET AGENT 912.368 and 919.368

Airline ticket agent. Careers. 1966. 2p. 20c

Career summary for desk-top file. Duties, qualifications, and outlook.

Ticket agent. Chronicle Guidance Publications. 1969. 4p. 35c

Occupational brief summarizing work performed, where employed, salary, personal qualifications, training required, and outlook.

**Traffic agents and clerks (civil aviation). One section of *Occupational Outlook Handbook.*

Nature of work, where employed, training, other qualifications, advancement, employment outlook, earnings, and working conditions.

TITLE SEARCHER 119.288

Title searcher. California State Department of Employment. 1966. 3p. Single copy free

Occupational guide describing work, requirements, training, and outlook.

TOBACCO INDUSTRY WORKER 920.885

Tobacco manufacturing workers. Science Research Associates. 1966. 4p. 45c

Occupational brief describing nature of work, requirements, earnings, advantages, disadvantages, and future outlook.

Tobacco products (manufacturing) occupations. Chronicle Guidance Publications. 1969. 4p. 35c

Occupational brief summarizing work performed, where employed, salary, personal qualifications, training required, and outlook.

TOOL AND DIE MAKER 601.280

Diemaker. Michigan Employment Security Commission. 1960. 2p. Single copy free

Job brief summarizing occupational data for use in Michigan.

Finding out about tool and die makers. Science Research Associates. 1967. 4p. 45c

Junior occupational brief containing some facts about the job and listing ways of finding out about the nature of the work. Includes suggestions for reading and titles of other occupational briefs on related topics.

Job grading standards for die sinker. Civil Service Commission. Supt. of Documents. 1970. 3p. 10c

This job classification outlines duties, skill, and knowledge requirements, responsibility, physical effort, and working conditions which determine job grade levels in accordance with the U.S. Civil Service Commission standards.

TOOL AND DIE MAKER—*Continued*

Learning the tool and die maker trade. U.S. Department of Labor. Supt. of Documents. 1970. 18p. 30c
Information concerning requirements and training.

Machine tools—America's muscles. National Machine Tool Builders Association. 1969. 20p. Free
Nature of work, opportunities, and outlook.

Tool designer. Careers. 1970. 2p. 20c
Career summary for desk-top file. Duties, qualifications, and outlook.

Tool designer. California State Department of Employment. 1967. 4p. Single copy free
Occupational guide describing work, requirements, training, and outlook.

Tool maker. Careers. 1968. 2p. 20c
Career summary for desk-top file. Duties, qualifications, and outlook.

Tool and die maker. California State Department of Employment. 1968. 3p. Single copy free
Occupational guide describing work, requirements, training, and outlook.

**Tool and die maker. Chronicle Guidance Publications. 1968. 4p. 35c
Occupational brief summarizing work performed, working conditions, earnings, personal qualifications, training requirements, opportunities, and employment outlook.

* Tool and die makers. Science Research Associates. 1968. 4p. 45c
Occupational brief describing nature of work, requirements, training, working conditions, earnings, and future outlook.

**Tool and die makers. One section of *Occupational Outlook Handbook.*
Nature of work, where employed, training, other qualifications, advancement, employment outlook, earnings, and working conditions.

Toolmaker. Guidance Centre. 1967. 4p. 35c postpaid
Definition, qualifications necessary for entry and success, preparation, earnings, advantages, disadvantages, how to get started, and related occupations.

Toolmaker. Michigan Employment Security Commission. 1960. 2p. Single copy free
Job brief summarizing occupational data for use in Michigan.

TRAFFIC AGENT. *See* Ticket agent; Traffic manager

TRAFFIC ENGINEER 019.188

**A career in traffic engineering. Institute of Traffic Engineers. 1968. 25p. Free
Development of the work, duties, training, rewards, opportunities, and fields of employment. Illustrated.

Finding out about traffic engineers. Science Research Associates. 1967. 4p. 45c

Junior occupational brief containing concise facts about the job.

**Opportunities in traffic engineering. Robinson, Carlton C. Vocational Guidance Manuals. 1966. 120p. $1.95 paper; library edition $3.75

Picturing this as a career field with challenging new opportunities, the author explains the difference between traffic engineering and highway management and describes in detail the work of the state traffic engineer and the city traffic engineer. Also discussed are requirements, preparation, and how to get started.

Traffic engineer. Careers. 1969. 2p. 20c

Career summary for desk-top file. Duties, qualifications, and outlook.

* Traffic engineers. Science Research Associates. 1968. 4p. 45c

Occupational brief describing nature of work, training, qualifications, opportunities, and outlook. Selected references.

TRAFFIC MANAGER 184.168

A career for you in traffic management. Academy of Advanced Traffic. No date. 8p. Free

Description of work, qualifications, opportunities, and training.

**Employment outlook for industrial traffic managers, purchasing agents. Bulletin No. 1650–5. Bureau of Labor Statistics, U.S. Department of Labor. Supt. of Documents. 1970. 8p. 10c

Reprint from the *Occupational Outlook Handbook*.

Finding out about traffic managers. Science Research Associates. 1967. 4p. 45c

Junior occupational brief describing work and opportunities.

**Industrial traffic managers. One section of *Occupational Outlook Handbook*.

Nature of work, where employed, training, other qualifications, advancement, employment outlook, earnings, and working conditions.

Traffic manager. Careers. 1969. 2p. 20c

Career summary for desk-top file. Duties, qualifications, and outlook.

Traffic manager. Chronicle Guidance Publications. 1968. 4p. 35c

Occupational brief summarizing work performed, working conditions, personal qualifications, training, opportunities, and outlook.

Traffic manager. Guidance Centre. 1969. 4p. 35c postpaid

History and importance, nature of work, qualifications, working conditions, preparation, remuneration, advancement, outlook, related occupations, and how to get started.

Traffic managers. Science Research Associates. 1966. 4p. 45c

Occupational brief describing duties, requirements, getting started and advancing, earnings, advantages, disadvantages, and future outlook.

TRAFFIC MANAGER—*Continued*

**Your future in traffic management. Heine, Robert. Richards Rosen Press. 1967. 160p. $4; library edition $3.78

Description of work, qualifications, and opportunities.

TRANSLATOR AND INTERPRETER. *See* Linguist

TRANSPORTATION AGENT 912.368

The wonderful world of transportation. Lee, Laurie and Lambert, David. Doubleday and Company. 1970. 96p. $3.95

The history and development of land, sea, and air transportation. For grades 5 to 7.

**Your career in transportation. Liston, Robert A. Julian Messner. 1966. 192p. $3.95; library binding $3.64

An analysis of job opportunities and their promise of future growth in the five areas of domestic transportation which offer the greatest outlook for employment: air transport, trucking, buses, railroads, and traffic by river and canal. Includes list of sixty-five colleges offering degrees or majors in transportation. Illustrated.

**Your future in the trucking industry. Eskow, Gerald W. Richards Rosen Press. 1964. Revised 1969. 157p. $2.95; library edition $2.79

Includes information about a wide variety of jobs ranging from the semi-skilled to the professional. The industry is presented as an expanding one which offers good opportunities for advancement.

See also Bus driver; Driver; Motor vehicle transportation worker; Truck driver

TRAVEL AGENCY WORKER 237.168

Finding out about sightseeing guides. Science Research Associates. 1967. 4p. 45c

Junior occupational brief describing work and opportunities.

Finding out about travel agents. Science Research Associates. 1967. 4p. 45c

Junior occupational brief containing concise facts about the job.

**Opportunities in travel careers. Short, Don. Vocational Guidance Manuals, Inc. 1966. 128p. $1.95 paper; $3.75 library edition

Discussion of work in commercial travel agency, automobile-club travel bureau, noncommercial travel bureau, governmental bureau, railroads, airlines, bus lines, sightseeing and tour companies, steamship lines, and hotels. Includes a discussion of salaries, opportunities, and how to get started. Includes lists of state and regional travel bureaus and travel promotion agencies, railroads, bus lines, steamship lines, and airlines.

* Travel agency workers. Science Research Associates. 1969. 4p. 45c
  Occupational brief describing nature of work, requirements, getting started and advancing, earnings and hours, advantages, disadvantages, and future outlook.

Travel agent. California State Department of Employment. 1966. 5p. Single copy free
  Duties, working conditions, wages, hours, promotion, training, and employment outlook in California.

Travel agent. Careers. 1968. 2p. 20c
  Career summary for desk-top file. Duties, qualifications, and outlook.

Travel agent. Guidance Centre. 1967. 4p. 35c postpaid
  History and importance, nature of work, qualifications, working conditions, preparation, remuneration, advancement, outlook, related occupations and how to get started.

Travel counselor. Chronicle Guidance Publications. 1969. 4p. 35c
  Occupational brief summarizing work performed, related jobs, qualifications, training, earnings, methods of entry, advantages, disadvantages, and outlook.

Travel industry jobs. Alumnae Advisory Center. 1964. 6p. 35c
  Reprint from *Mademoiselle* describing several case histories of young women who have succeeded in jobs related to travel.

**Your career in the world of travel. Dowdell, Dorothy and Dowdell, Joseph. Julian Messner. 1971. 192p. $4.50; library edition $4.92
  Discussion of the career fields that have direct contact with the touring public: tour operation, travel agencies, bus lines, sightseeing, airlines sales, railroad and steamship passenger service, hotel-motel management, auto associations, car rentals, and tourist-information bureaus.

TREE EXPERT 409.181

Finding out about tree experts. Science Research Associates. 1967. 4p. 45c
  Junior occupational brief describing work and opportunities.

* Tree experts. Science Research Associates. 1968. 4p. 45c
  Occupational brief describing nature of work, requirements, methods of getting started, earnings, advantages, disadvantages, and future outlook.

Tree surgeon. Careers. 1970. 2p. 20c
  Career summary for desk-top file. Duties, qualifications, and outlook.

Tree surgeon. Chronicle Guidance Publications. 1967. 4p. 35c
  Occupational brief describing the care of trees and shrubs, importance of the work, training, wages, benefits, and employment outlook.

TRUCK DRIVER 905.883

The changing image of the truck driver. Chronicle Guidance Publications. 1967. 4p. 35c
  Reprinted article from *Traffic Safety* discusses public image of the truck driver, work performed, and salaries.

TRUCK DRIVER—*Continued*

**Driving occupations. One section of *Occupational Outlook Handbook.*

Nature of work, qualifications, and employment outlook. Specific information for over-the-road truck driver, local truck driver, routeman, intercity bus driver, local transit bus driver, and taxi driver.

Finding out about long-distance truck drivers. Science Research Associates. 1967. 4p. 45c

Junior occupational brief describing work and opportunities.

**Local truck drivers. One section of *Occupational Outlook Handbook.*

Nature of work, where employed, qualifications, employment outlook, earnings, and working conditions.

* Long-distance truck and bus drivers. Science Research Associates. 1968. 4p. 45c

Occupational brief describing the kinds of trucking, driver duties, qualifications, training, how to become a driver, opportunities, earnings, advantages, disadvantages, and future outlook.

Long haul truck driver, motor transport. California State Department of Employment. 1967. 5p. Single copy free

Occupational guides summarizing duties, employment prospects, earnings, requirements for entry, and suggestions for locating a job.

On the road with the truckers. American Trucking Associations. 1968. 6p. Free

New insights into opportunities as a truck driver.

On the road with the truckers. Chronicle Guidance Publications. 1969. 4p. 35c

Reprinted article from *The Lamp* discusses the drivers of the nation's highways and new truck stops catering to truckers' needs.

**Over-the-road truck drivers. One section of *Occupational Outlook Handbook.*

Nature of work, where employed, qualifications, training, advancement, employment outlook, earnings, and working conditions.

Powered industrial truck operator. Chronicle Guidance Publications. 1967. 4p. 35c

Occupational brief summarizing nature of work, working conditions, training requirements, personal qualifications, earnings, hours, and outlook.

Truck and transport driver. Guidance Centre. 1968. 4p. 35c postpaid

Definition, history and importance, qualifications, employment, advancement, outlook, remuneration, and how to get started.

Truck driver. Chronicle Guidance Publications. 1967. 4p. 35c

Occupational brief containing work performed, working conditions, personal requirements, training requirements, outlook, methods of entry, and suggested activities.

Truck driver, heavy. Careers. 1970. 2p. 20c

Career summary for desk-top file. Duties, qualifications, and outlook.

Truck drivers. Michigan Employment Security Commission. 1958. 2p. Single copy free

Job brief summarizing occupational data for use in Michigan.

The trucks that haul by night. Stevens, Leonard A. Thomas Y. Crowell Company. 1968. 48p. $3.50

This account of one night's haul provides some insight into trucking procedures. Written for ages 6 to 10.

Union wages and hours for local truckdrivers and their helpers. U.S. Department of Labor. Supt. of Documents. 1969. 20p. 50c

Surveys of the wage and benefit information for sixty-eight cities.

See also Bus driver; Driver; Motor vehicle transportation worker; Transportation agent

TRUCK FARMER. ***See*** **Vegetable farmer**

TYPIST **203.138**

Finding out about typists and stenographers. Science Research Associates. 1967. 4p. 45c

Junior occupational brief summarizing what the work requires and offers.

Typist. California State Department of Employment. 1966. 6p. Single copy free

Occupational guide describing work, requirements, training, and outlook.

Typist. Careers. 1969. 8p. 35c

Career brief describing duties, working conditions, training, personal qualifications, earnings, advancement prospects, and outlook.

Typist. Chronicle Guidance Publications. 1966. 4p. 35c

Occupational brief summarizing work performed, working conditions, qualifications, training, opportunities, methods of entry, related jobs, and outlook.

Typist. Michigan Employment Security Commission. 1966. 2p. Single copy free

Job brief summarizing occupational data for use in Michigan.

Typists. Science Research Associates. 1970. 4p. 45c

Occupational brief describing work, training, qualifications, opportunities, and outlook.

Typists. One section of *Occupational Outlook Handbook.*

Nature of work, places of employment, training, qualifications, employment outlook, earnings, advancement, and working condtions.

See also Clerical worker; Secretary; Stenographer

UNDERTAKER. ***See*** **Funeral director**

UNSKILLED WORKER 89 and 92

Factory occupations not requiring specialized training. One section of *Occupational Outlook Handbook,* 1964 edition

Nature of work, employment outlook, earnings, and working conditions.

Laborers. Science Research Associates. 1969. 4p. 45c

Occupational brief describing work, training, opportunities, and outlook.

Unskilled workers (laborers), semiskilled workers (operatives). One section of *Occupational Outlook Handbook.*

Brief explanation of kinds of jobs held and the employment outlook in some manual occupations.

UPHOLSTERER. *See* Furniture upholsterer

URBAN PLANNER 199.168

* Careers in planning. Changing Times. 1963. 3p. 15c

Reprint describing the mounting problems of city growth, traffic, land use, highway locations, and the utilization of natural resources. Includes education, qualifications, and earnings.

Careers in urban affairs: six young people talk about their professions in the inner city. Asbell, Bernard. David McKay Company. 1970. 111p. $3.95

Urban specialists cite examples of the cases they handle, describe their satisfactions and frustrations, and indicate the qualifications needed and the remuneration to be expected. Of interest to students interested in careers in urban services.

**The challenge of urban planning. American Institute of Planners. 1970. 8p. Free

A discussion of the issues facing planners, why they are needed, nature of work, some special duties, preparation, and career possibilities.

City planners. Steinberg, Jane. Alumnae Advisory Center. 1969. 7p. 35c

This describes the work of some women city planners who are trying to correct urban problems.

City planners. Alumnae Advisory Center. 1960. 8p. 35c

Reprint from *Mademoiselle* describing the work of several young women who are working on urban problems.

**City planners. Science Research Associates. 1967. 4p. 45c

Occupational brief describing nature of work, requirements, training, methods of getting started, earnings, advantages, disadvantages, and future outlook.

**Employment outlook for urban planners. Bulletin No. 1650–48. Bureau of Labor Statistics, U.S. Department of Labor. Supt. of Documents. 1970. 8p. 10c

Reprint from the *Occupational Outlook Handbook.*

Finding out about city planners. Science Research Associates. 1967. 4p. 45c

Junior occupational brief summarizing what the work requires and offers.

List of colleges offering degrees in planning. American Institute of Planners. 1968. 2p. Free

Includes schools in the United States and Canada.

Planner (city and regional). California State Department of Employment. 1966. 7p. Single copy free

Duties, working conditions, salaries, hours, entrance requirements, promotion, training, and employment outlook in California.

Schools offering degree programs in planning and related fields. American Society of Planning Officials. 1969. 12p. Single copy free; price for multiple copies supplied upon request.

List of schools offering bachelor's, master's, and doctorate degree programs, and the two-year preprofessional programs.

Suggested reading for information on a career in planning. American Society of Planning Officials. 1969. 2p. Single copy free; price for multiple copies supplied upon request

Information on careers in planning.

Two for the see saw. Chronicle Guidance Publications. 1968. 8p. 50c

Reprinted article from *AIA Journal* discusses opportunities in urban design and building design.

Unusual careers. Munzer, Martha E. Alfred A. Knopf, Inc. 1962. 160p. $3

The author emphasizes the opportunities in the conservation of natural resources. The careers described are solar scientist, geologist, meteorologist, oceanographer, ecologist, sanitary engineer, research chemist, and city and regional planner.

Urban and regional planner. Guidance Centre. 1968. 4p. 35c postpaid

Definition, history and importance, nature of work, preparation, qualifications, working conditions, employment, advancement, outlook, remuneration, and how to get started.

Urban planner. American Society of Planning Officials. 1969. 20p. Single copy free

Contains an example of actual requests for professional planners received by the society, giving types of positions and earnings.

Urban planner. Careers. 1970. 2p. 20c

Career summary for desk-top file. Duties, qualifications, and outlook.

* Urban planner. Chronicle Guidance Publications. 1969. 4p. 35c

Occupational brief summarizing work performed, working conditions, salaries, qualifications, training, opportunities, and employment outlook.

** Urban planners. One section of *Occupational Outlook Handbook.*

Nature of work, where employed, training, other qualifications, advancement, employment outlook, earnings, and working conditions.

USHER 344.878

Usher. Careers. 1970. 2p. 20c

Career summary for desk-top file. Duties, qualifications, and outlook.

USHER—*Continued*

Usher. Chronicle Guidance Publications. 1966. 4p. 35c

Occupational brief summarizing work performed, working conditions, hours, wages, personal requirements, training requirements, and outlook.

Usher. Guidance Centre. 1966. 4p. 35c postpaid

History and importance, nature of work, qualifications, working conditions, preparation, remuneration, advancement, outlook, related occupations, and how to get started.

VARI-TYPIST 203.582

Varityper operator. California State Department of Employment. 1967. 3p. Single copy free

Occupational guide describing work, requirements, training, and outlook.

Varityper operator. Careers. 1967. 2p. 20c

Career summary for desk-top file. Duties, qualifications, and outlook.

VEGETABLE FARMER 403.181

Finding out about vegetable and fruit farmers. Science Research Associates. 1967. 4p. 45c

Junior occupational brief describing work and opportunities.

Mushroom grower. Guidance Centre. 1968. 4p. 35c postpaid

History and importance, nature of work, qualifications, working conditions, preparation, remuneration, advancement, outlook, related occupations, and how to get started.

Truck farmer. Careers. 1970. 2p. 20c

Career summary for desk-top file. Duties, qualifications, and outlook.

Truck farmer. Guidance Centre. 1969. 4p. 23c postpaid

Definition, nature of work, working conditions, qualifications, earnings, employment and advancement, getting started, and related occupations.

Vegetable farmers. Science Research Associates. 1967. 4p. 45c

Occupational brief describing nature of work, preparation, opportunities, advantages, disadvantages, and future outlook.

See also Farmer, General; Fruit grower

VENDING MACHINE ROUTEMAN AND MECHANIC 292.358 and 639.381

Automatic vending routemen. Science Research Associates. 1966. 4p. 45c

Occupational guide describing work, requirements, training, and outlook.

**Employment outlook for vending machine mechanics. Bulletin No. 1650–90. Bureau of Statistics, U.S. Department of Labor. Supt. of Documents. 1970. 8p. 10c

Reprint from the *Occupational Outlook Handbook*.

Finding out about automatic vending routemen. Science Research Associates. 1967. 4p. 45c

Junior occupational brief describing work and opportunities.

Vending machine mechanics. One section of *Occupational Outlook Handbook.*

Nature of work, places of employment, qualifications, outlook, earnings, and working conditions.

Vending machine operator. Careers. 1967. 2p. 20c

Career summary for desk-top file. Duties, qualifications, and outlook.

**Vending machine repairman and operator. Chronicle Guidance Publications. 1969. 4p. 35c

Occupational brief summarizing work performed, where employed, working conditions, qualifications, training, earnings, and outlook.

VETERINARIAN 073.108

Animal doctors; what do they do? Greene, Carla. Harper and Row. 1967. 64p. $1.95; library edition $2.19

Simple text and three-color drawings explore the work of veterinarians—animal doctors in city, country, zoo, and circus as well as the doctor who cares for animals sent into space.

**Career facts about veterinary medicine. American Veterinary Medical Association. 1968. 6p. Single copy free; additional copies 3c each

Brief description of opportunities in health services and science, qualifications, training, and a list of twenty-one colleges of veterinary medicine.

A career in animal sciences. American Society of Animal Sciences. No date. 8p. 20c

Description of the varied areas of work and the many opportunities in this field. Includes a list of schools which offer a major or degree in animal sciences.

**Employment outlook for veterinarians. Bulletin No. 1650–22. Bureau of Labor Statistics, U.S. Department of Labor. Supt. of Documents. 1970. 8p. 10c

Reprint from the *Occupational Outlook Handbook.*

Finding out about veterinarians. Science Research Associates. 1967. 4p. 45c

Junior occupational brief summarizing what the work requires and offers.

**Opportunities in veterinary medicine. Swope, Robert E. Vocational Guidance Manuals. 1965. 144p. $1.95 paper; library binding $3.75

Asserting that this is a highly scientific field offering new challenges and opportunities for young men and women, the author analyzes the opportunities. The scope of the work is described for the practitioner in private practice, public service, industry, institutional teaching, military service, or research.

VETERINARIAN—*Continued*

Report on educational qualifications of public health veterinarians. American Public Health Association. 1959. 6p. Single copy free

General scope of the field, future outlook, educational qualifications, personal qualities, and lines of promotion.

**Today's veterinarian. American Veterinary Medical Association. 1970. 22p. Free

Careers in agriculture, public health, research, industry, government, and the military service are discussed. Veterinary medical training is described, including names and locations of colleges of veterinary medicine.

Veterinarian. California State Department of Employment 1967. 6p. Single copy free

Occupational guide describing work, requirements, training, and outlook.

Veterinarian. Careers. 1968. 8p. 35c

Career brief describing nature of work, training, working conditions, personal qualifications, employment prospects, earnings, where employed, and related careers. Includes list of seventeen approved schools for training.

Veterinarian. Chronicle Guidance Publications. 1967. 4p. 35c

Occupational brief summarizing work performed, working conditions, earnings, personal qualifications, training requirements, opportunities, and employment outlook.

Veterinarian. Guidance Centre. 1968. 4p. 35c postpaid

Definition, history and importance, working conditions, qualifications, preparation, earnings, advantages, disadvantages, how to get started, and related occupations.

Veterinarians. Michigan Employment Security Commission. 1962. 2p. Single copy free

Job brief summarizing occupational data for use in Michigan.

Veterinarians. Science Research Associates. 1966. 4p. 45c

Occupational brief describing nature of work, requirements, training, getting started, earnings, advantages, disadvantages, and future outlook.

* Veterinarians. One section of *Occupational Outlook Handbook*.

Nature of work, where employed, training, other qualifications, advancement, employment outlook, earnings, and working conditions.

Veterinarians and their patients. May, Charles Paul. Nelson and Sons. 1964. 240p. $3.50

An account of the work in private practice, research laboratories, animal hospitals, the Armed Forces, and in circuses and zoos. Illustrated.

Veterinary medicine. Pages 226-31 of *Health Careers Guidebook*.

Nature of work, personal qualifications, training, licensing, opportunities, and prospects.

What does a veterinarian do? Compton, Grant. Dodd, Mead and Company. 1964. 64p. Library edition $2.99

Photographs and brief text describe the work of the doctor with animals of all kinds from house pets and farm animals to circus performers. For grades 3 to 7.

**Your future in veterinary medicine. Riser, Wayne. Richards Rosen Press. Revised 1969. 158p. $4; library edition $3.78

Presents career information concerning work on a governmental level as well as practice with small animals.

VOCATIONAL COUNSELOR. ***See*** **Counselor; Personnel and employment manager**

VOCATIONAL REHABILITATION COUNSELOR. ***See*** **Rehabilitation counselor**

WAC. ***See*** **Armed Forces**

WAITER AND WAITRESS **311.878**

Dining car waiters. One section of *Occupational Outlook Handbook.*

Nature of work, training, other qualifications, advancement, earnings, and working conditions.

Finding out about dining car waiters. Science Research Associates. 1967. 4p. 45c

Junior occupational brief describing work and opportunities.

Finding out about waiters and waitresses. Science Research Associates. 1967. 4p. 45c

Junior occupational brief describing work and opportunities.

Railroad dining car waiters. Science Research Associates. 1966. 4p. 45c

Occupational brief describing work, qualifications, earnings, things to consider, and outlook.

Waiter or waitress. Guidance Centre. 1968. 4p. 35c postpaid

History and importance, nature of work, qualifications, preparation, working conditions, employment, outlook, advancement, earnings, advantages, and disadvantages.

* Waiter-waitress. Careers. 1967. 8p. 35c

Career brief describing duties, working conditions, training requirements, personal qualifications, employment prospects, advantages, disadvantages, earnings, measuring one's interest and ability, and suggested high school program.

Waiter (waitress). Chronicle Guidance Publications. 1969. 4p. 35c

Occupational brief summarizing work performed, working conditions, qualifications, training, opportunities, outlook, methods of entry, related jobs, and suggested activities.

WAITER AND WAITRESS—*Continued*

**Waiter-waitress as a career. Belleau, Wilfrid. Park Publishing House. 1969. 15p. $1

Importance and nature of the work, kinds of restaurants, qualifications, training, working conditions, income, opportunities, and advancement.

Waiters and waitresses. Science Research Associates. 1970. 4p. 45c

Occupational brief describing nature of work, qualifications, opportunities, advantages, disadvantages, and future outlook. Selected references.

**Waiters and waitresses. One section of *Occupational Outlook Handbook.*

Nature of work, where employed, training, other qualifications, advancement, employment outlook, earnings, and working conditions.

Waitress. California State Department of Employment. 1968. 2p. Single copy free

Occupational guide describing work, requirements, training, and outlook.

WASTE WATER TREATMENT PLANT OPERATOR. *See* Sewage-plant operator

WATCHMAKER AND WATCH REPAIRMAN 715.281

**Aim for a job in watchmaking. Lipton, Benjamin. Richards Rosen Press. 1967. 128p. $4; library edition $3.78

Description of training requirements, opportunities, and outlook. Includes a section on training handicapped people for this work.

Careers in watch repairing. American Watchmakers Institute. No date. 8p. Free

Description of work, qualifications, earnings, and outlook.

Clocks, watches and allied products industry. Chronicle Guidance Publications. 1967. 4p. 35c

Occupational brief summarizing work performed, working conditions, hours and earnings, personal requirements, training opportunities, and outlook.

Finding out about watch repairmen. Science Research Associates. 1967. 4p. 45c

Junior occupational brief summarizing what the work requires and offers.

National roster of watchmaking schools. American Watchmakers Institute. 1967. 6p. Free

Names, addresses, and pertinent information of thirty-six schools of watchmaking in the United States.

Watch repairmen. Science Research Associates. 1967. 4p. 45c

Occupational brief describing work, qualifications, training, earnings, and outlook.

**Watch repairmen. One section of *Occupational Outlook Handbook.*

Nature of work, where employed, training, other qualifications, advancement, employment outlook, earnings, and working conditions.

Watchmaker. California State Department of Employment. 1966. 3p. Single copy free

Occupational guide describing work, requirements, training, and outlook.

**Watchmaker (repairman). Careers. 1967. 8p. 35c

Career brief describing duties, working conditions, training requirements, training opportunities, personal qualifications, employment prospects, advantages, disadvantages, earnings, related careers, measuring one's interest and ability, and suggested high school program.

Watchmaker. Chronicle Guidance Publications. 1966. 4p. 35c

Occupational brief summarizing work performed, qualifications, training, working conditions, wages, and opportunities.

Watchmaker. Guidance Centre. 1966. 4p. 35c postpaid

Nature of work, qualifications, preparation, employment and advancement, outlook, earnings, advantages, disadvantages, how to get started, and related occupations.

Your future and our school—courses in watchmaking and repairing. Bowman Technical School. 1968. 12p. Free

Illustrated recruiting bulletin describing careers and courses in watchmaking and repairing.

See also Jeweler

WEATHER FORECASTER. *See* Meteorologist

WELDER 810. thru 819.887

**Aim for a job in welding. Berg, Thomas. Richards Rosen Press. 1967. 156p. $4; library edition $3.78

Basic information on job requirements, opportunities, working conditions, and pay rates. Useful for its lists of colleges, trade and technical schools offering training in welding.

Employment outlook for welders, oxygen and arc cutters. Bulletin No. 1650–105. Bureau of Labor Statistics, U.S. Department of Labor. Supt. of Documents. 1970. 8p. 10c

Reprint from the *Occupational Outlook Handbook.*

Finding out about welders. Science Research Associates. 1967. 4p. 45c

Junior occupational brief containing concise facts about the job.

**Opportunities in the welding industry. American Welding Society. 1962. 6p. Free

Discussion of the industry in general, educational requirements, wages, opportunities, and specific job descriptions.

Welder. California State Department of Employment. 1965. 4p. Single copy free

Occupational guide describing work, requirements, training, and outlook.

Welder. Guidance Centre. 1967. 4p. 35c postpaid

History and importance, nature of work, qualifications, preparation, working conditions, earnings, advantages, disadvantages, how to get started, and related occupations.

WELDER–*Continued*

Welder, manual. Careers. 1969. 2p. 20c
Career summary for desk-top file. Duties, qualifications, and outlook.

Welders. Chronicle Guidance Publications. 1968. 4p. 35c
Occupational brief describing work of arc, gas, and resistance welders. Includes description of working conditions, qualifications, training, outlook, and where employed.

Welders. Michigan Employment Security Commission. 1958. 2p. Single copy free
Job brief summarizing occupational data for use in Michigan.

Welders. Science Research Associates. 1967. 4p. 45c
Occupational brief describing nature of work, requirements, training, earnings, and outlook.

**Welders and oxygen and arc cutters. One section of *Occupational Outlook Handbook*.
Nature of work, where employed, training, other qualifications, employment outlook, earnings, and working conditions.

Welders and oxygen cutters. Careers. 1970. 8p. 35c
Career brief describing duties, working conditions, training, personal characteristics, earnings, where employed, and outlook.

Welding machine operator, arc. Careers. 1967. 2p. 20c
Career summary for desk-top file. Duties, qualifications, and outlook.

WHARFINGER **184.388**

Wharfinger. California State Department of Employment. 1965. 2p. Single copy free
Occupational guide describing work, requirements, training, and outlook in water transportation.

WHOLESALER **185.168**

**Career opportunities in wholesaling. National Association of Wholesalers. 1969. 12p. Single copy free
Function of wholesaling, kinds of jobs, training, advancement, working conditions, and trends.

Exploring your future in merchandising. Sextant Systems, Inc. 1970. 96p. $8.95
One page is devoted to each of ninety-five jobs, summarizing duties, requirements for entering, promotional outlook, and pay and skill level. Accompanying the book is an organizational chart showing the beginning jobs and those to which one may be promoted.

* Wholesale salesmen. Careers. 1966. 8p. 35c
Career brief describing duties, working conditions, training, personal qualifications, earnings, and outlook.

**Wholesale trade sales workers. One section of *Occupational Outlook Handbook.*

Nature of work, where employed, training, employment outlook, earnings, and working conditions.

Your career in wholesale distribution. National Association of Wholesalers. 1969. 10p. Single copy free

Function of wholesaling, kinds of jobs, fringe benefits. working conditions, and trends.

WILDLIFE SPECIALIST 040.081

Finding out about wildlife managers. Science Research Associates. 1967. 4p. 45c

Junior occupational brief describing work and opportunities.

Fish and wildlife; the story of the work of the U.S. Fish and Wildlife Service. Colby, Carroll B. Coward-McCann, Inc. 1955. 48p. $2.50; library binding $2.97

Describes the work of protecting and conserving the wild birds, animals, and fish of our country. Written for grades 4 to 8.

Jobs in outdoor work. Science Research Associates. 1964. 48p. $1.15

Describes the variety of job prospects and opportunities in outdoor work, including the wildlife manager, treeman, forester, surveyor, and nurseryman.

John Muier, protector of the wilds. Haines, Madge and Morrill, Leslie. Abingdon Press. 1957. 128p. $2.25

Biography of the great naturalist who fought to preserve in national parks some of the wilderness he treasured.

**Nature's guardians; your career in conservation. Neal, Harry Edward. Julian Messner. 1963. 192p. Library binding $3.64

Kinds of work, opportunities, and training in wildlife management, fishery work, forestry, or soil and water conservation. Bibliography.

Park naturalist. Careers. 1965. 2p. 20c

Career summary for desk-top file. Duties, qualifications, and outlook.

Park rangers and game wardens the world over. Torbert, Floyd James. Hastings House. 1968. 64p. $3.96

An account of the protectors of natural wildlife reserves in sixteen countries. Includes descriptions of the duties of rangers and wardens. For grades 4 to 6.

The United States Department of the Interior; a story of rangeland, wildlife, and dams. Duell, Sloan and Pearce. 1963. 117p. $3.50

Describes the activities of various agencies such as the Fish and Wildlife Service, the Bureau of Indian Affairs, the Bureau of Mines, the Bureau of Land Management, the Bureau of Reclamation, and the National Park Service.

A wildlife conservation career for you. The Wildlife Society. 1968. 11p. Free

Description of the nature of work, training and education needed, personal requirements, places of work, and earnings.

WILDLIFE SPECIALIST—*Continued*

* Wildlife managers. Science Research Associates. 1970. 4p. 45c
Occupational brief describing nature of work, personal qualifications, educational requirements, earnings, advantages, disadvantages, and outlook.

Wildlife research problems, programs, progress. Government Printing Office. Supt. of Documents. 1970. 112p. $1.25
Gives an idea of kinds of work for which there may be demands.

Wildlife specialist. Careers. 1970. 8p. 35c
Career brief describing duties, working conditions, training, personal qualifications, earnings, advancement prospects, and outlook.

See also Fish and game warden; Conservation specialist

WINDOW TRIMMER. ***See*** **Display worker**

WINE MAKER **183.168**

Enologist (wine maker). California State Department of Employment. 1964. 6p. Single copy free
Job duties, working conditions, pay, hours, training, and employment outlook in California.

Vineyard manager (vineyard foreman). California State Department of Employment. 1964. 5p. Single copy free
Occupational guide describing work, requirements, training, and outlook.

WOMEN'S-CLOTHING DESIGNER. ***See*** **Clothes designer**

WOOD TECHNOLOGIST **040.081**

Colleges and universities and their professional education programs for careers in the forest products industries. National Forest Product Association. 1963. 4p. Free
Names and locations of schools.

Millman (woodworking). California State Department of Employment. 1967. 4p. Single copy free
Occupational guide describing work, requirements, training, and outlook of a wood machinist.

Wood technologist. California State Department of Employment. 1966. 5p. Single copy free
Occupational guide describing work, requirements, training, and outlook.

Woodworker. Guidance Centre. 1969. 4p. 35c postpaid
Nature of the work, preparation, qualifications, employment outlook, advancement, remuneration, related occupations, and how to get started.

WOODSMAN (LOGGING) 940.884

Woodsman (logging). Guidance Centre. 1965. 4p. 35c postpaid

Nature of work, history and importance, working conditions, qualifications necessary for entry and success, preparation, outlook, and how to get started.

WRITER 139.288

**Advertising: a career of action and variety for exceptional men and women. American Association of Advertising Agencies. 1970. 24p. 25c. Single copy free to counselors.

The booklet shows how advertising makes use of talents in writing, art, film making, selling, statistics, and economics. Copiously illustrated.

Edna St. Vincent Millay: America's best-loved poet. Shafter, Toby. Julian Messner. 1957. 192p. $3.50; library binding $3.34

Biography of the well-known poet.

Education for technical writers. Chronicle Guidance Publications. 1967. 4p. 35c

Reprinted article from *Society of Technical Writers and Publishers Review* discusses qualifications, training, and hirability of applicants for writing positions.

**Employment outlook for writing occupations. Bulletin No. 1650–49. Bureau of Labor Statistics, U.S. Department of Labor. Supt. of Documents. 1970. 12p. 15c

Reprint from the *Occupational Outlook Handbook*. Includes information about newspaper reporters, and technical writers.

Finding out about free-lance writers. Science Research Associates. 1967. 4p. 45c

Junior occupational brief describing work and opportunities.

Finding out about technical writers. Science Research Associates. 1967. 4p. 45c

Junior occupational brief describing work and opportunities.

* Free-lance writers. Science Research Associates. 1968. 4p. 45c

Occupational brief describing nature of work, training, qualifications, opportunities, advantages, disadvantages, and future outlook.

Free-lance writing. Alumnae Advisory Center. 1968. 6p. 35c

Reprint from *Mademoiselle* warning that to succeed one has to be a disciplined loner. However, the author points out many advantages in free-lance writing.

Jobs and opportunities for writers. Writer's Digest. 1968. 16p. $1

Description of various kinds of work and outlook.

Literary and library prizes. Weber, Olga S. R. R. Bowker Company. Revised 1967. 340p. $9.95

This frequently-revised directory gives the description, requirements, means of selection, and names of winners of international literary prizes from date of inception through 1966. Gives an idea of the rewards of literary work.

WRITER—*Continued*

Literary market place—the business directory of American book publishing. R. R. Bowker Company. 1970. 700p. $9.95

Includes names and addresses of book publishers, advertising agents, author's agents, national associations, book clubs, columnists and commentators, and organizations marketing literary material. Also includes a list of courses given by twelve institutions and associations on phases of the book trade and graphic arts, list of writer's conferences with addresses and dates, and list of major awards given to books and authors. Revised annually.

Literary writer (free lance). Chronicle Guidance Publications. 1969. 4p. 35c

Occupational brief summarizing work performed, where employed, working conditions, personal requirements, earnings, methods of entry, and outlook.

No whippings, no gold watches; the saga of a writer and his jobs. Kronenberger, Louis. Little, Brown and Company. 1970. 309p. $6.95

An American writer and critic looks back at a varied career that has encompassed a variety of jobs with several publishing houses, teaching sessions at a number of universities, and an interval as a university librarian.

**Opportunities in free-lance writing. Maxon, Hazel C. Vocational Guidance Manuals. 1964. 128p. $1.95 paper; $3.75 library edition

Discusses ability, expanding market, remuneration, opportunity, competition, education and experience desirable, how to keep in touch with the markets, how to begin and how to prepare a manuscript. Description of a seamy day and a sunny day.

Opportunities in technical writing. Gould, Jay R. Vocational Guidance Manuals. 1964. 160p. $1.95 paper; library edition $3.75

Pointing out that this is a new field with new challenges for those with writing ability and an interest in the sciences and engineering, the author describes the many projects of technical writers. Information is given concerning education and training and how to get started. A list is presented of employers of technical writers.

Report of the opportunities in free-lance writing as a career or as an avocation. National Writers Club. 1968. 16p. 15c. Single copy free

Information on the markets for original manuscripts.

Science writers. Science Research Associates. 1966. 4p. 45c

Occupational brief describing work, training, qualifications, opportunities, and outlook.

Scriptwriters. Science Research Associates. 1967. 4p. 45c

Occupational brief describing work, training, qualifications, opportunities, and outlook.

* Technical writer. Careers. 1968. 8p. 35c

Career brief summarizing duties, training, personal qualifications, earnings, advancement prospects, related careers, and outlook. Additional readings.

Technical writer. California State Department of Employment. 1968. 3p. Single copy free

Occupational guide describing work, requirements, training, and outlook.

Technical writer. Chronicle Guidance Publications. 1969. 4p. 35c
Occupational brief summarizing work performed, personal qualifications, training, opportunities, and outlook.

Technical writers. Science Research Associates. 1970. 4p. 45c
Occupational brief describing work, qualifications, earnings, advantages, disadvantages, and outlook. Selected references.

**Technical writers. One section of *Occupational Outlook Handbook*.
Nature of work, where employed, training, other qualifications, advancement, employment outlook, earnings, and working conditions.

Twelve writing jobs. Alumnae Advisory Center. 1963. 7p. 35c
Reprint from *Mademoiselle* describing the work of twelve writers of nonfiction, employed in a variety of commercial writing fields.

**Why not be a technical writer? Leaflet 47. Women's Bureau, U.S. Department of Labor. Supt. of Documents. 1968. 8p. 10c
Brief sketch of nature of work, duties, where employed, qualifications, earnings, and opportunities. Illustrated.

Writer. Careers. 1967. 8p. 35c
Career brief describing duties, working conditions, training requirements, personal qualifications, employment outlook, salaries, related careers, measuring one's interest and ability, and suggested high school program.

**Writing as a career. Lobsenz, Norman M. Henry Z. Walck, Inc. 1963. 128p. $4.50
This book tells how to prepare for, where to find, and what to expect in eleven major career areas for writers: newspapers, consumer magazines, industrial magazines, business publications, free-lance writing, advertising, public relations, technical journalism, radio and television journalism, and creative writing. Reading list.

Young women poets. Alumnae Advisory Center. 1969. 6p. 35c
Reprint from *Mademoiselle* describing typical activities, related work, and how to progress in this field.

See also Playwright

X-RAY TECHNICIAN. *See* Radiologic technologist

YMCA PROFESSIONAL WORKER 195.108

Exploring your future in recreation, parks, and youth services. Sextant Systems, Inc. 1971. 96p. $8.95
One page is devoted to each of ninety-five jobs, describing the duties, requirements for entering, promotional outlook, and the pay and skill level.

Make your life count. National Council of Young Men's Christian Association. 1968. 8p. Single copy free
Employment opportunities, educational requirements, methods of training, and list of regional offices.

YMCA secretary. Careers. 1970. 2p. 20c
Career summary for desk-top file. Duties, qualifications, and outlook.

YMCA PROFESSIONAL WORKER—*Continued*

**You and the YMCA. National Council of Young Men's Christian Association. 1968. 10p. Single copy free

Illustrated folder describing work for the YMCA, and the qualifications required.

YWCA PROFESSIONAL WORKER **195.108**

**Basic booklet on YWCA job opportunities. Young Women's Christian Association, National Board. 1967. 16p. Free

Information about professional work in the YWCA.

YWCA personnel administration manual. Young Women's Christian Association, National Board. 1966. 122p. $2.50

A comprehensive manual on recruitment, employment, and the development of professional staff. Appendix includes sample job description, personnel policies and records, and suggested salary ranges.

YWCA Professional workers. Careers. 1968. 2p. 20c

Career summary for desk-top file. Duties, qualifications, and outlook.

YOUTH ORGANIZATION WORKER. ***See* Group worker**

ZOOLOGIST **041.081**

**Careers in animal biology. American Society of Zoologists. 1961. 16p. 35c

This booklet describes the work of zoologists who specialize in the study of certain classes of animals. Includes the ornithologist's study of birds, the herpetologist's work with reptiles and amphibians, the ichthyologist's research with fishes, and the mammalogist's study of mammals.

Ichthyologist. Careers. 1968. 2p. 20c

Career summary for desk-top file. Describes duties, working conditions, qualifications, training, outlook, where employed, and related careers.

Jobs in zoos. Alumnae Advisory Center. 1967. 6p. 35c

Reprint from *Mademoiselle* describing typical jobs, how to begin, and case histories of some successful women who work in zoos.

**Opportunities for the ichthyologist. U.S. National Museum. 1964. 4p. Single copy free

Brochure containing information about the preparation, opportunities, and required training.

Zeke zoo keeper. Kaufman, Joe. Golden Press. 1968. 24p. 69c

A tall picture book, sixteen inches tall, prepared for nursery school and kindergarten children. Contains vivid color illustrations of typical activities, equipment, and uniforms, explained in simple caption texts.

Zoologist. Careers. 1968. 2p. 20c

Career summary for desk-top file. Duties, qualifications, and outlook.

Zoologist. Chronicle Guidance Publications. 1967. 4p. 35c

Occupational brief summarizing work performed, where employed, earnings, personal qualifications, training, methods of entry, and employment outlook.

Zoologist. Guidance Centre. 1967. 4p. 35c postpaid

Definition, nature of work, preparation, qualifications, working conditions, employment, advancement, outlook, remuneration, and how to get started.

**Zoologists. Science Research Associates. 1968. 4p. 45c

Occupational brief describing nature of work, requirements, preparation, opportunities, earnings, and outlook.

Zoologists. Brief section in *Occupational Outlook Handbook.*

Nature of work, training, and employment outlook.

See also Herpetologist

B. Books and Pamphlets Describing More Than One Occupation

**After college . . . what? A career exploration handbook. Brown, Newell. Lads Publishing Company. 1968. 246p. $2.95 paper

After offering the college student general guidelines to the choice of a career, the author describes six major fields of work and sixty-two specific jobs. Salary charts, sources of job information, and advice on applying for work are appended.

Beggar to king; all the occupations of biblical times. Duckat, Walter B. Doubleday and Company. 1968. 327p. $5.95

This unusual compilation brings together information on over two hundred occupations mentioned in the Bible. Contains several appendices.

* Career guide for young people. Moore, Mary Furlong. Doubleday and Company. 1963. 262p. 95c paper

Arranged alphabetically under professions, arts, sciences, and business are brief job descriptions. Each explains the qualifications the job requires and the earnings, advancement, and opportunities one may expect.

Career thresholds. U.S. Department of Labor. Supt. of Documents. 1970. 266p. $2

A longitudinal study of the educational and labor market experience of male youth.

**Careers for college graduates. Peterson, Clarence E. Barnes and Noble, Inc. 1968. 334p. $2.25 paper

Following a section on planning a career, preparation for employment, and obtaining a job, there are occupational digests for eighty-two kinds of work. Most of the digests describe nature of work, where employed, training, qualifications, and advancement. Good reading lists.

Careers for women. Texas Woman's University. 1967. 42p. Free

For each of twenty major fields there is a discussion of opportunities, positions held by graduates, and training. Illustrations of views and activities of the college.

Careers in the age of automation. Aulick, June and Cross, Wilbur. Hawthorn Books, Inc. 1969. 223p. $5.95

This book discusses the opportunities which automation has made possible, especially in science, finance, management, marketing, selling, and the arts. Also gives advice on where the jobs will be in the future. Gives sources of information on various professions.

B. Books and Pamphlets Describing More Than One Occupation—*Continued*

Careers in the national park service. National Park Service. 1968. 31p. Free

Describes permanent employment in the National Park Service. Discusses typical jobs, preparation, application procedure, and employee benefits. Illustrated.

The college graduate and General Motors. General Motors Corporation, Salaried Personnel Placement Activity. Revised 1968. 17p. Free

A pamphlet giving information concerning the types of work for which college students and graduates are employed in General Motors and the general procedure followed in their recruiting program.

A counseling aid for high school counselors and deans of girls. University of Cincinnati, College of Business Administration. Annual. 24p. Free to counselors

Contains sixteen career articles written by women graduates of the degree program in business administration.

**Dictionary of occupational titles. Third edition. Volume I. Definitions of titles. U.S. Employment Service. Supt. of Documents. Revised 1965. 809p. $5

Volume I presents alphabetically by job title the definitions and code numbers of 21,741 jobs. These are known by 13,809 additional titles, or alternate titles, making a total of 35,550 titles defined. This edition contains 6,432 jobs new to the *Dictionary*.

Dictionary of occupational titles. Third edition. Volume II. Occupational classification and industry index. U.S. Employment Service. Supt. of Documents. Revised 1965. 656p. $4.25

Volume II presents the new occupational classification structure consisting of two arrangements of jobs: (1) jobs grouped in numerical order according to some combination of work field, purpose, material, product, subject matter, generic term, and industry; (2) jobs grouped according to some combination of required educational development, specific vocational preparation, aptitudes, interests, temperaments, and physical demands. Also lists all titles by industry.

Dictionary of occupational titles. Supplement 1, 1966. Selected characteristics of occupations. U.S. Employment Service. Supt. of Documents. 1966. 280p. $2.75

Lists physical demands, working conditions, and training time requirements for each job defined in the *Dictionary*. Provides index for locating each job in the *Dictionary* where information about the range of aptitudes, interests, and temperaments required by groups of occupations is shown.

Dictionary of occupational titles. Supplement 2, 1968. Selected Characteristics of occupations by worker traits and physical strength. U.S. Employment Service. Supt. of Documents. 1968. 156p. $1.25

Rearranges the data of the supplement 1 by grouping together jobs with similar traits and abilities (worker trait groups), and subgrouping jobs according to physical strength needed.

**Earned degrees conferred: bachelor's and higher degrees. U.S. Office of Education. Supt. of Documents. 1968. 289p. $2

Analytic report of data relating to degrees conferred by major areas of study, by type of institution, by region, and by institution. Degree data are summarized at the bachelor's, master's, and doctor's level for each of 200 major fields of study and for each of 1,549 colleges conferring degrees.

* Education and jobs. Bureau of Labor Statistics, U.S. Department of Labor. Order from Supt. of Documents. 1968. 5 pamphlets. 8 pages each. Single copy 10c each. $6.75 per 100

This series of motivational pamphlets is designed as a guide to jobs that match different levels of education and training. Each pamphlet contains qualifications, training needed, trends, and employment opportunities for each occupation listed in each category. Titles:

Jobs for which apprenticeship training is available.
Jobs for which a high school education is generally required.
Jobs for which junior college technical institute or other specialized training is usually required.
Jobs for which a high school education is preferred, but not essential.
Jobs for which a college education is usually required.

**Encyclopedia of careers and vocational guidance. Hopke, William E., ed. Vol. I: Planning your career. 752p. Vol. II: Careers and Opportunities. 784p. 1967. Ferguson Publishing Company. $30 boxed set

Volume one's value lies in introductory material on topics such as defining personal goals, finding a job, and applying vocational test results. The remainder of the volume consists of a series of essays by authorities who give an overview of their vocations. Volume two consists of detailed information concerning jobs, including nature of work, requirements, potential earnings, advantages, and disadvantages.

**Exciting careers for home economists. Spencer, Lila. Julian Messner. 1967. 192p. $3.95; library binding $3.64

Describes opportunities and requirements in a variety of specialized areas in textiles, food, fashion, writing, art, chemistry, teaching, radio, and television. Includes a selected reading list and list of colleges offering majors or degrees in home economics.

Exploring your future in the professions. Sextant Systems, Inc. 1970. 96p. $8.95

One page is devoted to each of ninety-five jobs, summarizing duties, requirements for entering, promotional outlook, and pay and skill level. Accompanying the book is an organizational chart showing the various professions in the humanities and in the sciences.

Famous American women. Stoddard, Hope. Crowell, Collier and Macmillan. 1970. 461p. $7.50

Biographical sketches of forty-two women who have made significant contributions to many areas of American life, including the arts, industrial engineering, sports, medicine, social reform, and philosophy. A bibliography appears at the end of each sketch and the book contains a portrait of each woman.

B. Books and Pamphlets Describing More Than One Occupation—*Continued*

**Federal career directory: a guide for college students. U.S. Civil Service Commission. Supt. of Documents. 1968. 87p. $1.25

Includes ninety-two job briefs containing nature of work, qualifications required, and career opportunities. One index of job briefs is by position title and another by college major fields of study. For college graduates.

Film catalog. American Federation of Labor and Congress of Industrial Organizations. 1968. 6p. Free to teachers

List of three hundred educational films provided for members and available to schools for a service charge.

**Future jobs for high school girls. Pamphlet 7. Women's Bureau, U.S. Department of Labor. Supt. of Documents. 1966. 73p. 30c

Designed for high school graduates, this pamphlet provides information on a variety of occupations open to women, from the woman-dominated secretarial group to technical specialties where women are just beginning to make their marks.

Futures for college women in New York. Alumnae Advisory Center. 1968. 56p. $1

Discussion of prospects for the beginner including secretarial work, publishing, programming, advertising, and fashion. Special advice on job seeking.

Great Negroes, past and present. Third edition. Afro-American Publishing Company. 1969. 212p. $6.95; paper $3.95

Brief biographical sketches of 175 black men and women. Has simplified presentation and numerous illustrations.

**A guide to professional careers. Duckat, Walter. Julian Messner. 1970. 285p. $5.95; library binding $5.64

For each of eighty careers requiring considerable training beyond high school, the author has detailed the requirements, training, duties, income, and future outlook. A useful appendix lists jobs with the Federal Government based on college majors. Another lists free vocational literature for each of the careers covered.

**Handbook of job facts. Fourth edition. Thiemann, Norma. Science Research Associates. 1968. 134p. $4.25

Compilation of information in tabular form, containing concise summaries of the basic facts about three hundred major occupations. The ten headings include duties, number of workers, special qualifications, earnings, and supply and demand.

Hands that help. Dodge, Bertha. Little, Brown and Company. 1967. 247p. $4.75

A description and history of the various careers allied to the medical profession.

How to start a money-making business at home. Robertson, Laura. Frederick Fell, Inc. 1969. 144p. $4.95

The author explores the potentials of home businesses where one can be one's own boss, such as an art rental agency, personal shopping service, dressmaking service for the physically handicapped, handicraft marketing, and other unusual businesses.

How to travel and get paid for it. Ford, Norman. Harian Publications. 1969. 72p. $1.50

Describes the types of work and opportunities with the transportation lines, airlines, Government agencies, commerce, and services such as the American National Red Cross.

Indexes of output per man hour in selected industries. Bureau of Labor Statistics, U.S. Department of Labor. Supt. of Documents. 1969. 100p. $1

This bulletin presents, for thirty-five industries, marked changes in productivity trends, output per man-hour, unit labor requirements, and related data from 1939 through 1968. Includes selected manufacturing industries, mining industries, railroad transportation, air transportation, and gas and electric utilities.

**Industry profiles. U.S. Department of Commerce. Supt. of Documents. 1969. 184p. $1.50

Designed to provide users of industrial data with a convenient single source of comparable basic industry statistics, this presents a statistical picture of economic developments in each of 418 manufacturing industries covered. It presents sixteen basic data series relating to employment, payrolls, man-hours, value of shipments, capital expenditures, and selected averages.

**Job guide for young workers, 1969-1970 edition. Bureau of Employment Security, U.S. Department of Labor. Supt. of Documents. 1969. 200p. $1.50

Supplies young workers with information on a host of entry jobs, related topics, and the many job-training programs available for young job-seekers. Discusses nature of work, working conditions, training and other requirements, avenues of advancement, employment prospects, and location of jobs. Gives advice on how to seek work.

**Job horizons for college women. Bulletin 288. Women's Bureau, U.S. Department of Labor. Supt. of Documents. 1967. 91p. 35c

Briefly describes the nature of thirty-two of the many careers open to college women, indicates educational and training requirements for entry into various professions, and lists a number of continuing education programs available. Lists selected readings on employment and training opportunities in the professions.

Job opportunities for young Negroes. Paradis, Adrian. David McKay Company. 1969. 224p. $4.95

This covers job opportunities in selling, service businesses, insurance, banking, transportation, government, health services, sports, armed forces, and manufacturing. Information is included on financial assistance. Also contains good lists of sources of references about various types of work.

B. Books and Pamphlets Describing More Than One Occupation—*Continued*

Jobs after high school. Changing Times. 1964. 4p. 15c

A guide to many opportunities for those who do not go to college.

Jobs for women in the FBI. Federal Bureau of Investigation. 1968. 1p. Free

Qualifications for technical and clerical work, including laboratory aides, translators, stenographers, typists, and clerks.

Jobs in unusual occupations. Feingold, S. Norman and List, Harold. Science Research Associates. 1963. 48p. $1.15

Short descriptions of three jobs requiring each of the following: physical ability, manual dexterity, reasoning ability, handling detail, handling people, working with nature, and musical or dramatic ability.

**Jobs to take you places—here and abroad; a guide to vocational opportunities in each of the fifty states and positions in business, government, and voluntary agencies abroad. Paradis, Adrian A. David McKay Company. 1968. 276p. $4.95

Suggestions to young people who want meaningful careers in an unfamiliar environment. Suggested readings are listed throughout the book.

Manpower needs for national goals in the 1970's. Lecht, Leonard A. Frederick A. Praeger, Inc. 1969. 183p. $7.50

The director of the Center for Priority Analysis of the National Planning Association predicts the demand factors in regard to high, moderate, and low growth occupations.

Men at work in the mid-Atlantic states. Lent, Henry B. G. P. Putnam's Sons. 1961. 192p. $3.00

An overview of the occupations of those who work in the major industries and manufacturing plants in New York, New Jersey, Pennsylvania, West Virginia, Delaware, and Maryland. For younger readers, ages 8 to 12.

Other titles in the same series survey New England, the West Coast, Great Lakes States, Great Plains States, Mountain States, and the South.

Modern American career women. Clymer, Eleanor and Erlich, Lillian. Dodd, Mead and Company. 1959. 179p. $3

Eighteen biographical sketches illustrating the variety of careers in which American women have attained distinction.

* Modern vocational trends reference handbook. Angel, Juvenal L. Regents Publishing Company. 7th edition 1969. 520p. $17.50

Description of work, training, remuneration, and opportunities for each of forty careers currently most popular among young men and women. A second section lists occupational titles for those who have special interests and abilities.

Moments of decision. Olson, H. F. Scholastic Book Services. 1961. 192p. 60c paper

Explores great moments in the lives of exciting personalities, as well as problems of vocational choice. This title is available to schools, only, through the Scholastic Book Services.

**National survey of professional, administrative, technical, and clerical pay. Bureau of Labor Statistics, U.S. Department of Labor. Supt. of Documents. 1970. 80p. 75c

This survey, the tenth in an annual series, provides nationwide salary averages and distributions for seventy-eight work level categories covering twelve occupational groups. Includes accountants, attorneys, personnel management, buyers, engineers and chemists, engineering technicians, draftsmen, and office clerical, in private industry.

Negro employment in basic industry; a study of racial policies in six industries. Northrup, Herbert. University of Pennsylvania Press. 1970. 769p. $10

An analysis of employment of Negroes, both men and women, in United States industry in years past and at present. The reports in this volume cover the automobile, aerospace, steel, rubber tire, petroleum, and chemical industries.

New careers, jobs with a future and a profession. U.S. Department of Labor. Supt. of Documents. 1969. 8p. 10c

This leaflet briefly discusses the program which is designed to help the poor and unemployed find steady jobs by starting them as preprofessionals in fields where labor shortages exist.

Night people. Colby, C. B. Coward-McCann, Inc. 1961. 48p. Library edition $2.97

Photographs and facts revealing the world of those who work after dark. Written for grades 4 and up.

**1969 handbook on women workers. Bulletin 290. Women's Bureau, U.S. Department of Labor. Supt. of Documents. 1969. 384p. $1.50

Factual information covering the participation and characteristics of women in the labor force, patterns of their employment, occupations, income, education and training, and the State laws affecting the employment status of women. Lists professional and social organizations for women. A bibliography on American workers, classified by subject matter, also is included. Frequently revised.

**Occupational outlook for college graduates. Bulletin 1681. Bureau of Labor Statistics, U.S. Department of Labor. Supt. of Documents. 1971. 258p. $2

This guide to occupations for which a college education is necessary or useful contains reports on employment opportunities for one hundred professional and related jobs. It is designed to be a convenient source of vocational information for college students, counselors, and college placement officials. Job descriptions in the book cover nature of the work, employment outlook through the 1970's, educational and training requirements, earnings, and places of employment.

B. Books and Pamphlets Describing More Than One Occupation—*Continued*

**Occupational outlook handbook. Bureau of Labor Statistics, U.S. Department of Labor. Supt. of Documents. 1970. 859p. $6.25

Brief reports on more than seven hundred occupations and thirty major industries including professions, skilled trades, clerical, sales, service occupations, and the major types of farming. Each report describes the employment trends and outlook, qualifications required for a beginning position, prospects for advancement, earnings, and working conditions. Introductory sections summarize the major trends in population and employment as background for an understanding of the individual occupations. 310 photographs; 40 charts.

**Occupational outlook handbook in brief. Summer issue of *Occupational Outlook Quarterly,* 1970. 16p. 45c

In tabular form a brief summary of the *Handbook* presents the estimated employment, average number of annual openings to 1980, and employment prospects for about 225 occupations.

**Occupational outlook reprint series. Bureau of Labor Statistics, U.S. Department of Labor. Supt. of Documents. 1970. 10c to 20c. Set of 128 pamphlets $16.55

Series of 128 individual pamphlets reprinted from the *Occupational Outlook Handbook,* each giving nature of work, places of employment, training, employment outlook, earnings, working conditions, and list of all occupations covered in the series.

Occupations in Federal white-collar workers. U.S. Civil Service Commission. Supt. of Documents. 1968. 125p. $1.25

An occupational inventory of full-time Federal civilian white-collar employees by agency, grade, sex, and geographic area. Median grade and average salary for men and women within each occupation as of October 31, 1967 are included.

**Our world of work. Wolfbein, Seymour and Goldstein, Harold. Science Research Associates. 1961. 48p. 75c

Presents a panoramic view of what our work force is like today and of the various trends that forecast its future. Includes discussion of how the world of work has changed in the past fifty years, what industries employ over sixty million workers, the major occupational fields, and other data about the rapidly growing labor market.

Patterns of United States economic growth. Government Printing Office. Supt. of Documents. 1970. 41p. 50c

Presents projections of employment by industry for 1980.

Profiles and portraits of American presidents and their wives. Grosset and Dunlap, Inc. 1969. 449p. $10

A portrait and text about each president and portraits of all but eight of the wives.

Speaking of people. National Urban League. 1963. 32p. 10c

Pictures, brief biographical sketches, and description of work of fourteen successful Negro workers.

Tomorrow's jobs—where the best will be. Changing Times. 1966. 5p. 15c

A brief estimate of job futures in a number of industries.

The unabashed career guide. Sandman, Peter M. Macmillan Company. 1969. 253p. $5.95

Basing his report on responses of five hundred persons questioned concerning their jobs, the author presents his views to college graduates about their selections of careers. The amusing style will appeal to older teen-agers.

* Unusual careers. Munzer, Martha. Alfred A. Knopf, Inc. 1962. 160p. $3

This book emphasizes the opportunities in discovery, conservation, development, and care of the country's natural resources. Includes information about the career of the solar scientist, meteorologist, oceanographer, ecologist, geologist, sanitary engineer, research chemist, and regional and city planner. Good reading lists. For younger readers.

The U.S. economy in 1980. Bureau of Labor Statistics, U.S. Department of Labor. Supt. of Documents. 1970. 59p. 65c

In this bulletin, the Bureau of Labor Statistics looks ten years ahead at the growth and composition of the economy, the need for workers, and the likely supply of manpower.

Vocational training in New York City . . . where to find it. Vocational Foundations, Inc. 1967. 324p. $8.50

Information about training in 600 vocations afforded by approximately 850 schools and colleges in New York City. Arranged by occupation. Includes entrance requirements and tuition costs. Good indexes.

Want to help make the world better? One way is through a career in the rehabilitation professions. National Easter Seal Society for Crippled Children and Adults. 1968. 6p. $15 per 1000. Single copy free

Describes the work of specialists who help the disabled attain a better life. Includes the physical therapist, occupational therapist, speech pathologist, rehabilitation counselor, recreation therapist, and medical social worker.

Women at work; every woman's guide to successful employment. Winter, Elmer L. Simon and Schuster, Inc. Revised 1967. 350p. $5.95; paper $1.95

First published under the title, *A woman's guide to earning a good living.*

Women who made America great. Gersh, Harry. Lippincott Company. 1962. 224p. $4.75

Life stories of ten women whose interests carried them into fields previously open only to men. Illustrated.

You and the next decade. Paradis, Adrian. David McKay Company. 1965. 192p. $3.50

Introduction to the job opportunities which will be open in the next ten years, pointing out the vocations which will need trained personnel.

** Your career—if you're not going to college. Splaver, Sarah. Julian Messner. Revised 1971. 224p. $4.95

Discussion of the opportunities available to the high school graduate, ranging from the unskilled and semiskilled to the skilled, service, agricultural, clerical, sales, and technical occupations which may be entered without college training. The book also contains advice concerning techniques of searching for a job.

C. Apprenticeship

**Apprentice training—sure way to a skilled craft. U.S. Department of Labor. Supt. of Documents. 1970. 12p. 15c

Pamphlet describes apprentice training, how it operates, who qualifies, opportunities, earnings, and where to apply. Also lists seventy-nine jobs which require apprenticeship and number of years of required training in each.

Apprentices. Careers. 1968. 8p. 35c

Career brief describing training programs, outlook for apprenticeable occupations, and preparation. List of apprenticeable trades with number of years required for training.

Apprentices. Chronicle Guidance Publications. 1967. 4p. 35c

Occupational brief summarizing need for apprenticeships, terms of usual agreements, a typical program, list of trades for which apprenticeship is generally considered necessary, and state apprenticeship council addresses.

**Apprenticeship, past and present. Bureau of Apprenticeship and Training, U.S. Department of Labor. Supt. of Labor. 1970. 24p. 25c

Traces the development of apprenticeship from early days to the present time and points to some directions of future activity.

The apprenticeship route to craftsmanship. Chronicle Guidance Publications. 1968. 2p. 35c

Reprinted article from *American Vocational Journal* discusses in general terms aspects of apprenticeships.

Apprenticeships in America. Kursh, Harry. Norton and Company. 1958. 176p. $4.95

This book presents the advantages open to apprentice-trained skilled workers, the standard apprenticeship agreements and rates of pay, and the types of registered apprenticeship programs. An important feature of the book is the guide to thirty-four of the most popular crafts and the occupational outlook for each. Also given is a list of ninety-two of the apprenticeable occupations with the number of years of training required.

Bureau of apprenticeship and training. United States Department of Labor. 1966. 8p. Free

Describes the nature and purpose of the national apprenticeship program and the functions of the Bureau. Lists regional offices where further information and technical assistance for apprenticeship programs can be obtained. The Bureau also publishes a series of pamphlets listing the apprenticeship standards for specific trades.

*Can I be a craftsman? Let's find out. General Motors, Public Relations Staff. 1969. 24p. Free

Includes an explanation of the apprentice program.

Careers in the crafts. International Association of Machinists. 1961. 6p. Free

Information about the apprenticeable trades, including qualifications, earnings, length of apprenticeship, who supervises the training, and how to find apprenticeship openings.

Finding out about apprentices. Science Research Associates. 1967. 4p. 45c

Junior occupational brief describing work and opportunities.

Research on apprenticeship. Busby, Walter A. Michigan State University, College of Education. 1962. 45p. $1.25

An annotated and classified list of ninety-five research studies dealing with apprenticeship completed during the period from 1930 to 1962. Of interest to persons concerned with the training of apprentices or those who are doing research in this area.

* Why not be an apprentice and become a skilled craftsman? Women's Bureau, U.S. Department of Labor. Supt. of Documents. 1970. 10p. 10c

Leaflet describing the kinds of opportunities, earnings, qualifications, and how to get started.

D. Bibliographies and Indexes

Career guidance index. Careers. Monthly, September through May. $6 per year

Each issue contains annotated references to selected free and inexpensive career materials.

Career index. Chronicle Guidance Publications, Inc. Annual compilation with 4 supplements. $10 per year

Compilation of over 700 sources of occupational, educational, and professional information. Printed postcards are included with the supplements for use when requesting selected free materials. Each issue contains an alphabetic list of sources of materials. The Annual and the final supplement also contain a cross-reference index by subject.

The career information center; a working model. U.S. Office of Education. Supt. of Documents. 1969. 41p. 30c

A manual based on the experience of the Career Information Center of Northeastern University, Boston, Massachusetts.

**The career information service. A guide to its development and use. Career Information Service, Southeastern Regional Vocational Technical School. 1968. 391p. $3 paper

Sections on the career information library, the job placement service, the follow-up service, and the career guidance resource center developed in the schools of Newton, Massachusetts. Over two hundred pages are devoted to the bibliography of occupational materials for career planning.

Careers for college women—a bibliography of vocational materials. University of Michigan, Center for Continuing Education of Women. 1968. 61p. $1

Prepared especially for adult counseling offices and to assist mature women with educational and vocational decisions.

D. Bibliographies and Indexes—*Continued*

Counselor's guide to manpower information. Government Printing Office. Supt. of Documents. 1968. 101p. $1

Annotated bibliography of several hundred Federal and state publications on occupational outlook, job descriptions, training, financial aid, minorities, and other topics related to career planning.

**Counselor's information service. B'nai B'rith Vocational Service. Quarterly. $7

Annotated bibliography of recently published books, pamphlets, charts, and articles concerning occupations and vocational and educational guidance. Each issue describes about two hundred publications.

Education. Price list 31. Supt. of Documents. 1968. 45p. Free

Price list of publications available from the Superintendent of Documents, U.S. Government Printing Office, Washington, D.C., 20402, on the subject of education, with catalog number, title, brief description, and price.

Educators guide to free guidance materials. Educators Progress Service. 1969. 236p. $7.50

This eighth annual edition is an annotated schedule of free audiovisual and other guidance aids. It lists and classifies information on titles, sources, and contents of 599 films, 73 filmstrips, 28 tapes, and 227 other books, pamphlets, charts, and posters.

Encyclopedia of Associations (National Organizations of the United States). Gale Research Company. 1968. 1331p. $29.50

Directory of national organizations, most of which distribute information about careers.

**Guidance exchange. Splaver, Sarah, ed. Annual $15 per year

An annotated bibliography of guidance literature and a section devoted to counselors' exchange of noteworthy experiences. Each issue contains about four hundred entries. Published in January of each year.

Guide to Federal career literature. Civil Service Commission. Supt. of Documents. 1969. 32p. 55c

Designed to serve as a convenient reference guide to Federal recruiting literature. This directory contains brief descriptions of 246 publications from 40 different departments and agencies, used in nationwide recruiting for college-entry level positions.

Health careers bibliography for guidance counselors. New Jersey Health Careers Service. 1970. 119p. $2

Lists 1,100 publications under 116 headings. The introduction states that only materials which have motivational value for counseling young people were chosen.

Job hunters' bibliography. Alumnae Advisory Center. 1969. 8p. $1

An up-to-date list of 131 titles in 57 different career fields. Sources and prices are given.

Labor. Price list 33. Supt. of Documents. 1968. 24p. Free

Price list of publications available from the Superintendent of Documents, U.S. Government Printing Office, Washington, D.C., 20402, on the subject of labor, with catalog number, title, brief description, and price.

NEA information on careers in education. Future Teachers of America. 1970. 8p. Single copy free

Brochure which lists career information materials available from the National Education Association. About ninety publications are grouped by subject areas and special fields.

NVGA bibliography of current career information. National Vocational Guidance Association. 1969. 129p. $2

Compilation of lists which have appeared in the *Vocational Guidance Quarterly* from 1966-1968. Lists over 1,300 publications and indicates level of recommendation. Also contains guidelines for preparing and evaluating career literature and occupational films.

**Need a lift? To educational opportunities, careers, loans, scholarships, employment! American Legion. 1970. 128p. 50c prepaid

This annually revised handbook, published as a part of the American Legion's education and scholarship program, contains sources of career, scholarship, and college information not only for children of veterans but for all children. Sources of career information are given for 242 specific occupations.

**1969-1970 Cumulative career index, an annual compilation with quarterly supplements. Chronicle Guidance Publications. 1969. 219p. $11

About seven hundred sources of career publications of free or inexpensive materials are listed. For each source, items for vocational and educational guidance are described and cross-referenced by title and *Dictionary of Occupational Titles* code numbers.

Occupations filing plan and bibliography, with set of labels. Bennett, Wilma. Interstate Printers and Publishers. Revised 1968. 109p. Index only $3.95; index plus 1088 labels $14.95

A set of gummed printed labels for about four hundred fields of work and seven hundred cross-references which may be pasted on folders and arranged alphabetically. An index lists the subject headings alphabetically and explains the use of the plan.

Occupations, professions and job descriptions. Price list 33 A. Supt. of Documents. 1968. 17p. Free

Price list of publications available from the Superintendent of Documents, U.S. Government Printing Office, Washington, D.C., 20402, on the subject of occupations and careers, with catalog number, title, brief description, and price.

**People in books: a selective guide to biographical literature arranged by vocations and other fields of reader interest. Nicholsen, Margaret E. H. W. Wilson Company. 1969. 498p. $12

This is a guide to biographical material available on individuals in over two hundred vocational fields. Materials indexed were selected from seventeen major standard annotated lists recommended for libraries, and the grade level of interest is noted for each title. Included is a name index and an index to autobiographies.

D. Bibliographies and Indexes—*Continued*

Selected U.S. government publications. Supt. of Documents. Bi-weekly. Free

A list of current Government publications, with brief descriptions and prices. Usually two or three career items are included in each issue.

Sources of career information in scientific fields. Manufacturing Chemists' Association. 1969. 28p. Single copy free

Recent list of free and inexpensive materials about careers in major scientific fields.

Sources of engineering career information. Engineers' Council for Professional Development. 1969. 20p. Free

A bibliography of engineering career information, identified by field of specialty. Also contains a list of reference books and general guidance information.

A starter file of free occupational literature. Eisen, Irving and Goodman, Leonard, compilers. B'nai B'rith Vocational Service. 1969. 29p. $1.25

List of materials which can be ordered to organize a cost-free occupational file that may be used when counseling young people in career choice. For each of 103 careers, the pamphlet titles, year of publication, and name and address of publisher are included.

Supplemental career index. Chronicle Guidance Publications. Quarterly. $10 per year

As a supplement to the annual cumulative career index, each issue contains about thirty to forty annotated references to free and inexpensive material. About half of the material listed is free. Printed post cards are included so one can send for the free material by writing name and address only. Each issue contains an alphabetic list of sources included.

Vertical file index. H. W. Wilson Company. Monthly except August. $8 a year, U.S. and Canada; $10, Foreign

Look under subject heading "Occupations" for recently published pamphlets.

**Vocations in biography and fiction. Haebich, Kathryn A. American Library Association. 1962. 77p. $1.75

Annotated listing of 1,070 books, for grades 9 through 12, classified according to two hundred careers. The author included books "which interpret vocations in terms of the lives and times of outstanding, interesting, and colorful personalities." Easy-reading titles below eighth-grade reading level have been designated by an asterisk.

See also Periodicals

E. Charts, Posters, and Display Materials

Announcement of the annual competitive examination. U.S. Coast Guard Academy. 9″ x 12″. Free

Illustrated poster announcing the examination.

Career adjustment posters. Chronicle Guidance Publications, Inc. Monthly. 17″ x 22″. $6 a year

One poster is included each month in the Chronicle Guidance Service. Points out to students ideas to be considered about educational goals, the world of work, etc.

Career chart. National Commission for Social Work Careers. 1968. 22″ x 17″. 25c

This bulletin board display provides information about various fields of practice, several social work positions, employment opportunities, qualifications, requirements, and outlook.

Career courier. Chiropractic Education Commission. 1968. 128 booklets. $4.25

Booklets in a display box for career day or library display.

**Careers in business. South-Western Publishing Company. 1961. 18″ x 24″. Free

Two-color chart listing beginning and top jobs and fields of opportunity in four types of business work: bookkeeping and accounting, stenographic and secretarial, general clerical, and merchandising. Also list of qualities to help one succeed. A border of illustrations across the top adds to its attractiveness.

College charts. Chronicle Guidance Publications, Inc. Revised annually. 275p. $3.50

Current information summarized in chart form with added footnotes on more than 2,650 colleges in the United States. Information includes admissions requirements, enrollments, costs, financial aid programs, and general data on degrees, special programs, etc.

College facts chart. National Beta Club. 1969-70. 64p. $1

Information presented in tabular form.

Current Federal examination announcements. U.S. Civil Service Commission. Revised bi-monthly. 16″ by 21″. Free

List of Civil Service examinations currently open throughout the country, giving titles, salaries, location of positions, and brief information regarding each examination.

Dietetics career posters. American Dietetic Association. 8½″ x 11″. 4 posters. 50c

Two-color posters for bulletin board use. Each of the posters features one of the major areas of the profession of dietetics: hospitals, industry, universities, and health agencies.

Exhibit: What's your specialty? There's a place for it in library service. American Library Association. 8′ x 7′6″, weight 250 lbs. Round-trip shipping charges

Suitable for display at career conferences, career fairs, and wherever a commercial-size booth is available. Comes in self-contained unit; requires two men to set up.

E. Charts, Posters, and Display Materials—*Continued*

General Electric progress posters. General Electric Company. Semimonthly. 14″ x 17″. Free. Available only to heads of science departments

Drawings of current scientific developments, with description underneath, produced for science classroom bulletin boards.

Health tabletop exhibit of health careers. American Medical Association. 1968. 120-pound, 6 by 8 feet. Transportation costs, round-trip

Colorful folding exhibit which depicts twenty-five professional areas in the health field. Emphasizes the range of opportunities and ways of preparing for medical study.

Job opportunities in mathematics. J. Weston Walch, 1962. 8½″ x 11″. 20 posters. $1.50

The set consists of twelve pairs of posters. In each pair, one shows in cartoon form some of the vocational possibilities; its companion shows interesting facts about the same field. Sets are available in science, retailing, computers, and professional occupations, the more recent ones priced $3.

Jobservation posters. Chronicle Guidance Publications, Inc. 1 poster per month. 11″ x 17″ or 17″ x 22″. Color. $6 per year

One is included each month in the Chronicle Occupational and 3-in-1 Services. Illustrates some facet of an occupation as presented in the companion brief.

A map of four-year colleges and universities in the United States. National Association of College Admissions Counselors. 33″ by 24″. $1

This may pinpoint the locations of regionally accredited colleges across the United States. Colleges are designated as co-educational, men's, or women's by the use of symbols.

A map of two-year colleges in the United States. National Association of College Admissions Counselors. 33″ by 24″. $1

A companion map to the one described above.

Meet the young home economist. American Home Economics Association. 1963. 7 pictures. 8″ x 11″. 25c

Bulletin board type pictures depicting careers in fashion, communications, research, interior design, community service, and food service.

Need money for college? It's available to you in these four forms: Scholarships, grants, jobs, loans. College Scholarship Service of the Entrance Examination Board. 1970. 11″ x 17″. Free to counselors

Bulletin board poster in color.

Occupational subject posters. Chronicle Guidance Publications, Inc. 17″ x 22″. 21 posters. $10 per set. 75c each

These posters picture occupations to which the various school subjects may lead. They are effective in pointing out the occupations related to mathematics, industrial arts, economics, etc.

Photographic exhibit. National Commission for Social Work Careers. 1968. 9 photos. 8″ x 10″. $10

Photographs and preprinted captions for an easily assembled display answering the question, "Why choose social work?" Good for career conferences.

Pictorial desk calendar. Keystone Junior College. 1969. 24p. Free

A picture of a campus scene, together with a brief statement about the college, on each month's calendar. Available after August first each year.

Porta-panel displays. Could you be a librarian? American Library Association. Six 4′ x 2′ panels, which fold into a canvas carrying case 4′ x 2′. Weight 47 pounds. Round-trip shipping charges

May be displayed accordion-style or straight. Retractable legs may be used on either floor or table. Consists of life-size photographs of librarians in action.

Poster. American Occupational Therapy Association. 1968. 14″ by 18″. $1. With easel back $1.25

A four-color poster to attract interest in this work.

Public information exhibits. Office of Public Affairs, U.S. Civil Service Commission. 12′ x 8′ x 2′. Loaned to professional groups

The exhibits are made of plywood panels which are bolted together. One man can set up the exhibit in about half an hour. It is necessary to request them two months in advance. Costs of shipment are paid by the Office of Public Affairs. Current titles are: *Civil Service at your service, The challenge of social change, The college graduate in the Federal Civil Service.*

Table displays; librarianship . . . career of variety . . . get the facts here. American Library Association. 4″ x 8″ display $1 each; 7″ x 13½″ display $1.75 each

Accordion-folded and self-supporting, illustrated with photographs of librarians at work. May be used on tables or mounted on bulletin boards.

Tree of knowledge and basic sciences. Museum of Science and Industry. 1938. 25″ x 38″. 95c

Chart from the Century of Progress Exposition in attractive colors, suitable for framing. Chart shows basic importance of mathematics to other fields of knowledge. At the base of the tree are listed mathematics, botany, chemistry, and seven other basic sciences. At the top of the tree are listed fourteen applied sciences such as architectural engineering, public health and hygiene, agronomy, and medicine.

Your high school record—does it count? (New Series). South Dakota Press. 1956. 18″ x 22″. Complete with glassed frame, $22.75; without frame, $21.25; book, $2.90

Poster set, consisting of thirty-seven posters, adapted from book of same title is designed to prove to students that the records they are making in high school will count for or against them in later life.

F. Foreign Study or Employment

Employment abroad—facts and fallacies. Chamber of Commerce of the United States, International Group. 1964. 13p. 25c

Suggestions about how to seek employment abroad and some of the problems to be faced.

Excitement, travel, career as an overseas secretary. United Business Schools Association. 1967. 6p. Free

Brief descriptions of some of the opportunities.

Federal jobs overseas. U.S. Civil Service Commission. Supt. of Documents. 1969. 12p. 10c

Types of positions, salaries, and minimum experience and training requirements. Also includes list of addresses to which inquiries may be sent.

Financial planning for study in the United States: A guide for students from other countries. College Entrance Examination Board. 1970. 48p. 10c

This booklet provides foreign students with detailed information about the costs of study in the United States, what responsibilities they will be expected to assume in meeting these costs, and what help may be available from other sources.

Foreign teaching opportunities. Advancement and Placement Institute. 1969. 30 guides. $1 each

A guide to opportunities in several foreign countries.

General memorandum for those interested in foreign study. Institute of International Education. 1968. 4p. Free

Discussion of factors involved in preparing for a period of foreign study.

How to get the job you want overseas. Liebers, Arthur. Pilot Books. 1969. 64p. $2.95 paper

This book is rich in its listings of names of overseas companies and of employment agencies which specialize in this type of position. Also it includes the Federal Civil Service examinations for overseas positions. A useful chapter gives suggestions for preparing a résumé for an overseas job.

International exchange; a report of the Bureau of Educational and Cultural Affairs, U.S. Department of State. Supt. of Documents. 1969. 30p. 35c

Includes information concerning the number of exchanges with each country, fields of specialization by category of grantees, and distribution of grantees.

Job opportunities abroad. Institute of International Education. 1968. 3p. Free

Mimeographed list of eighteen sources of information.

Jobs to take you places—here and abroad. Paradis, Adrian. David McKay Company. 1968. 288p. $4.95

Information for the young man or woman who wants to live in foreign lands or see the world and get paid for it. Includes how to search for overseas employment and what to do to find the right opening.

Leads on jobs abroad. Cunningham, Ann Marie. Alumnae Advisory Center. 1969. 16p. 35c

Description of the job opportunities abroad with the various departments of the United States Government. Also includes some jobs with foreign govments and non-profit organizations.

**The new guide to study abroad. Garraty, John A. and others. Harper and Row. 1969. 431p. $7.95; paper $3.95

A comprehensive directory of summer and academic year study opportunities in other countries for high school students, college and university students, and teachers. In addition to evaluative descriptions of individual programs, the book includes a section of general information and advice on planning and preparing for study abroad.

**New horizons in education; the benefits of study abroad. Pan American World Airways. 1965. 222p. $6.95 hard cover; $3.95 paper

Information concerning the study program, costs, admission requirements, and other features of several universities in each of thirty-eight countries.

Opportunities abroad for teachers, 1971-72. Government Printing Office. Supt. of Documents. 1970. 28p. 20c

Describes the U.S. Government grants to be offered to American teachers either to teach for an academic year in elementary and secondary schools abroad or to attend summer seminars abroad under the International Educational and Cultural Exchange Program.

Overseas employment guide. National Employment Services Institute. 1969. 100p. $2

Directory of employers who offer summer jobs abroad in industry, resorts, education, and international organizations. Information about jobs expected to be available and where to apply.

Overseas opportunities for educators in Government dependent schools. Advancement and Placement Institute. 1962. 4p. 50c

Includes qualifications and salaries.

Overseas teacher. Gerard, Jane. Julian Messner. 1963. 192p. $3.50

Career fiction. Story of the challenges for the teacher in the overseas school system for Americans in the U.S. Air Force.

Schools abroad of interest to Americans. Porter Sargent Publisher. 1967. 352p. $4.40

Guide to assist those who wish to study abroad.

**Selective guide to overseas employment. Angel, Juvenal L. Regents Publishing Company. 1969. 217p. $6.95

A reference book which answers many questions about the approach to a job overseas.

Series of guides to assist you in obtaining employment overseas. Advancement and Placement Institute. 1969. 30 guides. $1 each

Guide for opportunities in thirty foreign countries.

F. Foreign Study or Employment—*Continued*

The student traveler: work, study, travel abroad. United States National Student Travel Association. 1968. 200p. $2.50

An annual publication presenting information on opportunities available to students who desire to study, work, or travel abroad. Includes helpful advice, description of travel aids, lists of travel programs, voluntary and paid jobs, and sources of information.

Students abroad. Council on International Educational Exchange. Annually. 3 booklets. Single copy free

Description of the overseas educational programs sponsored by the Council's member institutions. One booklet describes high school student programs, another summer study, and a third the academic year study, travel, and work opportunities.

Summer study abroad. Institute of International Education. 1969. 150p. 50c

This guide lists over two hundred courses sponsored by organizations in thirty-five foreign countries. The entries give course titles, dates, locations, and often tuition and living expenses. The guide also includes list of courses offered in some specialized fields, such as music and architecture. Reading references about summer study are added.

Summer study tours for teachers, counselors, university students, and educational groups. Study Abroad, Inc. 1970. 20p. Free

An annual compilation.

**Teacher exchange opportunities under the International Educational Exchange Program. Bureau of International Education, U.S. Office of Education. Published annually. Available August, September, and October. Free

Information about the exchange program and when and where to apply for the teaching positions and summer seminar grants available to go abroad under the Mutual Educational and Cultural Exchange Act of 1961 (Fulbright-Hays Act).

Teaching abroad. Institute of International Education. 1968. 7p. Free

Names and addresses of thirty administering agencies.

Your future in jobs abroad. Winter, Elmer. Richards Rosen Press. 1968. 191p. $4; library edition $3.78

Discussion of practical consideration of working abroad and suggestions on seeking a job.

Vacation study abroad; vacation courses and scholarships. UNESCO. 1970. 93p. $1.50

Listing of short term summer courses open to foreign students in countries around the world. Following a section of courses sponsored by international organizations, the schools are listed under country.

G. Information About Colleges, Schools for Vocational Training, and Other Educational Institutions

Accredited curricula leading to first degrees in engineering in the U.S. Engineers' Council for Professional Development. 1969. 20p. 25c

Lists all institutions giving accredited degrees.

Accredited curricula leading to degrees in engineering technology in the U.S. Engineers' Council for Professional Development. 1969. 12p. 25c

Lists all institutions giving accredited degrees.

Accredited institutions of higher education. American Council on Education. 1969. 247p. $4.50

Junior and senior colleges accredited as of September 1, 1969, or working toward that goal. Presents name, address, control, degrees, specialized accreditation in thirty-four fields, enrollment, and chief executive officer.

**Admissions and financial aid requirements and procedures at College Board member colleges. College Entrance Examination Board. 1970. 103p. $1

A tabular summary of the basic test requirements, preferred test dates, and admissions and financial aid application deadlines of the 870 member colleges. Also given are the dates colleges notify candidates about admission and financial aid and the candidates' reply requirements.

**American junior colleges. Gleazer, Edmund J., ed. American Council on Education. 7th edition. 1967. 957p. $14

Classified data for 751 two-year colleges recognized by regional or state accrediting agencies. Includes date organized, type of control, accreditation, enrollment, admission requirements, fees, curricula offered, size of campus, and terminal or occupational curricula.

American trade schools directory. Croner, Ulrich H. Croner Publications. Annually. 150p. With supplements, $12 per year plus postage

About 3,000 schools are classified according to trades taught and listed by states and cities. Loose-leaf edition permits use of a monthly amendment service.

**American universities and colleges. Singletary, Otis A. and Newman, Jane P., eds. American Council on Education. 10th edition. 1968. 1782p. $22

This is an authoritative guide to 1,291 accredited four-year colleges. The factual summary includes the nature of each institution, admission requirements, financial structure, enrollment, size of teaching staff, and academic characteristics of freshmen. Seventy-five new colleges have been added since the 9th edition. Arrangement is by states. Also given are lists of accredited schools in twenty-six professions.

G. Information About Colleges, Schools for Vocational Training, and Other Educational Institutions—*Continued*

**Annual guides to graduate study, 1970. Hegener, Karen, ed. Peterson's Guides, Inc. 1969. 12 volumes, bound in 2 library binders. $60

Contains pertinent data on programs of study, faculty, financial aid, research, facilities, and cost of 1,450 graduate programs in eighty-four academic areas. Arranged under ten broad areas such as biological sciences, business, communication engineering, library and information services, and physical sciences.

Baird's manual of American college fraternities. George Banta Company. 1968. 905p. $9

A directory of fraternities, sororities, and honor, professional, and recognition societies. This is the eighteenth edition.

Barron's handbook of college transfer information. Proia, Nicholas and Drysdale, Barbara. Barron's Educational Series, Inc. 1970. 295p. $3.95

Includes a state-by-state chart giving name and address of the college, admissions criteria, examinations and recommendations required, housing requirements, financial aids, application deadline date, and other pertinent information for students planning to transfer.

Barron's profiles of American colleges. Barron's Educational Series. 1969. 150 profiles. $1.50 each

Profiles have been prepared on 150 colleges, giving data on admissions, test scores, costs, programs, facilities, and social life. Provides a method of comparison of colleges under consideration.

Blue book of occupational education. CCM Information Corporation. 1970. 900p. $29.50

A listing of more than twelve thousand trade, technical, and vocational schools in the United States. Major sections include geographical listings of schools by state and city, alphabetical listing by curriculum offered, Veteran's Administration approved schools, and accredited special schools.

Camp directory. New York State Camp Directors Association. 1969. 30p. Free

Information concerning 105 camps in New York State. Revised annually.

Catholic colleges and universities. Catholic College Bureau. 1968. 223p. $1.50

Directory of two hundred colleges. For each school there is given the enrollment, admission requirements, fees, housing, curriculum, accreditation, and significant aspects. There also is a directory of programs of study, listing the colleges offering training in special fields such as music, dental hygiene, nursing, home economics, and teacher education.

Choosing a college. Hoy, John C. Delacorte Press. 1967. 192p. $5

The book is intended to help the student select the college most suitable to his aims, temperament, and capabilities. One section advises the student on judging the quality of a college.

College advanced placement policies. College Entrance Examination Board. 1969. 73p. $1

This book lists the colleges that may offer credit or placement or both to students who take advanced placement courses in high school. The examination grades normally accepted by each college are listed for each subject in which an Advanced Placement Examination is offered.

**College ahead! Revised edition. Wilson, Eugene S. and Bucher, Charles A. Harcourt, Brace and World. 1961. 202p. $4.50

Includes discussion of requirements for college admission, how colleges differ, how to visit a college, how to apply, and how to make the first year a good one. Bibliography.

**The college blue book. 13th edition. CCM Information Corporation. 1969. 10 volumes. 3600p. $99

Purchasers of the set may buy additional copies of Vol. 2 for $9.95. The contents has been organized into ten volumes as follows:

Volume

1. Guide and index
2. U.S. colleges, tabular data—admission requirements, costs
3. U.S. colleges, narrative descriptions of 3,439 colleges
4 and 5. College degrees offered—colleges at which they may be obtained
6. College atlas
7. Specialized educational programs
8. Professional careers and accreditations, professional and educational associations
9. Scholarships, fellowships and grants
10. Secondary schools in the United States

College choice. Careers. 1967. 8p. 35c

Things to consider in the selection of a college.

College costs. Life Insurance Agency Management Association. Published annually. 44p. 30c

Tuition, basic fees, room and board costs, and the total undergraduate enrollment are listed for approximately 1,000 colleges and universities.

College entrance guide. Einstein, Bernice W. Grosset and Dunlap, Inc. 7th edition. 1970. 327p. $3.95; paper $1.95

Contains sections with special advice for veterans, colleges for students with C averages, special opportunities for the disadvantaged students, help for rejected students, and colleges with summer college preparation programs. Also included is a listing of colleges with facilities for the handicapped.

College facts chart. National Beta Club. 1968-69. 64p. $1

Information about colleges in fifty states in tabular form including degrees offered, enrollment, number of teachers, average tuition, cost of board and room, and average total cost for the school year. Compiled annually.

G. Information About Colleges, Schools for Vocational Training, and Other Educational Institutions—*Continued*

College for your child, why not? Michigan State University, School of Labor and Industrial Relations. 1963. 15p. 10c

Discussion of the nature and purpose of a college education and what parents can do to help their children get ready for it.

College guide for Jewish youth. Feingold, S. Norman and Jospe, Alfred, eds. B'nai B'rith Vocational Service. 1968. 180p. $4

This book offers guidelines to assist students and their parents to select an appropriate college. Information is given on costs, scholarships, environment, enrollment, and Jewish social, educational, and religious life at more than 540 colleges.

**The college handbook. College Entrance Examination Board. 1969. 1360p. $4.75

Data on 832 member colleges of the Board. Described in section listing the Counselor's Professional Bookshelf.

College kit. American Personnel and Guidance Association. 1969. 4 booklets. $1.25

Contained in this kit are three booklets on college and one on career planning: *Career decisions, How to visit colleges, How about college?* and *How about college financing—for college-bound young people, their parents and counselors.*

College programs for high school students: summer 1970. Directory Publishers Company. 1970. 300p. $7

This directory, updated each year, is a listing of college programs that are available to high school students each summer. Each program is described in terms of calendar, costs, eligibility requirements, and the scope of the courses offered.

The college scene: students tell it like it is. Foley, James and Foley, Robert. Cowles Book Company. 1969. 224p. $4.95

A report of personal interviews with thousands of students on more than one hundred campuses. Topics cover the draft, riots, black studies, drugs, faculty, religion, and the world scene.

College student's handbook. Lass, Abraham H. and Wilson, Eugene S. David White Company. 1970. 201p. $6.95

Discussion of academic, financial, and social problems of college students. Some career information is included.

College: the life of a student. Engeman, Jack. Lothrop, Lee and Shepard Company. 1959. 128p. $4.95

More than 250 photographs, with informative text and captions, show many aspects of life in college and help prospective students know what lies in store for them during their college careers. Photographs were taken at fifty different colleges.

Colleges and universities in Pennsylvania. Department of Public Instruction, Commonwealth of Pennsylvania. 1969. 144p. $1

Information is compiled concerning 140 institutions, including entrance requirements, enrollment, costs, curriculum offered, living accommodations, accreditation, scholarships, and student loan funds.

Colleges classified—a guide for counselors, parents, and students. Nelson, A. Gordon. Chronicle Guidance Publications. 1968. 68p. $1

Colleges classified by various combinations of student body, enrollment, region, and cost. Useful in finding institutions which fit a student's expressed preferences.

Colleges with jobs for students. Changing Times. 1966. 15p. 75c

A survey of campus job openings in four-year and two-year accredited colleges. Frequently revised.

Colleges with room for students. Changing Times. 1968. 32p. 75c

Annual survey of openings in four-year accredited colleges. Summarizes responses from 663 colleges.

**Comparative guide to American colleges for students, parents, and counselors. Cass, James and Birnbaum, Max. Harper and Row. 3rd edition. 1969. 837p. $10; paper $4.95

Information concerning the four-year colleges in the United States, indexed by state, including selectivity in admission practices, religious affiliation, enrollment figures, and cultural environment. Descriptions of fifty-six newly accredited institutions have been added since the last edition.

**Comparative guide to two-year colleges and four-year specialized schools and programs. Cass, James and Birnbaum, Max. Harper and Row. 1969. 275p. $7.95; paper $3.95

A companion to their *Comparative Guide to American Colleges*, this volume covers non-residential and primarily local two-year colleges, residential junior colleges, and specialized schools and programs. Occupational indexes group institutions offering preparation in specific areas.

**Complete planning for college. Sulkin, Sidney. Harper and Row. 1968. 324p. $3.95

This revised edition discusses some major concerns for students who are planning on attending college. The section on financing an education has information about paying for college, estimating college costs, the types of financial aid available, and reducing college costs.

Concerned about college? Choosing a college? Changing colleges? Association of College Admissions Counselors. 1968. 10p. Free

Description of services offered by the non-profit clearinghouse which provides inter-communication between a student, his counselor, and the member colleges. This is accomplished with one application and a small fee.

A counselor's guide to home study training. National Home Study Council. 1970. 8p. Free

Information about the estimated growth of twenty-five occupational fields for which training is available through home study.

G. Information About Colleges, Schools for Vocational Training, and Other Educational Institutions—*Continued*

**Directory for exceptional children. 6th edition. Porter Sargent. 1969. 704p. $12

Descriptive listings of three thousand public and private schools, hospitals, clinics, and other facilities for the emotionally disturbed, the physically handicapped, and the mentally retarded. Included also are listings of associations and Federal and state agencies concerned with the education and welfare of the exceptional.

Directory issue. The Journalism Educator. 1968. 48p. $3

Bulletin of the American Society of Journalism School Administrators containing list of seventy schools and departments offering majors or degrees in journalism. Name of journalism unit is followed by year in which established, association affiliations, student organizations, facilities, and degrees offered.

Directory of accredited camps for boys and girls. American Camping Association. 1969. 300p. $1.50

List of three thousand camps arranged alphabetically by states. Includes location, affiliation, details of capacity, price, program, and facilities.

Directory of accredited private home study schools. National Home Study Council. 1970. 12p. Free

List of 120 schools with addresses and dates founded. The leaflet also contains a partial list of the home study subjects, with numbers referring to the schools which offer each.

Directory of business schools in the United States. United Business Schools Association. 1969. 24p. Free to counselors and librarians

List of private business schools that have met membership requirements in the association.

Directory of educational and training institutions. McCoy, Marion and Thoenen, Eugene. West Virginia State Department of Education. 1968. 100p. $1 paper

An example of a state directory of training facilities.

Directory of private trade and vocational schools in New York State. Private Vocational Schools Association of New York. 1969. 23p. Free to counselors

Directory of sixty-nine schools and the courses offered in each. Includes schools licensed as private trade and correspondence schools by the New York State Education Department.

**Earned degrees conferred: bachelor's and higher degrees. U.S. Office of Education. Supt. of Documents. 1968. 289p. $2

Useful to students for judging the extent of a college's program in a particular field of study. Degree data are summarized at the bachelor's, master's and doctor's level for each of two hundred major fields of study and for each of the 1,549 colleges conferring degrees. Also includes an analytic report of data relating to degrees conferred by major areas of study, type of institution, region, and institution. An annual report.

Education and jobs. Bureau of Labor Statistics, U.S. Department of Labor. Order from Supt. of Documents. 1968. 5 pamphlets. 8 pages each. $6.75 per 100. Single copy 10c each

This series of motivational pamphlets is designed as a guide to jobs that match different levels of education and training. Each pamphlet contains qualifications, training needed, trends, and employment opportunities for each occupation listed in each group. Titles:

Jobs for which apprenticeship training is available.
Jobs for which a high school education is generally required.
Jobs for which junior college technical institute or other specialized training is usually required.
Jobs for which a high school education is preferred, but not essential.
Jobs for which a college education is usually required.

Education of American leaders. Pierson, George W. Frederick Praeger, Inc. 1969. 295p. $17.50

The findings reveal the comparative contributions of U.S. colleges and universities as producers of leaders and men of exceptional distinction. Separate chapters summarize the various professions such as medicine, banking, and law.

Educational opportunities of Greater Boston for adults. Educational Exchange of Greater Boston. Annual. 200p. $2.95

Description of Boston's day and evening courses for adults. Price includes summer school supplement.

Eleven Corning College Day speeches. Corning Glass Works Foundation. 1954-1964. 99p. Free

Addresses given on College Days at Corning, New York, including Why go to College?; A college education is worth $500,000; A college education: the best investment for your future; Who should go to college?; Why go to college?; Your opportunity: is college the way? Excellent material.

Estimates of school statistics, 1968-1969. National Education Association. 1968. 36p. $1

Annual report providing, on a state-by-state basis, up-to-date information on school districts, pupils enrolled, teachers' salaries, revenues and expenditures, and numbers of high school graduates.

Evening college—the big second chance. McMahon, Ernest. Public Affairs Committee. 1968. 30p. 25c

Information concerning transfer, accreditation, certificates, and other important considerations. Includes suggested references.

**Facing facts about college admissions—a guide for pre-college students and their parents. Prudential Insurance Company. Revised 1969. 27p. Free

Useful information to assist young people to make suitable decisions about college admission. Includes explanation of what colleges consider in connection with admission and what the student can do to make practical preparation for college.

G. Information About Colleges, Schools for Vocational Training, and Other Educational Institutions—*Continued*

Facing facts about the two-year college. Prudential Insurance Company. Revised 1968. 32p. Free

The booklet traces the development of the two-year college and discusses the programs and courses of study available in them. It describes the junior college as a new college for a new society because four-year colleges will not be able to accommodate the millions who will be seeking entrance before the decade closes.

**Facing facts about your college career. Prudential Insurance Company. Revised 1968. 32p. Free

Advice to help insure the prospective college student that once in college he will stay there and succeed. Some topics discussed are: learning to be independent, being away from home, dealing with outside activities, dealing with academic work, and two big changes. Good reading lists.

Fact sheet for guidance counselors. New York University, Office of the Registrar and Supervisor of Admissions. 1968. 6p. Free

A convenient reference brochure giving information about the six undergraduate divisions of the university, admission procedures, financial aid, and prospects of admission in 1968.

Facts about New England colleges and universities. New England Board of Higher Education. 1968-69. 20p. Single copy free

Data about two hundred and forty institutions authorized by their state legislatures to grant academic degrees. The information includes costs, enrollment, accreditation, and general type of curriculum. Published annually.

Financial aid for graduate students. College Opportunities, Inc. 1970-71. 500p. $10

Information concerning 693 accredited graduate schools.

Financial aids for undergraduate students. College Opportunities, Inc. 1970-71. 1500p. $37.50

Information concerning academic standards, financial aids, and the focus of the educational experience offered by 1,801 accredited schools.

Financing equal opportunity in higher education. College Entrance Examination Board. 1970. 44p. $1

Papers presented at a colloquium concerning existing barriers to access to higher education encountered by low income and minority populations.

From high school to job. Gardner, John W. Carnegie Corporation of New York. 1960. 12p. Free

Reprint from the annual report suggesting that schools should provide continuing vocational and educational counseling for those who leave high school and those who do not go on to higher education.

The gifted: educational resources. Porter Sargent. 1961. 285p. $4

A nationwide survey of over eight hundred public and private school programs, nursery through college, designed to challenge and develop academically talented students. The school programs are arranged by geographic regions and classified by types of programs offered.

Graduate study in college student personnel work. American College Personnel Association. Order from American Personnel and Guidance Association. 1969. 53p. $1

This presents entrance, graduation, and major academic course requirements for the seventy-four institutions that submitted information.

* Guide to American graduate schools. Livesey, Herbert B. and Robbins, Gene A. Viking Press. 1967. 357p. $8.50

A directory of six hundred colleges, universities, and professional schools offering studies beyond the bachelor's degree. Individual institutional entries give information about fields of study and degrees offered, admissions and degree requirements, fees, possibilities of student aid, enrollments, and housing.

The guide to college life. Mitchell, Joyce S. Prentice-Hall, Inc. 1968. 295p. $3.50

This guide focuses on the college life at 286 colleges, giving information on academic life, academic emphasis in fields of study, student regulations, residential life, extracurricular activities, and financial aid. The major source of this data was the student handbook of each institution.

Guide to college-level independent study. Sabo, Alex. Chronicle Guidance Publications, Inc. Revised biennially. 180p. $3.50

Lists general fields of study which may be undertaken by correspondence. Each college description lists conditions of enrollment, costs, and course titles.

Guide to college majors. Chronicle Guidance Publications, Inc. Revised annually. 180p. $3.50

Lists institutions offering major programs of study in 170 four-year and 90 two-year subject areas. Colleges arranged by subject and state. Also indicates colleges offering master's and doctorate programs in each major.

**A guide to graduate study. Quick, Robert. American Council on Education. 1969. 637p. $15

This reference work in its fourth edition reviews objectives of graduate study for the prospective student with keys to selection, admission, and finance. Two hundred and fifty graduate schools leading to the Ph.D. degree are covered.

**Guide to independent study through correspondence study. National University Extension Association. 1970. 60p. 50c

Lists correspondence courses from sixty-four accredited universities and colleges, including those for college credit, self-interest, high school work, and vocational and technical interests. Key list indicates quarter or semester credits, cooperative contract with United States Armed Forces Institute, and graduate credit. Also, courses for college credit are grouped under forty careers.

G. Information About Colleges, Schools for Vocational Training, and Other Educational Institutions—*Continued*

Guide to summer camps and summer schools. Porter Sargent Publisher. 16th edition. 1969. 336p. $4.40; paper $2.20

Directory of about one thousand camps and summer schools.

Guiding your child toward college. Bucher, Charles and others. Barnes and Noble, Inc. 1967. 190p. $1.50 paper

Covers such topics as tests, extracurricular activities, choice of high school subjects, selecting the college, applying, financing, and the adjusting to college life. Good reading lists.

**Handbook for college admissions. National Association of College Admissions Counselors. 1967-70. 669p. $4.50 to members; $5.50 to others

In this handbook, published biannually, one page is devoted to each of 662 colleges, setting forth the programs of study, admissions requirements, opening dates, costs and housing, financial aid, and name of admissions officer. All listed colleges are fully accredited by their regional accrediting associations.

Handbook of adult education in the United States. Smith, Robert and others, eds. Adult Education Association. 1969. 600p. $6.95

Includes institutional programs and resources.

**Handbook of private schools. 50th edition. Porter Sargent. 1969. 1456p. $10

Information concerning 2,500 private schools. Includes tuition, faculty and enrollment data, graduate records, and some scholarship opportunities. Revised annually.

Helping your teenager choose a college. Klein, David. Child Study Association of America. 1963. 36p. 65c

An aid to parents in clarifying the ways of looking at college choice. Provides suggestions on how to avoid common fallacies and pitfalls in selecting a college.

**How about college? A guide for parents of college-bound students. American School Counselor Association. Order from American Personnel and Guidance Association. 1968. 16p. 25c

Revision of a popular leaflet explains how to choose a college, admission qualifications, applying for admission. Bibliography.

How an Ivy League college decides on admissions. Kinkead, Katharine. Norton and Company. 1961. 94p. $3.50

Description of the painstaking procedures by which Yale University selected its freshman class of 1960. Parents and candidates facing college committee decisions can gain an idea of the process they will encounter. Written by a magazine reporter.

**How to get into college. Bowles, Frank H. and others. Dutton and Company. Revised 1968. 160p. $4.95

Provides information on many aspects of college selection, preparation, admission, financing, and succeeding during the first year. Material is presented in question and answer form.

How to get into college and stay there. Diamond, Esther. Science Research Associates. Revised 1970. 89p. $2.75

Activity text which challenges students in grades 9 through 12 to consider plans for higher education.

How to go to high school or college by mail. Martin, Kevin. Frederick Fell, Inc. 1969. 254p. $5.95

A useful guide to correspondence study for those wanting to get a high school diploma or college degree. Basic details are given concerning admission, registration, programs of study, fees, and credits. All the members of the National University Extension Association are listed with requirements and subjects offered.

How to prepare for college. Lass, Abraham. Pocket Books. 1962. 497p. 95c paper

Includes a wide variety of topics, including how to choose a college, how to conduct the college interview, and how to stay in college. A final chapter contains do's and don'ts for parents.

How to put your husband through college. Debrodt, Barbars. Harper and Row. 1970. 192p. $5.95

The author has compiled a book of practical help in solving the problems of the wife of a student. She discusses many ways of assisting her husband in his new role as student. She offers advice on food, rent, and entertainment budgeting as well as on money and time required for the various degrees.

How to select a camp or summer school. Good Housekeeping. 1966. 14p. 20c

Addressed to parents, this is a guide to selecting a child's camp or summer school. Includes basic information on the many types of summer schools or camps available, what to look for when investigating camps, and costs.

How to select a school or college. Good Housekeeping. 1962. 21p. 25c

Addressed to parents, this booklet points out the problems to be considered in making this choice, suggests questions to be asked of oneself and of the schools under consideration, and presents some measures for comparison of colleges.

The insiders' guide to the colleges. Yale Daily News staff, compiler. 1970. 265p. $2.95

Candid and informal comments concerning one hundred colleges and universities. Each school is described by residents.

Introduction to college. Anderson, Bert B. Holt, Rinehart and Winston, Inc. 1969. 243p. $3.95

This book aims to acquaint college freshmen with the many demands made by their colleges and to help them achieve a desirable personal and social adjustment. Contains helpful suggestions on planning for the future.

G. Information About Colleges, Schools for Vocational Training, and Other Educational Institutions—*Continued*

The Ivy League guidebook. Tobias, Andres P. and others. Macmillan Company. 1969. 175p. $6.95; Collier Books, paper, $2.95

A pictorial guide designed to help young men who are thinking of attending one of the eight schools of the Ivy League, formed in 1954 to regulate football competition. The authors visited each of the schools and report on data such as tuition, size, library volume count, percentage of public school graduates admitted, median College Board scores, cost of room and board, social life, and coordinate women's divisions.

Junior college directory. American Association of Junior Colleges. 1969. 115p. $1.50

Information concerning both accredited and nonaccredited nonprofit institutions with symbols which indicate the type of accreditation or approval. Student enrollment, faculty size, type of control or affiliation, and type of school included.

List of cooperative education colleges and universities. 1970. 4p. Free; stamped, self-addressed envelope must be included.

A frequently revised list.

A listing of Catholic secondary schools in USA. United States Catholic Conference. 1967. 62p. $2

Names of 2,450 schools arranged alphabetically by states. Boarding schools, orphanages, and protectories are also indicated.

Looking at private trade and correspondence schools. National Vocational Guidance Association. 1963. 8p. 25c

This booklet is a guide for students who are considering continuing their education in private trade or correspondence schools. It provides information on whether this is the kind of education suitable for the student, how to evaluate a school, things to watch out for, and how to make the best decision. Examples illustrate successful and unsuccessful selection of a school.

**Lovejoy's career and vocational school guide—a handbook of job training opportunities. Lovejoy, Clarence E. Simon and Schuster, Inc. 1967. 176p. $6.50; $3.95 paper

The schools are grouped according to major interests: business, nursing and medical technical, barbering and cosmetology, arts, home study, mechanical and technical, flying, public vocational schools, and schools for miscellaneous vocations. Under each of the above sections the schools are listed geographically, first by state and then under the cities and towns in which they are located. An index of occupational titles lists each school by number.

**Lovejoy's college guide; a complete reference book to 3,368 American colleges and universities. Lovejoy, Clarence E. Simon and Schuster, Inc. 11th ed. 1970. 447p. $7.50; paper $4.95

Latest revision of an updated guide to colleges. The rating and description section constitutes the major portion but is preceded by practical information on costs, admissions, scholarships, and suggestions on selecting a school.

Lovejoy's prep school guide. Lovejoy, Clarence E. Simon and Schuster, Inc. 3rd edition 1969. 224p. $5.95; paper $3.95

Information concerning 2,272 independent secondary schools.

**Medical school admission requirements: U.S.A. and Canada. Association of American Medical Colleges. 1969-70. 332p. $4

Information concerning the admission, requirements, costs, and admission procedures of each of the 103 American and 16 Canadian medical schools. Contains recommendations on preparation for medical education and how to apply to medical schools. Revised annually.

**National directory of schools and vocations. Miller, Adeline E. and Brown, Betty I. State Schools Publications. 1967-68. 703p. $12.95

For each of three hundred occupations the schools that offer training are listed alphabetically by states. Includes professional, technical, trade, and business schools. Many trades are included.

**New American guide to colleges. Hawes, Gene R. New American Library, Inc. 1966. 560p. 95c

This is a compact reference giving basic facts about entrance examinations required, enrollment, expenses, number of majors offered, special majors, and average financial aid awarded.

A new social invention, the community college. Gleazer, Edmund J., Jr. American Association of Junior Colleges. 1962. 16p. 10c

Observations concerning the composition, objectives, and role of the two-year community college.

An opportunity for you . . . the junior college. National Education Association. 1967. 4p. 35 copies $1

Describes the junior college, explains some popular misconceptions, and tells why one out of every four high school graduates who continue their formal education does so in a junior college.

Parents' guide to summer camps. Shapiro, Charlotte M. and Jarmul, Lore. Harper and Row. 1968. $5.95; paper $2.95

Description of 411 private summer camps in New England, New York, New Jersey, and Pennsylvania. Includes sources for further information.

Patterson's American education. Educational Directories Inc. 1970. 800p. $25 plus postage

Most useful for the names and addresses of officials of colleges, universities, county and public school systems, and special, private, technical, and vocational schools. Also includes lists of schools, classified alphabetically, geographically, and by type of school.

Patterson's schools classified. Educational Directories Inc. Published annually. 184p. $3.50 plus postage, paper

Includes a listing of seven thousand schools classified as to type, such as agriculture, architecture, art, fashion, and mechanical trades.

G. Information About Colleges, Schools for Vocational Training, and Other Educational Institutions—*Continued*

Prep school guide for Jewish youth. Feingold, S. Norman and others. B'nai B'rith Vocational Service. 1966. 224p. $4.95

Information on six hundred prep schools in the United States and Canada. Provides admission requirements, special programs, costs, size of school, and location. Data on number of Jewish students and proximity of synagogues also included.

**Private independent schools. 22nd edition. Bunting and Lyon, Inc. 1969. 372p. $15

One section is a directory of 365 private schools for boys and girls including boarding schools, day schools, and military schools with or without church affiliations. Contains statistical information, requirements for admission, costs, and extracurricular activities. Another section is comprised of descriptive listings of 675 schools which hold membership in one of the educational associations that compose the National Association of Independent Schools. Good index. Revised annually.

Private schools illustrated—a select directory of private boarding schools, day and country day schools in the United States. Porter Sargent. 1962. 352p. $2

A reprint of one section of the *Handbook of Private Schools.*

Random House guide to graduate study in the arts and sciences. Wasserman, E. R. and Switzer, E. E. Random House. 1968. 361p. $6.95

This book provides a listing of courses of graduate study in the United States. For each area of study there is also a listing of the institutions offering Ph.D. degrees in the field, including the number of degrees awarded in the period from 1960-1965 and the enrollment in the specific department as of the fall of 1964.

Sargent guide to summer camps and summer schools. Porter Sargent, Publisher. 1969. 336p. $4.40 cloth; $2.20 paper

Directory of about one thousand foremost private resident camps and summer schools. Master listings give name and address, location, date of establishment, the director's name and his winter address, enrollment, fee, and special features.

Second semester. Swift, H. M. David McKay Company. 1961. 244p. $3.95

Career fiction. A picture of life in a small coeducational college, with overtones that will be of interest to young people embarking on their college careers.

The *Seventeen* guide to college choice. Klein, David. Macmillan Company. 1969. 278p. $5.95

The author has compiled material from his articles in *Seventeen* magazine giving advice to teen-age girls on how to get the most out of high school, how to select a college, how to apply for college admission, and how to adjust successfully to college life. Interviews with three admission directors help to clarify their admission policies.

Should you pay for advice on college? Changing Times. 6p. 15c

Information about the assistance offered by commercial agencies, colleges, and nonprofit agencies.

**Stay in high school. American School. 1964. 4p. Free

Reasons why young people should stay in school and graduate. Available in sets for class or homeroom use.

Summary report of 698 colleges interested in additional applications after April 15 for fall 1970 admission. Chronicle Guidance Publications. Prepared annually. 16p. $1

Arranged by states, this is a tabular report of openings for freshmen and for transfer students, for men and for women, as indicated by the colleges the previous March 1.

Summer studies in private independent schools: the programs of summer study in American private schools and camps. 5th edition. 1968. Bunting and Lyon, Inc. 310p. $6

Descriptive entries for about sixty summer school programs for boys and girls of elementary and high school age. Data usually include admission requirements, costs, regular academic and special programs, and recreational facilities.

Technician education yearbook. Prakken Publications. 3rd edition. 1967-68. 236p. $10

Directory of 1,024 institutions on high school and college levels. Arranged alphabetically within states, it gives curricula, accreditation, enrollment, admission, public or private.

**The teenager and home study; a practical guide to correspondence education for young people and guidance counselors. Wellman, Henry Q. Richards Rosen Press. 1970. 155p. $4; library edition $3.78

Designed to help potential students select a quality correspondence that can best meet the needs of students who can benefit from home study instruction. Contains lists of accredited correspondence schools offering training in a variety of career areas, suggestions for finishing high school by correspondence, list of colleges offering correspondence courses, and subjects available from accredited private home study schools.

Training opportunities—non-college. Careers. 1967. 8p. 35c

Career brief describing on-the-job training, junior colleges, technical and trade schools, business schools, apprenticeship, correspondence schools, and company schools.

Universities and colleges of Canada. Association of Universities and Colleges of Canada. 1969. 427p. $5

Detailed information regarding sixty-one universities and colleges in Canada, including enrollment, degrees conferred, fees and costs, admission requirements, and programs of study offered at each institution.

University; the students, faculty, and campus life at one university. Schwartz, Alvin. Viking Press. 1969. 175. $5.95; library edition $5.63

An informative description of the University of Pennsylvania as a representative institution evoking a sense of campus life in readable text and related photographs.

G. Information About Colleges, Schools for Vocational Training, and Other Educational Institutions—*Continued*

USAFI catalog. United States Armed Forces Institute. 1968. 150p. Free

Description of courses available to young men and women on active duty with the armed forces. Also information concerning individual study opportunities, testing service, applying for credit, special reference and resource materials available from USAFI, and services available after discharge to inactive duty.

Vocational training in New York City . . . where to find it. Vocational Foundation, Inc. 1970. 324p. $8.50

Information about training in approximately 600 subjects afforded by approximately 850 schools and colleges in New York City that give some form of training intended as preparation for a specific kind of work. Arranged by occupation. Good indexes. Includes entrance requirements and tuition costs.

What about college? Lehigh University. 1962. 14p. Free

Aimed to help and to encourage students to think about their abilities and limitations, their career objectives, and their further educational plans. Good advice about choice of a college and how to apply for admission. Revised biannually.

What type of college for what type of student. Hood, Albert B. University of Minnesota Press. 1968. 94p. $2.75 paper

A study analyzing the scholastic success of students during their college freshman year in relation to their high school marks, test scores, personality data, and type of institution attended.

What you must know about getting into college. Rubinfeld, William A. Vocational Guidance Manuals. 1964. 160p. $3.75; $1.95 paper

The chapter headings include: Preparation for college, Selection of a college, Getting into college, Scholarships and financial aid, Visiting colleges, Tests for admission to college, and Adjustment to college.

What's a good college? Changing Times. 1962. 5p. 15c

Reprint describing the many factors that make up a good college.

Why did you go to college, Linda Warren? Bonnell, Dorothy. Julian Messner. 1969. 192p. $3.50; library binding $3.34

Career fiction. From the security of home and friends to exposure to perplexing new ideas and fast-paced college competition, Linda's efforts reflect the struggle of young people to come to grips with themselves and their consciences.

World-wide graduate award directory. Advancement and Placement Institute. 1959. 56p. $3

Description of assistantships, fellowships, scholarships, and research grants contributed by over one thousand universities and foundations in forty-four states and fifty-five foreign countries. Arranged by country or state.

**Your college education—how to pay for it. Splaver, Sarah. Julian Messner. 1964. 288p. $4.95; library binding $4.64

Discussion of methods of increasing a student's financial resources, decreasing his college costs, and securing financial aid when need exists. Two sections of special interest to the counselor are the financial aid programs and informational materials provided by states and those available in the major fields of study.

Your first year at college: letters to a college freshman. McCabe, Joseph E. Westminster Press. 1967. 93p. $2.95

Although the author writes about careers, campus activities, and student unrest, his main emphasis is on the wise use of the college years to build a meaningful life.

Your introduction to Oklahoma State University. 1969. 92p. Free

An example of an illustrated college catolog suggesting the courses basic to 120 areas of study. Designed to furnish pertinent information to high school seniors and to college freshmen and sophomores.

H. Job Seeking

Agency training centers for Federal employees. Government Printing Office. Supt. of Documents. 1968. 84p. $1

This directory provides information on the number and variety of programs offered at agency operated training centers. Includes purpose of the training center, the type of program offered, who may attend, and other general information.

All about me. Bruer, J. M. American Technical Society. 1966. 72p. $1.10 paper

A booklet organized for recording those facts needed for insurance, applications, references, and certificates.

Are you a woman looking for a job? New York State Department of Labor, Division of Employment. 1967. 9p. Free to counselors and librarians

Designed to assist the employment-seeking woman who is without job experience.

**Can I get *the* job? Let's find out. General Motors Corporation, Public Relations Staff. 1954. 32p. Free

Suggestions to young people on preparation for the first job. Sections are entitled: What are my interests? What do I have to offer? What are employers looking for? How do I get an interview? Who does the talking? Available in classroom sets free of charge.

Career employment guide. National Employment Services Institute. 8th annual edition. 1969. 91p. $2

Directory of employers who offer summer jobs in industry, utilities, research laboratories, insurance, finance, retailing, and government. Gives nature of employer's business, kinds of summer jobs, and where to apply.

H. Job Seeking—*Continued*

Charm: the career girl's guide to business and personal success. Whitcomb, Helen and Lang, Rosalind. McGraw-Hill Book Company. 1964. 472p. $7.75

Includes practical suggestions on business etiquette, job finding techniques, and personal attributes which help the career girl achieve success.

College placement annual. College Placement Council. Annual. 696p. Available only through college placement offices or to subscribers to group of Journal Publications. $10

Articles written by experienced placement officers to give specific help to the job seeker in preparing for interviews. Contains a geographical and occupational index to aid students in determing where and with what employers they will be able to find opportunities in their chosen fields of interests. Directory of two thousand employers who normally recruit college graduates.

College placement directory. Zimmerman, O. T. and Zimmerman, Mildred K. Industrial Research Service. 4th edition. 1968. 643p. $17

Over one thousand employers who hire college graduates itemize their employment openings and the name of the personnel officer in charge. Another section lists the colleges with a description of type of institutions, size of enrollment, and the name of the placement officer. This directory acquaints the college graduate with the employment opportunities. Good indexes.

Cowles guide to summer jobs in Federal agencies. Cowles Book Company. 1969. 214p. $3.95

Of interest to students who wish to work for the Government during the summer vacations, this provides information about the opportunities and how to apply for the summer employment examination. Some specimen test questions are shown.

Directory of college placement officers. College Placement Council. Annual. 100p. Available only by subscription to the group of Journal Publications. $10

Listing of college placement officers including name and location of college; name, title, and telephone number of placement offices; date on which interviews begin for next school year; special requirements, if any, for scheduling of interviews; and months in which institution has graduating classes.

Do you want a job? U.S. Department of Labor, Manpower Administration. Supt. of Documents. 1970. 8p. 10c

This illustrated leaflet explains how local employment service offices help young people choose jobs, acquire work experience, or continue in school.

Employment agencies. Alumnae Advisory Center. 1969. 5p. 35c

This reveals the vices of some employment agencies and gives suggestions concerning the type of agency to avoid.

Employment opportunities for men and women after 60. Angel, Juvenal L. Regents Publishing Company. 1969. 180p. $10

Some of the topics covered are: Possibilities after 60, counseling the mature worker, opportunities according to aptitudes and abilities, part-time employment, starting your own business, and directory of Senior Centers in the United States.

Employment opportunities with National Park concessioners. National Park Service. Annually. 4p. Free

Names and addresses of individual concessioners.

Facts you should know about employment agencies. Better Business Bureau. 1963. 6p. Free

Details concerning services, fees, etc., are discussed, as well as unethical practices which might be encountered.

**Federal career directory: a guide for college students. U.S. Civil Service Commission. Supt. of Documents. 1968. 87p. $1.25

Includes description of thirty-eight Federal agencies and ninety-two job briefs containing nature of work, qualifications required, and career opportunities. One index of job briefs is by position title and another by college major fields of study. For college graduates.

The Federal merit promotion program. U.S. Civil Service Commission. Supt. of Documents. 1965. 6p. 5c

Describes merit principles and criteria which must be followed in promotion of Federal employees.

Finding jobs for Negroes: a kit of ideas for management. Government Printing Office. Supt. of Documents. 1970. 13p. 30c

A kit of ideas that can help an employer solve problems that he may face in efforts to employ workers from minority groups.

Finding your job. Wilson, Howard. Administrative Research Associates. 1963. 48p. $1

Prepared to aid the student in the job seeking process. Includes discussion of how to get leads, getting the interview, preparing for the interview, what to do during the interview, and the follow-up.

*Fitting yourself for business: what the employer wants beyond skills. MacGibbon, Elizabeth Gregg. McGraw-Hill Book Company. 1961. 416p. $7.25

Practical instruction on applying for a job, adjusting to office work and personalities, managing one's income, and maintaining standards for correct dress and grooming.

**Future jobs for high school girls. Pamphlet 7. Women's Bureau, U.S. Department of Labor. Supt. of Documents. 1966. 73p. 30c

Designed for high school graduates, this pamphlet provides information on a variety of occupations open to women and gives some tips on how to get additional training and experience.

H. Job Seeking—*Continued*

**Futures for college women in New York. Alumnae Advisory Center. 1968. 56p. $1

Guidebook of informative material for college graduates who are seeking work in New York City. Contains advice on job seeking procedures, names of some employers who hire college women, employment agency fees, street address guide, list of reliable residences for women, nature of payroll deductions, and fringe benefits. Good bibliography on job seeking.

Guide to preparing a résumé. New York State Department of Labor, Division of Employment. 1963. 39p. Single copies free to counselors and librarians

Prepared to assist the job seeker in evaluating and formulating his assets in an organized and logical manner. Good suggestions for planning the résumé, suggested outline, sample résumés, and pointers on the covering letters.

**Help wanted: female. The young woman's guide to job-hunting. King, Alice Gore. Charles Scribner's Sons. 1968. 123p. $1.00 paper; library edition $3.95

For the job-changer, the recent graduate, the returning wife or mother. Advice concerning where to look, interviews, employment agencies, letters of application, and why and how to change jobs.

How not to write letters of application. Alumnae Advisory Center. 1968. 12p. 35c

Terse statements and line drawings present practical reminders.

How to earn (a lot of) money in college: the student guide to employment. Harvard Student Agencies. 1968. 238p. $1.95

Advice from students on how to get term-time employment or starting one's own job.

How to find and apply for a job. Keily, Helen J. and Walters, R. G. South-Western Publishing Company. 1960. 91p. $1.36

This booklet has been prepared to help high school and college graduates to apply for positions in corporations and employment offices. It covers information on selling one's self, discovering opportunities, the personal interview, the application form, and the letter of application.

How to get a job. Stone, Elna. Bruce Publishing Company. 1969. 80p. $1.88 paper

A series of workbook-type exercises to help individuals become more effective in getting, holding, and progressing on the job.

How to get a job—a handy guide for jobseekers. The President's Committee on Employment of the Handicapped. 1967. 28p. Free

Written for the mentally retarded, the guide gives tips on how to find and keep the right job.

**How to get and hold the right job. New York State Department of Labor, Division of Employment. 1961. 16p. Free to counselors and librarians

Tips on getting and holding a job.

**How to get and hold the right job—facts from your employment service. U.S. Employment Service. Supt. of Documents. 1967. 20p. 10c

Clear and concise tips on getting and holding a job. Includes sections on the following: What to look for in a job, Take stock of yourself, Consider job requirements, Sources of job leads, Getting ready for the interview, What to do during the interview, Your letter of application, Why people sometimes fail to get the jobs they seek, Why workers lose their jobs, What employers say they want, and Getting ahead in your field of work.

How to get *the* job. Dreese, Mitchell. Science Research Associates. Revised 1968. 48p. 75c

Discussion of steps necessary to plan and carry out a successful job campaign, getting ahead on the job, and starting your own business.

How to hold your job. Fudell, Stanley and Peck, John. John Day Company. 1967. 249p. $6.95

A teacher's book and accompanying student workbook composed of twelve units of daily curriculum material for use with mentally retarded adolescents reading on a second-grade level. The emphasis is on teaching work values and personal attitudes.

How to look for a job in New York. King, Alice Gore. Alumnae Advisory Center. 1966. 26p. $2

Good practical advice which is applicable to any community concerning the search for a job and preparation for work.

How to make it in a man's world. Pogrebin, Letty Cotton. Doubleday and Company. 1970. 288p. $5.95

Describes how some women have distinguished themselves, adjusted to a variety of categories of bosses, and "moved into the executive suite."

How to move in and move up. Butler, E. A. Macmillan Company. 1970. 192p. $5.95

The president of an executive recruiting company discusses the insights he has gained during thirteen years of consultation with corporation executives. Of interest to potential executives.

How to "sell yourself" to an employer. New York State Department of Labor, Division of Employment. 1961. 4p. Free to counselors and librarians

A checklist of fifteen proven points helpful in landing a job.

How to succeed in job search—when really trying. Copy-Write Creations. 1968. 86p. $2.10

Helpful information on many phases of job hunting, including charts of fees which may legally be charged by employment agencies in all fifty states.

How to write your résumé. Alumnae Advisory Center. 1970. 22p. $1.50

Practical information about writing and using a sales sheet, followed by twelve sample forms for variations according to individual experiences.

H. Job Seeking—*Continued*

How you can get a better job. American Technical Society. 1964. 181p. $3.25

Discussion of the basic personal factors that make for success and promotion in a job. One section includes suggestions on how high school graduates can partially offset their lack of actual working experience. Separate sections are available at 40c each.

Improving your creativity on the job. Morgan, John S. American Management Association. 1968. 224p. $9

Suggestions for stimulating one's innate creative powers and cultivating original approaches to problem solving.

Interview! The executive's guide to selecting the right personnel. Hariton, Theodore. Hastings House, Publishers. 1970. 159p. $6.95

Although written as a practical guide for interviewers, the job applicant can learn what to expect in an interview. The sample interview and the interview rating form will be especially helpful.

The job finder: it pays to advertise. Feingold, S. Norman. Bellman Publishing Company. 1966. 37p. $2.25

Suggestions on how to use want ads in magazines, trade journals, and periodicals. Also includes help in writing the situation wanted ad.

**Jobfinding techniques for mature women. Women's Bureau, U.S. Department of Labor. Supt. of Documents. 1970. 40p. 30c

This pamphlet points out techniques for finding jobs available to mature women and is designed as a step-by-step guide to assist them to prepare for and to find employment. Topics covered include how to do a self-inventory, how to prepare a résumé, the job hunt, how to prepare a letter of application, guides to an effective interview, and training opportunities.

A job for you . . . sparetime, summer, Saturday. Peake, Miriam Morrison. Scholastic Book Services. 1964. 72p. 35c paper

Includes discussion of finding a job, making the most of an interview, behaving on the job, getting along with fellow employees, dealing with the public, and planning a budget. This title is available to schools, only through the Scholastic Book Services.

**Job guide for young workers, 1969-1970 edition. Bureau of Employment Security, U.S. Department of Labor. 1969. 200p. $1.50

Gives advice on how to seek work and presents information on different entry jobs.

Job hopping. Alumnae Advisory Center. 1967. 6p. 35c

This reprint from *Mademoiselle* presents many advantages of changing jobs and gives practical advice concerning it.

The job hunt; job-seeking behavior of unemployed workers in a local economy. Sheppard, Harold L. and Belitsky, A. Harvey. Johns Hopkins Press. 1966. 304p. $7.95

This is an investigation which explores the relationship of social-psychological factors to job-seeking patterns. For research workers on this subject.

Job hunters' bibliography. Alumnae Advisory Center. 1969. 8p. $1

A list of 131 titles in 57 different career fields. Sources and prices are given.

Job strategy: preparing for effective placement in business and industry. Rood, Allen. McGraw-Hill Book Company. 1961. 281p. $6.95

A guide to tested techniques for planning and conducting a successful job campaign.

Job training suggestions for women and girls. Leaflet 40. Women's Bureau, U.S. Department of Labor. Supt. of Documents. 1970. 16p. 15c

Gives a brief summary of various types of job training available to women and indicates where such programs are offered.

The Macmillan job guide to American corporations. McKay, Ernest A. Macmillan Company. 1967. 374p. $7.95

Information concerning 260 companies, with alphabetical, geographic, and academic indexes. Gives number of employees, job functions, training programs, degree requirements, opportunities, and employee benefits. Fewer employers but more detail than the *College Placement Annual.*

A manual for campus recruiters. College Placem nt Council. 1962. 39p. $1

Concise outline-type brochure covering the fundamentals of college recruiting. Includes the responsibilities of the employer, college, and student.

Memo on job-finding for the mature woman. Leaflet 13. Women's Bureau, U.S. Department of Labor. Supt. of Documents. 1963. 8p. 5c

Suggestions concerning the job hunt, the job interview, social security, importance of maturity, and obtaining job skills.

Merchandising your job talents. Manpower Administration. Supt. of Documents. Revised 1969. 26p. 25c

This pamphlet for job hunters tells them where they can learn more about jobs for which they are qualified, how to prepare a letter of application, and how to present their qualifications at job interviews. Some hints on taking tests are also presented.

Money in your pocket: a management guide for young adults. Patton, Price A. and Patton, Martha. David McKay Company. 1959. 192p. $3.75

Discussion of the management of one's salary, budgeting, saving, installment buying, insurance, and business practices for the teen-ager.

Nine ways to get the most out of your first job. Changing Times. 1964. 3p. 15c

Basic points to help make a good start.

Ninety-nine ways for teen-agers to earn money during the summer. Advancement and Placement Institute. 1962. 24p. 50c

A compilation of ideas which have been tested money-makers in many parts of the country.

H. Job Seeking—*Continued*

Occupations for men and women after 45. Angel, Juvenal L. World Trade Academy Press. 1963. 200p. $12.50

Suggestions are given for the mature worker. Topics include finding a position, jobs open to mature workers, make your own job by setting up a small business, part-time employment, and employment services for mature employees.

**On the job training and where to get it. Liston, Robert A. Julian Messner. 1967. 190p. $3.95; library binding $3.64

Addressed to the high school graduate with ambition who cannot go to college. The purpose of the book is to describe training opportunities and how one can qualify for that training either on the job or in formal, industrial training programs. Special emphasis is placed on the technical fields, but the building trades, industrial production, retail sales, and service occupations are included.

The opportunity explosion. Snelling, Robert O. Macmillan Company. 1969. 320p. $6.95

The president of a well-known employment agency asserts that those who really want jobs can find them. He explains how to go about finding suitable employment, emphasizing the importance of resiliency in changing jobs, of taking stock of oneself, of advance planning, and of achieving originality of approach.

Opportunity knocks books. Andrews, Margaret E. Gregg Division, McGraw-Hill Book Company. 1968. 6 booklets. $1.36 each

A series of prevocational paperback books aimed to give students practical suggestions for making the most of themselves both in their careers and their personal lives. Titles include *The job you want* and *It's up to you.*

Over forty—out of work? How to win at the job-hunting game. Albee, Lou. Prentice-Hall, Inc. 1970. 194p. $5.95

Inspirational in tone yet straightforward in detail, this guide is addressed to the middle-aged man who is looking for employment. Gives suggestions on securing value from interviews, selling one's employment attributes, and development of a satisfying mental attitude. The author is a former consultant to a Forty Plus Club.

Part-time employment—employer attitudes on opportunities for the college-trained woman. Alumnae Advisory Center. 1964. 62p. $1

Intended as a guide to women seeking less than full-time employment.

Part-time jobs and summer jobs. Sterling Publishing Company. 1966. 128p. $1.95

Advice concerning finding vacation or week-end jobs. Some are discussed in the light of maximum earnings over a short period of time, others as stepping-stones to lifetime employment.

Part-time summer, and volunteer jobs for Jewish and other minority groups. Sinick, Daniel. B'nai B'rith Vocational Service. 1969. 112p. $2.50

This book is specifically oriented toward minority groups, describing jobs in the part-time labor market. Information is included on how to choose jobs, how to find appropriate jobs, requirements for employment, cooperative education programs, and selected references that will provide further leads. Each section is subdivided into job listings for people of high school age, and for those of college age and older.

Pathway to your future: the job résumé and letter of application. Adler Kenneth R. Bellman Publishing Company. 1964. 33p. $1.75

Suggestions for effectively putting facts about oneself on paper when applying for a job. Includes sixteen sample résumés and eight letters of application.

**Planning your career. Calvert, Robert, Jr. and Steele, John E. McGraw-Hill Book Company. 1963. 152p. $1.95 paper

Includes model résumés, application letters, and other career-planning devices to help the reader develop skill in job-seeking techniques. Three phases of career development are presented: determination of career goals, location of suitable employment, and satisfactory progress in one's career.

Poise for the successful business girl. Parr, Mary. Dartnell Corporation. 1960. 61p. 50c

Ways of acquiring poise as an aid to success in business life.

Preparing the recruitment brochure. College Placement Council. 1964. 16p. $1

A booklet to assist employers in the preparation of effective college recruitment literature.

Principles and practices of college recruiting. College Placement Council. 1968. 6p. $5 per 100. Single copy free to counselors.

Compilation of accepted ethical concepts of college recruiting, providing a standard of conduct and procedure for the student, the college, and the employer.

Rate yourself. Rhodes, R. M. Executive Development Press. 1951. 14p. 30c

A number of self-rating check lists designed to point out personal strengths and weaknesses in attitudes, working characteristics, self-management, and taking it on the chin. Also included are suggestions for discovering strong points and "what to do about yourself."

Recreation employment guide. National Employment Services Institute. 8th annual edition. 1969. 113p. $2

Directory of employers who offer summer jobs in resorts, motels, hotels, restaurants, ranches, camps, marinas, beaches, parks, youth hostels, and churches. Information about when the jobs will be available and when and where to apply.

Seasonal employment in the National Park Service. National Park Service. 1968. 18p. Free

Types of positions, duties, qualifications required, salaries, and opportunities are followed by an explanation of how and when to apply.

H. Job Seeking—*Continued*

**Selective guide to overseas employment, Angel, Juvenal L. Regents Publishing Company. 1969. 224p. $6.95; paper edition $3.95

General information about the approach to a job overseas is followed by discussion of opportunities in each of twenty countries.

So you want to go back to work. Scofield, Nanette and Klaeman, Betty. Random House. 1968. 208p. $4.95

Helpful chapters for the housewife who seeks to return to work, for the widow, the divorcee, and the handicapped woman.

Success. Shafer, Robert and Bernd, Verlene, eds. Scholastic Book Services. 1964. 192p. 60c paper

Short stories and essays that illuminate the different kinds of success and the qualities needed to attain them. This title is available to schools, only, through the Scholastic Book Services.

Summer employment directory of the United States. National Directory Service. 1969. 208p. $4.95

Contains a list of 80,000 summer job openings with organizations which want to hire high school seniors, college students, and teachers. Published annually.

Summer job directory. Advancement and Placement Institute. 1969. 100p. $6

Annual listing of actual summer jobs, compensated projects, apprenticeships, and permanent jobs; those for high school students are so indicated. Includes a sampling of 58,000 opportunities in the United States and 24 foreign countries. Entries include job descriptions, openings, salaries, names and addresses of personnel directors, and employers.

Summer jobs in Federal agencies. U.S. Civil Service Commission. 1969. 31p. Single copy free

Examination announcement revised each year. Discusses the summer employment programs of various Federal agencies. Lists the occupations of summer employees by agencies and explains how to apply for jobs.

Summer opportunities for teenagers. Advancement and Placement Institute. 1963. 72p. $3

An annual compilation of opportunities in camping, hobbies, hosteling, farming, travel, reading, and volunteer service projects. Also features some job leads and ways by which the teenager can make his own job.

Summer resort jobs. Irving, Judy. Alumnae Advisory Center. 1969. 5p. 35c

Suggestions on methods of obtaining summer jobs at resorts and a description of some work opportunities.

The teenage employment guide. Goldenthal, Allan B. Regents Publishing Company. 1970. 128p. $4.95; paper $2.95

Intended as a guide for high school graduates and dropouts who are seeking jobs that do not require "too much training." Includes some part-time jobs, on-the-job training, apprenticeships, and discusses the accepted methods of applying for a job.

Thinking about your first job? Remember Uncle Sam when it comes to choosing an employer. U.S. Civil Service Commission. 1968. 8p. Single copy free

Brief information about Federal employment opportunities for high school graduates.

Twelve pointers that lead to promotion. Moulton, Richard H. Executive Development Press. No date. 16p. 30c

Practical suggestions for a man with managerial asperations to improve his relationships with those above him.

What industry looks for in the high school graduate. McMillan, John E. Eastman Kodak Company, Public Relations Department. No date. 7p. Free

Discussion of character traits considered important for success in industry.

**Why and how to prepare an effective résumé. Angel, Juvenal L. Regents Publishing Company. 4th edition 1965. 256p. $9

Information for persons planning to look for work or change positions. Some topics included are the necessity of a good résumé; the analytical, functional, and chronological résumé; work sheet; and examples.

Why young people fail to get and hold jobs. New York State Department of Labor, Division of Employment, New York State Employment Service. 1963. 12p. Single copies free to counselors and librarians

These cases illustrating why young people fail to get and hold jobs are examples of actual problems faced by young people in adjusting to their vocations after they leave school.

A woman's guide to earning a good living. Winter, Elmer. Simon and Schuster, Inc. 1961. 401p. $4.95

Addressed to the older woman who wishes to return to work, this book offers many suggestions for finding jobs and describes opportunities including self-employment and work for the handicapped.

World-wide summer placement directory. Advancement and Placement Institute. 1969. 100p. $6

An annual compilation of actual summer jobs, employment opportunities, projects, and awards available to college students, teachers, and librarians. Information includes opportunities listed by all stages and in many foreign countries.

The young woman in business. McLean, Beth and Paris, Jeanne. Iowa State University Press. 1962. 304p. $5

Practical advice on many of the problems concerning getting and holding a job.

Your first job. Kiwanis Club. 1964. 4p. 15c

Hints to young job seekers summarizing first steps, arranging for the interview, getting ready for the interview, selling one's self in the interview, and what to do after the interview.

H. Job Seeking—*Continued*

**Your future in your own business. Winter, Elmer L. Richards Rosen Press. 1966. 188p. $4; library edition $3.78

Basic information about going into business for one's self. Includes topics such as evaluating opportunities; finding, starting, or buying a business; financing; selecting employees; setting up long-range goals; and managing a business.

Your letter is you. Alumnae Advisory Center. 1968. 10p. 25c

Concise information to the job seeker on how to prepare the letter of application, what to say in it, errors to beware of, and the follow-up of the letter.

I. Legislation and Social Security

American women, 1963-1968. Report of the Interdepartmental Committee on the Status of Women. Supt. of Documents. 1968. 33p. 70c

Factual accounts of progress, grouped according to the major categories of the original report, noting action taken under public and private auspices.

American women, report of the President's Commission on the Status of Women. Supt. of Documents. 1963. 86p. $1.25

Presents findings and recommendations regarding the opportunities of American women in seven categories: education, employment, labor standards, security of basic income, equality of rights under the law, participation in government, and home and community.

Background facts on women workers in the United States. Women's Bureau, U.S. Department of Labor. 1968. 17p. Free

Contains statistical facts on women workers in the economy. Some topics covered are labor force status, industry of employment, occupation, earnings, and educational attainment.

Best places to live when you retire. Heusinkveld, Helen and Musson, Noverre. Frederick Fell, Inc. 1968. 111p. $6.95

A national directory of retirement residences. Several chapters give wise advice to those in search of retirement homes.

Compilation of the social security laws. Volumes I and II. Social Security Administration. Supt. of Documents. 1968. 1,523p. $1.75 each volume

Contains the Social Security Act, as amended, and related enactments through January 2, 1968. Compiled solely for reference purposes.

Continuing education programs and services for women. Pamphlet 10. Women's Bureau, U.S. Department of Labor. Supt. of Documents. 1968. 112p. 40c

Lists many programs designed for adult women to update their work skills or to obtain higher education. Includes a list of recommended readings on employment and training opportunities.

Employment certificates. Bureau of Labor Standards, U.S. Department of Labor. 1963. 6p. Free

Explanation of the usefulness of employment certificates, how and where they may be obtained, and what papers are necessary to get them.

Employment certificates help you help youth. Bulletin 183. Bureau of Labor Standards. Revised 1964. 21p. Free to counselors

Primarily addressed to persons who issue employment certificates. Shows how state labor departments, guidance and placement counselors, youth-serving agencies, and other community groups can cooperate with employment certificate issuing officers in helping young workers.

Federal benefits for veterans and dependents. Veterans Administration. Supt. of Documents. 1969. 70p. 30c

This fact sheet is designed to provide only general information concerning benefits for veterans, their dependents, and beneficiaries.

Federal labor laws and programs. Bulletin 262. Bureau of Labor Standards. Supt. of Documents. 1964. 180p. 55c

Provides a quick reference to the important Federal labor laws and regulations of general application.

Growth of labor law in the United States. U.S. Department of Labor. Supt. of Documents. 1968. 311p. $1.25

Gives history of major state labor laws in the United States. Examines and compares current state provisions. Includes chapters on child labor, hours and minimum wage, occupational health and safety, unemployment insurance, workmen's compensation, anti-discrimination, and other laws. Twenty-four tables.

Handbook for young workers. Bulletin 271. Bureau of Labor Standards. Supt. of Documents. 1965. 29p. 20c

Explains the kinds of adjustments required of new entrants into the labor force. Describes Federal laws and regulations that affect the age at which boys and girls may start to work, the numbers of hours and the times of the day or week during which they may work, and the kinds of jobs which are regarded as safe and suitable for them. Also discusses some other laws that affect young workers.

How to begin working. New York State Department of Labor, Division of Employment. 1961. 10p. Free to counselors and librarians

The legal requirements for the protection of young workers; working papers; tips on jobs and salaries; minimum wages; unemployment insurance.

If you become disabled. Social Security Administration. Supt. of Documents. 1968. 32p. 15c

Describes the disability provisions of the social security law and lists the requirements for disability insurance benefits. Available free from social security offices.

I. Legislation and Social Security—*Continued*

The intelligent woman's guide to future security. Kutner, Luis. Dodd, Mead and Company. 1970. 202p. $4.95

Prepared to reinforce rather than replace the assistance given by lawyers and advisers, this book discusses wills, probate procedures, estate planning, taxes, insurance, social security, real estate, the stock market, financing the funeral, and other matters of interest to women in charge of financial matters.

Managing your family finances. Lasser, J. K. Doubleday and Company. 1968. 264p. $5.95

Practical advice on estate planning, methods of increasing income, life and health insurance, mortgages, mutual funds, credit buying, social security, and other money management.

Negro women in the population and in the labor force. Women's Bureau, U.S. Department of Labor. Supt. of Documents. 1967. 41p. 30c

Facts concerning population trends, occupations, unemployment, income levels, and educational attainment.

1969 handbook on women workers. Women's Bureau, U.S. Department of Labor. Supt. of Documents. 1969. 384p. $1.50

The handbook assembles factual information such as the Federal and state laws affecting the employment of women, their occupations, income, earnings, education, and training. Includes a good topical bibliography.

Part-time employment of women. Women's Bureau, U.S. Department of Labor. 1968. 8p. Free

Indicates work experience by age, occupation, and marital status.

Reemployment rights of Federal employees who perform duty in the Armed Forces. Civil Service Commission. Supt. of Documents. 1968. 7p. 5c

Explains how and when Federal employees who leave their jobs to serve in the armed forces are eligible to return to their former status.

Security and medicare. Segal, Martin. Associated Press Newsfeatures. 1968. 36p. 50c

An explanation of the new social security and medicare provisions.

Social security benefits for students, 18-22. Government Printing Office. Supt. of Documents. 1969. 8p. 10c

Tells how a student from ages eighteen to twenty-two may now secure monthly cash social security benefits. Explains the requirements necessary to receive such benefits, the information needed when applying, and how and where to apply.

**Social security benefits—how you earn them . . . how much credit you need . . . how to estimate the amount. Social Security Administration. Supt. of Documents. 1969. 14p. 15c

This leaflet gives a simple explanation of what social security credits are, how one earns them, and how many are needed. It also contains a step-by-step explanation of how to estimate the amount of one's benefit. Available free from social security offices.

Social security handbook on retirement, survivors, disability, and health insurance. Social Security Administration. Supt. of Documents. 1969. 477p. $2.25

A detailed explanation of who is entitled to benefits and how to get them. Helpful information on coverage provisions, figuring the benefit rate, filing a claim, and establishing rights to benefits. Designed for professional people who help others with social security matters.

Social security information for young families. Social Security Administration. Supt. of Documents. 1970. 19p. 15c

This booklet is about the protection social security has for younger people, how a worker earns this protection, the benefits that can be paid, and other information of concern to younger workers.

Special information for self-employed farmers about reporting income for social security. Social Security Administration. Supt. of Documents. 1968. 8p. 10c

Specific information concerning how the self-employed farmer may earn social security credits and how to figure and report net earnings. Available free from social security offices.

Special information for self-employed people about reporting their income for social security. Social Security Administration. 1969. 6p. 10c

Specific information on how self-employed people earn social security credits and how to figure and report net earnings. Available free from social security offices.

State child-labor standards. Bulletin 158. Bureau of Labor Standards. Supt. of Documents. Revised 1965. 399p. $1.25

Summary of laws, state by state, affecting the employment of minors under eighteen years of age. Also includes hazardous occupations prohibited for minors, by state.

Teaching high school students about labor unions. American Federation of Labor and Congress of Industrial Organizations. 1960. 8p. 5c. Single copy free to teachers

A report of a unit of study on collective bargaining.

Teenagers can be hired. Bureau of Labor Standards. Revised 1965. 2p. Free to counselors

Gives examples of the kinds of jobs in which fourteen- to seventeen-year-olds may be employed.

Under 21; a young people's guide to legal rights. Dorman, Michael. Delacorte Press. 1970. 210p. $4.50

Discussion of rights of minors concerning business affairs, driving, voting, criminal law, drugs, drinking, marriage, relationships with parents, and the draft and military service.

Unions and what they do. Lens, Sidney. Putnam's Sons. 1968. 160p. $3.49

This explanation of the complex functions of unions includes how unions are formed, what constitutes collective bargaining, and what unions can offer their workers. Prepared for grades 8 to 11.

I. Legislation and Social Security—*Continued*

Who are the working mothers? Leaflet 37. Women's Bureau, U.S. Department of Labor. Supt. of Documents. 1968. 4p. 10c

Gives factual information about the number of working mothers, ages of their children, their reasons for working, their occupations, and family characteristics and income.

Your medicare handbook, health insurance under Social Security. U.S. Department of Health, Education, and Welfare. Supt. of Documents. 1969. 31p. 40c

Explains the benefits and regulations of the plan.

Your personal guide to successful retirement: the complete, step-by-step handbook of retirement planning. Margolius, Sidney. Random House. 1969. 160p. $6.95; paper $3.95

A concise guide for the person contemplating retirement. It advises on many financial aspects of retirement such as health-care costs, housing, income tax procedures, investments, budget planning, and handling such matters as wills and inheritance taxes. Includes a useful bibliography.

**Your social security. Social Security Administration. Supt. of Documents. 1969. 48p. 15c

Describing social security rights and responsibilities, this booklet provides details on retirement, survivors, disability, and health insurance; amount of work required; events that stop payment; kinds of work covered; and procedures for checking one's account. Available free from social security offices.

Your social security earnings record. Social Security Administration. Supt. of Documents. 1968. 32p. 10c

Explains how earnings records are kept, what benefits are payable, how much work is required for benefits, and how to get a statement of earnings.

The youth you supervise. Bulletin 174. Bureau of Labor Standards. Supt. of Documents. Revised 1965. 12p. 10c

Helps to explain why young workers sometimes find it so hard to adjust to the demands of the job and to meet the requirements of employers and fellow workers. Offers suggestions for helping them to make the needed adjustments in ways which help to lessen the tensions which may accompany the hiring of young workers and often limit their later progress as workers.

J. Occupations for the Handicapped

The blind on the go and at work. U.S. Rehabilitation Services Administration. 1966. 24p. Free

Selected articles from the rehabilitation record.

The blind person and employment. American Foundation for the Blind. 1968. 4p. Free

A leaflet briefly describing some of the types of jobs available to a blind person.

Blind workers in service occupations in hospitals. American Foundation for the Blind. 1967. 12p. Free

Guidelines for selection, training, and placement of blind workers in service departments of hospitals, such as dietary, laundry, and housekeeping.

Career opportunities in service to the disadvantaged and handicapped. Government Printing Office. Supt. of Documents. 1969. 39p. 30c

Describes various personnel training programs designed to train people to work with the disadvantaged. This pamphlet is intended to encourage persons to take advantage of the training possibilities offered by the Federal Government.

Career opportunities in the field of mental retardation. Government Printing Office. Supt. of Documents. 1969. 30p. 25c

This publication is addressed primarily to the high school and college student who is interested in working with the mentally retarded and wishes a general introduction to the opportunities in the field.

Careers for the blind in electronic data processing. Chronicle Guidance Publications. 1967. 4p. 35c

Reprinted article from *Occupational Outlook Quarterly* discusses programming, aids for the blind in computer work, qualifications of programmer, adjustment to blindness before training, how to get training, and who should seek training.

Careers in special education. Council for Exceptional Children, National Education Association. 1968. 32p. 25c

The professional preparation, job opportunities, and sources of information are summarized for the following fields: mental retardation, gifted, behavioral disorders, physical disabilities, visual handicaps, speech and language disorders, and hearing impairment.

Consult the personnel and training service. American Foundation for the Blind. 1967. 4p. Free

A flyer describing the services of the Foundation, a clearinghouse for jobs in the field of service to blind persons.

Counseling the disadvantaged youth. Amos, William E. and Grambs, Jean D., eds. Prentice-Hall, Inc. 1968. 438p. $7.95

Contains a helpful chapter on presenting educational and occupational information to the disadvantaged.

Directory for exceptional children. 6th edition. Porter Sargent. 1969. 1150p. $12

Descriptive listings of three thousand public and private schools, hospitals, clinics, and other facilities for the emotionally disturbed, the physically handicapped, and the mentally retarded. Included also are listings of associations and Federal and state agencies concerned with the education and welfare of the exceptional.

Employment assistance for the handicapped. The President's Committee on Employment of the Handicapped. 1967. 37p. Free to Counselors

A directory of Federal and state programs to help the handicapped person to employment.

J. Occupations for the Handicapped—*Continued*

Employment for the handicapped. Arthur, Julietta K. Abingdon Press. 1967. 272p. $5.95

The author stresses the need of the impaired person to be well-informed, realistic, and emotionally prepared to enter today's job market. She analyzes sources of help, training, higher education, and job opportunities in private industry, government service, and self-employment.

**Employment opportunities for the handicapped. Angel, Juvenal L. Regents Publishing Company. 1969. 325p. $12.50

In addition to a discussion of part-time and home-based employment opportunities, 350 occupations open to disabled men and women are presented. One section lists possibilities according to aptitudes and abilities. Good bibliography.

Financial assistance programs for the handicapped. Government Printing Office. Supt. of Documents. 1968. 98p. $1

This publication is a guide to the Department of Health, Education, and Welfare's financial assistance programs for the handicapped.

For your consideration: five careers. American Foundation for the Blind. Revised 1967. 12p. Free

Describes careers in social work, rehabilitation teaching, vocational rehabilitation counseling, orientation instruction, and education. Designed for high school students.

The Grove Park report—principles underlying nonmedical vocational training and rehabilitation; preparation services for blind persons. American Foundation for the Blind. 1961. 40p. 50c

Principles for vocational training and for personal adjustment training. Includes training of vending stand operators, transcribing machine operators, and homemaking.

Guide to job placement of the mentally restored. The President's Committee on Employment of the Handicapped. 1965. 41p. Free to counselors

Techniques of proper placement of former mental patients. Contains a discussion aimed at helping employers to better evaluate the prospective employee.

**Guide to job placement of mentally retarded. The President's Committee on Employment of the Handicapped. 1963. 16p. Free to counselors

A guide to assist in job placement of the mentally retarded.

Hearts courageous; twelve who achieved. Herman, William. Dutton and Company. 1949. 254p. $3.95

Inspirational life stories of twelve men and women who overcame physical handicaps to achieve greatness.

Help for the disabled through vocational rehabilitation. Social and Rehabilitation Service. 1961. 11p. Free

General information concerning the service of restoring the disabled to paid jobs through medical service, counsel and guidance, and training.

Home economics fellowships administered by American Home Economics Association. American Home Economics Association. 1969. 4p. Single copy free

Fellowships including grants for advanced study in the area of rehabilitation of physically and mentally handicapped.

How to get a job. The President's Committee on Employment of the Handicapped. 1967. 28p. Free

Written for the mentally retarded, this guide gives tips on how to find and keep the right job.

An introduction to the vocational rehabilitation process. Social and Rehabilitation Service. Supt. of Documents. Revised 1967. 201p. $1.75

A manual for orientation and in-service training of rehabilitation counselors.

Law as a profession for the blind. American Foundation for the Blind. 1954. 67p. 75c

Descriptions of the work of the blind lawyer in a variety of situations—law school; small town; suburb; city; in public life; and as a judge, a professor, and Federal employee. Each description was written by a blind lawyer.

Opportunities for blind persons and the visually impaired. Social and Rehabilitation Service. 1969. 24p. Free

General information concerning the rehabilitation program.

Opportunity for blind persons and the visually impaired through vocational rehabilitation. U.S. Rehabilitation Services Administration. 1969. 22p. Free

Includes eligibility and application procedures for vocational rehabilitation.

Opportunities for the hard of hearing and the deaf. Social and Rehabilitation Service. Revised 1968. 20p. Free

One section contains a report on kinds of jobs obtained.

Programs to employ the disadvantaged. Doeringer, Peter B., ed. Prentice-Hall, Inc. 1970. 160p. $7.50; paper $3.75

Presented here are six case studies describing recent efforts by private employers to provide job opportunities for disadvantaged persons. The employer programs were selected to deal with a variety of problems, including hiring and entry training, upgrading, and employment. Of interest to research workers.

Report to the President. The President's Committee on Employment of the Handicapped. 1968. 50p. Free to counselors

Gives various agency reports on the programs and progress of activities for the handicapped.

Scholarship Program: education of handicapped children, summer 1970 and academic year 1970-71. U.S. Office of Education. Supt. of Documents. 1970. 63p. Free to counselors

A directory assisting individuals seeking Federal scholarships for professional training in the education of handicapped children.

J. Occupations for the Handicapped—*Continued*

Scholarships. National Easter Seal Society for Crippled Children and Adults. Revised annually. 1p. Free

Terms of eligibility.

Selected references on the vocational counseling, placement, and employment of handicapped workers. National Easter Seal Society for Crippled Children and Adults. 1968. 18. Single copy free

An annotated bibliography of publications for counselors and employment professional workers.

So you're going to hire the mentally retarded. The President's Committee on Employment of the Handicapped. 1963. 6p. Free to counselors

Tips to employers who are about to hire former mental patients. A companion leaflet is entitled *So You're Going to Hire the Mentally Restored.*

A summary of selected legislation relating to the handicapped. U.S. Department of Health, Education, and Welfare. Supt. of Documents. 1969. 13p. 20c

Explains and underscores Federal Government's role.

Visually handicapped workers in service occupations in the food service and lodging industries. American Foundation for the Blind. 1967. 12p. Free

Guidelines for the selection, training, and placement of blind workers in various jobs in hotels, motels, and restaurants.

Wasted assets? The President's Committee on Employment of the Handicapped. 1965. 18p. Free to counselors

Describes seven volunteer community programs that provide guidance and assistance to former mental patients ready for employment.

**Your handicap—don't let it handicap you. Splaver, Sarah. Julian Messner. 1967. 224p. $3.95; library binding $3.64

Stressing that much depends on the attitudes and motivations of the individual and the assistance he seeks, many resources are pointed out which are available to the disabled with visual, auditory, speech, orthopedic, or somatic handicaps. Good reference lists.

K. Package Purchases

Careers desk-top career kit. Careers. For senior high school $125; for junior high school $114.50

Kit for counselors' desk-top use and students' library table-top use. Contains summaries, career briefs, a metal file box and a set of alphabetical tab cards. Includes a total of 1260 items.

Careers senior high school service subscription. Careers. Monthly, September through May. $40 per year. Without posters $33.50

Includes summaries, job briefs, college guides, and various career planning publications. A junior high school service subscription is available for $37.

Chronicle's occupational library. Chronicle Guidance Publications. $287 F.O.B. Moravia, N.Y.

Two-drawer mobile steel file cabinet in tan or gray; occupational filing plan of three hundred letter-size folders inserted in ninety "Pendaflex" hanging folders, tabbed with codes and titles of the *Dictionary of Occupational Titles.* The folders are stocked with Chronicle's briefs, reprints, and posters. The cost includes a year's advance subscription to the Chronicle 3-in-1 service.

Chronicle's ready reference to occupations. Chronicle Guidance Publications. Initial purchase $89.50. Annual supplement $20.25

This is a complete set of 395 occupational briefs filed in a handy desk-top carton. Arranged by *Dictionary of Occupational Titles* code numbers. Includes file dividers and index cards.

College admissions data service. Educational Research Corporation. 1969-1970. $75 annual subscription

This service includes a loose-leaf handbook with facts on 350 colleges, monthly bulletins to keep the information current, plus *Guidance Counselor's Calendar* with testing and conference dates of interest to counselors. Annual revisions are issued.

College kit. American Personnel and Guidance Association. 1969. 4 booklets. $1.25

One booklet on career planning and three on college preparation: *Career decisions, How to visit colleges, How about college?* and *How about college planning?*

College view-deck. Chronicle Guidance Publications, Inc., Moravia, N.Y. 110 data cards with Manual and related forms. Updated annually. $108 for initial deck. $40 annual updating service

A data retrieval system adapted for student use. Categorizes common college characteristics which students consider as they make their college selection. Information includes costs, enrollments, major fields of study and related areas. Includes data cards in separate two- and four-year college sections. Lighted viewer or unlighted desk set available for use with data cards.

Professional careers kit. Careers. $75

Kit contains about five hundred career items such as briefs, summaries, college guides, and training guides. Other kits are available in special subjects: Industrial careers kit, $42; Health careers kit, $34.50; Science careers kit, $34.50; and Semi-skilled careers kit, $42.

SRA career information kit. Science Research Associates. $199.50 in case. $284.50 in file

This kit consists of over 600 occupational pamphlets, selected from many sources. The materials are assembled in a sturdy corrugated case with lift-off cover and filed in 212 file folders. The contents of the kit may be inserted in a regular filing cabinet if desired. A manual and index accompany the kit.

SRA careers in science and math. Science Research Associates. $36.75

A selection of eighty-four junior occupational briefs, eight job family booklets, and related posters. For grades 7 to 12.

K. Package Purchases—*Continued*

SRA college occupational exploration kit. Science Research Associates. $84.95

Information for the college student to help direct him to occupations appropriate to his aspirations and abilities.

SRA guidance service subscription plan. Science Research Associates. $43.50 per year

This service provides four mailings during the academic year including eighty occupational briefs, eight job family booklets, twenty research reports, and related posters.

SRA occupational exploration kit. $99.50

This kit is aimed to help the student explore occupations in terms of his own abilities, interests, and goals. In this kit are four hundred occupational briefs, twenty job family booklets, twenty-five student record books, and an "OccuScan." For grades 9 to 12.

SRA widening occupational roles kit (WORK). Science Research Associates. $141.75

Teaching material for grades 6 to 9. Includes four hundred junior occupational briefs, fifty-one guidance filmstrips, thirty-five student workbooks, and a teacher's manual. May be used in the homeroom, for group guidance, or with English and social studies classes.

L. Periodicals

Career index. Chronicle Guidance Publications, Inc. Annual compilation with supplements. $10 per year

Compilation of over seven hundred sources of occupational, educational and professional information. Printed postcards are included with the supplements for use when requesting selected free materials. Each issue contains an alphabetic list of sources of materials. The Annual and final supplement also contain a cross-reference index by subject.

College admissions data service. Educational Research Corporation. $75 annual subscription

This service includes a loose-leaf handbook containing facts on 350 colleges, plus monthly bulletins to keep the information current.

Counselor education and supervision. Association for Counselor Education and supervision. Order from American Personnel and Guidance Association. 4 issues. $6 a year. Single copy $2

Focuses on theory, practices, and research of interest to those in counselor education and supervisory positions, especially on state departments of education and in colleges.

Crusade for education. Advancement and Placement Institute. Monthly. $6 individual membership; $12 institutional

Placement journal describing professional openings in the United States and abroad for teachers, librarians, administrators, and scientists. Also contains information on scholarships, awards, summer opportunities, and some part-time work.

Elementary school guidance and counseling. American School Counselor Association. Order from American Personnel and Guidance Association. 4 issues. $6 a year

Serves the special needs of those working in guidance with elementary grades from kindergarten to grade 8.

Employment and earnings. Bureau of Labor Statistics, U.S. Department of Labor. Supt. of Documents. Monthly. $10 a year; $1 a copy

Current national statistics on labor force, employment, unemployment, hours, earnings, and labor turnover; state and area statistics on employment by major industry division, and hours, earnings, and labor turnover for manufacturing. Data are presented in summary, charts, and tables.

Guidance exchange. Splaver, Sarah, ed. Annual. $15 per year

An annotated bibliography of guidance literature and a section devoted to counselors' exchange of noteworthy experiences. Each issue contains about four hundred entries. Published in January of each year.

Information bulletin. Vocational Foundation, Inc. Bi-weekly, September to June. $2

Mimeographed bulletin describing new educational and occupational materials and giving information to supplement *Vocational Training in New York City . . . Where to Find It.*

Journal of college placement. College Placement Council. Quarterly. Available only as part of a subscription to the group of Journal Publications. $10

Articles of interest to college placement officers who help students and graduates find employment. Also of interest to the industrial personnel representatives.

Journal of college student personnel. American College Personnel Association. Order from American Personnel and Guidance Association. 6 issues. $12. Single copy $3

Serves the common interests of all student personnel workers in higher education.

Journal of employment counseling. National Employment Counselors Association. Order from American Personnel and Guidance Association. 4 issues. $4 a year. Single copy $1.50

Encourages professional development of those who counsel in an employment setting or work in related areas of counselor education, research, administration, or supervision.

Journal of the National Association of College Admissions Counselors. National Association of College Admissions Counselors. Quarterly. $6

Professional publication devoted to articles in the field of counseling, admissions, and financial aid.

Journal of the Student Personnel Association for Teacher Education. (SPATE). Order from American Personnel and Guidance Association. 4 issues. $6.50 a year. Single copy $1.75

Reports on programs and research of interest to student personnel workers in teacher training institutions.

L. Periodicals—*Continued*

Lovejoy's guidance digest. Monthly, September through June. $15 per year

Current information about college entrance requirements, scholarships, curriculum changes, draft news, etc.

Measurement and evaluation in guidance. Association for Measurement and Evaluation in Guidance. Order from American Personnel and Guidance Association. 4 issues. $6 a year. Single copy $2

Offers help and an opportunity to share ideas and experiences to guidance users of tests at the various educational levels.

Monthly labor review. Bureau of Labor Statistics, U.S. Department of Labor. Supt. of Documents. Monthly. $9; per year; $11.25 outside the United States

This publication includes information on trends and levels of the labor force, employment, earnings, wages, hours, and related employer practices. Much of this information is available for particular industries, occupations, and localities. Also covers other aspects of labor economics and industrial relations, such as prices and cost of living, labor laws, trade union activities, collective bargaining agreement provisions, work stoppages, and labor turnover.

The occupational outlook quarterly. Bureau of Labor Statistics, U.S. Department of Labor. Supt. of Documents. $1.50 a year; 45c a copy

Supplements the *Occupational Outlook Handbook* and reports on current occupational outlook and trends. Information is based primarily on the continuous research and statistical program of the Bureau of Labor Statistics.

**The personnel and guidance journal. American Personnel and Guidance Association. 10 issues, September through June. $15 a year. Single copy $2

Official publication of APGA presenting current information on significant developments in guidance and counseling. Includes book reviews, letters, and comments.

Placement service bulletin. American Personnel and Guidance Association. 4 issues. Candidate's subscription, APGA members only, $6 a year. Employer's subscription $5. Single issue, employers only, $3

Clearinghouse for job opportunities and candidates in personnel and guidance.

Rehabilitation Counseling bulletin. American Rehabilitation Counseling Association. Order from American Personnel and Guidance Association. 4 issues. $7. Single issue $2

Reports of new research, techniques, and national and international developments of significance to those in rehabilitation counseling.

The school counselor. American School Counselor Association. Order from American Personnel and Guidance Association. 5 issues. $8 a year

Presents an overview of new concepts and practical suggestions to help school counselors in various settings meet increasing responsibilities.

**The vocational guidance quarterly. National Vocational Guidance Association. Order from American Personnel and Guidance Association. 4 issues. $8 a year. Single copy $2.50

The professional publication of the Association, containing reports of current studies and conferences. Also covers timely information on career selection and outlook. Intended for use throughout education, government, business, industry, labor, and management.

Washington counseletter. Dr. Joseph E. Barber. Chronicle Guidance Publications, Inc. Monthly September through April. $8 per year

An eight-page newsletter reporting current national events in education and guidance of interest to counselors.

See also Bibliographies and Indexes

M. Planning a Career

**Career decisions. Byrn, Delmont K. National Vocational Guidance Association. Order from the American Personnel and Guidance Association. 1969. 32p. 50c

Booklet designed to help today's teenagers and their parents plan for career success in tomorrow's world. Some topics discussed are: Your life priorities, Your emerging self, Potential abilities, Credentials for work, Values and standards, and Making right moves.

Career guidance and planning help a person achieve a successful career. Chronicle Guidance Publications. 1967. 4p. 35c

Reprinted article from *Chemical and Engineering News* discusses career guidance of the prospective chemical engineer from prehigh school through postcollege.

A career-planning guide: prepared for the World Book Encyclopedia. Edgerton, A. H. Field Enterprises. 1966. 48p. $1

Discussion and check lists for parents and their sons or daughters to work together on career selection. Includes material for estimating abilities and career interests.

* Careers. Lifton, Walter M. United Educators, Inc. 1969. 10p. 20c

A reprint from the *American Educator Encyclopedia,* containing information about planning a career. Includes a list of the 150 leading occupations in which the greater number of people engage.

Careers for you. Ferrari, Erma Paul. Abingdon Press. 1969. 160p. $1.75 paper

Information about opportunities and suggestions on self-evaluation. Also suggestions for acquiring the necessary training and experience.

**Careers—opportunities and preparation. General Electric Company. 1968. 5p. Free

Information about opportunities and preparation for careers, especially science and engineering. Answers questions frequently asked about choice of a college, ways of financing higher education, and the most important college subjects to take.

M. Planning a Career—*Continued*

Choosing an occupation: a guide for high school students. Bail, Joe P. and Nelson, A. Gordon. Cooperative Extension Service, New York College of Agriculture. Revised 1967. 12p. 10c

Discussion of the following topics: Planning for the future, What people do for a living, Understanding yourself, Self-inventory worksheet, Exploring an occupation, and Worksheet for studying an occupation.

Choosing your career. Wilson, Howard. Administrative Research Associates. 1963. 45p. $1

Prepared as an aid for analysis of one's self, the world of work, and a specific career. Topics include self-appraisal scales, the major occupations, and college and training institutions.

**Choosing your occupation—career guidelines for high school students from your state employment service. Bureau of Employment Security. Supt. of Documents. 1965. 16p. 15c

Suggestions for a self-inventory of interests and ability, list of occupations for which there is a demand for more workers, and some advice about approaching occupational choice.

College, careers, and you. Plummer, Robert and Blocker, Clyde. Science Research Associates. 1963. 48p. 75c

Discussion of career plans in a changing world, planning on graduate school, and what employers will consider.

College entrance guide. Einstein, Bernice W. Grosset and Dunlap, Inc. 1970. 327p. $3.95

This handbook offers pupils and parents details on career planning, preparation for college, examinations, application and admissions procedures, financial assistance, and special programs.

Exploring your future in the professions. Sextant Systems, Inc. 1970. 96p. $8.95

One page is devoted to each of ninety-five jobs, describing the duties, requirements for entering, promotional outlook, and the pay and skill level.

**Facing facts about career opportunities for the high school graduate. Prudential Insurance Company. 1965. 32p. Free

This booklet contains advice to the high school student that he will be graduating into a world of increasing opportunity for the capable, prepared worker and that he should use this time, while still in high school, to prepare well for a satisfying career and a rewarding life.

**Facing facts about choosing your life's work—a guide for students and counselors. Prudential Insurance Company. 1968. 32p. Free

To help young people in their transition from school to work, this explains what to look for in a career, how to make a career decision, and what employers are looking for.

Get ahead in business. Scheinfeld, Aaron. Hawthorn Books, Inc. 1969. 160p. $6.95

Frank insights on career planning, motivation, and ways to evaluate oneself in the job.

Getting the most out of high school. Scott, J. Irving. Oceana Publications. Revised 1968. 165p. $5.50

Contains a helpful chapter on school subjects and their relationship to possible occupational fields. Also includes charts showing the relationship between education and job and income, as well as self-tests to measure the effectivenes of study and work habits and to improve them. Good reading lists.

* Girls and their futures. Zapoleon, Marguerite W. Science Research Associates. Revised 1968. 48p. 75c

Chapter headings are: Will you drift or steer into your future? For what work should you plan? How your schooling affects your future, Planning for employment, and Planning with a total view. Selected readings.

**Guidance services. Humphreys, J. Anthony; Traxler, Arthur E; and North, Robert D. Science Research Associates. Revised 1967. 434p. $6.30

Discussion of principles and techniques. Includes chapters on making vocational choices, solving educational problems, and finding jobs.

A guide for parents and students—plan early for your future education. American Legion. 1969. 8p. 25c. $2.50 for 500 copies, prepaid

Some succinct suggestions for preparing for college or vocational training.

Helping rural youth choose careers. U.S. Department of Agriculture. Miscellaneous Publication 771. Supt. of Documents. 1963. 8p. 5c

Points up some of the shifts in the employment picture with special concern for the effects of recent social and economic trends.

How about college financing? A guide for parents of college-bound students. American School Counselor Association. Order from American Personnel and Guidance Association. 1964. 24p. 30c

Suggests ways to keep expenses down and explains methods of systematic planning through savings, loans, part-time work, scholarships, and grants.

How to visit colleges. National Vocational Guidance Association. 1965. 32p. 40c

Practical suggestions concerning why and how to visit colleges as one step in making a wise choice. Also, some general suggestions on preparation for college admission.

**Job horizons for college women. Bulletin 288. Women's Bureau, U.S. Department of Labor. Supt. of Documents. 1967. 91p. 35c

Briefly describes the nature of some of the many careers open to college women, indicates educational and training requirements for entry into various professions, and lists a number of continuing education programs available. Also lists selected readings on employment and training opportunities in the professions.

Looking ahead through spare time study. International Correspondence Schools. 1970. 96p. Free

A description of the courses offered in many major career fields.

M. Planning a Career—*Continued*

Money, jobs and futures: a guide for young people on the move. Roesch, Roberta. Macrae Smith Company. 1965. 192p. $3.95

The topics include part-time and summer jobs, turning hobbies to cash, how to study, and what to consider in planning one's life work.

The next five years. Glatthorn, Allan and Manone, Carl. Interstate Printers and Publishers. 1965. 120p. $2

A planning guide to help high school students and their parents develop effective plans for the future. Written specifically for the eleventh-grade student who is contemplating further education.

Opportunities to learn: a guide to countinuing education. Nelson, A. Gordon. Cooperative Extension Service, New York College of Agriculture. 1968. 12p. 20c

Educational opportunities such as on-the-job training, apprenticeships, correspondence courses, manpower development and training programs, and evening school courses are suggested.

Part-time, summer and volunteer jobs for Jewish and other minority group youth. Sinick, Daniel. B'nai B'rith Vocational Service. 1969. 112p. $2.50

Discussion of placement resources, finding a job, preparing resumes, and handling interviews. Part-time and temporary jobs are presented in two categories: for those of high school age and for college age and older.

Planning your career. Calvert, Robert, Jr. and Steele, John E. McGraw-Hill Book Company. 1963. 152p. $1.95 paper

Three phases of career development are presented: selecting a goal, organizing a job campaign, and evaluating one's progress.

**Stay in high school. American School. 1964. 4p. Free

Reasons why young people should stay in school and graduate. Available in sets for class or homeroom use.

Successful adjustment in college. Revised edition. Chandler, John R. and others. Prentice-Hall, Inc. 1958. 202p. $4.95

Prepared to assist the entering college student in making an adjustment to his new environment. Although personal growth is the major area considered, some sections are devoted to making a wise vocational choice, exploring vocations, and discovering vocational interests.

**Tomorrow's jobs. Reprint of the introduction to the *Occupational Outlook Handbook*. Bulletin 1650–1. Bureau of Labor Statistics, U.S. Department of Labor. Supt. of Documents. 1970. 9p. 15c

Discussion of the expected population and labor force growth, the changing occupational structure of the economy, and implications for education, training, and future employment. This reprint is directed to counselors, parents, teachers, and others who assist young people in making vocational choices.

Undergraduate announcement and career guide. Lehigh University. 1969. 160p. Free

Discussions of factors which should influence a choice of a career and a college are followed by twenty career areas. These describe briefly major careers associated with courses of instruction at Lehigh. Revised annually.

**Vocational planning for college students. Borow, Henry and Lindsey, Robert. Prentice-Hall, Inc. 1959. 186p. $4.75 paper

By means of a devlopmental series of written projects, laboratory exercises, discussion units, and reading assignments, the student is taught a systematic method for evolving a suitable career plan.

What to do after high school. Spiegler, Charles and Reiner, William. Science Research Associates. 1971. 75p. $2.25

This book provides information on occupational possibilities, education, and training available for those not planning to attend college.

What's ahead for your own boy or girl? National Urban League. No date. 9p. 5c

Booklet written for parents to help them understand how they can help their boy or girl choose a satisfying and profitable career.

You and tomorrow. General Electric Company. 1968. 16p. Free

Depicts the importance of a broad education in preparation for tomorrow's exciting careers. Relates the basic subjects to both technical and non-technical vocations. Available in classroom quantities of up to fifty. Illustrated.

**Your career—if you're not going to college. Splaver, Sarah. Julian Messner. 1971. 224p. $4.95

Discussion of the opportunities available to the high school graduate and advice concerning techniques of searching for a job.

Your job and career—where are you headed? Changing Times. 1964. 5p. 15c

Job prospects in various occupations.

Your life work. Kiwanis Club. 1964. 4p. 15c

Practical suggestions are grouped under the following headings: You should have a vocation; Decide on your vocation early; Study yourself first; Study the occupational fields; Make your choice on a sound basis; Plan your preparation carefully; Plan for your first job; Make good in your life work.

Your vocational adventure. Burt, Jesse C. Abingdon Press. 1959. 203p. $2.95; $1.65 paper

Suggestions for choosing the vocation which will be suitable and will open the doors of opportunities.

N. Preparing for Examinations

The art of being a successful student. Thompson, Helen M. Washington Square Press. 1964. 160p. 45c

Stresses organizing one's time, reading better and faster, increasing one's vocabulary, and using resources effectively.

N. Preparing for Examinations—*Continued*

Barron's how to prepare for the high school equivalency examination. Barron's Educational Series, Inc. 1968. 357p. $8; paper $3.95

Specific suggestions on reviewing for and taking the tests are followed by sample questions in the five areas covered—English, mathematics, social studies, science, and literature. Also includes a summary of state programs for issuance of these certificates.

College credit by examination through the college-level examination program. College Entrance Examination Board. 1970. 63p. Free

A general description of the plan of granting credit by examination. Explains the program that helps colleges evaluate the backgrounds of college applicants who have not had traditional schooling but have educated themselves in various non-traditional ways such as reading, on-the-job training, or correspondence courses.

College entrance reviews. Educators Publishing Service. 1967. 124p. $2 each

Aimed to provide practice exercises and many typical questions and answers to familiarize students with the form and content of objective tests. In mathematics, the exercises are graded according to progressive difficulty.

English review series. Educators Publishing Service. 1958-1962. 5 books. $1.15 each

Review exercises and test questions. The books have accompanying keys with answers only or guides with answers and explanations. Also available is a series of language review exercises (French, Latin, Spanish, German) and a vocabulary builder series.

How to get higher marks in school. Shefter, Harry. Washington Square Press. 1961. 264p. 60c

Suggestions to develop better study and work habits. Designed to help both the slower and the more advanced student make the most of the educational opportunities offered them.

How to improve your reading. Witty, Paul. Science Research Associates. 1963. 275p. $4.50

Aimed to help junior high school students to develop better reading skills through reading exercises. Includes a progress folder, and a reading list arranged by interest areas. A similar book prepared for persons above the ninth grade is entitled *How To Become a Better Reader.* (275p. $4.50).

How to prepare for college entrance examinations. Brownstein, Samuel C. and Weiner, Mitchel. Barron's Educational Series. 4th edition. 1969. 538p. $7.50; paper $3.95

Several new types of tests are included in this edition of sample tests and answers.

How to prepare talks and oral reports. Shefter, Harry. Washington Square Press. 1963. 239p. 60c

Stresses various means of making good preparation.

**How to score high on the Scholastic Aptitude Test and other college entrance tests. Genua, A. J. Hayden Book Co., Inc. 1962. 220p. $2.59

Each section contains material for study and review, practice exercises, and answers. A special feature is the section on word building and the study guide on prefixes, roots, and suffixes. A list of colleges with the entrance tests required by each is arranged alphabetically by states.

How to study. Preston, Ralph and Botel, Morton. Science Research Associates. 1967. 98p. $1.85

Activity text or workbook designed to help the high school and college student evaluate and improve his study habits. Includes a section on getting ready for and taking examinations.

How to study and take exams. Pettit, Lincoln. Hayden Book Company. 1960. 96p. $1.49

In addition to the mechanics of studying, this book aims to provide motivation for learning.

**How to study better and get higher marks. Ehrlich, Eugene H. Thomas Y. Crowell Company. 1961. 287p. $5.95

Includes discussions of improving one's memory, writing papers, studying effectively, and getting higher marks on examinations.

How to write a report. Brandt, Sue R. Franklin Watts, Inc. 1968. 66p. $2.65; library binding $1.98

Included is helpful information on understanding the subject, locating information, taking notes, preparing a bibliography, making an outline, and drafting the actual report. For grades 4 to 7.

It pays to increase your word power. Funk, Peter V. K. Funk and Wagnalls. 1969. 205p. $4.95

A self-help manual for readers who want to increase their vocabularies, consisting of a series of word tests and exercises accompanied by definitions and correct answers.

Learn how to study. Kelner, Bernard. Science Research Associates. 1961. 66p. $1.10

An easy-to-read workbook for grades 4 to 7 stressing the importance of good study habits, setting up good conditions for study, and how to organize and report information.

Meeting the test. Anderson, Scarvia and others. Four Winds Press. 1965. 192p. $3.95

Designed to help high school students succeed with tests by relieving their anxieties about them. Emphasizes the constructive use of the variety of tests used in education and industry.

National merit scholarship tests; the complete study guide for scoring high. Tarr, Harry A. Arco Publishing Company. 1968. 416p. $6.50; paper $4

This third edition contains suggestions for preparation for the test. The hundreds of questions are patterned after the actual tests.

N. Preparing for Examinations—*Continued*

Preparing for college study. Fedde, Norman A. Readers Press. 1962. 156p. 95c

Suggestions to help the student develop self-discipline under the new circumstances that college presents. Includes discussion of scheduling, concentration, how to study, note making, methods of reading, use of the library, academic writing, and preparing for examinations.

Preparing for the American College Testing Program. Orgel, Joseph R. Educators Publishing Service. 1962. 120p. $4

Suggestions and sample test questions of the type previously used in this test program.

Preparing for the Federal service entrance examination. Civil Service Commission. Supt. of Documents. 1966. 16p. 20c

This pamphlet provides background information on the examination, explains how it is used in filling Federal positions, and gives examples of the kinds of questions in the examination.

A study guide for the College Board Scholastic Aptitude Test. College Entrance Book Company. 1969. 188p. $1.50

In addition to sample tests and answers, there is a discussion of several questions. Stresses the types of quetions which have been used in the verbal and mathematics sections of the College Entrance Examination Board tests.

O. Professional Counseling Services

College Admissions Assistance Center, 461 Park Avenue South, New York 10016. $20

This is a nationwide nonprofit clearinghouse service designed to assist prospective college students find colleges with room for more students. It is sponsored by the Council of Higher Educational Institutions in New York City and serves students over a wide geographical area. The fee is $20 to be submitted with application. Authorized college officials review student records and contact those students in whom they are interested. Provides an opportunity for the student's records to be available for review by over three hundred colleges located throughout the country.

College Admissions Center, National Association of College Admissions Counselors, 801 Davis Street, Evanston, Ill. 60201. $20

Students register with this nonprofit admissions clearinghouse by filling out its registration form with a $20 fee. Representatives of colleges review the records of unplaced students and communicate directly with those who interest them for their colleges. The center is open on a year-round basis; students can thus be considered for admission at any semester or quarter of the year.

Directory of approved counseling agencies. American Board on Counseling agencies. Order from American Personnel and Guidance Association. 1969. 201p. $3

List of 191 counseling agencies which have met the standards of the American Board on Counseling Agencies. Relevant information includes address, telephone number, hours, fees, a description of the clientele served, and the professional qualifications of the staff.

Graduate Admissions Assistance Center, 461 Park Avenue South, New York 10016. $25

This is a nationwide nonprofit service to accredited graduate schools throughout the country and all masters' degree candidates in all fields except medicine, dentistry, and veterinary sciences. It is sponsored by the Council of Higher Educational Institutions in New York City. The fee is $25 to be submitted with the application. This is a service for those students experiencing difficulty in gaining admission through normal channels.

Graduate School Service, American College Admissions Center, Liberty Trust Building, Philadelphia, Pa. 19107. $20

A nonprofit service available to students wishing to enroll in a graduate school.

Independent School Admissions Advisory Center, 238 North Main St., Wallingford, Conn.

The authors of *Private Independent Schools* and *Summer Studies in Private Independent Schools* conduct an advisory center for parents of children in the primary, elementary, or high school grades. They advise parents of the enrollment situations in various schools where it might be to their advantage to make application. The expense of the consultations is covered by fees paid by the families.

National Scholarship Service and Fund for Negro Students, 6 E. 82nd St., New York, N.Y.

To enable Negro students to attend college, this organization assists them in obtaining admission and winning scholarship aid at a wide variety of colleges. Students are required to submit their scores on the National Merit Scholarship Test or the Preliminary Scholastic Aptitude Test during the junior year for the purpose of counseling.

Private College Admissions Center, 1740 N Street, N.W., Washington, D.C. $20

This national nonprofit admissions center has been established to help prospective freshmen find unfilled places in the country's 944 private colleges and universities. For a $20 fee this center will make applications available to member colleges seeking students.

P. Scholarships

Admissions and financial aid requirements and procedures at College Board member colleges. College Entrance Examination Board. 1970. 79p. $1

A tabular summary of the basic test requirements, preferred test dates, and admissions and financial aid application deadlines of the 870 member colleges. Also given are the dates colleges notify candidates about admission and financial aid and the candidates' reply requirements.

Awards for singers. Central Opera Service. 1969. 16p. 50c

Information, compiled by states, concerning financial aid and scholarships.

P. Scholarships—*Continued*

Bausch and Lomb awards. Bausch and Lomb, Incorporated. 1969. 12p. Free

Description of plan whereby the Bausch and Lomb science award winner in each high school may compete for scholarship aid at the University of Rochester.

College? But that takes bread, man. National Scholarship Service and Fund for Negro Students. 1968. 6p. Free

A brief description of the scope of the service.

Educational scholarships, loans, and financial aids. The Department of the Army. Supt. of Documents. 1969. 83p. $1

The Department of the Army has compiled some references to assist dependents of active, retired, and deceased army personnel to reach their educational goals. Contains some suggestions as to where to look for student aid information.

Educational scholarships, loans, and financial aids. U.S. Department of Defense. Supt. of Documents. 1969. 83p. $1

Educational opportunities for dependents of active, retired, or deceased army personnel.

Educational scholarships, loans and financial aids. U.S. Office of Education. Supt. of Documents. 1969. 30p. $1

A compilation of sources of student aids.

Federal aid for schools. Rowland, Howard and Wing, Richard. Macmillan Company. 1970. 400p. $15

This guide describes a step-by-step program for obtaining some of the Federal funds available to public and private schools.

Federal dollars for scholars. Toy, Henry, Jr. Nu-Toy, Inc. 1970. 216p. $4.20 paper

This book is designed to answer two questions, namely how to secure funds to attend college and what options exist in discharging one's military obligation. In the main part of the book, the author describes the Federal education programs for individuals and includes short sketches of the Government agencies which administer these programs.

Financial aid for graduate students. College Opportunities, Inc. 1970-71. 500p. $10

Information concerning academic standards and financial aids of 693 accredited graduate schools.

**Financial aid for higher education. U.S. Office of Education. Supt. of Documents. 1968. 110p. $1

An introduction to financial aid and the concept of financial need. Identifies various general and specific categories of financial assistance. Also lists those colleges participating in the Federal student aid program.

Financial aid for personnel and guidance graduate study, 1970-1971. American Personnel and Guidance Association. 1970. 60p. $3

This compilation of financial aids gives these data from more than 250 institutions: departments offering programs; persons to whom admission applications and applications for aid should be sent; dates for applications; program titles and degrees offered; financial aid by type, number, and amount; costs; entrance requirements; graduate enrollments; number of degrees granted; and hours required per degree program.

Financial aids for undergraduate students. College Opportunities, Inc. 1970-71. 1500p. $37.50

Information concerning academic standards and financial aids of 1801 accredited schools.

Financial assistance for library education. American Library Association. 1970. 56p. 50c. 100 copies $42

Lists scholarships and other aid available for the academic year 1969-70. Includes names of institutions, associations, or other organizations offering aid of $500 or more for training as a librarian.

Financing a college education—a guide for counselors. College Entrance Examination Board. 1970. 38p. 25c

This booklet explains the work of the College Scholarship Service and the procedures used in the analysis of the Parents' Confidential Statement. It describes the various kinds and sources of student financial aid and how colleges and agencies measure financial need and administer their aid funds. It includes a list of colleges and agencies using the Parents' Confidential Statement and the dates for filing it.

Foundation directory; edition 3. Russell Sage Foundation. 1967. 1198p. $12

Describes 6,803 foundations, their purposes, and current areas of interest. Includes information on scholarships or fellowships offered.

The General Henry H. Arnold Educational Fund. Air Force Aid Society. No date. 7p. Free

Information about loans and grants available through this fund for the college education of children of Air Force personnel.

Graduate fellowship program in educational research. Government Printing Office. Supt. of Documents. 1968. 66p. 65c

Summarizes the distinctive features of the graduate educational research training programs funded by the U.S. Office of Education.

Grants and aid to individuals in the arts. Washington International Arts Letter. 1970. 75p. $8.95 paper

Thirteen hundred sources of financial aid over $1,000 in the arts, music, and writing.

Guide to OE-administered programs, fiscal year 1970. U.S. Office of Education. Supt. of Documents. 1970. 6p. Single copy free from *American Education*. Multiple copies 20c each from Supt. of Documents

A chart indicates type of assistance, purpose, who may apply, and where to apply.

P. Scholarships—*Continued*

A guide to student assistance. Congress House Document number 91-221. Supt. of Documents. 1969. 129p. 60c

This guide contains information on financial aid programs for students in higher education and the procedures for applying for aid. Though the concentration is on Federally sponsored programs, it contains information on some others. It includes a list of colleges and universities by state, showing programs available, such as national defense student loan program and work-study and educational opportunity grant programs.

A guide to student assistance. Government Printing Office. Supt. of Documents. 1970. 64p. 60c

A comprehensive listing of what help is available from Government sources in financing college costs. Provides information concerning how to apply and to whom.

How the Office of Education assists college students and colleges. U.S. Office of Education. Supt. of Documents. 1969. 60p. 65c

This publication includes the provisions of numerous programs of aid to students, indicates who is eligible for benefits under them, how to obtain these benefits, and where to write for further information about them.

How to earn money in college. Harvard Student Agencies, Inc. 1968. 238p. $1.95

Written by students for college students, the book describes a variety of jobs that can provide money for college expenses. Contains information on financial aid, student-managed small businesses, summer employment, and how to get a job.

**How to get money for college. Fine, Benjamin and Eisenberg, Sidney. Doubleday and Company. 1964. 227p. $4.95

A compilation of sources of scholarships, loans, and grants.

How you can search for science talent. Science Clubs of America. 1969. 24p. Free

Facts about the annual science talent search for Westinghouse Science Scholarships and Awards. Explains the rules and regulations and gives sample examination questions.

Journalism scholarship guide. Newspaper Fund, Inc. 1969. 68p. Free

A listing of financial aids offered by schools, newspapers, and professional societies to college students who want to study journalism, totaling almost two million dollars. Good reference list included.

A letter to parents: financial aid for college. Margolius, Sidney. College Entrance Examination Board. 1969. 10p. Free

This leaflet offers general advice to parents on student aid programs and the way in which financial need is determined by many colleges. Copies of this publication are available in many schools.

Low cost-loans for education. United Student Aid Funds, Inc. 1969. 6p. Free

Explanation of the plan and how to participate.

**Lovejoy's scholarship guide. Second edition. Lovejoy, Clarence E. Simon and Schuster. 1964. 91p. $4.95; 2.95 paper

A useful reference book giving information about scholarships, fellowships, grant-in-aid, loan funds, assistantships, workshops, contests, and awards. Includes scholarships sponsored by industry; labor unions; welfare groups; professional associations; foundations; and fraternal, educational, religious, and patriotic groups.

National defense graduate fellowships: Graduate programs 1970-71. U.S. Office of Education. 1970. 26p. Free

A list of programs and fellowship allocations by state and participating institutions.

National Honor Society scholarship program: 185 scholarships, 185,000 dollars. National Association of Secondary School Principals. 1970. 2p. Free

Poster giving dates and student eligibility.

National scholarship program of the printing and publishing industry. Graphic Arts Industry, Inc. 1969. 16p. Free

Description of the scholarship program available to qualified students in the graphic communications field.

National Science Foundation graduate fellowships. National Academy of Sciences. 1968. 4p. Free

Conditions of appointment, eligibility, stipends, and application dates. For graduate study. A new brochure is prepared for each year's competition.

National Science Foundation grants and awards, 1968. Government Printing Office. Supt. of Documents. 1968. 274p. $1.25

Contains a list of grants and awards given by the National Science Foundation for the fiscal year ending June, 1968.

**Need a lift? To educational opportunities, careers, loans, scholarships, employment. American Legion. 1969. 128p. 50c

The handbook refers students to financial aid sources and describes the specific aid programs of colleges, foundations, states, and the Federal Government. Included are many reference sources of career information. Revised annually.

Need financial aid for college? Engineers' Council for Professional Development. No date. 8p. 3c. $12.50 per 500 copies

Advice to students for making early financial college plans; suggestions and information concerning such aid.

RCA aid to education—scholarships and fellowships. Radio Corporation of America. 1968. 4p. Free

This booklet presents information on the various plans under which the Radio Corporation of America assists college and university students through scholarships and fellowships.

Scholarship information. Boys' Clubs of America. 1969. 4p. Free

A general description of the various scholarship programs available for education and training to men planning a professional career in Boys' Club work.

P. Scholarships—*Continued*

Scholarships, fellowships, and work-study plans for graduate social work education for individuals interested in Jewish community center work as a career. National Jewish Welfare Board. 1963. 8p. Free

Issued annually.

Scholarships for children of deceased veterans. Amvets National Service Foundation. 1957. 4p. Free

Scholarships available to high school seniors who are children of deceased or totally disabled veterans of World War II or the Korean conflict.

Scholarships loans and awards offered by affiliated labor unions. Chronicle Guidance Publications. 1970. 26p. $1

Programs awarded on a national basis are followed by the state listings of council, district, and local labor unions awards.

Scholarships loans and awards offered by the fifty states. Chronicle Guidance Publications. 1970. 60p. $1

List of current sources of financial aid available from the states to students seeking assistance for education beyond the high school level.

Scholarships, loans, and self-help opportunities in West Virginia colleges. Trotter, Nancy. West Virginia State Department of Education. 1968. 146p. $1 paper

Prepared for high school students in West Virginia, the information has value to counselors and students in other states.

A selected list of major fellowship opportunities and aids to advanced education for foreign nationals. National Academy of Sciences. 1968. 19p. Free

Sources of graduate fellowships, revised annually.

A selected list of major fellowship opportunities and aids to advanced education for United States citizens. National Academy of Sciences. 1968. 36p. Free

Sources of graduate fellowships and loans. Revised annually.

Student aid annual and bulletins. Chronicle Guidance Publications. Revised annually. 300p. $10. Single copies of bulletins available at $1 each

Financial assistance programs available to entering freshmen and graduate students from non-collegiate sources. Includes private organizations in the Annual and state and labor union sources in the other Bulletins.

* Student financial aid: manual for colleges and universities. Babbidge, Homer D., Jr. American College Personnel Association. Order from American Personnel and Guidance Association. 1960. 56p. $1.50

Reissue of a popular aid in the effective administration of measuring student need, scholarships, loan assistance, student employment, and miscellaneous forms of financial aid.

Student information bulletin. National Merit Scholarship Corporation. Published annually. 80p. Free

Provides information of particular interest to high school students planning to take the National Merit Scholarship Qualifying Test. It includes eligibility rules and requirements and a descriptive list of currently available scholarships awarded by the 350 cooperating companies, foundations, unions, professional associations, and other sponsors of Merit Scholarships. Also includes a description of the National Achievement Scholarship program for outstanding Negro students.

Thousands of science projects. Science Clubs of America. 1957. 46p. 25c; 10 for $1

Suggestions for projects from the Science Talent Search Scholarship contest and the National Science Fair may be found in this listing of projects prepared by students during the past several years.

World-wide graduate award directory. Advancement and Placement Institute. 1959. 56p. $3

Description of assistantships, fellowships, scholarships, and research grants contributed by over one thousand universities and foundations in forty-four states and fifty-five foreign countries. Arranged by country or state.

**Your college education—how to pay for it. Splaver, Sarah. Julian Messner. 1964. 288p. $4.95; library binding $4.64

Includes financial aid programs and informational materials provided by states.

Q. Textbooks for Pupils

Building your life. 3rd edition. Landis, Judson T. and Landis, Mary G. Prentice-Hall, Inc. 1962. 350p. $6.36

Written for young people in their early teens. Sections are devoted to the following topics: You and your personality, Learning to understand others, Obligations to self and society, Family understanding, Physical and mental health, and Growing up economically. Self-evaluation tests have been included with each chapter to help the student understand his present development and social adjustment.

Career choice and career preparation. Schill, William J. and Nichols, Harold E. Interstate Printers and Publishers, Inc. 1970. 300p. $4.95

Called a programmed self-study guide, this is a work book for the pupil to proceed at his own rate. Its aim is to enable the young person to gain a knowledge of himself in relation to the decisions of career preparation.

Charting your job future. Giles, Lambert. Science Research Associates. Revised 1968. 72p. $1.80

Activity text aimed to help high school students make career plans, find out about job qualifications, and learn how to seek employment. Includes charts, self-quizzes, and checklists to help students analyze their interest and ability.

Choosing your career. Humphreys, J. Anthony. Science Research Associates. 1961. 48p. 75c

Shows how to analyze one's interests and abilities, how to find out the essential items about a great variety of jobs, and how to relate your knowledge of yourself to your knowledge of jobs.

Q. Textbooks for Pupils—*Continued*

Educational and vocational planning. Martinson, William D. Scott, Foresman and Company. 1959. 84p. $2.75

Textbook for a college course. Includes units on the need for planning, learning about jobs, reaching a decision, learning to know yourself, planning your education, and locating a job.

Essential aspects of career planning and development. Atherton, James C. and Humphrey, Anthony. Interstate Printers and Publishers. 1969. 307p. $5.95

The first half of the book contains guidelines on career planning and development. The remainder of the publication is devoted to job seeking, employment competency, and advancement in an occupation. Prepared for persons preparing for employment and for those who are exploring the world of work.

How to choose your work. Stone, Elna. Bruce Publishing Company. 1969. 64p. $1.80 paper

A workbook in three sections which will help the high school student analyze his individual preferences, his abilities, and the general job opportunities.

How to get a job. Stone, Elna. Bruce Publishing Company. 1969. 80p. $1.88 paper

A series of instructions and workbook-type exercises to help individuals become more effective in getting, holding, and progressing on the job.

**If you're not going to college. Spiegler, Charles and Hamburger, Martin. Science Research Associates. Revised 1970. $1.95

An activity-textbook for high school students who are not planning on four-year college training. Includes range of possibilities from semiprofessional and technical to trade and business education and on-the-job training opportunities.

The insight series—It's your education; It's your personality; It's your life; It's your future. Revised edition. Cribbin, James J.; McMahon, William J.; and Harris, Brother Philip. Harcourt, Brace and World. 1962. 4 books. $2.40 each

This four-book series is designed for group guidance in Catholic high schools. The first book provides insight into the high school experience, the second insight into one's personality and relations with others, the third encourages planning for the future, and the fourth concerns the immediate job horizon, parttime work in college, military obligations, and a lifetime career. Teachers' handbooks are available.

It's your life—a group guidance program for Catholic high schools. Revised edition. Cribbin, James J.; Harris, Brother Philip; and McMahon, William J. Harcourt, Brace and World. 1962. 348p. $2.40

Includes topics for group guidance, including choosing a career and planning one's education. The chapters on colleges contain information about the Catholic colleges only. A teacher's handbook is available for use with the text.

My career guidebook. Belman, Harry S. and Shertzer, Bruce. Bruce Publishing Company. Revised 1967. 64p. $1.20 paper

A workbook for making future educational and vocational plans. Prepared for students at the junior high school level. A *Teacher's Manual* is available for $1.75.

**Occupations and careers. Feingold, S. Norman and Swerdloff, Sol. McGraw-Hill Book Company. 1969. 372p. $6.96

The first eleven chapters deal with the significance of self-understanding, the relationship of school subjects to careers, and choosing and preparing for a job. The last eight chapters contain information about the major groups of occupations.

The Sextant series for exploring your future. Sextant Systems, Inc. Set of 12 volumes. Complete set with wall charts and profile forms $92.50; library set $75

Twelve books have been released, each combining job descriptions with a method of personal profiling. Each book contains job descriptions of the range of occupations particular to that industry, organizational charts, and a set of personal forms for individual pupil use.

**Vocational planning for college students. Borow, Henry and Lindsey, Robert. Prentice-Hall, Inc. 1959. 186p. $4.75 paper

Prepared as a textbook for a college course in orientation. Includes discussion of learning to explore occupations, delimiting the range of occupational choices, comparative study of two occupations, and understanding the world of work.

Your practical guide to college admission. Willard J. Dolman. Chronicle Guidance Publications, Inc. 68p. $1

A student workbook for use by high school juniors and seniors as they carry out their college selection program. Serves as a text and workbook. Is designed to be used with or without the Chronicle College View-Deck.

R. Use of Occupational Information and The Counselor's Professional Bookshelf

The American high school today. Conant, James B. McGraw-Hill Book Company. 1959. 140p. $3.50; paper $1.95

Contains specific recommendations for guidance in the secondary schools.

Answers to questions about guidance. National Education Association. 1963. 4p. 35 copies $1

Provides answers to twelve questions about objectives, methods, and results of modern school guidance programs. Prepared to use with parent meetings.

Audio visual market place; a multimedia guide. Bowker Company. 1969. 177p. $12.25

This brings together information on services dealing with films and other nonprint materials. Includes list of distributors, producers, film libraries, pertinent books, and other reference sources.

R. Use of Occupational Information and The Counselor's Professional Bookshelf—*Continued*

**Career decisions. Byrn, Delmont K. National Vocational Guidance Association. 1969. 32p. 50c

Advice on career planning for young people. Includes discussion of life priorities, personality factors, interests, motives, values, achievements, and making right moves.

**Career guidance practices in school and community. Hansen, Lorraine. National Vocational Guidance Association. Order from American Personnel and Guidance Association. 1970. 188p. $3.95 paper

Summarizes current thinking and practices in career planning, outlines courses, lists objectives, and provides other information for developing a workable program.

The career information center: a working model. U.S. Office of Education. Supt. of Documents. 1969. 41p. 30c

A manual based on the experience of the Career Information Center of Northeastern University in Boston, Massachusetts. Describes the methods of providing career information by means of career assemblies, career conferences, radio programs, tape recordings, filmstrip services, and television programs.

College Board score reports—a guide for counselors and admissions officers. College Entrance Examination Board. 1970. 38p. 25c

This guide is intended for school counselors and college admissions officers who use College Board scores in counseling students and admitting them to college. It provides current and appropriate information about the scores and their use.

**The college handbook. College Entrance Examination Board. 1969. 1360p. $4.75

This is a consolidation of two former publications, *The College Handbook* and the *Manual of Freshmen Class Profiles*. Presents data on 832 member colleges of the Board, including type of institution, location, enrollment, campus and facilities, programs of study offered, admissions requirements, college life, annual expenses, financial aid available, and other key information. For 618 of the colleges there is added tabular information concerning Scholastic Aptitude Test scores and class rank or grade-point average to assist a student to determine his chances of acceptance at a particular college. Also includes a list of 2,700 American undergraduate institutions offering at least a two-year program beyond grade twelve.

**Computer-assisted counseling. Super, Donald E. and others. Teachers College Press, Columbia University. 1970. 133p. $7.50; $4.50 paper

Descriptions and evaluative assessments of four system development projects which have applied the computer to vocational guidance services. Discussion of the present status and future developments of innovations utilizing the computer.

Computer-based vocational guidance systems. Government Printing Office. Supt. of Documents. 1969. 168p. $1.25

A collection of symposium papers presenting problems and accomplishments of computer systems designed to assist pupils to acquire self-knowledge, to make wise decisions, and to accept responsibility for them. Also reported are the progress of systems development projects, applications of technology in solving guidance problems, and difficulties in implementation. Summary of papers presented at fourth symposium on this subject.

Counseling and guidance: an exploration. Moser, L. E. and Moser, R. S. Prentice-Hall, Inc. 1963. 446p. $8.50

An introduction to current concepts, theories, and practices.

The counseling of college students. Siegel, Max, ed., Macmillan Company. 1968. 487p. $9.95

The eighteen selections focus on the history of counseling, its essential tools, and the roles of teacher and counselor. Helpful discussions are included on placement counseling and on vocational and career counseling.

**The counselor in a changing world. Wrenn, C. Gilbert. American Personnel and Guidance Association. 1962. 195p. $2.50

Report of the Commission on Guidance in American Schools, containing discussion of major elements in the school counselor's task, the nature of changes in the next decade, new social forces that are influencing young people, and personal and professional recommendations to the school counselor. Selected references.

The counselor in the schools. Boy, Angelico and Pine, Gerald J. Houghton Mifflin Company, 1968. 406p. $7.50

Analysis of the role of counselors who follow a client-centered point of view. Included are transcripts of four counseling sessions, accompanied by parallel comments which explain the dynamics of the counselor's role.

**Counselor's manual for *How About College Financing?* Feingold, S. Norman. American School Counselor Association. Order from American Personnel and Guidance Association. Revised 1968. 54p. $1

Discussion of trends in financial aid, counseling economically deprived students, and the development of local scholarship programs.

Dictionary of personnel and guidance terms: including professional agencies and associations. Hopke, William E., ed. Ferguson Publishing Company. 1968. 464p. $8.95

Following directions on how to use the book, the authors define more than three thousand terms. Also included are useful lists of professional organizations and a bibliography of sources.

Directory of approved counseling agencies, 1969-1970. American Board of Counseling Services. Order from American Personnel and Guidance Association. 1969. 201p. $3

One hundred and ninety-one approved agencies are listed with information on their services, hours, fees, clientele, and staff.

R. Use of Occupational Information and The Counselor's Professional Bookshelf—*Continued*

The discovery of talent. Wolfle, Dael, ed. Harvard University Press. 1969. 316p. $9.50

This volume gathers together the Walter Van Dyke Bingham lectures, by a distinguished group of pioneers, on the development of exceptional abilities and capacities. They provide a succinct reference work about human talents.

Economic report of the President transmitted to the Congress. Govt. Printing Office. Supt. of Documents. 1970. 284p. $1.50

Includes a report on unemployment, the economy, and statistical tables relating to income, employment, and production. The report lists past trends and future recommendations in many areas of economic concern.

Education and jobs: the great training robbery. Berg, Ivar. Frederick Praeger, Inc. 1970. 200p. $7.50

Urging that employers make a more realistic appraisal of job credentials, the author claims that many with less education perform as well as the more highly educated in comparable positions.

Education and training for full employment. Wolfbein, Seymour. Columbia University Press. 1967. 304p. $6.95

Sets forth ten basic policies underlying present manpower plans. Of interest to college students of economics.

Education, manpower and economic growth: strategies of human resource development. Harbison, Frederick and Myers, Charles A. McGraw-Hill Book Company. 1964. 229p. $8.95

The authors stress that the development of human resources is a more reliable indicator today of the growth of nations than any other measure. Methods of greater investment in people through education and training are suggested.

Education of the culturally different, a multi-cultural approach, a handbook for educators. U.S. Office of Education. Supt. of Documents. 1969. 64p. 35c

Distinguishes the concept of the culturally different pupil from that of the culturally disadvantaged. Discusses problems of minority populations.

The elementary school counselor. Van Hoose, William H.; Peters, Mildred; and Leonard, George E. Wayne State University Press. 1970. 96p. $1.95

Emphasizes the need for elementary school guidance and children's developmental needs. Discusses the emerging role of the elementary school counselor and career development at the elementary school levels.

Elementary school guidance. Detjen, Ervin W. and Detjen, Mary F. McGraw-Hill Book Company. 1963. 240p. $7.50

Provides an introduction to the guidance services of the elementary school, the functions of guidance personnel, and some of the techniques and methods which can be used by teachers.

Employment and earnings statistics for states and areas, 1939-68. Bureau of Labor Statistics, U.S. Department of Labor. Supt. of Documents. 1969. 621p. $5.25

Basic information on payroll employment for each of the states and 212 major labor areas, providing a geographic profile of the industrial complex. A special section containing analytical and summary data is included.

Employment and educational services in the mobilization for youth experience. Weissman, Harold H., ed. Association Press. 1969. 224p. $4.95; paper $2.95

Description of a pioneer project of a social agency located on New York's Lower East Side aimed to eradicate poverty. Efforts were made to increase the employability of lower-class youths, to increase the number of employment opportunities, and to increase the visibility for youths of the job opportunities available to them.

Equal educational opportunity. Harvard Educational Review. 1969. 273p. $5.95

Discussions concerning the effect of economic and social class on educational experience and response that contribute inequalities of educational opportunities and on the political, legal, and moral issues involved.

Guidance for children in elementary schools. Hill, George E. and Luckey, Eleanore B. Appleton-Century-Crofts. 1969. 598p. $7.95

Includes various factors which contribute to the effectiveness of guidance in the elementary schools, descriptions of existing programs, and considerations for improvement.

Guidance of the college-bound—problems, practices, and perspectives. Herr, Edwin L. and Cramer, Stanley H. Appleton-Century-Crofts. 1968. 305p. $3.95

Pertinent theory and related research are summarized in readable form. Recommendations are included regarding the application process, the format and use of a school profile sheet, and group methods of presenting information about colleges.

Guidance: program development and management. Peters, Herman J. and Schertzer, Bruce. Merrill Books, Inc. 1969. 658p. $9.50

This book presents plans for initiating, developing, and appraising a modern school guidance program. One chapter is devoted to developing a vocational guidance service and one to educational guidance.

Guidance services in the modern school. Ohlsen, Merle M. Harcourt, Brace and World. 1964. 515p. $8.75

One section focuses attention on educational and vocational planning.

Guidelines for preparing and evaluating occupational materials. National Vocational Guidance Association. Revised 1964. 11p. 40c

Includes a guide for preparing industrial careers brochures and standards for use in preparing and evaluating occupational literature.

R. Use of Occupational Information and The Counselor's Professional Bookshelf—*Continued*

Guidelines for the collection, maintenance, and dissemination of pupil records. Russell Sage Foundation. 1969. 48p. Single copy free. Additional copies 50c each

Report of a conference on the ethical and legal aspects of school record keeping. Suggests policies regarding use of information about students, the conditions under which such information is collected, and who may have access to it.

Guidelines to preparation and evaluation of occupational films. National Vocational Guidance Association. Order from American Personnel and Guidance Association. 1966. 8p. 25c

Criteria for production and evaluation of career films.

**The information service in guidance: occupational, educational, social. Norris Willa; Zeran, F. R.; and Hatch, R. N. Rand McNally and Company. Revised 1966. 600p. $9.50

The nature, scope, types, and sources of information are outlined, followed by chapters on the presentation of the information and programming the services.

Introduction to guidance: selected readings. Shertzer, Bruce and Stone, Shelley, eds. Houghton Mifflin Company. 1970. 459p. $5.95

Fifty-eight articles selected to complement and supplement the topics most commonly treated in textbooks for the beginning guidance course.

Learning for earning: new opportunities for paycheck education. U.S. Office of Education. Supt. of Documents. 1969. 16p. 25c

Highlights the provisions of the Vocational Education Amendments of 1968 and discusses Federal and state efforts to create, maintain, extend, and improve vocational education programs in an attempt to train and retrain persons for gainful employment.

The legal basis for college student personnel work. Bakken, Clarence. American College Personnel Association. Order from American Personnel and Guidance Association. 1968. 65p. $2

Explains legislation pertaining to guidance for those working in college personnel services. Selected court decisions illustrate the legal basis for authority for services, admissions, records, housing and food services, scholarships, loans, and student discipline.

Man, work and society. Nosow, Sigmund and Form, William H. Basic Books, Inc. 1962. 612p. $8.50

A collection of writings of men in the field of sociology about man's relationship to work and the society in which he lives. Good bibliography on the psychology of work.

Manpower report of the President. U.S. Department of Labor. 1970. 329p. $2.50

Annual report to the Congress, prepared by the Department of Labor, analyzing programs and activities in the manpower field. The statistical appendix provides data on the labor force, employment, unemployment, manpower programs, earnings, productivity, and gross national product.

National trade and professional associations of the United States. Columbia Books, Inc. 1970. 169p. $10

Names and locations of 4,300 associations, most of which are potential sources of occupational information. Listed alphabetically and indexed by subject and product, this directory also provides number of members, size of staff, executive officer, and publications. Revised annually in January.

Negroes and jobs. Ferman, Louis, ed. University of Michigan Press. 1969. 591p. $9

A study concluding that the unemployment rate of Negroes remains twice that of the white man and seeking the causes and cures.

New careers, jobs with a future and a profession. Govt. Printing Office. Supt. of Documents. 1969. 8p. 15c

This leaflet briefly describes the program administered by the Department of Labor's Manpower Administration, which is designed to help the poor and unemployed find steady jobs by starting them as preprofessionals in fields where labor shortages exist.

The 1969-70 directory of approved counseling agencies. American Board on Counseling Services. Order from American Personnel and Guidance Association. 1969. 200p. $3

The directory describes agencies that meet the board's criteria. Included are clientele, fees, hours, sponsor, name and professional qualifications of the director, and number of professional staff members in each agency. Includes 191 approved agencies.

Occupational employment patterns for 1960 and 1975. U.S. Department of Labor. Supt. of Documents. 1968. 283p. $2.25

Presents estimates of the occupational composition of employment by industry for 1960 and projections for 1975. Occupational profiles were prepared for 116 industries. The per cent of total employment in each industry was developed for about 160 occupational categories classified in ten broad occupational groups which comprise all types of work.

**Occupational information. 3rd edition. Hoppock, Robert. McGraw-Hill Book Company. 1967. 548p. $9.50

Includes discussions of basic theories of occupational choice, the use of occupational information in counseling, principles and methods of teaching courses in occupations, and suggestions for college instructors of courses in occupations. Also covers a review of the research in this area.

Occupational information: a career guidance view. Wolfbein, Seymour. Random House. 1968. 146p. $1.95

Discussion of topics which affect the economy: The people and their world of work, The social and economic setting, Population patterns and trends, Automation and education, Migration and mobility, Income and earnings, and Unemployment and poverty.

R. Use of Occupational Information and The Counselor's Professional Bookshelf—*Continued*

**Occupational information in the elementary school. Norris, Willa. Science Research Associates. 1968. 243p. $5.25

Includes theory and methods of presenting occupational information from kindergarten through sixth grade. The last half of the book contains lists of books, pamphlets, films, filmstrips, songs, and recordings suitable for use.

**Occupational information: the dynamics of its nature and use. Baer, Max F. and Roeber, Edward C. Science Research Associates. 1964. 495p. $7.10

Includes discussion of the use of occupational information in counseling interviews and with groups of students.

**Occupations and careers. Feingold, S. Norman and Swerdloff, Sol. McGraw-Hill Book Company. 1969. 372p. $6.96

Occupational choice is presented as a developmental process, taking place over an extended period of time. The last half of the book is devoted to the major groups of occupations.

Personalizing information processes: educational, occupational, and personal-social. Hollis, Joseph and Hollis, Lucile. Macmillan Company. 1969. 461p. $8.95

Ten chapters are devoted to implications of recent research, sources and types of educational and occupational information, its physical maintenance, making it available to users, and methods of utilizing it. Good selected references.

Pre-service and in-service preparation of school counselors for educational guidance. Cramer, Stanley, ed. Association for Counselor Education and supervision. Order from American Personnel and Guidance Association. 1970. 68p. $2

Report on counselors' attitudes toward their preparation.

Pupil personnel services in schools. Hummel, Dean L. and Bonham, S. J. Rand McNally and Company. 1968. 331p. $6

The authors of this book advocate a balanced and coordinated program of pupil services. They insist that the direction of such programs must be with the key leadership in the schools, that of the school superintendent, for effective administration.

Pupil personnel services in the modern school. Arbuckle, Dugold S. Allyn and Bacon, Inc. 1966. 404p. $6.75

An examination of the pupil personnel services and the personnel who staff these services. One section is devoted to the information service and another to a discussion of teachers and counselors in action.

School subjects and jobs. Brochard, John. Science Research Associates. Revised 1968. 48p. 75c

In chart form, this booklet shows how the different subjects taken in high school are related to different jobs.

Strategy for guidance, a point of view and its implications. Roeber, Edward C., Walz, Garry R., and Smith, Glenn E. Macmillan Company. 1969. 293p. $6.95

An approach to developing and implementing an effective school guidance program. Good discussion of the emerging roles and functions of school counselors.

Students enrolled for advanced degrees, summary data, fall 1968. U.S. Office of Education. Supt. of Documents. 1970. 66p. $1

Tenth in the series of surveys of enrollment for advanced degrees.

Teachers guide to group vocational guidance. Shertzer, Bruce and Knowles, Richard T. Bellman Publishing Company. 1964. 94p.

Presents twenty lesson plans for a unit on the world of work, ten for the unit on knowing oneself, and ten on securing a job and progressing in it. Suggested readings for most of the lesson plans.

**Teacher's role in career development. National Vocational Guidance Association. Order from American Personnel and Guidance Association. 1965. 107p. $1

Emphasizes the important contribution classroom teachers make in pointing out the relationship of the subject matter they teach to various careers. Many good reference lists of source materials.

Techniques of counseling. Warters, Jane. McGraw-Hill Book Company. 1964. 478p. $8.95

Discussion of tests, inventories, observation reports, self-reports, cumulative personnel records, case studies, and case conferences.

Theories of counseling. Stefflre, Buford, ed. McGraw-Hill Company. 1965. 298p. $7.50

Discusses the function and present status of counseling theory in the work of the high school and college counselor.

Tomorrow's manpower needs. United States Bureau of Labor Statistics. Supt. of Documents. 1969. 4 volumes. $4.80

Volume I. Developing area manpower projections. $1
Volume II. National trends and outlook. $1.25
Volume III. Occupational employment. 55c
Volume IV. National industry-occupational matrix. $2

Training and reference manual for job analysis. Bureau of Employment Security. Supt. of Documents. 1965. 91p. 60c

An operational and reference text that presents the principles and practices for obtaining information about jobs.

Training manual for the *Dictionary of Occupational Titles,* third edition. Bureau of Employment Security. Supt. of Documents. Part A, instructor's guide, 1965. 23p. 25c. Part B, trainee's workbook. 1965 323p. $1.75

A self-training program concerning the contents, structure, arrangement, and use of the *Dictionary.*

R. Use of Occupational Information and The Counselor's Professional Bookshelf—*Continued*

U.S. associations and societies. World Almanac. 1970. 952p. $2.25

Names of about one thousand organizations with addresses and names of executive officers. Many of them provide information about careers. List is revised annually.

Vocational counseling: a reappraisal in honor of Donald G. Paterson. Viteles, Morris S., Brayfield, Arthur H. and Tyler, Leona E. University of Minnesota Press. 1962. 70p. $1.50

Papers concerning the past, present, and future of vocational guidance.

Vocational education and occupations. U.S. Office of Education. Supt. of Documents. 1969. 292p. $2.25

Provides a means for evaluating, comparing, and improving the results of occupational education. Useful to point out the kinds of instructional programs that exist to prepare students for specific occupations which do not require a bachelor's degree.

Vocational guidance and career development: selected readings. Peters, Herman and Hansen, James., eds. Macmillan Company. 1971. 512p. $5.95

In this second edition three new sections have been added to include general trends, the disadvantaged, and career development of women.

What is an education worth? A dollar-and-sense evaluation. *Occupational Outlook Quarterly*, December, 1968. Supt. of Documents. 4p. 45c

A reprint reporting on the estimated lifetime earnings for males, ages eighteen to sixty-four, by occupational group and education. The Bureau of the Census report shows relationship between education and income.

Directory of Publishers and Distributors

Abelard-Schuman, Ltd., 257 Park Ave. South, New York, N.Y. 10010
Abingdon Press, 201 Eighth Ave., S., Nashville, Tenn. 37202
Academy of Advanced Traffic, 50 Broadway, New York, N.Y. 10004
Accounting Careers Council, National Distribution Center, P.O. Box 650, Radio City Station, New York, N.Y. 10019
Acoustical Society of America, 335 E. 45th St., New York, N.Y. 10017
Administrative Research Associates, Box 3, Deerfield, Ill. 60015
Adult Education Association, 1225 19th St., N.W., Washington, D.C. 20036
Advancement and Placement Institute, 169 N. 9th St., Brooklyn, N.Y. 11211
Aerospace Medical Association, Washington National Airport, Washington, D.C. 20001
Afro-American Publishing Company, 1727 S. Indiana Ave., Chicago, Ill. 60616
Air Conditioning and Refrigeration Institute, 1815 N. Fort Myer Drive, Arlington, Va. 22209
Air Force Aid Society, National Headquarters, Air Force, Stop 102, Washington, D.C. 20333
Air Transport Association of America, 1000 Connecticut Ave., N.W., Washington, D.C. 20036
Allied Trades of the Baking Industry, Inc., 541 Lexington Ave., New York, N.Y. 10022
Allyn and Bacon, Inc., 470 Atlantic Ave., Boston, Mass. 02210
Alpha Kappa Psi Fraternity, 111 E. 38th St., Indianapolis, Ind. 46205
Aluminum Company of America, 1501 Alcoa Bldg., Pittsburgh, Pa. 15219
Alumnae Advisory Center, Inc., Box A. C., 541 Madison Ave., New York, N.Y. 10022
American Academy of Political and Social Science, 3937 Chestnut St., Philadelphia, Pa. 19104
American Advertising Federation, 1225 Connecticut Ave., Washington, D.C. 20036
American Anthropological Association, 3700 Massachusetts Ave., N.W., Washington, D.C. 20016
American Apparel Manufacturers Association, 2000 K St., N.W., Washington, D.C. 20006
American Art Directory, Bowker Company, 1180 Ave. of the Americas, New York, N.Y. 10036
American Association for Health, Physical Education, and Recreation, 1201 16th St., N.W., Washington, D.C. 20036
American Association for Inhalation Therapy, 3554 9th St., Riverside, Calif. 92501

American Association for the Advancement of Science, 1515 Massachusetts Ave., N.W., Washington, D.C. 20005

American Association of Advertising Agencies, 200 Park Ave., New York, N.Y. 10017

American Association of Anatomists, Department of Anatomy, University of Michigan, East Medical Building, Ann Arbor, Mich. 48104

American Association of Dental Schools, 211 E. Chicago Ave., Chicago, Ill. 60611

American Association of Industrial Nurses, 79 Madison Ave., New York, N.Y. 10016

American Association of Junior Colleges, 1315 16th St., N.W., Washington, D.C. 20036

American Association of Medical Assistants, 200 E. Ohio St., Chicago, Ill. 60611

American Association of Nurse Anesthetists, Prudential Building, Prudential Plaza, Chicago, Ill. 60601

American Association of Nurserymen, 835 Southern Bldg., Washington, D.C. 20005

American Association of Theological Schools, 534 Third National Building, Dayton, Ohio 45402

American Astronomical Society, Executive Office, 211 FitzRandolph Road, Princeton, N.J. 08540

American Bakers Association, Industrial Relations Dept., 1700 Pennsylvania Ave., N.W., Washington, D.C. 20006

American Bankers Association, 90 Park Ave., New York, N.Y. 10016

American Bar Association, Information Service, 1155 E. 60th St., Chicago, Ill. 60637

American Board of Funeral Service Education, Committee on Scholarships, 201 Columbia Street, Fairmont, W. Va. 26554

American Board of Opticianry, 821 Eggert Road, Buffalo, N.Y. 14226

American Camping Association, Bradford Woods, Martinsville, Ind. 46151

American Cemetery Association, 329 E. Broad St., Columbus, Ohio 43215

American Ceramic Society, 4055 N. High St., Columbus, Ohio 43214

American Chamber of Commerce Executives, 1522 K Street, N.W., Washington, D.C. 20005

American Chemical Society, 1155 16th St., N.W., Washington, D.C. 20036

American College of Hospital Administrators, 840 N. Lake Shore Drive, Chicago, Ill. 60611

American Collegiate Retailing Association, Rochester Institute of Technology, College of Business, P.O. Box 3407, Rochester, N.Y. 14614

American Congress on Surveying and Mapping, 430 Woodward Bldg., 733 15th St., N.W., Washington, D.C. 20005

American Council on Education, 1785 Massachusetts Ave., N.W., Washington, D.C. 20036

American Council on Education for Journalism, Milton Gross, Secretary, 200 Neff Hall, University of Missouri, Columbia, Mo. 65201

American Council on Pharmaceutical Education, 77 W. Washington St., Chicago, Ill. 60602

American Culinary Federation, 221 West 57th St., New York, N.Y. 10019

American Dental Assistants Association, 211 E. Chicago Ave., Chicago, Ill. 60611

American Dental Association, Council on Dental Education, 211 E. Chicago Ave., Chicago, Ill. 60611

American Dental Hygienists Association, Suite 1616, 211 East Chicago Ave., Chicago, Ill. 60611

American Dietetic Association, 620 N. Michigan Ave., Chicago, Ill. 60611

American Education, U.S. Office of Education, Washington, D.C. 20202

American Federation of Labor and Congress of Industrial Organizations, Department of Education, 815 16th St., N.W., Washington, D.C. 20006

American Fisheries Society, 1404 New York Ave., N.W., Washington, D.C. 20005

American Forestry Association, 919 17th St., N.W., Washington, D.C. 20006

American Foundation for the Blind, 15 W. 16th St., New York, N.Y. 10011

American Foundrymen's Society, Golf and Wolf Roads, Des Plaines, Ill. 60016

American Geological Institute, 1444 N St., N.W., Washington, D.C. 20005

American Geophysical Union, 2100 Pennsylvania Ave., N.W., Washington, D.C. 20037

American Guild of Organists, 630 Fifth Ave., Room 2010, New York, N.Y. 10020

American Heart Association, 44 E. 23rd St., New York, N.Y. 10010

American Historical Association, 400 A St., S.E., Washington, D.C. 20003

American Home Economics Association, 1600 20th St., N.W., Washington, D.C. 20009

American Hospital Association, 840 N. Lake Shore Drive, Chicago, Ill. 60611

American Hotel and Motel Association, 221 W. 57th St., New York, N.Y. 10019

American Industrial Arts Association, 1201 16th St., N.W., Washington, D.C. 20036

American Industrial Hygiene Association, 25711 Southfield Road, Southfield, Mich. 48075

American Institute for Design and Drafting, 305 S. Andrews Ave., Suite 610, Fort Lauderdale, Florida 33301

American Institute of Architects, 1735 New York Ave., N.W., Washington, D.C. 20006

American Institute of Biological Sciences, 3900 Wisconsin Ave., N.W., Washington, D.C. 20016

American Institute of Certified Public Accountants, 666 Fifth Ave., New York, N.Y. 10019

American Institute of Cooperation, 1200 17th St., N.W., Washington, D.C. 20036

American Institute of Industrial Engineers, 345 E. 47th St., New York, N.Y. 10017

American Institute of Mining, Metallurgical, and Petroleum Engineers, 345 E. 47th St., New York, N.Y. 10017

American Institute of Nutrition, Public Information Committee, 9650 Rockville Pike, Bethesda, Md. 20014

American Institute of Physics, 335 E. 45th St., New York, N.Y. 10017

American Institute of Planners, 917 15th St., N.W., Room 800, Washington, D.C. 20005

American Iron and Steel Institute, 150 E. 42nd St., New York, N.Y. 10017

American Legion, Education and Scholarship Program, P.O. Box 1055, Indianapolis, Ind. 46206

American Library Association, Office for Recruitment, 50 E. Huron St., Chicago, Ill. 60611

American Management Association, 135 W. 50th St., New York, N.Y. 10020

American Marketing Association, 230 N. Michigan Ave., Chicago, Ill. 60601

American Mathematical Society, P.O. Box 6248, Providence, R.I. 02904

American Meat Institute, Dept. of Membership and Personnel Relations, 59 E. Van Burean St., Chicago, Ill. 60605

American Medical Association, 535 N. Dearborn St., Chicago, Ill. 60610

American Medical Technologists, 710 Higgins Road, Park Ridge, Ill. 60068

American Medical Women's Association, 1740 Broadway, New York, N.Y. 10019

American Meteorological Society, 45 Beacon St., Boston, Mass. 02108

American National Red Cross, National Headquarters, Personnel Services, Washington, D.C. 20006

American Newspaper Publishers Association Foundation, 750 Third Ave., New York, N.Y. 10017

American Nurses' Association, Division on Community Health Nursing Practice, 10 Columbus Circle, New York, N.Y. 10019

American Occupational Therapy Association, 251 Park Ave. South, New York, N.Y. 10010

American Optometric Association, 7000 Chippewa St., St. Louis, Mo. 63119

American Orthoptic Council, 3400 Massachusetts Ave., N.W., Washington, D.C. 20007

American Orthotic and Prosthetic Association, 919 18th St., N.W., Washington, D.C. 20006

American Osteopathic Association, 212 E. Ohio St., Chicago, Ill. 60611

American Paper Institute, 260 Madison Ave., New York, N.Y. 10016

American Personnel and Guidance Association, Publication Sales, 1607 New Hampshire Ave., N.W., Washington, D.C. 20009

American Petroleum Institute, 1271 Ave. of the Americas, New York, N.Y. 10020

American Pharmaceutical Association, 2215 Constitution Ave., N.W., Washington, D.C. 20037

American Physical Therapy Association, 1740 Broadway, New York, N.Y. 10019

American Physiological Society, 9650 Rockville Pike, Bethesda, Md. 20014

American Phytopathological Society, 1821 University Ave., St. Paul, Minn. 55104

American Podiatry Association, 20 Chevy Chase Circle, N.W., Washington, D.C. 20015

American Psychiatric Association, 1700 18th St., N.W., Washington, D.C. 20009

American Public Health Association, 1740 Broadway, New York, N.Y. 10018

American Public Welfare Association, 1313 E. 60th St., Chicago, Ill. 60637

American Registry of Radiologic Technologists, 2600 Wayzata Blvd., Minneapolis, Minn. 55405

American Road Builders' Association, 525 School St., S.W., Washington, D.C. 20024

American School, Drexel Avenue at 58th St., Chicago, Ill. 60637

American Society for Cell Biology, Dr. George D. Pappas, Secretary, Albert Einstein College of Medicine, Dept. of Anatomy, 1300 Morris Park Ave., Bronx, N.Y. 10461

American Society for Engineering Education, 2100 Pennsylvania Ave., N.W., Washington, D.C. 20037

American Society for Horticultural Science, P.O. Box 109, St. Joseph, Michigan 49085

American Society for Metals, Metals Park, Ohio 44073

American Society for Microbiology, 1913 Eye St., N.W., Washington, D.C. 20006

American Society for Personnel Administration, 52 E. Bridge St., Berea, Ohio 44017

American Society for Pharmacology and Experimental Therapeutics, Inc., 9650 Rockville Pike, Bethesda, Md. 20014

American Society of Agricultural Engineers, Saint Joseph, Mich. 49085

American Society of Agronomy, 677 S. Segoe Road, Madison, Wis. 53711

American Society of Animal Sciences, 113 N. Nell St., Champaign, Ill. 61820

American Society of Biological Chemists, 9650 Rockville Pike, Bethesda, Md. 20014

American Society of Civil Engineers, 345 E. 47th St., New York, N.Y. 10017

American Society of Heating, Refrigerating, and Air-Conditioning Engineers, 345 E. 47th St., New York, N.Y. 10017

American Society of Ichthyologists and Herpetologists, U.S. National Museum, Division of Reptiles, Washington, D.C. 20560

American Society of Internal Medicine, 525 Hearst Bldg., Third at Market, San Francisco, Calif. 94103

American Society of Landscape Architects, 2013 Eye St., N.W., Washington, D.C. 20006

American Society of Mechanical Engineers, 345 E. 47th St., New York, N.Y. 10017

American Society of Medical Technologists, Suite 1600, Hermann Professional Bldg., Houston, Texas 77025

American Society of Planning Officials, 1313 E. 60th St., Chicago, Ill. 60637

American Society of Plant Physiologists, P.O. Box 5706, Washington, D.C. 20014

American Society of Radiologic Technologists, 645 N. Michigan Ave., Chicago, Ill. 60611

American Society of Range Management, 2120 S. Birch St., Denver, Colo. 80222

American Society of Safety Engineers, 850 Busse Highway, Park Ridge, Ill. 60068

American Society of Zoologists, Box 2739 California Lutheran College, Thousand Oaks, Calif. 91360

American Sociological Association, 1001 Connecticut Ave., N.W., Washington, D.C. 20036

American Speech and Hearing Association, 9030 Old Georgetown Road, Washington, D.C. 20014

American Statistical Association, 810 18th St., N.W., Washington, D.C. 20006

American Technical Society, 848 E. 58th St., Chicago, Ill. 60637

American Textile Manufacturers Institute, 1501 Johnson Building, Charlotte, N.C. 28202

American Translators Association, P.O. Box 489, Madison Square Station, New York 10010

American Trucking Associations, Education Section, Public Relations Dept., 1616 P St., N.W., Washington, D.C. 20036

American Veterinary Medical Association, 600 S. Michigan Ave., Chicago, Ill. 60605

American Watchmakers Institute, Inc., P.O. Box 11011, Cincinnati, Ohio 45211

American Welding Society, 345 E. 47th St., New York, N.Y. 10017

American West Publishing Company, 599 College Ave., Palo Alto, California 94306

AMVETS National Service Foundation, 1710 Rhode Island Ave., N.W., Washington, D.C. 20036

Antioch College, Yellow Springs, Ohio 45387

Appleton-Century-Crofts, 440 Park Ave., South, New York 10016
Archaeological Institute of America, 260 W. Broadway, New York, N.Y. 10013
Arco Publishing Company, 219 Park Ave. South, New York, N.Y. 10003
Armstrong Cork Company, Public Relations Dept., Lancaster, Pa. 17604
Army Opportunities, U.S. Army Recruiting Command, Hampton, Va. 23369
Associated Press Newsfeatures, 50 Rockefeller Plaza, New York, N.Y. 10020
Association for Childhood Education International, 3615 Wisconsin Ave., N.W., Washington, D.C. 20016
Association of American Geographers, 1146 16th St., N.W., Washington, D.C. 20036
Association of American Medical Colleges, 2530 Ridge Ave., Evanston, Ill. 60201
Association of American Railroads, Public Relations Department, American Railroads Bldg., Washington, D.C. 20036
Association of College Admissions Counselors, 801 Davis St., Evanston, Ill. 60201
Association of Collegiate Schools of Architecture, 521 18th St., N.W., Washington, D.C. 20006
Association of Industrial Advertisers, 41 E. 42nd St., New York, N.Y. 10017
Association of Medical Illustrators, Johns Hopkins Medical School, Dept. of Art as Applied to Medicine, 725 N. Wolfe St., Baltimore, Md. 21205
Association of Universities and Colleges of Canada, 151 Slater, Ottawa 4, Ontario, Canada
Association of University Programs in Hospital Administration, Room 420, 1 DuPont Circle, Washington, D.C. 20005
Association Press, 291 Broadway, New York, N.Y. 10007
Atchinson, Topeka and Santa Fe Railway Company, Public Relations Dept., 80 E. Jackson Blvd., Chicago, Ill. 60604
Atheneum Publishers, 122 E. 42nd St., New York, N.Y. 10017
Atlantic-Little Brown. See Little, Brown and Company
Automobile Manufacturers Association, 320 Center Bldg., Detroit, Mich. 48202

Bankers Association of America. See American Bankers of America
Bankers Publishing Company, 89 Beach St., Boston, Mass. 02111
George Banta Company, Curtis Reed Plaza, Menasha, Wis. 54952
Barbizon School of Modeling, 574 Fifth Ave., New York, N.Y. 10036
Barnes and Noble, Inc., 105 Fifth Ave., New York, N.Y. 10003
Barron's Educational Series, Inc., 113 Crossways Park Drive, Woodbury, N.Y. 11797
Basic Books, Inc., 404 Park Ave. South, New York, N.Y. 10016

Bausch and Lomb, Incorporated, Science Award Committee, Rochester, N.Y. 14602

Bellman Publishing Company, P.O. Box 172, Cambridge, Mass. 02138

Beneficial Management Corporation, Beneficial Building, 200 South St., Morristown, N.J. 07960

Berklee School of Music, 1140 Boylston St., Boston, Mass. 02215

Bethany Press, 2640 Pine Blvd., P.O. Box 179, St. Louis, Mo. 63166

Better Business Bureau of Metropolitan New York, 220 Church St., New York, N.Y. 10013

Biophysical Society, Life Sciences Bldg., Pennsylvania State University, University Park, Pa. 16802

B'nai B'rith Vocational Service, 1640 Rhode Island Avenue, N.W., Washington, D.C. 20036

Board of Christian Education, United Presbyterian Church in the U.S.A., Division of Vocation, 808 Witherspoon Bldg., Philadelphia, Pa. 19107

Board of Missions of The United Methodist Church, 475 Riverside Drive, New York, N.Y. 10027

Bobbs-Merrill Company, 4300 W. 62nd St., Indianapolis, Ind. 46268

Botanical Society of America, Department of Botany, Indiana University, Bloomington, Inc. 47401

Bowker, R. R., Company, 1180 Ave. of the Americas, New York, N.Y. 10036

Bowman Technical School, Duke and Chestnut Streets, Lancaster, Pa. 17604

Boy Scouts of America, Personnel Division, New Brunswick, N.J. 08903

Boys' Clubs of America, 771 First Ave., New York, N.Y. 10017

Brotherhood of Painters, Decorators, and Paperhangers of America, 1925 K St., N.W., Washington, D.C. 20006

Bruce Publishing Company, 400 N. Broadway, Milwaukee, Wis. 53201

Bryant College of Business Administration, Providence, R.I. 02906

Bunting and Lyon, Inc., 238 N. Main St., Wallingford, Conn. 06492

Bureau of Labor Standards, U.S. Department of Labor, Washington, D.C. 20210

Bureau of Labor Statistics. Order from Supt. of Documents

Bureau of Public Assistance, Social Security Administration, U.S. Department of Health, Education, and Welfare, Washington, D.C. 20201

Burroughs Wellcome and Company, 1 Scarsdale Road, Tuckahoe, N.Y. 10707

California State Department of Employment, 800 Capitol Mall, Sacramento, Calif. 95814

Camp Fire Girls, Inc., 65 Worth St., New York, N.Y. 10013

Career Information Service, Southeastern Regional Vocational Technical School, 250 Foundry St., Route 106, South Easton, Mass. 02375

Careers, Inc., P.O. Box 135, Largo, Fla. 33540
Carnegie Corporation, 437 Madison Ave., New York, N.Y. 10022
Casualty Actuarial Society, 200 E. 42nd St., New York, N.Y. 10017
Catholic College Bureau, Room 626, 25 E. Jackson Blvd., Chicago, Ill. 60604
CCM Information Corporation, 909 Third Ave., New York, N.Y. 10022
Central Committee for Conscientious Objectors, Suite 300, 2016 Walnut St., Philadelphia, Pa. 19103
Central Opera Service, Metropolitan Opera Association, New York, N.Y. 10023
Chamber of Commerce of the United States, International Group, 1615 H St., N.W., Washington, D.C. 20006
Changing Times, The Kiplinger Magazine, School Services, 1729 H St., N.W., Washington, D.C. 20006
Child Study Association of America, 9 E. 89th St., New York, N.Y. 10028
Childrens Press, Inc., 1224 W. Van Buren St., Chicago, Ill. 00607
Chilton Book Company, 401 Walnut St., Philadelphia, Pa. 19106
Chiropractic Education Commission, Dept. C.G., 741 Brady St., Davenport, Iowa 52803
Chronicle Guidance Publication, Inc., Moravia, N.Y. 13118
Cincinnati College of Mortuary Science, 3200 Reading Road, Cincinnati, Ohio 45229
Club Managers Association of America, 1030 15th St., N.W., Washington, D.C. 20005
College Admissions Assistance Center, 461 Park Ave. South, New York, N.Y. 10016
College Entrance Book Company, 104 Fifth Ave., New York, N.Y. 10011
College Entrance Examination Board, Publication Order Office, Box 592, Princeton, N.J. 08540
College of Agriculture, Department of Dairy Technology, Ohio State University, 2121 Fyffe Road, Columbus, Ohio 43210
College of Earth and Mineral Sciences, 345 E. 47th St., New York, N.Y. 10017
College Opportunities, Inc., Box 4116, Cincinnati, Ohio 45204
College Placement Council, 35 E. Elizabeth Ave., Bethlehem, Pa. 18018
College Scholarship Service. See College Entrance Examination Board
Collier Books. See Crowell, Collier and Macmillan
Colorado School of Mines, Golden, Colo. 80401
Columbia Books, Inc., 917 15th St., N.W., Washington, D.C. 20005
Columbia University Press, 440 W. 110th St., New York, N.Y. 10025
Columbia University, School of Dental and Oral Surgery, Courses for Dental Hygiene, 630 W. 168th St., New York, N.Y. 10032
Committee on Careers, National League for Nursing, 10 Columbus Circle, New York, N.Y. 10019

Committee on Marine Research, Education, and Facilities, National Council on Marine Resources and Engineering Development, Bldg. 159E, Washington Navy Yard, Washington, D.C. 20390

Conference of Catholic Schools of Nursing, 1438 S. Grand Blvd., St. Louis, Mo. 63104

Connecticut Mutual Life Insurance Company, Dept. 316-D, Hartford, Conn. 06115

Cooperative Extension Service, New York State College of Agriculture, Cornell University, Ithaca, N.Y. 14850

Copy-Write Creations, 1865 77th St., Brooklyn, N.Y. 11214

Corning Glass Works Foundation, Corning, N.Y. 14830

Council for the Advancement of Small Colleges, 1346 Connecticut Ave., N.W., Washington, D.C. 20036

Council for Exceptional Children, National Education Association, 1201 16th St., N.W., Washington, D.C. 20036

Council for Professional Education for Business, American Association of Collegiate Schools of Business, 101 N. Skinker Blvd., St. Louis, Mo. 63130

Council on Hotel, Restaurant, and Institutional Education, Statler Hall, Cornell University, Ithaca, N.Y. 14850

Council on International Educational Exchange, 777 United Nations Plaza, New York, N.Y. 10017

Council on Medical Education of the American Medical Association, 535 N. Dearborn St., Chicago, Ill. 60610

Council on Opportunities in Selling, Inc., 630 Third Ave., New York, N.Y. 10017

Council on Social Work Education, 345 E. 46th St., New York, N.Y. 10016

Coward, McCann and Geoghegan, Inc., 200 Madison Ave., New York, N.Y. 10016

Cowles Book Company, 488 Madison Ave., New York, N.Y. 10022

Criterion Books, Inc., 6 West 57th St., New York, N.Y. 10019

Croner Publications, Inc., 211 Jamaica Ave., Queens Village, N.Y. 11428

Crowell, Collier and Macmillan, Inc., 866 Third Ave., New York, N.Y. 10022

Thomas Y. Crowell Company, 201 Park Ave. South, New York, N.Y. 10003

Crown Publishers, Inc., 419 Park Ave. South, New York, N.Y. 10016

Dartnell Corporation, 4660 Ravenswood Ave., Chicago, Ill. 60640

Data Processing Horizons, P.O. Box 99, South Pasadena, Calif. 91030

John Day Company, Inc., 62 W. 45th St., New York, N.Y. 10036

Delacorte Press, 750 Third Ave., New York, N.Y. 10017

Department of Home Economics, National Education Association, 1601 16th St., N.W., Washington, D.C. 20036

Department of Public Instruction, Commonwealth of Pennsylvania, Box 911, Education Building, Harrisburg, Pa. 17126
DeVry Institute of Technology, 4141 Belmont Ave., Chicago, Ill. 60641
Dial Press, Inc. 750 Third Ave., New York, N.Y. 10017
Directory Publishers Company, Hillsdale, N.J. 07642
Dodd, Mead and Company, 79 Madison Ave., New York, N.Y. 10016
Doubleday and Company, Garden City, Long Island, N.Y. 11530
Duell, Sloan and Pearce, Inc., 250 Park Ave., New York, N.Y. 10017

E. P. Dutton and Company, 201 Park Ave. South, New York, N.Y. 10003
Eastman Kodak Company, Public Relations Department, 343 State St., Rochester, N.Y. 14650
Ecological Society of America, Dr. S. I. Auerbach, Secretary, Oak Ridge National Laboratory, Oak Ridge, Tenn. 37830
Educational Directories Inc., P.O. Box 199, Mount Prospect, Ill. 60056
Educational Dimensions Corporation, Box 146, Great Neck, N.Y. 11023
Educational Exchange of Greater Boston, 18 Brattle St., Cambridge, Mass. 02138
Educational Research Corporation, 10 Craigie St., Cambridge, Mass. 02138
Educators Progress Service, Inc., Randolph, Wis. 53956
Educators Publishing Service, 75 Moulton St., Cambridge, Mass. 02138
Electronic Computer Programming Institute, Empire State Bldg., New York 10001
Electronic Industries Association, 2001 Eye St., N.W., Washington, D.C. 20006
Engineers' Council for Professional Development, 345 E. 47th St., New York, N.Y. 10017
Engineers Joint Council, 345 E. 47th St., New York, N.Y. 10017
Entomological Society of America, 4603 Calvert Road, College Park, Md. 20740
Evans and Company, 216 East 49th St., New York, N.Y. 10017
Executive Development Press, Littleton, N.H. 03581

Family Service Association of America, 44 E. 23rd St., New York, N.Y. 10010
Farm Electrification Company, Box 1008, Oakbrook, Ill. 50523
Federal Aviation Administration, Dept. of Transportation, Washington, D.C. 20590
Federal Bureau of Investigation, U.S. Dept. of Justice, Washington, D.C. 20535
Frederick Fell, Inc., 386 Park Ave. South, New York, N.Y. 10016
J. G. Ferguson Publishing Company, 6 N. Michigan Ave., Chicago, Ill. 60602

Fibre Box Association, 224 S. Michigan Ave., Chicago, Ill. 60604
Fidelity Mutual Life Insurance Company, Fairmount Ave., Philadelphia, Pa. 19101
Field Enterprises Educational Corporation, Merchandise Mart Plaza, Chicago, Ill. 60654
Financial Executives Institute, 50 W. 44th St., New York, N.Y. 10036
Finney Company, 3350 Gorham Ave., Minneapolis, Minn. 55426
Follett Publishing Company, 201 N. Wells St., Chicago, Ill. 60606
Four Winds Press, Division of Scholastic Magazines, 50 W. 44th St., New York, N.Y. 10036
The Free Press, 866 Third Ave., New York, N.Y. 10022
W. H. Freeman and Company, Publishers, 660 Market St., San Francisco, Calif. 94104
Fresno State College, Department of Criminology, Fresno, Calif. 93726
Friendship Press, 475 Riverside Drive, New York, N.Y. 10027
Funk and Wagnalls Company, 380 Lexington Ave., New York, N.Y. 10017
Future Teachers of America, National Commission on Teacher Education and Professional Standards, 1201 16th St., N.W., Washington, D.C. 20036

Gale Research Company, Book Tower, Detroit, Mich. 48226
Genealological Publishing Company, 521-23 St. Paul Place, Baltimore, Md. 21202
General Electric Company, Educational Relations Service, 1 River Road, Schenectady, N.Y. 12305
General Motors Corporation, Educational Relations Section, Public Relations Staff, 3044 W. Grand Blvd., Detroit, Mich. 48202
General Motors Corporation, Public Relations Staff, Detroit, Mich. 48202
General Motors Corporation, Salaried Personnel Placement Activity, General Motors Bldg., Detroit, Mich. 48202
General Motors Institute, Flint, Mich. 48502
Girl Scouts of the U.S.A., 830 Third Ave., New York, N.Y. 10022
Golden Gate Junior Books, 8344 Melrose Ave., Los Angeles, Calif. 90069
Golden Press, 850 Third Ave., New York, N.Y. 10022
Good Housekeeping Bulletin Service, 959 Eighth Ave., New York, N.Y. 10019
Gordon and Breach, Science Publishers, Inc. 150 Sunset Blvd., Pacific Palisades, Calif. 90272
Government Printing Office. Order from Supt. of Documents, Washington, D.C. 20402
Graduate Admissions Assistance Center, 461 Park Ave. South, New York, N.Y. 10016

Graduate School Service, American College Admissions Center, Liberty Trust Bldg., Philadelphia, Pa. 19107
Graphic Arts Industry, Inc., Educational Council, 4615 Forbes Ave., Pittsburgh, Pa. 15213
Gregg Division, McGraw-Hill Book Company, 330 W. 42nd St., New York, N.Y. 10036
Grosset and Dunlap, Inc., 51 Madison Ave., New York, N.Y. 10010
Guidance Centre, The College of Education, University of Toronto, 1000 Yonge Street, Toronto 289, Ontario, Canada
Guidance Exchange, 3310 Rochambeau Ave., Bronx, N.Y. 10457

Hammond, Inc., Maplewood, N.J. 07040
Harcourt, Brace and Jovanovich, Inc., 757 Third Ave., New York, N.Y. 10017
Harian Publications, Greenlawn, New York 11740
Harper and Row, Publishers, 49 E. 33rd St., New York, N.Y. 10016
Harvard Educational Review, Cambridge, Mass. 02138
Harvard Student Agencies, Cambridge, Mass. 02138
Harvard University Press, 79 Garden St., Cambridge, Mass. 02138
Hastings House, Inc., 10 E. 40th St., New York, N.Y. 10016
Hawthorn Books, Inc., 70 Fifth Ave., New York, N.Y. 10011
Hayden Book Company, 116 W. 14th St., New York, N.Y. 10011
D. C. Heath and Company, 125 Spring Street, Lexington, Mass. 02173
Hebrew Union College and Jewish Institute of Religion, 3101 Clifton Ave., Cincinnati, Ohio 45220
Holiday House, Inc., 18 E. 56th St., New York, N.Y. 10022
Holt, Rinehart and Winston, Inc., 383 Madison Ave., New York, N.Y. 10017
Houghton Mifflin Company, 2 Park St., Boston, Mass. 02107

Illinois Institute of Technology, 10 W. 33rd St., Chicago, Ill. 60616
Illuminating Engineering Society, 345 E. 47th St., New York, N.Y. 10017
Immigration and Naturalization Service, U.S. Dept. of Justice, 119 D St., N.E., Washington, D.C. 20536
Independent School Admissions Advisory Center, 238 N. Main St., Wallingford, Conn. 06492
Industrial Designers Society of America, 60 W. 55th St., New York, N.Y. 10019
Industrial Research Service, Masonic Building, Dover, N.H. 03820
Institute of Electrical and Electronics Engineers, 345 E. 47th St., New York, N.Y. 10017
Institute of Internal Auditors, 170 Broadway, New York, N.Y. 10038
Institute of International Education, 809 United Nations Plaza, New York, N.Y. 10017

Institute of Life Insurance, Educational Division, 277 Park Ave., New York, N.Y. 10017

Institute of Traffic Engineers, 2029 K St., N.W., Washington, D.C. 20006

Insurance Information Institute, Educational Division, 110 William St., New York, N.Y. 10038

Interior Design Educators Council, 84-44 120th St., Kew Gardens, N.Y. 11415

Internal Revenue Service, U.S. Treasury Department, 1111 Constitution Ave., N.W., Washington, D.C. 20224

International Accountants Society, 209 W. Jackson Blvd., Chicago, Ill. 60606

International Association of Chiefs of Police, 1319 18th St., N.W., Washington, D.C. 20036

International Association of Fire Chiefs, 232 Madison Ave., New York, N.Y. 10016

International Association of Machinists, 1300 Connecticut Ave., N.W., Washington, D.C. 20036

International Business Machines Corporation, Office Products Division, 590 Madison Ave., New York, N.Y. 10022

International Chiropractors Association, 741 Brady St., Davenport, Iowa 52808

International Correspondence Schools, Scranton, Pa. 18515

International Oceanographic Foundation, Rickenbacker Causeway, Virginia Key, Miami, Fla. 33149

Interstate Printers and Publishers, Inc., 19 N. Jackson St., Danville, Ill. 61832

Investment Bankers Association of America, 425 13th St., N.W., Washington, D.C. 20004

Iowa State University Press, Press Building, Ames, Iowa 50010

Johns Hopkins Press, Baltimore, Md. 21218

Journalism Educator, American Society of Journalism School Administrators, Long Island University, Department of Journalism, Brooklyn, N.Y. 11201

Kappa Epsilon, 1539 N. 51st St., Milwaukee, Wis. 53208

Keystone Junior College, Public Relations Department, La Plume, Pa. 18440

Kiwanis Club of Long Beach, Lafayette Hotel, 140 Linden Ave., Long Beach, Calif. 90802

Alfred A. Knopf, Inc., 501 Madison Ave., New York, N.Y. 10022

M. W. Lads Publishing Company, 1250 Broadway, New York, N.Y. 10001

Lehigh University, Office of Admission, Bethlehem, Pa. 18015
Life Insurance Agency Management Association, 170 Sigourney St., Hartford, Conn. 06105
J. B. Lippincott Company, East Washington Square, Philadelphia, Pa. 19105
Little, Brown and Company, 34 Beacon St., Boston, Mass. 02106
Long's College Book Company, 1836 N. High St., Columbus 1, Ohio 43201
Lothrop, Lee and Shephard Company, 381 Park Ave. South, New York, N.Y. 10016
Lovejoy's Guidance Digest, 443 Broad Street, Red Bank, N.J. 07701
Lutheran Church in America Vocational Services, 231 Madison Ave., New York, N.Y. 10016

Macmillan Company, 866 Third Ave., New York, N.Y. 10022
McGraw-Hill Book Company, 330 W. 42nd St., New York, N.Y. 10036
McGraw-Hill Book Company, Junior Book Division, 330 West 42nd St., New York, N.Y. 10036
David McKay Company, Inc., 750 Third Ave., New York, N.Y. 10017
Macrae Smith Company, 225 S. 15th St., Philadelphia, Pa. 19102.
Manufacturing Chemists Association, 1825 Connecticut Ave., N.W., Washington, D.C. 20009
Mathematical Association of America, 1225 Connecticut Ave., N.W., Washington, D.C. 20036
Medical Library Association, 919 N. Michigan Ave., Chicago, Ill. 60611
Melmont Publishers, 1224 W. Van Buren St., Chicago, Ill. 00607
Meredith Press, 250 Park Ave., New York, N.Y. 10017
Charles E. Merrill Publishing Company, 1300 Alum Creek Drive, Columbus, Ohio 43216
Julian Messner, 1 West 39th St., New York, N.Y. 10018
Metallurgical Society, 345 E. 47th St., New York, N.Y. 10017
Methods and Materials Press, 6 S. Derby Road, Springfield, N.J. 07081
Michigan Employment Security Commission, 7310 Woodward Ave., Detroit, Mich. 48202
Michigan State University, College of Education, Educational Publications Services, Erickson Hall, East Lansing, Mich. 48823
Michigan State University, Dept. of Forestry, East Lansing, Mich. 48823
Michigan State University, School of Labor and Industrial Relations, East Lansing, Mich. 48823
Modern Language Association, Materials Center, 62 Fifth Ave., New York, N.Y. 10011
William Morrow and Company, 425 Park Ave. South, New York, N.Y. 10016
Museum of Science and Industry, Jackson Park, Chicago, Ill. 60637
Music Educators National Conference, 1201 16th St., N.W., Washington, D.C. 20036

Mycological Society of America, Care of New York Botanical Garden, Bronx, N.Y. 10458

National Academy of Sciences, National Research Council, 2101 Constitution Ave., Washington, D.C. 20418

National Aerospace Education Council, 806 15th St., N.W., Washington, D.C. 20005

National Architectural Accrediting Board, 521 18th St., N.W., Washington, D.C. 20006

National Art Education Association, 1201 16th St., N.W., Washington, D.C. 20036

National Assembly for Social Policy and Development, 345 E. 46th St., New York, N.Y. 10017

National Association for Mental Health, 10 Columbus Circle, New York, N.Y. 10019

National Association for Music Therapy, P.O. Box 610, Lawrence, Kansas 66044

National Association for Practical Nurse Education and Service, 535 Fifth Ave., New York, N.Y. 10017

National Association of Accountants, 505 Park Ave., New York, N.Y. 10022

National Association of Bank-Women, Inc., Public Relations Office, 60 E. 42nd St., New York, N.Y. 10017

National Association of Broadcasters, 1771 N St., N.W., Washington, D.C. 20036

National Association of Certified Dental Laboratories, 210 Thomas House, 1330 Massachusetts Ave., N.W., Washington, D.C. 20005

National Association of Chain Drug Stores, 1625 Eye Street, N.W., Washington D.C. 20006

National Association of College Admissions Counselors, 801 Davis St., Evanston, Ill. 60201

National Association of Cosmetology Schools, 125 Halsey St., Newark, N.J. 07102

National Association of Food Chains, 1725 Eye St., N.W., Washington, D.C. 20006

National Association of Direct Selling Companies, 165 Center St., Winona, Minn. 55987

National Association of Legal Secretaries, 29 S. La Salle St., Chicago, Ill. 60603

National Association of Motor Bus Owners, 839 17th St., N.W., Washington, D.C. 20006

National Association of Plumbing-Heating-Cooling Contractors, 1016 20th St., N.W., Washington, D.C. 20036

National Association of Purchasing Management, 11 Park Place, New York, N.Y. 10007

National Association of Real Estate Boards, 155 E. Superior St., Chicago Ill. 60611

National Association of Retail Druggists, 1 E. Wacker Drive, Chicago, Ill. 60611

National Association of Retail Grocers of the United States, 360 Michigan Ave., Chicago, Ill. 60601

National Association of Sanitarians, 1550 Lincoln St., Denver, Colo. 80203

National Association of Schools of Art, 1424 16th St., N.W., Washington, D.C. 20036

National Association of Secondary School Principals, 1201 16th St., N.W., Washington, D.C. 20036

National Association of Social Workers, 2 Park Ave., New York, N.Y. 10016

National Association of State Universities and Land Grant Colleges, Dean of Agriculture, Land Grant College of each state

National Association of Wholesalers, 1725 K St., N.W., Washington, D.C. 20006

National Automobile Dealers Association, Public Relations Department, 2000 K St., N.W., Washington, D.C. 20006

National Beta Club, Box 730, Spartanburg, S. C. 29301

National Better Business Bureau, 230 Park Ave., New York, N.Y. 10017

National Broadcasting Company, Department of Information. 30 Rockefeller Plaza, New York, N.Y. 10020

National Career Center, 3839 White Plains Road, Bronx, N.Y. 10467

National Coal Association, Education Division, 1130 17th St., N.W., Washington, D.C. 20036

National Commission for Cooperative Education, 52 Vanderbilt Ave., New York, N.Y. 10017

National Commission for Social Work Careers, 2 Park Ave., New York, N.Y. 10016

National Commission on Teacher Education and Professional Standards, National Education Association, 1201 16th St., N.W., Washington, D.C. 20036

National Consumer Finance Association. 1000 16th St., N.W., Washington, D.C. 20036

National Council of Churches, Division of Christian Education, 475 Riverside Drive, New York, N.Y. 10027

National Council of Teachers of Mathematics, 1201 16th St., N.W., Washington, D.C. 20036

National Council of Young Men's Christian Association, Recruiting Services, 291 Broadway, New York, N.Y. 10007

National Council on Crime and Delinquency, 44 E. 23rd St., New York, N.Y. 10010

National Directory Service, Box 32065, Cincinnati, Ohio 45232

National Easter Seal Society for Crippled Children and Adults, 2023 W. Ogden Ave., Chicago, Ill. 60612

National Education Association, 1201 16th St., N.W., Washington, D.C. 20036

National Employment Services Institute, 1100 Connecticut Ave., N.W., Washington, D.C. 20036

National Executive Housekeepers Association, Business and Professional Bldg., Gallipolis, Ohio 45631

National Federation of Licensed Practical Nurses, Inc., 250 W. 57th St., Suite 1511, New York, N.Y. 10019

National Forest Products Association, Technical Services Division, 1619 Massachusetts Ave., N.W., Washington, D.C. 20036

National Funeral Directors Association, 135 W. Wells St., Milwaukee, Wis. 53203

National Geographic Society, 17th and M Sts., N.W., Washington, D.C. 20036

National Health Council, 1740 Broadway, New York, N.Y. 10019

National Home Study Council, 1601 18th St., N.W., Washington, D.C. 20009

National Institute of Drycleaning, Silver Spring, Md. 20910

National Institute of Mental Health, 5454 Wisconsin Ave., Chevy Chase, Md. 20015

National Jewish Welfare Board, Bureau of Personnel and Training, 15 E. 26th Street, New York, N.Y. 10010

National Landscape Nurserymen's Association, 832 Southern Bldg., Washington, D.C. 20005

National League for Nursing, Committee on Careers, 10 Columbus Circle, New York, N.Y. 10019

National League of Cities, 1612 K Street, N.W., Washington, D.C. 20006

National LP-Gas Association, 79 W. Monroe St., Chicago, Ill. 60603

National Machine Tool Builders Association, 2139 Wisconsin Ave., N.W., Washington, D.C. 20007

National Medical Fellowships, Inc., 3935 Elm St., Downers Grove, Ill. 60515

National Merit Scholarship Corporation, 990 Grove St., Evanston, Ill. 60201

National Oceanographic Foundation, 10 Rickenbacker Causeway, Virginia Key, Miami, Florida. 33149

National Park Service, U.S. Department of the Interior, Washington, D.C. 20240

National Plastering Industry's Joint Apprenticeship Trust Fund, 1000 Vermont Ave., N.W., Washington, D.C. 20005

National Recreation and Park Association, 1700 Pennsylvania Ave., N.W., Washington, D.C. 20006

National Rehabilitation Counseling Association, 1522 K St., N.W., Washington, D.C. 20005

National Restaurant Association, 1530 N. Lake Shore Drive, Chicago, Ill. 60610

National Retail Merchants Association, 100 W. 31st St., New York, N.Y. 10001

National Scholarship Service and Fund for Negro Students, 1776 Broadway, New York, N.Y. 10019

National Science Teachers Association, 1201 16th St., N.W., Washington, D.C. 20036

National Secretaries Association, Suite 410, 1103 Grand Ave., Kansas City, Mo. 64106

National Selected Morticians, 1616 Central St., Evanston, Ill. 60201

National Service Board for Religious Objectors, 550 Washington Bldg., 15th and New York Ave., N.W., Washington, D.C. 20005

National Shorthand Reporters Association, Executive Secretary, 25 W. Main St., Madison, Wis. 53703

National Social Welfare Assembly, Inc., 345 E. 46th St., New York, N.Y. 10017

National Society of Interior Designers, 315 E. 62nd St., New York, N.Y. 10021

National Society of Professional Engineers, 2029 K St., N.W., Washington, D.C. 20006

National Society of Public Accountants, 1717 Pennsylvania Ave., N.W., Washington, D.C. 20006

National Tuberculosis and Respiratory Disease Association, 1740 Broadway, New York, N.Y. 10019

National University Extension Association, One Dupont Circle, Suite 360, Washington, D.C. 20036

National Urban League, 55 E. 52nd St., New York, N.Y. 10022

National Vocational Guidance Association, 1607 New Hampshire Ave., N.W., Washington, D.C. 20009

National Vocational Guidance Association. Order from American Personnel and Guidance Association.

National Wildlife Federation, 1412 16th St., N.W., Washington, D.C. 20036

National Writers Club, 745 Sherman St., Denver, Colo. 80203

Thomas Nelson and Sons, Copewood and Davis Streets, Camden, N.J. 08103

New American Library, Inc., 1301 Ave. of the Americas, New York, N.Y. 10019

New Brunswick Secretarial, Accounting, and Business Machines School, 110 Albany St., New Brunswick, N.J. 08901

New England Board of Higher Education, 20 Walnut St., Wellesley, Mass. 02181

New Jersey Education Association, 180 W. State St., Trenton, N.J. 08608

New Jersey Health Careers Service, 375 W. State St., Trenton, N.J. 08615

New Mexico Institute of Mining and Technology, Campus Station, Socorro, New Mexico 87801

New York Mergenthaler Linotype School, 244 W. 23rd St., New York, N.Y. 10011

New York State Camp Directors Association, 2112 Broadway, P.O. Box 723, Ansonia Station, New York, N.Y. 10023

New York State Department of Civil Service, State Office Building Campus, Albany, N.Y. 12226

New York State Department of Labor, Division of Employment, 370 Seventh Ave., New York 10001

New York State University College of Forestry, Syracuse University, Syracuse, N.Y. 13210

New York University, Office of the Registrar and Supervisor of Admissions, Washington Square, New York 10003

New York University, School of Education, Prosthetics and Orthotics Curriculum, 317 E. 34th St., New York, N.Y. 10016

Newark College of Engineering, Public Relations Office, 323 High St., Newark, N.J. 07102

Newspaper Fund, Inc., P.O. Box 300, Princeton, N.J. 08540

W. W. Norton and Company, 55 Fifth Ave., New York, N.Y. 10003

Oak Ridge Associated Universities, P.O. Box 117, Oak Ridge, Tenn. 37831

Occupational Outlook Quarterly. Order from Supt. of Documents, Government Printing Office, Washington, D.C. 20402

Oceana Publications, Inc., 75 Main St., Dobbs Ferry, N.Y. 10522

Ohio Department of Health, Office of Career Information, Columbus, Ohio 43216

Oklahoma State University, Stillwater, Okla. 74074

Olin Mathieson Chemical Corporation, 460 Park Ave., New York, N.Y. 10022

Optical Society of America, 2100 Pennsylvania Ave., N.W., Washington, D.C. 20037

Paint Industry Education Bureau, 1500 Rhode Island Ave., N.W., Washington, D.C. 20005

Pan American World Airways, Pan Am Building, New York, N.Y. 10017

Park Publishing House, 516 Viewridge Drive, Angwin, California 94508

Peace Corps, Washington, D.C. 20525

Pennsylvnia State University, College of Earth and Mineral Sciences, Experiment Station, University Park, Pa. 16802

Peterson's Guides, Inc., P.O. Box 123, Princeton, N.J. 08540

Charles Pfizer and Company, 235 E. 42nd St., New York, N.Y. 10017

Philadelphia College of Art, Broad and Pine Streets, Philadelphia, Pa. 19102
Philadelphia College of Textiles and Science, School House Lane, Philadelphia, Pa. 19144
Pilot Books, 347 Fifth Ave., New York, N.Y. 10016
Platt and Munk Company, 200 Fifth Ave., New York, N.Y. 10010
Pocket Books, Inc., 1 West 39th Street, New York, N.Y. 10018
Frederick A. Praeger, Inc., 111 Fourth Ave., New York, N.Y. 10003
Prakken Publications, Inc., 416 Longshore Drive, Ann Arbor, Mich. 48107
Pratt Institute, De Kalb Ave. and Hall St., Brooklyn, N.Y. 11205
Prentice-Hall, Inc., Englewood Cliffs, N.J. 07632
President's Committee on Employment of the Handicapped, U.S. Employment Service, Bureau of Employment Security, U.S. Department of Labor, Washington, D.C. 20210
Theodore Presser Company, Presser Place, Bryn Mawr, Pa. 19010
Printing Industries of Metropolitan New York, Inc., 461 Eighth Ave., New York, N.Y. 10001
Printing Industries Technical Institute, 1514 South Street, Nashville, Tenn. 37212
Private College Admissions Center, 1740 N St., N.W., Washington, D.C. 20036
Private Vocational Schools Association of New York, Box 297, Marlboro, N.Y. 12542
Professional Photographers of America, 1090 Executive Way, Oak Leaf Commons, Des Plaines, Ill. 60018
Prudential Insurance Company, Public Relations Department, Box 36, Prudential Plaza, Newark, N.J. 07101
Public Affairs Committee, 381 Park Ave. South, New York, N.Y. 10016
Public Health Service, U.S. Department of Health, Education, and Welfare, 8120 Woodmont Ave., Bethesda, Md. 20014
Public Personnel Association, 1313 E. 60th Street, Chicago, Ill. 60637
Public Relations Society of America, 845 Third Ave., New York, N.Y. 10022
Pulp and Paper Foundation, Inc., College of Forestry, Syracuse University, Syracuse, N.Y. 13210
Purdue University, Office of University Editor, Lafayette, Ind. 47907
G.P. Putnam's Sons, 200 Madison Ave., New York, N.Y. 10016

Quill and Scroll, International Honor Society for High School Journalists, School of Journalism, University of Iowa, Iowa City, Iowa 52240

Radio Corporation of America, Educational Aid Committee, Research Center, Princeton, New Jersey 08540

Rand McNally and Company, College Department, P.O. Box 7600, Chicago, Ill. 60680

Random House, Inc., 201 E. 50th St., New York, N.Y. 10022

Readers Press, 130 Bristol St., New Haven, Conn. 06511

Regents Publishing Company, Distributed by Simon and Schuster, Inc., 1 West 39th St., New York, N.Y. 10018

Registry of Medical Technologists, 445 N. Lake Shore Drive, Chicago, Ill. 60611

Rehabilitation Services Administration, Social and Rehabilitation Service, U.S. Department of Health, Education, and Welfare, Washington, D.C. 20201

Reilly and Lee, 114 W. Illinois St., Chicago, Ill. 60610

Richards Rosen Press, 29 E. 21st St., New York, N.Y. 10010

Ritter Equipment Company, P.O. Box 848, Rochester, N.Y. 14603

Rittners School, 345 Marlborough St., Boston, Mass. 02115

Rochester Institute of Technology, Public Relations Office, Rochester, N.Y. 14608

Ronald Press Company, 79 Madison Ave., New York, N.Y. 10016

Roy Publishers, Inc., 30 E. 74th St., New York, N.Y. 10021

Royal Typewriter Company, Division of Litton Industries, 150 Park Ave., Hartford, Conn. 06106

Russell Sage Foundation, 230 Park Ave., New York, N.Y. 10017

Sales and Marketing Executives-International, Career Service Division, 630 Third Ave., New York, N.Y. 10017

Porter Sargent, Publisher, 11 Beacon Street, Boston, Mass. 02108

Scholastic Book Services, Division of Scholastic Magazines, 50 W. 44th St., New York, N.Y. 10036

Science Clubs of America, 1719 N St., N.W., Washington, D.C. 20036

Science Research Associates, Inc., 259 East Erie St., Chicago, Ill. 60611

Science Service, 1719 N St., N.W., Washington, D.C. 20036

Scientific Manpower Commission, 2101 Constitution Ave., N.W., Washington, D.C. 20418

Scott, Foresman and Company, 199 E. Lake Ave., Glenview, Ill. 60025

Charles Scribner's Sons, 597 Fifth Ave., New York, N.Y. 10017

Sextant Systems, Inc., 3048 N. 34th St., Milwaukee, Wis. 53210

Simon and Schuster, Inc., 630 Fifth Ave., New York, N.Y. 10020

Alfred P. Sloan Foundation, 630 Fifth Ave., New York, N.Y. 10020

Small Business Administration, Office of Procurement and Management Assistance, Washington, D.C. Order from Supt. of Documents.

Social and Rehabilitation Service, Rehabilitation Services Administration, U.S. Department of Health, Education, and Welfare, Washington, D.C. 20201

Society of Actuaries, 208 S. LaSalle St., Chicago, Ill. 60604

The Society of American Archivists, Care of State Historical Society of Wisconsin, Madison, Wis. 53706

Society of American Florists and Ornamental Horticulturists, Sheraton-Park Hotel, Washington, D.C. 20008

Society of American Foresters, 1010 16th St., N.W., Washington, D.C. 20036

Society of Exploration Geophysicists, P.O. Box 3098, Tulsa, Oklahoma 74101

Society of Fire Protection Engineers, 60 Batterymarch St., Boston, Mass. 02110

Society of Mining Engineers, 345 E. 47th St., New York, N.Y. 10017

Society of Petroleum Engineers, 6200 North Central Expressway, Dallas, Texas 75206

Society of Plastics Engineers, 65 Prospect St., Stamford, Conn. 06902

Society of the Plastics Industry, Inc., 250 Park Ave., New York, N.Y. 10017

Society of Reproduction Engineers, 305 S. Andrews Ave., Suite 610, Fort Lauderdale, Florida 33301

Society of Women Engineers, United Engineering Center, Room 305, 345 E. 47th St., New York, N.Y. 10017

Soil Conservation Society of America, 7515 N.E. Ankeny Road, Ankeny, Iowa 50021

South Dakota Press, Vermillion, S.D. 57069

South-Western Publishing Company, 5101 Madison Road, Cincinnati, Ohio 45227

Southeastern Regional Vocational Technical School, 250 Foundry St., Route 106, South Easton, Mass. 02375

Southern Illinois University Press, Carbondale, Ill. 62901

Special Libraries Association, 235 Park Ave. South, New York, N.Y. 10003

Sport Fishing Institute, Dept. CI, Suite 503, 719 13th St., N.W., Washington, D.C. 20005

State of California Department of Employment. See California State Department

State Schools Publications, North Springfield, Erie County, Pa. 16430

State University of New York College of Forestry, Syracuse, N.Y. 13210

State University of New York, Maritime College, Fort Schuyler, Bronx, N.Y. 10465

Stein and Day Publishers, 7 E. 48th St., New York, N.Y. 10017

Sterling Publishing Company, 419 Park Ave. South, New York, N.Y. 10016

Stewardess Careers, Box 460 L, Hialeah, Florida, 33010

Structural Clay Products Institute, Mason Relations Department, 1750 Old Meadow Road, McLean, Va. 22101

Study Abroad, Inc., 250 W. 57th St., New York, N.Y. 10019

Superintendent of Documents, U.S. Government Printing Office, Washington, D.C. 20402

Syracuse Pulp and Paper Foundation, State University College of Forestry at Syracuse University, Syracuse, N.Y. 13210

Teacher Exchange Section, Institute of International Studies, U.S. Office of Education, Department of Health, Education, and Welfare, Washington, D.C. 20201

Teachers College Press, Columbia University, 1234 Amsterdam Ave., New York, N.Y. 10027

Texas Woman's University, Admissions Office, University Hill Station, Denton, Texas 76204

Textile Distributors Association, Inc., 1040 Ave. of the Americas, New York, N.Y. 10018

Tri-State College, Registrar's Office, College Hill, Angola, Ind. 46703

Tupper and Love, Inc., P.O. Box 48000, Doraville, Ga. 30340

Underwood Corporation, Education Dept., 1 Park Ave., New York, N.Y. 10016

UNESCO. Distributed by UNIPUB, Inc., P.O. Box 433, New York, N.Y. 10016

United Air Lines, Personnel Department, Kennedy International Airport, Jamaica, N.Y. 11430

United Business Schools Association, 1101 17th St., N.W., Washington, D.C. 20036

United Educators, Inc., Tangley Oaks Educational Center, Lake Bluff, Ill. 60044

United Methodist Church, Interboard Committee for Enlistment for Church Occupations, P.O. Box 871, Nashville, Tenn. 37202

U.S. Air Force Academy, USAF Academy, Colorado 80840

U.S. Air Force Recruiting Service, Randolph Air Force Base, Texas 78148

U.S. Armed Forces Institute, Department of Defense, Madison, Wis. 53703

U.S. Army Recruiting Command, Hampton, Va. 23369

U.S. Atomic Energy Commission, Division of Nuclear Education and Training, Washington, D.C. 20545

U.S. Atomic Energy Commission, Division of Technical Information, Oak Ridge, Tenn. 37830

U.S. Atomic Energy Commission, Special Projects Office, Oak Ridge, Tenn. 37830

United States Catholic Conference, Department of Education, 1312 Massachusetts Ave., N.W., Washington, D.C. 20005

U.S. Civil Service Commission, Washington, D.C. 20415

U.S. Coast Guard Academy, New London, Conn. 06320

U.S. Coast Guard, Dept. of Transportation, Washington, D.C. 20591

U.S. Department of Agriculture. Order from Supt. of Documents, Government Printing Office, Washington, D.C. 20402

U.S. Department of Commerce. Order from Superintendent of Documents, Government Printing Office, Washington, D.C. 20402

U.S. Department of Defense, High School News Service, Building 1-B, Great Lakes, Ill. 60088

U.S. Department of Defense, Office of the Assistant Secretary of Defense, Manpower and Reserve Affairs, The Pentagon, Washington, D.C. 20301

U.S. Department of Labor. Order from Government Printing Office, Supt. of Documents 20402

U.S. Department of State, Employment Division, Washington, D.C. 20520

U.S. Department of the Navy, Naval Ship Systems Command, Washington, D.C. 20360

U.S. Department of the Navy, Recruiting Aids Division, Bureau of Naval Personnel, Washington, D.C. 20390

U.S. Department of Transportation. Order from Superintendent of Documents, Government Printing Office, Washington, D.C. 20402

U.S. Geological Survey, Washington, D.C. 20242

U.S. Marine Corps, Department of the Navy, Procurement Aids Section, Washington, D.C. 20380

U.S. National Museum. Inquire of local museums

United States National Student Travel Association, 70 Fifth Ave., New York, N.Y. 10011

U.S. Naval Institute, Annapolis, Maryland 21402

U.S. Rehabilitation Services Administration, Department of Health, Education, and Welfare, Washington, D.C. 20201

U.S. Securities and Exchange Commission, Director of Personnel, Washington, D.C. 20549

United Student Aid Funds, Inc., 5259 N. Tacoma Ave., Indianapolis, Ind. 46220

University of Chicago Press, 5750 Ellis Ave., Chicago, Ill. 60637

University of Cincinnati, College of Business Administration, Cincinnati, Ohio 45221

University of Georgia Press, Athens, Ga. 30601

University of Illinois Press, Urbana, Ill. 61801

University of Michigan, Center for Continuing Education of Women, 330 Thompson St., Ann Arbor, Mich. 48108

University of Michigan Press, Ann Arbor, Mich. 48106

University of Minnesota Press, 2037 University Ave., S.E., Minneapolis, Minn. 55455

University of Missouri, Admissions Office, Rolla, Mo. 65401

University of Missouri, School of Forestry, Columbia, Mo. 65201

University of Notre Dame Press, Notre Dame, Ind. 46556

University of Pennsylvania Press, 3933 Walnut St., Philadelphia, Pa. 19104

Upjohn Company, Employment Office, 7000 Portage Road, Kalamazoo, Mich. 49001

Van Nostrand Reinhold Company, 450 W. 33rd St., New York, N.Y. 10001
Vanguard Press, 424 Madison Ave., New York, N.Y. 10017
Veterans Administration, Washington, D.C. 20420
Veterans Administration, Forms and Publications Depot, Arlington, Va. 22206
Viking Press, Inc., 625 Madison Ave., New York, N.Y. 10022
Virginia Polytechnic Institute, College of Agriculture, Blacksburg, Va. 24061
Vocational and Technical Education Division, U.S. Office of Education. Order from Supt. of Documents.
Vocational Foundation, Inc. 333 Park Ave. South, New York, N.Y. 10010
Vocational Guidance Manuals, 235 E. 45th St., New York, N.Y. 10017
Vocational Rehabilitation Services Administration. See Rehabilitation Services Administration

J. Weston Walch, Publisher, Portland, Maine 04104
Henry Z. Walck, Inc., 19 Union Square W., New York, N.Y. 10003
Walker and Company, 720 Fifth Ave., New York, N.Y. 10019
Ives Washburn, Inc., 750 Third Ave., New York, N.Y. 10017
Washington International Arts Letter, 115 Fifth St., S.E., Washington, D.C. 20003
Washington Square Press, 630 Fifth Ave., New York, N.Y. 10020
Watson-Guptill Publications, 165 W. 46th St., New York, N.Y. 10036
Franklin Watts, Inc., 845 Third Ave., New York, N.Y. 10022
Wayne State University Press, Detroit, Mich. 48202
West Virginia State Department of Education, State Capitol, Charleston, W. Va. 25305
Westminster Press, Witherspoon Bldg., Philadelphia, Pa. 19107
David White Company, 60 East 55th Street, New York, N.Y. 10022
Wildlife Management Institute, 709 Wire Bldg., Washington, D.C. 20005
The Wildlife Society, Suite S-176, 3900 Wisconsin Ave., N.W., Washington, D.C. 20016
Wiley and Sons, Inc., 605 Third Ave., New York, N.Y. 10016
H. W. Wilson Company, 950 University Ave., Bronx, N.Y. 10452
Women's Bureau, U.S. Department of Labor, Washington, D.C. 20210
World Almanac, Newspaper Enterprise Association, 230 Park Ave., New York, N.Y. 10017
World Publishing Company, 110 E. 59th St., New York, N.Y. 10022
World Trade Academy Press. Distributed by Simon and Schuster, Inc., 1 West 39th St., New York, N.Y. 10018

Writer's Digest, 22 East 12th Street, Cincinnati, Ohio 45210
Peter H. Wyden, Inc., 750 Third Ave., New York, N.Y. 10017

Yale Daily News Staff, New Haven, Conn. 06511
Young Women's Christian Association, National Board, Bureau of Communications, 600 Lexington Ave., New York, N.Y. 10022

Zondervan Publishing House, 1415 Lake Drive, S.E., Grand Rapids, Mich. 49506

Index

Alumnae Advisory Center, 13-14
Aim high vocational guidance series, 30
American Art Directory, 82
Annotated bibliography, 45-589
Apprenticeship, 512-13
Arco-Rosen career guidance series, 31

Bibliographies and indexes, 513-16
Bibliography, annotated, 45-589
B'nai B'rith occupational brief series, 15-16
B'nai B'rith Vocational Service, 15-16
Books and pamphlets describing more than one occupation, 508-12
Books for personal counseling, 27-8
Bureau of Labor Statistics, 36-7
Busy people books, 23

California State Department of Employment, 34-5
Careers briefs, Careers, 15-16
Career briefs, Pratt Institute, 29
Career guidance service, Careers, 15-16
Career opportunities for women, 39-40
Career pamphlets, Veterans Administration, 40-1
Career romances for young moderns, 26
Career summaries, Careers, 16
Careers, desk-top file, 15
Careers for tomorrow series, 41
Careers in depth series, 29-30
Careers, Inc., Publishers, 15-16
Changing Times, 16-17
Changing Times reprints 16-17
Charting your course series, 22-3
Charts and posters, 516-19
Children's Press, 17-18
Chronicle Guidance Publications, Inc., 18-19
Chronicle occupational brief service, 18-19
Chronicle "3 in 1" guidance service, 18-19
Chronicle's occupational library, 559
Colby books, 19
Come to work with us series, 17-18
Community helper series, 20
College directories, 523-39
College information, 523-39
Contents of annotations, 8
Counselor's professional bookshelf, 579, 589
Coward, McCann, and Geoghegan, Inc., 19
Criteria used in compilation of bibliography, 9-10

Description of series of books and pamphlets, 13-43
Dictionary of Occupational Titles, 504
Directory of Publishers and Distributors, 589-614
Display materials, 516-19
Dodd, Mead and Company, 20-1
Dodd, Mead career books, 20-1
Dutton and Company, 21-2
Dutton books on careers, 21-2

Earned Degrees Conferred, 505
Educational institutions, 523-39
Employment abroad, 520-2
Employment and scholarship handbooks, 43
Employment opportunities for women, 39
Encyclopedia of Careers and Vocational Guidance, 505
Examination guides, 566-70
Exploring your future series, 34

Finding your job series, 22-3
Finney Company, 22, 23
Foreign study or employment, 520-2

Goals of bibliography, 7, 10, 583
Golden Press, 23-4
Guidance Centre, 24

Guidelines for evaluating occupational material, 583

Handicapped, occupations for, 554-8
Health Careers Guidebook, 300

"I want to be" series, 17
Indexes and bibliographies, 513-16
Informal vocational studies, 25
Information about colleges, 523-39
Information about job seeking, 539-50
Information about scholarships, 571-8

Job seeking, 539-50
Juvenile titles, 19-21

Labor laws, 550-54
Legislation and social security, 550-4
Let's go community books, 19-20
Lippincott titles, 24-5

Macmillan career books, 25-6
Macmillan Company, 25-6
Mademoiselle college and career reprints, 13-14
Melmont Publishers, 17-18
Messner biographies, 26-7
Messner career books, 27
Messner, Julian, 26-8
Michigan Employment Security Commission, 28
Michigan job briefs, 28

National Vocational Guidance Association, 583
Number of headings, 8
Number of publications free of charge, 10
Number of publishers, 10
Number of references, 8, 10
Number of series, 8
Occupational guidance charting your course series, 22-3
Occupational guidance series, 22
Occupational guide series, 35-6
Occupational indexes and bibliographies, 513-16
Occupational information, use of, 579-88
Occupational outlook briefs, 42
Occupational outlook excerpts, 38
Occupational Outlook Handbook, 36-7
Occupational Outlook Handbook reprints, 37-8
Occupational titles, 8
Occupations for the handicapped, 554-8
Ontario College of Education, The Guidance Centre, 24

Package purchases, 558-60
Paperbacks, 31
Park Publishing House, 28
Periodicals, 560
Planning a career, 563-7
Posters, list of, 516-19
Pratt Institute, 29
Preparing for examinations, 567-70
Prices, 8
Primary social studies enrichment materials, 17
Professional counseling services, 570
"Professions and what they do" books, 43
Publications issued in series, 13-43
Purpose of bibliography, 7

Reprints from *Occupational Outlook Handbook,* 37-8
Rochester Institute of Technology, 31
Richards Rosen Press, 29-31

Science Research Associates, 31-4
SRA career information kit, 559
SRA guidance service subscription plan, 31
SRA occupational briefs, 32
Scholarship information, 571, 578
Schools for vocational training, 523-39
Seeking a job, 539-50
Series of pamphlets and books, 13-43
Several occupations, 508-12
Sextant series for exploring your future, 34
Sextant Systems, Inc., 34
Small Business Administration, 34-5
Social security, 550-4
Standards for evaluating occupational literature, 10-11

Stars and double stars, 10
Starting and managing series, 34-5
State of California Department of Employment, 34-5
Study abroad, 520-2

Textbooks for pupils, 578-9
Titles with largest number of references, 10
Toronto, University of, The Guidance Centre, 24

U.S. Civil Service Commission, 36
U.S. Department of Labor, 36-9
Use of occupational information, 578-88

Veterans Administration, 40-1
Vocational monographs, 28-9
Vocational Guidance Manuals, Inc., 41-2
Vocational guidance series, 31
Vocational training, 538

Wage and Labor Standards Administration, 38-40
Walck, Henry Z., Inc., 42
Watts, Franklin, Inc., 42
"Why not be?" series, 39
Women's Bureau, U.S. Department of Labor, 38-40
World Trade Academy Press, 43